NEW VENTURE CREATION

ENTREPRENEURSHIP IN THE 1990s

NEW VENTURE CREATION

ENTREPRENEURSHIP IN THE 1990s

THIRD EDITION

Jeffry A. Timmons, A.B., M.B.A., D.B.A.
Frederic C. Hamilton Professor
of Free Enterprise Studies
Babson College
Babson Park, Massachusetts

and

Class of 1954 Professor of New Ventures
Harvard University Graduate School
of Business Administration
Boston, Massachusetts

with

Leonard E. Smollen, B.S., M.S.
Executive Vice President
Venture Founders Corporation
Waltham, Massachusetts

Alexander L.M. Dingee, Jr.
President
Venture Founders Corporation
Waltham, Massachusetts

IRWIN

Homewood, IL 60430
Boston, MA 02116

Associate publisher: Martin F. Hanifin
Developmental editor: Kama Brockmann
Project editor: Gladys True
Production manager: Ann Cassady
Designer: Robyn Basquin
Artist: Rolin Graphics Inc.
Compositor: Graphic World, Inc.
Typeface: 11/13 Times Roman
Printer: Patterson Printing

Library of Congress Cataloging-in-Publication Data

Timmons, Jeffry A.
New venture creation : entrepreneurship in the 1990s / Jeffry A.
Timmons—3rd ed.
    p.   cm.
Includes bibliographical references.
ISBN 0-256-07879-3
1. New business enterprises—Handbooks, manuals, etc.
2. Entrepreneurship—Handbooks, manuals, etc. 3. Small business-
-Handbooks, manuals, etc. I. Title.
HD62.5.T55   1990
658.1′1—dc20   89–37898
                                                        CIP

Printed in the United States of America
    4 5 6 7 8 9 0 P 6 5 4 3 2 1

To Frederic C. Hamilton, Founder and Chairman of Hamilton Brothers Oil Company, first to succeed in extracting oil from the North Sea, ahead of the world's giant oil companies. His generosity and support created the Frederic C. Hamilton Professorship in Free Enterprise Studies at Babson College which made this revised edition possible.

Preface

A BOOK FOR THE SILENT REVOLUTION

Nearly two decades have passed since work began on the first edition of this book. During that time an explosion has occurred in entrepreneurship in America, and around the world, and the *extraordinary power of the entrepreneurial process* has been seen.

We are now, I believe, in the midst of an unusual revolution, a revolution of the human spirit, which I have called the "Silent Revolution." By creating and seizing opportunities; by providing imagination, tenacity, and leadership; and by insisting on the higher ethical ground of square dealing, successful entrepreneurs play for the long haul. In this complicated process, they create and allocate value and benefits for individuals, groups, organizations, and society. Entrepreneurs, it turns out, are the fuel, engine, and throttle for the economic engines of this and other countries.

Introduced in my three recent books, this notion of a Silent Revolution is compelling. And, it can be said that a cultural imperative exists in the minds of millions of Americans—that of the entrepreneurial dream of working for oneself and "growing up big."

Entrepreneurship is, however, not just the domain of new and small firms. It can also happen in old and large companies (though we see it far less frequently), in slower-growing and even troubled companies, and in nonprofit organizations.

Further, entrepreneurship is apolitical and thereby capable of transcending ideological and political borders. This engine of economic progress is now being discovered worldwide and shows unprecedented promise of a sustained global revolution, including China and other Eastern bloc nations. Lighting the flame of the entrepreneurial spirit empowers nations and peoples with "the knowledge and ability to fish, rather than just giving them a fish."

New Venture Creation is thus a book about entrepreneurship, and how it is fueling the Silent Revolution.

A BOOK ABOUT THE PROCESS OF ENTREPRENEURSHIP

New Venture Creation is a book about the actual process of getting a new venture started, growing the venture, successfully harvesting it, and starting again.

There is a substantial body of knowledge, concepts, and tools that entrepreneurs need to know, prior to and while taking the start-up plunge and after, if they are to get the odds in their favor. Accompanying the explosion in entrepreneurship has been a significant increase in research and knowledge about the entrepreneurial process. Much of what was known previously has been reinforced and refined, some has been challenged, and numerous new insights have emerged.

New Venture Creation has been the product of experience and considerable research in this field, rooted in real-world application, nearly two decades of research, and refinement in the classroom. The third edition updates and refines the best of the first two editions and includes new insights which have emerged.

As before, the design and flow of the book is aimed at creating knowledge, skills, awareness, and involvement in the process and the critical aspects of creating a new venture and then making it grow. In a pragmatic way—through text, case studies, and hands-on exercises—the book guides students in discovering the concepts of entrepreneurship and the competencies, skills, know-how and experience, attitudes, resources, and networks that are sufficient to pursue different entrepreneurial opportunities. No doubt about it: there is no substitute for the real thing—actually starting a company. But short of that, it is possible to expose students to many of the vital issues and immerse them in key learning experiences, such as the development of a business plan.

The book is divided into six parts. The first three parts detail the driving forces of entrepreneurship—the opportunity recognition, the team, and resource requirements. Part I addresses the process by which *real* opportunities—not just ideas—can be discovered and selected. This section concerns opportunities around which higher potential ventures can be built, where the risks and trade-offs are acceptable, and where entrepreneurs will be able to exit their businesses, profitably and when they want to, rather than when they have to or, worse, not at all.

Part II concerns the team and what makes entrepreneurs tick—how they think and act—and what they do to get the odds of success in their favor.

Part III is about resources and developing a business plan.

The next two parts concern some details. Part IV concerns entrepreneurial finance and the process of financing new ventures. Part V talks about start-up, strategies for success and managing rapid growth, and harvest issues.

Part VI helps in crafting a personal entrepreneurial strategy. Once an entrepreneur knows how winning entrepreneurs think, act, and perform, then he or she can establish goals to practice emulating those actions, attitudes, habits, and strategies. This section asks entrepreneurs to think of the process of becoming an entrepreneur, much as a coach of an athlete would in preparing for a winning season, and also to consider the following: What are my real talents, strengths, and weaknesses and how can my talents and strengths be exploited (and my weaknesses minimized)? What are the opportunities to use my strengths and to capitalize on the competition's weaknesses?

New Venture Creation seeks to enable entrepreneurs to immerse themselves in the dynamics of launching and growing a company and to address the following practical issues:

- What does an entrepreneurial career take?
- What is the difference between a good opportunity and just another idea?
- Is the opportunity I am considering the right opportunity for me, now?
- Why do some firms grow quickly to several million dollars in sales but then stumble, never growing beyond a single-product firm?
- What are the critical tasks and hurdles in seizing an opportunity and building the business?
- How much money do I need and when, where, and how can I get it—on acceptable terms?
- What financing sources, strategies, and mechanisms can I use from prestart, through the early growth stage, to the harvest of my venture?

- What are the minimum resources I need to gain control over the opportunity, and how can I do this?
- Is a business plan needed, and, if so, what kind is needed and how and when should I develop one?
- Who are the constituents for whom I must create or add value to achieve a positive cash flow and to develop harvest options?
- What is my venture worth and how do I negotiate what to give up?
- What are the critical transitions in entrepreneurial management as a firm grows from $1 million to $5 million to $25 million in sales?
- What are some of the pitfalls, minefields, and hazards I need to anticipate, prepare for, and respond to?
- What are the contacts and networks I need to access and to develop?
- Do I know what I do and do not know, and do I know what to do about it?
- How can I develop a personal "entrepreneurial game plan" to acquire the experience I need to succeed?
- How critical and sensitive is the timing in each of these areas?
- Why do entrepreneurs who succeed long term seek to maintain reputations for integrity and ethical business practices?
- Why do entrepreneurship and entrepreneurial management seem surrounded by paradoxes, well-known to entrepreneurs, such as:
  - Ambiguity and uncertainty versus planning and rigor.
  - Creativity versus disciplined analysis.
  - Patience and perseverance versus urgency.
  - Organization and management versus flexibility.
  - Innovation and responsiveness versus systemization.
  - Risk avoidance versus risk management.
  - Current profits versus long-term equity?

AN APPROACH WITH REAL-WORLD RESULTS

New Venture Creation is about the dignity of practical knowledge and the utility of the question: *Is entrepreneurship for me, and, if so, how do I get the odds in my favor?*

The domain is you and the whole is integrated, or woven together, like beads and threads. The interrelationships among the functional parts of a business are studied with an eye for achieving a winning balance.

New Venture Creation will help you achieve this winning balance by assisting you in addressing these central, yet very practical, questions about new ventures and entrepreneurship. One result will be a *compression and acceleration of learning* that, if left to the school of hard knocks alone, would be far more costly and time consuming than is either necessary or desirable.

The approaches taught here have been used by successful entrepreneurs, investors, and students who have gone forth to start their own businesses. The content and material have won accolades from experienced graduate students, college seniors, and hundreds of founders and owners of new and emerging companies pursuing their entrepreneurial dreams. Earlier editions of *New Venture Creation* (1977 and 1985) became leading books for courses on entrepreneurship and starting new ventures courses worldwide. According to *The Wall Street Journal,* October 1987, *New Venture Creation* is a "textbook classic." The consensus of real world entrepreneurs and students about the material in the book is: It works!

HISTORY OF *NEW VENTURE CREATION*

New Venture Creation has roots going back over 20 years, reflected best in a feature article about the author in a Babson College alumni bulletin entitled, "This Professor Practices What He Teaches."

Numerous experiences have been important testing grounds for applying and refining approaches to launching and growing higher-potential ventures, and much of what is here in *New Venture Creation* has been tempered and enhanced by my "postgraduate degree" working directly with entrepreneurs and entrepreneurial firms.

Since 1971, and even earlier doing doctoral research at the Harvard Business School, I have been immersed in the world of entrepreneurs and the start-up, development, and financing of new and growing (and sometimes shrinking) companies as a student, researcher, teacher, and scholar and as an investor, advisor, director, and founding shareholder.

In 1971, I became a founding shareholder of Venture Founders Corporation, a Boston venture capital firm with subsidiaries in the United Kingdom and Belgium that manages over $65 million. I worked closely with Venture Founders from 1971 through 1982 in developing ways to identify, evaluate, and finance seed-stage and stage-up ventures. Of particular note, these investing activities spanned a range of high-, low-, and no-technology businesses and product and service businesses in the United States, Canada, the United Kingdom, and Europe.

Through my own firm, Curtis-Palmer & Company, Inc., which I founded in 1981, I have consulted with presidents and partners of venture capital firms and emerging companies in the United States, the United Kingdom, and Sweden. From 1981 to 1982, I accepted a full-time assignment in Stockholm with one of the first venture capital firms there. Clients have included Investkontakt & Svetab, Venture Founders Corporation, Zero Stage Capital, Venture Economics (publisher of *Venture Capital Journal*), Vlasic Foods (part of Campbell Soup), and the Sunmark Companies, a $160 million-plus private firm in St. Louis recently acquired by Nestlé. In 1984, as the first outside member of the partnership committee of Cellular One in Boston, I became actively involved in starting and building the first independent car phone company in New England. In 1986, I became a founding shareholder and director of Boston Communications Group, which at this writing owns and operates cellular phone systems in southern Maine and New Hampshire, cellular phone installation and service centers, and Cellular Express, a credit-card cellular phone system for limousine services nationwide. Since 1985, I have assisted Ernst & Young's national Privately Owned Emerging Business Group to develop and implement professional development programs in emerging businesses and entrepreneurship and in financing alternatives for partners in this leading Big Eight accounting firm. This effort is now expanding in a similar effort for Thorne Ernst & Whinney in Canada and for Ernst & Young in the United Kingdom. In 1988, I joined the advisory board of Bridge Capital Investors, a $150 million bridge fund in Teaneck, New Jersey, which specializes in providing growth capital for emerging companies with sales in the $5 million to $100 million range.

In addition to the practical experience noted above, I have conducted research in entrepreneurship on new and emerging firms and venture financing; this research has resulted in nearly 100 papers and articles that have been published in such publications as the *Harvard Business Review, Journal of Business Venturing,* and in proceedings of national and international conferences, including *Frontiers of Entrepreneurship Research: 1981–1987.* I authored and co-authored several books, including *The Entrepreneurial Mind, New Business Opportunities,* and *Planning and Financing a New Business* (all three Acton, Mass.: Brick House Publishing, 1989), *The Encyclopedia of Small Business Resources* (Harper & Row, 1984), *The Insider's Guide to Small Business Resources* (Doubleday, 1982), and *A Region's Struggling Savior* (Small Business Administration, 1980). I co-edited *Frontiers of Entrepreneurship Research: 1983–1985* (Babson College, 1983–1985). In addition, my speaking and consulting assignments have included travels throughout the United States, Austria, Australia, Canada, the Philippines, the United Kingdom, Scandinavia, Spain, and elsewhere, and contact with entrepreneurs in these places.

Currently holding a joint appointment at Babson College and Harvard Business School as the first Frederic C. Hamilton Professor of Free Enterprise Studies and the first Class of 1954 Professor of New Ventures at Babson and Harvard, respectively, I have continued with my love for and study of entrepreneurship. I joined Babson College in 1982, as Paul T. Babson Professor, and have served as director of the Center for Entrepreneurial Studies and as co-chairman of the Babson Entrepreneurship Research Conference. I am a founder and director of the Price–Babson College Fellow Program. I have developed and teach courses on starting new ventures and financing entrepreneurial ventures for students in colleges and graduate schools and for the presidents and executives of emerging businesses in the Entrepreneurial Management Program at Babson College.

I received an A.B. from Colgate University and my M.B.A. and D.B.A. from the Harvard Business School.

New Venture Creation thus has a rich background in practical experience, research, and education.

Jeffry A. Timmons

Acknowledgments

The third edition of this book, as was the original book and the second edition, is a cumulative effort, reflecting the encouragement, thinking, and achievements of many—associates, entrepreneurs, investors, teachers, students, colleagues, and friends. But first and foremost I want to thank Bonnie Van Slyke for her superb effort in making the third edition possible. Her thoroughness, her skillful editorial eye, her extraordinary sense of organization, and her attention to the details set a new standard for quality control. My only hope is that she will be available for the fourth!

The original book (1977) stemmed from materials and concepts in my doctoral dissertation at the Harvard Business School and from work with co-authors of the first two editions, Alec Dingee and Leonard Smollen, my co-founders and associates at Venture Founders Corporation of Lexington, Massachusetts. Their busy entrepreneuring and investing schedules prohibited them from contributing to this edition; but I am most grateful for their earlier contributions, still evident in chapters on the business plan, financing, and success strategies. Earlier course development work at Northeastern University and later during the 1980s at Babson College was an important contributor. Early inspirations to pursue this area of interest and eventually to share my work can be credited to many, especially Paul R. Lawrence, Arthur N. Turner, and David McClelland of Harvard University, and John J. Bray, Richard C. Whiteley, and John Humphrey of The Forum Corporation, Boston.

There are many roots and contributors to the ideas behind the third edition from whom I have drawn intellectual capital and from whom I have received support and encouragement, as well as inspiration. To list them all might well comprise a chapter by itself. Short of that, I wish to express special thanks to those who have been so helpful in recent years. First, my colleagues at Babson College and the Harvard Business School who have been a constant source of encouragement, inspiration, and friendship—Bill Bygrave, Alan Cohen, Neil Churchill, Jeff Ellis, Ned Goodhue, Dan Muzyka, Bob Reiser, Natalie Taylor, Bill Wetzel, J. B. Kassarjian, Tom Moore, and Gordon Prichett—and our Price–Babson College Fellows—Stan Rich, Chuck Schmidt, Randy Wise, and, especially, Les Charm, for his generous giving of time, entrepreneurial energy, and resources to Babson. A special thanks to Bill Dill, president of Babson College through June 1989, for his support of the entrepreneurial studies mission over the past eight years. And thanks to all of the inductees into Babson's Academy of Distinguished Entrepreneurs who have shared their entrepreneurial lives with us and have contributed so much to the legend and legacy of entrepreneurship at Babson College. Without the backup and hard work of Bonnie Pandya, coordinator of the Price–Babson College Fellows Program, and Barbara Ward, it is unlikely this project would have been completed.

My dear friend and colleague Howard H. Stevenson, first Sarofim-Rock Professor at the Harvard Business School, stands alone for his support and for his generous sharing of his "world class" intellectual capital and extraordinary wit. Howard, more than anyone else, has caused the academic community to focus on the role of opportunity in the entrepreneurial process and the centrality of entrepreneurship in general management. Others at HBS who have been instrumental in furthering the entrepreneurial management mission and being supportive include Ron Fox; Bill Fruhan; Rosabeth Moss Kanter, first Class of 1960 Professor; John Kao; Paul Lawrence; Marty Marshall; John McArthur, Dean; Tom Piper; Mike Roberts; Bill Sahlman; and the Class of 1954.

Outside Babson and Harvard, several key people have given more to this effort than they shall ever know. Paul J. Tobin, president of Cellular One, Boston, and the Boston Communications Group, has been a model entrepreneur and entrepreneurial manager in pioneering the car phone industry in America, along with the superb team at Cell-One (Bob, Jean, and Kim). I "go to school" and learn new lessons on entrepreneurial creativity and the "nose for an opportunity" each time I work with P.J. and see him, and the team, in action. Invaluable exchanges of ideas with several other entrepreneurs and venture capitalists have been both sources of encouragement and my educators: Brian Applegate, Gordon Baty, Karl Baumgartner, Bill Egan, Dave Gumpert, Doug Kahn, Paul Kelley, Earl Linehan, Jack Peterson, and The Fabb. Included are a special thanks to John Van Slyke for sharing his knowledge and experience and to my colleagues at Bridge Capital: Don Remey, Bart Goodwin, Hoyt Goodrich, Bill Spencer, and Geoff Wadsworth, and advisors Craig Foley, Bill Foxley, and Dick Johnson.

A great debt of appreciation is perpetually due to all my former students from whom I learn with each encounter, and I marvel both at their accomplishments and how little damage I imparted! Especially, Peter Altman, Avrum Belzar, Jeff Brown, Everett Dowling, Brian Dwyer, Joe Harris, Carl Hedberg, Greg Hunter, Jody Kosinski, Frank Mosvold, Greg Murphy, Steve Orne, Gerry Peterson, Steve Richards, Jim Turner, and Marc Wallace, to name a few.

The work of over 250 researchers who have contributed to the Babson Entrepreneurship Research Conferences, begun in 1981 by Karl Vesper while he was Paul T. Babson Professor, and reported in *Frontiers of Entrepreneurship Research,* 1981 through 1989 (Babson College), have added to my thinking. A driving force behind entrepreneurship research, these conferences were sponsored by Babson College beginning in 1981 and later were co-sponsored by Georgia Tech's School of Management (1984), the Wharton Center for Entrepreneurship (1985), Pepperdine University (1987), University of Calgary (1988), and St. Louis University (1989). While the names of these researchers are too numerous to note, I am especially mindful of the work of Professors Birley, Block, Boyd, Brockhaus, Brown, Bruno, Tyebjee, Bygrave, Churchill, Cooper, Dunkleberg, Feigen, Gasse, Hornaday, Hoy, Krasner, MacMillan, Miner, Mitton, Muzyka, Peterson, Roberts, Sahlman, Sexton, Shapero, Smith, H. Stevenson, Tarpley, Vesper, and Wetzel.

Research studies reported elsewhere, such as the Baylor Conference (1980) and the 75th Anniversary Entrepreneurship Symposium held at Harvard Business School in 1983, have also been invaluable.

Practical knowledge and earlier research of the venture capital industry has been enhanced by the publications and work of my friends and colleagues, Stanley E. Pratt and

Norman D. Fast, founders of Venture Economics and publishers of *Venture Capital Journal.* The founding management teams of Investkontakt AB and Svetab in Sweden made innumerable innovations in applying my earlier concepts and approaches to their venture capital and business development activities there. These include: Hakan Raihle, Morgan Olsson, Ingvar Svenson, Gunnar Olofgors, Lars Bostrom, Per Wahlstrom, and their staffs. Further fine-tuning of earlier concepts and approaches occurred in practice in the United Kingdom. Contributing to this effort were the late Brian Haslett, Jack Peterson, Jack Hayes, and Paul Croke of Ventures Founders Corporation and Joseph Frye of VF Limited in the United Kingdom. Professor Chris Harling of Cranfield Business School was an extraordinary co-worker in these efforts.

Entrepreneurs and others whose experience and insight have touched me over the years are many. Any list would be lengthy, and I am most appreciative of them all. I especially want to thank Doug Kahn, Brian Dwyer, Michael Harde, John Bray, J. C. Egnew, John Moore, Art Beisang, Ken DaFoe, Fred Alper, Karl Baumgartner, Don Spigarelli, Bill Egan, Harry Healer, Kevin Rhone, Jan Pirrong, Dan Gregory, Arthur Little, Jim Morgan, Bill Congleton, Earl Linehan, Jim Hindman and Ed Kelley, Allan Harle, Colin Chapman, Ken Fisher, Bill Poduska, Bill Foster, Richard Testa, Burt McMurtry, Brent Rider, Howard Head, Paul Kelley, and Gordon Baty.

My work with my good friend and colleague David Gumpert of the *Harvard Business Review* on two other books and articles helped to make easier the writing of this manuscript. I am grateful to Wendy C. Handler, assistant professor, Babson College, who wrote the material for Chapter 8, "The Family Venture."

I am also most appreciative of Richard J. Testa of Testa, Hurwitz & Thibeault, Boston, for contributing his excellent article "The Legal Process of Venture Capital Investment," reproduced as Appendix III, from *Pratt's Guide to Venture Capital Sources,* 8th edition. I am grateful also to Kenneth Goodpaster, professor, Harvard Business School, for permission to use his material on ethics in Chapter 9. I also wish to acknowledge the earlier contributions to Chapter 9 of Grace M. Dingee, Nancy Tieken, and David Boyd, professor and dean of the College of Business, Northeastern University, Boston. I am thankful also to Robert Morris Associates of Philadelphia for permission to use information about their statement studies (Appendix I).

Harold Price, founder and benefactor; Gloria Appel; and the late Edwin M. Appel of the Price Institute have been staunch and unwavering champions of entrepreneurship at Babson College and across America. Their generous, pioneering support of the Price–Babson Fellows Program has made a major contribution toward cloning entrepreneurial minds—in both faculty and students—at colleges and universities worldwide. They have exceeded their previous extraordinary generosity by making a half-million-dollar Challenge Grant to Babson's Center for Entrepreneurial Studies to help us continue the mission and our work.

Hal Seigle, retired chairman of the Sunmark Companies, St. Louis, and now a professional director and advisor to growing companies, has taught me a great deal about the difference between working hard and working smart and in appreciating the difference between an idea and an opportunity. Watching him do both, always with a lot of class and integrity, has been a postgraduate course by itself.

My colleagues at Ernst & Young's national office in the Privately Owned and Emerging Business Group have opened my eyes to a whole new perspective on how it is possible for a Big Eight firm to be very entrepreneurial in seeking out new business opportunities and building their own business. They include Herb Braun, Gary Dando, Bill Casey, and Bruce Mantia (all in Cleveland); partners Ron Diegelman (Baltimore), Gayle Goodman (San Francisco), Dick Haddrill (Atlanta), Carl Mayhall (Dallas), Dick Nigon (Minneapolis), Ralph Sabin (Newport Beach), and Dale Sander (San Diego); and

Hy Shweil (Stamford) and members of the POEB Task Force. In the United Kingdom, Alan Clarke, Will Rainey, David Wilson, and David Wilkinson; and at Thorne Ernst & Whinney (Canada), Don Brown, Howard Crofts, Jim Harper, and Don MacClean have all worked with me to build a culture, a strategy, and the know-how for providing value-added service opportunities as general business advisors to privately owned and emerging businesses.

Research for and preparation of the third edition were made possible by the generous support of the Frederic C. Hamilton Chair at Babson College, endowed by Mr. Hamilton (founder of the first firm to successfully retrieve oil from the North Sea for commercial sale). Without this support such an undertaking would not have been possible.

Last, a special personal thank you is extended to Gladys True, project editor at Richard D. Irwin, for her highly professional effort in bringing the book to press. Her calmness, patience, and professionalism in the face of many deadlines and my burdened schedule were greatly appreciated.

                                                                                      J.A.T.

Contents

PART I   OPPORTUNITY RECOGNITION   1

1   The Entrepreneurial Process   3
  The Silent Revolution   3
  What is Entrepreneurship?   5
  The Problem of Survival   7
  Exceptions to the Failure Rule   9
  An Analytical Framework   12
  Implementation   19
  Creation of Value   19
  Myths and Realities   19
  The Entrepreneurial Mind   22
  Case – Outdoor Scene, Inc.   24
  Exercise – Take an Entrepreneur to Dinner   32

2   New Venture Ideas   37
  The Role of Ideas   37
  Pattern Recognition   40
  Finding Ideas   43
  Case – Halsey & Halsey Inc.   46
  Exercise – Creative Squares   63
  Exercise – Idea Generation Guide   65

3   Opportunity Recognition   71
  Recognizing Opportunities   71
  Screening Opportunities   75
  Gathering Information   83
  Case – Fibercom Applications, Inc.   87

4   Screening Venture Opportunities   117
  Screening Venture Opportunities   117
  Exercise – Venture Opportunity Screening Guide   118

PART II   THE FOUNDERS   159

5   The Entrepreneurial Mind in Thought and Action   **161**
The Search for Understanding   161
Converging on the Entrepreneurial Mind   165
A Look at Intrapreneuring   172
The Concept of Apprenticeship   172
Entrepreneur's Creed   175
Case—Kevin Mooney   176

6   The Entrepreneurial Manager   **181**
The Entrepreneurial Domain   181
Stages of Growth   184
Management Competencies   190
Case—PMI, Inc.   196
Exercise—Management Competency Inventory   209

7   The New Venture Team   **227**
The Importance of the Team   227
Forming/Building Teams   228
Rewards and Incentives   236
Case—Beantown Seafoods, Inc.   239
Exercise—Rewards   261

8   The Family Venture   **269**
Popular and Numerous   269
The Impact of Goals   270
The Family Venture Team   274
Strategies for Success   277
Case—Family Venture Partners, Inc.   279

9   Personal Ethics and the Entrepreneur   **283**
Exercise—Ethics   285
Overview of Ethics   291
Ethical Stereotypes   292
Should Ethics Be Taught?   293
Thorny Issues for Entrepreneurs   298
Ethics Exercise Revisited   300

PART III   RESOURCE REQUIREMENTS   303

10   Resource Requirements   **305**
The Entrepreneurial Approach to Resources   305
Outside People Resources   307
Financial Resources   316
General Sources of Information   323
Exercise—Financial Statements   327

11   The What, Whether, and Why of the Business Plan   **329**
Planning and the Business Plan   329
Pitfalls of Effective Planning   333
A Closer Look at the What   336
Case—Rapidrill Business Plan   340

12   The Business Plan Guide   **377**
Preparing a Business Plan   377
Exercise—The Business Plan Guide   378

PART IV   FINANCING ENTREPRENEURIAL VENTURES   399

13   Entrepreneurial Finance   **401**
        Venture Financing   401
        Crafting Financial and Fund-Raising Strategies   406
        Case — Hindman & Company   411
14   Risk Capital   **421**
        Obtaining Risk Capital   421
        The Entrepreneur and Friendly Investors   422
        Informal Investors   422
        Professional Investors   425
        Types of Risk Investment   435
        Case — Bridge Capital Investors, Inc.   439
15   Valuing, Negotiating, and Structuring the Deal   **453**
        Structuring the Deal   453
        Negotiating   454
        Valuation   454
        The Deal   456
        Common Deal Documents   460
        Common Investment Instruments   462
        Sand Traps   463
16   Obtaining Debt Capital   **469**
        Borrowing Debt Capital   469
        Traditional Debt Sources   470
        Other Creative and Off-Balance-Sheet Sources   479
        Case — Michigan Lighting, Inc.   480

PART V   START-UP AND AFTER   491

17   Entrepreneurs in Action   **493**
        Anatomy of the Iterative Process   493
        Strategies for Success   505
        Setting up a Business   507
        Creditability Builders   507
18   Managing Rapid Growth   **511**
        Growing Up Big   511
        The Importance of Culture and Organizational Climate   517
        Anticipating and Coping with Problems   519
        Solving Problems   525
19   The Entrepreneur and the Troubled Company   **529**
        When the Bloom is off the Rose   529
        The Gestation Period of Crisis   532
        Predicting Trouble   533
        The Threat of Bankruptcy   535
        Intervention   537
20   The Harvest and Beyond   **543**
        The Journey   543
        Getting to the Final Destination   544
        Harvest Options   546
        Beyond the Harvest   549
        Seven Secrets of Success   550

PART VI   CRAFTING A PERSONAL ENTREPRENEURIAL STRATEGY   551

21 Crafting a Personal Entrepreneurial Strategy   **553**
Planning Revisited   **553**
Crafting an Entrepreneurial Strategy   **555**
Exercise – Personal Entrepreneurial Strategy   **558**

APPENDIXES   605

I   Information about RMA "Projection of Financial Statements" and RMA Statement Studies   **606**
II   Information about Industry Norms and Key Business Ratios, Published by Dun & Bradstreet   **618**
III   "The Legal Process of Venture Capital Investment" by Richard J. Testa   **620**
IV   Sample Terms Sheet   **635**
V   Outline of an Investment Agreement   **637**
VI   Sample Vesting and Stock Restriction Agreement   **640**
VII   Sample Loan Agreement   **644**
VIII   Vases and Faces Exercise   **651**

Annotated Bibliography   **653**

Index   **667**

THE OPPORTUNITY | PART I

One often hears, especially from younger, newer entrepreneurs, the exhortation: "Go for it! You have nothing to lose now. So what if it doesn't work out. You can do it again. Why wait?" While the spirit reflected in these comments is commendable and while there can be no substitute for doing, such itchiness can be a real mistake unless it is focused on a solid opportunity.

Most entrepreneurs who start businesses, particularly if they are their first, run out of cash at a faster rate than they bring in customers and profitable sales. While there are many reasons for this, the first is that they have not focused on the right opportunities. Unsuccessful entrepreneurs usually equate an idea with an opportunity; successful entrepreneurs know the difference.

While there are boundless opportunities for those with the entrepreneurial zest, the fact of the matter is that a single entrepreneur will be able to launch and build only a few good businesses—probably no more than three or four—during his or her energetic and productive years. (Fortunately, all you need to do is grow and harvest one quite profitable venture whose sales have exceeded several million dollars. The result will be a most satisfying professional life, as well as a quite financially rewarding one.)

How important is it then that you screen and choose an opportunity with great care? Very important. It is no accident that venture capital investors have consistently invested in just 1 percent to 3 percent of all the ventures they review.

As important as it is to find a good opportunity, each good opportunity has its risk and problems as well. The perfect deal has yet to be seen. Identifying risks and problems before you start so steps can be taken, early on, to eliminate them or reduce any negative effects is another dimension of opportunity screening.

The Entrepreneurial Process 1 ⟩

> *Anyone [can be an entrepreneur] who wants to experience the deep, dark canyons of uncertainty and ambiguity; and who wants to walk the breathtaking highlands of success. But I caution, do not plan to walk the latter, until you have experienced the former.*
>
> **An Entrepreneur**

RESULTS EXPECTED

Upon completion of this chapter, you will have:

1. Examined evidence of and trends in the "Silent Revolution."
2. Developed a definition of entrepreneurship and looked at its practical, intellectual, and policy agenda.
3. Determined how successful entrepreneurs define and measure success.
4. Looked at the failure rule and examined why there are exceptions to the failure rule and the types of new businesses that succeed.
5. Discussed briefly a framework for analyzing new ventures.
6. Analyzed the proposed start-up of Outdoor Scene, Inc.
7. Conducted an interview with a successful entrepreneur.

THE SILENT REVOLUTION

The Entrepreneurial Wave

Among the adult working population in the United States, which in 1988 numbered 120 million, more than one in seven is self-employed, and it can be said that the dream of working for oneself exists in the minds of millions of other Americans. Compared to managers and those working for others, as many as three times more plan never to retire.[1]

And it is no wonder that so many have the dream—a dream of walking the breathtaking highlands of success mentioned in the opening quotation.[2] The self-employed feel good about themselves, about their work lives, and about the economic rewards they earn. Uniformly, the self-employed report the highest levels of personal satisfaction, challenge, pride, and remuneration. They seem to love the entrepreneurial game for its own sake. They love their work because it is invigorating, energizing, and meaningful.

The vast majority of the nearly 2 million millionaires in the United States in 1988 accumulated their wealth through entrepreneurial acts.

What may be more surprising is that even graduates of the Harvard Business School, which has long been thought of as the West Point for the Fortune 500, thrive on this

---

[1] Howard H. Stevenson, "Who Are the Harvard Self-Employed?" *Frontiers of Entrepreneur Research: 1983,* ed. J. A. Hornaday et al. (Babson Park, Mass.: Babson College, 1983), p. 233.

[2] The quotation is from an interview with his father, an entrepreneur, conducted by Gian Perotti, Babson College, class of 1984.

entrepreneurial dream. About one third end up working for themselves, and the vast majority of all graduates 10 years after graduation work for smaller companies employing fewer than 1,000 persons. Ninety percent of the second-year MBA candidates say they want to work for themselves.[3]

The entrepreneurial wave has also spread to colleges and high schools in recent years. Over 400 colleges and universities offer courses in starting new ventures and entrepreneurship, compared to as few as 50 in 1975. A 1987 Roper survey showed that 46 percent of all college freshmen surveyed felt owning one's own business was an attractive career alternative.

The entrepreneurial wave in America in the past decade has brought unprecedented benefits not just to individuals but to society as a whole. Entrepreneurs, it turns out, are the fuel, engine, and throttle for the economic engine of the country. Consider the following:

- About 1.3 million *new enterprises,* from one-person operations and up, were launched in the United States in 1988. By the year 2000, demographers estimate there will be 30 million firms in the United States, up significantly from the 18 million firms in existence in 1988.[4]

- Virtually all of the net new jobs created in this country come from these *new and expanding firms* — not from large, established companies. It has been found that, from 1984 to 1987, the top 5 percent of all new companies accounted for 87 percent of all new jobs, the top 10 percent created 96 percent, and the top 15 percent created 98 percent. Also, from 1980 to 1987, the Fortune 500 eliminated a net 3.1 million people from their payrolls. At the same time, the non-Fortune 500 firms — predominantly new and smaller firms — created 17 million new jobs, and the public sector contributed 1.3 million.[5]

- In the United States, 36 million jobs have been created in the last 20 years, whereas in Europe there has been a net loss.

- In the United States, women have been starting two to three times more businesses as men, and these businesses are growing faster. By 1990, nearly 5 million businesses (representing one fourth of all businesses) will be owned by women.

- Since World War II, 50 percent of all innovations, and 95 percent of all radical innovations, have come from *new and smaller firms.* These have included, for example, the microcomputer, the pacemaker, overnight express packages, the quick oil change, fast food, oral contraceptives, the X-ray machine, and so forth.[6]

- The companies of 37 individual entrepreneurs who were inducted into the Babson College Academy of Distinguished Entrepreneurs from 1977 to 1988 have combined sales in 1988 equalling the GNP of the *20th largest country in the world.*[7] Many of these entrepreneurs built their companies from nothing, and their names include entrepreneurial legends,[8] as well as others with equal deeds but less public familiarity.

- Between $50 billion and $60 billion of informal risk capital exists in our economy in 1988, and another $30 billion of venture capital funds are available from professional sources

---

[3] Stevenson, "Who Are the Harvard Self-Employed?"

[4] Frank Swain, Office of Advocacy, Small Business Administration, Washington, D.C. (speech in Dallas at Ernst & Whinney's Privately Owned and Emerging Businesses, "Current Matters," October 6, 1988).

[5] Various studies for the Small Business Administration by David Birch, reported in *INC.* and elsewhere.

[6] Several studies by the United States Department of Commerce.

[7] Compiled by John Marthinsen, Professor, Babson College, Founder's Day, 1988.

[8] Royal Little of Textron, Inc.; An Wang, Wang Laboratories, Inc.; Frank Purdue, Purdue Farms, Inc.; Ken Olsen, Digital Equipment Corporation; Sochio Honda, Honda Motor Company, Ltd.; Ray Kroc, McDonald's Corporation; Fred Smith, Federal Express Corporation; Nolan Bushnell, Pizza Time Theatre, Inc.; Trammel Crow, Trammel Crow Company; J. Willard Marriott, Jr., The Marriott Corporation; Ed Lowe, Ed Lowe Enterprises (The Kitty-Litter Company); Wally Amos, The Famous Amos Chocolate Chip Cookie Corporation; H. R. Bloch, H & R Block, Inc.; Don Burr, People Express; John Cullinane, Cullinet Software, Inc.; Rupert Murdoch, New America Publishing, Inc.; Peter Sprague, National Semiconductor Corporation; and John Templeton, The Templeton Funds.

seeking to back small-company entrepreneurs.[9] The availability of such funds is now a worldwide phenomenon occurring in the United Kingdom, the countries of Western Europe and Scandinavia, Kenya, Spain, Brazil, Australia, the Philippines, Japan, Korea, and elsewhere.

- In the United States, a recent national survey by the Yankalovich organization found two significant trends: (1) Women are questioning the traditional world of work and seeking alternatives to it by exploring opportunities for *entrepreneurship* and (2) people in their 50s and 60s are not planning to retire but rather to pursue second careers in smaller, more *entrepreneurial settings.*

- *Entrepreneurship is not just the domain of new and small firms.* It can also happen in older and larger companies (although it is seen far less frequently), in slower growing and even troubled companies, in nonprofit organizations, and in Eastern, Western, and developing economies.

- Entrepreneurship also happens in all types of economies. For the first time, in June and July of 1987, 46 senior policy makers, researchers, entrepreneurs, and executives from 26 countries met in Salzburg, Austria, for an eight-day seminar in *entrepreneurship.*[10] In 1988, the newly organized European Foundation for Entrepreneurship Research held its first annual conference of researchers and practitioners at IMEDE in Lausanne, Switzerland, and, in 1989, in Paris.

Dawn of a New Era

This source of economic progress is now being discovered worldwide, and there exists the unprecedented promise of a sustained global entrepreneurial effort. Again, lighting the flame of the entrepreneurial spirit empowers nations and people who, as Mark Twain said, know "the difference between lightning and a lightning bug."

In short, we are in the midst of what can be called the *Silent Revolution.* It is entirely possible that the Silent Revolution will affect the 21st century as much and probably more than the Industrial Revolution affected the 20th.[11]

WHAT IS ENTREPRENEURSHIP?

A Definition

Entrepreneurship is creating and building something of value from practically nothing. That is, entrepreneurship is the process of creating or seizing an opportunity and pursuing it regardless of the resources currently controlled.[12] Entrepreneurship involves the definition, creation, and distribution of value and benefits to individuals, groups, organizations, and society. Entrepreneurship is very rarely a get-rich-quick proposition; rather, it is one of building long-term value and durable cash flow streams.

Fundamentally, entrepreneurship is a human creative act. It involves finding personal energy by initiating and building an enterprise or organization, rather than by just watching, analyzing, or describing one. Entrepreneurship usually requires a vision and the passion, commitment, and motivation to transmit this vision to other stakeholders, such as partners,

---

[9] Estimates based on research by William E. Wetzel, Jr., 1987/88 Paul T. Babson Professor, Babson College.

[10] Led by the author and Howard H. Stevenson, Sarofim-Rock Professor, Harvard Business School.

[11] Jeffry A. Timmons, *The Entrepreneurial Mind* (Acton, Mass.: Brick House Publishing, 1989).

[12] The definition of entrepreneurship has evolved over the past few years from work done at the Harvard Business School and at Babson College. Particular credit is due to Howard H. Stevenson of the Harvard Business School. Credit is also due to other colleagues of the author at the Harvard Business School and at Babson College.

customers, suppliers, employees, and financial backers. It also requires a willingness to take calculated risks—both personal and financial—and then doing everything possible to influence the odds.

Entrepreneurship involves building a team of people with complementary skills and talents; of sensing an opportunity where others see chaos, contradiction, and confusion; and of finding, marshalling, and controlling resources (often owned by others) to pursue the opportunity.

And, entrepreneurship involves making sure the venture does not run out of money when it needs money most.

The Stark Urgency of Entrepreneurship

Entrepreneurship has been likened to athletics or medicine, where the entrepreneur is to business what a decathlete or surgeon is to the Olympics or to an operation. In all, winning strategies require intense, active, and creative involvement. There are challenges, uncertainty, calculated risk taking, and risk minimizing. And disaster can pounce with unexpected suddenness.

Entrepreneurship can be compared to the Boston Marathon which, like an entrepreneurial endeavor, is a race with an especially punishing series of long hills, called in the marathon *Heart Break Hill.*

Or, the successful entrepreneurial act is reminiscent of the improvisation and resourcefulness of a star football running back or of a downhill ski racer speeding like a projectile. A downhill ski racer is always at the edge of disaster but just as close to victory, and the balance shifts to victory if his or her talents and abilities exceed those of the competition and if split second judgments and mental calculations result in actions that keep him or her pointed toward victory. And, as with the racer, disaster for an entrepreneur can pounce unexpectedly. Just ask Adam Osborne, who in 1981 developed and marketed the first portable minicomputer. By 1985, Osborne Computer, having made the wrong move at the wrong time, was displaced by another firm, Compaq, and went out of business.

Still others have likened entrepreneurship to a symphony orchestra, where people with diverse skills and personalities are so blended by the conductor, with mastery and balance, that the whole is greater than the sum of the parts. Or it has been compared to juggling, where, because of adroitness under stress and pressure, the skillful juggler can keep many balls in the air at once and recover quickly from the slightest miscast.

Entrepreneurship parallels other activities having similar demands and unknowns. Take, for instance, the unknowns and urgency to act faced by the first pilot to break the sound barrier, the legendary Chuck Yeager, as documented in *The Right Stuff:*

In the thin air at the edge of space, where the stars and the moon came out at noon, in an atmosphere so thin that the ordinary laws of aerodynamics no longer applied and a plane could skid into a flat spin like a cereal bowl on a waxed Formica counter and then start tumbling, end over end like a brick . . . you had to be "afraid to panic." In the skids, the tumbles, the spins there was only one thing you could let yourself think about: What do I do next?[13]

All the acts above are artistic and creative. Their outcomes also tend to be either highly rewarding successes or painful and visible misses. And common to all is that stark urgency—What do I do next?

---

[13] Tom Wolfe, *The Right Stuff* (New York: Bantam Books, 1980), pp. 51–52.

The Practical Agenda

Entrepreneurship is holistic and integrated; that is, entrepreneurship concerns the business and its managers/founders in the entirety, not just piecemeal.

Thus, entrepreneurship is akin to the problem-solving task of constructing a jigsaw puzzle. In the process of creating the puzzle, pieces will invariably be missing or obscure, and the trick is to see and anticipate patterns—before others.

The educational focus of the practical agenda centers on the question: *What are the concepts, skills, know-how and know-who, information, attitudes, alternatives, and resources that entrepreneurs and entrepreneurial managers need?*

The Intellectual and Policy Agenda

The study of entrepreneurship also seeks to understand a rich, complex, and challenging intellectual agenda. A provocative intellectual question, which has important policy implications, is: *Why does entrepreneurship occur—and fail to occur—in new firms and old; in small firms and large; in fast- and slow-growing firms; in the private and public sectors; and in the East, the West, and developing economies?*

As was suggested by the working definition earlier, entrepreneurship is not just the domain of new and emerging businesses. The intellectual and policy agenda addresses at least the following issues:

- Recognition, creation, and pursuit of opportunity in new and existing firms.
- Building, survival, and renewal of companies.
- Financing of new, emerging, and submerging organizations.
- Entrepreneurship's role in larger organizations.
- Public policy.

The intellectual and policy domain will grow in importance in the decade ahead, and entrepreneurs need to be aware of and may well contribute to this area of entrepreneurship.

THE PROBLEM OF SURVIVAL

Failure Rule

An extraordinary variety of people, opportunities, and strategies characterize the approximately 18 million corporations, partnerships, and proprietorships in this United States.[14] There has been an unprecedented number of new company formations in the United States in the past few years. In 1988, for example, 1.3 million new businesses were started, according to government estimates.

Not only can almost anyone start a business, a great many succeed. While it certainly helps, a person does not have to be a genius to create a successful business. As Nolan Bushnell has asserted, "if you are not a millionaire or bankrupt by the time you are thirty, you are not really trying."[15]

And, while its rigors may favor the young, age is no barrier to entry. One study showed that nearly 21 percent of the founders were over 40 when they embarked on their

---

[14] Only nonfarm businesses are included in the figure.

[15] In response to a question from a student at Founder's Day, Babson College, 1983.

entrepreneurial careers, the majority were in their 30s, and just over one quarter did so by the time they were 25. Further, numerous examples exist of founders who were over 60. Take, for instance, Colonel Sanders of Kentucky Fried Chicken. Another example, although perhaps less well known, is that of Stanley Rich,[16] who is over 70 years old and has started at least seven businesses since the age of 60.

Discussed above in the definition of entrepreneurship is the idea of value creation and distribution, not just for the owners but also for other stakeholders, such as partners, customers, suppliers, employees, and backers. Even for those businesses which survive, realizing a capital gain or at least deriving sufficient income from the business is decidedly more difficult.

This ability to generate sufficient income or potential for capital gain is a critical measure of success and separates those businesses which fail or which merely survive as a job substitute from those which succeed.

For the vast majority of new businesses in the country, the odds of survival definitely are not in their favor. While government data, research, and "business mortality" statisticians may not agree on the precise failure and survival figures for new businesses, they do agree that failure is the rule, not the exception.

Complicating efforts to obtain precise figures is the fact that it is not easy to define and identify failures, and reliable statistics and databases just are not available. However, the Small Business Administration estimated in 1983 that, for every three new businesses formed, two close their doors.[17]

There is also wide variation in failure rates across industries. In 1980, for instance, even though retail trade, construction, and service businesses accounted for just 3 of 21 categories reported by Dun & Bradstreet, they accounted for 70 percent of all failures and bankruptcies in that year.[18] What is worse, smaller firms—those employing fewer than 100 persons—suffered the most. In 1981 and 1982, approximately 99 percent of all businesses filing for bankruptcy were these smaller firms.[19]

Exhibit 1.1 is a distillation of a number of studies of failure rates over the last 50 years. Illustrated are the facts that (1) failure rates are high and (2) although the majority of the failures occur in the first two to five years, it may take considerably longer for some to fail. This picture is supported by the findings of several different studies.[20]

Another study of business failures and bankruptcies found that, for those businesses which failed, over 53 percent of the failures occurred in the first 5 years; nearly 30 percent occurred in years 6 through 10; and the remaining 17 percent involved firms in existence more than 10 years.[21]

To make matters worse, most people think that the failure rates are actually much higher. Since most would argue that actions are governed, more often than not, by perceptions rather than facts alone, this perception of failure, in addition to the dismal record, can be a serious obstacle to aspiring entrepreneurs.

[16] A Price–Babson College Fellow, Stanley Rich is a founder of the M.I.T. Enterprise Forum[SM].

[17] *The State of Small Business: A Report of the President, Transmitted to the Congress, March 1983* (Washington, D.C.: Small Business Administration, 1983).

[18] Dun & Bradstreet, Business Economics Division, *The Business Failure Record, 1980* (New York, 1982).

[19] *The State of Small Business*, pp. 156–57.

[20] Summaries of these are reported by Albert N. Shapero and Joseph Giglierano, "Exits and Entries: A Study in Yellow Pages Journalism," *Frontiers of Entrepreneurship Research: 1982*, ed. K. Vesper et al. (Babson Park, Mass.: Babson College, 1982), pp. 113–41; and Arnold C. Cooper, William C. Dunkelberg, and Carolyn Y. Woo, "Survival and Failure: A Longitudinal Study," *Frontiers of Entrepreneurship Research: 1988*, ed. B Kirchhoff et al. (Babson Park, Mass.: Babson College), pp. 225–37.

[21] Dun & Bradstreet, p. 10.

Exhibit 1.1
Overall New Business Failure Rates

By the End of	Percentage that Fail
1st year	40%
2nd year	60
10th year	90

Sources: Commerce Department; SBA; Dun & Bradstreet.

Innovation, Economic Renewal, and Learning

A certain level of failure is part of "creative self-destruction" described by Joseph Schumpeter. It is part of the dynamics of innovation and economic renewal, a process which requires both births and deaths.

More important, it is also part of the learning process inherent in gaining an entrepreneurial apprenticeship. If a business fails, no other country in the world has laws, institutions, and social norms that are more forgiving. Firms go out of existence, but entrepreneurs do not.

EXCEPTIONS TO THE FAILURE RULE

Higher Potential Ventures

A majority of the new businesses started each year are traditional, very small businesses employing one or two people who are willing to sacrifice income for the lifestyle they are afforded. These firms are called *mom and pop* businesses, marginal firms, or lifestyle firms.[22]

Remember, however, that the idea of value creation and distribution is implicit in the definition of entrepreneurship. The lifestyle firms described above do not succeed in this way. Separating lifestyle firms from the pool of new businesses, two other types of firms remain. First, there are high potential firms, firms having the potential for significant capital gain. The second type includes foundation firms, or attractive small companies, which generate enough income to compensate fully those involved.[23] These two types of firms—the higher potential ventures—have sales of at least $500,000 to $1 million and grow at a rate of at least 10 percent per year. It is interesting to note that, according to government data, only about 1 business in 5 had annual sales in 1980 of over $1 million, 1 in 10 over $2 million, 1 in 80 over $10 million, and 67 of 1,000 greater than $25 million.[24] Further, the 500 largest service companies earned, in 1988, net income as a percent of sales typically in the 3 percent to 5 percent range, and these companies outperformed the 500 largest companies in the industrial group.[25]

Success, rather than failure, is the rule among higher potential ventures and attractive small companies. They are driven by talented and experienced founders pursuing attractive opportunities who are able to attract both the right people and the necessary financial and other resources to make the venture work.

---

[22] Patrick R. Liles, *New Business Ventures and the Entrepreneur* (Illinois: Richard D. Irwin, 1974), pp. 4–5.

[23] Ibid., p. 10.

[24] *The State of Small Business: A Report of the President* (Washington, D.C.: United States Government Printing Office, 1989), p. 47.

[25] *Fortune*, June 11, 1984, pp. 170–94.

Exhibit 1.2
One-Year Survival Rates by Firm Size

Firm Size (employees)	Survival Percent
0–9	77.8%
10–19	85.5
20–99	95.3
100–249	95.2
250+	100.0

Source: Michael B. Teitz et al., "Small Business and Employment Growth in California," Working Paper No. 348, University of California at Berkeley, March 1981, p. 42.

Threshold Concept

There appears to be a minimum threshold size of at least 5 to 10 employees—and 20 is even better—and of sales of $500,000 to $1 million. *Exhibit 1.2* shows, based on a cross-section of all new firms, one-year survival rates for new firms jump from approximately 78 percent for firms having up to 9 employees to approximately 95 percent for firms with between 20 and 99 employees.

After four years, as shown in *Exhibit 1.3*, the survival rate jumps from approximately 37 percent for firms with less than 19 employees to about 54 percent for firms with 20 to 49 employees.

Although any estimates based on sales per employee vary considerably from industry to industry, this minimum threshold translates roughly to a threshold of $50,000 to $100,000 of sales per employee annually. But highly successful firms can generate much higher sales per employee. Take Apple Computer, for instance which, by 1988, had sales per employee of $329,000, well above IBM's figure of $127,000.[26]

Promise of Growth

The definition of entrepreneurship implies the promise of expansion and the building of long-term value and durable cash flow streams as well.

But, as will be discussed later, it takes a long time for new companies to become established and grow. A recent Small Business Administration study, summarized in *Exhibit 1.4*, covering the period from 1976 to 1986, found that two of every five small firms founded survived six or more years but that few achieved growth during the first four years.[27] The study also found that survival rates more than double for firms which grow and, the earlier in the life of the business that growth occurs, the higher the chance of survival.[28]

Other data also confirm this exception. A study done by INC. shows that, between 1982 and 1987, the average growth in sales of the INC. 500 was 96 percent per year. The study also finds that, of the 7 million corporations in the United States, approximately 7 percent—or just under 500,000 firms—grew over 20 percent per year and just over 1 percent—or approximately 80,000 firms—grew 50 percent per year.

Some of the true excitement of entrepreneurship lies in conceiving, launching, and building firms such as these.

[26] From annual reports to shareholders.

[27] Bruce D. Phillips and Bruce A. Kirchhoff, "An Analysis of New Firm Survival and Growth," *Frontiers in Entrepreneurship Research: 1988*, ed. B. Kirchhoff et al. (Babson Park, Mass.: Babson College, 1982), p. 266–67.

[28] This confirms this exception to the failure rule noted above and in the original edition of this book in 1977.

Exhibit 1.3
Four-Year Survival Rates by Firm Size

Firm Size (employees)	D&B Study (1969–76)	California Study (1976–80)
0–19	37.4%	49.9%
20–49	53.6	66.9
50–99	55.7	66.9
100–499	67.7	70.0

Sources: David L. Birch, *MIT Studies, 1979–1980;* and Michael B. Teitz et al., "Small Business and Employment Growth in California," Working Paper No. 348, University of California at Berkeley, March 1981, table 5, p. 22.

Exhibit 1.4
Percentage of New Small Firms Surviving Six or More Years*

Industry	All Classes (percent)	Zero Growth 0%	Low Growth 1–4%	Medium Growth 5–9%	High Growth 10%+
Total, All Industries	39.8%	27.5%	66.3%	75.5%	78.4%
Agriculture, Forestry, Fishing	43.1	35.0	74.7	80.7	82.8
Mining	39.1	27.1	67.8	61.5	57.0
Construction	35.3	24.1	65.0	72.2	74.3
Manufacturing	46.9	27.0	66.9	73.5	76.0
Transportation, Utilities, Communications	39.7	25.7	68.5	72.4	75.6
Wholesale Trade	44.3	28.3	66.5	74.9	77.2
Retail Trade	38.4	27.1	62.7	74.4	76.8
Finance, Insurance, Real Estate	38.6	28.7	68.7	76.4	78.5
Services	40.9	28.7	69.1	79.4	83.5

* Ranked by number of jobs created from 1976–86.
Source: U.S. Small Business Administration, August 29, 1988; B. D. Phillips and B. A. Kirchhoff, "An Analysis of New Firm Survival and Growth, *Frontiers in Entrepreneurship Research: 1988,* ed. B. Kirchhoff et al., pp. 266–67.

Venture Capital Backing

Another notable pattern of exception to the failure rule is found for businesses which have attracted start-up financing from private venture capital companies. Instead of the 70 percent to 90 percent failure rate shown when all types of new firms are considered, these new ventures enjoy a *survival* rate nearly that high.

Studies of success rates of venture capital portfolios, summarized in *Exhibit 1.5,* show that, in the portfolios of experienced professional venture capital firms, typically about 15 percent to 20 percent of the companies will result in total loss of the original investments and further that it is unusual for the loss rates for portfolios of experienced venture capital firms to exceed 30 percent to 35 percent and for the loss rates to fall below 10 percent.[29]

Another recent study, which analyzed 218 investments made by five prominent venture capital firms during the 1970s, found that 14.7 percent of those portfolio companies resulted in complete losses and another 24.8 percent experienced partial losses.[30]

[29] J. A. Timmons et al., *New Venture Creation* (Homewood, Ill.: Richard D. Irwin, 1977), pp. 10–11; E. B. Roberts, "How to Succeed in a New Technology Enterprise," *Technology Review* 2, no. 2 (1970); C. Taylor, "Starting-Up in the High Technology Industries in California," commissioned by the Wells Fargo Investment Company, 1969; R. B. Faucett, "The Management of Venture Capital Investment Companies," Sloan School master's thesis, M.I.T., 1971; and R. B. Faucett, "Venture Capital: Fact and Myth," Foothill Group, 1972.

[30] T. Dehudy, N. D. Fast, and S. E. Pratt, *Venture Economics,* Needham, Mass., 1981.

Exhibit 1.5
Studies of Success Rates of Venture Capital Portfolios

	Success Rates (percent)
Venture Capital Journal survey (1983)—232 portfolio companies and 32 venture capital firms	85%
International venture capital firm results (1972–88)—$60 million funds in U.S., U.K., Canada, and Belgium	85
Wells Fargo Bank study (1972)—279 high technology firms	65
Studies by M.I.T. and other studies	80–82

Thus, about 40 percent of the portfolio involved losses of some kind. It is interesting to note that offsetting these losses were spectacular successes. Among the 218 investments in the 10-year period of the study, 3.8 percent returned 10 times or more the original investment, after taxes, and another 8.3 percent returned 5 to 10 times, again after taxes. This translates into about 25 percent compounded return on investment after taxes.

Even higher returns have been achieved by such spectacular successes as Apple Computer, Lotus, Digital Equipment, Intel, Compaq, and the like.

This compelling data has led some to conclude that there is a threshold core of 10 percent to 15 percent of new companies which will become the winners in terms of size, job creation, profitability, innovation, and potential for harvesting (and thereby realizing a capital gain). And, eventually, from among these 10 percent to 15 percent of all new firms emerge the "winning performers."[31] As shown in *Exhibit 1.6*, the top 25 percent among all medium-sized companies achieved records of growth from 1978 to 1983 that exceeded the growth of the top quarter of the economy, the top quarter of the Fortune 500, and firms classified as "excellent companies."

AN ANALYTICAL FRAMEWORK

Driving Forces

What is going on here? What do these talented entrepreneurs and companies backed by venture capital do differently? What is accounting for this exceptional record? Are there some lessons here for aspiring entrepreneurs?

The conclusion is there are some central, fundamental forces that drive the entrepreneurial process and account for these success rates. Granted, there are almost as many different approaches, philosophies, and nuances to the art and craft of new venture creation as there are entrepreneurs, private investors, and venture capital companies. Yet, time and again, central themes rise to the surface.

Professional venture capital investors follow a unique approach in their businesses, and successful entrepreneurs who grow multimillion-dollar firms, often from scratch and sometimes with little money, also understand that *entrepreneurial achievement is driven by people who search for and shape superior opportunities*.

Most important, an understanding of these fundamental forces is not the monopoly of venture capitalists or the entrepreneurs they back. Thousands of examples confirm the universal nature of the forces driving the entrepreneurial process.

Take, for example, the following:

[31] Donald K. Clifford, Jr., and Richard E. Cavanagh, *The Winning Performance* (New York: Bantam Books, 1985), p. 3.

Exhibit 1.6
Compound Annual Growth Rates, 1978–83

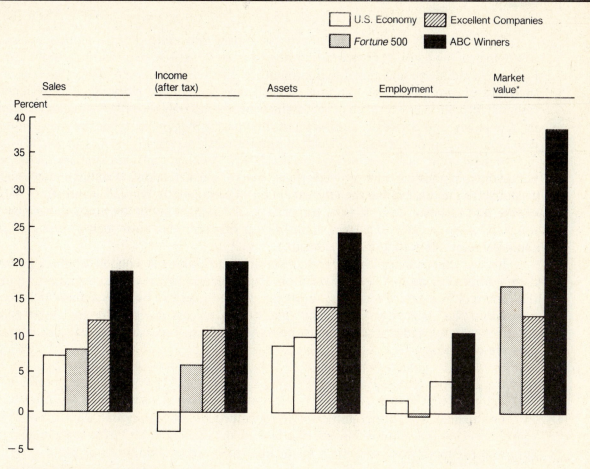

*Does not apply to U.S. economy

Growth Rates, 1978–83 (percent)

Performance Measure	U.S. Economy	Fortune 500	Excellent Companies	ABC Winners
Sales	7.1%	7.9%	12.0%	18.4%
After-tax income	−2.7	5.9	10.4	19.7
Assets	8.3	9.5	13.5	23.6
Employment	1.0	−0.5	3.6	10.0
Market value	NA	16.3	12.5	37.8

Source: Donald K. Clifford, Jr., and Richard E. Cavanagh, *The Winning Performance* (New York: Bantam Books, 1985).

■ Tony Harnett came to this country from his native Ireland as a young high school dropout. He had a lot of ambition and was in search of opportunity. In 1976, he and his wife Susan bought a small natural foods store in Brookline, Massachusetts, with annual sales of a meager $110,000 per year. By paying a lot of attention to the critical driving forces, those that venture capitalists also seem to concentrate on, they have built Bread And Circus into a multistore venture whose annual sales in 1988 exceeded $35 million. Interestingly, they did this without having to raise a dime of venture capital.

■ Another entrepreneur started and built a small company, without venture capital, which became the leading firm manufacturing and selling metal picture frames. By 1983, the company had about 70 percent of the North American market, yet did only $15 million in very profitable sales. The company was acquired by a European firm for over $20 million in cash.

In analyzing the entrepreneurial process, relying only on traditional models, such as a psychological model or a competitive strategy model, to analyze new ventures is not useful. First, any unidimensional model that attempts to distill the common basis for the collective successes of entrepreneurial ventures can tell only part of the story. Second, systematic research into the characteristics of successful ventures has only recently begun, and research in economics and strategic management has barely begun to focus on new venture development and performance. Third, entrepreneurship typically occurs in a real-world environment that lacks certainty, predictability, stability, and smoothness. Risk and uncertainty, paradoxes and contradictions, market imperfections, and asymmetries and vacuums are the rules, rather than the exceptions. Consequently, confusing and often chaotic change and turbulence in markets, technology, and availability of resources is business as usual. (It is no wonder that large, multilayered organizations have such a dismal record competing and innovating in this domain.)

Instead, the analytical framework, illustrated in *Exhibit 1.7*, isolates the three primary driving forces behind new venture creation: the founders, opportunity recognition, and the resource requirements. Experience shows that these forces can be assessed and influenced to improve the chances of succeeding. The key to success in new venture creation is a continual, careful, and realistic assessment of these driving forces and the real time in which they are occurring.

The Importance of Fit

Throughout, it is a trial-and-error iterative process of finding out what it takes, the "gaps" faced as the venture unfolds, and how to shape a good "fit." Not surprisingly, this approach seems to work well for a lot of innovative undertakings. After all, the Wright brothers flew over 1,000 glider flights in the efforts to find out what worked before attaching a motor-driven propeller to their airplane.

The key elements of successful new ventures (i.e., the founders, the opportunity, and the resources) fit one another — rarely perfectly, but reasonably so — within the context of the real world. The potential of the venture will depend on fit of the lead entrepreneur with his or her management team and of the lead entrepreneur and his or her management team with the opportunity.

A question which should be answered, then, is: For whom is the opportunity desirable? It should be recognized that the personal values and lifestyles of the founders enter heavily into whether there is a fit.

In turn, the lead entrepreneur, the management team, and the opportunity must fit with the ability to marshall and control the necessary resources.

Thus, realistically evaluating the merits and deficiencies of each element and accurately judging the potential fit of each element are essential.

The Importance of Timing

Every entrepreneurial event occurs in *real time,* where the clock can be either enemy or friend, or both.

Thus, timing is crucial in every entrepreneurial situation. Recognizing and seizing an opportunity is often a precarious race with an hour glass — when the disappearing sand is the cash running out.

Exhibit 1.7
Real-World Environmental Context and Central Driving Forces of Entrepreneurship

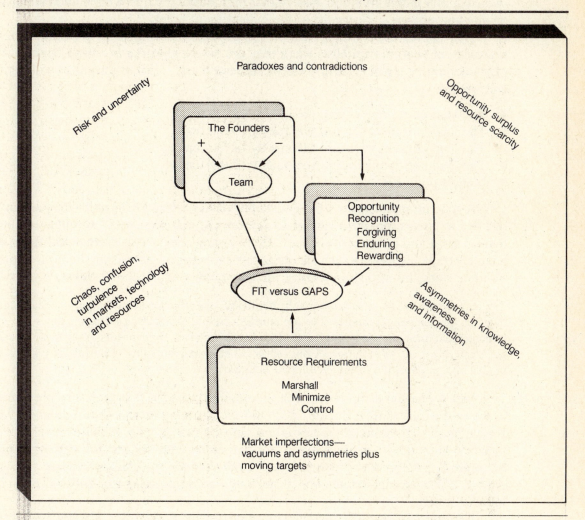

The Founders

Lead Entrepreneur and the Management Team

Several studies, including a recent study of the 50 most active venture capital firms in the United States, have confirmed the view that one of the central forces driving the entrepreneurial process is the founders.[32]

Recent research on high-technology companies formed in this country since 1967 — highly innovative technological ventures, where one would expect the elegance of the technology to have special importance — shows that the founders are more important than the technology.[33] Of course, the high-tech game cannot be won without innovative

---

[32] J. A. Timmons and D. E. Gumpert, "Discard Many Old Rules for Raising Venture Capital," *Harvard Business Review,* January–February 1982.

[33] Jeffry A. Timmons, Norman D. Fast, and William D. Bygrave, "The Flow of Venture Capital to Highly Innovative Technological Ventures," *Frontiers of Entrepreneurship Research: 1983,* ed. J. A. Hornaday et al. (Babson Park, Mass.: Babson College, 1983), p. 316.

technology; but venture capitalists, who are among the most active and prominent investors in the country in this area, still insisted that they placed greatest weight and emphasis on the quality and proven track record of the management team.

That the team is a driving force of the entrepreneurial process is demonstrated in the responses of venture capitalists when they are asked what the five most important factors which determine if a new venture will be successful are. Venture capitalists will state plainly and simply:

- The lead entrepreneur and the quality of the team.
- The lead entrepreneur and the quality of the team.
- The lead entrepreneur and the quality of the team.
- The lead entrepreneur and the quality of the team.
- Market potential.

A good example of this is the philosophy of Burr Egan Deleage & Company of Boston, one of the largest and most successful venture capital firms, with over $200 million under management and investments in over 100 emerging companies. Partner Bill Egan, who has been centrally involved in such successes as Continental Cablevision, Federal Express, and Tandon, states his strong preference for high-quality management this way:

The management team must have quality, depth and maturity. It must be experienced in the industry in which the company competes. The top manager should have had prior profit center responsibility. Management must possess intimate knowledge of the market for its products and have a well thought out strategy for the penetration of this market. The strength of the management team is the most important consideration in the investment decision.

Ideally, having a top-notch idea or innovation and a first-rate entrepreneurial team is the best of all worlds. But this does not happen very often. The founder of American Research & Development Corporation and father of the American venture capital industry, General Georges Doriot,[34] is often quoted for his insistence that he preferred a Grade A entrepreneurial team with a Grade B idea to a Grade B team with a Grade A idea. This view has become one of the standard operating axioms of the venture capital industry today.[35]

Another famous entrepreneur who expressed such a position is Arthur Rock, founder of a firm that was the lead capital investor in such new ventures as Fairchild Semiconductor, Teledyne, Scientific Data Systems, Intel, and Apple Computer. He put it this way: "If you can find good people, they can always change the product. Nearly every mistake I've made has been I picked the wrong people, not the wrong idea."[36]

Further, the management team is critically important to the chances of survival and expansion of new ventures, whether or not they are candidates for venture capital. As was seen earlier, those firms who grew beyond 20 employees and roughly $1 million in sales were most likely to survive and prosper. In a majority of cases, it is quite difficult to do this without a team of at least two key contributors.

---

[34] In 1946, General Doriot, a retired Harvard Business School professor noted for encouraging entrepreneurship among his students, founded American Research and Development Corporation in Boston, the first institutional U.S. venture capital firm. The company put venture capital on the map when its investment of about $70,000 in 1957 in four young M.I.T. engineers with an idea for a new computer grew to about $350 million—as shares in Digital Equipment Corporation, today America's second largest computer firm.

[35] J. A. Timmons, N. D. Fast, S. E. Pratt, and W. D. Bygrave, "Venture Capital Investing in Highly Innovative Technological Ventures," published by *Venture Economics,* Needham, Mass., March 1984, for the National Science Foundation.

[36] Arthur Rock, "Strategy vs. Tactics from a Venture Capitalist," *Harvard Business Review,* November–December 1987, pp. 63–67.

A Word about Solo Entrepreneurs

A substantial amount of research, as well as practical experience, confirms that a team grows a business while a solo entrepreneur makes a living. If an entrepreneur's aspirations include growing a business large and profitable enough to realize a capital gain, then he or she needs to think team.

But teams are not for everyone. Numerous examples exist of solo entrepreneurs carving out small niches for themselves, earning substantial six-figure incomes, and building wealth by wise financial planning and investing.[37]

In these instances, the fundamental driving forces are at work, without a team.

Opportunity Recognition

Ideas Are Not Necessarily Opportunities

If there is any single spark that ignites an entrepreneurial explosion, it is the opportunity.[38]

There certainly does not seem to be a lack of ideas for new or improved products or services. Entrepreneurs, inventors, innovators, and college students abound with new ideas. However, there are far more ideas than good business opportunities.

This is because—and it cannot be repeated enough—*an idea is not necessarily an opportunity.*[39] While at the center of an opportunity is always an idea, not all ideas are opportunities.

In understanding the difference between an opportunity and just another idea, it is crucial to understand that entrepreneurship is a market-driven process.

An opportunity is attractive, durable, and timely and is anchored in a product or service that creates or adds value for its buyer or end user. Opportunities are created because there are changing circumstances, inconsistencies, chaos, lags or leads, information gaps, and a variety of other vacuums, and because there are entrepreneurs who can recognize and seize them. And, successful new ventures are invariably anchored in opportunities with rewarding, forgiving, and durable gross margins and profits.

The challenge then is recognizing an opportunity buried in often contradictory data, signals, and the inevitable noise and chaos of the marketplace, since the more *imperfect* the market (i.e., the greater the gaps, asymmetries, and inconsistencies of knowledge and information), the more abundant the opportunities. A skillful entrepreneur can shape and create an opportunity where others see little or nothing—or see it too early or too late.

After all, if recognizing and seizing an opportunity were simply a matter of using available techniques, checklists, and other screening and evaluation methods, we might have

---

[37] Sources of information about solo entrepreneurs and small enterprises include the following magazines: *Entrepreneur, In-Business,* and *Home-Based Business.*

[38] Opportunity recognition was originally identified as a driving force in new venture creation in the 1977 edition of this text. The conceptual framework developed by Howard H. Stevenson at the Harvard Business School, and his helpful suggestions have both reinforced and refocused this identification of opportunity recognition as central. See also Howard H. Stevenson, "A New Paradigm for Entrepreneurial Management," *Entrepreneurship: What It Is and How to Teach It,* ed. John J. Kao and Howard H. Stevenson (Boston: Harvard Business School, 1984). Empirical research bearing on the question of opportunity screening and evaluation and any common characteristics of successful entrepreneurial ventures is documented in a paper by Jeffry A. Timmons, Daniel F. Muzyka, Howard H. Stevenson, and William D. Bygrave, "Opportunity Recognition: The Core of Entrepreneurship," *Frontiers of Entrepreneurship Research: 1987,* ed. Neil Churchill et al. (Babson Park, Mass.: Babson College, 1987), p. 409.

[39] See Jeffry A. Timmons, *New Business Opportunities* (Acton, Mass.: Brick House Publishing, 1989).

far more than the one-in-five businesses that had sales in 1980 of over $1 million. Why? Because the literature on techniques for screening and evaluating ideas indicates that over 200 such methods have been developed and documented.

Another Look at Fit and Timing

Recent work has lent even further support to the hypothesis that an opportunity is quite situational and depends on the mix and match of the key players and on how promising and forgiving the opportunity is, given the team's strengths, advantages, and shortcomings.

Further, the vast majority of those founding new businesses run out of money *before* they find enough customers for their "good ideas." Thus, for entrepreneurs, timing can be everything.

Another critical question is, therefore: If there really is a business opportunity, rather than just a product or two, is there time to seize the opportunity? If there is an opportunity, whether an entrepreneur can seize the opportunity in time depends on movements in technology and competitors' thrusts, among other factors.

Thus, an opportunity is also a constantly moving target, and there exists a "window of opportunity."

Resource Requirements

Control of Minimum Resources

Identifying, attracting, and managing the resources required to execute the opportunity, both inside and outside the business, is the third driving force in entrepreneurship.[40]

Entrepreneurs have a quite different mentality when it comes to resources. First, entrepreneurs manage to get more out of less; that is, their approach often is to find ways to push ahead with *minimum resources.* To accomplish this, they often invest "sweat equity" and use customer advances, barter, and other "bootstrapping" techniques.

Also, successful entrepreneurs know that they can get the odds in their favor and even improve the chances of attaining their business plan if they utilize resources differently. They position themselves to commit and decommit quickly, thereby avoiding commitment to future resources until necessary.

Thus, entrepreneurs seek to *control resources* rather than own them. They would rather borrow, rent, or lease these resources. For example, finding and properly using outside resources, such as bankers, CPAs, lawyers, informal advisors, board members, and other experts, is one way of controlling, rather than owning, resources and one of the most easily overlooked challenges entrepreneurs face.

By reducing the resources required to a minimum and controlling, rather than owning, those resources, the risk and capital required are minimized.

Financial Resources

When initially asked what the most critical ingredients needed to successfully launch a new company are, most people include money among the top three items, if not list it first. No doubt about it, a venture cannot go far without it. After all, it is the fuel in the gas tank of a car that makes it go.

But, in truth, the capacity to raise the money is a result of having the other parts of the act together. *Financing follows* from identifying good people to pursue a good opportunity who demonstrate that they clearly grasp the driving forces that will govern success.

---

[40] The role of outside resources as a key success factor was contributed early by Patrick R. Liles, doctoral dissertation, Harvard Business School, 1970.

In fact, it seems that one of the worse things that can happen to an entrepreneur is having *too much money too early*. Take, for instance, Howard Head's approach to developing the very first metal ski. He left his job at a large aircraft manufacturer after World War II, and, working with his own savings on a shoe string and literally out of his own garage, he began to develop his metal ski. It took over 40 iterations before he finally developed a marketable metal ski. Head feels that, had he insisted on having all the right talent and financing in place before he started to develop the product, he would have failed by wasting them prematurely. Head Ski subsequently dominated the international ski industry through the late 1960s and was sold to AMF.[41]

IMPLEMENTATION

It is in the implementation that the real work and challenge begin. In this regard, a business plan is a key tool in the process of identifying gaps and fits and pulling the vision together and transmitting the passion to others.

However, having a superbly prepared document describing a timely opportunity may be a necessary condition for launching and building a successful venture, but it is far from sufficient. The lead entrepreneur and the management team must be able to implement it. Arthur Rock has said:

Most entrepreneurs have no problem coming up with a good strategy . . . but they usually need all the help they can get in developing and implementing the tactics that will make them successful in the long run.[42]

CREATION OF VALUE

Creation of value—creating a "value pie"—is the ultimate end product of the entrepreneurial process for an entrepreneur, his or her backers, and the other stakeholders (i.e., partners, employees, customers, suppliers, and service providers).

Clearly, harvesting value or dividing the pie is a nonissue until something begins to sprout or until the pie is big enough to go around.

Starting a venture, growing a venture, and then harvesting a venture successfully are not the same. In that respect, we are reminded of the comment by George Bernard Shaw, taken from a different context: "Any darned fool can start a love affair, but it takes a real genius to end one successfully."

MYTHS AND REALITIES

Folklore and stereotypes about entrepreneurs and entrepreneurial success are remarkably durable, even in these informed and sophisticated times. There is more known about the founders and the process of entrepreneurship than ever before.

However, certain myths enjoy recurring attention and popularity. Part of the problem is that, while generalities may apply to certain types of entrepreneurs and particular situations, the great variety of founders tends to defy generalization. *Exhibit 1.8* shows myths about entrepreneurs that have persisted and realities that are supported by research.

Studies have indicated that 90 percent or more of founders start their companies in the

---

[41] Howard Head subsequently followed the same approach in developing the Prince tennis racket, which he sold in 1982.

[42] Rock, "Strategy vs. Tactics from a Venture Capitalist," pp. 63–67.

Exhibit 1.8
Myths about Entrepreneurs

Myth 1 — Entrepreneurs are born, not made.

Reality — While entrepreneurs are born with certain native intelligence, a flair for creating, and energy, by themselves these talents are like unmolded clay or an unpainted canvas. The making of an entrepreneur occurs by accumulating the relevant skills, know-how, experiences, and contacts over a period of years and includes large doses of self-development. The creative capacity to envision and then pursue an opportunity is a direct descendent of at least 10 or more years of experience that lead to pattern recognition.

Myth 2 — Anyone can start a business.

Reality — Entrepreneurs who recognize the difference between an idea and an opportunity, and who think big enough, start businesses that have a better chance of succeeding. Luck, to the extent it is involved, requires good preparation. And the easiest part is starting up. What is hardest is surviving, sustaining, and building a venture so its founders can realize a "harvest." Perhaps only one in 10 to 20 new businesses that survive five years or more result in a capital gain for the founders.

Myth 3 — Entrepreneurs are gamblers.

Reality — Successful entrepreneurs take very careful, calculated risks. They try to influence the odds, often by getting others to share risk with them and by avoiding or minimizing risks if they have the choice. Often they slice up the risk into smaller, quite digestible pieces; only then do they commit the time or resources to determine if that piece will work. They do not deliberately seek to take more risk or to take unnecessary risk, nor do they shy away from unavoidable risk.

Myth 4 — Entrepreneurs want the whole show to themselves.

Reality — Owning and running the whole show effectively puts a ceiling on growth. Solo entrepreneurs usually make a living. It is extremely difficult to grow a higher potential venture by working single-handedly. Higher potential entrepreneurs build a team, an organization, and a company. Besides, 100 percent of nothing is nothing, so, rather than taking a large piece of the pie, they work to make the pie bigger.

Myth 5 — Entrepreneurs are their own bosses and completely independent.

Reality — Entrepreneurs are far from independent and have to serve many masters and constituencies. These stakeholders include partners, investors, customers, suppliers, creditors, employees, families, and those involved in social and community obligations. Entrepreneurs, however, can make free choices of whether, when, and which they care to respond to. It is extremely difficult, and rare, to build a business beyond $1 million to $2 million in sales single-handedly.

Myth 6 — Entrepreneurs work longer and harder than managers in big companies.

Reality — There is no evidence that all entrepreneurs work more than their corporate counterparts. Some do, some do not. Some actually report that they work less.

Myth 7 — Entrepreneurs experience a great deal of stress and pay a high price.

Reality — No doubt about it: Being an entrepreneur is stressful and demanding. But, there is no evidence that it is any more stressful than numerous other highly demanding professional roles, and entrepreneurs find their jobs more satisfying. They have a high sense of accomplishment, are healthier, and are much less likely to retire than those who work for others. Three times as many entrepreneurs as corporate managers said they plan never to retire.

Exhibit 1.8 *(concluded)*

Myth 8 — Starting a business is risky and often ends in failure.

Reality — Talented and experienced entrepreneurs — because they pursue attractive opportunities and are able to attract the right people and necessary financial and other resources to make the venture work — often head successful ventures. Further, businesses fail, but entrepreneurs do not. Failure is often the fire that tempers the steel of an entrepreneur's learning experience and street savvy.

Myth 9 — Money is the most important start-up ingredient.

Reality — If the other pieces and talents are there, the money will follow; but it does not follow that, if an entrepreneur has enough money, he or she will succeed. Money is one of the least important ingredients in new venture success. Money is to the entrepreneur what the paint and brush is to the artist — an inert tool, which, in the right hands, can create marvels. Money is also a way of keeping score, rather than just an end by itself. Entrepreneurs thrive on the thrill of the chase; and, time and again, even after he or she has made a few million dollars or more, an entrepreneur will work incessantly on a new vision to build another company.

Myth 10 — Entrepreneurs should be young and energetic.

Reality — While these qualities may help, age is no barrier. The average age of entrepreneurs starting high potential businesses is in the mid-30s, and there are numerous examples of entrepreneurs starting businesses in their 60s. What is critical is possessing the relevant know-how, experience, and contacts that greatly facilitate recognizing and pursuing an opportunity.

Myth 11 — Entrepreneurs are motivated solely by the quest for the almighty dollar.

Reality — Entrepreneurs seeking high potential ventures are more driven by building enterprises and realizing long-term capital gains than by instant gratification through high salaries and perks. A sense of personal achievement and accomplishment, feeling in control of their own destinies, and realizing their vision and dreams are also powerful motivators. Money is viewed as a tool and a way of keeping score.

Myth 12 — Entrepreneurs seek power and control over others.

Reality — Successful entrepreneurs are driven by the quest for responsibility, achievement, and results, rather than for power for its own sake. They thrive on a sense of accomplishment and of outperforming the competition, rather than a personal need for power expressed by dominating and controlling others. By virtue of their accomplishments, they may be powerful and influential, but these are more by-products of the entrepreneurial process than a driving force behind it.

Myth 13 — If an entrepreneur is talented, success will happen in a year or two.

Reality — An old maxim among venture capitalists says it all: The lemons ripen in two and a half years, but the pearls take seven or eight. Rarely is a new business established solidly in less than three or four years.

Myth 14 — Any entrepreneur with a good idea can raise venture capital.

Reality — Of the ventures of entrepreneurs with good ideas who seek out venture capital, only 1 to 3 out of 100 are funded.

Myth 15 — If an entrepreneur has enough start-up capital, he or she can't miss.

Reality — The opposite is often true; that is, too much money at the outset often creates euphoria and a spoiled-child syndrome. The accompanying lack of discipline and impulsive spending usually leads to serious problems and to failure.

same marketplace, technology, or industry they have been working in.[43] Others have found that founders are likely to have from 8 to 10 years of experience, and they are likely to be well-educated. It also appears that successful entrepreneurs have wide experience in products/markets and across functional areas.[44]

Studies also have shown that most successful entrepreneurs start companies in their 30s. One study of founders of high-tech companies on Route 128 in Boston from 1982 to 1984 showed that the average age of the founders was 40.

It has been found that entrepreneurs work both more and less than their counterparts in large organizations, that they have high degrees of satisfaction with their jobs, and that they are healthier.[45] Another study showed that nearly 21 percent of the founders were over 40 when they embarked on their entrepreneurial career, the majority were in their 30s, and just over one quarter did so by the time they were 25.

THE ENTREPRENEURIAL MIND[46]

What Successful Entrepreneurs Do

Most of the research about entrepreneurs has focused on the influences of genes, family, education, career experience, and so forth, but no psychological model has been supported. Successful entrepreneurs seem to be of both sexes and in as many sizes, shapes, colors, and descriptions imaginable. Perhaps, one Price–Babson College Fellow phrased it best when he said, "One does not want to overdo the personality stuff, but there is a certain ring to it."[47]

However, the real question is: *What do successful entrepreneurs do?* That is, how do they think, what actions do they initiate, and how do they go about starting and building businesses? It is the result that counts, and, by understanding the attitudes, behaviors, management competencies, experience, and know-how that contribute to entrepreneurial success, one has some useful benchmarks for gauging what to do and what to do differently.

Successful entrepreneurs share common attitudes and behaviors. They work hard and are driven by an intense commitment and determined perseverance; they see the cup half full, rather than half empty; they strive for integrity; they burn with the competitive desire to excel and win; they are dissatisfied with the status quo and seek opportunities to improve almost any situation they encounter; they use failure as a tool for learning and eschew perfection in favor of effectiveness; and they believe they can personally make an enormous difference in the final outcome of their ventures and their lives.

Those who have succeeded speak of these attitudes and behaviors time and again.[48] For example, two famous entrepreneurs have captured the intense commitment and determined perseverance of entrepreneurs. Wally Amos, famous for his chocolate chip cookies, said, "You can do anything you want to do."[49] And John Johnson of Johnson Publishing Company

---

[43] A good summary of some of these studies is provided by Robert H. Brockhaus, "The Psychology of the Entrepreneur," in *Encyclopedia of Entrepreneurship,* ed. C. Kent, D. Sexton, and K. Vesper (Englewood Cliffs, N. J.: Prentice-Hall, 1982), pp. 50–55.

[44] Over 65 studies in this area have been reported in *Frontiers of Entrepreneurship Research* (Babson Park, Mass.: Babson College) for the years 1981 through 1989.

[45] Stevenson, "Who Are the Harvard Self-Employed?" p. 233.

[46] See Jeffry A. Timmons, *The Entrepreneurial Mind* (Acton, Mass.: Brick House Publishing, 1989).

[47] Comment made during a presentation at the June 1987 Price–Babson College Fellows Program by Jerry W. Gustafson, Coleman–Fannie May Candies Professor of Entrepreneurship, Beloit College, at Babson College.

[48] See the excellent summary of a study of the first 21 inductees into Babson College's Academy of Distinguished Entrepreneurs by John A. Hornaday and Nancy Tieken, "Capturing Twenty-One Heffalumps," in *Frontiers of Entrepreneurship Research: 1983,* pp. 23–50.

[49] Made during a speech at his induction in 1982 into the Academy of Distinguished Entrepreneurs, Babson College.

Exhibit 1.9
Who Is the Entrepreneur?

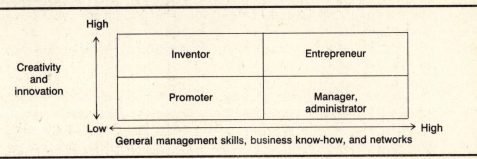

(publisher of *Ebony*) expressed it this way: "You need to think yourself out of a corner, meet needs, and never, never accept 'no' for an answer."[50]

It seems that entrepreneurs who succeed possess not only a creative and innovative flair and other attitudes and behaviors but also solid general management skills, business know-how, and sufficient contacts. *Exhibit 1.9* demonstrates this relationship. Inventors, noted for their creativity, often lack the necessary management skills and business know-how. Promoters usually lack serious general management and business skills and true creativity. Administrators govern, police, and ensure the smooth operation of the status quo; their management skills, while high, are tuned to efficiency as well, and creativity is usually not required. Although the management skills of the manager and the entrepreneur overlap, the former is more driven by conservation of resources and the latter is more opportunity-driven.[51]

Apprenticeship

However, during the past several years, studies about entrepreneurs have tended to confirm what practitioners have known all along: that some attitudes, behaviors, and know-how can in fact be acquired and that some of these attributes are more desirable than others.[52]

Increasingly, evidence from research about the career paths of entrepreneurs and the self-employed suggests that the role of experience and know-how is central in successful venture creation.[53] Evidence also suggests that success is linked to thoughtful preparation and planning.[54]

Most successful entrepreneurs follow a pattern of apprenticeship, where they prepare for becoming entrepreneurs by gaining the relevant business experiences needed from parents who are self-employed or through job experiences. They do not leave acquisition of experience to accident or osmosis. As entrepreneur Harvey "Chet" Krentzman has said, "Know what you know and what you *don't* know."

---

[50] Made during a speech at his induction in 1979 into the Academy of Distinguished Entrepreneurs, Babson College.

[51] Timmons, Muzyka, Stevenson, and Bygrave, "Opportunity Recognition: The Core of Entrepreneurship," pp. 42–49.

[52] See studies cited in footnote 44.

[53] Karl H. Vesper, "New Venture Ideas: Don't Overlook the Experience Factor," *Harvard Business Review,* reprinted in *Growing Concerns: Building and Managing the Smaller Business,* ed. D. E. Gumpert (New York: John Wiley & Sons, 1984), pp. 28–55.

[54] See Robert Ronstadt's and Howard Stevenson's studies reported in *Frontiers of Entrepreneurship Research: 1983,* ed. J. A. Hornaday et al. (Babson Park, Mass.: Babson College, 1983).

Role Models

Further, there is no more powerful teacher than a good example. Numerous studies show a strong connection between the presence of role models and the emergence of entrepreneurs.

For instance, one recent study showed that over half of those starting new businesses had parents who owned businesses.[55] The authors summarized it this way:

People who start companies are more likely to come from families in which their parents or close relatives were in business for themselves. These older people were examples or "models" for the children. Whether they were successful or not probably didn't matter. However, for the children growing up in such a family, the action of starting a new business seems possible—something they can do.

CASE—OUTDOOR SCENE, INC.*

Preparation Questions

1. What are the strengths and weaknesses of the entrepreneurs, individually and as a team?
2. What is the opportunity?
3. Would you invest in the entrepreneurs if you were convinced that the opportunity was sound, and why or why not?
4. What are the critical skills and resources necessary to succeed in the business?
5. What do you think the entrepreneurs should do and why?

OUTDOOR SCENE, INC.

In early 1976, at age 31, J. C. Egnew was employed as vice president of manufacturing by Wilderness Products, Inc., a large tent producer. He was responsible for the overall planning and administration of the company's manufacturing operations. The company's sales were about $12 million per year, and it employed over 350 people at three plants. Although the company was growing, Egnew began to encounter basic differences of opinion and philosophy with the owners and top management of the company, particularly over issues of new product development and expansion. Prompted by these differences, Egnew became increasingly intrigued with the possibility of starting his own tent manufacturing company. He discussed his ideas with a co-worker, John F. Moore, the sales service manager.

Wilderness Products had experienced substantial growth in unit volume and dollar sales, but Egnew was troubled about its apparent lack of concern for profits. Drawing from his business school training, he also observed other problems in the company:

There is not one page of formal planning. There is no real organization—everyone is just doing his own thing. And the techniques being used to manage the company aren't keeping up with the rate of growth. They may be appropriate for $1–2 million tent manufacturer, but not one doing $12 million.

There were still other problems with the way the company was being managed. As Egnew put it:

---

[55] Arnold Cooper and William Dunkelberg, "A New Look at Business Entry" (San Mateo, Calif.: National Federation of Independent Businesses, March 1984).

* Copyright © 1986 by Jeffry A. Timmons; for discussion purposes only, not to reflect either effective or ineffective entrepreneurial practices.

If I ask the production manager, the sales manager, and the president what our capacity is and for a sales forecast, I get three very different answers. The company is very sales oriented in a seller's market. So we fill up with orders which required too much overtime to produce, and we end up with missed delivery schedules and unprofitable sales. It has gotten to the point where I honestly feel that something is way out of balance.

During the three years since joining Wilderness Products, Egnew had gained experience in and knowledge of the tent manufacturing industry. He felt that there was a substantial national market for tents and that his current employer was not competing as effectively as it could. In particular, he felt that there was significant potential to manufacture and market a line of camping tents and accessories having broad-based consumer appeal. He felt that such trends as more discretionary income and more leisure time were favorably affecting consumer demand for tents. Further, a U.S. Department of the Interior study estimated that Americans went camping 97 million times a year; it also predicted that camping frequency would increase by more than twice the rate of population growth.[1] Also, federal and state governments were making more public land accessible for public recreation, and many private firms were entering the campground business.[2]

Egnew's operating experience in the industry was confirming the impact of these trends. During the previous four years, for example, the six major tent manufacturers had been continually delinquent to customers because they were unable to keep pace with the growing market. Poor deliveries prevailed in this period, while production by the "big six" was expanding at an annual rate of 20 percent. Egnew also knew that strong retail demand had led to a severe erosion of product quality as a result of haphazard industry expansion.

In response to the situation, Egnew decided to try to convince the management that a coordinated plan was needed to pull the business together and make it profitable. During evenings and weekends he and Moore drew up what they considered a sensible long-range plan, and Egnew then discussed the plan with his employer. "I got them to agree to it, but in six months it all went out the window." He concluded: "I didn't have what it takes to convince them to run the business the way I wanted to."

This left him with what he felt were three principal alternatives:

1. Quit and get another job.
2. Get the president fired.
3. Start his own tent manufacturing company.

Egnew had little net worth and only three years in the business. He was married and had a son. His salary of $26,000 per year provided him with a comfortable standard of living. He wondered whether he wasn't kidding himself, whether it was realistic to go out on his own, and how he might pursue the idea since he had never started a company previously.

Determined to resolve their future, Egnew and Moore agreed to meet again for an entire weekend to decide on a strategy.

Personal Backgrounds

J. C. Egnew.   J. C. Egnew was born and raised in Indiana. He recalled some of his attitudes, which he attributed to his upbringing:

---

[1] U.S. Department of the Interior, *Outdoor Recreation Trends* (Washington, D.C.: U.S. Government Printing Office, 1967).
[2] Clayne R. Jensen, *Outdoor Recreation in America* (Minneapolis: Burgess, 1970), chap. 4.

My dad was a teacher, but a farmer at heart. I remember his thoroughness—"if you're going to do something, do it well." He believed in sticking with things. Both my parents developed in me a high regard for my individual freedom.

This independence apparently also included emancipation from the classroom and attraction to the world of work and basketball. By the time Egnew was 16 he was working full-time after school. He noted, "I learned a sense of self-responsibility and how to support myself. I made most of my own decisions concerning school and other things. I found work a lot more interesting than school."

In addition to working full-time in high school, J. C. also played basketball. His schoolwork suffered. "I always did what I had to do to get by, and I wasn't sure I wanted to go to college." He graduated from high school 401st out of a class of 439 students.

Following graduation from high school, J. C. entered the University of Evansville, where he received his bachelor of science in mechanical engineering in 1967. He described himself as a loner during college, without a large circle of friends. He became very interested in the cooperative education program, which allowed students to alternate between full-time schooling and work. During co-op he worked for NASA in Huntsville, Alabama, rising from the rank of GS-3 to GS-5 in two years. He graduated in the lower third of his class after an erratic academic performance that included both dean's list and probation. He summed it up: "I hated to take tests, and I was not a crammer."

After graduation he joined NASA in Huntsville as a flight systems test engineer, GS-7, and rose to GS-9 by July 1969. He served as lead test engineer responsible for the conduct of hardware development test programs. This included coordinating and directing about 20 engineers and technicians in formulating, conducting, and evaluating tests and test results. In July 1969, he was promoted to production test manager for NASA and moved to Bay St. Louis, Mississippi. His responsibilities included the supervision of flight vehicle tests. By August 1972, he had risen to GS-13. He commented on his work:

I enjoyed getting involved in things where there was no established solution. I liked to find the solutions. I especially liked the new position since it involved work that hadn't been done before. But in about two years most of the problems were solved and it got boring. So I decided to return to school for my master's in industrial management at the University of Tennessee, Knoxville.

John F. Moore.   John Moore was born and raised in Columbus, Ohio, one of two sons of a navy career officer who had worked his way up through the ranks. Though his father ran the house "like the commander of a ship," he was quite permissive with his two sons. "He taught us right from wrong. But what he really gave me was the motivation to do things on my own."

In high school John Moore was captain of the swimming, baseball, and football teams. At the same time he worked about 15 hours a week after school in a shoe store, and each summer he worked full-time paving driveways. He graduated in the lower third of his high school class, noting that "I did what I had to do to stay eligible and graduate." His considerable athletic promise earned him a full baseball scholarship to Ohio State University. The lure of fraternity life, particularly its social activities, detracted further from his less than enthusiastic interest in academics. Repeated academic probation caused him to lose his scholarship, so he entered the navy in April 1965. He was honorably discharged in April 1969.

In July 1969, Moore joined North American Rockwell Corporation as a materials requirements analyst, and in early 1972 he became supervisor in the Support Operations Division. In September 1972, he returned to college and was met with greater academic success: "Once I went back, I got A's and B's and even won an honors medal in physics."

Upon graduating in June 1974 with a B.S. in industrial management from the University of Tennessee, Knoxville, Moore returned to North American Rockwell for three months as logistics staff assistant in Bay St. Louis, Mississippi. In October 1974, after much urging by J. C. Egnew, he joined Wilderness Products, Inc., as sales service manager.

At Wilderness, he was responsible for customer service, inventory control, transportation, and warehouse activities. This included factory sales to key "house accounts," developing product mix and initiating marketing plans, supervising 30 employees in office areas and transportation and warehousing facilities, and purchasing some accessory products and equipment.

Discussions between Egnew and Moore

In early 1976, Egnew and Moore began a series of thoughtful discussions about what their future might hold. The first topic they raised was a very basic one: the reasons that each of them had for wanting to start his own business.

Egnew felt:

As long as my professional talents are being challenged, I have an opportunity to grow, and the rewards for my contributions are commensurate with the marketplace, I'm happy. Everybody likes to have their future tied to a winner. Nobody likes to be in a losing operation. I have begun to look at alternatives. I see tremendous opportunities in the tent business that aren't being properly taken care of. I feel that there is room for another firm. Now I'm trying to decide what to do next.

I never really think about the chance to make a big killing. If I'm on target in 5, 8, or 10 years, at the end of that time I'll be able to do what I want to do. I'll have a new sense of freedom, a sense of independence to do my own thing. Ownership and growth will provide the real rewards. We all dream about making something happen. If you succeed in building your own business, there's no question about who's responsible.

Moore shared similar views:

J. C. is the only one at Wilderness doing anything with any principles in mind or using what we learned in school instead of just shooting from the hip. If we could get organized, we could do it. I feel that I have been exposed to the business. It is dynamic, something new every day, and I like this. I am excited by the challenge of doing it ourselves. I keep thinking to myself, we can do it!

In addition to challenge, both men appreciated the need to make a total commitment to the business if it was to be a success. Egnew believed:

The commitment to go into business is made when you sever whatever ties you have and say "my livelihood is dependent on this enterprise"—that's when the commitment is made. If the two or three people aren't willing to use most of their key assets for the business, then I wouldn't touch them. So the commitment is also shown when you get everybody to put their bucks in. That's when it all starts.

He also believed that starting salaries were a useful measure of commitment and that investors were right to expect personal and financial commitment from the key team members:

Starting salaries should be lean. A new business needs every possible advantage it can find. If key personnel won't make sacrifices up front, then they won't make them when it gets tough. You should be prepared to make a substantial personal commitment to your business if you haven't already done so. I would be naive to think, "Well, I have this fine educational background, and I have some pretty relevant experience—after all, I'm putting my professional reputation on the line here. What else can you ask for?" "But if the milk turns sour," an investor would point out, "all you have to do is move to some place as far away as southwest Texas and get a 10 or 20 percent salary increase in a new job and you're off and running again, while we're sitting here holding all the empty baskets." That's when it really hit me. If I were investing money in a new business and the two or three key people weren't able to make a significant commitment based on their personal assets, then I sure wouldn't be willing to commit a dime to them. That's the commitment that makes you work a little bit harder and makes you determined that you're going to find a way to succeed. Any investor with sense is going to look for this kind of commitment.

Risks and Rewards

Next, Egnew and Moore discussed their attitudes about risks and rewards in starting a new business. Egnew stated:

If we were to start our own business, I wouldn't waste much time thinking about "what if it doesn't work out?" My thinking is positive. If we can ever afford to blow something, now is the time—we are young and have no heavy debts. The idea or dream of having your own business is one many people have, and here is our opportunity. We are frustrated with the way things are going at Wilderness; the opportunity for a better way to do things looks real; and we have a chance to build something.

Moore's comments reflected his confidence in Egnew's optimism:

If we decide to go ahead, I won't have time to worry or think about not making it. I don't feel that it's that much of a risk when we sit here talking about it, I am so hyped up thinking it could work. I guess if we'd both been fired from Wilderness and had to start our own company, I would do a bit more worrying. Whenever I am ready to throw in the towel, J. C. keeps the momentum going. It looks like an opportunity to make a lot of money. Wilderness went public in 1972, and one owner with 7 percent of the stock made $600,000. I feel J. C. has it all together, more than any other person I've ever met. I have tremendous respect for him. I am willing to gamble on a good guy, and therefore I feel it is a good gamble.

Taking the Plunge—Or Not

By spring 1976, J. C. Egnew and John F. Moore had continued to investigate the idea of starting their own tent manufacturing business. Recognizing the difficulties of starting a new venture and their own inexperience in business, they began to assess their entrepreneurial and management strengths and weaknesses, and to analyze the feasibility of the new business idea. Time was also becoming a serious factor and Egnew and Moore were faced with a serious dilemma: how to start their business in time to take advantage of the 1977 spring market.

From their previous business training, both Egnew and Moore were aware of the high failure rates of new businesses. Egnew expressed his opinions on this issue:

Most new companies begin with an idea for a new product or service. Few of them survive, and rarely, if ever, does one excel on the strength of the product alone. You have to put it all together. You can't just have a great idea that's better than anything on the market and have a winner. You also need an organization and a plan. Getting the movement going is the hardest thing. That's what makes a start-up so risky. All these things have to get moving at the same time—it's like the inertia of a large train. You've got to devote a lot of energy just to get things going.

Part of the process of "taking the plunge" included assessing the opportunity. Although committed to the venture psychologically, they did not want to launch a venture that had a poor chance of succeeding. A principal aim of their initial work was to determine whether any major flaws existed in their idea and to decide whether the business was worth pursuing. *Exhibit A* summarizes the industry and financial data Egnew and Moore have gathered to investigate the potential for their new tent manufacturing business.

More Dilemmas

Their preliminary investigation provided Egnew and Moore with a substantial amount of data. Since they began their investigation, several more weeks had passed. They wondered whether their idea was worth pursuing.

Some new developments of which they had been previously unaware emerged from their investigations. First, they found that the industry was "closed to outsiders," making it very difficult to get useful market information. Second, they found that the sales of the major canvas suppliers for tents had been declining steadily in recent years. Third, they discovered, to their surprise, that no new firms had entered the tent business in the past five to six years, in spite of what they estimated as a growing, seller's market. Further, they learned that a handful of small tent manufacturers had actually failed and gone out of business during this period. (See *Exhibit A*.)

Exhibit A

June 10, 1976

To: John Cohen

From: J. C. Egnew
 John Moore

Re: Feasibility Information for a New Tent Manufacturing Company

The Industry

The significant tent-producing companies in the continental United States are ranked below, based on 1976 sales:

Kellwood Company:	
Sears	$10,000,000
Wentzel	8,000,000
	18,000,000
Hettrick (Olin Corporation)	15,000,000
Wilderness Products	10,000,000
National Canvas Products	7,000,000
Coleman	4,000,000
Eureka Tent and Awning	3,000,000
Other	3,000,000
Total	$60,000,000

The Thomas Register lists a good many other firms in the tent business. Most of these firms are small mom 'n' pop operations consisting of those who "custom-produce" (make to order) awnings and tents and other canvas items such as "show tents" and circus-type carnival tents. Others are primarily in the repair business. Some of these have a national market, while others have a regional market only.

Approximately 10 percent of this total tent market consists of tents designed for specific uses (e.g., mountain climbing and backpacking). This factor will limit the general tent market potential for the coming year to $54 million (not accounting for an anticipated 1977 growth factor of 20 percent in the market as a whole).

Following is an estimated geographic breakdown of the national tent market that is based on observed industry sales patterns:

	Percent	
New England States	22%	
Metropolitan New York City	13	
Mideast (New York, Pennsylvania)	8	
Midwest (Corn Belt, Plains)	26	
Central Atlantic Coast	4	
Southeast	9	
Southwest	6	
Far West (Coastal)	8	
Other	4	
Total	100%	($60,000,000)

It has been an industry practice for retailers to start taking deliveries of tents after January 1, since tents are not usually "Christmas" items. To encourage early order commitments and deliveries, the industry has been allowing "net April 1st" payment terms on tents delivered prior to April. Because delivery service has been poor in the past, it is not unusual for customers to place orders in October and November for tents desired in March or April. Projected sales trends by month for the total tent market follow:

Month	Percent of Annual Sales
January	16%
February	21
March	15
April	11
May	10
June	6
July	4
August	2
September	3
October	3
November	4
December	5
Total	100%

The Competition

Listed below is a comparison of prices among three of the industry leaders for some of the main types of tents available to the consumer. Profit margins do not vary significantly from one type of tent to another.

Prices of the Major Products for Three Major Competitors (1976 published prices)

Style	Size	Wilderness	Hettrick	National
Cabin	7 × 7	$30.80	$ —	$33.02
	8 × 10	40.00	47.35	50.58
	9 × 12	47.95	55.75	58.48
	10 × 16	55.95	65.90	—
Cabin-screen	10 × 16	69.75	76.80	—
Umbrella	7 × 7	21.90	21.00	23.82
	9 × 9	32.25	36.80	41.12
Canopy	10 × 10	12.75	—	15.71
	12 × 12	15.45	15.75	18.40
Screenhouse	10 × 10	28.95	33.65	—
Pup tent	5 × 7	4.79	4.75	5.18
	5 × 7	10.80	10.50	10.00
Jvc. umbrella	7 × 7	8.75	9.25	11.16
Tri. awning	8 × 10	13.75	15.80	17.20
	8 × 12	16.35	18.20	18.60

— means not offered by that competitor.

All prices listed are for the 1976 season and are expected to increase from 10 percent to 12 percent on the average for the upcoming 1977 season.

The next table presents a comparison of the number of models of each type of tent produced by some of the leading manufacturers.

Comparison of the Number of Models* Offered by Five Major Tent Producers

Company	Cabin	Umbrella	Play	Canopy and Screen	Awnings	Nylon	Other
Wilderness:							
Regular	20	4	5	8	9	6	2
Special	32	3	2	9	2	—	—
Hettrick:							
Regular	12	4	9	7	10	2	6
National	9	6	17	6	14	1	4
Coleman	18	2	2	3	—	1	13
Eureka	9	9	14	11	31	7	13

* Includes ice tents, "flies," wind curtains, etc.

Financial Considerations

The following is a summary of industry practices relating to the manufacture and sale of tents.

Accounts receivable:	75 percent of all sales prior to April 1 billing. Further, 50 percent of the accounts will be paid on or before April 1, 35 percent will be 30 days past due, 10 percent will be 60 days past due, and 5 percent will be 90 or more days past due when paid.
Inventories:	Monthly inventories will peak in February and be at a minimum level in June.
Work in process:	20 percent of monthly production.
Finished goods:	9.3 percent of monthly sales.
Accounts payable:	80 percent of monthly purchases.
Cost of goods sold:	76 percent of sales.
Gross profit:	24 percent of sales.
General, selling, and administration:	Industry average is 15 percent of sales.

EXERCISE — TAKE AN ENTREPRENEUR TO DINNER

Over the years, students have found it valuable to interview entrepreneurs who have, within the past 5 to 10 years, started firms whose sales now exceed $1 million and which are profitable. Through such an interview, you can gain insight into an entrepreneur's reasons, strategies, approaches, and motivations for starting and owning a business.

Gathering information through interviewing is a valuable skill to practice. You can learn a great deal in a short time through interviewing—if you prepare thoughtfully and thoroughly.

The Take an Entrepreneur to Dinner Exercise has been used by students to interview successful entrepreneurs. While there is no right way to structure an interview, the interview in the exercise has merit because it is chronological and it has been tested successfully on many occasions.

EXERCISE
TAKE AN ENTREPRENEUR TO DINNER

STEP 1: CONTACT THE PERSON YOU HAVE SELECTED AND MAKE AN APPOINTMENT. Be sure to explain why you want the appointment and to give a realistic estimate of how much time you will need.

STEP 2: IDENTIFY SPECIFIC QUESTIONS YOU WOULD LIKE TO HAVE ANSWERED AND THE GENERAL AREAS ABOUT WHICH YOU WOULD LIKE INFORMATION. (SEE SUGGESTED INTERVIEW IN **STEP 3.**) Using a combination of open-ended questions, such as general questions about how the entrepreneur got started, what happened next, and so forth, and closed-ended questions, such as specific questions about what his or her goals were, if he or she had to find partners, and so forth, will help to keep the interview focused and yet allow for unexpected comments and insights.

STEP 3: CONDUCT THE INTERVIEW. If *both* you and the person you are interviewing are comfortable, using a small tape recorder during the interview can be of great help to you later. Remember, too, that you most likely will learn more if you are an "interested listener."

Interview

Questions for Gathering Information

- Would you tell me about yourself before you started your first venture:

  - Were your parents, relatives, or close friends entrepreneurial? How so?

  - Did you have any other role models?

  - What was your education/military experience? In hindsight, was it helpful? In what specific ways?

  - What was your previous work experience? Was it helpful? What particular "chunks of experience" were especially valuable or irrelevant?

  - In particular, did you have any sales or marketing experience? How important was it or a lack of it to starting your company?

- How did you start your venture:

  - How did you spot the opportunity? How did it surface?

  - What were your goals? What were your lifestyle or other personal requirements? How did you fit these together?

  - How did you evaluate the opportunity in terms of: the critical elements for success? The competition? The market?

  - Did you find or have partners? What kind of planning did you do? What kind of financing did you have?

  - Did you have a start-up business plan of any kind? Please tell me about it.

  - How much time did it take from conception to the first day of business? How many hours a day did you spend working on it?

— How much capital did it take? How long did it take to reach a positive cash flow and break-even sales volume? If you did not have enough money at the time, what were some ways in which you "bootstrapped" the venture (i.e., bartering, borrowing, and the like). Tell me about the pressures and crises during that early survival period.

— What outside help did you get? Did you have experienced advisors? Lawyers? Accountants? Tax experts? Patent experts? How did you develop these networks and how long did it take?

— What was your family situation at the time?

— What did you perceive to be your own strengths? Weaknesses?

— What did you perceive to be the strengths of your venture? Weaknesses?

— What was your most triumphant moment? Your worst moment?

— Did you want to have partners or do it solo? Why?

■ Once you got going, then:

— What were the most difficult gaps to fill and problems to solve as you began to grow rapidly?

— When you looked for key people as partners, advisors, or managers, were there any personal attributes or attitudes you were especially seeking because you knew they would fit with you and were important to success? How did you find them?

— Are there any attributes among partners and advisors that you would definitely try to avoid?

— Have things become more predictable? Or less?

— Do you spend more/same/less time with your business now than in the early years?

— Do you feel more managerial and less entrepreneurial now?

— In terms of the future, do you plan to harvest? To maintain? To expand?

— Do you plan ever to retire? Would you explain.

— Have your goals changed? Have you met them?

— Has your family situation changed?

Questions for Concluding (choose one)

■ What do you consider your most valuable asset—the thing that enabled you to "make it"?

■ If you had it to do over again, would you do it again, in the same way?

- Looking back, what do you feel are the most critical concepts, skills, attitudes, and know-how you needed to get your company started and grown to where it is today? What will be needed for the next five years? To what extent can any of these be learned?

- Some people say there is a lot of stress being an entrepreneur. What have you experienced? How would you say it compares with other "hot seat" jobs, such as the head of a big company or a partner in a large law, consulting, or accounting firm?

- What are the things that you find personally rewarding and satisfying as an entrepreneur? What have been the rewards, risks, and trade-offs?

- Who should try to be an entrepreneur? Can you give me any ideas there?

- What advice would you give an aspiring entrepreneur? Could you suggest the three most important "lessons" you have learned? How can I learn them while minimizing the tuition?

STEP 4: EVALUATE WHAT YOU HAVE LEARNED.   Write down the information you have gathered in some form that will be helpful to you later on. Be as specific as you can. Jotting down direct quotes is more effective than statements such as "highly motivated individual." And, be sure to make a note of what you did *not* find out.

STEP 5: WRITE A THANK YOU NOTE.   This is more than a courtesy; it will also help the entrepreneur to remember you favorably should you want to follow up on the interview.

New Venture Ideas

Nothing is more dangerous than an idea, when it's the only one we have.

Alain Emile Chartier

RESULTS EXPECTED

At the conclusion of the chapter, you will have:

1. Examined the role of ideas in entrepreneurship.
2. Discussed the creative process and how experience and trial-and-error iteration can aid in pattern recognition.
3. Examined ways to enhance creativity and its role in the development of ideas.
4. Identified some source for locating new business ideas.
5. Analyzed the Halsey & Halsey, Inc., case.
6. Generated some new venture ideas using the Idea Generation Exercise.

THE ROLE OF IDEAS

Ideas As Tools

It is worth emphasizing again that *a good idea is nothing more than a tool in the hands of an entrepreneur.* Finding a good idea is the *first* step in the task of converting an entrepreneur's creativity into an opportunity.

The importance of the idea is most often overrated, usually at the expense of underemphasizing the need for products, or services, or both, which can be sold in enough quantity to real customers.

Further, the new business that simply bursts from a flash of brilliance is rare. What is usually necessary is a series of trial-and-error iterations, or repetitions, before a crude and promising product or service fits with what the customer is really willing to pay for. After all, Howard Head made 40 different metal skis before he finally made 1 which worked consistently.

In fact, with surprising frequency, major businesses are built around totally different products than those originally envisioned. Consider these examples:

- F. Leland Strange, the founder and president of Quadram, a maker of graphics and communications boards and other boards for microcomputers, told the story of how he developed his marketing idea into a company with $100 million in sales in three years.[1] He stated that he had developed a business plan to launch his company, and the company even hit projected revenues for the first two years. He noted, however, that success was achieved with completely *different* products than those in the original plan.

[1] Keynote address at the 1984 Babson Entrepreneurship Research Conference, cosponsored by the School of Management, Georgia Institute of Technology, April 23–25, 1984, Atlanta, Georgia.

- Polaroid Corporation was founded with a product based on the principle of polarizing light waves, a discovery by Dr. Land that he patented. Polarized head lamps, it was reasoned, would have the compelling safety feature of reducing head-on collisions caused at night by the "blinding" by oncoming lights. Conceivably, such polarized lamps could be installed by car manufacturers in every vehicle manufactured. However, the company grew to its present $2 billion-plus size through a quite different application of the original technology—instant photography.
- IBM began in the wire and cable business and later expanded to time clocks. Sales in the 1920s were only a few million dollars a year. Its successful mainframe computer business and then its successful personal computer business emerged much later.

The Great Mousetrap Fallacy

Perhaps no one did a greater disservice to generations of would-be entrepreneurs than Ralph Waldo Emerson in his oft-quoted line:

If a man can make a better mousetrap than his neighbor, though he builds his house in the woods the world will make a beaten path to his door.

What can be called the "great mousetrap fallacy" was thus spawned. Indeed, it is often assumed that success is possible if an entrepreneur can just come up with a new idea. And, in today's changing world, if the idea has anything to do with technology, success is certain—or so it would seem.

The truth of the matter is that ideas are inert and, for all practical purposes, worthless. Further, the flow of ideas is really quite phenomenal. Venture capital investors, for instance, during the investing boom of the 1980s, received as many as 100 to 200 proposals and business plans each month. Only 1 to 3 percent of these actually received financing, however.

Yet, the fallacy persists despite the lessons of practical experience noted long ago in the insightful reply to Emerson by O. B. Winters:

The manufacturer who waits for the world to beat a path to his door is a great optimist. But the manufacturer who shows this "mousetrap" to the world keeps the smoke coming out his chimney.

Contributors to the Fallacy

One cannot blame it all on Ralph Waldo Emerson. There are several reasons for the perpetuation of the fallacy.

One is the portrayal in oversimplified accounts of the ease and genius with which such ventures as Xerox, IBM, and Polaroid have made their founders wealthy. Unfortunately, these exceptions do not provide a useful rule to guide aspiring entrepreneurs.

Another is that inventors seem particularly prone to mousetrap myopia. Perhaps they are, like Emerson was, substantially sheltered in viewpoint and experience from the tough, competitive realities of the business world. Consequently, they underestimate, if not seriously downgrade, the importance of what it takes to make a business succeed. Frankly, inventing and brainstorming may probably be a lot more fun than the careful and diligent observation, investigation, and nurturing of customers that are often required to sell a product or service.

Contributing also to the great mousetrap fallacy is the tremendous psychological ownership attached to an invention or, later, to a new product. This attachment is different from attachment to a business. The intense and highly involved personal identity and commitment to an invention or new "widget" tends to weaken, or preclude entirely, realistic assessment of the other crucial aspects of the business. While an intense level of psychological ownership and involvement is certainly a prerequisite for creating a new business, the fatal flaw in attachment to an invention or product is the narrowness of its focus. The focal point needs to be the building of the business, rather than just one aspect of it, the idea.

Another source of mousetrap myopia lies in a technical and scientific orientation; that is, a desire to do it better. A good illustration of this is the experience of a Canadian entrepreneur who founded, with his brother, a company to manufacture truck seats. The entrepreneur's brother had developed a new seat for trucks that was a definite improvement over other seats. The entrepreneur knew he could profitably sell the seat his brother had designed, and they did so. When they needed more manufacturing capacity, one brother was not as interested in manufacturing more of the first seat as he was in the several ideas he had on how to improve the seat. The first brother stated, "If I had listened to him, we probably would be a small custom shop today, or out of business. Instead, we concentrated on making seats that would sell at a profit, rather than just making a better and better seat. Our company has several million dollars of sales today and is profitable."

The Best Idea

Consider the following examples, which drive the point home that having the best technology or idea often does not make the critical difference in success:

- UNIVAC had the early elegance and technology lead over IBM in computers, but it was never able to seize the emerging, significant opportunities in the computer industry.
- In 1967 and 1968, a lead investor, Fred Adler, received over 50 business plans from entrepreneurs who proposed to start minicomputer firms. Several minicomputer companies were started at that time, and several of the firms actually had a better idea in the form of more advanced technology than the one that most attracted Adler's attention. Data General's lead entrepreneur and his team had an entrepreneurial flair and market focus, which Adler bet on.[2] In 1988, the company had sales of $1.3 billion.
- In 1969, the then-fledgling Cullinet, Inc., raised $500,000 in the then-hot new issues market. Two years later, the firm had spent this initial capital, and, according to its founder, John Cullinane, still had a payroll of $8,500 to meet. Cullinane said the money had been spent unwisely through "programmer anarchy." He turned the company around by firing his programmers since, he said, they did not understand what happiness was. "Happiness," Cullinane said, "is a satisfied customer."[3] He then developed customer-anchored software products and a plan for growth that led to a substantial venture capital investment during a lean time for venture capital.
- Finally, Lotus and its product, Lotus 1-2-3, the first integrated package for the personal computer to include spreadsheet, graphics, and database management capabilities, is a good example. Critics and reviewers have since reported that some new software products are indeed more elegant and sophisticated than Lotus 1-2-3, but new entrants probably require $5 million and up to fund the marketing necessary to launch new software products and gain attention and distribution in this tumultuous marketplace.

[2] The story of the entrepreneurial culture at Data General was told in a best-seller by Tracy Kidder, *The Soul of a New Machine* (Boston: Little, Brown, 1981).

[3] Speaking at his induction in 1984 into the Babson College Academy of Distinguished Entrepreneurs.

Being There First

Further, having the best idea first by no means is a guarantee of success. Again, just ask Adam Osborne, or Dan Bricklin, who was first with the spreadsheet software VisiCalc.

Also, unless having the best idea first also includes the capacity to preempt other competitors by capturing a significant share of the market or by erecting insurmountable barriers to entry, being there first can mean proving for the competition that the market exists to be snared.

PATTERN RECOGNITION

The Experience Factor

However, since ideas are building tools, one cannot build a successful business without them, as one could not build a house without a hammer. In this regard, experience is vital in looking at new venture ideas. Those with experience have been there before.

Time after time, experienced entrepreneurs exhibit an ability to recognize quickly a pattern—and an opportunity—while it is still taking shape. Herbert Simon of the Department of Psychology at Carnegie-Mellon University described the recognizing of patterns as a creative process that is not simply logical, linear, and additive; he says, rather, the process often is intuitive and inductive, involving the creative linking, or cross-association, of two or more in-depth "chunks" of experience, know-how, and contacts.[4] Simon contends that it takes 10 years or more for people to accumulate what he calls the "50,000 chunks" of experience, and so forth, that enable them to be highly creative and recognize patterns—familiar circumstances that can be translated from one place to another.

Thus, the process of sorting through ideas and recognizing a pattern also can be compared to the process of fitting pieces into a three-dimensional jigsaw puzzle. It is impossible to assemble such a puzzle by looking at it as a whole unit. Rather, one needs to see the relationships between and be able to fit together seemingly unrelated pieces before the whole is visible.

Recognizing ideas which can become entrepreneurial opportunities stems from a capacity to see what others do not—that one plus one equals three, or more. Consider the following examples of the common thread of pattern recognition and creating new businesses by linking knowledge in one field or marketplace with quite different technical, business, or marketing know-how:

- A middle manager employed by a larger company was on a plant tour of a small machinery manufacturer, a customer, in the Midwest. A machinist was mechanically cutting metal during a demonstration of a particular fabricating operation. Shockingly, the machinist accidentally sliced his hand in the cutting machine, removing two fingers. Instantly, the manager recognized that the application of new laser technology for this cutting operation was a significant business opportunity which would make it possible to eliminate such horrible accidents as he had just witnessed. He subsequently launched and built a multimillion-dollar company. Here linking the knowledge of the capabilities of lasers to an old, injury-prone metal-cutting technology yielded an opportunity.

- During travel throughout Europe, the eventual founders of Crate & Barrel frequently saw stylish and innovative products for the kitchen and home that were not yet available in the United States. When they returned home, the founders created Crate & Barrel to offer these products, for which market research had, in a sense, already been conducted

---

[4] Described in a working paper by Herbert A. Simon, "What We Know about the Creative Process," (Carnegie-Mellon University, 1984).

in the United States. This knowledge of consumer buying habits in one geographical region, Europe, was applied to a previously untapped consumer market in another country, the United States.

■ Howard Head had been an aeronautical design engineer working with new light metal alloys to build more efficient airfoils during World War II. Head transferred knowledge of metal bonding technology from the aircraft manufacturing business to a consumer product, metal skis, and then to another, tennis rackets. In the first case, although he had limited skiing experience, he had concluded that, if he could make a metal ski, there would be a significant market as a result of the limitations of wooden skis. His company dominated the ski industry for many years. In talking about his decision to develop the oversized Prince tennis racket after he saw a need for ball control among players learning tennis, Head said, "I saw the pattern again that had worked at Head Ski. . . . I had proven to myself before that you can take different technology and know-how and apply it to a solution in a new area."[5] He had set about learning enough about the physics of tennis rackets and surfaces and developed the Prince racket.

■ In Texas, a young entrepreneur launched a modular home sales business in the late 1970s. First, he parlayed experience as a loan officer with a large New York City bank into a job with a manufacturer of mobile and modular homes in Texas. This enabled him, over a three-year period, to learn the business and to understand the market opportunity. He then opened a sales location in a growing suburb about 25 miles from booming larger cities. By studying his competitors and conducting an analysis of how customers actually went about purchasing new modular homes, he spotted a pattern that meant opportunity. Customers usually shopped at three different locations, where they could see different models and price ranges before making a purchase decision. Since his market analysis showed there was room in the city for three or four such businesses, he opened two additional sites, each with a different name and with different but complementary lines. Within two years, despite record high interest rates, his business had nearly tripled to $17 million in annual sales, and his only competitor was planning to move.

Enhancing Creative Thinking

The creative thinking described above is of great value in recognizing opportunities, as well as other aspects of entrepreneurship.

The notion that creativity can be learned or enhanced holds important implications for entrepreneurs who need to be creative in their thinking.

Most people can certainly spot creative flair. Children seem to have it, and many seem to lose it. Several studies suggest that creativity actually peaks around the first grade because a person's life tends to become increasingly structured and defined by others and by institutions. Further, the development in school of intellectual discipline and rigor in thinking takes on greater importance than during the formative years, and most of our education beyond grade school stresses a logical, rational mode of orderly reasoning and thinking. Finally, social pressures may tend to be a taming influence on creativity.

There is evidence that one can enhance creative thinking in later years. Take, for instance, a group called Synectics of Cambridge, Massachusetts, one of the first organizations in the early 1950s to investigate systematically the process of creative thinking and to conduct training sessions in applying creative thinking to business. Underlying the Synectics approach to developing creativity were the following theories:[6]

---

[5] Keynote address at the first annual Entrepreneur's Night of UCLA Graduate School of Business, April 18, 1984, Westwood, California.

[6] William J. J. Gordon, *Synectics* (New York: Harper & Row, 1961), p. 6.

- The efficiency of a person's creative process can be markedly increased if he or she understands the psychological process by which the process operates.
- The emotional component in the creative process is more important than the intellectual, and the irrational more important than the rational.
- The emotional, irrational elements need to be understood in order to increase the probability of success in a problem-solving situation.

The author participated in one of these training sessions, and it became evident during the sessions that the methods did unlock the thinking process and yielded very imaginative solutions.

Two Interesting Approaches

Since the 1950s, a good deal has been learned about the workings of the human brain. Today, there is general agreement that the two sides of the brain process information in quite different ways.

The left side performs rational, logical functions, while the right side operates the intuitive and nonrational modes of thought. A person uses both sides, actually shifting from one mode to the other.

How to control modes of thought is of interest to entrepreneurs and they can, perhaps, draw on two interesting approaches.

In 1979, Betty Edwards, an art teacher, wrote a book on drawing that became very popular. In this book, she compared the characteristics of the left mode and the right mode, listed in *Exhibit 2.1*. She counselled her art students on how to foster the shift from one mode of thought to another:

Exhibit 2.1
Comparison of Left-Mode and Right-Mode Characteristics

L-Mode	R-Mode
Verbal: Using words to name, describe, define.	*Nonverbal:* Awareness of things, but minimal connection with words.
Analytic: Figuring things out step-by-step and part-by-part.	*Synthetic:* Putting things together to form wholes.
Symbolic: Using a symbol to *stand for* something. For example, the sign + stands for the process of addition.	*Concrete:* Relating to things as they are at the present moment.
Abstract: Taking out a small bit of information and using it to represent the whole thing.	*Analogic:* Seeing likenesses between things; understanding metaphoric relationships.
Temporal: Keeping track of time, sequencing one thing after another: Doing first things first, second things second, etc.	*Nontemporal:* Without a sense of time.
Rational: Drawing conclusions based on *reason* and *facts.*	*Nonrational:* Not requiring a basis of reason or facts; willingness to suspend judgment.
Digital: Using numbers as in counting.	*Spatial:* Seeing where things are in relation to other things, and how parts go together to form a whole.
Logical: Drawing conclusions based on logic: one thing following another in logical order—for example, a mathematical theorem or a well-stated argument.	*Intuitive:* Making leaps of insight, often based on incomplete patterns, hunches, feelings, or visual images.
Linear: Thinking in terms of linked ideas, one thought directly following another, often leading to a convergent conclusion.	*Holistic:* Seeing whole things all at once; perceiving the overall patterns and structures, often leading to divergent conclusions.

Source: Betty Edwards, *Drawing on the Right Side of the Brain* (Boston, Mass.: Houghton Mifflin, 1979), p. 40.

It's important that you experience the shift from one mode to the other—the shift from the ordinary verbal, analytic state to the spatial, nonverbal state. By setting up the conditions for this mental shift and experiencing the slightly different feeling it produces, you will be able to recognize and foster this state in yourself—a state in which you will be able to draw.[7]

The exercises she designed to help her art students shift from one mode to another are fun to try. (See Appendix VIII for a Vases and Faces Exercise.)

Another lighthearted but workable approach is taken by Roger von Oech in a book on creativity. He states there are 10 "mental locks" that interfere with creative thinking and suggests ways to unlock them. His creativity blockers are worth considering in the process of looking for the right idea:[8]

1. There is a right answer.
2. That's not logical.
3. Follow the rules.
4. Be practical.
5. Avoid ambiguity.
6. To err is wrong.
7. Play is frivolous.
8. That's not my area.
9. Don't be foolish.
10. I'm not creative.

Team Creativity

It seems teams of people can generate creativity that may not exist in a single individual. Continually, the creativity of a team of people is impressive, and comparable or better creative solutions to problems evolving from the collective interaction of a small group of people have been observed.

A good example of the creativity generated by using more than one head is that of a company founded by a Babson College graduate with little technical training. He teamed up with a talented inventor, and the entrepreneurial and business know-how of the founder complemented the creative and technical skills of the inventor. The result has been a rapidly growing multimillion-dollar venture in the field of video-based surgical equipment.

Students interested in exploring this further may want at this time to do the exercise called "Creative Squares" at the end of the chapter.

FINDING IDEAS

Ideas can come from a wide variety of sources, contacts, and experiences. Karl Vesper suggests, in addition to work experience, such potential sources as hobbies, social encounters, self-employment, moonlighting, and deliberate search.[9]

Suggested below are some sources of and places to find new ideas:[10]

- ■ *Existing businesses.* Purchasing an on-going business is an excellent way to find a new business idea. Such a route to a new venture can save time and money and can reduce risk as well. Investment bankers and business brokers are knowledgeable about

---

[7] Betty Edwards, *Drawing on the Right Side of the Brain* (Boston: Houghton Mifflin, 1979).

[8] Roger von Oech, *A Whack on the Side of the Head* (New York: Warner Books, 1983).

[9] Karl H. Vesper, *New Venture Strategies* (Englewood Cliffs, N.J.: Prentice-Hall, 1980), chap. 5.

[10] See also David E. Gumpert and Jeffry A. Timmons, *The Encyclopedia of Small Business Resources* (New York: Harper & Row, 1984).

businesses for sale, as are trust officers. It is worth noting, however, that the very best private businesses for sale are not advertised by or given to brokers, and the real gems are usually bought by individuals or firms closest to them, such as management, directors, customers, suppliers, or financial backers. Bankruptcy judges have a continual flow of ventures in serious trouble. There can be some excellent opportunities buried beneath all the financial debris of a bankrupt firm.

■ *Franchises.* Franchising is another way to enter an industry, by either starting a franchise operation or becoming a franchisee. That this is a fertile area is indicated by the fact that the number of franchisors nationally now stands at over 2,000, according to the International Franchise Association and the Department of Commerce, and that franchisors account for well over $300 billion in sales annually and nearly one third of all retail sales.[11] The following sources can provide a useful start for a search in this field:

Franchise Opportunity Handbook, U.S. Department of Commerce.
The Franchise Annual Handbook and Directory, edited by Edward L. Dixon.
Franchising: Proven Techniques for Rapid Company Expansion and Market Dominance,
  by David Seltz.
Franchising World, published by the International Franchise Association.
Franchising Today, published by Franchise Technologies.
Listings of opportunities and ads in such publications as *INC., Venture,* and *The Wall Street Journal.*
International Franchise Handbook.
Databases, such as Dialog and CompuServe.

■ *Patents.* Patent brokers specialize in marketing patents that are owned by individual inventors, corporations, universities, or other research organizations to those seeking new commercially viable products. Some brokers specialize in international product licensing, and, occasionally, a patent broker will purchase an invention and then resell it. Although, over the years, the patent broker's image has been tarnished by a few unscrupulous brokers, acquisitions effected by reputable brokers have resulted in significant new products. Notable among these was Bausch & Lomb's acquisition, through the National Patent Development Corporation, of the United States rights to hydron, a material used in contact lenses. Some patent brokers are:

MGA Technology, Inc., Chicago, Illinois.
New Product Development Services, Inc., Kansas City, Missouri.
University Patents, Chicago, Illinois.
Research Corporation, New York, New York.
Pegasus Corporation, New York, New York.
National Patent Development Corporation, New York, New York.

■ *Product licensing.* A good way to obtain exposure to a large number of product ideas available from universities, corporations, and independent investors is to subscribe to information services, such as the *American Bulletin of International Technology, Selected Business Ventures* (published by General Electric Company), *Technology Mart, Patent Licensing Gazette,* and the National Technical Information Service. In addition, corporations, not-for-profit research institutes, and universities are sources of ideas:

Corporations. Corporations engaged in research and development develop inventions or services that they do not exploit commercially. These inventions either do not fit existing product lines or marketing programs or do not represent sufficiently large markets to be interesting to large corporations. A good number of corporations

---

[11] Ibid., p. 177

license these kinds of inventions, either through patent brokers, product-licensing information services, or their own patent marketing efforts. Directly contacting a corporation with a licensing program may prove fruitful. Among the major corporations known to have active internal patent marketing efforts are the following:

— Gulf and Western Invention Development Corporation.
— Kraft Corporation, Research and Development.
— Pillsbury Company, Research and Development Laboratories.
— Union Carbide Corporation, Nuclear Division.
— RCA Corporation, Domestic Licensing.
— TRW Corporation, Systems Group.
— Lockheed Corporation, Patent Licensing.

Not-for-profit research institutes.   These nonprofit organizations do research and development under contract to the government and private industry as well as some internally sponsored research and development of new products and processes that can be licensed to private corporations for further development, manufacturing, and marketing. Perhaps the most famous example of how this works is Battelle Memorial Institute's participation in the development of xerography and the subsequent license of the technology to the Haloid Corporation, now Xerox Corporation. Some nonprofit research institutes with active licensing programs are:

— Battelle Memorial Institute.
— ITT Research Institute.
— Stanford Research Institute.
— Southwest Research Institute.

Universities.   A number of universities are active in research in the physical sciences and seek to license inventions that result from this research, either directly or through an associated research foundation that administers its patent program. Massachusetts Institute of Technology and the California Institute of Technology publish periodic reports containing abstracts of inventions they own which are available for licensing. In addition, since a number of very good ideas developed in universities never reach formal licensing outlets, another way to find these ideas is to become familiar with the work of researchers in an area of interest. Among universities that have active licensing programs are:

— Massachusetts Institute of Technology.
— California Institute of Technology.
— University of Wisconsin.
— Iowa State University.
— Purdue University.
— University of California.
— University of Oregon.

■ *Industry and Trade Contacts.*

Trade shows and association meetings.   Trade shows and association meetings in an industry can be an excellent way to examine the products of many of the potential competitors, meet distributors and sales representatives, learn of product and market trends, and identify potential products. The American Electronics Association is a good example of an association which holds such seminars and meetings.

Customers.   Contacting potential customers of a certain type of product can help determine what their needs are and where existing products are deficient or inadequate. For example, discussions with doctors who head medical services at leading hospitals might lead to product ideas in the biomedical equipment business.

Distributors and wholesalers.   Contacting people who distribute a certain type of product can yield extensive information about the strengths and weaknesses of existing products and the kinds of product improvements and new products that are needed by customers.

Competitors.   Examining products offered by companies competing in an industry can show whether an existing design is protected by patent and whether it can be improved or imitated.

- *Former employers.*   A number of businesses are started with products or services, or both, based on technology and ideas developed by entrepreneurs while they were employed by others. In some cases, research laboratories were not interested in commercial exploitation of technology; or the previous employer was not interested in the ideas for new products, and the rights were given up or sold. In others, the ideas were developed under government contract and were in the public domain. In addition, some companies will help entrepreneurs set up companies in return for equity.

- *Professional contacts.*   Ideas can also be found by contacting such professionals as patent attorneys, accountants, commercial bankers, and venture capitalists who come into contact with those seeking to license patents or to start a business using patented products or processes.

- *Consulting.*   A method for obtaining ideas that has been successful for technically trained entrepreneurs is to provide consulting and one-of-a-kind engineering designs for people in fields of interest. For example, an entrepreneur wanting to establish a medical equipment company can do consulting or design experimental equipment for medical researchers. These kinds of activities often lead to prototypes that can be turned into products needed by a number of researchers. For example, this approach was used in establishing a company to produce psychological testing equipment that evolved from consulting done at the Massachusetts General Hospital and, again, in a company to design and manufacture oceanographic instruments which were developed from consulting done for an oceanographic research institute.

- *Networking.*   Networks can be a stimulant and source of new ideas, as well as a source of valuable contacts with people. Much of this requires personal initiative on an informal basis; but around the country, organized networks can facilitate and accelerate the process of making contacts and finding new business ideas. Consider, for example, in the Boston area, a high-density area of exceptional entrepreneurial activity, several networks have emerged in recent years, including the Babson Entrepreneurial Exchange, the Smaller Business Association of New England (SBANE), the M.I.T. Enterprise Forum, the 128 Venture Group, and the Boston Computer Society. Similar organizations can be found in all other of the United States, such as: the American Women's Economic Development Corporation in New York City; the Association of Women Entrepreneurs; the Entrepreneur's Roundtable of the UCLA Graduate Student Association; and the Association of Collegiate Entrepreneurs at Wichita State University.

CASE—HALSEY & HALSEY, INC.

Preparation Questions

1. What do you think of the HHI venture opportunity?
2. Would you consider going to work for the Halseys?
3. Would you consider investing in it?

HALSEY & HALSEY, INC.*

In early 1977, as part of a new venture course in college, George Halsey developed a business plan for Halsey & Halsey, Inc. (HHI), a fresh fish distribution company started in 1976 by his father.

Following graduation, George joined a large international conglomerate as a product manager. He was successful in his job but frustrated by working in a corporate environment. George saw a lack of focus and direction in the company's marketing attempts. He felt they were in the wrong market at the wrong time and believed new products flopped because they were not carefully researched.

George believed he saw an opportunity to focus his attention on new markets for fresh fish. George was convinced the business plan defined HHI's market, determined goals, and outlined a plan to meet targets. He told his father he was going to build HHI into a million dollar sales operation. Daniel Halsey, questioning the worth of formal business plans, replied in disbelief, "A million dollars, are you crazy?" George wondered whether he should take the plunge. After all, wasn't this a good time in his career to "go for it"?

Halsey & Halsey, Inc.'s original business plan follows:

Part 1: HHI and the Industry

In February 1976, Daniel Halsey registered Halsey & Halsey, Inc., as a profit-oriented proprietorship. After 21 years with a national manufacturer of consumer and institutional packaged frozen fish products, Mr. Halsey established the company to meet the increasing national demand for fresh fish.

With two of the nation's largest ocean perch processors morally backing his efforts, the search for potential customers began in the Midwest—an area of the country where perch is heavily consumed.

Today, HHI successfully acts as a broker/wholesaler within the fresh fish segment of the commercial fishing industry.

The industry is divided into two major marketing categories: the industrial category and the edible products category. Among the end products of the industrial category are such items as pet foods and fish oils. As *Exhibit A* demonstrates, this category of the industry has steadily declined over the years, now processing only 33 percent of the industry's total supplies.

The other category of the industry, edible products, is divided into three subsegments: frozen, canned, and fresh (the segment HHI competes in). Unfortunately, the U.S. Department of Commerce—the major source of this report's marketing statistics—does not numerically differentiate the fresh and frozen segments. It is estimated, however, that of all edible products, fresh fish represents 17 percent of the total category, while frozen and canned generate 39 percent and 44 percent respectively of the category's business. *Exhibit B* reflects the physical segmentation of the industry.

Recently, the United States implemented a more stringent conservation effort to help protect our waters from being overfished—a move primarily designed to curtail the activities of foreign fishing fleets (i.e., in particular the Russian and Japanese fleets), in hopes of revitalizing the American fleet. Within the last 10 years for instance (1965–75), the total fish

---

* This case is based upon the business plan prepared by a student at Northeastern University in May 1977 and is used with his permission.

The plan was submitted to Professor Jeffry A. Timmons of Northeastern University as partial fulfillment of the requirements in the New Venture Creation course.

The case is intended to convey a real entrepreneurial event and is not intended to illustrate either effective or ineffective entrepreneurial intuition and decision making.

Exhibit A
Supply of Fishery Products (in millions of pounds)

Year	Industrial	Percent Change	Edible	Percent Change	Total	Percent Change
1975	3,289	+2.3%	6,559	−6.8%	9,848	−3.9%
1974	3,215	−54.0	7,037	+4.0	10,252	−25.4
1973	6,989	+20.9	6,764	+12.3	13,753	+16.5
1972	5,781	+9.9	6,023	−3.1	11,804	+2.9
1971	5,261	−14.8	6,213	+9.5	11,474	−3.1
1970	6,173	−47.7	5,674	+1.7	11,847	−31.8
1969	11,802	+29.1	5,579	+15.1	17,381	+24.2
1968	9,142	+29.9	4,849	−10.7	13,991	+12.2
1967	7,037	+30.9	5,432	+5.2	12,469	+18.4
1966	5,372	—	5,163	—	10,535	—

Source: U.S. Department of Commerce.

Exhibit B
Supply Segmentation of the Commercial Fishing Industry

Total Supply

Industrial   Edible Products

Canned   Meal   Oils   Solubles

Frozen   Fresh   Canned

Finfish   Shellfish

Cod   Haddock   Perch   Flounder, etc.   Lobster   Clams   Scallops, etc.

Exhibit C
Supply of Edible Commercial Fishery Products (in millions of pounds)

Year	Domestic	Percent	Imported	Percent
1975	2,417	36.8%	4,142	63.2%
1974	2,328	33.1	4,709	66.9
1973	2,310	34.2	4,454	65.8
1972	2,441	40.5	3,583	59.5
1971	2,537	40.8	3,676	59.2
1970	2,321	40.9	3,353	59.1
1969	2,347	42.1	3,232	57.9
1968	2,368	48.8	2,481	51.2
1967	2,573	47.4	2,859	52.6
1966	2,587	50.1	2,576	49.9

Source: U.S. Department of Commerce

supply for the United States has actually increased an average of 3.2 percent per year; imports, however, have represented a larger share of the U.S. market each year.

As *Exhibit C* reflects, imports accounted for 63 percent of the U.S. edible products supply in 1975 but, in 1965, had 50 percent of the category. Accordingly, while the foreign fleets have consistently supplied more product, the U.S. fleet has historically harvested the same number of pounds. It is projected,[1] however, that with the 200 mile limit domestic production should substantially increase over the next five years. (A more complete discussion of the 200 mile limit and its effect on HHI will be covered later in this report.)

[1] *A Baseline Economic Forecast of the U.S. Fishing Industry,* 1975.

Exhibit D
Per Capita Consumption (in pounds)

Year	Total*	Percent Change	Fresh and Frozen	Percent Change	Steaks and Fillets	Percent Change
1975	46.5	−4.5%	6.8	−6.9%	2.12	−16.5%
1974	48.7	−26.1	7.3	+2.8	2.54	+10.9
1973	65.9	+16.0	7.1	+6.0	2.29	+12.2
1972	56.8	+1.4	6.7	−2.9	2.04	−6.0
1971	56.0	−4.1	6.9	+4.5	2.17	+8.0
1970	58.4	−32.6	6.6	+6.4	2.01	+8.1
1969	86.6	+23.0	6.2	+6.9	1.86	+13.4
1968	70.4	+11.0	5.8	−4.9	1.64	−5.7
1967	63.4	+17.0	6.1	+1.7	1.74	+3.6
1966	54.2	−13.6	6.0	+1.7	1.68	+3.7

* Includes both industrial and edible product categories.
Source: U.S. Department of Commerce.

Over the years, consumer demand for edible fish has increased, too, but at a slower rate than supplies.

Over the last five years, per capita consumption has increased an average of 1.6 percent per year. However, a subsegment within the fresh and frozen category (see *Exhibit D*), entitled "fillets and steaks," has increased an average of 2.3 percent over the same period. This is important because all fresh fish falls within this subsegment of per capita consumption.

Part 2: What Is Halsey & Halsey, Inc.?

In Part 1 HHI was described as a "broker/wholesaler," perhaps a somewhat abstract definition. Therefore, look at this in more detail.

HHI is classified as a service—presently, simply buying and selling processed fresh fish. Unlike a broker, HHI actually takes possession of the merchandise; it does not, however, have any inventory. Accordingly, HHI doesn't buy fish unless a customer has previously committed to a specific quantity and species of fish. This can work in a number of ways:

1. *Source initiated.* Here, the suppliers offer "x" amount of a specific species to HHI at "x" price. HHI in turn calls its portfolio of customers, probing their demands and confirming orders. After the final customer has been called, HHI telephones the supplier with the specific orders. About 65 percent of HHI business is transacted in this manner.

2. *Customer initiated.* In a conversation with a customer a request may be made for HHI to purchase a certain species of fish. Subsequently, HHI first checks existing suppliers for product availability and pricing, and/or explores new suppliers. At the conclusion of the search, HHI recalls the customer with the results (i.e., the price and if supplies enabled HHI to fill the entire order) and confirm the order. About 30 percent of HHI business falls within this category.

3. *HHI initiated.* Occasionally HHI will solicit new business from an existing customer by recommending a further diversification of the customer's product line. However, this is a difficult selling task and occurs in only about 5 percent of all transactions.

What are HHI's customers' characteristics? Of the customers now served, 95 percent are fish and/or poultry distributors, while the remaining 5 percent are composed of direct retail accounts. The direct retail accounts include a cross section of primarily supermarket chains, but also include a chain of retail fish stores. The bulk of customers, however, distribute to small retail and fish stores, restaurants, and to supermarkets, too.

Last year HHI tried to survey potential customers, but the results were disappointing and inconclusive. *Exhibit E* is a sample questionnaire.

Geographically, HHI customers are as near as Boston and as far west as Denver. The majority of customers are located in the Midwest, however.

Exhibit E
Customer Questionnaire No. 1, February 1976

1. Does your company presently handle fresh fish?
   _____YES
   _____NO (Please skip to question 12)

2. Does your company sell: _____Freshwater fish?
   _____Ocean fish?
   _____Both freshwater and ocean?
   If "both," what percentage of your
   sales are from: fresh_____%
   ocean_____%

3. How many total pounds of fresh fish do you sell in a week?   _____lbs.

4. In regards to your answer to #3, what percentage would you estimate are sold to the:
   Institutional trade _____%
   Retail trade _____%

5. What species of fresh fish are you presently selling?
   Species   *Pounds Sold per Week*
   _____   _____lbs.
   _____   _____lbs.
   _____   _____lbs.
   _____   _____lbs.
   _____   _____lbs.

6. What percentage of your total 1975 sales did fresh fish represent?   _____%

7. How often do you presently obtain fresh fish deliveries?
   _____ times a week
   or
   _____ times a month

8. Are these deliveries _____ flown in?
   _____ trucked in?

9. Does the majority of the fresh fish you sell come from:
   (Please check one)
   _____the East Coast
   _____the Gulf
   _____the West Coast
   _____the Midwest
   _____Canada
   _____any other source

10. On an average, what's the lapse time between ordering and delivery?   _____days

11. Is this considered a problem for you in any way? If "Yes," why is that so?   _____Yes   _____No

12. At this point in time, what type of an order might you be interested in?
    Species   *Pounds per Week*
    _____   _____lbs.
    _____   _____lbs.
    _____   _____lbs.
    _____   _____lbs.
    _____   _____lbs.

13. What would you prefer in a pack-out for your fresh fish orders?
    (Please check the one best for you.)
    Total lbs. per Case   *Units per Case*
    _____   1 to   10 lbs.   _____1 unit
    _____ 25 to   50 lbs.   _____2 to 3 units
    _____ 50 to   75 lbs.   _____4 units
    _____ 75 to 100 lbs.   _____5 to 6 units
    _____100 to 125 lbs.   _____7 units
    _____over 125 lbs.   _____other

Exhibit E *(concluded)*

14. What type (frequency) of delivery service would be best for you?
_____ daily
_____ 3 to 4 times weekly
_____ 2 times per week
_____ 1 time a week
_____ once every 6 to 10 days

15. What day of the week would you like delivery?
_____ Monday
_____ Tuesday
_____ Wednesday
_____ Thursday
_____ Friday
_____ Saturday/Sunday
_____ no preference

16. In this area, how many competitors do you have?
_____ 1 to 2
_____ 3
_____ 4
_____ 5 to 6
_____ 7 to 10
_____ more than 10

17. What would you estimate is your share of market?
_____ $

Finally, for statistical purposes, we would like to ask you the following questions.

18. Is your company listed in Dun and Bradstreet?
_____ Yes _____ No
If "Yes," what is the company's rating?
_____

19. For 1975, was the total dollar sales of your firm?
_____ MORE or _____ LESS than $1,000,000
if "MORE":
Is it _____ MORE or _____ LESS than $5,000,000
if "LESS":
Is it _____ MORE or _____ LESS than $500,000

We greatly appreciate your time. Thank you.

Initially HHI offered only ocean perch to its customers. As noted earlier, this was primarily because the only suppliers at that time handled perch on an almost exclusive basis.

In HHI's first 9 to 10 months in business, approximately 95 percent of volume was generated through the sale of perch. Within the last five months, however, HHI successfully extended its product line. There were three key factors initiating this change:

1. *Profitability.* To gain recognition within the industry, HHI entered the market on a strategy of low price. Accordingly, its net margin on perch was almost minimal (i.e., 5 percent). Other species, however, offered a higher margin—once obtaining the customers' orders for the lower-priced perch.

2. *Customer demand.* Like HHI, many of its customers too sought new and/or alternate sources of supply. HHI, therefore, tried to meet customers' demands, often resulting in an extension of its product line.

3. *Market opportunity.* As HHI matured, it saw that many of its competitors maltreated the customers it shared. It was HHI's belief that a possible key to future success was to emphasize service and ambition. One way of accomplishing this would be by showing the customers HHI's full-line capabilities.

Overall, the major HHI objective was to lure new business by demonstrating to existing customers that it was willing to do most anything to help its customers—in other words, to develop credibility within the industry.

Part 3: The Fresh Fish Market

The product — one of the most important aspects of success in this segment of the industry is product availability. As mentioned earlier, HHI has two of the nation's largest perch processors on an almost exclusive basis. This has played an essential role in its success to date, especially when considering the dwindling availabilities of perch on the open market.

To give better perspective of those items HHI sells, *Exhibits F, G,* and *H* outline the products' availability and pricing trends. *Exhibit H* indexes the percent change of price to the percent change of supply.

Over the last five years, fish prices have risen an average of 18.7 percent per year. Per capita consumption of fillets and steaks, however, has increased an average of 2.3 percent per year during that same period *(Exhibit D)*. The rise in consumption despite the outpaced rise in prices can be attributed to several key factors:

1.   There appears to be more aggressive campaigning on behalf of the national frozen fish manufacturers to introduce consumers to a historically flat section of the freezer case. Companies among these crusaders include Gorton's (now a subsidiary of General Mills), Mrs. Paul's (a subsidiary of RCA), and a host of regional brands (e.g., Van de Kamps in the West, Booth's in the Midwest, plus heavier promotional plans of the chains' private labels).

2.   Many families looked for main meal alternatives during the meat boycotts in the mid-1970s — many of which found the lower cost/high protein benefits of fish.

3.   As a result of the products' overall increase in demand, distribution has increased at the retail level. Some retailers, which historically carried one brand of frozen fish, are now carrying two, while many supermarkets are now adding fresh fish in their deli sections.

To maintain momentum at the retail level, supplies of domestic production, the primary source of fresh fish, must increase in the upcoming years. Accordingly, in 1975, the National Marine Fisheries Service (a department within the U.S. Department of Commerce) and an independent consultant jointly published a 22-page summary forecasting supplies and prices through 1985. Their projections include:

Exhibit F
Fish Supplies (in million pounds)

Species	1976 lbs.	Percent Change vs. Year Ago				
		1976	1975	1974	1973	1972
Fish:						
Butterfish	3.1	−29%	+8%	+18%	+109%	−54%
Cod	55.8	NC	−5	+17	+8	−12
Cusk	2.8	−9	+5	+3	+32	+22
Flounder	110.6	+4	−3	−5	−1	+4
Haddock	12.8	−21	+97	−1	−29	−46
Hake	14.1	+27	+1	+9	+6	+20
Halibut	20.6	−5	+17	−24	−10	−6
Perch	32.1	NC	−23	−22	−9	−2
Pollock	24.3	+18	+6	+38	+10	+18
Scup	16.0	−5	+9	−7	+31	−8
Total fish	292.2	+2%	NC	−1%	−1%	−4%
Shell:						
Clams	81.0	−28	−6	+12	+19	+8
Lobster	31.7	+9	+3	+1	−1	−12
Scallops	22.0	+88	+36	+6	+8	−3
Total shell	134.7	−12	−2	+9	+14	+2
Total all	426.9	−3%	−1%	+2%	+4%	−3%

Exhibit G
Whole Fish Prices

Species	1976 ¢/lb.	Percent Change vs. Year Ago				
		1976	1975	1974	1973	1972
Fish:						
Butterfish	28.2¢	+17%	−2%	NC	NC	+41%
Cod	25.7	+10	+21	+7%	+6%	+42
Cusk	17.8	+26	+5	+16	+17	+13
Flounder	37.8	+11	+33	+11	+15	+23
Haddock	43.5	+33	−11	−3	+4	+41
Hake	11.6	+24	+11	−8	+26	+25
Halibut	94.2	+40	+32	−2	+6	+109
Perch	13.7	+33	+27	+5	+37	+10
Pollock	13.4	+11	+12	+5	+15	+17
Scup	21.3	NC	+16	−35	+22	−1
Total fish	32.6	+16	+31	+2	+11	+34
Shell:						
Clams	77.4	+114	+13	−1	−9	−3
Lobster	$1.660	−2	+13	+4	+17	+17
Scallops	$1.809	−2	+21	−13	−3	+23
Total shell	$1.152	+58	+18	−5	−2	+4
Total all	58.6¢	+34%	+24%	NC	+7%	+17%

Exhibit H
Price Index*

Species	1976	1975	1974	1973	1972
Fish:					
Butterfish	165	91	85	48	306
Cod	110	127	91	98	161
Cusk	138	100	113	89	93
Flounder	107	137	117	116	118
Haddock	168	45	98	146	261
Hake	98	110	84	119	104
Halibut	147	113	129	118	222
Perch	133	165	136	150	112
Pollock	94	106	76	104	99
Scup	105	106	70	93	108
Total fish	114	131	103	112	140
Shell:					
Clams	297	120	88	76	90
Lobster	90	110	103	118	143
Scallops	52	89	82	90	126
Total shell	179	120	87	86	102
Total all	138	125	98	103	121

* An index of "100" would represent the percent change in price equalling the percent change in supply. Below "100" would be interpreted as the percent change in supply surpassing the percent change in price (e.g., supply +8 percent, price −2 percent would equal an index of "91").

1. *Total* supplies to increase an average 3.4 percent per year, while prices rise only 3.7 percent.

2. Total *edible product* supplies to increase an average 2.4 percent per year, while their associated prices rise 3.3 percent per year.

3. *Per capita consumption* of total edible products to increase from 35.2 pounds per person in 1975 to 39.7 by 1985 — an increase of 13 percent in per capita consumption.

In the final paragraphs of this report, it is stated that these projections were made under the assumption that the United States *did not* implement its 200-mile fishing limit. Subsequently, its authors state that these figures would be conservative if the pending legislation passed. Therefore, the assumption is made that supplies of domestic production will increase substantially within the next 10 years, and that there is a greater probability of increasing per capita consumption, especially within the fillets and steak category.

The customer — as previously stated, HHI's customers are a combination of fresh fish distributors and direct retail accounts. Most are located in the Midwest, but extend as far east as Boston and as far west as Denver.

In obtaining a sale from these customers, the most important factor is a combination of price and product availability. But unlike 5 to 10 years ago, another element is growing in importance. Today's retailers are beginning to actively promote their fresh fish sections. Accordingly, service and reliability are playing more of an important role each year within the industry.

Service — an important element today, because buyers have a multitude of responsibilities, in addition to buying the merchandise. **Reliability,** too, is essential — an embarrassing situation for a buyer to set up a fresh fish promotion for the chain, only to find out his supplier cannot obtain any product!

HHI has recently obtained most of the fresh fish business of a chain of supermarkets in the Rochester, New York, market. According to the head buyer, there were a number of reasons why:

1. Commonly, HHI presented merchandising and promotional ideas to the chain, many of which were accepted and were successful when implemented. Of the chain's current suppliers, HHI was the only supplier offering assistance in the field of marketing.

2. In the recent past, suppliers had shorted the chain on sale items; however, HHI had established itself as being reliable in this area. Often, as an emergency favor, HHI was able to secure the supply the competitors could not obtain.

3. HHI's prices have always been competitive — frequently parity priced and occasionally lower priced but consistently an excellent product.

There were other factors mentioned, but these appeared to be HHI's most salable attributes.

The **competition** — HHI has classified competition into two categories: primary and secondary. These are further classified by being either just a wholesaler, such as HHI, or as a wholesaler/processor, having its own production facilities in addition to selling its own output.

HHI's primary competitors are located on Boston's fish pier and its nearby ports. (This would include Fall River, New Bedford, Gloucester, and Massachusetts' other smaller ports.) Its secondary competitors would subsequently be found in the other areas of New England, primarily in Maine. HHI considers these firms secondary for the following reasons:

1. On those items on which HHI competes, there is occasionally a difference in quality and pricing. For instance, Gulf of Maine perch is more desirable than Atlantic perch on the open market and has historically brought a higher price.

2. Most secondary competitors are frozen fish processors and prefer to maintain a low-key profile of their fresh production.

3. Since most of these secondary competitors are outside of the Boston market, fishermen are subjected to a local market's pricing policies. Accordingly, there may be a substantial difference in pricing in those locations of HHI's secondary competitors. Frequently, many fishermen in these smaller ports are forced to Boston to obtain money for their catch.

There is a third group of competitors, but they are competitive with HHI only under certain circumstances. These competitors are found in the West Coast and Canada and normally serve as a very last alternate source for HHI's customers.

Inherent of Canada's fish, the country is perplexed by a problem of distribution of fresh fish. The largest port, St. John's, is many road-hours away from the American market. Subsequently, American fresh fish buyers have traditionally had problems with importing fresh Canadian fish.

Although the West Coast has many of the distribution problems solved (attributed to wide-body jets), its quality of fish falls far below that of the East Coast. This is because the Pacific is a warmer body of water, subsequently producing a softer fish. Therefore, to help offset this product disadvantage, West Coast fish tends to be much lower priced than Atlantic fish.

As outlined earlier in this report, it is contended that the key element of future success for HHI is its competitive advantage in service. This includes consistently offering a quality product at a competitive price.

It is, of course, difficult to measure success in this segment of the industry. Although sales would be a good indication of success, most firms within the industry are privately held and, therefore, are scrupulous in regard to whom their financial position is known. To further complicate the benchmarking problem, the only market trends available are those released by the Commerce Department. As earlier documented, these reports do not numerically differentiate fresh and frozen production. Subsequently, a wholesaler, such as HHI, could only have 0.0001 percent of the total market, yet generate a million dollars in sales. It is, therefore, because of these problems that HHI must use its own sales in relation to itself to gauge its relative success or failure in today's marketplace.

Part 4: Marketing and Sales Strategy

In developing a strategy, two factors are important: the customer and seasonality.

For marketing purposes, marketing areas are classified into two categories: developed and expansion markets.

A *developed market* is an area where fish has a high level of distribution, supplying the market with a wide variety of species at competitive prices. Examples of these markets would include the New England region, New York State, Cleveland, Chicago, and Detroit. Another characteristic of the developed market is that its buyers are keenly aware of the market's current status—they shop extensively for the lowest price/highest quality. Presently, about 98 percent of HHI's business is in these developed markets.

In an *expansion market,* fresh fish is distributed on a very limited scale, although it may have already developed a strong frozen fish franchise. Examples of these markets would be Davenport, Minneapolis, and Phoenix/Tucson.

Obtaining distribution in the expansion markets is difficult. First, a distributor and wholesaler must be found who has both the physical capabilities and the ambition to take on this new product. Second, through very different selling, they have to be convinced that

HHI is *the* company to act as their liaison to the fresh fish market and whose judgment is completely trusted (i.e., when and what species to buy).

Since these are two separate and distinct marketing groups, HHI has employed two strategies.

Developed markets. This strategy has these objectives: (1) To increase the volume of existing customers. (2) To develop customer confidence and loyalty. (3) To find new customers.

Strategy and tactics. In discovering new customers, HHI has used two resources very successfully: trade references and local truckers.

When shipping product, it is common for a trucker to drop-ship a number of fresh fish orders within a specific geographic region. Through a little probing, this was learned: (1) the customers he's making deliveries for and (2) what species the customer has bought.

Another source for leads has been the existing customers. Again, through probing, customers' competitors and their product line have been learned. Although as a policy HHI offers its customers product exclusivity within the trading area, the competitor provides an alternate source of sales. This has proven to be an effective way of increasing both HHI's sales and customer portfolio.

Another method of increasing HHI's volume, in addition to finding new customers within the developed markets, is by increasing the volume of existing accounts. To accomplish this objective, two strategies are being used:

1. Obtain increased volume of existing items. For instance, if a customer is currently purchasing 5,000 pounds of perch from HHI each week, HHI will try to increase the order to 8,000 to 10,000 pounds.
2. Diversify the product line. Utilizing the above example, HHI would attempt to maintain the perch volume while recommending a new species (i.e., use HHI as a new source of product).

Within the developed market, price plays an essential role in obtaining the sale. When the market is glutted with product, HHI sometimes marks up the product no more than 2 cents to 4 cents per pound. In a shortage situation, however, HHI mark ups have been as high as 25 cents per pound. In either case, HHI will not forfeit volume for profit. At this point in HHI's history, the strategy is to obtain increased volume through repeat purchase, hoping to develop credibility and loyalty with each account. Therefore, to greedily overprice the product may severely limit HHI's future growth and profit potential.

Expansion markets. Soon after HHI was formed, a five-week customer recruitment process was initiated. Traveling by car, each major market between Boston and Denver was investigated. Among the findings of the field trip was the realization and substantiation of fresh fish potential in key underdeveloped markets.

An essential element of success in developing markets where fresh fish has potential is obtaining distribution within supermarkets. The success in Denver, for instance, is attributed to helping the chains' distributors develop a program to market the new product. Included in the program were point-of-sale materials (tear-off pads with recipes and display cards), in addition to recommending a promotion theme, schedule, and merchandising tactics (i.e., how much shelf space to allocate to each species and how to package and display the product).

For HHI to develop an expansion market, much time and investment is required. It offers, however, a very high profit potential. Unlike the developed markets, expansion markets are less price sensitive because of the market's lack of experience within the category. This translates into a higher profit margin for both the chain and HHI, offering a quick payback for the initial marketing expenditures. Yet, despite the potential, HHI has decided not to actively pursue expansion markets until 1979 or 1980. There are four key reasons for this delay:

1. At this time, HHI's personnel are occupied full time in developing existing business and an associated cash base.

2. It's important for HHI to develop a good name with its existing customers to help ensure future growth. Service is the primary selling attribute.

3. As noted earlier, to develop these markets HHI must be on a sound financial base. The strategy, therefore, is to utilize the profits from existing accounts to finance future developmental programs.

4. Through more exposure to the industry, HHI hopes to better understand the intricacies and existing problems of fresh fish to better programs and presentation to the expansion markets.

Seasonality. Like many products, fresh fish is affected by the seasons, segmented by spring and fall. From April through October, suppliers scurry for customers, while the remainder of the year, November through March, fish supplies are limited. It is, however, during these winter months that HHI realizes its higher margins.

As noted earlier, HHI is on an almost exclusive basis with this country's largest perch processors. Subsequently, the company is one of the only wholesalers selling perch during the winter months. In many cases HHI has developed new customers by them calling for a product. Therefore, in light of the products' seasonality, two strategies are used:

1. Spring. During the spring months, HHI looks for new sources of supply that will provide product during the fall months. Once finding a supplier with fall potential, the strategy is to give the processor as much business as possible, in hopes of gaining both credibility and loyalty with the supplier.

2. Fall. Once securing supplies for the fall, HHI turns its attention to recruiting new customers and business within existing accounts. Historically, HHI will not accept new customers unless they agree to maintain their account with HHI through the spring/summer months. HHI has had much success with the strategy of having a continual supply of product in the fall—a selling point many primary competitors cannot make.

Part 5: Overall Schedule for 1977–79

Timing	*Activity*
1977:	
May–October	1. Seek new sources of supply for fall.
	2. Diversify product line.
November–December	1. Begin legal proceedings for incorporation effective 1/1/78.
	2. Field trip to review suppliers and find new sources.
	3. Begin design of chains' spring program.
	4. Hire part-time shipping clerk and bookkeeper.
1978:	
January–March	1. Incorporate.
	2. Customer-related field trip to present spring programs and for customer relations activities.

Timing		Activity
April–June	1.	Hire full-time assistant.
	2.	Move to larger facilities.
	3.	Begin expansion program.
1979:		
January–December	1.	Continuation of expansion program.
	2.	Further diversification of product lines.
	3.	Execute normal seasonal activities.

Part 6: The Management Team

A good management team is composed of individuals who can effectively draw and build from each other's talents and experiences. Accordingly, another factor attributed to HHI's success is its management team.

Currently, the company's only full-time employee is the company's proprietor, Daniel Halsey. After 22 years with a national consumer and institutional frozen fish packaged goods corporation, Daniel Halsey established HHI to meet the increasing national demand for fresh fish — a trend his former employer wished to ignore.

In his former position, Daniel was national sales and promotion manager. His duties included the design and execution of both consumer and trade promotions, in addition to managing the corporation's national brokerage force.

To further strengthen the HHI team, Daniel's two sons, Michael and George, serve as part-time consultants. Michael, a securities salesman in Chicago, serves as HHI's key financial advisor. George, presently employed as a product manager in New York, is involved in consumer marketing and subsequently provides HHI with guidance on specific marketing and sales problems.

HHI is essentially a one-man show at this time. Daniel, therefore, is responsible for each aspect of the company — sales, distribution, finance, and accounting. It's normally a 75- to 80-hour work week. It is planned, however, that by mid-1977 two part-time staff members will join HHI — a shipping clerk and a bookkeeper. As mentioned earlier, a full-time assistant will be hired in 1979 whose primary responsibilities will include the development of an expansion program, in addition to handling the various aspects of the business.

Among HHI's supporting staff is a local CPA and an attorney.

Part 7: Critical Risks and Assumptions

As a service, HHI is highly susceptible to risks that are marketing or personnel oriented, or both. It is, however, with the following risks that HHI operates:

1. As a sole proprietorship and a one-man operation, it is essential that Daniel Halsey retain his health.

2. As a one-man operation, it is estimated that HHI is now at its optimal sales level.

3. To expand the company's sales base, a full-time employee will be hired within the next 12 to 18 months and will be trained as an assistant to Daniel Halsey.

4. As a broker/wholesaler, HHI is susceptible to a more unloyal customer attempting to buy directly from the HHI source. Although this has attempted in the recent past, HHI has successfully put down the customers' attempts by applying gentle pressure on the supplier.

5. That supplies and prices remain stable (i.e., there are no catastrophic natural disasters).

6.   That all HHI customers pay their bills. (At any one time, a customer may be in debt for $10,000 to $30,000. Although HHI thoroughly checks a customer's credit history before accepting an order, a nonpayment of a very large invoice may put a severe financial strain on HHI.)

7.   That there are no legal proceedings implicating HHI in a food poisoning case subsequently finding the company liable.

8.   If a fresh fish price war started (yet to happen, however, in the history of this segment of the market), HHI may be one of the first casualties, given the company's present small financial base.

Part 8:   The Income Statement

Financial records are shown in *Exhibits I* and *J.*

1976   HHI's first 10 months in business resulted in a profit of over $13,000 on sales of $335,800.

1977   First quarter sales and income are actual.
The second quarter's projections were based on the trends of the company's short financial history.
Sales in the third quarter are projected to decline in light of the quarter's increased competitive activities.

1978   Sales for the year are projected to grow, 12 percent to 7.5 percent of which is inflation. Profits for the year decline to reflect increased expenditures in administrative costs and in developing the expansion program.

1979   For the year, sales are projected to increase 18 percent. The growth is to be primarily attributed to the attainment of new business through the expansion program.
The company's profits (retained earnings) appear weak for the year. Actually, the reduced profits are a result of a combination of increased overhead, investment in expansion programs, and an increase in the owner's withdrawal.

1980   Now beginning to materialize sales within the expansion markets, sales are projected to increase 27 percent, while profits increase 154 percent.

Part 9:   Cash Flow and Proposed Financing

In addition to the items noted in the income statement, the cash flow projections include the cash requirements needed for HHI's expansion program through 1980. See *Exhibit K.*

Based on these estimates, HHI's future will be self-financed and, therefore, will not require outside financial assistance to obtain its objectives.

Exhibit I
Income Statement

	1976	1977					1978				
	Total Year	1st Q.	2nd Q.	3rd Q.	4th Q.	Total	1st Q.	2nd Q.	3rd Q.	4th Q.	Total
Sales	$335.8	$191.6	$321.9	$285.0	$330.0	$1,128.5	$214.6	$360.5	$319.2	$369.6	$1,263.9
Less: Cost of goods	308.3	181.6	286.5	265.0	306.7	1,039.8	198.8	335.6	302.7	332.7	1,169.8
Gross profit	$ 27.5	$ 10.0	$ 35.4	$ 20.0	$ 23.3	$ 28.7	$ 15.5	$ 24.9	$ 16.5	$ 36.9	$ 94.1
(as a percent of sales)	(8.2%)	(5.2%)	(11.0%)	(7.0%)	(7.1%)	(7.9%)	(7.4%)	(6.9%)	(5.2%)	(10.0%)	(7.4%)
Less: Telephone	$ 1.9	$ 0.5	$ 0.7	$ 0.7	$ 0.7	$ 2.6	$ 0.8	$ 0.8	$ 0.8	$ 0.8	$ 3.2
Distribution	5.9	4.3	6.4	5.6	6.6	23.0	4.0	8.3	7.3	8.5	29.0
General & admin. expenses	5.7	1.1	1.4	1.7	1.8	6.0	1.6	2.7	7.4	7.7	19.4
Total expenses	$ 13.5	$ 5.9	$ 8.5	$ 8.0	$ 9.1	$ 31.6	$ 7.3	$ 11.8	$ 15.5	$ 17.0	$ 51.6
Operating profit	$ 14.0	$ 4.1	$ 26.9	$ 11.9	$ 14.2	$ 57.1	$ 8.5	$ 13.1	$ 1.0	$ 20.0	$ 42.6
(as a percent of sales)	(4.2%)	(2.1%)	(8.4%)	(4.2%)	(4.3%)	(5.1%)	(4.0%)	(3.6%)	(0.3%)	(5.4%)	(3.4%)
Less: Owner's withdrawal	$ 6.3	$ 2.7	$ 7.3	$ 2.3	$ 5.1	$ 17.4	$ 4.0	$ 6.2	$ 0.5	$ 9.3	$ 20.0
Retained earnings	$ 7.7	$ 1.4	$ 19.6	$ 9.6	$ 9.1	$ 39.7	$ 4.5	$ 6.9	$ 0.5	$ 10.5	$ 22.4
(as a percent of sales)	(2.8%)	(0.7%)	(6.1%)	(3.4%)	(2.7%)	(3.5%)	(2.1%)	(1.9%)	(0.2%)	(2.8%)	(1.8%)

Exhibit J
Income Statement

	1979					1980
	1st Q.	2nd Q.	3rd Q.	4th Q.	Total	Total Year
Sales	$234.3	$408.8	$375.3	$474.6	$1,493.0	$1,896.3
Less: Cost of goods	213.3	281.5	348.1	428.9	1,371.7	1,728.3
Gross profit	$ 21.1	$ 27.3	$ 27.2	$ 45.7	$ 121.3	$ 168.0
(as a percent of sales)	(9.0%)	(6.7%)	(7.2%)	(7.5%)	(8.1%)	(8.8%)
Less: Telephone	$ 1.0	$ 1.0	$ 1.0	$ 1.0	$ 4.0	$ 5.0
Distribution	6.7	11.7	10.8	13.6	42.8	56.9
General & admin. expenses	7.3	9.1	8.7	9.7	34.8	41.7
Total expenses	$ 15.0	$ 21.8	$ 20.5	$ 24.3	$ 81.6	$ 103.6
Operating profit	$ 6.1	$ 5.5	$ 6.7	$ 21.4	$ 39.7	$ 64.4
(as a percent of sales)	(2.6%)	(1.3%)	(1.8%)	(4.5%)	(2.7%)	(3.4%)
Less: Owner's withdrawal	$ 4.6	$ 4.2	$ 5.1	$ 16.2	$ 30.0	$ 40.0
Retained earnings	$ 1.5	$ 1.3	$ 1.6	$ 5.2	$ 9.6	$ 24.4
(as a percent of sales)	(0.5%)	(0.3%)	(0.4%)	(1.1%)	(0.6%)	(1.3%)

Exhibit K
Cash Flow

	Cash Flow	1977				1978				1979			
	1976	1st	2nd	3rd	4th	1st	2nd	3rd	4th	1st	2nd	3rd	4th
Cash balance	$ -0-	$ 9.7	$ 10.6	$ 30.2	$ 38.8	$ 46.5	$ 48.9	$ 54.8	$ 51.6	$ 51.6	$ 47.8	$ 35.6	$ 24.9
Add: Cash receipts	310.9	168.6	263.9	250.8	290.4	188.8	320.2	280.9	325.2	206.2	359.7	330.3	417.6
Collection of accounts rec.	24.9	23.0	38.6	34.2	39.6	25.7	40.3	38.3	44.3	28.1	49.1	45.0	56.9
Invested cap.	2.0	-0-	-0-	-0-	-0-	-0-	-0-	-0-	-0-	-0-	-0-	-0-	-0-
Total receivables	$337.8	$201.3	$332.5	$315.2	$368.8	$261.0	$409.4	$374.0	$421.1	$285.9	$456.6	$410.9	$499.4
Less: Trade payable	$314.2	$185.9	$292.9	$270.7	$313.3	$203.7	$343.9	$310.0	$341.2	$219.9	$393.2	$358.9	$442.5
Administr.	7.6	1.6	2.1	2.4	2.9	3.4	3.5	9.6	12.9	11.3	17.9	18.3	18.1
Leased equip.	-0-	-0-	-0-	1.0	1.0	1.0	1.0	1.4	1.4	2.3	3.7	3.7	3.7
Fixed assets	-0-	0.5	-0-	-0-	-0-	-0-	-0-	0.9	-0-	-0-	-0-	2.0	-0-
Owner's withdrawal	6.3	2.7	7.3	2.3	5.1	4.0	6.2	0.5	9.3	4.6	4.2	5.1	16.2
Total disbursements	$328.1	$190.7	$302.3	$276.4	$322.3	$212.1	$354.6	$322.4	$364.8	$238.1	$421.0	$386.0	$480.5
Cash balance	$ 9.7	$ 10.6	$ 30.2	$ 38.8	$ 46.5	$ 48.9	$ 54.8	$ 51.6	$ 56.3	$ 47.8	$ 35.6	$ 24.9	$ 18.9

EXERCISE – CREATIVE SQUARES

The Creative Squares Exercise can show group creativity in action.

EXERCISE
CREATIVE SQUARES

STEP 1: DIVIDE YOUR GROUP BY (1) SEPARATING INTO A NUMBER OF GROUPS OF THREE OR MORE PERSONS EACH AND (2) HAVING AT LEAST FIVE INDIVIDUALS WORK ALONE.

STEP 2: SHOW THE FOLLOWING FIGURE TO EVERYONE AND ASK THE GROUPS AND THE INDIVIDUALS TO COUNT THE TOTAL NUMBER OF SQUARES IN THE FIGURE.   Assume that the figure is a square box on a single flat plane. In counting, angles of any square must be right angles, and the sides must be of equal length.

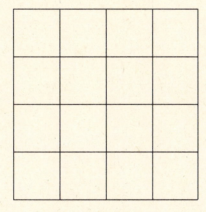

STEP 3: DISCUSS THE CREATIVE PROCESS BY WHICH THE GROUPS AND THE INDIVIDUALS REACHED THEIR ANSWERS.

EXERCISE—IDEA GENERATION GUIDE

Before beginning the process of generating ideas for new ventures, it is useful to reflect on an old German proverb that says, "Every beginning is hard." If you allow yourself to think creatively, you will be surprised with the number of interesting ideas you can generate once you begin.

The Idea Generation Guide is an exercise in generating ideas. The aim is for you to generate as many interesting ideas as possible. *While generating your ideas, do not evaluate them or worry about their implementation.* Discussion and exercises in the rest of the book will allow you to evaluate these ideas to see if they are opportunities and to consider your own personal entrepreneurial strategy.

And, remember, in any creative endeavor there are no "right" answers.

EXERCISE
IDEA GENERATION GUIDE

NAME:

DATE:

STEP 1:   GENERATE A LIST OF AS MANY NEW VENTURE IDEAS AS POSSIBLE.   Thinking about any unmet or poorly filled customer needs of which you know that have resulted from regulatory changes, technological changes, knowledge and information gaps, lags, asymmetries, inconsistencies, and so forth, will help you generate such a list. Also, think about various products and services (and their substitutes) and the providers of these products or services. If you know of any weaknesses or vulnerabilities, you may discover new venture ideas.

STEP 2:   EXPAND YOUR LIST IF POSSIBLE.   Think about your personal interests, your desired lifestyle, your values, what you feel you are likely to do very well, and contributions you would like to make.

STEP 3:   ASK AT LEAST THREE PEOPLE WHO KNOW YOU WELL TO LOOK AT YOUR LIST, AND REVISE YOUR LIST TO REFLECT ANY NEW IDEAS EMERGING FROM THIS EXCHANGE.   See discussion about getting feedback in Chapter 21.

STEP 4: JOT DOWN INSIGHTS, OBSERVATIONS, AND CONCLUSIONS THAT HAVE EMERGED ABOUT YOUR BUSINESS IDEAS OR YOUR PERSONAL PREFERENCES:

Opportunity Recognition

I was seldom able to see an opportunity until it had ceased to be one.

Mark Twain

RESULTS EXPECTED

At the conclusion of the chapter, you will have:

1. Defined the differences between an idea and an opportunity.
2. Examined opportunity in the context of the real world and real time and how opportunity fits within a framework for analysis.
3. Examined criteria used by successful entrepreneurs and investors to evaluate opportunities.
4. Looked at some personal criteria that can be used in evaluating opportunities.
5. Identified how to find information that can be used in screening opportunities.

RECOGNIZING OPPORTUNITIES

Good Ideas Are Not Necessarily Good Opportunities

If an idea is not an opportunity, what is an opportunity?[1] *An opportunity has the qualities of being attractive, durable, and timely and is anchored in a product or service which creates or adds value for its buyer or end user.*

For an opportunity to have these qualities, the "window of opportunity" is opening, rather than closing, and remains open long enough. Further, entry into a market with the right characteristics is feasible (and the management team is able to achieve it). The venture has or is able to achieve a competitive advantage (i.e., to achieve leverage). Finally, the economics of the venture are rewarding and forgiving and allow significant profit and growth potential.

To repeat, opportunities that have the qualities named above are anchored in a product or service that creates or adds value for its buyer or end user. The most successful entrepreneurs, venture capitalists, and private investors are opportunity-focused; that is, they start with what customers and the marketplace want and do not lose sight of this.

The Real World

Opportunities are created, or built, using ideas and entrepreneurial creativity. Yet, while the image of a carpenter or mason at work is useful, in reality the process is more like the collision of particles in the process of a nuclear reaction or like the spawning of hurricanes over the ocean.

[1] See Jeffry A. Timmons, *New Business Opportunities* (Acton, Mass.: Brick House Publishing, 1989).

71

Ideas interact with real-world conditions and entrepreneurial creativity at a point in time. The product of this interaction is an opportunity around which a new venture can be created.

The business environment in which an entrepreneur launches his or her venture is usually given and cannot be altered significantly. And, with the exception of perhaps some businesses established as social or nonprofit organizations, businesses in the United States operate in a free enterprise system characterized by private ownership and profits.

In a free enterprise system, *opportunities* are spawned when there are changing circumstances, chaos, confusion, inconsistencies, lags or leads, knowledge and information gaps, and a variety of other vacuums in an industry or market.

Changes in the business environment and, therefore, anticipation of these changes, are so critical in entrepreneurship that constant vigilance for changes is a valuable habit. It is thus that an entrepreneur with credibility, creativity, and decisiveness can seize an opportunity while others study it.

Opportunities are situational. Some conditions under which opportunities are spawned are entirely idiosyncratic, while, at other times, they are generalizable and can be applied to other industries, products, or services. In this way, cross-association can trigger in the entrepreneurial mind the crude recognition of existing or impending opportunities.

Consider the following broad range of examples that illustrate the phenomenon of vacuums in which opportunities are spawned:

- Deregulation of telecommunications and airlines led to the formation of tens of thousands of new firms in the 1980s.
- Microcomputer hardware in the early 1980s far outpaced the development of software. The development of the industry was highly dependent on the development of software, leading to aggressive efforts by IBM, Apple, and others to encourage software entrepreneurs to close this gap.
- Many opportunities exist in fragmented, traditional industries that may have a craft or "mom and pop" character and where there is little appreciation or know-how in marketing and finance. Consider such possibilities as fishing lodges, inns, and hotels; cleaners/laundries; hardware stores; pharmacies; waste management plants; flower shops; nurseries; tents; and auto repairs.
- In our service-dominated economy (where 70 percent of businesses are service business versus 30 percent just 25 years ago), customer service, rather than the product itself, can be the critical success factor. One recent study by The Forum Corporation in Boston showed that 70 percent of customers leave because of poor service and only 15 percent because of price or quality.
- Sometimes existing competitors cannot, or will not, increase capacity as quickly as the market is moving. For example, the tent industry, as seen in the Outdoor Scene case earlier, was characterized by this capacity stickiness in the mid-1970s. In the late-1970s, some steel had a 90-week delivery lag, with the price to be determined, and foreign competitors certainly took notice.
- The tremendous shift to off-shore manufacturing of labor-intensive and transportation-insensitive products in Asia and Mexico, such as computer-related and microprocessor-driven consumer products, is an excellent example.
- In a wide variety of industries, entrepreneurs sometimes find they are the only ones who can perform. Such fields as consulting, software design, financial services, process engineering, and technical and medical products and services abound with examples of know-how monopolies. Sometimes a management team is simply the best in an industry and irreplaceable in the near term, just as is seen with great coaches with winning records.

Exhibit 3.1
The Window of Opportunity

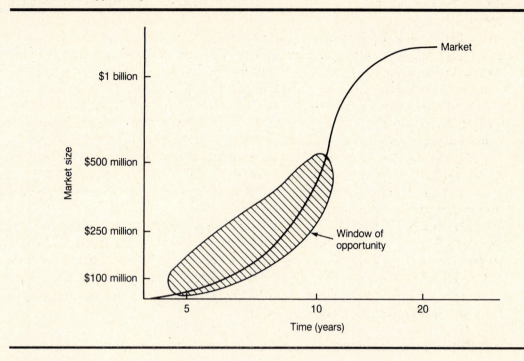

Real Time

Opportunities exist, or are created, in real time and have what is called a window of opportunity. For an entrepreneur to seize an opportunity requires that the window be opening, not closing, and that it remain open long enough.

Exhibit 3.1 illustrates, for a generalized market, a window of opportunity. Markets grow at different rates over time, and as a market quickly becomes larger, more and more opportunities are possible. As the market becomes larger and established, conditions are not as favorable. Thus, at the point where a market starts to become sufficiently large and structured (e.g., at five years in *Exhibit 3.1*), the window opens; the window begins to close as the market matures (e.g., at 15 years in the exhibit).

The curve shown describes the rapid growth pattern typical of such new industries as microcomputers and software, cellular car phones, quick oil changes, and biotechnology. For example, in the cellular car phone industry, most major cities began service between 1983 and 1984 for the very first time. By 1989, there were over 2 million subscribers in the United States, and the industry continued to experience significant growth. In other industries, such as a mature industry, where growth is not so rapid, the slope of a curve would be less steep and the possibilities for opportunities fewer.

Finally, in considering the window of opportunity, the length of time the window will be open is important. It takes a considerable length of time to determine whether a new venture is a success or a failure. And, if it is to be a success, the benefits of that success need to be harvested.

Exhibit 3.2 shows that, for venture-capital-backed firms, the lemons (i.e., the losers) ripen in about two and a half years, while the pearls (i.e., the winners) take seven or eight

Exhibit 3.2
Lemons and Pearls

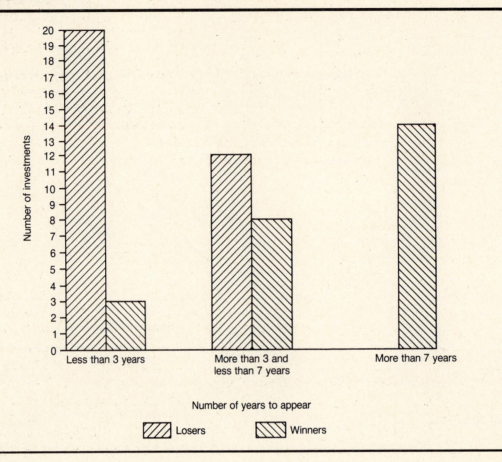

years. An extreme example of the length of time it can take for a pearl to be harvested is the experience of a Silicon Valley venture capital firm that invested in a new firm in 1966 and was finally able to realize a capital gain in early 1984.

Another way to think of the process of creating and seizing an opportunity in real time can be thought of as a process of selecting objects, opportunities, from a conveyor belt moving through an open window, the window of opportunity. The speed changes at which the conveyor belt moves, and the window through which it moves is constantly opening and closing. That the window is continually opening and closing and that the speed of the conveyor belt is constantly changing represents the volatile and dynamic nature of the marketplace and the importance of timing. For an opportunity to be created and seized, it needs to be selected from the conveyor belt before the window closes.

The ability to recognize a potential opportunity when it appears and the sense of timing to seize it as the window is opening, rather than slamming shut, are critical. That opportunities are a function of real time is illustrated in a statement made by the president and founder of Digital Equipment Corporation in 1977. At that time, Ken Olsen said, "There is no reason for any individual to have a computer in their home."

Relation to the Framework of Analysis

And finally, it is important to remember that, once recognized, successful opportunities fit with the other forces of new venture creation.

This iterative process of assessing and reassessing the fit among the central driving forces in the creation of a new venture was shown in *Exhibit 1.6* in Chapter 1. Of utmost importance when talking of opportunity recognition is the fit of the lead entrepreneur and the management team with an opportunity. Good opportunities are both *desirable* to and *attainable* by those on the team using the resources that are available.

SCREENING OPPORTUNITIES

Opportunity Focus

Opportunity focus is also the most fruitful point of departure for screening opportunities. The screening process[2] should not begin with strategy (which derives from the nature of the opportunity), with financial and spreadsheet analysis (which flow from the former), or with estimations of how much the company is worth and who will own what shares.

These starting points, and others, usually place the cart before the horse. Perhaps the best evidence of how the cart is often placed before the horse comes from the tens of thousands of tax-sheltered investments that turned sour in the mid-1980s. Also, as has been noted, a good number of entrepreneurs who start businesses—particularly those for whom the ventures are their first—run out of cash at a faster rate than they bring in customers and profitable sales. There are lots of reasons why this happens, but one thing is certain: These entrepreneurs have not focused on the right opportunity.

Over the years, those with experience in business and in specific market areas have developed rules of thumb to guide them in screening opportunities. For example, one such rule of thumb was used by a firm with approximately $1 billion in sales in evaluating start-ups in the minicomputer industry in the mid-1980s. This firm believed, based on an analysis of performance data relating to 60 computer-related start-ups in the United States from 1975 to 1984, that one leading indicator of the progress of new firms and a good boundary measure of positive performance and a healthy start was sales per employee of $75,000 or more. To this firm, sales of less than $50,000 per employee signaled serious trouble.

While there is always the risk of oversimplification in using rules of thumb, it is true also that one can miss the fundamentals while searching for subtleties.

Screening Criteria

Venture capitalists, savvy entrepreneurs, and investors also use this concept of boundaries in screening ventures. *Exhibit 3.3* summarizes criteria used by venture capitalists to evaluate opportunities. These criteria are used by this group to evaluate a select group of opportunities that tend to have a high technology bias. As will be seen later, venture capital investors reject 60 percent to 70 percent of the new ventures presented to them very early in the review process, based on how the entrepreneurs satisfy these criteria.

However, these criteria are not the exclusive domain of venture capitalists. The criteria are based on plain good business sense that is used by successful entrepreneurs, private investors, and venture capitalists.

---

[2] See J. A. Timmons, D. F. Muzyka, H. H. Stevenson, and W. D. Bygrave, "Opportunity Recognition: The Core of Entrepreneurship," *Frontiers of Entrepreneurial Research: 1987,* ed. Neil Churchill et al. (Babson Park, Mass.: Babson College, 1987), p. 409.

Exhibit 3.3
Criteria for Evaluating Venture Opportunities

Criterion	Attractiveness	
	Higher Potential	*Lower Potential*
Market Issues		
Market:		
Need	Identified	Unfocused
Customers	Reachable; receptive	Unreachable or loyal to others
Payback to user	Less than one year	Three years plus
Value added or created	High	Low
Product life	Durable; beyond time to recover investment plus profit	Perishable; less than time to recover investment
Market structure	Imperfect competition or emerging industry	Perfect Competition or highly concentrated or mature industry or declining industry
Market size	$100 million sales	Unknown or less than $10 million sales or multibillion
Market growth rate	Growing at 30% to 50% or more	Contracting or less than 10%
Gross margins	40% to 50% or more; durable	Less than 20%; fragile
Market share attainable (year 5)	20% or more; leader	Less than 5%
Cost structure	Low-cost provider	Declining cost
Economic/Harvest Issues		
Profits after tax	10% to 15% or more; durable	Less than 5%; fragile
Time to:		
Break even	Under 2 years	More than 3 years
Positive cash flow	Under 2 years	More than 3 years
ROI potential	25% or more/year; high value	Less than 15%–20%/year; low value
Value	High strategic value	Low strategic value
Capital requirements	Low to moderate; fundable	Very high; unfundable
Exit mechanism	Present or envisioned harvest options	Undefined; illiquid investment
Competitive Advantages Issues		
Fixed and variable costs:		
Production	Lowest	Highest
Marketing	Lowest	Highest
Distribution	Lowest	Highest
Degree of control:		
Prices	Moderate to strong	Weak
Costs	Moderate to strong	Weak
Channels of supply/resources	Moderate to strong	Weak
Channels of distribution	Moderate to strong	Weak
Barriers to entry:		
Proprietary protection/ regulation adv.	Have or can gain	None
Response/lead time advantage in technology, product, market innovation, people, location, resources, or capacity	Resilient and responsive; have or can gain	None
Legal, contractual advantage	Proprietary or exclusivity	None
Contacts and networks	Well-developed; high quality; accessible	Crude; limited; inaccessible
Management Team Issues		
Team	Existing, strong proven performance	Weak or solo entrepreneur
Competitor's mind set and strategies	Competitive; few; not self-destructive	Dumb
Fatal Flaw Issue		
Fatal flaws	None	One or more

The point of departure here is opportunity and, implicitly, the customer, the marketplace, and the industry. *Exhibit 3.3* shows how higher and lower potential opportunities can be placed along an attractiveness scale. The criteria provide some quantitative way in which an entrepreneur can make judgments about industry and market issues, competitive advantage issues, economic and harvest issues, management team issues, and fatal flaw issues and whether these do or do not add up to a compelling opportunity. For example, *dominant* strength in any one of these criteria can readily translate into a winning entry, whereas a flaw in any one can be fatal.

Entrepreneurs contemplating opportunities that will yield attractive companies, not high potential ventures, can also benefit from paying attention to these criteria. These entrepreneurs will then be in a better position to decide how these criteria can be compromised.

As outlined in *Exhibit 3.3*, business opportunities with the greatest potential will possess many of the following, or they will so dominate in one or a few that the competition cannot come close:

■ *Industry and Market Issues*

Market.   *Higher potential* businesses can identify a market niche for a product or service that meets an important customer need and provides high value-added or value-created benefits to customers. Customers are reachable and receptive to the product or service, with no brand or other loyalties. The potential payback to the user or customer of a given product or service through cost savings or other value-added or created properties is one year or less and is identifiable, repeatable, and verifiable. Further, the product or service life exists beyond the time needed to recover the investment, plus a profit. And the company is able to expand beyond a one-product company. Take, for example, the growing success of cellular car phone service. At prevailing rates, one can talk for about $25 an hour, and many providers of professional services can readily bill more than the $25 an hour for what would otherwise be unused time. If benefits to customers cannot be calculated in such dollar terms, then the market potential is far more difficult and risky to ascertain.

Lower potential opportunities are unfocused regarding customer need, and customers are unreachable and/or have brand or other loyalties to others. A payback to the user of more than three years and a low value added or created also makes an opportunity unattractive. Being unable to expand beyond a one-product company also can make for a lower potential opportunity. The failure of one of the first portable computer companies, Osborne Computer, is a good example of this.

Market structure.   Market structure, such as evidenced by the number of sellers, size distribution of sellers, whether products are differentiated, conditions of entry and exit, number of buyers, cost conditions, and sensitivity of demand to changes in price, are significant.

A fragmented, imperfect market or emerging industry often contains vacuums and asymmetries that create unfilled market niches—for example, markets where resource ownership, cost advantages, and the like can be achieved. In addition, those where information or knowledge gaps exist and where competition is profitable, but not so strong as to be overwhelming, are attractive. An example of a market with an information gap is that of the experience a Boston entrepreneur encountered with a large New York company that wanted to dispose of a small, old office building in downtown Boston. This office building, because its book value was about $200,000, was viewed by the financially oriented firm as a "low value asset," and the company wanted to dispose of it so the resulting cash could be put to work for a higher return. The buyer, who had done more homework than the out-of-town sellers, bought the building for $200,000 and resold it in less than six months for over $8 million.

Industries that are highly concentrated, that are perfectly competitive, or that are mature or declining industries are typically unattractive. The capital requirements and costs to achieve distribution and marketing presence can be prohibitive, and such behavior as price cutting and other competitive strategies in highly concentrated markets can be a significant barrier to entry. (The most blatant example is organized crime and its life-threatening actions when territories are invaded.) Yet, revenge by "normal" competitors who are well-positioned through product strategy, legal tactics, and the like also can be punishing to the pocketbook.

The airline industry, after deregulation, is an example of a perfectly competitive market and one where many of the recent entrants will have difficulty. That perfectly competitive industries are unattractive is captured by the comment of one prominent Boston venture capitalist, William Egan, who put it this way: "I want to be in a non-auction market."[3]

Market size.   An attractive new venture sells to a market that is large and growing (i.e., one where capturing a small market share can represent significant and increasing sales volume).

A minimum market size of over $100 million in sales is attractive. Such a market size means it is possible to achieve significant sales by capturing roughly 5 percent or less and not threaten competitors. For example, to achieve a sales level of $1 million in a $100 million market requires capturing only 1 percent of the market. Thus, a recreational equipment manufacturer entered a $60 million market that was expected to grow at 20 percent per year to over $100 million by the third year. The founders were able to create a substantial smaller company without obtaining a major market share and possibly incurring the wrath of existing competitors.

However, such a market can be too large. A multibillion-dollar market may be too mature and stable, and such a level of certainty can translate into competition from Fortune 500-type firms and, if highly competitive, translate into lower margins and profitability. Further, an unknown market or one that is less than $10 million in sales also is unattractive. To understand the disadvantage of a large, more mature market, consider the entry of a firm into the microcomputer industry today versus the entry of Apple Computer into that market in 1975.

Growth rate.   An attractive market is large and growing (i.e., one where capturing a good share of the increase is less threatening to competitors and where a small market share can represent significant and increasing sales volume). An annual growth rate of 30 percent to 50 percent creates new niches for new entrants, and such a market is a thriving and expansive one, rather than a stable or contracting one, where competitors are scrambling for the same niches. Thus, for example, a $100 million-plus market growing at 50 percent per year has the potential to become a $1 billion industry in a few years, and, if a new venture is able to capture just 2 percent of sales in the first year, it can attain sales in the first year of $1 million. If it just maintains its market share over the next few years, sales will grow significantly.

The microcomputer industry was just such a market, with plenty of room for innovative entrants targeting sales of $50 million to $100 million. Compaq, the portable microcomputer firm, achieved sales of $110 million in its very first year and, by 1988, reached nearly $2 billion in sales. Sun Microsystems, a 1983 start-up in CAD/CAM work stations, grew to $1.2 billion by 1988. Conversely, a market which is growing at a rate less than 10 percent or one that is contracting is unattractive.

Gross margins.   The potential for high and durable gross margins (i.e., the unit

---

[3] Comments made during a presentation at Babson College, May 1985.

selling price less all direct and variable costs) is important. Gross margins exceeding 40 percent to 50 percent provide a tremendous built-in cushion that allows for more error and more flexibility to learn from mistakes than do gross margins of 20 percent or less. High and durable gross margins, in turn, mean that a venture can reach breakeven earlier, an event that preferably occurs within the first two years. Thus, for example, if gross margins are just 20 percent, for every $1 increase in fixed costs (e.g., insurance, salaries, rent, and utilities), sales need to increase $5 just to stay even. If gross margins are 75 percent, however, a $1 increase in fixed costs requires a sales increase of just $1.33. An example of the cushion provided by high and durable gross margins is provided by an entrepreneur who built the international division of an emerging software company to $17 million in highly profitable sales in just five years (when he was twenty-five years of age). He stresses there is simply no substitute for outrageous gross margins, by saying, "It allows you to make all kinds of mistakes that would kill a normal company. And we made them all. But our high gross margins covered all the learning tuition and still left a good profit."[4]

Gross margins of less than 20 percent, particularly if they are fragile, are unattractive.

Market share. The potential to be a leader in the market and capture at least a 20 percent share of the market is important. The potential to be a leader in the market and capture at least 20 percent can create a very high value for a company that might otherwise be worth not much more than book value. For example, one such firm, with less than $15 million in sales, became the dominant factor in its small market niche with a 70 percent market share. The company was acquired for $23 million in cash.

A firm that will be able to capture less than 5 percent of a market is unattractive in the eyes of most investors seeking a higher potential company.

Cost structure. A firm that can become the low cost provider is attractive, whereby a firm that continually faces declining cost conditions is less so. Attractive opportunities exist in industries where economies of scale are not significant (or work to the advantage of the new venture). Attractive opportunities boast of low costs of learning by doing. Where costs per unit are high when small amounts of the product are sold, existing firms that have low promotion costs can face attractive market opportunities.

■ *Economic and Harvest Issues*

Profits after tax. High and durable gross margins usually translate into strong and durable after-tax profits. Attractive opportunities have potential for durable profits of at least 10 percent to 15 percent, and often 15 percent to 20 percent or more. Those generating after-tax profits of less than 5 percent are quite fragile.

Time to breakeven and positive cash flow. As mentioned above, breakeven and positive cash flow for attractive companies is possible within two years. Once the time to breakeven and positive cash flow is greater than three years, the attractiveness of the opportunity diminishes accordingly.

ROI potential. An important corollary to forgiving economics is reward. Very attractive opportunities have the potential to yield a return on investment of 25 percent or more per year. After all, during the 1980s, many venture capital funds only achieved single-digit returns on investment. High and durable gross margins and high and durable after-tax profits usually yield high earnings per share and high return on stockholders' equity, thus generating a satisfactory "harvest" price for a company. This

---

[4] R. Douglas Kahn, president, Interactive Images, Inc., speaking at Babson College about his experiences as international marketing director at McCormack & Dodge from 1978 through 1983.

is most likely true whether the company is sold through an initial public offering or privately or whether it is acquired.

Given the risk typically involved, a return on investment potential of less than 15 percent to 20 percent per year is unattractive.

Value.   New ventures that are based on strategic value, such as valuable technology, in an industry are attractive, while those with low or no strategic value are less attractive. For example, most observers contend, a product technology of compelling strategic value to Xerox was owned, in the mid-1980s, by a small company with about $10 million in sales and showing a prior-year loss of $1.5 million. Xerox purchased the company for $56 million. Opportunities with extremely large capital commitments, whose value on exit can be severely eroded by unanticipated circumstances, are less attractive. Such an example would be nuclear power.

Capital requirements.   Ventures that can be funded and have capital require-ments that are low to moderate are attractive. Realistically, most higher potential businesses need significant amounts of cash — several hundred thousand dollars and up — to get started. However, a business that can be started with little or no capital is rare, but they do exist. One such venture was launched in Boston in 1971 with $7,500 of the founder's capital and grew to over $30 million in sales by 1989. In today's venture capital market, the first round of financing is typically $1 million to $2 million or more for a start-up.[5] Some higher potential ventures, such as those in the service sector or "cash sales" businesses, have lower capital requirements than do high-technology manufacturing firms with continual large research and development expenditures.

If the venture needs too much money or cannot be funded, it is unattractive. An extreme example is a venture that a team of students recently proposed to repair satellites. The students believed that the required start-up capital was in the $50 million to $200 million range. Projects of this magnitude are in the domain of the government and the very large corporation, rather than that of entrepreneurs and venture capitalists.

Exit mechanism.   Businesses that are eventually sold — privately or to the public — or acquired usually are started and grown with a harvest objective in mind. Attractive companies that realize capital gains from the sale of their businesses have, or envision, a harvest or exit mechanism. Unattractive opportunities do not have an exit mechanism in mind.

■ *Competitive Advantages*

Variable and fixed costs.   An attractive opportunity has the potential for being the lowest-cost producer and for having the lowest costs of marketing and distribution. For example, Bowmar was unable to remain competitive in the market for electronic calculators after the producers of large-scale integrated circuits, such as Hewlett-Packard, entered the business. Being unable to achieve and sustain a position as a low-cost producer shortens the life expectancy of a new venture.

Degree of control.   Attractive opportunities have potential for moderate-to-strong degree of control over prices, costs, and channels of distribution. Fragmented markets where there is no dominant competitor — no "IBM" — have this potential. These markets usually have a market leader with a 20 percent market share *or less.* For example, sole control of the source of supply of a critical component for a product or

---

[5]   J. A. Timmons, W. Bygrave, and N. Fast, "The Flow of Venture Capital to Highly Innovative Technological Ventures," a study for the National Science Foundation; reported in *Frontiers of Entrepreneurship Research: 1984,* ed. J. A. Hornaday et al. (Babson Park, Mass.: Babson College, 1984).

of channels of distribution can give a new venture market dominance even if other areas are weak.

Lack of control over such factors as product development and component prices can make an opportunity unattractive. For example, in the case of Viatron, its suppliers were unable to produce several of the semiconductors that the company needed at low enough prices to permit Viatron to make the inexpensive computer terminal that it had publicized extensively.

A market where a major competitor has a market share of 40 percent, 50 percent, or, especially, 60 percent usually implies a market where power and influence over suppliers, customers, and pricing create a serious barrier and risk for a new firm. Such a firm will have few degrees of freedom. However, if a dominant competitor is at full capacity, is slow to innovate or to add capacity in a large and growing market, or routinely ignores or abuses the customer (remember "Ma Bell"), there may be an entry opportunity. However, entrepreneurs usually do not find such sleepy competition in dynamic, emerging industries dense with opportunity.

Entry barriers.   Having a favorable window of opportunity is important. Having or being able to gain proprietary protection, regulatory advantage, or other legal or contractual advantage, such as exclusive rights to a market or with a distributor, is attractive. Having or being able to gain an advantage in response/lead times is important since these can create barriers to entry or expansion by others. For example, advantages in response/lead times in technology, product innovation, market innovation, people, location, resources, or capacity make an opportunity attractive. Possession of well-developed, high-quality, accessible contacts that are the products of years of building a top-notch reputation and that cannot be acquired quickly is also advantageous. In fact, there are times when this competitive advantage may be so strong as to provide dominance in the marketplace, even though many of the other factors are weak or average. An example of how quickly the joys of start-up may fade if others cannot be kept out is the experience of firms in the hard disk drive industry that were unable to erect entry barriers in the United States in the early to mid-1980s. By the end of 1983, some 90 hard disk drive companies were launched, and severe price competition led to a major industry shakeout.

If a firm cannot keep others out or if it faces already existing entry barriers, it is unattractive. An easily overlooked issue is a firm's capacity to gain distribution of its product. As simple as it may sound, even venture-capital-backed companies fall victim to this market issue. Air Florida apparently assembled all the right ingredients, including substantial financing, yet was unable to secure sufficient gate space for its airplanes. Even though it sold passenger seats, it had no place to pick the passengers up or drop them off.

■ **Management Team Issues**

Entrepreneurial team.   Attractive opportunities have teams which are existing and strong and contain industry superstars. The team has proven profit and loss experience in the same technology, market, and service area, and members have complementary and compatible skills. An unattractive opportunity does not have such a team in place or has no team.

■ **Fatal Flaw Issues**

Fatal flaws.   Basically, attractive ventures have no fatal flaws, and one or more fatal flaws render an opportunity unattractive. Usually, these relate to one of the above criteria, and examples abound of markets which are too small, which have overpowering competition, where the cost of entry is too high, where an entrant is unable to produce at a competitive price, and so on. One such example of an entry barrier being a fatal flaw was the inability of the same Air Florida to get its flights listed on reservation computers.

Personal Criteria

One of the most challenging parts of screening opportunities is applying personal criteria:

- **Upside/downside issues.** An attractive opportunity does not have excessive downside risk. The upside and the downside of pursuing an opportunity are not linear, nor are they on the same continuum. The upside is easy, and it has been said that success has a thousand sires. The downside is quite another matter, since it has also been said that failure is an orphan. An entrepreneur needs to be able to absorb the financial downside in a way that he or she can rebound, without becoming indentured to debt obligations. If an entrepreneur's financial exposure in launching the venture is greater than his or her net worth, the resources he or she can reasonably draw upon, and his or her alternative disposable earnings stream if it does not work out, the deal may be too big. While today's bankruptcy laws are extremely generous, the psychological burdens of living through such an ordeal are infinitely more painful than the financial consequences. An existing business needs to consider if a failure will be too demanding to the firm's reputation and future credibility, aside from the obvious financial consequences.[6]
- **Opportunity cost.** In pursuing any venture opportunity, there are also opportunity costs. An entrepreneur who is skilled enough to grow a successful, multimillion-dollar venture has talents that are highly valued by medium- to large-sized firms as well. While assessing benefits that may accrue in pursuing an opportunity, an entrepreneur needs to take a serious look at other alternatives, including potential "golden handcuffs," and account honestly for any "cut" in salary that may be involved in pursuing a certain opportunity.

  Further, pursuing an opportunity can shape an entrepreneur in ways it is hard to imagine. An entrepreneur will probably have time to execute between two to four mulitmillion-dollar ventures between the ages of 25 and 50. Each of these experiences will position him or her, *for better or for worse,* for the next opportunity. Since it is important for an entrepreneur, in his or her early years, to gain relevant management experience and since building a venture (either one that works out or one that does not) takes a lot more time than is commonly believed, it is important to consider alternatives while assessing an opportunity.
- **Desirability.** A good opportunity is not only attractive but also desirable (i.e., a good opportunity "fits"). An example of an intensely personal criterion would be the desire for a certain lifestyle. This desire may preclude pursuing certain opportunities (i.e., certain opportunities may be opportunities for someone else). The founder of a major high-technology venture in the Boston area was asked why the headquarters of his firm were located in downtown Boston, while those of other such firms were located on the famous Route 128 outside of the city. His reply was that he wanted to live in Boston because he loved the city and wanted to be able to walk to work. He said, "The rest did not matter."

---

[6] This point was made by J. Willard Marriott, Jr., at Founder's Day, Babson College, 1988.

GATHERING INFORMATION

The data available about market characteristics, competitors, and so on, is frequently inversely related to the real potential of an opportunity; that is, if market data are readily available and if the data clearly show significant potential, then a large number of competitors will enter the market and the opportunities will diminish.

The good news is that most data will not only be incomplete, inaccurate, and contradictory but also their meaning will be ambiguous. For entrepreneurs, gathering the necessary information and seeing possibilities and making linkages where others see only chaos is essential.

Leonard Fuld defined competitor intelligence as highly specific and timely information about a corporation.[7] Finding out about competitors' sales plans, key elements of their corporate strategies, the capacity of their plants and the technology used in them, who their principal suppliers and customers are, and a good bit about the new products that rivals have under development is difficult, but not impossible, even in emerging industries, when talking to intelligence sources.[8]

Using published resources is one source of such information. Interviewing people and analyzing data also is critical. Fuld believes that, since business transactions generate information which flow then into the public domain, one can locate intelligence sources by understanding the transaction and how intelligence behaves and flows.[9]

This can be done legally and ethically. There are, of course, less than ethical tactics, which include conducting phony job interviews, getting customers to put out phony bid requests, and lying, cheating, and stealing. Entrepreneurs need to be very careful to avoid such practices and are advised to consult an attorney when in doubt.

Note that the sources of information given below are just a start. Much creativity, work, and analysis will be involved to find intelligence and to extend the information obtained into useful form. For example, a competitor's income statement and balance sheet will rarely be handed out. Rather, they most likely must be derived from information in public filings or news articles or from credit reports, financial ratios, and interviews.[10]

Published Sources

The first step is a complete search of material in libraries. There exists a huge amount of published information, databases, and other sources about industry, market, competitor, and personnel information. Some of this information will have been uncovered in searching for ideas (see the list of sources in Chapter 2). Listed below are additional sources for gathering information to help you get started.

■ *Guides and company information.* Information is available in special issues of *Forbes* and *Fortune* and the following:
  — *Thomas Register.*
  — *Directory of Corporate Affiliations.*
  — *Standard & Poor's Register of Corporations, Directors and Executives.*
  — *Standard & Poor's Corporation Records.*
  — *Dun & Bradstreet Million Dollar Directory.*

---

[7] Leonard M. Fuld, *Competitor Intelligence: How to Get It; How to Use It* (New York: John Wiley & Sons, 1985), p. 9.

[8] An excellent resource is Fuld, *Competitor Intelligence.* See also David E. Gumpert and Jeffry A. Timmons, *The Encyclopedia of Small Business Resources* (New York: Harper & Row, 1984); *Fortune,* "How to Snoop on Your Competitors," May 14, 1984, pp. 28–33; and information published by accounting firms, such as *Sources of Industry Data,* published by Ernst & Whinney.

[9] Fuld, ibid., pp. 12–17.

[10] Fuld, ibid., p. 325.

- *Dun & Bradstreet Billion Dollar Directory; America's Corporate Families.*
- *Dun & Bradstreet Principal International Businesses.*
- *Dun & Bradstreet Business Information Reports.*
- *Moody's Manuals.*
- *World Almanac.*
- *Encyclopedia of Business Information Sources,* edited by Paul Wasserman.
- *Business Information Sources,* by Lorna Daniels.
- *Directory of Industry Data Sources,* by Harfax.
- *Business Information,* by Michael Lavin.
- *Financial Analyst's Handbook,* by Sumner Levine.
- *Value Line Investment Survey.*
- *Encyclopedia of Small Business Resources,* by David E. Gumpert and Jeffry A. Timmons.

- **Overviews and general industry information.** Overviews of American industries, such as:
  - *Moody's Investors Industrial Review.*
  - *Standard & Poor's Industry Surveys.*
  - *U.S. Industrial Outlook,* U.S. Department of Commerce.
  - *Current Industrial Reports,* U.S. Department of Commerce.
  - Census Information from U.S. Department of Commerce.
  - *County Business Patterns,* U.S. Department of Commerce.
  - *Industry Surveys,* Standard & Poor's Corporation.
  - *Forbes Annual Report on American Industry.*
  - *The Wall Street Transcript.*
  - *Inside U.S. Business,* by Philip Mattera.

- **Statistics and financial and operating ratios.** Industry statistics listed under the subject, statistics, in library catalogs, and under Standard Industrial Classification (SIC) code numbers in publications (see the *Standard Industrial Classification Manual*). Such information also can be obtained from trade associations. There are also guides to statistics, general collections of industry statistics, and sources of composite financial and operating ratios, such as:
  - *Statistical Abstract of the United States,* U.S. Bureau of the Census.
  - *Encyclopedia of Business Information Sources,* edited by Paul Wasserman.
  - *Economic Indicators.*
  - *Statistical Reference Index.*
  - *American Statistics Index.*
  - *Statistics Sources.*
  - *Basebook,* Predicasts.
  - *Statistical Service,* Standard & Poor's Corporation.
  - *County Business Patterns,* U.S. Bureau of the Census.
  - U.S. Bureau of the Census publications on certain industries.
  - Competitive assessments of certain industries in the United States by the U.S. International Trade Administration.
  - *Summary of Trade and Tariff Information,* U.S. International Trade Administration.
  - Studies of media and markets by Simmons Market Research Bureau, Inc. (New York, New York).
  - *Industry Norms and Key Business Ratios,* Dun & Bradstreet Corporation.
  - *Annual Statement Studies,* Robert Morris Associates.
  - *Analysts Handbook,* Standard & Poor's Corporation.
  - *Almanac of Business and Industrial Financial Ratios,* published by Prentice-Hall.

- **Projections and forecasts.** Projections and forecasts listed under the subject in library catalogs and publications, such as:

- *Predicasts Forecasts.*
- *Predicasts F&S Index.*
- **Market data.** An overall guide to sources of data on consumer and industrial markets can be found in such publications as:
  - *Data Sources for Business & Market Analysis,* Scarecrow Press.
  - *Basebook,* Predicasts.
  - *U.S. Industrial Outlook Handbook.*
  - *Findex* (Find/SVP).
- **Consumer expenditures.** Data on consumer expenditures can be found in such publications as:
  - *Editor & Publisher Market Guide.*
  - *U.S. Census Reports* (*Business, Housing,* etc.).
  - *Survey of Buying Power,* published by Sales Management, Inc.
- **Market studies.** Market studies of particular industries and products available from such companies as:
  - Predicasts (Cleveland, Ohio).
  - Simmons Market Research Bureau (New York, New York).
  - Arthur D. Little, Inc. (Cambridge, Massachusetts).
  - Business Communications Company (Stamford, Connecticut).
  - Frost & Sullivan, Inc. (New York, New York).
  - Morton Research Corporation (Merrick, New York).
  - Theta Technology Corporation (Wethersfield, Connecticut).
- **Data services.** A listing of on-line databases appeared in the June 1984 *Personal Software.* Data services and databases, such as:[11]
  - Dialog Information Service, Inc. (Knight-Ridder, Inc.).
  - CompuServe Information Service Company (H&R Block, Inc.).
  - Dow Jones News/Retrieval Service (Dow Jones & Company).
  - *Lexis, Nexis, Mesis* (Mead Corporation).
  - The Information Bank (Parsipanny, New Jersey).
  - Information Data Search, Inc. (Brookline, Massachusetts).
  - Economic Information Systems (New York, New York).
- **Articles.** Magazine and newspaper articles published by trade associations, government agencies, and commercial publishers. Lists can be found by consulting periodical indexes and directories, such as:
  - *The Directory of Directories.*
  - *Predicasts F&S Index.*
  - *Business Periodicals Index.*
  - *Guide to Special Issues and Indexes of Periodicals.*
  - *Public Affairs Information Service Bulletin.*
  - *Applied Science and Technology Index.*
  - *The Wall Street Journal Index.*
  - *New York Times Index.*
  - *Encyclopedia of Business Information Sources.*
  - *Standard Periodical Directory.*
  - Library directories of current periodical publications.
- **Other sources:**
  - *Wall Street Transcript.*
  - *CIRR: Company & Industry Research Reports.*
  - *Encyclopedia of Associations.*

---

[11] Gumpert and Timmons, *The Encyclopedia of Small Business Resources,* pp. 376–79.

- *National Trade and Professional Associations of the United States and Canada and Labor Unions.*
- *Ayer Directory of Newspapers, Magazines, and Trade Publications.*
- Brokerage house reports.
- Trade association material.
- Books and other material listed in library catalogues under the name of the industry.
- NASA Industrial Applications Centers and several universities, such as Southeastern Oklahoma State University, the University of New Mexico, the University of Southern California, and the University of Pittsburgh provide technically oriented reports, studies, and literature searches.
- Company annual reports.
- ■ *Biographical:*
  - *Standard & Poor's Register of Corporations, Directors and Executives.*
  - *Dun & Bradstreet Reference Book of Corporation Managements.*
  - *Who's Who* directories.

Other Intelligence

Everything entrepreneurs need to know will not be found in libraries, since this information needs to be "highly specific" and "current." This information is most likely available from people—industry experts, suppliers, and the like.

Summarized below are some useful sources of intelligence.

- ■ *Trade associations.* Trade associations, especially the editors of their publications and information officers,[12] are good sources of information. Especially, trade shows and conferences are prime places to discover the latest activities of competitors.
- ■ *Employees.* Employees who have left a competitor's company often can provide information about the competitor, especially if the employee departed on bad terms. Also, a firm can hire people away from a competitor. While consideration of ethics in this situation is important, certainly the number of experienced people in any industry is limited, and competitors must prove that a company hired a person intentionally to get specific trade secrets in order to challenge any hiring legally. Students who have worked for competitors are another source of information.
- ■ *Consulting firms.* Consulting firms frequently conduct industry studies and then make this information available. Frequently, in such fields as computers or software, competitors use the same design consultants, and these consultants can be sources of information.
- ■ *Market research firms.* Firms doing the market studies, such as those listed under published sources above, can be sources of intelligence.
- ■ *Key customers, manufacturers, suppliers, distributors, and buyers.* These groups are often a prime source of information.
- ■ *Public filings.* Federal, state, and local filings, such as filings with the Securities and Exchange Commission (SEC) or Freedom-of-Information Act Filings, can reveal a surprising amount of information. There are companies that process inquiries of this type.
- ■ *Reverse engineering.* Reverse engineering can be used to determine costs of production

---

[12] Ibid., pp. 46 and 48.

and sometimes even manufacturing methods. An example of this practice is the experience of Advanced Energy Technology, Inc., of Boulder, Colorado, which learned first-hand about such tactics. No sooner had it announced a new product, which was patented, when it received 50 orders, half of which were from competitors asking for only one or two of the items.

- *Networks.* The networks mentioned in Chapter 2 as sources of new venture ideas also can be sources of competitor intelligence.
- *Other.* Classified ads, buyers guides, labor unions, real estate agents, courts, local reporters, etc., can provide clues.[13]

CASE — FIBERCOM APPLICATIONS, INC.

Preparation Questions

1. Evaluate the business opportunity, the business plan, and the start-up strategy.
2. What should Smith and McCormack do now?
3. What fund-raising strategy and sources of financing should they consider and not consider, and why?
4. As a private investor, what would your position be in negotiating with Fibercom? As a venture capitalist?

FIBERCOM APPLICATIONS, INC.

In late January 1985, Gary Smith contacted his former professor to seek some advice on his and his partners' efforts to launch a company in the rapidly emerging fiber optics industry. After catching up on the prior 10 years, Smith summarized their situation:

"My partner, Tom McCormack, and I had worked together at BIW Cable for several years, and had off and on talked about the idea of starting our own company. After BIW went public in 1983 the place seemed to slide into a fat 'n' happy approach to the business. It was difficult to get top management interested in some niches in the market that Tom and I believed existed. So last spring we decided to put a business plan together, raise $750,000, and do it. Tom actually resigned in May of 1984 and began concentrating on this full time. The plan was for me to stay on until we raised the money. Tom, myself, and four other partners put up about $100,000 of seed money to enable us to raise the rest."

"So when will you run out of cash?" the professor queried.

After a considerable silence, and some modest clearing of the throat, Smith reckoned, with eyes now glued to an apparent object on the floor, "We are about out now." He said that no other money was in sight, and that's why he had come in to visit.

"What do you think we should do now?" Smith asked.

"Did you bring a copy of your business plan?"

"Yes" was the reply as he passed the latest version of the plan to the professor, conspicuously dated January 1985.

Attached is a copy of the Fibercom Applications, Inc., start-up business plan.

---

[13] Fuld, ibid., pp. 369—418.

Fibercom Applications, Inc., Business Plan, January, 1985

COMPANY

Fibercom Applications, Inc.
1625 Aero Drive
Raleigh, NC 27623
919-555-8200

CONTACT

Mr. Thomas J. McCormack, President

BUSINESS

Fibercom Applications was formed in May 1984, to manufacture fiber optic cables and cable assemblies for the data communication, process control, and other specialty markets.

Sales are forecast to grow to $50,000,000 within 5 years.

Manufacturing fiber optic cables requires special equipment and highly skilled, competent, and experienced design, production, and management personnel. Fibercom Applications has proprietary knowledge of the design, manufacture, and marketing of fiber optic cables.

The company will make use of unique materials to custom design fiber optic cables for use by specific market segments. By choosing these segments, the management's experience is that the company can sell its products at higher margins than those available in other parts of the fiber optic cable market.

There are only a small number of competitors serving the company's target industries. The company will compete with these firms by offering a variety of cable types and by possessing an in-depth knowledge of its customers' requirements. Because of the experience and specialized skills necessary to produce fiber optic cables it is difficult for other companies to readily enter the fiber optic cable business.

SELECTED FINANCIAL DATA
(dollars in 000s)

Year	1	2	3	4	5
Sales	1,750	3,500	10,000	25,000	50,000
Earnings	(25)	244	1,017	3,507	7,394

MANAGEMENT

The company has three key managers. Together, they sold and produced more than $2,000,000 of specialty fiber optic cable in 1983, representing about 10% of the available market in that year. The management is exceptionally experienced in manufacturing specialty fiber optic cables.

Thomas J. McCormack, founder and President, has more than 6 years experience in specialty cable manufacturing, including 4 years in fiber optics. He has been General Manager of the Fiber Optics Division of BIW Cable Systems, a specialty cable manufacturer, where he started their fiber optic efforts. He has sold to and produced cable for all the company's targeted markets.

Gary A. Smith, Vice President—Sales and Marketing, has more than 4 years experience in the sales and marketing of specialty cables, including fiber optic cable. He has sold to all of the company's targeted markets. In 1983, at BIW Cable Systems, he was the top-ranked sales manager in the country, increasing his territory's sales by 21%, to $7.1 million.

Clint M. Owens, Vice President — Engineering, has 20 years experience with wire and cable, including 6 years with fiber optics. He started the fiber optics group at Brand Rex Company, and directed the growth of his division to more than $2,000,000 in 1984. He has extensive experience in selling to and producing fiber optic cables for the company's targeted markets.

FUNDS REQUIRED

Fibercom Applications requires $750,000 of additional funding to begin operations. The company proposes to issue 300,000 shares of common stock, representing 10.7% ownership, for this funding. Alternate structuring will be considered.

USE OF FUNDS

The funds will be used as follows:

Capital equipment	$530,000
Working capital	220,000

Business Plan — Table of Contents

Title	Section
Summary	1
Financing Requirements	2
Business	3
Market Size and Competition	4
Sales Projections	5
Capital Equipment	6
Year 0 Operations	7
Years 2–5 Operations	8
Risk Factors	9
Appendix A: Financial Projections	10
Appendix B: Management Résumés	11

1. Summary

Fibercom Applications (the "company") will design, manufacture, and market fiber optic cables and cable assemblies. Fiber optic cables use hair-thin flexible glass fibers to transmit information as light pulses or as a modulated beam of light. Fiber optic cable assemblies have fiber optic connectors attached to the ends of the cable.

The company will serve selected segments of the rapidly growing fiber optic market. The company's targeted market segments are the computer interconnection/local area network and process control areas. These emerging market niches are not being adequately served by current suppliers and provide the best opportunities for highly profitable sales of the company's unique and proprietary cables.

Manufacturing fiber optic cables requires special equipment, along with highly skilled, competent, and experienced design, manufacturing, and management personnel. Fibercom

Applications has extensive experience in and possesses proprietary knowledge of the design, manufacture, and marketing of fiber optic cables.

Fibercom Applications will manufacture fiber optic cables for specialty applications. By providing custom engineered products, Fibercom Applications will be recognized as the technical expert in each market. Through its technical superiority, the company will be better able to anticipate market needs, to identify potential market niches, and to sell at premium margins.

The management of the company is exceptionally experienced in providing fiber optic cables to these markets. The company's three key employees have combined experience of more than 15 years in the design, manufacture, marketing, and selling of fiber optic cables to the target markets. Two of the key employees have previous experience in starting up a specialty fiber optic cable manufacturing operation. In 1983, the three key employees sold more than $2,000,000 of specialty fiber optic cables, representing about 10 percent of the available market.

The company will have a limited number of competitors in its target industries (see Market Size and Competition, section 4). Some of these competitors are larger than the company and have access to more financial resources than the company. Others, while having current sales in excess of the company's, do not possess the technical and marketing skills of Fibercom Applications. Because manufacturing fiber optic cables requires special equipment and unique skills, it is very difficult for new manufacturers, including existing electrical wire and cable companies, to enter the market. The management of the company believes it can successfully compete with both existing and possible future manufacturers in its targeted markets on the basis of superior technology and variety of fiber products, and by providing outstanding service to its customers.

The company's sales are forecast to grow to $50 million in year 5. To permit operations as outlined herein, $750,000 of capital is required immediately. This capital will be used for the following:

A.	Purchase of equipment	$530,000
B.	Working capital	220,000
	Total	$750,000

This capital will fund the company's operations for 18 months, when additional capital is required. This additional capital may have to be raised to by selling additional equity.

2. Financing Requirements

Fibercom Applications has completed seed financing totaling $150,000 and requires additional equity capital of $750,000. The company will use short-term debt, provided by commercial banks, to meet cash flow requirements.

Fibercom Applications, a Delaware corporation, was incorporated in May 1984. The company has an authorized level of 2,000 shares of common stock, of which 1,250 shares are currently issued and outstanding and 110 shares are reserved for sale under existing warrant and option agreements.

Existing ownership of the company is:

Shareholder	Number of Shares
Thomas J. McCormack	325
Gary A. Smith	325
Clint M. Owens	100
All others (total = 6 people)	500
Reserved for issue	110
Total	1,360

Prior to raising the additional capital, the company intends to split its stock at a ratio of 2,000 new shares for each currently existing share, to reserve 250,000 shares for an incentive stock plan for future employees, and to raise the company's authorized level of stock to 5 million shares.

The company proposes to raise $750,000 by selling 300,000 shares of newly issued common stock at a price of $2.50 per share. After issuing these shares, the company's capitalization will be:

2.8 million shares of common stock, issued and outstanding:		
Par value, $0.01 per share		$ 28,000
Additional paid in capital		827,000
Total capital		$900,000
The ownership of the company will then be:		
Existing shareholders	2,500,000	$150,000
New shareholders	300,000	750,000
Total	2,800,000	$900,000

3. Business

Fibercom Applications designs, manufactures, and markets fiber optic cables to a select number of market segments. In the broadest sense, fiber optic cables are used by two distinct markets — the telephone industry and specialty markets. These two areas are different, both technically and commercially. While cables for the telephone industry offer state-of-the-art optical performance, the cables are sold as a commodity at low margins. In the specialty market, the cables may have less stringent optical requirements, but there are other performance needs that must be met. Fibercom Applications will serve selected areas of the specialty market. The company will treat each market niche independently, both in terms of cable design and in selling techniques. Fibercom Applications will be recognized as the expert in each segment, will be able to anticipate market needs, and will identify and participate in the profitable niches of each.

Communication technology has rapidly changed in the last decade. The increasing use of telephone systems, computers, and other systems that utilize low-power digital signals, in place of systems where high-power analog signals convey information, has imposed stringent new requirements on the communication media.

For these modern systems, conventional electrical interconnections may not be satisfactory without extensive equipment modification or costly installation changes, or both. The low-power digital signals are particularly susceptible to electromagnetic interference.

Further, all electronic equipment radiates electromagnetic noise, and the U.S. government has recently established strict limits on the amount of radiation that can be emitted from electronic equipment. Electrical interconnecting cables accentuate this emission problem. Fiber optic communication systems overcome this and other problems associated with electrical equipment.

Fiber optics is a relatively new technology offering a number of advantages over the traditional electrical method of transmitting information. Fiber optic systems (see Fiber Optic Systems, below) can carry more information than electrical systems and are immune to electromagnetic and radio frequency interference. Fiber optic cables do not radiate electromagnetic signals as electrical cables do. Fiber optic cables are smaller and lighter than electrical cables, thereby reducing installation costs. Fiber optic cables also have lower losses than the electrical cables they replace, and can therefore transmit signals of a given strength longer distances than electrical cables.

Fiber Optic Markets

The market for fiber optic cables is expected to grow to $1 billion by 1990 (see Market Size and Competition, section 4). Fibercom Applications has divided the total market into four segments.

1. Telecommunications. The telecommunications market may be subdivided into two areas.

(a) Long-haul Communications. This market segment is characterized by high capacity, high fiber count cables. These cables usually contain over 24 signal mode fibers. The cables are installed with long distances between terminals, so the cables must be produced in the longest practical lengths, 2 kM or more. Optical performance of these cables is state of the art, and cable performance is the most important evaluation criteria.

(b) Subscriber Loop. This part of the telephone market uses cables with relatively high fiber counts, ranging from 6 to 24 fibers per cable. The cables contain either single mode or high performance graded index fibers. These applications are growing rapidly as terminal equipment, connecting devices, and splicing equipment becomes more readily available.

The telephone market segment is by far the largest, accounting for up to 75 percent of the total market. There are seven suppliers to this market area, and the company does not intend to capture a significant part of this market. It is likely that the company will have limited sales to the telephone industry, in those applications where special performance is needed, or where a special design is required.

2. Computer Interconnection/Local Area Networks. The interconnection of mainframe, minicomputers, and microcomputers and peripherals by local area networks is predicted to grow explosively in the next few years. The success of the "office of the future" depends upon reliable, secure, and high speed transmission of data between the CPU and peripheral devices.

Electrical interconnections are limited in their ability to meet these criteria. Electrical cable is limited in the amount of data that can be carried and in the distance the data can be sent without amplification. The data also is subject to error from interference picked up by the cable, and the cables themselves radiate electromagnetic noise. Fiber optics eliminates these problems.

The cables for this market have relatively low fiber counts, ranging from 2 to 12 fibers per cable, and are installed in a wide variety of environments. The cables typically use larger core fibers than the telecommunications products.

The management of Fibercom Applications has experience in serving this market area. The company has designed and developed a unique product for interoffice connections and intends to aggressively promote this product to the computer interconnection market. The company intends to fully serve this market. Competitors and market size are discussed in Section 4.

3. Process Control. With the expanding use of microprocessor-based control systems and programmable controllers in factory and plant environments, fiber optics is making significant inroads into the process control industry primarily because of its noise immunity and high data transfer capacity.

The cables for this market usually have low fiber counts, from 1 to 12 fibers per cable, and must be custom designed for each application. For example, a process control system may have a basic requirement for a two-channel cable. If the control system is being installed in a nuclear generating station the cable must be radiation resistant, while if the control system is being installed in a chemical refinery the cable may have to withstand exposure to hazardous vapors. While the same basic design may be used for each cable, different materials may have to be used in each application to meet the specific environmental requirements.

Fibercom Applications' management has extensive experience in serving many different parts of the process control industry. Using its specialized knowledge of materials and constructions, the company has designed a number of unique cables for use in industrial environments. The company will supply a significant portion of the fiber optic cable used in this market.

The size and competition in this market segment are discussed in Section 4.

4. Military. The military market presents a variety of applications. The cables are characterized by low fiber counts, 1 to 12 fibers, and frequently use special radiation resistant large core fibers. The cables are subject to stringent performance requirements, including low temperature, severe bending and twisting, and fungus attack.

The company intends to serve the military market where special performance is needed. The company will provide extremely rugged, gas and/or water blocked cables, and cables suitable for performance over a wide temperature range. Again, competition and market size are discussed in Section 4.

In each of its target markets, the company's management has successful prior experience in designing, manufacturing, and selling cables. The target markets are growing rapidly, as shown in Section 4. In the target markets, the management's experience is that higher gross margins are available, and that the company's extensive knowledge of special materials and cable design can be sold at a premium.

Fiber Optics Systems

Fiber optic cable is one part of an overall fiber optic system. Fiber optic communications requires a system consisting of three parts—an optical transmitter, an optical fiber cable, and an optical receiver. The transmitter takes incoming electrical signals and converts them to optical pulses. The fiber optic cable carries the light pulses from the transmitter to the receiver. The receiver reverses the process, converting the optical pulses back to electrical signals. Operational failure of any one part of the system is catastrophic. Any individual part is useless unless the other parts are functional. Transmitters and receivers with outstanding reliability are now commercially available at low cost. Cable technology, however, has not been highly developed for nontelephone applications. Fibercom Applications will provide the highly reliable cables that will assure high system reliability.

Great progress has been made in designing and manufacturing optical fiber, the primary component of the cable. Cost reductions of 90 percent and more have been made over the last three years, while, during the same time, quality and performance of the fiber has improved.

Because of their delicate structure, optical fibers cannot be used without the protection of properly designed cable. Fiber optic cable development efforts have been limited to cables used for long distance telecommunications. The design of cables containing optical fibers for specialty market applications has not progressed.

The designer of cables for use in the specialty markets must consider many parameters, including installation conditions, environmental temperatures, flame retardency, radiation resistance, water resistance, and chemical resistance. In fact, to maximize cable reliability, specific and unique cables must be designed for each application.

The lack of properly designed cables has impeded the use of fiber optics in the nontelephone market. For instance, local area networking of computers is an application that can benefit from using fiber optics. In recognition of this need, the American National Standards Committee has formed a working group to write a standard for fiber optics in the local area network. This committee is of national stature, and its work will accelerate the use of fiber in LANs. In reporting on the committee's work, the *Electronic Engineering Times* of May 14, 1984, quotes the committee as saying "the lack of satisfactory commercially available fiber optic cable" is the main reason for slow implementation of fiber optics in this application.

Once a suitable cable has been developed, it may not be usable for all applications in a market. In one system the fiber optic cable may be installed beneath carpets, in air handling ducts, in walls, in conduit, in cable trays, and under floors. The cable design must be tailored to make the cable suitable for each application. This entails selecting alternate materials, changing the relative position of the fibers, or varying the strength characteristics.

Fiber Optic Cable Design

The design of fiber optic cables is similar to that of electrical cables, but with several salient yet significant differences. In most electrical cables no consideration is given to the physical strength of the cable, since the electrical conductor provides sufficient strength. Electrical cables are simply designed to provide a dielectric covering over the conductor, either by using an insulating material applied to the conductor, by physically separating the conductors, or a combination of both.

In comparison, many factors must be considered when designing a fiber optic cable. The glass optical fiber has little inherent strength and is easily damaged by external forces. Therefore, a fiber optic cable must be designed to maximize the protection of the fiber. Excessive coiling or stretching will damage the fiber. Thermal expansion and contraction of the other cable materials relative to the optical fiber may damage the fiber. Materials must be selected in view of their physical and thermal performance, and the fiber must be precisely located in the cable to achieve maximum isolation from its environment.

Fibercom Applications has designed cables with a variety of materials that are thermally compatible with the optical fiber and that provide a high level of protection to the fiber. These designs provide a higher level of protection than provided by cables made by our competition.

Fibercom Applications will custom design fiber optic cables to meet its customers' service requirements. The company will provide features in its products that are not available from its competitors. These features include:

1. Unique Applications of Materials

Fibercom Applications will manufacture cables using the widest variety of materials available in the fiber optic market.

Every material must be processed in a different manner, and small variations in processing will cause scrap. Process development for each material is both costly and time consuming and requires considerable experience both in extrusion and in fiber optics. For this reason, most companies do not offer a wide range of materials.

The management of Fibercom Applications has extensive experience in processing a variety of materials. The company is experienced in developing methods and techniques to utilize many materials in fiber optic cables. Using its methods, the company will continue to develop these processes. Where practical, the company will seek to protect its processes with patents.

2. Heavy Wall Loose Tubes

The company's targeted markets demand cables that are extremely rugged and highly reliable.

To provide these features, Fibercom Applications will manufacture fiber optic cables that have a thick loose tube protecting the fiber. Extruding thick loose tubes over optical fibers is very difficult and requires careful attention to processing. All the residual stress in the materials must be eliminated, and the loose tubes must be made under precise and controlled conditions. Moreover, the company will manufacture these tubes in a variety of materials.

The heavy wall loose tube feature makes the cable slightly more expensive to build, but its higher reliability permits it to be sold at a higher price.

The management of the company has experience in designing and building cables with heavy wall loose tubes. This experience will be used to efficiently produce this product with little or no scrap.

3. Flame Retardancy

Many of the company's target markets demand cables with a high degree of flame retardancy. The company will manufacture highly flame retardant cables for "plenum" use at a lower cost than its competition. The company, therefore, can achieve a higher profit margin on this product.

Fibercom Applications also will manufacture cables that meet the stringent flame test requirements for Type TC cable, allowing the company's product to be used in the same way as electrical cables and without the extra costs associated with installing a separate cable mounting system.

Other companies produce flame retardant fiber optic cables. However, their choice of materials is very limited. To differentiate its products, Fibercom Applications will work with our customers to select a material that achieves all the customer's needs, and to convince the customer to specify the company's unique materials for its cables.

4. Specialization in Large Core Fibers

Fibercom Applications will manufacture cables with large core optical fibers. Large core fibers are used extensively in short distance applications that are typical of many of the company's targeted markets. Large core fibers are very subject to damage from handling, and, therefore, manufacturing cables incorporating these fibers is more difficult than making cables with small core fibers. Because of the manufacturing difficulties, many manufacturers of fiber optic cables do not offer cables with large core fibers.

The management of Fibercom Applications has extensive experience in successfully building cables with large core fibers. The company is experienced with these fibers and in selecting machinery and processes compatible with them. By choosing the proper equipment, and specializing in making these cables, the company will be more efficient than others and, therefore, more profitable.

Fibercom Applications will also provide many other features in its products. The company's management has many years of experience in designing and manufacturing fiber optic cables. The company has already designed cables that consider these properties for specific applications, and it has perfected techniques to economically manufacture the cables. These products include:

1. *Undercarpet cables.* The company has designed and built a fiber optic cable for use in undercarpet office applications. This special design uses a unique material and construction that has been successfully tested by a major supplier of undercarpet systems.
2. *Molded cable assemblies.* The company has designed an assembly with connectors molded to the end of the cable that promises to be more rugged, durable, and reliable than existing assemblies. The company believes this product will have great acceptance in the computer interconnection market and in the process control industry.
3. *Plenum cables.* The company has designed a series of plenum cables using less-expensive materials than other cables of this type. Prototype cables must be built and tested to make this product commercial.

Manufacturing

Fiber optic cable manufacturing is significantly different than making electrical cables. Because the fiber is delicate and cannot be reclaimed if damaged, properly designed, operated, and maintained equipment must be used in making fiber optic cables. This equipment must have precise tension controls, along with other sensitive control mechanisms, to achieve a high-quality thermally stable covering over the fiber. Profitability depends upon error-free manufacturing with little scrap.

Satisfactory performance of the finished cable depends upon achieving a uniform material over the optical fiber. The uniformity of the material depends on many factors, but of primary importance is the proper extrusion process. Control of the entire extrusion process is critical. Extrusion tool design must be tailored to the material and its dimensions. Temperature of the melting extrudate must be precisely controlled to avoid residual stress. Cooling characteristics must be tailored to each material. These controls are not normally imposed, or are they needed, for electrical cable manufacturing.

Fiber optic cables must be manufactured in a cleaner environment than electrical cables. Moreover, fiber optic cables cannot be made in the same area with electrical cables. Any airborne contaminants that come in contact with the optical fiber may damage it, with resulting scrap.

The company has developed a unique method of manufacturing one- and two-channel optical cables more efficiently than its competitors. Both cable types are widely used in many of the company's targeted markets, and the company expects to capture a large portion of this business.

Fibercom Applications will only manufacture fiber optic cables. The company will be expert in the handling of optical fiber. It will enforce housekeeping and cleanliness standards that could not be enforced in a plant making both electrical and optical cables.

The management of the company has combined experience of more than 10 years in building fiber optic cables and in designing and installing the proper equipment to make them efficiently. The company's specialization, experience, and efficiency will be its competitive advantage.

Marketing and Sales

Fibercom Applications will market its products primarily on the basis of technical superiority. The company will establish a reputation of supplying a high-quality product, delivered on time.

A major goal of the company's marketing plan is to produce the company's products as specified by its customers. To accomplish this, it will identify specific customers in each target market area and work closely with the customer's engineers in preparing performance specifications for their cables.

Repeat orders from a customer are an important part of the company's growth philosophy. To promote good will and allegiance, and, therefore, obtain repeat orders, the company will organize and direct its efforts to provide outstanding service to its customers.

To achieve brand recognition, the company will actively promote its products through advertising and trade show participation. The company plans regular mailings of informational literature to its customers.

Fibercom Applications will sell its products through an integrated network of direct salespeople, manufacturers' agents, and distributors.

The company will hire direct salespeople to serve several areas where the use of agents and distributors is impractical. They will be responsible for sales to computer manufacturers (IBM, DEC, Wang), to process control manufacturers (Honeywell, Foxboro), and to other large customers (architect-engineers, electric utilities).

Manufacturers' agents will sell to all other accounts, particularly those which buy smaller quantities of cable and those that do not require continuous technical sales efforts. The vice president of sales and marketing will supervise these agents and monitor their progress. The company expects that it will take at least a year to complete a representative network.

The company also will support distributor sales to those industries that prefer to buy in this way.

The company does not intend to serve all the targeted markets at once. The company will concentrate its efforts in the process control and computer markets. These markets promise the fastest returns on the sales efforts for several reasons. First, the company's management has extensive experience in selling to both the process control and computer markets. Second, both areas are currently purchasing sufficient volumes of cable to permit the company's revenue targets to be met. Third, the markets are not being adequately served by the existing suppliers.

4. Market Size and Competition

Fibercom Applications will serve selected areas of the market for specialty fiber optic cable assemblies. The company's target markets include the computer interconnection, process control, military, and broadband markets.

All areas of the fiber optic cable market are experiencing extremely high growth rates that are expected by many market research firms to continue for the next decade. Several market research organizations (Kessler Marketing Intelligence, Gnostic Concepts, A. D. Little, Frost and Sullivan) have made predictions about the growth. These studies estimate that the total market for fiber optic cables in 1984 was about $240 million. The studies also indicate that telephone industry accounts for about 80 percent of the 1984 market and that the market for the company's products was between $40 and $60 million in 1983.

The company believes that in 1984 the market for its products was approximately $48 million, up 85 percent from 1983. The company's estimate was determined by consolidating internal estimates with the published figures of several sources. The internal estimates were made by personal knowledge of the market, evaluating competitors' size, and discussions with fiber manufacturers.

The market for fiber optic cables is growing at a rapid pace. Published growth rates range from 40 to 65 percent per year. The company's own estimate is on the conservative

Table 4–A
Projected Size of the Company's Market

Year	Estimated target market
1983	$ 26,000,000
1984	48,000,000
1985	70,000,000
1986	100,000,000
1987	160,000,000
1988	220,000,000
1989	300,000,000
1990	400,000,000

end of this range; Fibercom Applications estimates that its targeted markets will grow at an annual rate of 40 percent. The size of the company's market is shown in *Table 4–A*.

Competition

Fibercom Applications will have several competitors for the nontelephone market. The three largest competitors are Siecor, Belden, and ITT.

Siecor. Siecor is a joint venture of Corning Glass Works and the Siemens Corporation. Corning is the second largest supplier of optical fiber in the United States (after AT&T Technologies) and Siemens is a German-based cable manufacturer. With the exception of AT&T Technologies, Siecor is the largest manufacturer of fiber optic cables in the United States.

Siecor concentrates its efforts in the telephone business; but with excess cable capacity to date, it is also the largest supplier of nontelephone cables. The explosive growth of sales to the telephone market, however, has impaired Siecor's ability to serve the specialty market and opens this part of their business to invasion by other manufacturers.

Siecor offers a variety of cables and currently competes in many of Fibercom's targeted markets. Siecor builds both loose and tight buffered cables and uses a relatively large number of materials in its cables. However, Fibercom Applications believes it can compete with Siecor on a customer service and delivery basis.

Belden. Belden is a unit of Cooper Industries. It does not manufacture fiber optic cables for the telephone industry but concentrates its efforts in markets similar to Fibercom's. Belden's fiber optic sales in 1984 were between $5 million and $8 million. Belden is well known in the fiber optic cable business.

Belden produces both tight and loose buffered cables but uses only a small number of materials. It, therefore, is at a disadvantage when competing with Fibercom Applications. It has an established sales and distribution network, which will help it in competing with Fibercom.

ITT. ITT acquired Valtec Corporation, which was a division of U.S. Philips, in September 1984. Combined with its own fiber optic cable business, ITT became a major supplier of fiber optic cable. Valtec concentrates its major sales efforts in the telephone industry, with lesser efforts in the military and computer interconnection markets. Prior to its acquisition, Valtec had several ownership changes in the last few years, and the continuity of management, necessary in the specialty business, has been difficult to maintain. Fibercom Applications estimates Valtec's total sales in 1984 to be $15 million, with nontelephone sales of between $4 million and $6 million. ITT had nontelephone sales of between $1 million and $2 million in 1984, so the combined company has nontelephone sales of between $5 million and $8 million.

Table 4–B
Sales to the Nontelephone Markets

Company	1984 Estimated Sales	
	Low	High
Siecor	$15,000,000	$20,000,000
ITT-Valtec	5,000,000	8,000,000
Belden	5,000,000	8,000,000
General Cable	2,000,000	4,000,000
Times Fiber	2,000,000	3,000,000
Brand Rex	1,500,000	2,000,000
Phalo	1,000,000	2,500,000
Mohawk	1,000,000	2,000,000
Maxlight	1,000,000	2,000,000
Pirelli	1,000,000	2,000,000
Anaconda-Ericcson	1,000,000	2,000,000
Optical Cable	750,000	1,500,000
BIW Cable	250,000	500,000
Whitmore	250,000	500,000
Others	500,000	1,000,000
Total	$37,250,000	$59,000,000

ITT will concentrate its efforts in the long distance telecommunications field, with a lesser effort in the military area. Fibercom Applications does not expect to compete directly against ITT in the data communications or process control markets.

Other Competitors.   Several other companies sell fiber optic cables to the company's targeted markets. These companies include Times Fiber Communications, Phalo (a division of Transitron), Mohawk (a division of Conductron), BIW Cable Systems, Brand Rex, Pirelli, General Cable, Anaconda-Ericcson, Optical Cable Corporation, and Whitmore. While the exact size of each company is unknown, Fibercom Applications' estimates of 1984 sales for each are shown in *Table 4–B,* above. Based on this analysis, the total size of the company's targeted nontelephone markets was between $37 million and $59 million.

Of these companies, General Cable and Anaconda-Ericcson continue to concentrate their sales efforts in the telephone industry and will play ever smaller roles in the specialty markets. Fibercom Applications' superior market knowledge and variety of materials will be used in competing with these companies.

Brand Rex, BIW Cable Systems, Phalo, Mohawk, and Whitmore have not made the commitment of manufacturing and engineering resources that is necessary to compete in the fiber optic market. Brand Rex and BIW have extensive skills in processing many materials. However, unless they make major investments in plant and personnel for the fiber optic business, they will not be able to challenge Fibercom on a performance basis. Of the other companies, Phalo and Whitmore do not possess the technical or material processing skills of the company.

Mohawk has withdrawn from the fiber optic business. Fibercom Applications will use its knowledge and experience in fiber optics to compete against these companies.

Optical Cable Corporation is a relatively new company, formed in 1983, and, by virtue of its specialization in fiber optics, will be a factor in Fibercom's markets. The management of Fibercom Applications has more experience in the company's target markets, however, and their specialized marketing skills will be used in competition with OCC.

At the present time, the company is aware of only three other potential competitors, Madison Wire and Cable, Berk-Tek, and Celwave Technologies. The company anticipates that one or more of these companies could become a major competitor.

5. Sales Projections

Fibercom Applications has established the following five-year sales forecast (see *Table 5–A*):

Table 5–A
Sales Forecast

Year	Fibercom Applications' Forecast
1	$ 1,750,000
2	3,500,000
3	10,000,000
4	25,000,000
5	50,000,000

This is a compound annual growth rate of more than 130 percent and requires substantial investment in plant, the hiring of extremely talented personnel, and an effective sales effort.

The sales projections result in a year 5 market penetration of more than 10 percent. This market share can be achieved within the company's marketing and manufacturing resources. The availability of trained design engineers and qualified sales personnel may make it difficult to attain higher growth rates in the specialty markets.

The company's potential customers range from large industrial and utility companies, with multibillion dollar revenues, to small privately owned companies, with sales under $1 million. These potential customers will be contacted through an integrated marketing and sales campaign, including space advertising, trade show participation, and direct sales contact. More information concerning the company's marketing and sales efforts are in Section 3.

6. Capital Equipment Requirements

Special equipment must be employed to produce the highest-quality fiber optic cables. Of particular importance, tension controls must be present on all fiber handling equipment to avoid damaging the fiber.

Fibercom Applications has extensive capital equipment requirements. Initial capital expenditures include the following:

1. A small plastic extrusion line, approximately 1.5 inches, for the primary application of buffering material over the fiber. The extruder must be able to process high-temperature fluoropolymer materials. Support equipment includes a water bath, fiber payoff and tensioning equipment, extrusion tools, pullout equipment, and a traversing takeup.
2. A medium-size plastic extrusion line for secondary extrusion of cable jackets. This equipment also must be able to handle fluoropolymer resins, plus conventional jacketing materials. Similar support equipment to that on item 1 is required.
3. A fiber optic cabler, capable of stranding 18 fibers in one operation. Each payout bay

must have precise tension controls. The line also will include taping equipment to apply both metallic and nonmetallic coverings over the cable's core.

4. A serving head, for use in the cabling machine or in the extrusion lines, to apply strength members to the cable.
5. Test equipment for performing bandwidth, attenuation, numerical aperture, and pulse dispersion measurements on optical fiber. Mechanical testing equipment, to test both cables and cable materials, and an optical time domain reflectometer are also needed.

The primary extrusion equipment (item 1, above) and test equipment (item 5, above) will be purchased as new equipment. Used equipment suitable for these purposes is not available. A used jacket extrusion line and cabler will be purchased for the initial operations.

The lead time for the equipment ranges from one to 4 months. The first equipment that must be installed is the small, primary extrusion line. After this line is installed, the secondary extrusion line and the fiber optic cabler will be installed.

With the use of overtime and multiple shifts, the initial equipment will support shipments through year 1. To support the projected sales in years 2 through 5, additional equipment is needed.

7. Year 0 Operations

The company's initial year (ending July 31, 1985) is an organizational year. Because of the high growth rates the company will experience, it is essential that proper systems and procedures be implemented immediately to achieve the financial goals that have been established. Efforts in this year will be concentrated in seven key areas:

1. Obtaining capital.
2. Recruiting key personnel.
3. Locating manufacturing space.
4. Purchasing and installing equipment.
5. Manufacturing trial products for internal and external evaluation.
6. Designing and executing an advertising campaign.
7. Obtaining initial production orders.

Meeting the sales forecast depends upon meeting several milestones in the initial year, shown in *Table 7–A*. Failure to meet these milestones may have an adverse effect on later operations.

Initial sales of the company will be produced by other manufacturers on a private label basis. These sales will generate cash flow and establish Fibercom Applications in the marketplace. However, because others will be manufacturing the product, none of the company's proprietary cables can be sold at this time.

Year 0 operating expenses are in four areas:

Table 7–A
1985 Milestones (year 0)

Date	Milestone
March 1	Receive startup capital
March 1	Begin advertising campaign
May 1	Install primary extruder
June 1	Begin trial extrusions
June 30	Produce initial production orders

1. Salaries of executive officers.
2. Design and implementation of an advertising campaign.
3. Salaries of startup production and test personnel.
4. Materials used in product trial manufacturing.

Pro forma financial statements for year 0 are included in Appendix A.

8. Years 1–5 Operations and Organization

Appendix A contains pro forma financial statements for years 1 through 5. These projections have been made using the assumptions outlined below.

A. Cost of Goods Sold

The actual material costs for the assumed product mix were calculated. Also from the product mix, machine loadings were calculated and the labor necessary to operate the machinery was determined.

B. Operating Expenses

Engineering.   Engineering and R&D are the responsibility of and under the direction of the vice president–engineering.

The vice president–engineering is responsible for all technical operations of the company and fulfills five functions. First, he maintains contact with chemical, compound, and other raw material suppliers to be aware of new materials as they become available. Second, he is responsible for all cable designs. Third, he recruits, trains, and supervises all application and process engineers. Fourth, he recruits, trains, and supervises all test personnel. Last, because the marketing of the company's products will be technically oriented, he has extensive customer contact.

The company initially will employ an experienced process engineer. He or she will report to the vice president–engineering and be responsible for all process development. This person must be highly skilled, with a strong technical background in plastic extrusion and possess hands-on experience with extrusion equipment. He or she also will participate in the company's development efforts to evaluate new materials and their applicability to fiber optic cables.

Test personnel and application engineers will be added as needed to support the production and sales efforts. By year 5, the company expects to employ 56 engineers and technicians.

Sales.   The vice president–sales and marketing is responsible for the sales, marketing, and customer service operations of the company.

The vice president–sales and marketing is technically knowledgeable about fiber optics and is experienced with the sales and marketing of products by manufacturers' agents, direct sales personnel, and distributors.

The vice president recruits and trains all sales personnel. He or she plans and directs the company's marketing plan, including an aggressive advertising campaign. He or she writes sales literature, prepares technical and commercial proposals, and sets price levels.

The company's initial sales efforts will be made through a network of manufacturers' agents, directed and coordinated by the vice president. The vice president is directly responsible for sales to the larger customers until a direct sales force is put in place.

Advertising and trade show participation are important parts of the company's sales efforts. Brand recognition will be gained by regular advertising in user-oriented industrial trade publications and by participation in trade shows.

The company will employ direct salespeople as quickly as possible. The vice president will coordinate the efforts of both the direct salespeople and the manufacturer's agents. Inside sales efforts will be organized and staffed to compliment the outside sales efforts.

By year 5, the company expects to employ 35 people in sales and have a national network of manufacturer's agents.

Administrative.   Administrative overhead includes manufacturing management, accounting, bookkeeping, purchasing, and production coordination.

Initially, the president will directly supervise the administrative and manufacturing efforts. A vice president–manufacturing is added to the company in year 1, who will be responsible for all manufacturing operations.

Additional overhead expenses include telephone and telex service, office expenses (copying, postage, stationery, etc.), legal and accounting services, and insurance costs.

Depreciation.   Depreciation is calculated on a five-year, straight-line basis.

9. Risk Factors

There are several risk factors to consider in making an investment in the company.

No Operating History

Fibercom Applications is a start-up company and has no operating history. All financial statements presented herein are estimates of future operations. If anticipated revenues are not received, if actual costs exceed projections, or if delays are encountered in developing the company's products, additional financing may be necessary.

To minimize this risk, strict controls will be imposed over material costs, labor costs, inventories, and other costs. Operations will be managed to maximize cash flow.

Limited Management Experience

The management of the company, while experienced in the manufacturing and sales of fiber optic cables, has no experience in organizing and starting up a new venture.

Mr. McCormack's experience with his former employer, where he started a fiber optics division, and Mr. Owens's experience with his former employer, where he started a fiber optics manufacturing operation, will be used to offset this risk. Both of these people have extensive contacts in the fiber optics and cable manufacturing business, and this experience will be used to the company's benefit. Additionally, outside directors and advisors will be sought to provide management guidance and assistance.

Market Growth

The success of the company depends on the projected growth of the overall market for fiber optic systems.

To minimize this risk, the company has based its projections on the low end of the projected growth of the industry. If this growth level is not achieved, a higher level of market share, sales to other markets, and sales of other specialty cables will be sought.

Raw Material Availability

The company will depend on outside sources for its major raw material, optical fiber. Disruption of this supply will adversely affect the company's ability to produce its products.

The company will attempt to negotiate annual supply contracts for optical fiber with one or more suppliers. There is no assurance that these contracts can be negotiated, or that they can be made on terms favorable to the company. Alternately, significant additional investments will have to made in both equipment and personnel to manufacture optical fiber.

Dependence upon Key Employees

The success of the company depends upon the continued employment of Messrs. McCormack, Smith, and Owens. Employment and noncompetition agreements will be negotiated with each to assure this continuity.

Other key employees must be hired, and the company will offer favorable compensation programs to attract and retain these employees.

10.   Appendix A: Financial Projections

The financial projections were made using the following assumptions:

Income Statement

Sales.   Sales projections were made based upon the company's estimate of the current market size and its growth projections. Conservative estimates were made of the company's market share.

Cost of Goods.   Cost of goods were calculated from actual cable constructions. Material costs were determined from suppliers of these materials. Labor costs were estimated at current labor rates, increased at 5 percent per year to represent a "real" increase. Inflation has not been considered.

Operating Expenses.   The actual staffing needed to produce the estimated sales was determined, and actual labor costs were used to determine expenses in each category. Labor costs were escalated at 5 percent per year, as above.

Depreciation.   Depreciation on all equipment was calculated on a five-year, straight-line basis.

Interest Income.   Interest income was calculated at 5 percent of the year earlier cash balance.

Taxes.   Taxes were calculated at 46 percent of pretax income, less investment tax credits and operating loss carryforwards.

Balance Sheet

Accounts Receivable.   Accounts receivable were estimated at 3.75 times the average monthly sales. With sales growing at a large annual rate, this is reasonable because the monthly sales at year end is much larger than the average monthly sales. Consequently, the receivables on a current basis will be more reasonable.

Inventory.   Inventory is estimated at three times the average monthly fiber and other materials.

Plant, Property, and Equipment.   Equipment costs are in accordance with those shown in capital equipment.

Accounts Payable.   Accounts payable are estimated at one month of the average monthly cost of goods sold, plus one week operating expenses.

Accrued Expenses.   Accrued expenses were estimated.

FIBERCOM APPLICATIONS, INC.
Projected Income Statement
Years Ending July 31, 1985–1990

	1985 (7 months)	1986	1987	1988	1989	1990
Sales	$ 146,500	$1,750,000	$3,500,000	$10,000,000	$25,000,000	$50,000,000
Cost of goods sold:						
Fiber	12,000	583,333	1,166,667	3,333,333	8,333,333	16,666,667
Other material	3,238	157,407	314,815	899,471	2,248,677	4,497,354
Direct labor	3,033	110,673	265,356	588,206	1,414,618	2,825,323
Indirect labor	10,250	51,000	53,550	145,530	482,730	1,050,197
Space	21,000	40,000	40,000	40,000	80,000	80,000
Benefits	2,657	32,335	63,781	146,747	79,469	775,104
Purchased products	89,100	0	0	0	0	0
Total cost of goods sold	141,278	974,748	1,904,169	5,153,287	12,938,827	25,894,645
Gross profit	5,222	775,252	1,595,831	4,846,713	12,061,173	24,105,355
Operating expenses:						
Engineering	31,975	161,815	280,050	495,772	993,702	1,859,440
Sales	42,513	221,362	452,575	902,861	1,750,760	3,007,343
Lease Costs	5,018	60,217	60,217	60,217	60,217	60,217
Administration	78,900	219,280	377,363	720,028	1,195,356	1,965,908
Depreciation	21,625	102,252	166,000	401,000	1,061,000	2,266,000
Total operating expenses	180,031	764,926	1,336,204	2,579,878	5,061,035	9,158,908
Operating profit	(174,809)	10,326	259,627	2,266,835	7,000,138	14,946,447
Interest expense (income)	(11,663)	33,156	14,704	384,171	504,864	1,253,177
Net income before taxes	(163,146)	(22,830)	244,924	1,882,664	6,495,274	13,693,270
Taxes	0	0	27,116	866,025	2,987,826	6,298,904
Net income after taxes	$(163,146)	$ (22,830)	$ 217,808	$ 1,016,639	$ 3,507,448	$ 7,394,366

Projected Cash Flow
Years Ending July 31, 1985–1990

	1985 (7 months)	1986	1987	1988	1989	1990
Sources of cash:						
Increase in equity	$ 750,000	$ 0	$ 0	$5,000,0000	$ 0	$ 0
Increase in debt	0	0	240,000	940,000	(1,180,000)	0
Net income	(163,146)	(22,830)	217,808	1,016,639	3,507,448	7,394,366
Depreciation	21,625	102,252	166,000	401,000	1,061,000	2,266,000
Increase in current liabilities	109,635	408,619	494,331	1,785,078	4,155,616	6,934,111
Total sources	718,114	488,041	1,118,139	9,142,717	7,544,064	16,594,477
Uses of cash:						
Capital expenditures	325,000	200,000	450,000	1,175,000	3,300,000	6,025,000
Increase in accounts receivable	30,000	470,000	593,750	2,031,250	4,687,500	7,812,500
Increase in inventory	50,794	62,434	257,142	687,831	1,587,302	2,645,503
Total uses	405,794	732,434	1,300,892	3,894,081	9,574,802	16,483,003
Cash flow	312,320	(244,393)	(182,753)	5,248,636	(2,030,738)	111,474
Beginning cash	70,000	382,320	137,927	(44,827)	5,203,809	3,173,071
Ending cash	$ 382,320	$ 137,927	$ (44,827)	$ 5,203,809	$ 3,173,071	$ 3,284,545

Projected Balance Sheet
July 31, 1985–1990

	1985	1986	1987	1988	1989	1990
			Assets			
Current assets:						
Cash	$ 382,320	$ 137,927	$ (44,827)	$ 5,203,809	$ 3,173,071	$ 3,284,545
Accounts receivable	30,000	500,000	1,093,750	3,125,000	7,812,500	15,625,000
Inventory	50,794	113,228	370,371	1,058,201	2,645,503	5,291,005
Total current assets	463,114	751,155	1,419,294	9,387,010	13,631,074	24,200,550
Property, plant, and equipment						
At cost	330,000	530,000	980,000	2,155,000	5,455,000	11,480,000
Less accumulated depreciation	21,625	123,877	289,877	690,877	1,751,877	4,017,877
	308,375	406,123	690,123	1,464,123	3,703,123	7,462,123
Total assets	$ 771,489	$1,157,278	$2,109,417	$10,851,133	$17,334,197	$31,662,673
			Liabilities and Shareholders' Equity			
Current liabilities:						
Accounts payable	$ 69,238	$ 211,640	$ 260,525	$ 686,062	$ 1,694,278	$ 3,369,386
Accrued expenses	0	0	20,000	20,000	30,000	60,000
Short-term debt	40,397	306,614	732,060	2,091,601	5,229,001	10,458,003
Total current liabilities	109,635	518,254	1,012,585	2,797,663	6,953,279	13,887,389
Long-term debt			240,000	1,180,000		
Shareholders' equity:						
Contributed capital	870,000	870,000	870,000	5,870,000	5,870,000	5,870,000
Retained earnings	(208,146)	(230,976)	(13,168)	1,003,470	4,510,918	11,905,284
	661,854	639,024	856,832	6,873,470	10,380,918	17,775,284
Total liabilities and shareholders' equity	$ 771,489	$1,157,278	$2,109,417	$10,851,133	$17,334,197	$31,662,673

Projected Income Statement
Seven Months Ending July 31, 1985

	Jan.	Feb.	March	April	May	June	July
Sales	$ 3,500	$ 7,500	$ 13,500	$ 28,500	$ 23,500	$ 20,000	$ 50,000
Cost of goods sold:							
Fiber						2,000	10,000
Other material						540	2,698
Direct labor						1,517	1,517
Indirect labor					1,750	4,250	4,250
Space	3,000	3,000	3,000	3,000	3,000	3,000	3,000
Benefits					350	1,153	1,153
Purchased products	0	3,600	9,000	22,500	18,000	13,500	22,500
Total cost of goods sold	3,000	6,600	12,000	25,500	23,100	25,960	45,118
Gross profit	500	900	1,500	3,000	400	(5,960)	4,882
Operating expenses:							
Engineering	4,525	4,525	4,525	4,525	4,525	4,575	4,775
Sales	5,888	5,888	5,888	5,888	5,888	6,438	6,638
Lease costs	0	0	0	0	0	0	5,018
Administration	8,850	10,850	10,850	10,850	12,500	12,500	12,500
Depreciation	83	83	83	5,292	5,292	5,292	5,500
Total operating expenses	19,346	21,346	21,346	26,555	28,205	28,805	34,431
Operating profit	(18,846)	(20,446)	(19,846)	(23,555)	(27,805)	(34,765)	(29,549)
Interest expense (income)	(350)	(309)	(278)	(4,028)	(2,545)	(2,236)	(1,919)
Net income before taxes	(18,496)	(20,137)	(19,568)	(19,527)	(25,260)	(32,529)	(27,630)
Taxes	0	0	0	0	0	0	0
Net income after taxes	$(18,496)	$(20,137)	$(19,568)	$(19,527)	$(25,260)	$(32,529)	$(27,630)

Projected Income Statement
Seven Months Ending July 31, 1985

	Jan.	Feb.	March	April	May	June	July
Sources of cash:							
Increase in equity	$ 0	$ 0	$750,000	$ 0	$ 0	$ 0	$ 0
Increase in debt	0	0	0	0	0	0	0
Net income	(18,496)	(20,137)	(19,568)	(19,527)	(25,260)	(32,529)	(27,630)
Depreciation	83	83	83	5,292	5,292	5,292	5,500
Increase in current liabilities	10,250	13,851	19,250	33,385	(22,792)	17,794	37,897
Total sources	(8,163)	(6,202)	749,765	19,150	(42,760)	(9,443)	15,767
Uses of cash:							
Capital expenditures	0	0	0	312,500	0	0	12,500
Increase in accounts receivable	0	0	0	0	0	5,000	25,000
Increase in inventory	0	0	0	1,270	7,619	16,508	25,397
Total uses	0	0	0	313,770	7,619	21,508	62,897
Cash flow	(8,163)	(6,202)	749,765	(294,620)	(50,379)	(30,951)	(47,130)
Beginning cash	70,000	61,837	55,635	805,400	510,780	460,401	429,450
Ending cash	$ 61,837	$ 55,635	$805,400	$ 510,780	$460,401	$429,450	$382,320

Projected Balance Sheet
Seven Months Ending July 31, 1985

	Jan.	Feb.	March	April	May	June	July
				Assets			
Current assets:							
Cash	$ 61,837	$ 55,635	$ 805,400	$ 510,780	$ 460,401	$ 429,450	$ 382,320
Accounts receivable						5,000	30,000
Inventory				1,270	8,889	25,397	50,794
Total current assets	61,837	55,635	805,400	512,050	469,290	459,847	463,114
Property, plant, and equipment:							
At cost	5,000	5,000	5,000	317,500	317,500	317,500	330,000
Less accumulated depreciation	83	167	250	5,542	10,834	16,125	21,625
	4,917	4,833	4,750	311,958	306,666	301,375	308,375
Total assets	$ 66,754	$ 60,468	$ 810,150	$ 824,008	$ 775,956	$ 761,222	$ 771,489
			Liabilities and Shareholders' Equity				
Current liabilities:							
Accounts payable	$	$ 3,600	$ 12,600	$ 35,100	$ 49,500	$ 56,540	$ 69,238
Accrued expenses							
Accrued salaries	10,250	20,500	30,750	41,000			
Short-term debt				635	4,444	15,198	40,397
Total current liabilities	10,250	24,100	43,350	76,735	53,944	71,738	109,635
Shareholders' equity:							
Contributed capital	120,000	120,000	870,000	870,000	870,000	870,000	870,000
Retained earnings	(63,496)	(83,632)	(103,200)	(122,727)	(147,988)	(180,516)	(208,146)
	56,504	36,368	766,800	747,273	722,012	689,484	661,854
Total liabilities and shareholders' equity	$ 66,754	$ 60,468	$ 810,150	$ 824,008	$ 775,956	$ 761,222	$ 771,489

Projected Income Statement
Twelve Months Ending July 31, 1986

	Aug.	Sep.	Oct.	Nov.	Dec.	Jan.	Feb.	Mar.	Apr.	May	June	July
Sales	$ 50,000	$100,000	$150,000	$150,000	$150,000	$150,000	$165,000	$165,000	$170,000	$165,000	$165,000	$170,000
Cost of goods sold:												
Fiber	16,667	33,333	50,000	50,000	50,000	50,000	55,000	55,000	56,667	55,000	55,000	56,667
Other materials	4,497	8,995	13,492	13,492	13,492	13,492	14,842	14,842	15,291	14,842	14,842	15,291
Direct labor	2,687	5,373	10,053	10,053	10,053	10,053	10,053	10,053	11,093	10,053	10,053	11,093
Indirect labor	4,250	4,250	4,250	4,250	4,250	4,250	4,250	4,250	4,250	4,250	4,250	4,250
Space	3,333	3,333	3,333	3,333	3,333	3,333	3,333	3,333	3,333	3,333	3,333	3,333
Benefits	1,387	1,925	2,861	2,861	2,861	2,861	2,861	2,861	3,069	2,861	2,861	3,069
Total cost of goods sold	32,821	57,209	83,989	83,989	83,989	83,989	90,339	90,339	93,703	90,339	90,339	93,703
Gross profit	17,179	42,791	66,011	66,011	66,011	66,011	74,661	74,661	76,297	74,661	74,661	76,297
Operating expenses:												
Engineering	11,330	11,829	13,767	13,766	13,766	13,766	13,916	13,916	13,966	13,915	13,915	13,966
Sales	9,618	12,889	18,660	18,910	19,160	19,410	19,810	20,060	20,360	20,560	20,810	21,110
Administration	15,484	17,984	18,484	18,484	18,484	18,484	18,684	18,684	18,684	18,634	18,634	18,657
Lease cost	5,018	5,018	5,018	5,018	5,018	5,018	5,018	5,018	5,018	5,018	5,018	5,018
Depreciation	8,208	8,208	8,208	8,417	8,417	8,417	8,625	8,625	8,625	8,834	8,834	8,834
Total operating expenses	49,658	55,928	64,137	64,595	64,845	65,095	66,003	66,253	66,653	66,961	67,211	67,585
Operating profit	(32,479)	(13,137)	1,874	1,416	1,166	916	8,658	8,508	9,644	7,700	7,450	8,712
Interest expense (income)	(1,012)	340	1,147	2,461	3,275	3,669	3,704	3,827	3,891	3,955	3,965	3,935
Net income before taxes	(31,467)	(13,477)	727	(1,045)	(2,109)	(2,753)	4,954	4,581	5,753	3,745	3,485	4,777
Taxes	0	0	0	0	0	0	0	0	0	0	0	0
Net income after taxes	$(31,467)	$(13,477)	$ 727	$ (1,045)	$ (2,109)	$ (2,753)	$ 4,954	$ 4,581	$ 5,753	$ 3,745	$ 3,485	$ 4,777

Projected Cash Flow
Twelve Months Ending July 31, 1986

	Aug.	Sep.	Oct.	Nov.	Dec.	Jan.	Feb.	Mar.	Apr.	May	June	July
Sources of cash:												
Increase in equity	$ 0	$ 0	$ 0	$ 0	$ 0	$ 0	$ 0	$ 0	$ 0	$ 0	$ 0	$ 0
Increase in debt	0	0	0	0	0	0	0	0	0	0	0	0
Net income	(31,467)	(13,477)	727	(1,045)	(2,109)	(2,753)	4,954	4,581	5,753	3,745	3,485	4,777
Depreciation	8,208	8,208	8,208	8,417	8,417	8,417	8,625	8,625	8,625	8,834	8,834	8,834
Increase in current liabilities	39,804	71,870	103,294	92,328	47,752	3,174	14,378	14,378	17,407	528	1,587	2,116
Total sources	16,545	66,601	112,229	99,700	54,060	8,838	27,957	27,584	31,786	13,107	13,906	15,727
Uses of cash:												
Capital expenditures	162,500	0	0	12,500	0	0	12,500	0	0	12,500	0	0
Increase in accts. rec.	50,000	70,000	150,000	100,000	50,000	0	15,000	15,000	20,000	0	0	0
Increase in inventory	23,279	21,164	0	0	3,175	6,349	1,058	1,058	(2,116)	1,058	3,175	4,233
Total uses	235,779	91,164	150,000	112,500	53,175	6,349	28,558	16,058	17,884	13,558	3,175	4,233
Cash flow	(219,234)	(24,563)	(37,771)	(12,800)	885	2,489	(601)	11,526	13,902	(451)	10,731	11,494
Beginning cash	382,320	163,086	138,523	100,752	87,952	88,837	91,326	90,725	102,251	116,153	115,702	126,433
Ending cash	$ 163,086	$138,523	$100,752	$ 87,952	$88,837	$91,326	$90,725	$102,251	$116,153	$115,702	$126,433	$137,927

Projected Balance Sheet
Twelve Months Ending July 31, 1986

	Aug.	Sep.	Oct.	Nov.	Dec.	Jan.	Feb.	Mar.	Apr.	May	June	July
Assets												
Current assets:												
Cash	$ 163,086	$ 138,523	$ 100,752	$ 87,952	$ 88,837	$ 91,326	$ 90,725	$ 102,251	$ 116,153	$ 115,702	$ 126,433	$ 137,927
Accounts receivable	80,000	150,000	300,000	400,000	450,000	450,000	465,000	480,000	500,000	500,000	500,000	500,000
Inventory	74,073	95,238	95,238	95,238	98,413	104,762	105,820	106,878	104,763	105,820	108,995	113,228
Total current assets	317,159	383,761	495,990	583,190	637,250	646,088	661,545	689,129	720,916	721,522	735,428	751,155
Property, plant, and equipment:												
At cost	492,500	492,500	492,500	505,000	505,000	505,000	517,500	517,500	517,500	530,000	530,000	530,000
Less accumulated depreciation	29,833	38,042	46,250	54,667	63,084	71,501	80,126	88,751	97,377	106,210	115,044	123,877
	462,667	454,458	446,250	450,333	441,916	433,499	437,374	428,749	420,128	423,790	414,956	406,123
Total assets	$ 779,826	$ 838,219	$ 924,240	$1,033,523	$1,079,166	$1,079,587	$1,098,919	$1,117,878	$1,141,039	$1,146,312	$1,150,384	$1,157,278
Liabilities and Shareholders' Equity												
Current liabilities:												
Accounts payable	$ 72,402	$ 98,690	$ 126,984	$ 169,312	$ 190,477	$ 190,476	$ 196,825	$ 203,175	$ 211,640	$ 211,640	$ 211,640	$ 211,640
Accrued expenses	0	0	0	0	0	0	0	0	0	0	0	0
Short-term debt	77,037	122,619	197,619	247,619	274,206	277,381	285,410	293,439	302,381	302,910	304,497	306,614
Total current liabs.	149,439	221,309	324,603	416,931	464,683	467,857	482,235	496,614	514,021	514,550	516,137	518,254
Shareholders' equity:												
Contributed capital	870,000	870,000	870,000	870,000	870,000	870,000	870,000	870,000	870,000	870,000	870,000	870,000
Retained earnings	(239,613)	(253,090)	(252,363)	(253,408)	(255,517)	(258,270)	(253,316)	(248,736)	(242,982)	(239,238)	(235,753)	(230,976)
Total equity	630,387	616,910	617,637	616,592	614,483	611,730	616,684	621,264	627,018	630,762	634,247	639,024
Total liabilities and shareholders' equity	$ 779,826	$ 838,219	$ 942,240	$1,033,523	$1,079,166	$1,079,587	$1,098,919	$1,117,878	$1,141,039	$1,145,312	$1,150,384	$1,157,278

11.   Appendix B: Management Résumés

Thomas J. McCormack

Professional Experience

BIW Cable Systems, Inc.

July 1983 – May 1984

General Manager – Fiber Optics Division

Promoted to general manager – Fiber Optics Division in July 1983. Managed all efforts of the company in fiber optics. Prepared and executed a business plan that saw sales grow from less than $150,000 in 1982 to over $400,000 in 1983. Purchased and supervised the installation of initial extrusion lines and cabling equipment. Hired and trained test technician and production personnel. Managed all engineering, marketing, and sales activities of the company's fiber optic products. Developed new product for interoffice data communications.

Worked closely with the national sales manager, vice president–marketing, and marketing managers to set sales targets and direct the sales efforts.

Had full P&L responsibility beginning in January 1984. Prior to this time, I had complete control over the fiber optics operations, but the division operations were not separately stated. I worked closely with the controller in determining and instituting procedures to define the division operation.

In this position, I worked closely with major fiber suppliers to determine acceptable products. Met with major foreign manufacturers to determine potential license arrangements.

1978–1983

Marketing Manager – Utility and Fiber Optic Products

Responsible for all marketing activities of the company for both electrical products to electric utility companies and for fiber optic products to all the company's customers.

Utility Products

Doubled the company's sales of all products to electric utility companies, while at the same time increasing the gross margin from 30 percent to over 50 percent. Responsible for developing and executing yearly marketing plans, setting five-year sales goals, outlining new product needs, producing sales literature, setting price levels, supervising application engineering activities, monitoring development of new materials and products, preparing quotations, and administering contracts. Introduced three major lines of new products, including standard cables that came to account for 50 percent of utility sales. Decreased utility related overhead by 25 percent. Expanded customer base from only architect-engineers to include direct sales to major utilities. Negotiated the largest contract in the company's history. As a matrix organization, participated with manufacturing in production planning for both short- and long-term needs. Supervised the utility sales efforts of 10 district sales managers.

Fiber Optic Products

Participated in company task force in 1979–80 to determine potential involvement with fiber optic products. Recommended to president to proceed with fiber optic business on a limited basis. The recommendation was accepted and I was designated to spend part-time in continuing investigation, and to secure limited initial orders. Sold first fiber optic cable in 1981. Recommended increased marketing activities in 1982 and planned initial capital expenditures made in 1982. Wrote company's first marketing plan in 1982, identifying target markets and setting five-year sales projections. Supervised the engineering and development efforts in fiber optics. Directed the sales activities of district sales managers. Made direct sales presentations to all categories of customers – process control, television networks, electric utilities, computer OEMs, etc. Prepared sales literature, set price levels, and wrote sales quotations. Had production, sales, marketing, and engineering people reporting to me on a matrix basis.

Public Service Electric and Gas Company

1970–1978

Senior Staff Engineer — Systems Engineering Group

Worked in Systems Engineering for a large, integrated utility company. Varied technical responsibilities, including:

Wire and Cable

Determined acceptable materials and construction for all low-voltage cables used in power generating stations. Acted as consultant to operating division to investigate problems or service failures. Performed engineering studies related to cable materials and design features (ampacity, temperature rating, environmental qualification). Prepared specifications for purchase.

Determined acceptable vendors and evaluated bids. Purchased materials worth approximately $5 million per year.

Worked closely with purchasing, legal, and construction departments within the company, and with manufacturers, other utilities, and architect-engineers outside the company.

Major accomplishments included expansion of acceptable vendors list, with an estimated cost savings of over $1 million in 1976–77, and qualified alternate constructions with estimated cost savings of over $500,000 per year.

Power Transformers

Similar duties and responsibilities as for wire and cable. Performed engineering studies to determine acceptable parameters and designs. Prepared specifications and evaluated manufacturer's proposals. Worked closely with operating departments regarding field service problems, and with the construction department on installation of large transformers.

Purchased and installed more than $10 million of power transformers per year.

Major accomplishments included the expansion of the acceptable vendors list, with subsequent savings of over $1 million per year. Specified and purchased the largest power transformers installed in the United States.

Other Responsibilities

Prepared general construction specifications for labor and materials. Prepared the general terms and conditions required for purchase of all engineered equipment. Performed special studies regarding power system operations.

Education

Rensselaer Polytechnic Institute, Troy, New York
   Master of Electrical Engineering, 1970
   Philip Sporn Fellowship
   Bachelor of Science, Electrical Engineering, 1969
   Eta Kappa Nu

Personal

Member — IEEE
       — IEEE Power Engineering Society
       — IEEE Industry Applications Society
       — IEEE Communications Society
Voting Member — IEEE PES Insulated Conductors Committee

Chairman — IEEE Working Group 12-32
           — IEEE Standard 383
           — Qualification of Nuclear Power Plant Cables
Chairman — IEEE Working Group 14-2
           — Fiber Optics in Power Plants

Gary A. Smith

Professional Experience

BIW Cable Systems
Manufacturing, Boston, MA

May 1982–present

District Sales Manager

Reporting to the vice president of sales and marketing, responsible for sales of all product lines in seven-state region, including New England and New York State (1983 sales $7.1 million). Direct interface with target markets and accounts. Establish forecasts, set key accounts, and formulate overall strategy for various product classes in territory. Supervise and manage three representative agencies (nine field salespeople).

March 1980–May 1982

Inside Sales Manager, Utility and Fiber Optic Products

Complete responsibility for proposals, contract administration, and customer service for market segment with annual sales of $6–7 million.
Supervise support personnel with dotted-line responsibility for customer service department.
Review proposals, establish pricing levels and directions. Establish programs for major contracts and monitor performance of various internal disciplines until completion. Interface with customers on all contract-related matters and advise and direct engineering, manufacturing, and quality assurance departments.

RCA Corporation — Automated Systems Division
Manufacturing, Burlington, MA

January 1979–March 1980

Senior Level Product Specialist

Responsible for procurement of $1–2 million annually of highly specialized optical and precision fabricated components for combat and field support devices.

Texas Instruments Inc.
Manufacturing, Attleboro, MA

June 1976–January 1979

Buyer

Responsible for procurement of $4–5 million annually of contracted services for Facilities Group, electromechanical components and capital equipment. Direct interaction with engineering and manufacturing. Preparation of technical specifications. Responsible for vendor selection and development, contract negotiation, quality and delivery assurance, and cost reduction programs.

Education

Northeastern University, Boston, MA
  Master of Business Administration/Finance awarded June 1976
Bucknell University, Lewisburg, PA
  Bachelor of Science in Civil Engineering awarded June 1974

Clint M. Owens

Qualifications in Brief

Successful development and marketing of new Fiber Optic products. Successfully managed the production scale-up of new ideas developed in the laboratory.

Extensive experience in solving engineering problems in high temperature wire and cable, including Kapton and Teflon insulations.

Employment

1975–1984

Brand Rex Company, Willimantic, CT

1975–1976

R&D Engineer — Responsible for new product development, principally high-temperature wire and cable.

1976–1982

Senior Product Engineer — Developed new products, principally for the military market. During this time, products developed accounted for an increase in sales from $1 million to $10 million per year.

1978–1982

Fiber Optics

Product Engineer — Was the company leader in their entry into fiber optics. I planned, had funds authorized, purchased equipment, and set up the fiber optics operations. Designed and sold fiber optic cables for the data communications industry. Current annual sales over $2 million. Hold a patent for transmission cable aimed at the computer market.

1982–1984

New Product Marketing Manager, Fiber Optics — Promoted to marketing manager while retaining my engineering responsibilities. Work closely with customers in new designs, determine if new products can be made. Thrust is toward proprietary products. Designed and marketed a major new product for LAN use.

1972–1975

Hitemp Wires, Inc., Happauge, NY

Director, Technical Services — Principally charged with maintaining an accurate material usage vs. estimated costs. Established cost accounting, manufacturing engineering specifications, and departmental procedures. Twenty-five percent of the time was spent with sales, reporting to the vice president — sales and engineering. My sales experience involved working closely with customers on new products. Developed many new products, including Power Buss Assembly (extruded Tefzel bonded to flat cable), Shurheat Heater Cable, Fire Alarm Cable (NY Law 5), and Ullage Cable (Tefzel insulated cable for measuring amount of oil in tankers).

Experience in screw extrusion, cabling, cable assembly, braiding, and quality control.

1972

Dor-Flex Electronics of California, Santa Ana, CA

Director of Engineering — Designed new equipment for maximum efficiency for polyimide dispersions, taping, sealing, and etching. Maintained liaison with equipment manufacturers and production group to maximize production output. Dor-Flex purchased Carolina Wire and Cable in December 1971.

1969–1971

Carolina Wire and Cable, Inc., Santa Ana, CA

Wire & Cable Engineer — Developed new Teflon dispersion, high-speed Liquid II applications, new taping methods, and instituted new QC test methods. Designed the power cable system for the Grumman F-14. Also developed the cables used by Sperry Flight Systems and TRW on the Pioneer spacecraft. All polyimide insulations used by General Dynamics, Fort Worth, TX, for Aerojet (GTR-22) were my developments.

1965–1969

E.I. Dupont de Nemours & Co., Inc., Wilmington, DE

Senior Technical Assistant — Worked directly for Dr. Lewis on the development and testing of Kapton. The airframe wiring used by Lockheed on the L-1011 was the primary project. All testing for the "Orange" report was performed by me. Developed new splice methods for Kapton. Also worked on electrical applications of films, including Mylar, polypropylene, fluorocarbons, etc.

Education

Penn Morton College   2½ years General Engineering

Screening Venture Opportunities

Greater than the tread of mighty armies is an idea whose time has come.

Victor Hugo

RESULTS EXPECTED

At the conclusion of the chapter, you will have:

1. Looked at what can be gained through opportunity screening.
2. Applied screening criteria to your own venture opportunities.

SCREENING VENTURE OPPORTUNITIES

While the above quote may well be true, it bears repeating that there are two classes of ventures: (1) those that promise to be profitable enough to provide for a harvest or, at least, to generate enough income to compensate fully those involved; (2) and all the rest. To illustrate, approximately 1.3 million new enterprises were launched in the United States in 1988, or roughly 100,000 each month. Of those, only 10 percent to 15 percent were likely to become "good" opportunities that will grow and achieve sales over $1 million.

The process of screening opportunities is a key step in determining the opportunity around which a business plan, and a business, should be developed. Applying screening criteria to your venture opportunities allows an entrepreneur to so focus on key issues that he or she can determine which opportunities may have higher potential. In other words, he or she can answer such key questions as: Why does the planet need another product *x* or service *x*? Time will then not be wasted developing a business plan for an idea whose time has *not* come.

Whether or not an entrepreneur plans to seek venture capital to execute an opportunity, it is vital also to have a realistic view of the vulnerabilities and fragilities of a venture, as well as its strengths. Often, the analytical process of screening opportunities triggers creative ideas and insights about how a concept or strategy can be modified in order to enhance significantly the profit potential of an opportunity.

Work done in screening opportunities can be used to draft a business plan should an opportunity pass the screening process. Involving potential partners or members of a management team in the task of evaluating opportunities is an excellent way to "try out the marriage."

However, since the question of whether an opportunity is an opportunity has another dimension. A key question is whether any opportunity is *an opportunity for you*. This is a very personal matter. The exercise on crafting a personal entrepreneurial strategy (Part VI) is recommended as an important companion exercise to complete the process of screening opportunities.

EXERCISE – VENTURE OPPORTUNITY SCREENING GUIDE

The Venture Opportunity Screening Guide (VOSG) is based on the screening criteria discussed in Chapter 3.

As you proceed through the VOSG, you will come to checkpoints. At each checkpoint, you can evaluate whether to proceed with your evaluation, change the definition of your opportunity in some way, or abandon it. When you pass all checkpoints in the VOSG, it should be much more apparent to what extent your opportunity is attractive. Rarely is it simply cut and dried, however. Most of the time, there will be considerable uncertainty and numerous unknowns and risk involved even at this point. What the process can do is help you to understand those uncertainties and risks in making your decision and to devise ways to make them acceptable for you. If they cannot be made acceptable, then you keep searching.

Deciding where your opportunity falls will take a considerable amount of work. Plan to spend at least 20 to 30 hours in completing the VOSG. Depending upon the nature of your opportunity and your knowledge and access to critical information, completing the VOSG may require more effort, but probably not less. While this time commitment may seem large, the amount of time ultimately consumed in evaluating an opportunity by trial and error is almost always greater, and the tuition is much higher.

Every venture is unique. Operation, marketing, cash flow cycles, and so forth, vary a good bit from company to company, from industry to industry, and from region to region, or country to country. As a result, you may find that not every issue pertinent to your venture will be covered in the VOSG or that some questions are irrelevant. Here and there, you may have to add to or tailor the VOSG to your particular circumstances.

It is suggested that you and each of the members of your team should fill out a VOSG.

As with other exercises in the book, feel free to make as many Xerox copies of the VOSG as you need.

EXERCISE
VENTURE OPPORTUNITY SCREENING GUIDE

NAME:

VENTURE:

DATE:

STEP 1: BRIEFLY DESCRIBE YOUR OPPORTUNITY "CONCEPT" WITHOUT MEN-
TIONING THE SPECIFIC PRODUCT(S) OR SERVICE(S).   An example of an
opportunity concept would be the one seen by the founders of Outdoor Scene via delivery,
quality, and service in the leisure-time industry. Such a summary will usually be between
50 and 100 words in length and include what compelling conditions and circumstances are
propelling the opportunity and why the opportunity exists, now, for you. Most concepts
begin in a fuzzy, ill-defined way, which is normal and acceptable. Once you have completed
the remaining sections of the guide, you can return to this summary and refine it.

STEP 2: FILL IN THE VENTURE OPPORTUNITY PROFILE BELOW BY INDICATING FOR EACH INDIVIDUAL CRITERION WHERE YOUR VENTURE IS LOCATED ON THE "POTENTIAL" CONTINUUM. Make an "x" to indicate your best estimate of where your idea stacks up. Be as specific as possible. (If you have trouble, relevant trade magazines and newsletters, other entrepreneurs, trade shows, fairs, or other sources can help.)

Venture Opportunity Profile

Higher Potential ← — — — — — — — — → *Lower Potential*

MARKET

Criterion	Higher Potential	Lower Potential
Need	Identified	Unfocused
Customers	Reachable, Receptive	Unreachable, Loyal to Others
Payback to User	Less than One Year	Three Years or More
Value Added or Created	High	Low
Product Life	Durable, Beyond Time to Recover Investment Plus Profit	Perishable Less than Time to Recover Investment
Market Structure	Imperfect Competition or Emerging Industry	Perfect Competition or Highly Concentrated or Mature/Declining Industry
Market Size	$100 Million Sales	Unknown; or Less $10 Million Sales or Multibillion
Market Growth Rate	Growing, 30%–50% or More	Contracting or Less than 10%
Gross Margins (e.g., selling price less direct, variable cost)	40%–50% or More, Durable	Less than 20%, Fragile
Market Share Attainable (year 5)	20% or More (Leader)	Less than 5%
Cost Structure	Low-cost Provider	Declining Cost

ECONOMIC & HARVEST ISSUES

Profits after Tax

10%–15% or More,
Durable

Less than 5%,
Fragile

Time to:

Breakeven

Under 2 years

More than 2 Years

Positive Cash Flow

Under 2 years

More than 2 Years

ROI Potential

25% or More/Year,
High Value

Less than 15% to
20%/Year, Low Value

Capital Requirements

Low

Very High

Exit Mechanism

Present or Envisioned
Harvest Options

Undefined,
Illiquid Investment

Value

High Strategic Value

Low Strategic Value

COMPETITIVE ADVANTAGES ISSUES

Fixed & Variable Costs:

Production

Lowest

Highest

Marketing

Lowest

Highest

Distribution

Lowest

Highest

Degree of Control:

Prices

Moderate to Strong

Weak

Costs

Moderate to Strong

Weak

Channels of
Distribution

Moderate to Strong

Weak

Ability to Erect Barriers to Entry:

Response/Lead Time Advantages— Technology, Product, Market Innovation, People, Location, or Capacity

Have or Can Gain Edge	None

Legal, Contractual Advantage

Proprietary or Exclusive	None

Contacts and Networks

Well-developed, High Quality, and Accessible	Crude, Limited, Inaccessible

Necessary Resources

Adequate	Weak or Inadequate

MANAGEMENT TEAM ISSUES

Entrepreneurial Team

Existing, Strong, Proven Performance	Weak, Solo Entrepreneur

Competitor's Mind Set and Strategies

Competitive, Focused Strategies not Self-destructive	Dumb Self-destructive

FATAL FLAW/RISK ISSUES

Existence of Fatal Flaws

None	Many

Risk

Low	High

STEP 3: ASSESS THE EXTERNAL ENVIRONMENT SURROUNDING YOUR VENTURE OPPORTUNITY.　　Include the following:

- An assessment of the characteristics of the opportunity window, including its perishability:

- A statement of what entry strategy suits the opportunity, and why:

- A statement of evidence of and/or reasoning behind your belief that external environment and the forces creating your opportunity described in **Step 1** and in the Venture Opportunity Profile "fit":

- A statement of your exit strategy and an assessment of the prospects that this strategy can be met, including a consideration of whether the risks, rewards, and trade-offs are acceptable:

CHECKPOINT: BEFORE YOU PROCEED, BE SURE THE OPPORTUNITY YOU HAVE OUTLINED IS COMPELLING AND YOU CAN ANSWER THE QUESTION: WHY DOES THE OPPORTUNITY EXIST NOW? IT IS JUST POSSIBLE YOU OUGHT TO ABANDON OR ALTER THE PRODUCT OR SERVICE IDEA BEHIND YOUR VENTURE AT THIS POINT. THE AMOUNT OF MONEY AND TIME NEEDED TO GET THE PRODUCT OR SERVICE TO MARKET, AND TO BE OPEN FOR BUSINESS, MAY BE BEYOND YOUR LIMITS. REMEMBER, EVEN IN THE ABUNDANT VENTURE CAPITAL MARKET OF THE MID-1980S, ONLY 1 PERCENT TO 3 PERCENT OF ALL VENTURES RECEIVED FUNDING. REMEMBER, ALSO, THAT THE FIRST ROUND OF FINANCING IS TYPICALLY IN THE $1 MILLION TO $2 MILLION RANGE AND, TO RAISE OVER $5 MILLION, YOU NEED A TRULY EXCEPTIONAL MANAGEMENT TEAM AND A CONCEPT WHOSE POTENTIAL REWARDS ARE LARGE COMPARED TO THE RISKS AND VULNERABILITIES TO OBSOLESCENCE AND COMPETITION.

STEP 4: ASSESS THE ATTRACTIVENESS OF YOUR VENTURE OPPORTUNITY BY APPLYING SCREENING CRITERIA.   Include the following:

■ A brief description of the market(s) or market niche(s) you want to enter:

■ An exact description of what product(s) or service(s) will be sold and, if a product, what the eventual end use(s) will be. (If your product(s) or service(s) are already commercially available or exist as prototypes, attach specifications, photographs, samples of work, and so forth.)

■ An estimate of how perishable the product(s) or service(s) are, including if it is likely to become obsolete and when:

■ An assessment of whether there are substitutes for the product(s) or services(s):

■ An assessment of the status of development and an estimate of how much time and how much money will be required to complete development, test the product(s) or service(s), and then introduce the product(s) or service(s) to the market:

Development Tasks		
Development Task	$ Required	Months to Complete

■ An assessment of any major difficulties in manufacturing the product(s) or delivering the service(s) and how much time and money will be required to resolve them:

■ A description of the customer support, such as warranty service, repair service, and training of technicians, salespeople, service people, or others, which will be needed:

■ An assessment of the strengths and weaknesses, relative to the competition, of the product(s) or service(s) in meeting customer need, including a description of payback of and value added by the product(s) or service(s):

■ An assessment of your primary customer group:
  − A description of the main reasons why your primary group of customers will buy your product or service, including whether customers in this group are reachable and receptive and how your product or service will add or create value, and what this means for your entry or expansion strategy:

— A list of 5 to 10 crucial questions you need to have answered and other information you need to know to identify good customer prospects:

— An indication of how customers buy products or services (e.g., from direct sales, either wholesale or retail; through manufacturers' representatives or brokers; through catalogs; via direct mail; etc.):

— A description of the purchasing process (i.e., where it occurs and who is ultimately responsible for approving expenditures; what and who influence the sale; how long does it take from first contact to a close, to delivery, and to cash receipt; and your conclusions about the competitive advantages you can achieve and how your product or service can add or create value):

■ An assessment of the market potential for your venture's product or service, the competition, and what is required to bring and sell the product or service to the customer. (Such an analysis need not be precise or comprehensive but should serve to eliminate from further consideration those ventures that have obvious market difficulties.) Include the following information:

— An estimate, for the past, present, and future, of the *approximate* size of the *total* potential market, as measured in units and in dollars or number of customers. In making your estimates, use available market data to estimate *ranges* of values, identify the area (country, region, locality, etc.) and, if the market is segmented, data for each segment:

Total Market Size				
Year				
19	19	19	19	19

Sales of Units/
   Number of Customers

Sales in Dollars

Sources of Data:

Researcher:

Confidence in Data:

— An assessment of the type of market in terms of price, quality, and service; degree of control, etc.; and your conclusions about what approaches are necessary to enter, survive, and win:

■ An assessment, based on a survey of customers, of how your customers do business, and of what investigatory steps are needed next:

	Customer Survey		
	Customer		
	No. 1	No. 2	No. 3
Nature of Customers			
Business or Role			
Reactions: Positive Negative Questions			

Specific Needs/Uses

Acceptable Terms—Price,
  Support, Etc.

Basis of Purchase Decisions:
  Time Frame

Who Makes Decision

Dollar Limits

Substitutes/Competitive
  Products or Services Used

Names of Competitors:

Competitive Products

Substitute Products

Customers Surveyed	
No.	Name

- An assessment of how your product or service will be positioned in the market, including:
  - A statement of any proprietary protection, such as patents, copyrights, or trade secrets, and what this means in the way of a competitive advantage:

— An assessment of any competitive advantages you can achieve in the level of quality, service, and so forth, including an objective description of any strengths (and weaknesses) of the product or service:

— An assessment of your pricing strategy versus those of competitors:

	Pricing Strategy		
	Highest Price	Average Price	Lowest Price
Retail			
Wholesale			
Distributor			
Other Channel			
Manufacturing			

— An assessment of where competitors in your industry or market niche are in terms of price versus performance/benefits/value added:

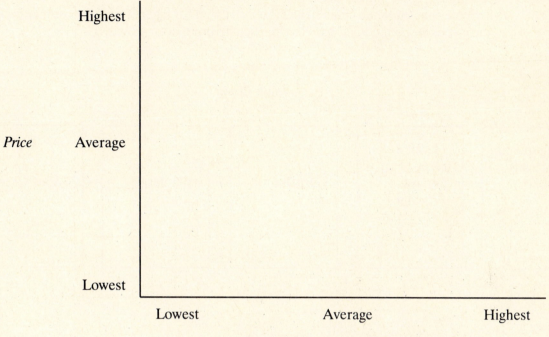

Performance/Benefits/Value Added

— An indication of how you plan to distribute and sell your product or services (e.g., through direct sales, mail order, manufacturers' representatives, etc.) and the likely sales, marketing, and advertising/trade promotion costs:

— A distribution plan for your product(s) or service(s), including any special requirements, such as refrigeration, and how much distribution costs will be as a percent of sales and of total costs:

■ Map the value chain for your product or service (i.e., indicate how your product or service will get to the end user or consumer; the portion of the final selling price realized in each step; and the dollar and percentage markup and the dollar and percentage gross margin per unit).

  (Note that the value chain below is constructed for a generalized consumer product and needs to be modified for your particular product or service.)

Value Chain

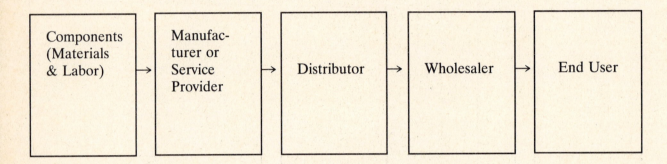

Price/Unit:
  Dollars
  Percent

Markup/Unit:
  Dollars
  Percent

Gross Margin:
  Dollars
  Percent

■ A realistic estimate of *approximate* sales and market share for your product or service for your *market area* which your venture can attain in each of your first five years:

Product/Service Sales and Market Share

	Year				
	1	2	3	4	5
Total Market: Units Dollars					
Est. Sales: Units Dollars					
Est. Market Share (percent):					
Est. Market Growth: Units Dollars					

Source of Data:

Researcher:

Confidence in Data:

CHECKPOINT: CONSIDER WHETHER YOU SUFFER FROM MOUSETRAP MYOPIA OR WHETHER YOU LACK ENOUGH EXPERIENCE TO TACKLE THE VENTURE AT THIS STAGE. IT IS POSSIBLE THAT, IF YOUR VENTURE DOES NOT STAND UP TO THIS EVALUATION, YOU MAY SIMPLY NOT BE AS FAR ALONG AS YOU HAD THOUGHT. REMEMBER, THE SINGLE LARGEST FACTOR CONTRIBUTING TO STILLBORN VENTURES AND TO THOSE WHO WILL RIPEN AS LEMONS IS LACK OF OPPORTUNITY FOCUS. IF YOU WERE UNABLE TO RESPOND TO MANY OF THE ABOVE QUESTIONS, OR DO NOT HAVE MUCH OF AN IDEA OF HOW TO ANSWER THEM, IT IS POSSIBLE THAT YOU NEED TO DO MORE WORK.

■   An assessment of the costs and profitability of your product or service:

Product/Service Costs and Profitability

Product/Service:

Sales Price:

Sales Level:

	$/Unit	Percent of Sales Price/Unit
Production Costs (i.e., labor and material costs) or Purchase Costs		
Gross Margin		
Fixed Costs		
Profit before Taxes		
Profit after Taxes		

■ An assessment of the minimum resources required to "get the doors open and revenue coming in," the costs, dates required, alternative means of gaining control (but not necessarily owning) these, and what this information tells you:

Resource Needs

	Minimum Needed	Cost ($)	Date Required	Probable Source
Plant, Equipment, and Facilities				
Product/Service Development				
Market Research				
Set-up of Sales and Distribution (e.g., brochures, demos, and mailers)				
One-time Expenditures (e.g., legal costs)				
Lease Deposits and Other Prepayments (e.g., utilities)				

Overhead (e.g., salaries, rent, and insurance)

Sales Costs (e.g., trips to trade shows)

Other Start-up Costs

TOTAL

COMMENTS

- A rough estimate of requirements for manufacturing and/or staff, operations, facilities, including:
  - An assessment of the major difficulties for such items as equipment, labor skills, and training, and quality standards in the manufacture of your product(s) or the delivery of your service(s):

—   An estimate of the number of people who will be required to launch the business and the key tasks they will perform:

—   An assessment of how you will deal with these difficulties and what is your estimate of the time and money needed to resolve them and begin saleable production:

▪   An identification of the cash flow and cash conversion cycle for your business over the first 15 months (including a consideration of leads/lags in getting sales, producing your product or service, delivering your product or service, and billing and collecting cash). Show as a bar chart the timing and duration of each activity below:

Cash Flow, Conversion Cycle, and Timing of Key Operational Activities

Development of
   Forecasts

Manufacturing

Sales Orders

Billing:

   Invoice

   Collect

Selling Season

```
        1    2    3    4    5    6    7    8    9    10   11   12   13   14   15
                                    Months
```

■ A preliminary, estimated cash flow statement for the first year, including considerations of resources needed for start-up and your cash conversion cycle:

■ An estimation of (1) the total amount of asset and working capital needed and peak months and (2) the amount of money needed to reach positive cash flow and the amount of money needed to reach breakeven, and an indication of the months when each will occur:

■ Create a breakeven chart similar to the following:

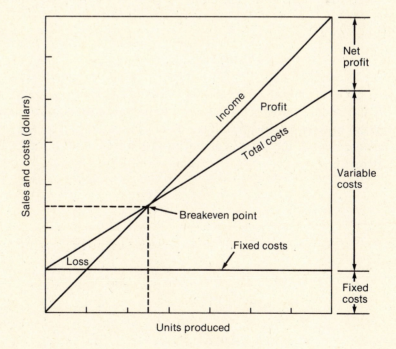

■ An estimate of the capital required for asset additions and operating needs (and the months in which these will occur) to attain the sales level projected in five years:

■ An statement of how you intend to raise capital, including all types (e.g., venture capital, financing raised through asset lenders, financing against inventory, receivables, equipment, and real estate); when; and from whom:

■ A statement of whether you intend to harvest your venture, how and when this might occur, and the prospects. (If you do not intend to harvest the venture, include instead a statement of the prospects that profits will be both durable and large enough to be attractive.)

■ An assessment of the sources of value, such as strategic, to another firm already in the market or one contemplating entry and an indication if there is a logical buyer(s) of your venture:

■ An assessment of how much it would take to liquidate the venture if you decided to exit and whether this is high:

CHECKPOINT:	RECONSIDER IF YOUR VENTURE OPPORTUNITY IS ATTRACTIVE. BEWARE OF COMPROMISING ON WHETHER YOUR OPPORTUNITY HAS "FORGIVING" AND "REWARDING" ECONOMICS. FOR EXAMPLE, ARE YOU CONVINCED THAT THE AMOUNT YOU NEED TO RAISE IS REASONABLE WITH RESPECT TO THE VENTURE'S POTENTIAL AND RISK? ARE OTHERS CONVINCED, AND, IF THEY ARE NOT, WHAT DO YOU KNOW THAT THEY DO NOT (AND VICE VERSA)? MOST START-UPS RUN OUT OF CASH BEFORE THEY SECURE ENOUGH PROFITABLE CUSTOMERS TO SUSTAIN A POSITIVE CASH FLOW. YOUR PRELIMINARY ESTIMATES OF FINANCIAL REQUIREMENTS NEED TO BE WITHIN THE AMOUNT THAT AN INVESTOR, VENTURE CAPITALIST, OR OTHER LENDER IS WILLING TO COMMIT TO A SINGLE VENTURE OR THAT YOU CAN PERSONALLY RAISE. EVEN IF YOUR IDEA IS NOT A CANDIDATE FOR VENTURE CAPITAL FINANCING, IT IS WORTH LOOKING AT YOUR VENTURE IN THIS WAY.

■ An assessment of competitors in the market, including those selling substitute products:

Competitor No.	Name	Products/Services That Compete Directly	Substitutes

■ A profile of the competition:

Competitor Profile

	Competitor No.			
	1	2	3	4
Estimated Sales/Year ($)				
Estimated Market Share (%)				
Description of Sales Force				

Marketing Tactics:

   Selling Terms

   Advertising/Promotion

   Distribution Channel

   Service/Training/Support

   Pricing

Major Strengths

Major Weaknesses

■ A ranking of major competitors by market share:

No.	Competitor	Estimated Market Share

- A Robert Morris Associates statement study:

RMA Study

RMA Data for Period Ending	Estimates for Proposed Venture				
Asset Size	Under $250M	$250M and Less than $1MM	$1MM and Less than $10MM	$10MM and Less than $50MM	All Sizes
Number of Statements					

Assets:
  Cash
  Marketable securities
  Receivables net
  Inventory net
  All other current
    Total current
  Fixed assets net
  All other noncurrent
    Total
	%	%	%	%	%

Liabilities:
  Due to banks—short-term
  Due to trade
  Income taxes
  Current maturities long-term debt
  All other current
    Total current debt
  Noncurrent debt, unsubordinated
    Total unsubordinated debt
  Subordinated debt
  Tangible net worth
    Total					

Income data:
  Net sales
  Cost of sales
  Gross profit
  All other expense net
  Profit before taxes					

Ratios:
  Quick
  Current
  Fixed/worth
  Debt/worth
  Unsubordinated debt/capital funds
  Sales/receivables
  Cost sales/inventory
  Sales/working capital
  Sales/worth
  Percent profit before taxes/worth
  Percent profit before taxes/total
    assets
Net sales/total assets					

■ An assessment of whether there are economies of scale in production and/or cost advantages in marketing and distribution:

■ An assessment, for *each* competitor's product or service, its costs and profitability:

Competitor Costs and Profitability			
Product/Service			
Sales Price			
Sales Level			

For Each:

	Dollars/Unit	Percent of Sales Price/Unit
Production Costs (i.e., labor and material costs) or Purchase Costs		
Gross Margin		
Fixed Costs		
Profit before Taxes		
Profit after Taxes		

■ An assessment of the history and projections of competitors' profits and industry averages:

Competitor Profits — Historical and Projected				
	Competitor			
Industry Average	1	2	3	4
Profits (percent of sales)				
Past Two Years				
Current Year				
Projected Next Two Years				
Sales/Employee				
Profit/Employee				

■ A ranking of competitors in terms of cost:

No.	Competitor

■   A profile for the current year of your competitors in terms of price and quality and of market share and profitability. Place competitors (using small circles identified by names) in the appropriate locations in the boxes below:

Array of Competitors

Highest	
Price	
Lowest	
Last	Leader

Quality

Largest	
Market Share	
Smallest	
Lowest	Highest

Profitability

- An assessment of the degree of control in the market (including that over prices, costs, and channels of distribution and by suppliers, buyers, etc.) and the extent to which you can influence these or will be subject to influence by others:

- An assessment of current lead times for changes in technology, capacity, product and market innovation, and so forth:

- An assessment of whether your venture will enjoy cost advantages or disadvantages in production and in marketing and distribution, and an indication of whether your venture will have the lowest, average, or highest costs of production, marketing, and distribution:

- An assessment of other competitive advantages which you have or can gain, how you would secure these, and what time and money is required, including:
  - An indication of whether your product or service will benefit from or be subject to any regulations and of the status of any copyrights, trade secrets, or patents or licenses and distribution or franchise agreements:

— An indication if you enjoy advantages in response and lead times for technology, capacity changes, product and market innovation, and so forth:

— An indication if you enjoy other "unfair" advantage, such as a strategic advantage, people advantage, resource advantage, location advantage, etc.:

— An assessment of whether you think you can be price competitive and make a profit, or other ways, such as product differentiation, in which you can compete:

■ A ranking of your venture in terms of price and quality and of market share and profitability relative to your competitors. Add your venture to the Arrays of Competitors above:

■ An assessment of whether any competitors enjoy competitive advantages, such as legal or contractual advantages:

■ An assessment of whether any competitors are vulnerable, the time period of this vulnerability, and the impact in terms of market structure of their succumbing to vulnerabilities:

> **CHECKPOINT:** DO YOU HAVE SUFFICIENT COMPETITIVE ADVANTAGE? REMEMBER, A SUCCESSFUL COMPANY SELLS TO A MARKET THAT IS LARGE AND GROWING; WHERE CAPTURING A SMALL MARKET SHARE CAN BRING SIGNIFICANT SALES VOLUME; WHERE IT DOES NOT FACE SIGNIFICANT BARRIERS TO ENTRY; AND WHERE ITS COMPETITION IS PROFITABLE, BUT NOT SO STRONG AS TO BE OVERWHELMING. FURTHER, A SUCCESSFUL COMPANY HAS A PRODUCT OR SERVICE THAT SOLVES SIGNIFICANT PROBLEMS THAT CUSTOMERS HAVE WITH COMPETITIVE PRODUCTS, SUCH AS POOR QUALITY, POOR SERVICE, POOR DELIVERY, ETC., AND A SALES PRICE THAT WILL ENABLE IT TO PENETRATE THE MARKET.

- An assessment of your partners and/or management team, including:
  - An evaluation of whether the founders and/or the management team are sufficiently committed to the opportunity and how much they are personally willing to invest in time, money, personal guarantees, and so forth:

  - An assessment of whether the founders and/or the management team possess the industry knowledge, experience, know-how, and skills required for the venture's success; if additional personnel is necessary and if these can be attracted to the venture; and if anyone on the team has managed previously what you are trying to undertake:

  - An assessment of whether the founders and/or management team have the necessary vision and entrepreneurial zest and whether they will be able to inspire this in others:

— An assessment of the level of trust felt among the founders and/or management team:

— A statement about who will do what—roles, responsibilities, and tasks:

— A statement about the contributions each founder and team member is expected to make:

— A statement about who will get what salary, what benefits, and what ownership share:

> **CHECKPOINT:**   CAN DO? REMEMBER, THE TEAM IS A PRIMARY FORCE DRIVING SUCCESSFUL ENTREPRENEURIAL VENTURES. IT IS IMPORTANT TO QUESTION THE ASSUMPTIONS ON WHICH YOUR TEAM HAS BEEN SHAPED; FOR EXAMPLE, EQUAL SALARIES AND STOCK OWNERSHIP CAN INDICATE THAT ASSUMPTIONS AS TO TASKS, ROLES, AND RESPONSIBILITIES ARE NAIVE. SOMEONE ON YOUR TEAM NEEDS TO BE EXPERIENCED AND COMPETENT IN THESE AREAS, OR THE TEAM NEEDS TO BE ABLE TO ATTRACT SOMEONE WHO IS.

STEP 5:   INCLUDE ANY OTHER VITAL ISSUES OR CONSIDERATIONS THAT ARE UNIQUE TO YOUR VENTURE OPPORTUNITY AND THAT HAVE NOT BEEN COVERED IN THE VOSG.   For example, a location analysis is necessary for retail establishments or real estate:

STEP 6:   ASSESS IF YOUR VENTURE OPPORTUNITY HAS ANY FATAL FLAWS:

STEP 7: LIST SIGNIFICANT ASSUMPTIONS (E.G., ASSUMPTIONS ABOUT CUSTOMER ORDERS, SALES PROJECTIONS, ETC.), INCLUDING:

■ A consideration of significant trade-offs that you have made:

■ A consideration of the major risks (e.g., unreliability of customer orders; overoptimistic sales projections; inability to achieve cost and time estimates; underestimating the magnitude, intensity, and vindictiveness of competitors' responses; etc.):

STEP 8: RANK ASSUMPTIONS ACCORDING TO IMPORTANCE:

STEP 9: EVALUATE THE DOWNSIDE CONSEQUENCES, IF ANY, WHEN YOUR ASSUMPTIONS ARE PROVED INVALID, HOW SEVERE THE IMPACT WOULD BE, AND IF AND HOW THESE CAN BE MINIMIZED, INCLUDING:

■ The cost and consequences of (1) lost growth opportunities and (2) liquidation or bankruptcy to the company, to you, and to other stakeholders:

STEP 10: RATE THE RISK OF THE VENTURE AS HIGH, MEDIUM, OR LOW:

STEP 11: LIST CHRONOLOGICALLY THE 10 TO 15 MOST CRITICAL ACTIONS YOU NEED TO TAKE DURING THE NEXT SIX MONTHS AND THE HURDLES THAT NEED TO BE OVERCOME IN ORDER TO CONVERT YOUR IDEA INTO A REAL OPPORTUNITY.   It is a good idea to have another person review what you have listed and adjust the list, if warranted.

Date	Action

STEP 12:   MAKE A WEEK-BY-WEEK SCHEDULE OF KEY TASKS TO BE PERFORMED, WHEN THEY ARE TO BE PERFORMED, AND BY WHOM.   Break larger tasks into their smallest possible components. Be alert for conflicts.

Week No.	Task	Date Completed	Person Responsible

CHECKPOINT: IT IS IMPORTANT TO TAKE A HARD LOOK AT THE ASSUMPTIONS YOU HAVE MADE, BOTH IMPLICIT AND EXPLICIT, AND TO ASSESS THE RISK OF THE VENTURE. TIME AND AGAIN. FIRST-TIME ENTREPRENEURS OVERESTIMATE SALES AND DELIVERY DATES AND UNDERESTIMATE COSTS, EFFORT, AND TIME RE-QUIRED TO EXECUTE THE OPPORTUNITY AND TO REACH A POSITIVE CASH FLOW. ALSO, WHILE EACH NEW BUSINESS HAS ITS RISKS AND PROBLEMS, AS WELL AS ITS OPPORTUNITIES, DIFFICULTIES NEED TO BE IDENTIFIED AS SOON AS POSSIBLE SO THEY CAN BE AVOIDED OR ELIMINATED OR THEIR IMPACT MINIMIZED.

STEP 13: RETURN TO **STEPS 1** AND **2** TO REFINE YOUR OPPORTUNITY SUMMARY AND MAKE ANY ADJUSTMENTS TO YOUR VENTURE OPPORTUNITY PROFILE. Attach to your VOSG a list of the names, addresses, and phone numbers of relevant sources of industry and market data.

CHECKPOINT: YOUR RESPONSES TO THE "VENTURE OPPORTUNITY SCREENING GUIDE" WILL HELP YOU TO DETERMINE WHETHER YOU WANT TO CONTINUE WITH YOUR VENTURE AND DEVELOP A COMPLETE BUSINESS PLAN. IF YOUR VENTURE HAS PASSED, A CRUCIAL QUESTION TO CONSIDER BEFORE PROCEEDING IS: WHAT DO I WANT TO GET OUT OF THE BUSINESS? YOU WILL WANT TO THINK TWICE ABOUT WHETHER THE VENTURE PROVIDES A STRONG FIT WITH YOUR PERSONAL GOALS, VALUES, AND NEEDS, IS WHAT GIVES YOU ENERGY, LEADS YOU DOWN THE PATH YOU WANT TO BE ON AND TO FURTHER AND EVEN BETTER OPPORTUNITIES. REMEMBER, YOU ARE WHAT YOU DO. IF YOU HAVE BEEN ABLE TO COMPLETE THE GUIDE, ARE SATISFIED THAT MOST OF THE RESULTS ARE POSITIVE, AND IF THE ANSWERS TO THE PERSONAL ISSUES ARE YES (SEE PART VI), THEN *GO FOR IT*.

THE FOUNDERS

PART II

Survival odds for a venture go up once sales of at least $1 million are reached and employees number approximately 20. Launching or acquiring and then building a business that will exceed 20 employees is more fun and more challenging than being involved in the vast majority of small one- or two-person operations. But, perhaps most important, a business of this magnitude achieves the critical mass necessary to attract good people, and, as a result, the prospects of realizing a harvest are significantly enhanced.

A leader who thinks and acts with an "entrepreneurial mind" can make a critical difference between a business destined to be a traditional very small lifestyle firm, or a stagnant or declining large one, and a higher potential venture. Practicing certain mental attitudes and acting in a certain way can stimulate, motivate, and reinforce the kind of zest and entrepreneurial culture whose self-fulfilling prophecy is success.

It is almost certainly impossible to take a number of people, give them a test, and determine which possess entrepreneurial minds and which do not. Rather, it is useful for would-be entrepreneurs and others involved in entrepreneurship to study how successful entrepreneurs think, feel, and respond and how those factors that are significant can be developed and strengthened—as a decathlete develops and strengthens certain muscles to compete at a certain level.

Entrepreneurs who create or recognize opportunities and then seize and shape them into higher potential ventures *think and do things differently*. They operate in an entrepreneurial domain, a place governed by certain modes of acting and dominated by certain principal driving forces.

External and internal pressures mandate that the entrepreneur be a manager as his or her venture grows beyond being founder-driven and dominated by the need to survive. The development of competencies as an entrepreneurial manager are critical. Thus, not only do acquired skills and relevant experience position entrepreneurs to see opportunities that others do not see or cannot grasp, these acquired skills and experience are key to achieving longer-term sustained growth and an eventual harvest.

It makes a lot of sense for entrepreneurs to pay particular attention to picking partners, key business associates, and managers with an eye for complementing their own weaknesses and strengths and the needs of the venture. As will be seen, they seek people who *fit*. The reason for this is that, not only can a weakness be an Achilles' heel for new ventures, but also the whole is almost always greater than the sum of its parts. For example, Ken Fisher joined Prime Computer in 1975 as president when the company had sales of just $7 million and employed 150 people. In six years the company grew to $365 million in sales and 4,500 employees. Sales grew at a compounded annual rate of 88 percent and net income by 108 percent, while return on shareholder's equity reached a high of 48.8 percent and topped 35.0 percent for four consecutive years. During his stay, Prime's share price increased 126 times to its 1981 high, just prior to his resignation. He subsequently formed Encore Computer Corporation with two industry leaders. In talking about his experiences, Fisher said a lead entrepreneur has need for " . . . an ego that sustains and drives a person to achieve, stress tolerance, controlled empathy, ability to resolve conflicts, keeping everything in perspective between the business and personal life, and least important of all these, intelligence."

Finally, ethics are terribly important in entrepreneurship. In highly unpredictable and fragile situations, ethical issues cannot be handled according to such simplistic notions as "always tell the truth."

The Entrepreneurial Mind in Thought and Action

Nothing that sends you to the grave with a smile on your face comes easy. Work hard doing what you love. Find out what gives you energy and improve on it.

Betty Coster, Entrepreneur

RESULTS EXPECTED

Upon completion of this chapter, you will have:

1. Examined ways to help you discover whether being an entrepreneur gives you sustaining energy, rather than takes it away.
2. Explored the entrepreneurial mind[1] — the strategies, approaches, attitudes, and behaviors that work for entrepreneurs who build higher potential ventures.
3. Developed concepts for evaluating a personal entrepreneurial strategy and an apprenticeship.
4. Developed an entrepreneur's "Creed."
5. Analyzed a case, Kevin Mooney.
6. (Optional) Crafted a personal entrepreneurial strategy.

THE SEARCH FOR UNDERSTANDING

Who Can Be an Entrepreneur?

The opening quote in Chapter 1 eloquently answered this question. But, as was noted in Chapter 1, there is much more behind "walking the breathtaking highlands of success."

The lead entrepreneurs who find and seize opportunities and grow higher potential ventures *do* things differently. Recall from *Exhibit 1.9* and the discussion in Chapter 1 that entrepreneurs — in thought and action — are anchored by certain attitudes and behaviors and by the "chunks" of experience, skills, know-how, and contacts they possess. They are thus positioned to see what others do not and seize opportunities and grow higher potential ventures.

Beyond Psychological Makeup

As was outlined in the first chapter, a psychological model of entrepreneurship has not been supported by research. However, behavioral scientists, venture capitalists, investors, and entrepreneurs share the opinion that the eventual success of a new venture will depend a great deal upon the talent and behavior of the lead entrepreneur and of his or her team.

Also mentioned in the first chapter was that a number of myths persist about entrepreneurs.

[1] Jeffry A. Timmons, *The Entrepreneurial Mind* (Acton, Mass.: Brick House Publishing, 1989).

Foremost among these myths is the belief that leaders are born, not made. The roots of much of this thinking reflect the assumptions and biases of an earlier era when rulers were royal and leadership was the prerogative of the aristocracy. Fortunately, such notions have not withstood the tests of practice and time, nor the inquisitiveness of researchers of leadership and management. It is widely accepted today that leadership is an extraordinarily complex subject, depending more on the interconnections among the leader, the task, the situation, and those being led than on inborn or inherited characteristics alone.

There are numerous ways of thinking about and accounting for human behavior and so, too, in trying to understand the entrepreneurial mind. These many theories of human behavior have implications in the study of entrepreneurship.

For example, for over 35 years Dr. David C. McClelland of Harvard University and Dr. John W. Atkinson of the University of Michigan and their colleagues have been seeking to understand individual motivation.[2] Their theory of psychological motivation is a generally accepted part of the literature on entrepreneurial behavior and has been used to a considerable extent in actual research, evaluation, and training efforts.

The theory states that people are motivated by three principal needs: (1) need for achievement, (2) need for power, and (3) need for affiliation. The *need for achievement* is the need to excel and for measurable personal accomplishment. A person competes against a self-imposed standard that does not involve competition with others. The individual sets realistic and challenging goals and likes to get feedback on how well he or she is doing in order to improve performance. The *need for power* is the need to influence others and to achieve an "influence goal" (i.e., the goal of outperforming someone else or establishing a reputation or position according to an externally derived and oriented standard). (While it is sometimes easier to see the negative aspects of power motivation, bear in mind that socialized and civilized power needs have played an important role in influencing people and institutions.) The *need for affiliation* is the need to attain an "affiliation goal" (i.e., the goal to build a warm relationship with someone else and/or to enjoy mutual friendship).

In thinking about this and other theories of human behavior, it is useful to keep in mind that what a person says and what a person does often are not the same thing. Further, it is easy for someone to confuse his or her own motivations with those of another person, whether a superior, partner, friend, or peer. There is also a tendency for one person to attribute motivations to an individual when there are none. There must be some activity or concern before any motivation is indicated. Also, people often have some of all the motivations described above, for example, and, in different circumstances, these will be more or less prominent. Finally, motivations in themselves are neither good nor bad. They are simply ways of describing why people do the things they do. But, the effect of the relative strengths of the certain needs and the fact that certain strengths and weaknesses may be associated with certain needs is of interest.

Other Research

Other research has come at the question from other directions and is converging on what these common attitudes and behaviors are.

---

[2] See John W. Atkinson, *An Introduction to Motivation* (Princeton, N.J.: van Nostrand, 1964); J. W. Atkinson, *Motives in Fantasy, Action and Society* (Princeton, N.J.: van Nostrand, 1958); D. C. McClelland, *The Achieving Society* (Princeton, N.J.: van Nostrand, 1961); J. W. Atkinson and N. T. Feather, eds., *A Theory of Achievement Motivation* (New York: John Wiley & Sons, 1966); and D. C. McClelland and D. G. Winter, *Motivating Economic Achievement* (New York: Free Press, 1969).

Exhibit 5.1
Characteristics of Entrepreneurs

Date	Author(s)	Characteristics	Normative	Empirical
1848	Mill	Risk-bearing	X	
1917	Weber	Source of formal authority	X	
1934	Schumpeter	Innovation; initiative	X	
1954	Sutton	Desire for responsibility	X	
1959	Hartman	Source of formal authority	X	
1961	McClelland	Risk-taking; need for achievement		X
1963	Davids	Ambition; desire for independence, responsibility; self-confidence		X
1964	Pickle	Drive/mental; human relations; communication ability; technical knowledge		X
1971	Palmer	Risk measurement		X
1971	Hornaday and Aboud	Need for achievement; autonomy; aggression; power; recognition; innovative/independent		X
1973	Winter	Need for power	X	
1974	Borland	Internal locus of control		X
1974	Liles	Need for achievement		X
1977	Gasse	Personal value orientation		X
1978	Timmons	Drive/self-confidence; goal-oriented; moderate risk-taker; locus of control; creativity/innovation	X	X
1980	Sexton	Energetic/ambitious; positive setbacks		X
1981	Welsh and White	Need to control; responsibility seeker; self-confidence/drive; challenge taker; moderate risk taker		X
1982	Dunkelberg and Cooper	Growth-oriented; independence-oriented; craftsman-oriented		X

Source: James W. Carland, Frank Hoy, William R. Boulton, and Jo Ann C. Carland, "Differentiating Entrepreneurs from Small Business Owners: A Conceptualization," *Academy of Management Review* 9, no. 2 (1984), p. 356.

One study proposed a stages model for entrepreneurs and their enterprises and found a relationship between attitudes and behaviors of successful entrepreneurs and various stages of development of their firms.[3] Another study found that entrepreneurs were distinguished from the rest of the pack.[4] For example, this study found that, "What is characteristic is not so much an overall type as a successful, growth-oriented entrepreneurial type. . . . It is the company builders who are distinctive."[5] The work of 18 researchers, shown in *Exhibit 5.1,* distinguishes the attitudes and behaviors of entrepreneurs and small business owners.[6] Other researchers report there are differences between franchised and independent entrepreneurs.[7]

In a study which involved 60 practicing entrepreneurs attending the Smaller Company Management Program at the Harvard Business School in January 1983, questions about attitudes and behaviors needed in entrepreneurship were addressed.[8] One message of

[3] Neil C. Churchill, "Entrepreneurs and Their Enterprises: A Stage Model," in *Frontiers of Entrepreneurship Research: 1983,* ed. J. A. Hornaday et al. (Babson Park: Mass.: Babson College, 1983), pp. 1–22.

[4] N. R. Smith and John B. Miner, "Motivational Considerations in the Success of Technologically Innovative Entrepreneurs," in *Frontiers of Entrepreneurship Research: 1984,* ed. J. Hornaday et al. (Babson Park, Mass.: Babson College, 1984), pp. 448–95.

[5] Ibid., pp. 448–95.

[6] James W. Carland, Frank Hoy, William R. Boulton, and Jo Ann C. Carland, "Differentiating Entrepreneurs from Small Business Owners: A Conceptualization," *Academy of Management Review* 9, no. 2 (1984), pp. 354–59.

[7] R. Knight, "A Comparison of Franchisers and Independent Entrepreneurs," in *Frontiers of Entrepreneurship Research: 1983,* ed. J. A. Hornaday et al. (Babson Park, Mass.: Babson College, 1983), pp. 167–91.

[8] J. A. Timmons and H. H. Stevenson, "Entrepreneurship Education in the 80s: What Entrepreneurs Say," in *Entrepreneurship: What It Is and How to Teach It,* ed. J. J. Kao and H. H. Stevenson (Boston, Mass.: Harvard Business School, 1985), pp. 115–34.

this study was that these entrepreneurs felt there was a need to focus on certain fundamentals in entrepreneurship: responsiveness, resiliency, and adaptiveness in seizing new opportunities. Similarly, many respondents recognized and endorsed the importance of people management issues. One described one of the most challenging tasks in five years as "a leadership role in attracting high quality people; imparting your vision to them; and holding and motivating them."

Many focused on the importance of building an organization and teamwork. For example, the head of a manufacturing firm with $10 million in sales said, "Understanding people and how to pull them together toward a basic goal will be my main challenge in five years." The head of a clothing manufacturing business with 225 employees and $6 million in sales shared a view of many that one of the most critical areas where an entrepreneur has leverage and long-term impact is in managing employees. He said, "Treating people honestly and letting them know when they do well goes a long way."

A number of respondents felt that the ability to conceptualize their business and do strategic planning would be of growing importance, particularly when thinking five years ahead.

Other attitudes they spoke of included a willingness to learn about and invest in new techniques, to be adaptable, to have a professional attitude, and to have patience. They talked about the importance of "enjoying and being interested in business" and also of the business "as a way of life." They mentioned an ability to "activate vision."

When asked directly which attitudes and philosophies are crucial today and five years hence, the acceptance of risk stood out for many. As one executive put it:

Success will go to the honest risk taker who has overcome greed and fear, faces reality, and makes decisions. You must have no fear to admit error and mistakes, but use these to learn and proceed.

The 40-year-old head of a general construction business with 325 employees called it being "risk sensitive within limits; you have to enjoy taking risks, rather than avoiding them." Nonetheless, a handful talked about risk avoidance.

Several talked about positive mental attitude and a sense of optimism. Still others cautioned that there is a need for humility; yet a handful noted a prominent role of "greed," a "desire to have things," and "more is better" as important attitudes.

The ageless importance of sensitivity to and respect for employees was stressed by a 49-year-old chief executive officer of a firm with $40 million in sales and 400 employees. He put it this way:

It is essential that the separation between management and the average employee be eliminated. Students should be taught to respect employees all the way down to the janitor and accept them as knowledgeable and able persons.

A recent consulting study by McKinsey of medium-size growth companies (i.e., companies with sales between $25 million and $1 billion and with sales or profit growth of more than 15 percent annually over five years) confirms that the chief executive officers of winning companies were notable for three common traits: perseverance, a builder's mentality, and a strong propensity for taking calculated risks.[9]

---

[9] Donald K. Clifford, Jr., and Richard E. Cavanagh, *The Winning Performance* (New York: Bantam Books, 1985), p. 3.

CONVERGING ON THE ENTREPRENEURIAL MIND

Desirable and Acquirable Attitudes and Behaviors

Distinguished entrepreneurs coming to Babson College over 12 years have emphasized that, while successful entrepreneurs have initiative and take charge, are determined and persevere, and are resilient and able to adapt, it is not just a matter of their personalities, *it is what they do.*[10]

While there is an undeniable core of such inborn characteristics as energy and raw intelligence, which an entrepreneur either has or does not, it is becoming apparent that possession of these characteristics does not necessarily an entrepreneur make. And, there is also a good deal of evidence that entrepreneurs are born and made better and that certain attitudes and behaviors can be acquired, developed, practiced, and refined—through a combination of experience and study.[11]

While not all attitudes and behaviors can be acquired by everyone at the same pace and with the same proficiency, entrepreneurs are able to improve significantly their odds of success by concentrating on those that work, by nurturing and practicing them, and by eliminating, or at least mitigating, the rest. Painstaking effort may be required, and much will depend upon the motivation of an individual to grow, but it seems people have an astounding capacity to change and learn if they are motivated and commited to do so.

Testimony given by successful entrepreneurs also confirms there are attitudes and behaviors that successful entrepreneurs have in common. Take, for instance, the first 21 inductees into Babson College's Academy of Distinguished Entrepreneurs, including such well-known entrepreneurs as Ken Olsen of DEC, An Wang of Wang Computers, Wally Amos of Famous Amos' Chocolate Chip Cookies, Bill Norris of Control Data, Sochiro Honda of Honda Motors, and the late Ray Kroc of McDonald's. All 21 of the inductees mentioned the possession of three attributes as the principal reasons for their successes: (1) the ability to respond positively to challenges and learn from mistakes, (2) taking personal initiative, and (3) great perseverance and determination.[12]

There are "themes" that have emerged from what successful entepreneurs do and how they perform. In discussing these themes, it is important to emphasize there are undoubtedly many attitudes and behaviors characterizing the entrepreneurial mind and there is no single set of attitudes and behaviors that every entrepreneur must have for every venture opportunity. Further, the fit concept argues that what is required in each situation depends on the mix and match of the key players and how promising and forgiving the opportunity is, given the founders' strengths and shortcomings. And, a team might collectively show many of the desired strengths. Even then, there is no such thing as a perfect entrepreneur—as yet.

Six Dominant Themes

A consensus has emerged around six dominant themes, shown in *Exhibit 5.2:*

- *Commitment and Determination.* Commitment and determination are seen as more important than any other factor. With commitment and determination, an entrepreneur can overcome incredible obstacles and also compensate enormously for other weaknesses.

[10] What attitudes and behaviors in entrepreneurs are "acquirable and desirable" represents the × synthesis of over 50 research studies compiled for the first and second editions of this book. See extensive references in J. A. Timmons, L. E. Smollen, and A. L. M. Dingee, Jr., *New Venture Creation,* 2nd ed. (Homewood, Ill.: Richard D. Irwin, 1985).

[11] David C. McClelland, "Achievement Motivation Can Be Developed," *Harvard Business Review,* November–December 1965; David C. McClelland and David G. Winter, *Motivating Economic Achievement* (New York: Free Press, 1969); and Jeffry A. Timmons, "Black Is Beautiful—Is It Bountiful?" *Harvard Business Review,* November–December 1971, p. 81.

[12] John A. Hornaday and Nancy B. Tieken, "Capturing Twenty-One Heffalumps," in *Frontiers of Entrepreneurship Research: 1983,* ed. J. A. Hornaday et al. (Babson Park, Mass.: Babson College, 1983), pp. 23–50.

Exhibit 5.2
Six Themes—Desirable and Acquirable Attitudes and Behaviors

Theme	*Attitude or Behavior*
Committment and Determination	Tenacity and decisiveness
	Discipline
	Persistence in solving problems
	Willingness to undertake personal sacrifice
	Total immersion
Opportunity Obsession	Having intimate knowledge of customers' needs
	Market-driven
	Obsessed with value creation and enhancement
Tolerance of Risk, Ambiguity, and Uncertainty	Calculated risk taker
	Risk minimizer
	Risk sharer
	Tolerance of uncertainty and lack of structure
	Tolerance of stress and conflict
	Ability to resolve problems and integrate solutions
Creativity, Self-reliance, and Ability to Adapt	Nonconventional, open-minded, lateral thinker
	Restlessness with status quo
	Ability to adapt
	Ability to learn
	Lack of fear of failure
	Ability to conceptualize and "sweat details" (helicopter mind)
Motivation to Excel	Goal-and-results orientation
	Drive to achieve and grow
	Low need for status and power
	Interpersonally supporting (vs. competitive)
	Aware of weaknesses and strengths
	Having perspective and sense of humor
Leadership	Self-starter
	Internal locus of control
	Integrity and reliability
	Patience
	Team builder and hero maker
	Experience
	Not lone wolf

All of the distinguished entrepreneurs referred to earlier said these attitudes were critical. Carl Sontheimer, president and founder of Cuisinarts, Inc., said: "Entrepreneurs come in all flavors, personalities, degrees of ethics, but one thing they have in common is they never give up." Franklin P. Purdue, president of Purdue Farms, Inc., said: "Nothing, absolutely nothing, replaces the willingness to work. You have to be willing to pay the price."

Total commitment is required by almost all entrepreneurial ventures. Almost without exception, entrepreneurs live under huge, constant pressures—first for their firms to survive start-up, then for them to stay alive, and finally for them to grow. A new venture demands top priority for the entrepreneur's time, emotions, and loyalty. Thus, involved in commitment and determination is usually personal sacrifice. An entrepreneur's commitment can be measured in several ways—through willingness to invest a substantial portion of his or her net worth in the venture, through willingness to take a cut in pay since he or she will own a major piece of the venture, and through other major sacrifices in lifestyle and family circumstances.

Entrepreneurs who successfully build new enterprises desire to overcome hurdles, solve problems, and complete the job, and they are disciplined, tenacious, and persistent in solving problems and in performing other tasks. They are not intimidated by difficult situations and, in fact, seem to view that the impossible just takes a little longer. However, they are neither aimless nor foolhardy in their relentless attack on a problem or obstacle that can impede their business. If a task is unsolvable, an entrepreneur actually will give up sooner than others. Most researchers share the opinion that, while entrepreneurs are extremely persistent, they are also realistic in recognizing what they can and cannot do, and where they can get help to solve a very difficult but necessary task.

■ *Opportunity Obsession.*   Successful entrepreneurs are obsessed – with opportunity. They are oriented to the goal of pursuing and executing an opportunity for accumulating resources or money per se. Much has been said about opportunity in the first chapters of this book. The obsession of entrepreneurs is manifested in total immersion in the opportunity. They are discriminating, realizing that ideas are a dime a dozen. They are intimately familiar with their industries, customers, and competition. This obsession with opportunity is what guides how an entrepreneur deals with important issues. It is noteworthy that the Chinese characters for crisis and problem, when combined, mean opportunity.

■ *Tolerance of Risk, Ambiguity, and Uncertainty.*   Since high rates of change and high levels of risk, ambiguity, and uncertainty are almost a given, successful entrepreneurs tolerate risk, ambiguity, and uncertainty.

Entrepreneurs risk money and much more than that – reputation. Successful entrepreneurs are not gamblers; they take calculated risks. Like the parachutist, they are willing to take a risk; however, in deciding to take a risk, they calculate the risk carefully and thoroughly and do everything possible to get the odds in their favor. Entrepreneurs get others to share inherent financial and business risks with them. Partners put up money and put their reputations on the line; investors do likewise; creditors join the party; as do customers who advance payments and suppliers who advance credit. For example, one researcher studied three very successful entrepreneurs in California who initiated and orchestrated actions which, while not risky to themselves, had risk consequences.[13] It was found that, while they shunned risk, they sustained their courage by the clarity and optimism with which they saw the future. They limited the risks they initiated by carefully defining and strategizing their ends and by controlling and monitoring their means – and by tailoring them both to what they saw the future to be. Further, they managed risk by transferring it to others.

Similarly, another study reported the results of an objective test administered to 71 entrepreneurs that showed motives involving self-achievement, avoiding risk, seeking feedback, personal innovation, and a positive orientation to the future are relatively strong in the most successful entrepreneurs.[14]

Entrepreneurs also tolerate ambiguity and uncertainty and are comfortable with conflict. Ask someone working in a large company how sure he or she is that he or she will receive a paycheck this month, in two months, in six months, and next year. Invariably, he or she will say that it is virtually certain and will muse at the question. Start-up entrepreneurs face just the opposite; there may be no revenue at the beginning, and, if there is, a 90-day backlog in orders would be quite an exception. To make matters worse, lack of organization, structure, and order is a way of life. Constant changes introduce ambiguity and stress into every part of the enterprise. Jobs are undefined and changing continually, customers are new, co-workers are new, and setbacks and surprises are inevitable. And there never seems to be enough time.

Successful entrepreneurs maximize the good "higher performance" results of stress and minimize the negative reactions of exhaustion and frustration. Two surveys

---

[13] Daryl Mitton, "No Money, Know-How, Know-Who: Formula for Managing Venture Success and Personal Wealth," *Frontiers of Entrepreneurship Research: 1984,* ed. J. Hornaday et al. (Babson Park, Mass.: Babson College, 1984), p. 427.

[14] Smith and Miner, "Motivational Considerations," p. 495.

have suggested that very high levels of both satisfaction and stress characterize founders, to a greater degree than managers, regardless of the success of their ventures.[15]

- *Creativity, Self-reliance, and Ability to Adapt.* The high levels of uncertainty and very rapid rates of change that characterize new ventures require fluid and highly adaptive forms of organization. An organization that can respond quickly and effectively is a must.

Successful entrepreneurs believe in themselves. They believe that their accomplishments (and setbacks) lie within their own control and influence and that they can affect the outcome. Successful entrepreneurs have the ability to see and "sweat the details" and also to conceptualize (i.e., they have "helicopter minds"). They are dissatisfied with status quo and are restless initiators.

The entrepreneur has historically been viewed as an independent, a highly self-reliant innovator, and the champion (and occasional villain) of the free enterprise economy. More modern research and investigation have refined considerably the ways of focusing on this self-reliance. There is considerable agreement among researchers and practitioners, alike, that effective entrepreneurs actively seek and take initiative. They willingly put themselves in situations where they are personally responsible for the success or failure of the operation. They like to take the initiative to solve a problem or fill a vacuum where no leadership exists. They also like situations where personal impact on problems can be measured. Again, this is the action-oriented nature of the entrepreneur expressing itself.

Successful entrepreneurs are adaptive and resilient. They have an insatiable desire to know how well they are performing. They realize that, to know how well they are doing and how to improve their performance, they need to actively seek out and use feedback. Seeking and using feedback is also central to the habit of learning from mistakes and setbacks, and of responding to the unexpected. For the same reasons, these entrepreneurs often are described as excellent listeners and quick learners.

Entrepreneurs are not afraid of failing; rather, they are more intent on succeeding. People who fear failure will neutralize whatever achievement motivation they may possess. They will tend to engage in a very easy task, where there is little chance of failure, or, in a very difficult situation, where they cannot be held personally responsible if they do not succeed.

Further, successful entrepreneurs have the ability to use failure experiences as a way of learning and to undertand better, not only their roles but also the roles of others, in causing the failure to avoid similar problems in the future. There is an old saying to the effect that the cowboy who has never been thrown from a horse undoubtedly has not ridden too many! The iterative, trial-and-error nature of becoming a successful entrepreneur makes serious setbacks and disappointments an integral part of the learning process.

- *Motivation to Excel.* Successful entrepreneurs are motivated to excel. Entrepreneurs are self-starters, who appear driven internally by a strong desire to compete against their own self-imposed standards and to pursue and attain challenging goals. This need to achieve has been well established in the literature on entrepreneurs since the pioneering work of McClelland and Atkinson on motivation in the 1950s and 1960s. Seeking out the challenge inherent in a start-up and responding in a positive way, noted by the distinguished entrepreneurs mentioned above, is achievement motivation in action.

Conversely, these entrepreneurs have a low need for status and power, and they derive personal motivation from the challenge and excitement of creating and building

---

[15] D. Boyd and D. E. Gumpert, "Loneliness of the Start-up Entrepreneur," in *Frontiers of Entrepreneurship Research: 1982 and 1983,* ed. J. A. Hornaday et al. (Babson Park, Mass.: Babson College, 1983), pp. 478–87.

enterprises. They are driven by a thirst for achievement, rather than by status and power. Ironically, their accomplishments, especially if they are very successful, give them power. But it is important to recognize that power and status are a result of their activities.

Setting high but attainable goals enables entrepreneurs to focus their energies, be very selective in sorting out opportunities, and know what to say "no" to. Having goals and direction also helps define priorities and provides measures of how well they are performing. Having an objective way of keeping score, such as changes in profits, sales, or stock price, is also important. Thus, money is seen as a tool, and a way of keeping score, rather than the object of the game by itself.

Successful entrepreneurs insist on the highest personal standards of integrity and reliability. They do what they say they are going to do, and they pull for the long-haul. These high personal standards are the glue and fiber that binds successful personal and business relationships and makes them endure. A recent study involving 130 members of the Small Company Management Program at Harvard Business School confirmed how important this issue is. Most simply said it was the single most important factor in their *long-term* successes.[16]

The best entrepreneurs have a keen awareness of their own strengths and weaknesses and those of their partners and of the competitive and other environments surrounding and influencing them. They are coldly realistic about what they can and cannot do and do not delude themselves; that is, they have "veridical awareness" or "optimistic realism." It also is worth noting that successful entrepreneurs believe in themselves. They do not believe the success or failure of their venture will be governed by fate, luck, or other powerful, external forces. They believe that they personally can affect the outcome. This attribute is also consistent with achievement motivation, which is the desire to take personal responsibility, and self-confidence.

This veridical awareness often is accompanied by other valuable entrepreneurial traits—perspective and a sense of humor. The ability to retain a sense of perspective, and to "know thyself," in both strengths and weaknesses, makes it possible for an entrepreneur to laugh, to ease tensions, and—frequently—to get an unfavorable situation set in a more profitable direction.

■ *Leadership.* Successful entrepreneurs are experienced, including having intimate knowledge of the technology and marketplace in which they will compete, have sound general management skills, and have a proven track record. They are self-starters and have an internal locus of control.

They are patient leaders, capable of installing tangible visions and managing for the longer-haul. The entrepreneur is at once a doer and a visionary. The vision of building a substantial enterprise that will contribute something lasting and relevant to the world while realizing a capital gain requires the patience to stick to the task for 5 to 10 years or more. There is among successful entrepreneurs a well-developed capacity to exert influence *without* formal power. These people are adept at conflict resolution. They know when to use logic and when to persuade, when to make a concession, and when to exact one. To run a successful venture, an entrepreneur learns to get along with many different constituencies, often with conflicting aims—the customer, the supplier, the financial backer, the creditor, as well as the partners and others on the inside. Success comes when the entrepreneur is a mediator, a negotiator rather than a dictator.

Successful entrepreneurs are interpersonally supporting and nurturing—not interpersonally competitive. When a strong need to control, influence, and gain power over others characterizes the lead entrepreneur, or where he or she has an insatiable appetite for putting an associate down, more often than not the venture gets into trouble.

---

[16] Timmons and Stevenson, "Entrepreneurship Education in the 80s: What Entrepreneurs Say," pp. 115–34.

A dictatorial, adversarial, and domineering management style makes it very difficult to attract and keep people who thrive on a thirst for achievement, responsibility, and results. Compliant partners and managers often are chosen. Destructive conflicts often erupt over who has the final say, who is right, and whose prerogatives are what.

Entrepreneurs who create and build substantial enterprises are not lone-wolves and super-independent. They do not need to collect all the credit for the effort. Not only do they recognize the reality that it is rarely possible to build a substantial business working all alone, they actively build a team. They have an uncanny ability to make heroes out of the people they attract to the venture by giving responsibility and sharing credit for accomplishments.

In the corporate setting, this "hero-making" ability is identified as an essential attribute of successful entrepreneurial managers.[17] These hero-makers, of both the independent and corporate varieties, try to make the pie bigger and better, rather than jealously clutching and hoarding a tiny pie that is all theirs. They have a capacity for objective interpersonal relationships as well, which enables them to smooth out individual differences of opinion by keeping attention focused on the common goal to be achieved.[18]

Other Desirable (But Not So Acquirable) Attitudes and Behaviors

The list of characteristics that most experts and observers would argue are more innate than acquired is, fortunately, much shorter. Even here researchers debate extensively whether these can be learned or nurtured to some degree. A friend who is a pediatrician provided a very appropriate explanation of the extent to which certain aspects of our personalities and makeup can be changed. It is like working with fine sandpaper on a large and very hard piece of wood. The surface of the wood can be modified by smoothing and refining it, but to alter its shape is an enormous undertaking.

The following five areas are of this nature. While these, too, are highly desirable givens for any aspiring entrepreneur with which to begin, it is possible to find quite successful entrepreneurs that may be lacking some or possess only a modest degree of each of these. Once again, few entrepreneurs—or others—have exceptional capacities in each of these areas. If these describe a particular entrepreneur's innate talents, then he or she possesses a tremendous potential to be harnessed.

- *Energy, Health, and Emotional Stability.* The extraordinary work loads and stressful demands faced by entrepreneurs place a premium on energy and on physical and emotional health. While each has strong genetic roots, they can also be fine-tuned and preserved by careful attention to eating and drinking habits, exercise, and relaxation.
- *Creativity and Innovativeness.* Creativity once was thought of as an exclusively inherited capacity, and most would agree that its roots are strongly genetic. But that may be a surprisingly culture-bound notion, judging by the level of creativity and innovation in the United States, compared with other equally sophisticated cultures that are not as creative and innovative. And, again, as noted in Chapter 2, a growing school of thought believes that creativity can actually be learned.
- *Intelligence.* Intelligence and conceptual ability are great advantages for an entrepreneur. There is most likely no successful higher potential venture whose founder would be described as "dumb" or even of "average intelligence." But "street smarts" (i.e., a nose

[17] David L. Bradford and Allan R. Cohen, *Managing for Excellence: The Guide to Developing High Performance in Contemporary Organizations* (New York: John Wiley & Sons, 1984).

[18] Churchill, "Entrepreneurs and Their Enterprises: A Stage Model," pp. 1–22.

for business), the entrepreneur's gut feel and instincts, and "rat-like cunning"[19] are special kinds of intelligence. Also, there are many examples of school dropouts who go on to become truly extraordinary entrepreneurs.

Take, for instance, the late Colonel Sanders of Kentucky Fried Chicken fame. He has been quoted as saying, "When I got to the point in school where they said *X* equals the unknown quantity, *Y,* I decided I had learned as much as I could, and decided I needed to quit school and go to work!" Needless to say, this is not intended to encourage anyone to leave school. The point is that an individual may have a kind of intelligence that will serve him or her well as an entrepreneur but not so well in some other situations.

■ *Capacity to Inspire.* "Vision" is that natural leadership quality that is charismatic, bold, and inspirational. All great leaders through the ages share vision, as do many truly extraordinary entrepreneurs. It is difficult to get anyone to argue that such exceptional personal qualities are other than inborn. Yet, though an entrepreneur's "charisma quotient" may be low, he or she is still the leader, and his or her vision is conveyed by the style of leadership. The entrepreneur's goals and values will establish the atmosphere within which all subsequent activity will unfold, and his or her inspiration, regardless of the form it takes, will shape the venture.

■ *Values.* Personal and ethical values seem to reflect the environments and backgrounds from which entrepreneurs have come and are developed early in life. These values are an integral part of an individual.

A Look at the Nonentrepreneurial Mind

There also appears to be a nonentrepreneurial mind that spells trouble for a new venture, or can be fatal. There is apparently no research on this topic, other than broad-brush abstractions about "management as the leading cause of failure."

Findings about hazardous thought patterns of pilots that may contribute to bad judgment are intriguing.[20] There may well be some parallels between the piloting task and leading an emerging company. Such feelings as invulnerability, being macho, being anti-authoritarian, being impulsive, and having outer control have been shown by researchers to be hazardous to pilots. To this list have been added three others—being a perfectionist, being a know-it-all, and being counter-dependent.

■ *Invulnerability.* This is a thought pattern of people who feel nothing disastrous could happen to them. They are likely to take unnecessary chances and unwise risks. This behavior obviously has severe implications when flying an airplane or launching a company.

■ *Being Macho.* This describes people who try to prove they are better than and can beat others. They may try to prove themselves by taking large risks, and they may try to impress others by exposing themselves to danger (i.e., they are adrenaline junkies). While it is associated with overconfidence, this thought pattern goes beyond that definition. Foolish head-to-head competition and irrational take-over battles may be good examples of this behavior.

■ *Being Anti-authoritarian.* Some people resent control of their actions by any outside authority. Their approach is summed up by the following: "Do not tell me. No one can tell me what to do!" Contrast this thought pattern with the tendency of successful entrepreneurs to seek and use feedback to attain their goals and to improve their

---

[19] The author thanks Phillip Thurston of Harvard Business School for this insightful term.
[20] Berl Brechner, "A Question of Judgement," *Flying,* May 1981, pp. 47–52.

performance, and with their propensity to seek team members and other necessary resources to execute an opportunity.

■ *Impulsivity.* Facing a moment of decision, certain people feel they must do something, do anything, and do it quickly. They fail to explore the implications of their actions and do not review alternatives before acting.

■ *Outer Control.* This is the opposite of the internal locus of control characteristic of successful entrepreneurs. People with the outer-control trait feel they can do little, if anything, to control what happens to them. If things go well, they attribute it to good luck and vice versa.

■ *Perfectionist.* Time and again, perfectionism is the enemy of the entrepreneur. The time and cost implications of attaining perfection invariably result in the opportunity window being slammed shut by a more decisive and nimble competitor, or disappearing altogether by a leapfrog in technology. (Being a perfectionist and having high standards are not the same, however.)

■ *Know It All.* Entrepreneurs who think they have all the answers usually have very few. To make matters worse, they often fail to recognize what they do *not* know. Good people and good opportunities find their way elsewhere.

■ *Counterdependency.* An extreme and severe case of independence can be a limiting mind-set for entrepreneurs. Bound and determined to accomplish things all by themselves, without a particle of help from anyone, these entrepreneurs often end up accomplishing very little. But it is all theirs to claim.

A LOOK AT INTRAPRENEURING

The existence of entrepreneurship in larger corporations will be addressed in the next chapter. Of interest, since it relates to the entrepreneurial mind discussed here, is what Rosabeth Moss Kanter found out about the following entrepreneurial attitudes and behaviors by the middle managers in a study:[21]

■ *Tolerance of change.*   These managers are comfortable with change and see unmet needs as opportunities.

■ *Direction and vision.*   These managers have clarity in their direction, carefully select projects, possess long time horizons, and see setbacks as temporary.

■ *Preparation and management style.*   These managers are known for their thoroughness of preparation and operate with a team-oriented, participative management style.

■ *Perseverance, persistence, and discretion.*   These managers practice perseverance, persistence, and discretion.

THE CONCEPT OF APPRENTICESHIP

Shaping and Managing an Apprenticeship

When one looks at successful entrepreneurs, one sees profiles of careers rich in experience. While there are some outstanding exceptions, such as Steven Jobs, founder of Apple Computer, or Mitch Kapor, founder of Lotus, most entrepreneurs acquire substantial relevant business experience before founding new ventures. As was shown in Chapter 1, they are likely to be older and to have at least 8 to 10 years of experience. They are likely to have accumulated enough net worth to contribute to funding the venture or to have a track record impressive enough to give investors and creditors the necessary confidence. Finally, they

---

[21] Rosabeth Moss Kanter, "Middle Manager as Innovator," *Harvard Business Review,* July–August 1982.

usually have found and nurtured relevant business and other contacts and networks that ultimately contribute to the success of their ventures.

It is fair to say that the first 10 or so years of an entrepreneur's career after he or she leaves school can make or break him or her in terms of how well he or she is prepared for serious entrepreneuring. Evidence suggests that the most durable entrepreneurial careers, those found to last 25 years or more, were begun across a broad age spectrum, but after the person selected prior work or a career to prepare specifically for an entrepreneurial career.

Having relevant experience, know-how, attitudes, behaviors, and skills appropriate for a particular venture opportunity can dramatically improve the odds for success. The other side of the coin is that, if an entrepreneur does not have these, then he or she will have to learn them while launching and growing the business. The tuition for such an approach is often greater than most entrepreneurs can afford.

Since entrepreneurs frequently evolve from an entrepreneurial heritage or are shaped and nurtured by their closeness to entrepreneurs and others, the concept of an apprenticeship can be a useful one. And, no doubt about it, a lot of what an entrepreneur needs to know about entrepreneuring comes from learning by doing. Knowing for what to prepare, where the windows for acquiring the relevant exposure lie, how to anticipate these, where to position oneself, and when to move on, can be quite useful.

As Howard Stevenson of the Harvard Business School has said:

You have to approach the world as an equal. There is no such thing as being supplicant. You are trying to work and create a better solution by creating action among a series of people who are relatively equal. We destroy potential entrepreneurs by putting them in a velvet-lined rut; by giving them jobs that pay too much, and by telling them they are too good, before they get adequate intelligence, experience, and responsibility.

Windows of Apprenticeship

Exhibit 5.3 summarizes the key elements of an apprenticeship and experience curve and relates these to age windows.[22] Age windows are especially important because of the inevitable time it takes to create and build a successful activity, whether it is a new venture or within another organization.

There is the saying in the venture capital business that the "lemons," or losers, in a portfolio ripen in about two and one half years and that the "pearls," or winners, on the other hand, usually take seven or eight years to come to fruition (see *Exhibit 3.2*). Therefore, seven years is a realistic time frame to expect to grow a higher potential business to a point where a capital gain can be realized. Interestingly, seven years is often described by presidents of large corporations, presidents of colleges, and by self-employed professionals as the time it takes to do something significant.

The implications of this are quite provocative. First, time is precious. Assume an entrepreneur spends the first five years after college or graduate school gaining relevant experience. He or she will be 25 to 30 years of age (or maybe as old as 35) when he or she launches a new venture. By the age of 50, there will have been time for starting, at most, three successful new ventures. What is more, it is not uncommon for entrepreneurs to go through false starts or even a failure at first in the trial-and-error process of learning the entrepreneurial ropes. As a result, his or her first venture may not be launched until later (i.e., in his or her mid- to late-30s). This would leave time to grow the current venture and maybe one more. (There is, of course, always the possibility of staying with a venture and growing it to a larger company of $50 million or more in sales.)

---

[22] The author wishes to acknowledge the contributions to his thinking by Mr. Harvey "Chet" Krentzman, entrepreneur, lecturer, author, and nurturer of at least three dozen growth-minded ventures over the past 20 years.

Exhibit 5.3
Windows of the Entrepreneurial Apprenticeship

Elements of the Apprenticeship and the Experience Curve	Age Window			
	20s	30s	40s	50s
1. Relevant business experience	Low	Moderate to high	Higher	Highest
2. Management skills and know-how	Low to moderate	Moderate to high	High	High
3. Entrepreneurial goals and commitment	Varies widely	Focused high	High	High
4. Drive and energy	Highest	High	Moderate	Lowest
5. Wisdom and judgment	Lowest	Higher	Higher	Highest
6. Focus of apprenticeship	Discussing what you enjoy; learning business, sales, marketing key; profit and loss responsibility.	General management Division management Founder	Growing and harvesting	Reinvesting
7. Dominant life-stage issues*	Realizing your "dream" of adolescence and young adulthood.		Personal growth and new directions and ventures.	Renewal, regeneration, reinvesting in the "system."

* Adapted from Daniel J. Levinson et al., *The Seasons of a Man's Life* (New York: Alfred A. Knopf, 1978).

Reflecting on *Exhibit 5.3* will reveal some other paradoxes and dilemmas. For one thing, just when an entrepreneur's drive, energy, and ambition are at a peak, the necessary relevant business experience and management skills are least developed. And those critical elements labeled wisdom and judgment are in their infancy. Later on, when an entrepreneur has gained the necessary experience in the "deep, dark canyons of uncertainty" and has thereby gained wisdom and judgment, mother nature has begun to recall the vast energy and drive that got him or her so far. Also, patience and perseverance to pursue relentlessly a long-term vision need to be balanced with the urgency and realism to make it happen. Flexibility to stick with the moving opportunity targets and to abandon some and shift to others is also required. However, flexibility and the ability to act with urgency disappear as the other commitments of life are assumed.

A Personal Strategy

An apprenticeship can be an integral part of the process of shaping an entrepreneurial career.

One principal task for an entrepreneur is to determine what kind of an entrepreneur he or she is likely to become, based on background, experience, and drive. Through an apprenticeship, an entrepreneur can shape a strategy and action plan to make it happen. Part VI addresses this issue more fully.

Despite all the work involved in becoming an entrepreneur, the bottom line is revealing. Evidence about the careers and job satisfaction of entrepreneurs all points to the same conclusion: If they had to do it over, not only would more of them become entrepreneurs again, but they would do it sooner.[23] And, they would also do it earlier

---

[23] Stevenson, "Who Are the Harvard Self-Employed?" *Frontiers of Entrepreneurship Research: 1983*, ed. J. A. Hornaday et al. (Babson Park, Mass.: Babson College, 1983), pp. 233–54.

in their careers.[24] They report higher personal satisfaction with their lives and their careers than their managerial counterparts. Nearly three times as many say they plan never to retire, according to Stevenson, than do managers. Numerous other studies show that the satisfaction from independence and living and working where and how they want to is a source of great satisfaction.[25] And, financially, there is no doubt that successful entrepreneurs enjoy higher incomes and net worths than career managers in large companies. In addition, the successful harvest of a company usually means a capital gain of several million dollars or more, and, with it, an entire new array of very attractive options and opportunities to do whatever they choose to do with the rest of their lives.

ENTREPRENEUR'S CREED

So much time and space would not be spent on the entrepreneurial mind if it was just of academic interest. But, they are, entrepreneurs themselves believe, in large part responsible for success. When asked an open-ended question about what they believed are the most critical concepts, skills, and know-how for running a business—today and five years hence—their answers were very revealing. Most mentioned mental attitudes and philosophies based on entrepreneurial attributes, rather than specific skills or organizational concepts. These answers are gathered together in what might be called "an entrepreneur's creed."

- DO WHAT GIVES YOU ENERGY—HAVE FUN.
- FIGURE OUT HOW TO MAKE IT WORK.
- SAY "CAN DO," RATHER THAN "CANNOT" OR "MAYBE."
- *ILLEGITIMI NON CARBORUNDUM:* TENACITY AND CREATIVITY WILL TRIUMPH.
- ANYTHING IS POSSIBLE IF YOU BELIEVE YOU CAN DO IT.
- IF YOU DON'T KNOW IT CAN'T BE DONE, THEN YOU'LL GO AHEAD AND DO IT.
- THE CUP IS HALF-FULL, NOT HALF-EMPTY.
- BE DISSATISFIED WITH THE WAY THINGS ARE—AND LOOK FOR IMPROVEMENT.
- DO THINGS DIFFERENTLY.
- DON'T TAKE A RISK IF YOU DON'T HAVE TO—BUT TAKE A CALCULATED RISK IF IT'S THE RIGHT OPPORTUNITY FOR YOU.
- BUSINESSES FAIL; SUCCESSFUL ENTREPRENEURS LEARN—BUT KEEP THE TUITION LOW.
- IT IS EASIER TO BEG FOR FORGIVENESS THAN TO ASK FOR PERMISSION IN THE FIRST PLACE.
- MAKE OPPORTUNITY AND RESULTS YOUR OBSESSION—NOT MONEY.
- MONEY IS A TOOL AND A SCORECARD AVAILABLE TO THE RIGHT PEOPLE WITH THE RIGHT OPPORTUNITY AT THE RIGHT TIME.
- MAKING MONEY IS EVEN MORE FUN THAN SPENDING IT.
- MAKE HEROES OUT OF OTHERS—A TEAM BUILDS A BUSINESS; AN INDIVIDUAL MAKES A LIVING.
- TAKE PRIDE IN YOUR ACCOMPLISHMENTS—IT'S CONTAGIOUS!

[24] Boyd and Gumpert, "Loneliness of the Start-up Entrepreneur," p. 486.

[25] Robert C. Ronstadt, "The Decision Not to Become an Entrepreneur," in *Frontiers of Entrepreneurship Research: 1983*, ed. J. Hornaday et al. (Babson Park, Mass.: Babson College, 1983), pp. 192–212; and Robert C. Ronstadt, "Ex-Entrepreneurs and the Decision to Start an Entrepreneurial Career," *Frontiers of Entrepreneurship Research: 1983*, ed. J. Hornaday et al. (Babson Park, Mass.: Babson College, 1983), pp. 437–60.

- SWEAT THE DETAILS THAT ARE CRITICAL TO SUCCESS.
- INTEGRITY AND RELIABILITY EQUAL LONG-RUN OIL AND GLUE.
- MAKE THE PIE BIGGER—DON'T WASTE TIME TRYING TO CUT SMALLER SLICES.
- PLAY FOR THE LONG HAUL—IT IS RARELY POSSIBLE TO GET RICH QUICKLY.
- ONLY THE LEAD DOG GETS A CHANGE OF VIEW.

CASE—KEVIN MOONEY

Preparation Questions

1. What should Kevin Mooney do, and why?
2. What criteria and considerations should be weighed, and how?
3. What are the relevance, risks, and rewards of the two opportunities and their implications in terms of Kevin Mooney's "apprenticeship"?

KEVIN MOONEY

As the elevator descended silently to the lobby, Kevin Mooney* mused confidently about the decision he was facing: whether or not to resign from Price Waterhouse, the prestigious accounting firm, and accept a position with a new, still quite small, software company. He wondered how many of his colleagues at Price Waterhouse would opt to leave the security of a big business for a challenge like the one at Softcorp, Inc. He would be director of international marketing at a small software firm specializing in financial and accounting software packages for mainframe computers. The company's sales were just over $1 million, and it had no international customers. Nobody in the company even had a passport! Kevin thought this opportunity was filled with chances to exercise his entrepreneurial talents. He liked the founders of the company; its products had growth potential; and he would be an important part of the management team, so they said. Yet, the future at Price Waterhouse was very bright. He wondered what he should do.

His Background

Kevin gave his father much of the credit for forging his entrepreneurial spirit. Nothing Kevin did was ever quite good enough for his father. His constant criticism made Kevin fiercely independent and willing to take on challenging tasks just to prove to himself that he could do them. Consequently, he often recognized opportunities where others didn't.

During high school in Philadelphia, the ham radio club he had organized needed money to buy equipment. Kevin figured the club could raise the money doing what it knew best—working with electrical equipment. He founded his first venture: Rapid Radio Repair at Reasonable Rates, a company which repaired small appliances for neighbors, offering reliable service, pickup, and delivery. The neighbors liked the service, and the venture kept the club running.

After high school Kevin Mooney enrolled at Cornell University as an engineering major. In the early 70s, engineering wasn't a very popular profession, or even a lucrative one, but Kevin thought he needed the discipline engineering offered. His four years at Cornell were successful, although his studies didn't excite him. His real interest was his position as

* This case was prepared by Loretto Crane, Research Assistant, under the direction of Professor Jeffry A. Timmons, as a basis for class discussion rather than to illustrate either effective or ineffective handling of an administrative situation. Copyright © 1984 by Babson College.

chairman of the Student Finance Commission, which had the responsibility of allocating a $130,000 budget among all the student organizations and activities on campus.

Immediately after graduation Kevin married his high school sweetheart and enrolled in Stanford Business School. He recalled his decision to enroll:

Stanford advised students entering directly from undergraduate school to work for several years before beginning the MBA. I figured that most of the younger students probably followed Stanford's advice. So I decided to enroll right away, learn from *their* work experiences, and save myself some time!

During his two years at Stanford Kevin chose courses which he thought would help him run a small business of his own. Then, before job interviews began, Kevin and his wife decided that the Pacific Northwest was the place they wanted to live; he planned his company interviews accordingly. (See *Exhibit A.*)

Exhibit A
Kevin Mooney's Résumé

KEVIN MOONEY
Blackwelder 5–G
Stanford, California   94305
(555) 321–6877

JOB OBJECTIVE: To secure a consulting or staff position in corporate or financial planning.

EDUCATION:
1974–1976   STANFORD GRADUATE SCHOOL OF BUSINESS
                   Candidate for MBA degree in June 1976. Concentration in finance. Selected to represent the Stanford Graduate School of Business on the Journey for Perspective Foundation 1975 international study program abroad. Traveled to Eastern and Western Europe for seminars with business and political leaders. Member of Investment Club and Business Development Association.

1970–1974   CORNELL UNIVERSITY, Ithaca, New York
                   BS degree in Industrial Engineering and Operations Research in June 1974. Dean's list. Chairman of Cornell Student Finance Commission. Responsibilities included financial planning for more than 100 organizations, allocation of $130,000 of student fees, hiring and directing office staff, and administration of accounts. President of Quill & Dagger Society (senior honorary).

BUSINESS
EXPERIENCE:
Summer 1975   PEAT, MARWICK, MITCHELL & CO., San Francisco, California
                   Management Consultant. Performed conceptual design and implementation of a centralized purchase order system. Developed complete cost accounting system and contributed in formulating approach and preparing written proposal for a consulting engagement.

Summer 1974   CORNELL UNIVERSITY, Ithaca, New York
                   Summer Conference Coordinator. Administrative responsibility for summer conference programs. Duties included computer information system development and implementation, personnel administration, and coordination of university departments and facilities.

Summers   DECISION DATA COMPUTER CORPORATION, Horsham, Pennsylvania
1972, 1973   Manufacturing Engineer. Responsibilities included plant layout, tool design, and writing manufacturing instructions.

Additional   Married. Private pilot, currently pursuing additional ratings. Other interests include skiing,
Information   photography, swimming, and bicycling.

References   Personal references are on file with the Placement Office and will be forwarded upon request.

Exhibit B
Softcorp, Inc., Performance, 1974–1976 ($000)

	1974	1975	1976
Annual revenue	$357	$734	$1,217
Installations (cumulative)	383	449	530
Total employees	11	23	29

Price Waterhouse was interviewing students interested in working in its newly created small business division in Seattle. Although Kevin never planned to be an accountant, the location appealed to him and he thought the job would give him the opportunity to get to know the region's business community. He took the job, and within three months he was generating all his own work, often attending business breakfasts to drum up prospective clients. During the first year he brought five new clients to the firm.

Softcorp, Inc.

One of his many clients was Softcorp, Inc. Founded in 1969 by two men who had worked together at Hewlett-Packard, the company was just beginning to build a reasonable customer base. In the beginning the two founders, Joe Hegarty and Bob Wilson, designed the company's accounting applications packages themselves. Accounts Payable and Fixed Asset Accounting were the company's flagship products and contributed about 90 percent of Softcorp's revenue. Entirely internally funded except for a small line of credit at the bank, Softcorp dedicated its efforts to product development, marketing, and customer support and training. By 1976, it had 29 employees and sales of $1.2 million. (See *Exhibit B.*)

Hegarty and Wilson first came to Price Waterhouse for help in enhancing their fixed-asset system to incorporate the latest IRS depreciation rules. After three years and no solution, Softcorp's executives were understandably frustrated. Kevin Mooney took over their account and resolved the outstanding problems within three months. Mooney's manner and competence impressed the two men, and their relationship thrived. Then, in late 1977, Hegarty and Wilson approached Kevin about the job as director of international marketing.

The Job Negotiations

The offer intrigued Mooney. He saw the opportunities inherent in this small company. He knew little about the general markets for software packages and even less about the international markets. Softcorp was small and undercapitalized, and Kevin wondered what resources would be available to him to launch an international marketing effort.

Kevin worked well with the two founders. He and his wife had been guests at Hegarty's home. In December 1977, Kevin Mooney met with Hegarty and Wilson to discuss the details of the job.

I remember asking them if they knew of any international customers out there who wanted their products. Hegarty just shrugged his shoulders and said, "If there are, we know you'll find them."

I reminded them that I didn't have any operating experience, but that didn't seem to bother them. They seemed very impressed with my competence and my education. Frankly, I don't think I would have hired me!

They offered me a nice salary (a 20 percent increase over what I was making at PW) plus a bonus which would be tied to performance. I raised the question of equity participation. Both men were reluctant to give me any equity up front. They cited examples of two employees who had been given stock, but only after each had demonstrated his commitment and loyalty to the company. They told me that once I had done the same, equity would be a possibility.

The elevator stopped at the lobby. Kevin had just had a last meeting with his boss, Bob Baker. His mentor at Price Waterhouse was disappointed that Kevin would throw away his promising future at Price Waterhouse.

Baker reminded Kevin that promotions would be announced in a few months, and he thought Kevin had a very good shot at being promoted to manager. Baker asked him several questions he couldn't answer: What resources would Softcorp make available to build the international division? How were they planning to measure his performance? What would constitute success or failure?

When the meeting ended, Baker shook Kevin Mooney's hand and said, "Do you realize if you go to Softcorp, you are probably going to fail? Are you prepared for that?" Mooney left the building with Baker's questions running through his mind. Softcorp's offer letter and nondisclosure agreement were in his briefcase, ready for his signature. He had two weeks to make his decision.

EXERCISE (OPTIONAL)

If desired, the Personal Entrepreneurial Strategy Exercises in Chapter 21, Part VI, may be done at this point. Before proceeding with the exercises, however, be sure to read the material on planning and obtaining feedback in Chapter 11.

The Entrepreneurial Manager   6

It's rare to find a leader who can carry a growing company through all its phases. When you get into the $1- to $2-billion range, then you may find leaders with entrepreneurial tendencies; but, in addition, they have real management and people skills.

Peter J. Sprague,
Chairman of the Board,
National Semiconductor Corporation

RESULTS EXPECTED

Upon completion of this chapter, you will have:

1. Studied different views about "entrepreneurial managers" and discovered that an individual can be both an entrepreneur and a manager.
2. Identified the stages of growth entrepreneurial ventures go through, the "domain" occupied, the venture modes characteristic of the entrepreneurial domain, and the principal forces acting in the domain.
3. Identified specific skills entrepreneurs need to know in order to manage start-up, survival, and growth.
4. Analyzed the case of PMI, Inc.
5. Evaluated your own skills and developed an action plan.

THE ENTREPRENEURIAL DOMAIN

Converging on the Entrepreneurial Manager

There are convergent pressures on being an entrepreneur and being a manager as a venture accelerates and grows beyond founder-driven and founder-dominated survival. Key to achieving longer-term sustained growth, and an eventual harvest, is the ability of an entrepreneur to have or to develop competencies as an entrepreneurial manager.

In the past, those studying entrepreneuriship and others active in starting new ventures, such as venture capitalists, have generally felt that the kind of person with the entrepreneurial spirit required to propel a new venture through start-up to a multimillion-dollar annual sales level is different from the kind of person who has the capacity to manage the new firm as it grows from $5 million to $20 million or $30 million in sales. Further, it has long been thought that the entrepreneur who clings to the lead role too long during the maturation process will subsequently limit company growth, if not seriously retard it.

In short, there is a belief that a good entrepreneur is usually not a good manager, since he or she lacks the management skill and experience necessary. Likewise, it is assumed that a manager is not an entrepreneur, since he or she lacks some intense personal qualities and the orientation required to launch a business from ground zero.

Increasingly, however, evidence suggests that new ventures that flourish beyond start-up and grow to become substantial, successful enterprises can be headed by entrepreneurs who are also effective managers. For instance, a 1983 survey by *INC.* magazine of the heads of the top 100 new ventures showed that the majority of these companies had founders who were still chief executive officers after several years and after their companies had attained sales of at least $10 million (and some as much as $50 million or more).

These and other data seem to defy the notion that entrepreneurs can start but cannot manage growing companies. While the truth is probably somewhere in between, one thing is apparent: Growing a higher potential venture requires management skills.

Clearly, a complex set of factors goes into making someone a successful entrepreneurial manager. Launching a new venture and then managing rapid growth involves managerial roles and tasks not found in most mature or stable environments. Further, one of the greatest strengths of successful entrepreneurs is that they know what they do and do not know. They have disciplined intellectual honesty, which prevents their optimism from becoming myopic delusion and their dreams from becoming blind ambition. No individual has all the skills discussed below, and the presence or absence of any single skill does not guarantee success or failure. That an entrepreneur knows whether he or she does not have a certain skill and where to get it is clearly as valuable as knowing whether he or she already has it.

Principal Forces and Venture Modes

Companies, whether they are new, growing, or mature, occupy a place in either an administrative or entrepreneurial "domain," an area which is influenced by certain principal forces and which is characterized by ways of acting, called "venture modes." *Exhibits 6.1* and *6.2* illustrate graphically the entrepreneurial and administrative domains and the dynamic of the principal forces acting in the domains and the dominant venture modes which result.[1]

In the exhibits, the four cells are defined by the stage of the venture (upper axis), the extent of change and uncertainty accompanying it (right axis), and the degree to which a venture is administrative (bottom axis) or entrepreneurial (left axis). Clearly, the entrepreneurial domain is the two upper cells in both exhibits, and the domains are functions both of the change and uncertainty facing a venture and the stage of growth of the venture.

Each venture mode (i.e., ways of acting) for firms in each cell is driven by certain principal forces. These forces are shown in *Exhibit 6.1.*

Shown in *Exhibit 6.2* are dominant venture modes characteristic of firms in each cell. Organizations at different stages are characterized by differing degrees of change and uncertainty and are, therefore, more or less entrepreneurial or more or less administrative. Thus, for example, a new venture in the seed/start-up stage, which is characterized by high change and uncertainty is most entrepreneurial. These firms will be new, innovative, or backbone ventures; will be led by a team; will be driven by their founders' goals, values, commitment, and perceptions of the opportunities; and will minimize the use of resources. At the other extreme is a mature firm, one which is in the maturity stage and characterized by low change and uncertainty, one which is stable or contracting, one which is led by an administrator or custodian, one which is driven by resource ownership and administrative efficiency, and one which is reactive. Other firms fall in between.

---

[1] These exhibits are built on work by Timmons and Stevenson: See Howard H. Stevenson, "A New Paradigm for Entrepreneurial Management," *Entrepreneurship: What It Is and How to Teach It* (Boston: Harvard Business School, 1985), pp. 30–61; and Jeffry A. Timmons and Howard H. Stevenson, "Entrepreneurship Education in the 80s: What Entrepreneurs Say," *Entrepreneurship: What It Is and How to Teach It* (Boston: Harvard Business School, 1985), pp. 115–34.

Exhibit 6.1
Dominant Venture Modes

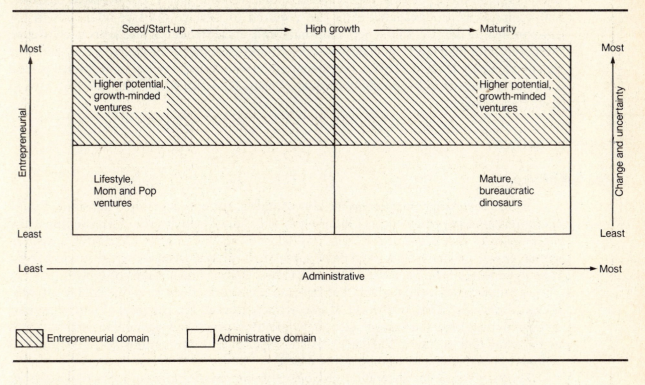

Exhibit 6.2
Principal Driving Forces

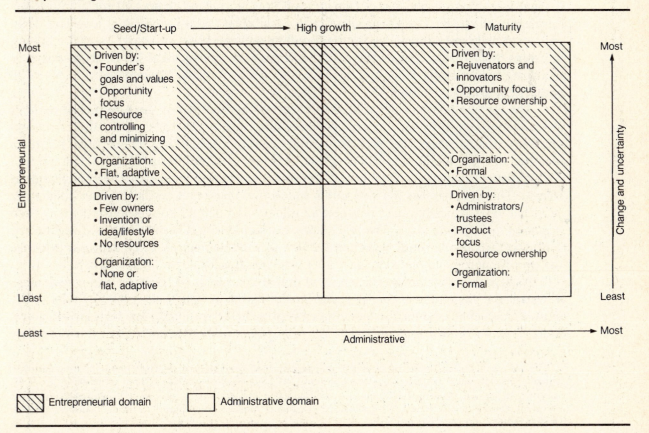

The managerial skills required of the firms in each cell are more evident upon examination of these principal forces and dominant venture modes. For example, creativity and comprehensive managerial skills are required to manage firms in both cells in the entrepreneurial domain. In the upper left-hand cell, entrepreneurial managers need to cope effectively with high levels of change and uncertainty, whether their management skills can be affectionately labeled MBWA (management by wandering around, of Hewlett-Packard fame) or management by muddling through. Certainly, as the firm enters the high growth stage, this changes.

STAGES OF GROWTH

A Theoretical View

As has been said before and as the above implies, entrepreneurship is not static. *Exhibit 6.3* represents a *theoretical* view of the process of gestation and growth of new ventures and the transitions that occur at different "boundaries" in this process.[2] Ventures are sown, sprout, grown, and harvested. Even those successful ventures which are not grown to harvest (i.e., those which have been defined as "attractive") go through stages of growth.

It cannot be stressed enough that this smooth, S-shaped curve in the exhibit is rarely, if ever, replicated in the real world. If one actually tracked the progress of most emerging companies over time, the "curve" actually would be a ragged and jagged line with many ups and downs; that is, these companies would experience some periods of rapid progress followed by setbacks and accompanying crises.

For the purposes of illustration, *Exhibit 6.3* shows venture stages in terms of time, sales, and number of employees. It is at the boundaries between stages that new ventures seem to experience transitions. Several researchers have noted that the new venture invariably goes through transition and will face certain issues.[3] Thus, the exhibit shows the crucial transitions during growth and the key management tasks of the chief executive officer or founders. Most important and most challenging for the founding entrepreneur, or a chief executive officer, is coping with crucial transitions and the change in management tasks, from doing to managing to managing managers, as a firm grows to roughly 20 employees, to 50 to 75 employees, and then to over 75.

The *start-up stage,* a stage that usually covers the first two or three years but perhaps as many as seven, is by far the most perilous stage and is characterized by the direct and exhaustive drive, energy, and entrepreneurial talent of a lead entrepreneur and a key team member or two. Here, the critical mass of people, market and financial results, and competitive resiliency are established, and investor, banker, and customer confidence is earned. The level of sales reached varies widely and may reach several million dollars per year, but sales typically range between $2 million and $20 million. A new company then begins its high-growth stage. The exact point at which this occurs can rarely be identified by a date on the calendar until well after the fact. It is in this stage that new ventures evidence the over 60 percent failure rate; that is, it is in this stage that the lemons ripen.

As with the other stages, the length of time it takes to go through the *high-growth stage,* as well as the magnitude of change occurring during the period, varies greatly. Probably the most difficult challenge for the founding entrepreneur occurs during the high-growth stage, when he or she finds it is necessary to let go of power and control (through veto) over key

---

[2] For another useful view of the stages of development of a firm and required management capabilities, see Carroll V. Kroeger, "Management Development and the Small Firm," *California Management Review* 17, no. 1 (Fall 1974), pp. 41–47.

[3] L. A. Griener, "Evolution and Revolution as Organizations Grow," *Trials and Rewards of the Entrepreneur* (Boston: Harvard Business Review, 1977), pp. 47–56; and H. N. Woodward, "Management Strategies for Small Companies" (Boston: Harvard Business Review, 1981), pp. 57–66.

Exhibit 6.3
Stages of Venture Growth, Crucial Transitions, and Core Management Mode

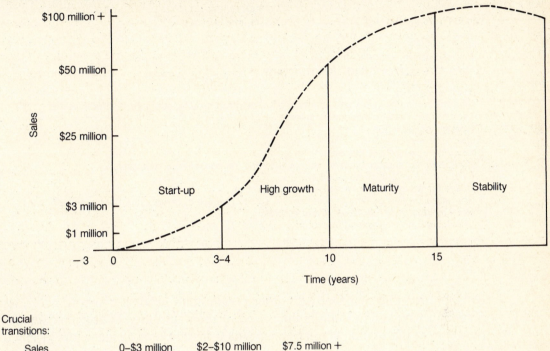

Crucial transitions:			
Sales	0–$3 million	$2–$10 million	$7.5 million +
Employees	0 to 20–25	25–75	75–100 +
Core management mode	Doing	Managing	Managing managers

decisions that he or she has always had, and when key responsibilities need to be delegated without abdicating ultimate leadership and responsibility for results. But the challenges do not end there. For example, in 1981, sales of Litton's microwave oven division had reached $13 million, and it had 275 employees. The long-range plan called for building sales volume to $100 million in five to seven years (i.e., growing at 40 percent per year, compounded). The head of the division said, "Having studied the market for the previous two years I was convinced that the only limit on our growth was our organization's inability to grow as rapidly as the market opportunities."[4]

From the high-growth stage, a company then moves to what is called the *maturity stage*. In this stage, the key issue for the company is no longer survival; rather, it is one of steady, profitable growth. The *stability stage* usually follows.

Managing for Rapid Growth

Managing for rapid growth involves a management orientation not found in mature and stable environments. (This topic will be addressed again in Chapter 18.)

For one thing, the tenet that one's responsibility must equal one's authority is often very counterproductive in a rapid-growth venture. Instead, results usually require close

---

[4] William W. George, "Task Teams for Rapid Growth," *Harvard Business Review*, March–April 1977.

Exhibit 6.4
Entrepreneurial Transitions

DOING ─────────────────→ MANAGING ──────────────────→ MANAGING MANAGERS
(Up to 20–25 employees)   (25–75 employees)   (over 75 employees)

Notable Characteristics of Doing Mode:
    Founder-driven creativity.
    Constant change, ambiguity, and uncertainty.
    Time compression.
    Nonlinear events.
    Informal communications and counterintuitive decision making, structure, and procedures.
    Lack of formal controls and mechanisms.
    Relative inexperience.
Probable Crises:
    Erosion of creativity of founders.
    Confusion and resentment over ambiguous roles, responsibilities, and goals.
    Failure to be able to clone founders.
    Desire for delegation versus autonomy and control.
    Specialization and eroding of collaboration versus practice of power, information, and influence.
    Need for operating mechanisms and controls.
    Conflict and divorce among founders.

---

collaboration of a manager with other people than his or her subordinates, and managers invariably have responsibilities far exceeding their authority. Politics and personal power can be a way of life in many larger and stagnant institutions, as managers jockey for influence and a piece of a shrinking pie in a zero-sum game; but, in rapid-growth firms, power and control are delegated. Everyone is committed to making the pie larger, and power and influence are derived from achieving not only one's own goals but also from contributing to the achievements of others as well. Influence also is derived from keeping the overall goals in mind, from resolving differences, and from developing a reputation as a person who not only gets results but can manage others and grow managerial talent as well.

Exhibit 6.4 characterizes probable crises that growing ventures will face, including erosion of creativity by founders and team; confusion or resentment, or both, over ambiguous roles, responsibilities, and goals; failure to be able to clone founders; specialization and eroding of collaboration; desire for autonomy and control; need for operating mechanisms and controls; and conflict and divorce among founders and members of team. It further delineates issues that confront entrepreneurial managers:

■ *Compounding of Time and Change.* In the high-growth stage, change, ambiguity, and uncertainty seem to be the only things that remain constant. Change, which is constant, creates higher levels of uncertainty, ambiguity, and risk, which, in turn, compound to shrink time, an already precious commodity. One result of change is a series of shock waves rolling through a new and growing venture by way of new customers, new technologies, new competitors, new markets, and new people. In industries characterized by galloping technological change, with relatively miniscule lead and lag times in bringing new products to market and in weathering the storms of rapid obsolescence, the effects of change and time are extreme. For example, the president of a rapidly growing small computer company said, "In our business it takes 6 to 12 months to develop a new computer, ready to bring to the market, and product technology obsolescence is running about 9 to 12 months." This time compresson has been seen in such industries as electronics and aerospace in the 1960s; small computers, integrated circuits, and silicon chips in the 1970s; and telecommunications and microcomputers in the 1980s.

■ *Nonlinear and Nonparametric Events.* Entrepreneurial management is characterized by nonlinear and nonparametric events. Just as the television did not come about by a succession of improvements in the radio and the jet plane did not emerge from engineers and scientists attempting to develop a better and better piston engine plane, so, too, within firms, events do not follow straight lines, progress arithmetically, or even appear related. Rather, they occur in bunches and in step-wise leaps. For example, a firm may double its sales forces in 15 months, rather than over eight years, or another may triple its manufacturing capacity and adopt a new materials resource planning system immediately, rather than utilizing existing capacity by increasing overtime, then adding a third shift nine months later, and finally adding a new plant three years hence.

- *Relative Inexperience.* In addition, the management team may be relatively inexperienced. The explosive birth and growth of these firms are usually unique events that cannot be replicated, and most of the pieces in the puzzle — the technology, applications, customers, the people, the firm itself — are usually new. Take Prime Computer as an example. Sales of this manufacturer of minicomputers grew rapidly in five years from $100 million per year to nearly $1.2 billion per year. The average age of all employees in the company was reported at less than 29 years, and the firm was barely 10 years old.

- *Counterintuitive, Unconventional Decision Making.* Yet another characteristic of rapidly growing ventures in the entrepreneurial domain is counterintuitive, unconventional patterns of decision making. For example, a computer firm needed to decide what approach to take in developing and introducing three new products in an uncertain, risky marketplace. Each proposed new product appeared to be aimed at the same end-user market, and the person heading each project was similarly enthusiastic, confident, and determined about succeeding. A traditional approach to such a problem would have been to determine the size and growth rates of each market segment; evaluate the probabilistic estimates of future revenues costs and capital requirements for their accuracy; compare the discounted, present-value cash flow streams that will emerge from each project; and select the project with the highest yield versus the required internal rate of return. Sometimes overlooked in such an analysis are the facts that most rapid growth companies have many excellent alternatives and, more commonly, the newness of technology, the immaturity of the marketplace, and the rapid discovery of further applications make it virtually impossible to know which of any product proposals is best. The computer firm decided to support all three new products at once, and a significant new business was built around each one. New market niches were discovered simultaneously, and the unconventional approach paid off.

- *Fluid Structures and Procedures.* Most rapid-growth ventures also defy conventional organizational patterns and structures. It is not uncommon to find a firm that has grown $25 million, $50 million, or even $150 million per year in sales and that still has no formal organizational chart. If an organizational chart does exist, it usually has three distinguishing features: First, it is inevitably out of date. Second, it changes frequently. For example, one firm had eight major reorganizations in its first five years as it grew to $5 million. And, third, the organizational structure is usually flat (i.e., it has few management layers), and there is easy accessibility to the top decision makers. But the informality and fluidity of organization structures and procedures do not mean casualness or sloppiness when it comes to goals, standards, or clarity of direction and purpose. Rather, it translates into responsiveness and readiness to absorb and assimilate rapid changes while maintaining financial and operational cohesion.

- *Entrepreneurial Culture.* There exists in growing new ventures a common value system, which is difficult to articulate, which is even more elusive to measure, and which is evident in behavior and attitudes. There is a belief in and commitment to growth, achievement, improvement, and success and a sense among members of the team that they are "in this thing together." Goals and the market determine priorities, rather than whose territory or whose prerogatives are being challenged. Managers appear unconcerned about status, power, and personal control. They are more concerned about making sure that tasks, goals, and roles are clear than whether the organizational chart is current or whether their office and rug reflect their current status. Likewise, they are more concerned about the evidence, competence, knowledge, and logic of arguments affecting a decision than the status given by a title or the formal position of the individual doing the arguing. Contrast this with a multibillion-dollar, but stagnant, firm in England. There are reportedly no less than 29 different makes and models of automobiles used in the firm to signify one's position.

This entrepreneurial climate, or culture, exists in larger firms also. Such a climate attracts and encourages the entrepreneurial achievers, and it helps perpetuate the intensity and pace so characteristic of high-growth firms. *Exhibit 6.5* shows how five companies studied by Rosabeth Moss Kanter, author of *The Change Masters,* range from most to least entrepreneurial. Kanter distinguished these firms in terms of the percentage of effective managers with entrepreneurial achievements, current economic trends, current "change" issues, organizational structure, information flow, communication emphasis, culture, and current emotional rewards. Another example of a large firm fostering an entrepreneurial culture is that of Pepsi Cola Corporation, North America. Roger Enrico, chief executive officer, summarized the critical factors for entrepreneurial managers, in addition to maintaining commitment and integrity, which Pepsi has encouraged:[5]

— Understanding the business and staying in that business.
— Setting high performance standards by developing short-run objectives which do not sacrifice long-run results.
— Providing responsive, personal leadership (i.e., not managing through memos and computer printouts but eyeball to eyeball) and energizing ideas.
— Encouraging individual initiative.
— Helping others to succeed.
— Developing individual networks for success.

The following section is based heavily on the work of Howard H. Stevenson and Jeffry A. Timmons.[6]

What Entrepreneurial Managers Need to Know

Much of business education traditionally has emphasized and prepared students for life in the administrative domain. There is nothing wrong with that; but education preparing students to start and manage vibrant, growing new ventures cannot afford to emphasize administrative efficiency, maintenance tasks, resource ownership, and institutional formalization. Rather, such a program needs to emphasize skills necessary for life in the entrepreneurial domain. For example, effective entrepreneurial managers need to be especially skillful at managing conflict, resolving differences, balancing multiple viewpoints and demands, and building teamwork and consensus. These skills are particularly difficult when working with others outside one's immediate formal chain of command.

The study of 60 practicing entrepreneurs described in the last chapter found that, in addition to the attitudes and behaviors noted there, practicing entrepreneurs felt an intimate knowledge of customers and market(s) was vitally important and needed to be emphasized

---

[5] Based on a talk given by Roger Enrico (Babson, class of 1965) on March 22, 1984, as Executive in Residence at Babson College.

[6] See Timmons and Stevenson, "Entrepreneurship Education in the 80s: What Entrepreneurs Say," pp. 115–34. Additionally, the author has benefited from pioneering research in growing firms done by colleagues at the Forum Corporation in Boston and from his work with founders of firms seeking venture capital to propel rapid growth.

Exhibit 6.5
Characteristics of Five Companies Ranging from Most to Least Entrepreneurial

	Chipco	Radco	Medco	Finco	Utico
Percentage of effective managers with entrepreneurial accomplishments	71%	69%	67%	47%	33%
Current economic trend	Steadily up	Trend up but currently down	Up		
Current "change" issues	Change "normal"; constant change in product generation; proliferating staff and units.	Change "normal" in products, technologies; recent changeover to second management generation with new focus.	Reorganized about 3–4 years ago to install matrix; "normal" product, technology changes.	Change a "shock"; new top-management group from outside reorganizing and trying to add competitive market posture.	Change a "shock"; undergoing reorganization to install matrix and add competitive market posture while reducing staff.
Organization structure	Matrix	Matrix in some areas; product lines act as quasi divisions.	Matrix in some areas.	Divisional; unitary hierarchy within division; some central services.	Functional organization; currently overlaying a matrix of regions and markets.
Information flow	Decentralized	Mixed	Mixed	Centralized	Centralized
Communication emphasis	Free Horizontal	Free Horizontal	Moderately free Horizontal	Constricted Vertical	Constricted Vertical
Culture	Clear, consistent, favors individual initiative.	Clear, though in transition from emphasis on invention to emphasis on routinization and systems.	Clear, pride in company, belief that talent will be rewarded.	Idiosyncratic; depends on boss and area.	Clear, but top management would like to change it; favors security maintenance, protection.
Current "emotional"	Pride in company, team feeling.	Uncertainty about changes.	Pride in company, team feeling.	Low trust, high uncertainty.	High certainty, confusion.
Rewards	Abundant; include visibility, chance to do more challenging work in the future and to get bigger budget for projects.	Abundant; include visibility, chance to do more challenging work in future and to get budgets for projects.	Moderately abundant, conventional.	Scarce; primarily monetary.	Scarce; promotion, salary freeze; recognition by peers grudging.

Source: Rosabeth Moss Kanter, "Middle Managers as Innovators," *Harvard Business Review,* July–August 1982.

above traditional management fare.[7] Leadership skills were considered important, and many respondents recognized and endorsed the importance of people management issues. One described a most challenging task of an entrepreneurial manager in the first five years as "a leadership role in attracting high-quality people; imparting your vision to them; and holding and motivating them." Many focused on the importance of building an organization and teamwork. The head of a manufacturing firm with $10 million in sales said, "Understanding

[7] Ibid.

people and how to pull them together toward a basic goal will be my main challenge in five years." The head of a clothing manufacturing business with 225 employees and $6 million in sales shared a view of many that one of the most critical areas where one has leverage and long-term impact is in managing employees. He stated, "Treating people honestly and letting them know when they do well goes a long way." Financial skills, and most especially the ability to understand cash flow and when a business will run out of money, were also considered important.

In talking of larger firms, Kanter identifies power and persuasion skills, skill in managing problems accompanying team and employee participation, and skill in understanding how change is designed and constructed in an organization as necessary. Kanter notes:

In short, individuals do not have to be doing "big things" in order to have their cumulative accomplishments eventually result in big performance for the company. . . . They are only rarely the inventors of the "breakthrough" system. They are only rarely doing something that is totally unique or that no one, in any organization, ever thought of before. Instead, they are often applying ideas that have proved themselves elsewhere, or they are rearranging parts to create a better result, or they are noting a potential problem before it turns into a catastrophe and mobilizing the actions to anticipate and solve it.[8]

A recent study of mid-sized-growth companies having sales between $25 million and $1 billion and a sales or profit growth of more than 15 percent annually over five years confirms the importance of many of these same fundamentals of entrepreneurial management.[9] For one thing, these companies practiced opportunity-driven management. According to the study, they achieved their first success with a unique product or distinctive way of doing business and often become leaders in market niches by delivering superior value to customers, rather than through low prices. They are highly committed to serving customers and pay very close attention to them. For another thing, these firms put great emphasis on financial control and managing every element of the business.

In a book that follows up on the implementation issues of how one gets middle managers to pursue and practice entrepreneurial excellence (first made famous in *In Search of Excellence* by Tom Peters and Bob Waterman), two authors note that some of the important fundamentals practiced by team-builder entrepreneurs, who are more intent on getting results than just getting their own way, also are emulated by effective middle managers.[10] The authors distinguish between the "heroic manager," whose need to be in control in many instances actually may stifle cooperation, and the "post-heroic manager," a developer who actually brings about excellence in organizations by developing entrepreneurial middle management. They find the lagging growth of a cadre of effective middle managers often becomes a bottleneck for the business.

MANAGEMENT COMPETENCIES

Entrepreneurs who build substantial companies that grow to over $10 million in sales and over 75 to 100 employees are both good entrepreneurs and good managers. Typically, they will have developed a solid base and a wide breadth of management skills and know-how over a number of years working in different areas (e.g., sales, marketing, manufacturing, and finance). It would be unusual for any single entrepreneur to be outstanding in all areas. More

---

[8] Rosabeth Moss Kanter, *The Change Masters* (New York: Simon & Schuster, 1983), pp. 354–55.

[9] The study was done by McKinsey & Company. See "How Growth Companies Succeed," reported in *Small Business Report,* July 1984, p. 9.

[10] David L. Bradford and Allan R. Cohen, *Managing for Excellence* (New York: John Wiley & Sons, 1984), pp. 3–4.

likely, a single entrepreneur will have strengths in one area, such as strong people management, conceptual and creative problem-solving skills, and marketing know-how, as well as some significant weaknesses. While it is risky to generalize, often entrepreneurs whose background is technical are weak in marketing, finance, and general management. Entrepreneurs who do not have a technical background are, as you might expect, often weakest in the technical or engineering aspects, manufacturing, and finance.

What has been stressed throughout this book is the concept of "fit." Having a management team whose skills are complementary, not the possession by an individual of a single, absolute set of skills or a profile, is important. Instead, the art and craft of entrepreneuring involves recognizing the skills and know-how needed to succeed in a venture, knowing what each team member does or does not know, and then compensating for shortcomings, either by getting key people on board to fill voids or by an individual accumulating the additional "chunks" before he or she takes the plunge.

Skills in Building a Climate and Leading

Managers of firms that are entrepreneurial need to recognize and cope with innovation, taking risk, and responding quickly, as well as with absorbing major setbacks. The most effective managers seem to thrive on the hectic, and at times chaotic, pace and find it challenging and stimulating, rather than frustrating or overwhelming. They use a consensus approach to build a motivated and committed team, they balance conflicting demands and priorities, and they manage conflicts especially adroitly.

These managers thus need interpersonal/team work skills that involve: (1) the ability to create, through management, a climate and spirit conducive to high performance, including pressing for performance while rewarding work well done and encouraging innovation, initiative, and calculated risk taking; (2) the ability to understand the relationships among tasks and between the leader and followers; and (3) the ability to lead in those situations where it is appropriate, including a willingness to manage actively, supervise and control activities of others through directions, suggestions, and the like.

These interpersonal skills can be called "entrepreneurial influence" skills, since they have a great deal to do with the way these managers exact influence over others:

■ *Leadership/Vision/Influence.* These managers are skillful in creating a clarity out of confusion, ambiguity, and uncertainty. These entrepreneurial managers are able to define adroitly and gain agreement on who has what responsibility and authority. Further, they do this in a way that builds motivation and commitment to cross-departmental and corporate goals, not just parochial interests. But this is not perceived by other managers as an effort to jealously carve out and guard personal turf and prerogatives. Rather, it is seen as a genuine effort to clarify roles, tasks, and responsibilities and to make sure there is accountability and appropriate approvals. This does not work unless the manager is seen as willing to relinquish his or her priorities and power in the interest of an overall goal. It also requires skill in making sure the appropriate people are included in setting cross-functional or cross-departmental goals and in making decisions. When things do not go as smoothly as was hoped, the most effective managers work them through to an agreement. Managers who are accustomed to a traditional line/staff, or functional, chains of command are often baffled and frustrated in their new role. While some may be quite effective in dealing with their own subordinates, it is an entirely new task to manage and work with peers, the subordinates of others, and even superiors outside one's chain of command.

- *Helping/Coaching and Conflict Management.* The most effective managers are more creative and skillful in handling conflicts, generating consensus decisions, and sharing their power and information. They are able to get people to open up, instead of clamming up; they get problems out on the table, instead of under the rug; and they do not become defensive when others disagree with their views. They seem to know that high-quality decisions require rapid flow of information in all directions and that knowledge, competence, logic, and evidence need to prevail over official status or formal rank in the organization. The way they manage and resolve conflicts is intriguing. For one thing, they are able to get potential adversaries to be creative and to collaborate by seeking a reconciliation of viewpoints, rather than emphasizing differences, and by blending ideas, rather than playing the role of hard-nose negotiator or devil's advocate to force their own solution. They are more willing to risk personal vulnerability in this process—often by giving up their own power and resources—than less-effective managers. The trade-offs are not easy: At the outset, such an approach involves more managers, takes more time, often appears to yield few immediate results, and seems like a more painful way to manage. Later on, however, the gains from the motivation, commitment, and teamwork anchored in consensus are striking. For one thing, there is swiftness and decisiveness in actions and follow through, since the negotiating, compromising, and accepting of priorities is history. For another, new disagreements that emerge generally do not bring progress to a halt, since there is both high clarity and broad acceptance of the overall goals and underlying priorities. Without this consensus, each new problem or disagreement often necessitates a time-consuming and painful confrontation and renegotiation simply because it was not done initially. Apparently, the Japanese understand this quite well.

- *Teamwork and People Management.* Another form of entrepreneurial influence has to do with encouraging creativity, innovativeness, and the taking of calculated risks. Simply stated, entrepreneurial managers build confidence by encouraging innovation and calculated risk taking, rather than by punishing or criticizing whatever is less than perfect. For another, they breed independent, entrepreneurial thinking by expecting and encouraging others to find and correct their own errors and to solve their own problems. This does not mean they follow a throw-them-to-the-wolves approach. Rather, they are perceived by their peers and other managers as accessible and willing to help when needed, and they provide the necessary resources to enable others to do the job. When it is appropriate, they go to bat for their peers and subordinates, even when they know they cannot always win. An ability to make "heroes" out of other team members and contributors and to make sure others are in the limelight, rather than accept these things oneself, is another critical skill.

  The capacity to generate the oil and glue that binds an organization or relationship together—trust—is critical. The most effective managers are perceived as trustworthy; they behave in ways that create trust. How do they do this? For one thing, they are straightforward: They do what they say they are going to do. They are not the corporate rumor carriers. They are open and spontaneous, rather than guarded and cautious with each word. And they are perceived as being honest and direct. Also, it is not too difficult to envision the kind of track record and reputation these entrepreneurial managers build for themselves. They have a reputation of getting results, because they understand that the task of managing in a rapid-growth company usually goes well beyond one's immediate chain of command. They become known as the creative problem solvers who have a knack for blending and balancing multiple views and demands. Their calculated risk taking works out more often than it fails. And they have a reputation for developing human capital (i.e., they groom and grow other effective growth managers by their example and their mentoring).

Other Management Competencies

Entrepreneurial managers need a sound foundation in what are considered traditional management skills. It is interesting to note that, in the study of practicing entrepreneurs mentioned earlier, there was a lack of importance assigned to virtually all of the prevailing and highly touted "new management techniques"; that is, no one mentioned capital asset-pricing models, beta coefficients, linear programming, and so forth.[11]

The list below is divided into two cross-functional areas—administration and law and taxation—and four key functional areas—marketing, finance, production and operations, and microcomputers. Technical skills unique to each venture are also necessary.

- *Administration*
  - *Problem Solving.* Ability to anticipate potential problems; ability to gather facts about problems, analyze them for *real* causes, and plan effective action to solve them; and ability to be very thorough in dealing with details of particular problems and to follow through.
  - *Communications.* Ability to communicate effectively and clearly—orally and in writing—to media, public, customers, peers, and subordinates.
  - *Planning.* Ability to set realistic and attainable goals, identify obstacles to achieving the goals, and develop detailed action plans to achieve those goals, and the ability to schedule personal time very systematically.
  - *Decision Making.* Ability to make decisions on the best analysis of incomplete data.
  - *Project Management.* Skills in organizing project teams, setting project goals, defining project tasks, and monitoring task completion in the face of problems and cost/quality constraints.
  - *Negotiating.* Ability to work effectively in negotiations, and the ability to balance quickly value given and value received.
  - *Managing Outside Professionals.* Ability to identify, manage, and guide appropriate legal, financial, banking, accounting, consulting, and other necessary outside advisors.
  - *Personnel Administration.* Ability to set up payroll, hiring, compensation, and training functions.
- *Law and Taxes*
  - *Corporate and Securities Law.* Familiarity with the uniform commercial code, including forms of organization and the rights and obligations of officers, shareholders, and directors; and familiarity with Security and Exchange Commission, state, and other regulations concerning the securities of your firm, both registered and unregistered, and the advantages and disadvantages of different instruments.
  - *Contract Law.* Familiarity with contract procedures and requirements of government and commercial contracts, licenses, leases, and other agreements, particularly employment agreements and agreements governing the vesting rights of shareholders and founders.
  - *Law Relating to Patent and Proprietary Rights.* Skills in preparation and revision of patent applications and the ability to recognize a strong patent, trademark, copyright, and privileged information claims, including familiarity with claim requirements, such as to intellectual property.

---

[11] Timmons and Stevenson, "Entrepreneurship Education in the 80s: What Entrepreneurs Say," pp. 115–34.

— *Tax Law.* Familiarity with state and federal reporting requirements, including specific requirements of a particular form of organization, of profit and other pension plans, and the like.
— *Real Estate Law.* Familiarity with leases, purchase offers, purchase and sale agreements, and so on, necessary for the rental or purchase and sale of property.
— *Bankruptcy Law.* Knowledge of bankruptcy law, options, and the forgivable and nonforgivable liabilities of founders, officers and directors.

■ *Marketing*
— *Market Research and Evaluation.* Ability to analyze and interpret market research study results, including knowing how to design and conduct studies and to find and interpret industry and competitor information, and a familiarity with questionnaire design and sampling techniques. One successful entrepreneur stated that what is vital "is knowing where the competitive threats are and where the opportunities are and an ability to see the customers' needs."
— *Marketing Planning.* Planning skills in planning overall sales, advertising, and promotion programs and in deciding on and setting up effective distributor or sales representative systems.
— *Product Pricing.* Ability to determine competitive pricing and margin structures and to position products in terms of price and ability to develop pricing policies that maximize profits.
— *Sales Management.* Ability to organize, supervise, and motivate a direct sales force, and the ability to analyze territory and account sales potential and to manage a sales force to obtain maximum share of market.
— *Direct Selling.* Skills in identifying, meeting, and developing new customers and in closing sales. Without orders for a product or service, a company does not really have a business.
— *Monitoring Customers and Delivery of Service.* Ability to perceive service needs of particular products and to determine service and spare-part requirements, handle customer complaints, and manage a service organization.
— *Distribution Management.* Ability to organize and manage the flow of product from manufacturing through distribution channels to ultimate customer, including familiarity with shipping costs, scheduling techniques, and so on.
— *Product Management.* Ability to integrate market information, perceived needs, research and development, and advertising into a rational product plan, and the ability to understand market penetration and breakeven.
— *New-product Planning.* Skills in introducing new products, including marketing testing, prototype testing, and development of price/sales/merchandising and distribution plans for new products.

■ *Operations/Production*
— *Manufacturing Management.* Knowledge of the production process, machines, manpower, and space required to produce a product and the skill in managing production to produce products within time, cost, and quality constraints.
— *Inventory Control.* Familiarity with techniques of controlling in-process and finished goods inventories of materials.
— *Cost Analysis and Control.* Ability to calculate labor and materials costs, develop standard cost systems, conduct variance analyses, calculate overtime labor needs, and manage/control costs.
— *Quality Control.* Ability to set up inspection systems and standards for effective control of quality of incoming, in-process, and finished materials.

- *Production Scheduling and Flow.* Ability to analyze work flow and to plan and manage production processes, the ability to manage work flow, and the ability to calculate schedules and flows for rising sales levels.
- *Purchasing.* Ability to identify appropriate sources of supply, to negotiate supplier contracts, and to manage the incoming flow of material into inventory, and familiarity with order quantities and discount advantages.
- *Job Evaluation.* Ability to analyze worker productivity and needs for additional help, and the ability to calculate cost-saving aspects of temporary versus permanent help.

Finance

- *Raising Capital.* Ability to decide how best to acquire funds for start-up and growth; ability to forecast funds needs and to prepare budgets; and familiarity with sources and vehicles of short- and long-term financing, formal and informal.
- *Managing Cash Flow.* Ability to project cash requirements, set up cash controls, and manage the firm's cash position, and the ability in identifying how much capital is needed and when and where you will run out of cash.
- *Credit and Collection Management.* Ability to develop credit policies and screening criteria, the ability to age receivables and payables, and an understanding of the use of collection agencies and when to start legal action.
- *Short-term Financing Alternatives.* Understanding of payables management and the use of interim financing, such as bank loans, factoring of receivables, pledging and selling notes and contracts, bills of lading, and bank acceptance; and familiarity with financial statements and budgeting/profit planning.
- *Public and Private Offerings.* Ability to develop a business plan and an offering memo that can be used to raise capital; a familiarity with the legal requirements of public and private stock offerings; and the ability to manage shareholder relations and to negotiate with financial sources.
- *Bookkeeping, Accounting, and Control.* Ability to determine appropriate bookkeeping and accounting systems as the company starts and grows, including various ledgers and accounts and, possibly, insurance needs.
- *Other Specific Skills.* Ability to read and prepare an income statement and balance sheet, and the ability to do cash flow analysis and planning, including breakeven analysis, contribution analysis, profit and loss analysis, and balance sheet management.

Microcomputers

- *Spreadsheet Analysis.* Ability to perform spreadsheet analysis using the microcomputer, including databases.
- *Other.* Knowledge of word processing, electronic mail, and so forth is extremely helpful.

Technical Skills

- These are unique to each venture.

As has been said before, not all entrepreneurs will find they are greatly skilled in the areas listed above; and, if they do not, they will most likely need to acquire these skills, either through apprenticeship, through partners, or through the use of advisors. However, it is useful to assume that, while there are many outstanding advisors, such as lawyers and accountants, who are of enormous benefit to entrepreneurs, these people are not always businesspeople and they often cannot make the best business judgments for those they are advising. For example, in the case of lawyers, their judgments, in many cases, are so contaminated by a desire to provide "perfect" or "fail-safe" protection that they are totally risk-averse.

CASE – PMI, INC.

Preparation Questions

1. Should Kevin Mooney sign the PMI agreement, and why or why not?
2. What are the rights, obligations, liabilities, and responsibilities of the parties to the agreement?
3. What do you see as Kevin's bargaining position? What should be his strategy for dealing with the increasing pressure?
4. What are the consequences of his *actions* for himself, for Softcorp, and for the top management teams of both Softcorp and PMI?
5. What other opportunities should he consider?

PRENTISS-MCGRAW, INC. (PMI)*

In March 1978, Kevin Mooney was hard at work in his new job at Softcorp, enjoying the task of setting up the international marketing division. (See *Exhibits A* and *B* for original offer letter and employment agreement.) He reported directly to Joe Hegarty, the president, who Kevin knew had enormous confidence in him. Within three months his responsibilities were expanded to include all of the company's domestic marketing, a function previously managed by Softcorp's vice president, Bob Wilson. Kevin took the new challenge and began developing relationships with advertising agencies and planning the direct mail program.

Problems

Within two months, Kevin Mooney's enthusiasm was brought up short with an invitation to lunch with Bob Wilson. During the lunch Wilson expressed shock at the changes Kevin had made in the U.S. marketing policies and anger at not having been consulted. Kevin listened attentively, stunned to see how hurt Wilson was. It had never occurred to him to check with Wilson.

Once he had learned what marketing areas were important to Wilson, he didn't tamper with them. Several months later, it was Kevin's turn to invite Wilson to lunch. The lunch was very pleasant; Wilson was surprised and pleased with how much better the U.S. marketing picture looked and complimented Kevin on his job.

Although Kevin Mooney had succeeded in smoothing the relationship between himself and the vice president, he did not spend much time working on building relationships with the other managers at his peer level. He enjoyed his job and liked watching his department succeed, but he didn't like the interdepartmental politics that some of the managers seemed to thrive on.

Personalities

Lack of leadership from both Hegarty and Wilson contributed significantly to the role that politics played. Hegarty, the president, was the creative thinker. Personable and charming, he was the idea generator and was comfortable dealing with the big picture, always avoiding the details. Bob Wilson's personality complemented Hegarty's. He was the detail

---

* This case was prepared by Loretto Crane, Research Assistant, under the direction of Professor Jeffry A. Timmons, as a basis for class discussion, rather than to illustrate either effective or ineffective handling of an administrative situation. Copyright © 1984 by Babson College.

January 27, 1978

Mr. Kevin Mooney
560 Hillside Avenue
Seattle, Washington   98115

Dear Kevin:

I enjoyed our meeting Tuesday evening, which was obviously due to the seemingly rapid passage of time. As a result of our conversations, I am writing to formalize an invitation to join Softcorp as its Director of International Marketing.

This position would require the development of a reasonably thorough understanding of all of our existing and planned products, as well as the complete marketing approach that is currently being used successfully in the United States.

Following that effort would be a research project to evaluate the various foreign markets in terms of their potential sales volume and concluding in the selection of those markets that could most readily and profitably be undertaken by Softcorp, Inc.

The focus of the position would then shift to one of structuring the type of organization that would be required to implement an effective non-U.S. marketing effort, and would eventually become one of administering the ongoing activities implied by the position's lofty title.

The position would carry an initial starting salary of $26,000 per year. Since the function is new to the company, we would want to review the initial results six months after initial date of employment. Thereafter, such reviews would be annual.

You also would be invited to participate in a medical reimbursement plan that would commence with your initial date of employment. This plan reimburses you for medical expenses not covered by insurance to a limit of $1,000 per year.

We would have no objection to your continued instructional efforts at local educational institutions. The obvious indication here is that such activities would not interfere with the functional requirements of the position.

To the extent that your efforts are successful, in that they generate sales, you would be provided with an overriding level of compensation based on the volume of those sales. That compensation is defined as follows:

Sales	Bonus Percentage
$0–100,000	1
$100,000–300,000	3
$300,000 up	2

This bonus is subject to change on a year-to-year basis as we see what our experience will be. It will be paid quarterly based upon what has been collected.

To preserve and enhance your personal domestic tranquility, the company is willing to absorb the expenses of your spouse should she elect to accompany you on two of your trips each year. It is assumed that the trips mentioned would aggregate approximately two weeks each year.

The position that we are defining is very critical to the future of Softcorp, Inc. We feel that it will take a strong effort over at least a two-year period to accomplish the objectives that we have defined. For this reason, we would ask that you contemplate your acceptance of this offer in the light of a minimum commitment of two years. This would avoid the many problems that we feel would occur if there were to be a break in the continuity of events that we have described.

Exhibit A *(concluded)*

The last point to be covered is that of equity participation in the company. Both Joe and I are open-minded with regard to stockholder expansion. The issue itself is open for discussion in any performance review that occurs after you have joined the company. Specifically, Kevin, when we recognize that a significant and continuing contribution is being made to the basic strength of the company itself, we would be of a frame of mind to structure an equity position for the individual responsible for that contribution.

We hope you will accept the position that we have offered, because we feel that the company can truly benefit from the talents and skills that you would bring to bear on the outlined function. We also feel that this position offers you an outstanding opportunity for personal and professional growth.

Please be in touch if you have any questions.

Sincerely,

Robert W. Wilson

Robert W. Wilson
President

---

man and very good at making Hegarty's ideas work. Wilson's leadership style was not to issue clear directives to his managers. Instead, he worked to get a consensus, preferring that his managers work out their differences among themselves. Kevin recalled:

Wilson's problem-solving style really was pretty ineffective. Split fights began to occur between the international and domestic divisions. Splits happen when two or more departments have to split a sales commission. I never had any problem splitting commission within my department, and I don't think the VP of domestic had any problem within his. But there was always trouble when we had to split it between us. I just got frustrated, sat down and wrote a memo to Wilson suggesting ideas for ways to alleviate the problem. I didn't think my solution was the only one, but I felt it was a start. Instead of getting back to me with his reaction, Wilson sent my memo on to the domestic VP. And nothing was ever resolved!

The International Department

Although Kevin Mooney was not inclined to interact with the other vice presidents, he did have the skills needed to build an international customer base. From the first day, he built the department brick by brick. By early 1979, he had signed the first two agent agreements (companies appointed to represent Softcorp in foreign countries) in England and Australia. Kevin selected companies, which he called "affiliates," already established in the computer service industry. By year-end the international division revenues accounted for almost 100 percent of Softcorp's profits.

By 1980, Scandinavia and Mexico were added to the list of international customers. Kevin Mooney recalled:

We were 120 percent over our plan for the year. I felt that I had demonstrated my commitment to the company and went to Hegarty to see about my getting some equity participation. I was surprised that he didn't remember our conversation about equity during the interview process.

Employment Agreement

This agreement dated 3-13-78 between Softcorp, Inc., a Washington Corporation, having its principal place of business at 381 East Street, Seattle, Washington (hereinafter called the "Company"), and Kevin Mooney, residing at 560 Hillside Avenue, Seattle, Washington 98115 (hereinafter called the "Employee").

In consideration of the mutual covenants herein contained, the parties agree as follows:

Section 1: The Company will employ the Employee and the Employee will serve the Company upon the terms and conditions provided herein, unless terminated as provided herein.

Section 2: During the term of employment hereunder the Employee shall devote his full time during business hours and use his best efforts in furtherance of the business of the Company.

Section 3: At the Company's request, the Employee agrees to assist the Company in every proper way to obtain for its or their own benefit patents for discoveries, inventions, or improvements thereof in any and all countries and all discoveries, inventions, or improvements are to remain the property of the Company whether patented or not.

Section 4: The Employee shall not divulge or communicate to any person or entity other than customers of the Company without the express written consent of the Company any trade secrets, trade knowledge, discoveries, inventions, innovations, computer programs, and other information obtained or conceived by the Company along all lines of work of said Company. During the term of employment hereunder and for a period of two years after the termination of this agreement by any means whatsoever, the Employee shall not within the territorial limits of the United States of America engage in business dealings competitive with the business of the Company with any persons, corporations, or associations and shall not engage as an Employee, Officer, Director, Partner, or Consultant in any business competitive with that of the Company. In the event that this section shall be determined by any court of competent jurisdiction to be unenforceable by reason of its extending for too great a period of time or over too large a geographic area or over too great a range of activities, it shall be interpreted to extend only over the maximum period of time, geographic area, or range of activities as to which it may be enforceable.

Section 5: Any and all notices under this agreement shall be in writing.

Section 6: This agreement supersedes all prior agreements written or oral between the Employee and the Company as of the date of the commencement of employment hereunder and shall constitute the only agreement between the parties for the period of employment hereunder. No provisions of this agreement shall be changed or modified nor shall this agreement be discharged in whole or in part except by an agreement in writing signed by the party against whom such change, modification, or discharge is claimed or sought to be enforced.

Section 7: This agreement shall inure to the benefit of and be binding upon the Company or its successors and assigns. All obligations of the Employee arising under this agreement shall survive the termination of this agreement and shall be binding upon his heirs, executors, and administrators.

Section 8: In the event the Employee leaves the Company voluntarily or is discharged by the Company, this agreement will be terminated except that Section 4 hereof shall survive such termination.

Softcorp, Inc.   Employee

By _Robert W. Wilson_   By _Kevin Mooney_

Exhibit C

Joseph Hegarty
381 East Street
Seattle, Washington   98115

3-17-80
Personal

Dear Joe,

It's 12:45 A.M., and I'm at 30,000 feet en route to San Francisco. I'll attend our seminar there tomorrow and then on to Australia. This flight has been a long one (and I've just started the journey), but it's given me a chance to think about SOFTCORP and the opportunities I've had here.

Let me first thank you sincerely for putting into place the equity plan that Bob described to me last week. Obviously, I appreciate it from a financial standpoint, but equally important, I appreciate the confidence you must have in me to justify such a program.

As you know, equity is something I have felt strongly about since I joined SOFTCORP, and I believe the plan you are implementing is well designed to meet both your objectives and mine. The quantity of stock is sufficient to meet my personal goals as long as we continue our tremendous growth over the next few years. Obviously, this provides strong motivation for me to dedicate my best talents and efforts to this pursuit.

This is also a good opportunity to thank you for the confidence you and Bob have shown in me over the past few years. The experience I've had has been terrific. I hope you've been as satisfied with my performance as I've been with the job. It's been a lot of hard work, but I can't imagine a better place to have done it. I hope the next few years can be as interesting, challenging, and successful as the past few. I'm confident that the international division will continue to grow and prosper and that there's still lots of room for improvement in the U.S. marketing activities.

Thank you for the opportunities you've provided and once again, thank you for the "precious" equity.

Kevin

Kevin

P.S. I've sent a similar letter to Bob.

Several weeks later I was flying to Dallas with Bob Wilson. Luckily, I had dug out the letter they had sent me. I showed Bob the letter and told him that I didn't want to pressure him, that the company certainly didn't have to give me any equity, but if that was their decision, Softcorp wasn't the place I wanted to work.

Seeing the letter was apparently quite significant for Wilson. Kevin Mooney was given 1 percent stock participation in Softcorp. (*Exhibit C* is a letter Mooney sent to Hegarty and Wilson.)

In 1981, Mooney was promoted to vice president; Wilson moved to president of Softcorp and Hegarty to chairman. By 1982, the international division had grown to include South Africa, Southeast Asia, and Venezuela; by 1983, new countries included New Zealand, France, Brazil, and Argentina. (See *Exhibit D.*)

Exhibit D
Softcorp, Inc., Performance, 1977–1983 ($ millions)

	1977	*1978*	*1979*	*1980*	*1981*	*1982*	*1983*
Total sales	$1.7	$3.1	$7.5	$15.6	$26.2	$39.0	$56.0
Profit	$0.048	$0.221	$0.775	$0.910	$1.02	$2.1	$3.6
International			$0.75	$1.5	$3.7	$8.7	$17.0
Employees	57	85	138	251	350	400	640

The Acquisition

Since 1980, Softcorp had considered the idea of going public. Each year, however, these plans were scratched because the company profile was never good enough to attract a market. It lacked timely financial statements; its profits weren't very good; and its performance was erratic. In 1983, however, Softcorp received a bona fide offer from a Fortune 500 firm, Prentiss-McGraw, Inc. (PMI). The firm thought Softcorp fitted well into its portfolio of companies; it saw Softcorp as a growth company with little need to generate healthy profits each year. Furthermore, its deal promised a hands-off approach. It was content to let the founders continue to manage the company. The purchase price was a range between $50 million and $80 million, depending on the company's performance over the next three years. The acquisition, however, had different harvest implications for several members of the management committee, as shown by the equity distribution among the eight management committee members. (See *Exhibit E.*)

As a part of the deal, the buyer asked all of us—Hegarty, Wilson, and the six vice presidents—to sign a noncompete agreement and an employment contract guaranteeing that we would work for them for three years. They explained that the employment contract was designed to protect us and that the noncompete agreement was meant to protect them. Everyone but me seemed very ready to sign. One of the VPs wanted the contract to be for five years!

Three of the vice presidents had received their stock options just eight months before the offer, and they weren't entitled to the capital gains tax treatment. PMI promised to provide them with additional compensation because their options would be taxed as ordinary income.

The other two VPs, who each owned 8 percent each in the form of stock, and Hegarty and Wilson were set for life. There I was, standing alone with my 1 percent, now diluted to 0.8 percent, stock, certainly not enough to retire on.

Exhibits F and *G* are the employment and noncompete agreements drawn up by PMI's attorneys for execution by Softcorp's executives.

Kevin Mooney's Dilemma

Kevin knew that he was pretty much alone in his reluctance to sign. But he had to consider what was most important to him. He was a young man with a young family. Right now, his job required lots of travel and he wasn't sure he wanted to continue traveling so much. In addition, he loved the job because he could be his own boss and run his own show. He had no idea how PMI's presence would affect that. Whether or not to sign the contract weighed heavily on Kevin's mind.

I thought I had better see a lawyer if for no other reason than to be able to use him as "the bad guy" in all of this. He confirmed my feelings about signing. He told me that I had built a good reputation

Exhibit E
Softcorp, Inc., Distribution of Equity

Joe Hegarty, Chairman	25% stock
Bob Wilson, President	25% stock
Dave Cassidy, VP, Operations	8% stock
Jonathan Latham, VP, Research and Development	8% stock
Richard White, VP, Marketing	0.8% stock (options)
Roger Fineman, VP, Sales	0.8% stock (options)
Stephen Marx, VP, Finance and Treasurer	0.8% stock (options)
Kevin Mooney, VP, International	0.8% stock

in the industry and that I could leverage that reputation elsewhere. He told me, "Unless they give you something, don't sign."

Then, at a sales meeting in Hawaii, Wilson cornered me, referring to my reluctance to sign as "the Mooney problem." He told me I was ruining it for the rest of them—that the deal wouldn't go through without my signature.

Kevin wondered how he should proceed.

EXERCISE—MANAGERIAL SKILLS AND KNOW-HOW ASSESSMENT

The purposes of the Management Skills and Know-how Assessment are three.

First, the assessment is intended to introduce important management competencies and skills in more detail. However, a complete treatment of traditional management skills is outside the scope of this book, and there are many excellent texts covering each fundamental area.

The second purpose of the assessment is that of enabling a lead entrepreneur or a member of a management team to so evaluate his or her strengths and weaknesses and those of potential team members that the needs in a venture can be evaluated.

Another important purpose is to enable an entrepreneur to diagnose his or her deficiencies in certain areas of management, to assess his or her strengths, and to begin to develop an agenda for learning. This self-knowledge is vital, whether an individual is to be a lead entrepreneur or whether he or she is considering becoming a member of an entrepreneurial management team now or in the future. In this regard, the assessment can be seen as an integral part of developing a personal entrepreneurial strategy and of the Personal Strategy Exercises in Chapter 21, Part VI.

The assessment is arranged as a list of management skills, divided into key areas, those requiring functional skills (i.e., marketing, finance, production and operations, and computers) plus areas requiring cross-functional skills (i.e., administration and law and taxation). The individual is asked to decide if he or she has thorough knowledge of the specific skills, some knowledge and experience, or no knowledge or experience.

As with any other decision process, the process of assessing management skills, whether a person's own or those of others, is most productive when it is done with the benefit of the most complete information available.

An assumption behind the format of the assessment is that a systematic recording and analysis of experiences can help an individual see where he or she has been and provide some direction for the future. Once the assessment has been completed, a determination can be made of whether a particular skill is required and when. In any case, the job of assessment is iterative in nature and requires continual review and adjustment.

Exhibit F

Shaw & Cartwright
Counselors at Law
60 City Square, N.W.
Seattle, Washington 98100
(206) 227-9740

March 25, 1983

Hand Delivered

R. Kevin Mooney, Vice President
Softcorp, Inc.
381 East Street
Seattle, WA 98115

Dear Kevin:

As promised earlier this week, I am enclosing copies of the following documents, which constitute *all* of the documents to be signed by senior Softcorp officers in connection with the Prentiss-McGraw, Inc., acquisition:

1. *Sellers Agreement.* This has already been signed by the seven senior officers. It contains a covenant not to compete on page 5, with a reference to Appendix A, which lists the termination dates of the covenant for each senior officer.

2. *Sellers' Agent Agreement.* I believe you have not yet seen this agreement, which also has already been signed by all senior officers. Basically, it constitutes a power of attorney granted to Bob and Joe to act on behalf of all sellers throughout the mechanics of the closing, distribution of cash proceeds, etc. and the earn-out period over the next three years. It grants no authority to negotiate or amend individual employment agreements whatsoever.

3. *Employment Agreement.* This has not yet been signed by anyone, but it is proposed that on or immediately before the closing (approximately April 26), all individuals in "tier two" would sign an employment agreement in the form of Exhibit 7, with individual treatment for salaries only. You will especially want to note Section 2 providing for a term of the Agreement through December 31, 1985, and Section 6(c) containing another covenant not to compete continuing for four months after such termination date (i.e., until April 30, 1986).

I would be pleased to attempt to answer any questions you may have regarding any of the above three agreements. If it appears likely that you may be signing any one or more of them, then you will undoubtedly want to secure your personal attorney's views.

I expect to be talking with you next week.

Very truly yours,

John J. Marshall

John J. Marshall

JJM:akl
Enclosures

Exhibit G

Employment Agreement

This AGREEMENT, dated as of May 4, 1983, between Softcorp, Inc. ("Company") and R. Kevin Mooney ("Executive").

Witnesseth:

Whereas, the Company, the Prentiss-McGraw, Inc. ("Buyer"), P&M Merger Corporation, a wholly owned subsidiary of Buyer ("Merger Corp."), and Robert W. Wilson and Joseph M. Hegarty, collectively as agent ("Sellers' Agent") for holders, including Executive, of the outstanding shares of capital stock and options to purchase capital stock of the Company ("Sellers"), have entered into an Agreement and Plan of Merger, dated as of March 21, 1983 (the "Merger Agreement"), pursuant to which Buyer will acquire the Company as a result of the merger of the Merger Corp. with and into the Company (the "Merger");

Whereas, Executive is and has been employed by the Company for more than five years and is currently Vice President—International of the Company;

Whereas, Executive possesses an intimate knowledge of the business and affairs of the Company, its policies, methods, personnel, and problems;

Whereas, the Board of Directors of the Company recognizes that Executive's contribution to the growth and success of the Company has been substantial and desires to assure the Company of Executive's continued employment and to compensate him therefor;

Whereas, Executive desires to be so employed by the Company, on the terms and conditions herein set forth;

Now, therefore, in consideration of the premises and the terms hereinafter set forth, but subject to the consummation of the Merger under the aforesaid Merger Agreement, the parties agree as follows:

1. *Employment.* After the Effective Date, as that term is defined in the Merger Agreement (the "Effective Date"), the Company shall employ Executive pursuant to the terms of this Agreement. Executive shall hold the office of Vice President—International and, in addition to the duties prescribed for such office, shall have such other duties, responsibilities, and powers as shall be consistent with such office and as may be prescribed from time to time. Executive shall devote substantially all of his business time and attention to the business of the Company. Executive hereby accepts said employment and agrees faithfully to perform said duties in compliance with the policies and procedures applicable to Executive's positions and to render said services for the term of his employment. During the term of this Agreement, Company shall not require Executive to change his current domicile to another state.

2. *Term.* The term of this Agreement shall commence as of the Effective Date and shall continue until December 31, 1985 (the "Termination Date"), unless sooner terminated pursuant to Paragraph 5 hereof. The provisions of Executive's previous employment arrangements with the Company shall continue in effect until the Effective Date, at which time such employment arrangements shall terminate.

3. *Compensation.*

(a) During the term of this Agreement, Executive shall be paid, as compensation for his services under this Agreement, as follows:

(i) Salary at the rate of $100,000 per annum, payable by check not less often than monthly and not later than the fifteenth day following the expiraton of the month in which services are rendered hereunder; and

(ii) Bonus, payable within three (3) months after the end of each year, and based upon the Company's Compensation and Bonus Plan in effect from year to year.

(iii) All salaries and bonuses hereunder shall be reviewed by the Company annually, which reviews shall not result in any reduction of the salaries hereunder.

(b) Executive shall be entitled to four weeks' vacation during each calendar year of this Agreement.

(c) As an employee of the Company, Executive shall be entitled to the employee welfare benefit, pension, and other benefit plans available to the employees of the Company, which shall not be less than those presently enjoyed by Executive.

4. *Confidential Information.* In the course of his employment with the Company prior to the date hereof Executive had, and in the course of his employment hereunder Executive will have, access to confidential information and records, data, formulas, specifications, and other trade secrets of the Company, Buyer, and Buyer's affiliates. During and after his employment by the Company, Buyer, or any of Buyer's affiliates, Executive shall not directly or indirectly disclose such information to any person or use any such information, except as required in the course of such employment. All records, files, drawings, documents, models, equipment, and the like relating to the Company's, Buyer's, or any of Buyer's affiliates' business, which Executive shall prepare or use or come in contact with, shall be and remain such company's sole property and shall not be removed from such company's premises without its written consent, except as required in the course of such employment.

5. *Termination.*

(a) Termination for Cause. The Company may terminate this Agreement for cause at any time without notice, and thereby cancel all rights and obligations of the parties hereto, except those set forth in Paragraphs 4 and 6*(c)* hereof. For purposes of this Agreement, "cause" shall mean action by Executive involving material breach of the terms of this Agreement which shall not have ceased within ten (10) days after written notice thereof, dishonesty, moral turpitude, or gross obstruction of business operations. If, however, Executive shall dispute whether he was discharged for "cause," then such dispute shall promptly be referred for final determination to binding arbitration in Seattle, Washington, in accordance with the rules and regulations of the American Arbitration Association. Pending such final determination of such dispute, Executive shall continue to participate in the employee welfare benefit, pension, and other benefit plans available to the employees of the company to the extent that such continued participation is permitted under such plans and applicable law, and all compensation which would have been payable to Executive under Paragraph 3 hereof if the Agreement had not been terminated for cause by the Company shall be deposited as it would have become payable in an interest-bearing bank account in any commercial bank doing business in the City of Seattle, Washington, to be held by such bank as escrowee pending such final determination and to be released (together with any interest earned thereon) in accordance with the instructions set forth in such final determination.

(b) Termination upon Disability. If, during the term of this Agreement, Executive shall become incapable of fulfilling his obligations hereunder because of injury or physical or mental illness, and such incapacity shall exist or may reasonably be expected upon competent medical opinion to exist for more than six (6) months in the aggregate during any period of twelve (12) consecutive months, the Company may, upon at least thirty (30) days' prior written notice to Executive, terminate all rights and obligations of the parties hereto, except those set forth in Paragraphs 4 and 6*(c)* and except as to payment of compensation in accordance with the terms of the Agreement for a period of at least six (6) months after the commencement of such injury or physical or mental illness.

(c) Termination by Death. If Executive dies during the term of his employment hereunder, this Agreement shall terminate immediately and any payments due Executive hereunder shall be paid to his legal representative.

6. *General Provisions.*

(a) Assignability. The rights and duties of the parties hereunder shall not be assignable, except that this Agreement and all rights and obligations hereunder may be assigned by the Company to, and assumed by, any corporation or other business entity which succeeds to all or substantially all of the business of the Company through merger, consolidation, acquisition of assets, or other transaction, upon condition that such assignee or successor assumes all of the obligations of the Company hereunder.

(b) Integration. This Agreement contains the entire agreement among the parties regarding the employment of Executive and supersedes all prior agreements and undertakings whether oral or written. No amendment to this Agreement may be made except by a writing signed by the party to be bound.

(c) Noncompetition; Specific Enforcement. Executive agrees that, prior to the applicable date set forth below, he will not directly or indirectly (as a director, officer, partner, employee, manager, consultant, independent contractor, advisor, or otherwise) engage in competition with, or own any interest in, provide any financing for, or perform any service for any business or organization which directly or indirectly engages in competition with any business conducted by the Company or any subsidiary or division of the Company in any area where such business is then conducted:

(i) if Executive's employment with the Company terminates on or after the Termination Date, four months after such date of termination;

(ii) if Executive's employment with the Company either terminates for "cause" or by voluntary termination prior to the Termination Date, the later of (A) the Termination Date or (B) four months after such date of termination.

The foregoing provisions shall not prohibit Executive's ownership of not more than 1 percent of the outstanding shares of any publicly held corporation or not more than 3 percent of the outstanding shares of any privately held corporation, partnership, or other business entity. In the event of a breach of the provisions of this subparagraph, Executive agrees that the remedy at law may be inadequate and that the Company, in addition to any other remedies, shall be entitled to temporary or permanent injunctive or mandatory relief without the necessity of proving damages. Notwithstanding any of the foregoing to the contrary, if Executive shall be discharged without "cause," there shall immediately upon such termination be no restrictions whatsoever upon the freedom of Executive to engage in competition with the business of the Company.

(d) Waiver. The waiver by any party of a breach of any provision of this Agreement shall not operate or be construed as a waiver of any subsequent breach of the same provision or of any other provision of this Agreement.

(e) Notices. Any notice to the Company or Executive hereunder shall be given in writing either by personal delivery or by registered or certified mail, postage prepaid, return receipt requested, addressed to the Company at its principal place of business or to Executive at his home address as then shown on the records of the Company. For purposes of determining compliance with any time limit herein, notice shall be deemed given when personally delivered or on the third business day after the day of such mailing.

(f) Severability. If, for any reason whatsoever, any one or more of the provisions of this Agreement shall be finally determined to be inoperative, unenforcable, or invalid, by a court of competent jurisdiction, in a particular case or in all cases, such determination shall not render such provision invalid in any other case or render any of the other provisions of this Agreement inoperative, unenforceable, or invalid.

(g) Applicable Law. The exercise, validity, construction, operation, and effect of the terms and provisions of this Agreement shall be determined in accordance with the laws of the State of Washington.

(h) Captions. The captions to the paragraphs of this Agreement are for convenience only and shall not be considered or referred to in resolving questions of interpretation.

(i) Counterparts. This Agreement may be executed in one or more counterparts, each of which shall be deemed an original, but all of which together shall constitute one and the same agreement.

In witness whereof, the parties have executed this Agreement as of the date first above written.

Softcorp, Inc.

_____Robert W. Wilson_____   By: _____
Executive

Finally, a complex set of factors clearly goes into making someone a successful entrepreneur. As with personal qualities, attitudes, and behaviors described in the last chapter, no individual has all the managerial skills defined in the exercise. The presence or absence of any one does not guarantee success or failure as an entrepreneur. Again, for an entrepreneur to know that he or she does not have a certain skill and to know how to acquire it are clearly as valuable as knowing that you already have a skill.

EXERCISE
MANAGERIAL SKILLS AND KNOW-HOW ASSESSMENT

NAME:

VENTURE:

DATE:

PART I—MANAGEMENT COMPETENCY INVENTORY

Part I of the exercise involves filling out the Management Competency Inventory and evaluating how critical certain management competencies are either (1) for the venture or (2) personally over the next one to three years.   *How you rank the importance of management competencies, therefore, will depend on the purpose of your managerial assessment.*

STEP 1:   COMPLETE THE MANAGEMENT COMPETENCY INVENTORY ON THE FOL-LOWING PAGES. For each management competency, place a check in the column that best describes your knowledge and experience. Note that a section is at the end of the inventory for **unique skills** required by your venture; for example, if it is a service or franchise business, there will be some skills and know-how that are unique. Then rank from 1 to 3 particular management competencies as follows:

> 1 = Critical
> 2 = Very Desirable
> 3 = Not Necessary

Competency Inventory				
Rank	Thorough Knowledge & Experience (Done Well)	Some Knowledge & Experience (So-so)	No Knowledge or Experience (New Ground)	Importance (1–3 Years)
MARKETING				
Market Research and Evaluation *Finding and interpreting industry and competitor information; designing and conducting market research studies; analyzing and interpreting market research data; etc.*				
Market Planning *Planning overall sales, advertising, and promotion programs; planning and setting up effective distributor or sales representative systems; etc.*				

Product Pricing

Determining competitive pricing and margin structures and break-even analysis; positioning products in terms of price; etc.

Sales Management

Organizing, supervising, and motivating a direct sales force; analyzing territory and account sales potential; managing sales force; etc.

Direct Selling

Identifying, meeting, and developing new customers; closing sales; etc.

Direct Mail/ Catalog Selling

Identifying and developing appropriate direct mail and catalog sales and related distribution; etc.

Telemarketing

Identifying, planning, implementing appropriate telemarketing programs; etc.

Customer Service

Determining customer service needs and spare-part requirements; managing a service organization and warranties; training; technical back-up; etc.

Distribution Management

Organizing and managing the flow of product from manufacturing through distribution channels to customer, etc.

Product Management

Integrating market information, perceived needs, research and development, and advertising into a rational product plan; etc.

New Product
Planning

*Planning the
introduction of
new products,
including mar-
keting testing,
prototype test-
ing, and devel-
opment of price,
sales, merchan-
dising, and dis-
tribution plans;
etc.*

**OPERATIONS/
PRODUCTION**

Manufacturing
Management

*Managing pro-
duction to pro-
duce products
within time,
cost, and qual-
ity constraints;
knowledge of
MRP; etc.*

Inventory
Control

*Using tech-
niques of con-
trolling in-
process and
finished goods
inventories, etc.*

Cost Analysis and Control

Calculating labor and materials costs; developing standard cost systems; conducting variance analyses; calculating overtime labor needs; managing and controlling costs; etc.

Quality Control

Setting up inspection systems and standards for effective control of quality in incoming, in-process, and finished goods; etc.

Production Scheduling and Flow

Analyzing work flow; planning and managing production processes; managing work flow; calculating schedules and flows for rising sales levels; etc.

Purchasing

Identifying appropriate sources of supply; negotiating supplier contracts; managing the incoming flow of material into inventory, etc.

Job Evaluation

Analyzing worker productivity and needs for additional help; calculating cost-saving aspects of temporary versus permanent help; etc.

FINANCE

Accounting

Determining appropriate bookkeeping and accounting systems; preparing and using income statements and balance sheets; analyzing cash flow, breakeven, contribution, and profit and loss; etc.

Capital
Budgeting

*Preparing bud-
gets; deciding
how best to ac-
quire funds for
start-up and
growth; fore-
casting funds
needs; etc.*

Cash Flow
Management

*Managing cash
position, in-
cluding project-
ing cash require-
ments; etc.*

Credit and
Collection
Management

*Developing
credit policies
and screening
criteria, etc.*

Short-term
Financing

*Managing pay-
ables and re-
ceivables; using
interim financ-
ing alternatives;
etc.*

Public and Private Offering Skills

Developing a business plan and offering memo; managing shareholder relations; negotiating with financial sources; etc.

ADMINISTRATION

Problem Solving

Anticipating problems and planning to avoid them; analyzing and solving problems, etc.

Communications

Communicating effectively and clearly, both orally and in writing, to customers, peers, subordinates, and outsiders; etc.

Planning

*Ability to set re-
alistic and at-
tainable goals,
identify obsta-
cles to achiev-
ing the goals,
and develop
detailed action
plans to achieve
those goals.*

Decision Making

*Making deci-
sions based on
the analysis of
incomplete data,
etc.*

Project
Management

*Organizing pro-
ject teams; set-
ting project goals;
defining project
tasks; monitor-
ing task com-
pletion in the
face of prob-
lems and cost/
quality con-
straints; etc.*

Negotiating

*Working effec-
tively in nego-
tiations; etc.*

Personnel
Administration

Setting up payroll, hiring, compensation, and training functions; identifying, managing, and guiding appropriate outside advisors; etc.

Management
Information
Systems

Knowledge of relevant management information systems available and appropriate for growth plans; etc.

Computer

Using spreadsheet, wordprocessing, and other relevant software; using electronic mail; etc.

**INTERPERSONAL/
TEAM**

Leadership/
Vision/Influence

*Actively leading,
instilling vision
and passion in
others, and man-
aging activities of
others; creating a
climate and spirit
conducive to high
performance; etc.*

Helping

*Determining when
assistance is war-
ranted and asking
for or providing
such assistance*

Feedback

*Providing effective
feedback or receiv-
ing it; etc.*

Conflict
Management

*Confronting differ-
ences openly and
obtaining resolution;
using evidence and
logic; etc.*

Teamwork and People Management

Working with others to achieve common goals; delegating responsibility and coaching subordinates, etc.

LAW

Corporations

Understanding the uniform commercial code, including that regarding forms of organization and the rights and obligations of officers, shareholders, and directors; etc.

Contracts

Understanding the requirements of government and commercial contracts, licenses, leases, and other agreements; etc.

Taxes

Understanding state and federal reporting requirements; understanding tax shelters, estate planning, fringe benefits, and so forth; etc.

Securities

Understanding regulations of Security and Exchange Commission and state agencies concerning the securities, both registered and unregistered; etc.

Patents and Proprietary Rights

Understanding the preparation and revision of patent applications; recognizing strong patent, trademark, copyright, and privileged information claims; etc.

Real Estate

> *Understanding agreements necessary for the rental or purchase and sale of property; etc.*

Bankruptcy

> *Understanding options and the forgivable and nonforgivable liabilities of founders, officers, directors, and so forth; etc.*

UNIQUE SKILLS

> *Unique competencies required.*

PART II—MANAGERIAL ASSESSMENT

Part II involves assessing management strengths and weaknesses, deciding which areas of competence are most critical, and developing a plan to overcome or compensate for any weaknesses and to capitalize on management strengths.

STEP 1: ASSESS MANAGEMENT STRENGTHS AND WEAKNESSES:
— Which management skills are particularly strong?

— Which skills are particularly weak?

— What patterns are evident?

STEP 2: CIRCLE THE AREAS OF COMPETENCE MOST CRITICAL TO THE SUCCESS OF THE VENTURE, AND CROSS OUT THOSE THAT ARE IRRELEVANT.

STEP 3: CONSIDER THE IMPLICATIONS FOR YOU AND FOR THE VENTURE:
— What are the implications of this particular constellation of management strengths and weaknesses?

— What specific actions can overcome or compensate for each critical weakness?

— What specific actions can be taken on critical strengths?

— What are the time implications of the above actions?

— What areas need to be explored further?

STEP 4: OBTAIN FEEDBACK.   If you are evaluating your management competencies as part of the development of a personal entrepreneurial strategy and planning your apprenticeship, it is recommended you read Chapter 21 and complete the management assessment and feedback exercises in Part VI at this time.

The New Venture Team

7

Behind every truly successful entrepreneur I know of, there stands an organization equipped to help convert ideas into purposeful action, to help accomplish the mission the entrepreneur has set for his enterprise, to help implement his strategy.

Gustavo A. Cisneros
Organizacion Diego Cisneros

RESULTS EXPECTED

Upon completion of the chapter, you will have:

1. Identified and examined the role and significance of teams in building successful new ventures.
2. Examined successful entrepreneurial philosophies and attitudes which can anchor vision in forming and developing effective new venture teams.
3. Identified the critical issues and hurdles, including common pitfalls, faced by entrepreneurs in forming and building new venture teams.
4. Examined issues of reward that new teams face in slicing the equity pie.
5. Analyzed the Beantown Seafoods, Inc., case.
6. Developed a reward system for your own venture.

THE IMPORTANCE OF THE TEAM

The Connection to Success

Entrepreneurial team building is addressed in light of both the author's experience and recent research that has brought some facts and thoughtful analysis to this least understood aspect of new venture creation.

Accumulating evidence suggests that a management team can make quite a difference in venture success. There is a strong connection between the growth potential of a new venture (and its ability to attract capital beyond the founder's resources from private and venture capital backers) and the quality of its management team.

The existence of a quality management team is one of the major differences between a firm that provides its founder simply a job substitute and the ability to employ perhaps a few family members and others and a higher potential venture. The lone-wolf entrepreneur may make a living, but the team builder creates an organization and a company—a company where substantial value, and harvest options, are created.

Ventures that do not have teams are not necessarily predestined for the new venture graveyard. Yet, building a higher potential venture without a team is extremely difficult. It is true that some entrepreneurs have acquired a distaste for partners and that some lead entrepreneurs can be happy only if they are in complete control; that is, they want employees, not partners, either internally or in outside investors. Take, for instance, an entrepreneur who founded a high-technology firm that grew steadily, but slowly, over 10 years to nearly $2 million in sales. As new patents and technological advances in fiber optics drew much interest from venture capitalists, he had more than one offer of up to $5 million of funding, which he turned down because the investors wanted to own 51 percent or more of his venture. Plain and simply, he said, "I do not want to give up control of what I have worked so long and hard to create." While clearly the exception to the rule, this entrepreneur has managed to grow his business to more than $20 million in sales.

As was noted in the first chapter, there is a lot of evidence which suggests the team can make quite a difference in venture success.[1] The studies cited indicated that venture capitalists believe teams are important, that the survival rate among venture capital-backed firms was the inverse of national averages, and that returns on these investments were high. A study of 104 high-technology ventures launched in the 1960s reported that 83.3 percent of high-growth companies, which achieved sales of $5 million or more annually, were launched by teams, while only 53.8 percent of the 73 discontinued companies had several founders.[2] This pattern is apparent from an even more recent study of the "Route 128 One Hundred" (i.e., the top firms comprising the new venture phenomenon in the greater Boston area along Route 128).[3] Typically, these firms averaged impressive annual sales of $16 million for ventures up to 5 years old, $49 million for those 6 to 10 years old, and several hundred million for more mature firms. It was found that *70 percent* of these had multiple founders. Among 86 firms, 38 percent actually had three or more founders, 17 percent had four or more, and 9 percent had five or more. One firm was launched by a team of eight.

Not only is the existence of a team important, but so, too, is the quality of the team. Because of this, venture capital investors have become even more active in helping to shape, and reshape, management teams. One recent study showed a significant shift toward this activity during the boom period in venture capital in the 1980s in contrast with practices in the 1970s.[4] Another study, examining the nature of venture capital investing in highly innovative technical ventures, revealed this role can be quite active.[5]

There is then a valuable role that the right partner(s) can play in a venture. In addition, mounting evidence suggests that entrepreneurs face loneliness, stress, and other pressures.[6] At the very least, finding the right partner can serve to mitigate these pressures.

The key, then, is getting, and working with, the "right" partner or partners. Getting the right partners and working with them successfully usually involves anticipating and dealing with some very critical issues and hurdles, when it is neither too early nor too late.

FORMING/BUILDING TEAMS

Anchoring Vision in Team Philosophy and Attitudes

The most successful entrepreneurs seem to anchor their vision of the future in certain entrepreneurial philosophies and attitudes (i.e., attitudes about what a team is, what its mission is, and how it will be rewarded). The heart and soul of this vision concerns what the founder or founders are trying to accomplish and the unwritten ground rules that become the fabric,

---

[1] Jeffry A. Timmons, "Careful Self-Analysis and Team Assessment Can Aid Entrepreneurs," in *Growing Concerns,* ed. D. E. Gumpert (New York: John Wiley & Sons, 1984), pp. 43–52.

[2] Arnold C. Cooper and Albert V. Bruno, "Success among High Technology Firms," *Business Horizons,* April 1977, p. 20.

[3] Jeffry A. Timmons and Susan Skinner, research assistant, "The Route 128 One Hundred," working paper, Babson College, Wellesley, Mass., 1984.

[4] Jeffry A. Timmons, "Discard Many Old Rules about Raising Venture Capital," in *Growing Concerns,* ed. D. E. Gumpert (New York: John Wiley & Sons, 1984), pp. 273–80.

[5] Jeffry A. Timmons, "Venture Capital: More than Money?" in *Pratt's Guide to Venture Capital Sources,* 8th ed. (Wellesley Hills, Mass.: Venture Economics, 1984), pp. 39–43.

[6] David Boyd and David Gumpert, "The Loneliness of the Start-up Entrepreneur," in *Frontiers of Entrepreneurship Research, 1982* and *1983,* ed. J. A. Hornaday et al. (Babson Park, Mass.: Babson College), pp. 478–87.

character, and purpose guiding how a team will work together, succeed and make mistakes together, and realize a harvest together. The rewards, compensation, and incentive structures rest on this philosophy and attitudes.

This fundamental mind-set is often evident in later success. The anchoring of this vision goes beyond all the critical nuts and bolts issues covered in the chapters and cases on the opportunity, the business plan, financing, and so forth. Each of these nuts and bolts is vital, but each, by itself, may not lead to success. A single factor rarely, if ever, does.

The capacity of the lead entrepreneur to craft a vision, and then to lead, inspire, persuade, and cajole key people both to sign up for and deliver the dream makes an enormous difference between success and failure, between loss and profit, and between substantial harvest and "turning over the keys" to get out from under large personal guarantees of debt. Instilling a vision, and the passion to win, occurs very early on, often during informal discussions, and seems to trigger a series of self-fulfilling prophecies that lead to success, rather than to "almosts" or to failure.

Thus, lead entrepreneurs and team members who understand team building and teamwork have a secret weapon. Many with outstanding technical or other relevant skills, educational credentials, and so on, will be at once prisoners and victims of the highly individualistic competitiveness that got them to where they are. They may be fantastic lone achievers, and some may even "talk a good team game." But when it comes to how they behave and perform, their egos can rarely fit inside an airplane hanger. They simply do not have the team mentality.

What are these team philosophies and attitudes that the best entrepreneurs have and are able to identify or instill in prospective partners and team members? These can be traced to the entrepreneurial mind-set discussed in Chapter 5—a mind-set that can be seen actively at work around the team-building challenge. While there are innumerable blends and variations, most likely the teams of those firms that succeed in growing up big will share in common many of the following:

- *Cohesion.* Members of a team believe they are all in this together, and, if the company wins, everyone wins. Members believe that no one can win unless everyone wins, and, conversely, if anyone loses, everyone loses. Rewards, compensation, and incentive structures rest on building company value and return on capital invested, no matter how small or sizable.
- *Teamwork.* A team that works as a team, rather than one where individual heroes are created, may be the single most distinguishing feature of the higher-potential company. Thus, on these teams, efforts are made to make others' jobs easier, to make heroes out of partners and key people, and to motivate people by celebrating their successes. As the highly successful, now retired, president and chief executive officer of The Sunmark Companies, Harold J. Seigle, likes to put it, "High performance breeds strong friendships!"
- *Integrity.* Hard choices and trade-offs are made in terms of what is good for the customer, the company, and value creation, rather than being based on purely utilitarian or Machiavellian ethics or narrow personal or departmental needs and concerns. There is a belief in and commitment to the notion of getting the job done without sacrificing quality, health, or personal standards.
- *Commitment to the long haul.* Like most organizations, new ventures thrive or wither depending on the level of commitment of their teams. Members of a committed team believe they are playing for the long haul and that the venture is not a get-rich-quick drill. Rather, the venture is viewed as a delayed—not instant—gratification game in which it can take 5, 7, or even 10 or more years to realize a harvest. *No one gets a windfall profit by signing up now but bailing out early or when the going gets tough.* Stock vesting agreements reflect this commitment. For example, stock will usually be so vested over five or seven

years that anyone who leaves early, for whatever reasons, can keep stock he or she has earned to date, but he or she is required to sell the remaining shares back to the company at the price originally paid. Of course, such a vesting agreement usually provides that, if the company is unexpectedly sold or if a public offering is made long before the five- or seven-year vesting period is up, then stock is 100 percent vested automatically with that event.

- *Harvest mind-set.* A successful harvest is the name of the game. This means that eventual capital gain is viewed as the scorecard, rather than the size of a monthly paycheck, the location and size of an office, a certain car, or the like.

- *Commitment to value creation.* Team members are committed to value creation; that is, making the pie bigger for everyone, including adding value for customers, enabling suppliers to win as the team succeeds, and making money for the team's constituencies and various stakeholders.

- *Equal inequality.* In successful emerging companies, democracy and blind equality generally do not work very well, and diligent efforts are made to determine who has what responsibility for the key tasks. The president is the one to set the ground rules and to shape the climate and culture of the venture. Bill Foster, founder and president of Stratus Computer, was asked if he and his partners were all equal. He said, "Yes, we are, except I get paid the most and I own the most stock."[7] For example, stock is usually not divided equally among the founders and key managers. In one company of four key people, stock was split as follows: 34 percent for the president, 23 percent each for the marketing and technical vice presidents, and 6 percent for the controller. The remainder went to outside directors and advisors. In another company, seven founders split the company as follows: 22 percent for the president, 15 percent for each of the four vice presidents, and 9 percent for each of the two other contributors. An example of how failure to differentiate in terms of ownership impacts a business is seen in a third firm, where four owners each had equal share. Yet, two of the owners contributed virtually everything, while the other two actually detracted from the business. Because of this unresolved problem, the company could not attract venture capital and never was able to grow dramatically.

- *Fairness.* Rewards for key employees and stock ownership are based on contribution, performance, and results *over time.* Since these can only be roughly estimated in advance, and since there will invariably be surprises and inequities, both positive and negative, as time goes on, adjustments are made. One good example is a company that achieved spectacular results in the rather short time period of two years in the cellular-car phone business. When the company was sold, it was evident that two of the six team members had contributed more than was reflected in their stock ownership position. To remedy this, another team member gave one of the two team members stock worth several hundred thousand dollars. Since the team was involved in another venture, the president made adjustments in the various ownership positions in the new venture, with each member's concurrence, to adjust for past inequities. In addition, it was decided to set aside 10 percent of the next venture to provide some discretion in making future adjustments for unanticipated contributions to ultimate success.

- *Sharing of the harvest.* This sense of fairness and justness seems to be extended by the more successful entrepreneurs to the harvest of a company, even when there is no legal or even ethical obligation whatsoever to do so. For example, as much as 10 percent to

[7] Remarks made at a Babson College Venture Capital Conference, June 1985.

20 percent of the "winnings" is frequently set aside to distribute to key employees. In one such recent harvest, employees were startled and awash with glee when informed they would each receive a year's salary after the company was sold. However, this is not always the case. In another firm, 90 percent of which was owned by an entrepreneur and his family, the president, who was the single person most responsible for the firm's success and spectacular valuation, needed to expend considerable effort to get the owners to agree to give bonuses to other key employees of around $3 million, an amount just over 1 percent of the $250 million sale price. (It is worth considering how this sense of fairness, or lack of it, affects future flows of quality people and opportunities from which these entrepreneurs can choose new ventures.)

A Process of Evolution

An entrepreneur considering issues of team formation will rarely discover black-and-white, bullet-proof answers that hold up over time. Nor is it being suggested than an entrepreneur need answers to *all* questions of what the opportunity requires, and when, before moving ahead. Emphasis on the importance of new venture teams also does not mean every new venture need start with a *full* team that plunges into the business. It may take some time for the team to come together as a firm grows, and there will also always be some doubt, a hope for more than a prospective partner can deliver, and a constant recalibration. Again, creative acts, such as running a marathon or entrepreneuring, will be full of unknowns, new ground, and surprises. Preparation is an insurance policy, and thinking through these team issues and team building concepts in advance is very inexpensive insurance.

The combination of the right team of people and a right venture opportunity can be a most powerful one. The whole is, in such instances, greater than the sum of the parts.

However, the odds for highly successful venture teams are rather thin. And, even if a venture survives, the turnover among team members during the early years probably exceeds the national divorce rate. Studies of new venture teams seeking venture capital show many never get off the ground. These usually exhaust their own resources and their commitment prior to raising the venture capital necessary to launch their ventures. Of those that are funded, about 1 in 20 will become very successful in three to five years, in that they will return in excess of five times the original investment in realizable capital gains.

The formation and development of new venture teams seems to be idiosyncratic, and there seem to be a multitude of ways in which venture partners come together. Some teams form by accidents of geography, common interest, or working together. Perhaps the common interest is simply that the team members want to start a business, while in others cases the interest is an idea that it is felt responds to a market need. Others form teams by virtue of past friendships. For example, roommates or close friendships in college or graduate school frequently lead to business partnerships. This was the case with two of the author's classmates in the MBA program at the Harvard Business School. Concluding that they would eventually go into business together after rooming together for a week, Leslie Charm and Carl Youngman have been partners for over 20 years as owners of three national franchise companies, Doktor Pet Centers, Command Performance, and Eye-Natural.

In the evolution of venture teams, two distinct patterns are identifiable. In the first, one person has an idea (or simply wants to start a business), and then as many as three or four associates join him or her over the next one to three years as the venture takes form. Or, an entire team forms at the outset based on such factors as a shared idea, a friendship, an experience, and so forth.

Filling the Gaps

There is no simple cookbook solution to team formation; rather, there are as many approaches to forming teams as there are ventures with multiple founders.

Successful entrepreneurs search out people and form and build a team based on what the opportunity requires, and when.[8] Team members will contribute high value to a venture if they complement and balance the lead entrepreneur—and each other. Yet, ironically, while a substantial amount of thought usually accompanies the decision of people to go into business together, an overabundance of the thinking, particularly among the less experienced, can focus on less-critical issues, such as titles, corporate name, letterhead, or what kind of lawyer or accountant is needed. Thus, teams are often ill-conceived from the outset and can easily plunge headlong into unanticipated and unplanned responses to crises, conflicts, and changes.

A team starts with a lead entrepreneur. In a start-up situation, the lead entrepreneur usually wears many hats. Beyond that, comparison of the nature and demands of the venture and the capabilities, motivations, and interests of the lead entrepreneur will signal gaps that exist and that need to be filled by other team members or by accessing other outside resources, such as members of a board of directors, consultants, lawyers, accountants, and so on.

Thus, for example, if the strengths of the lead entrepreneur or a team member are technical in nature, other team members, or outside resources, need to fill voids in marketing, finance, and such. Realistically, there will be an overlapping and sharing of responsibilities; but team members need to complement, not duplicate, the lead entrepreneur's capabilities and those of other team members.

Note that a by-product of forming a team may be alteration of an entry strategy if a critical gap cannot be filled. For example, a firm may find that it simply cannot assault a certain market because it cannot hire the right marketing person. (But it may find it could attract a top-notch person to exploit another niche with a modified product or service.)

Most important, the process of evaluating and deciding who is needed and when is dynamic and is not a one-time event. What know-how, skills, and expertise are required; what key tasks and action steps need to be taken; what the requisites for success are; what the firm's distinctive competence is; what external contacts are required; how extensive and how critical the gaps are; how much the venture can afford to pay; whether the venture can gain access to the expertise it needs through additions to its board of directors or outside consultants; and the like, determine when and how these needs could be filled. And answers to such questions will change over time.

The following, organized around the analytical framework shown in *Exhibit 1.1,* can guide the formation of new venture teams:

- **The Founder.** What kind of team is needed depends upon the nature of the opportunity and what the lead entrepreneur brings to the game. One key step in forming a team is for the lead entrepreneur to assess his entrepreneurial strategy. (The personal entrepreneurial strategy exercise in Chapter 21 is a valuable input in approaching these issues.) Thus, the lead entrepreneur needs to first consider whether he or she really wants a team and whether he or she wants to grow a higher-potential company. He or she then needs to assess what talents, know-how, skills, track record, contacts, and resources he or she brings to the table; that is, what "chunks" have been acquired. (See the Management Skills and Know-how Assessment in Chapter 6.) Once this is determined, the lead entrepreneur needs to consider what the venture has to have to succeed, who is needed to complement him or her, and when. The best entrepreneurs are optimistic realists and have a real desire to improve their performance. They work at knowing what

[8] See J. A. Timmons, "The Entrepreneurial Team," *Journal of Small Business Management,* October 1975, pp. 36–37.

they do and do not know and are honest with themselves. The lead entrepreneur needs to consider issues, such as:

—What relevant industry, market, and technologic know-how and experience are needed to win, and do I bring these to the venture?

—Are my personal and business strengths in those specific areas that are critical to success in the proposed business?

—Do I have the contacts and networks needed (and will the ones I have make a competitive difference), or do I look to partners in this area?

—Can I attract a "first team" of all-star partners, and can I manage these people and other team members effectively?

—Why did I decide to pursue this particular opportunity now, and what do I want out of the business (i.e., what are my goals and my income and harvest aspirations)?

—Do I know what the sacrifices and commitment will be, and am I prepared to make these?

—What are the risks involved, am I comfortable with them, and do I look for someone with a different risk-taking orientation?

■ *The Opportunity.* The need for team members is something an entrepreneur constantly thinks about, especially in the idea stage before start-up. What is needed in the way of a team depends on the match-up between the lead entrepreneur and the opportunity, and how fast and aggressively he or she plans to proceed. (See the Venture Opportunity Screening Guide in Chapter 4.) While most new ventures plan to "bootstrap" it and bring on additional team members only as the company can afford them, the Catch-22 is that, if a venture is looking for venture capital or serious private investors, the more it has the team in place in advance the higher will be its valuation and the smaller the ownership share that will have to be parted with. Some questions which need to be considered are:

—Have I clearly defined the value added and the economics of the business, and have I considered how (and with whom) the venture can make money in this business? For instance, whether a company is selling razors or razor blades makes a difference in the need for different team members.

—What are the critical success variables in the business I want to start, and what (or who) is needed to influence these variables positively?

—Do I have, or have access to, the critical external relationships with investors, lawyers, bankers, customers, suppliers, regulatory agencies, and so forth, that are necessary to pursue my opportunity, or do I need help in this area?

—What competitive advantage and strategy should I focus on, and what people are necessary to pursue this strategy or advantage?

■ *Outside Resources.* Gaps can be filled by accessing outside resources,[9] such as boards of directors, accountants, lawyers, consultants, and so forth. Usually, tax and legal expertise can best be obtained initially on a part-time basis. Other expertise (e.g., expertise required to design an inventory control system) is specialized and needed only once. Generally, if the resource is a one-time or periodic effort, or if the need is peripheral to the key tasks, goals, and activities required by the business, then such an alternative as using consultants makes sense. However, if the expertise is a must for the venture at the outset and the lead entrepreneur cannot provide it, or learn it quickly, then one or more people will have to be acquired. Some questions are:

—Is the need for specialized, one-time or part-time expertise peripheral or on the critical path?

—Will trade secrets be compromised if I obtain this expertise externally?

---

[9] See William A. Sahlman and Howard H. Stevenson, "Choosing Small Company Advisors," *Harvard Business Review,* March–April 1987.

Additional Considerations

Forming and building a team is, like marriage, a rather unscientific, occasionally unpredictable, and frequently surprising exercise — no matter how hard one may try to make it otherwise! The analogy of marriage and family, with all its accompanying complexities and consequences, is a particularly useful one. Forming a team has many of the characteristics of the courtship and marriage ritual, involving decisions based in part on emotion. There may well be a certain infatuation among team members and an aura of admiration, respect, and often fierce loyalty. Similarly, the complex psychological joys, frustrations, and uncertainties that accompany the birth and raising of children (here, the product or service) are experienced in entrepreneurial teams as well.

Thus, the following additional issues need to be considered:

■ *Values, Goals, and Commitment.* It is critical that a team be well anchored in terms of values and goals. In any new venture the participants establish psychological contracts and climates. While these are most often set when the lead entrepreneur encourages standards of excellence and respect for team members' contributions, selection of team members whose goals and values are in agreement can greatly facilitate establishment of a psychological contract and an entrepreneurial climate. In successful companies, the personal goals and values of team members align well, and the goals of the company are championed by team members as well. While this alignment may be less exact in large publicly owned corporations and greatest in small closely held firms, significant overlapping of a team member's goals with those of other team members and the overlap of corporate goals and team members' goals is desirable. Practically speaking, these evaluations of team members are some of the most difficult to make.

■ *Definition of Roles.* A diligent effort needs to be made to determine who is comfortable with and who has what responsibility for the key tasks so duplication of capabilities or responsibilities is minimized. Roles cannot be pinned down precisely for all tasks, since some key tasks and problems simply cannot be anticipated and since contributions are not always made by people originally expected to make them. Indeed, maintaining a loose, flexible, and flat structure with shared responsibility and information is desirable for utilizing individual strengths, flexibility, rapid learning, and responsive decision making.

■ *Peer Groups.* The support and approval of family, friends, and co-workers can be helpful, especially when adversity strikes. Reference group approval can be a significant source of positive reinforcement for a person's career choice and, thus, his or her entire self-image and identity.[10] Ideally, the peer group support for each team member should be there. (If it is not, the lead entrepreneur may have to accept the additional burden of encouragement and support in hard times — one which can be sizable.) Therefore, questions of whether a prospective team member's spouse is solidly in favor of his or her decision to pursue an entrepreneurial career and the "sweat equity" required and of whether the team member's close friends will be a source of support and encouragement or of detraction or negativism needs to be considered.

---

[10] Reference groups — groups consisting of individuals with whom there is frequent interaction (such as family, friends, and co-workers), with whom values and interests are shared, and from whom support and approval for activities are derived — have long been known for their influence on behavior. See John W. Thibault and Harold H. Kelley, *The Social Psychology of Groups* (New York: John Wiley & Sons, 1966).

Common Pitfalls

There can be difficulties in the practical implementation of these philosophies and attitudes, irrespective of the venture opportunity and the people involved. The company then may come unglued before it gets started, may experience infant mortality, or may live perpetually immersed in nasty divisive conflicts and power struggles that, even if they do not eventually kill the company, will certainly cripple its potential.

Often, a team lacks skill and experience in dealing with such difficult start-up issues, does not take the time to go through an extended "mating dance" among potential partners during the moonlighting phase prior to actually launching the venture, or does not seek the advice of competent advisors. As a result, such a team may be unable to deal with such sensitive issues as who gets how much ownership, who will commit what time and money or other resources, how disagreements will be resolved, and how a team member can leave or be let go. Thus, crucial early discussions among team members sometimes lead to a premature disbanding of promising teams with sound business ideas. Or, in the rush to get going, or because the funds to pay for help in these areas are lacking, a team may stay together but not work through, even in a rough way, many of these issues. Such teams do not take advantage of the moonlighting phase to test the commitment and contribution made by team members. For example, to build a substantial business, a partner needs to be totally committed to the venture. The success of the venture is the partner's most important goal, and other priorities, including his or her family, come second.[11] Another advantage of using such a shakedown period effectively is that the risks inherent in such factors as premature commitment to permanent decisions regarding salary and stock are lower.

The "common approach" to forming a new venture team also can be a common pitfall for new venture teams. Here, two to four entrepreneurs, usually friends or work-acquaintances, decide to demonstrate their equality with such democratic trimmings as equal stock ownership, equal salaries, equal office space and cars, and other items symbolizing their peer status. Left unanswered are questions of who is in charge, who makes the final decisions, and how real differences of opinion are resolved. While some overlapping of roles and a sharing in and negotiating of decisions are desirable in new venture teams, too much looseness is debilitating. Even sophisticated buy-sell agreements among partners often fail to resolve the conflicts.

Another pitfall is a belief that there are no deficiencies in the lead entrepreneur or the management team. Or, a team is overly fascinated with or overcommitted to a product idea. For example, a lead entrepreneur who is unwilling or unable to identify his own deficiencies and weaknesses and to add appropriate team members to compensate for these, and who further lacks an understanding of what is really needed to make a new venture grow into a successful business, has fallen into this pitfall.[12]

Failing to recognize that creating and building a new venture is a dynamic process is a problem for some teams. Therefore, such teams fail to realize that initial agreements are likely not to reflect actual contributions of team members over time, regardless of how much time one devotes to team-building tasks and regardless of the agreements team members make before start-up. In addition, they fail to consider that teams are likely to change in composition over time. Richard Testa, a leading attorney whose firm has

---

[11] This has been shown, for example, by Edgar H. Schein's research about entrepreneurs, general managers, and technical managers who are M.I.T. alumni. See the *Proceedings* of the Eastern Academy of Management meeting, May 1972, Boston.

[12] J. A. Timmons presented a discussion of these entrepreneurial characteristics at the First International Conference on Entrepreneurship. See "Entrepreneurial Behavior," *Proceedings,* First International Conference on Entrepreneurship, Center for Entrepreneurial Studies, Toronto, November 1973.

dealt with such ventures as Lotus Development Corporation and with numerous venture capital firms, recently startled those attending a seminar[13] on raising venture capital by saying:

The only thing that I can tell you with great certainty about this start-up business has to do with you and your partners. I can virtually guarantee you, based on our decade plus of experience, that five years from now at least one of the founders will have left every company represented here today.

Such a team, therefore, fails to put in place mechanisms that will facilitate and help structure graceful divorces and that will provide for the internal adjustments required as the venture grows.

Destructive motivations in investors, prospective team members, or the lead entrepreneur spell trouble. Teams that are not alert to signs of potentially destructive motivations, such as an early concern for power and control by a team member, suffer.

Finally, new venture teams may take trust for granted. Integrity is important in long-term business success, and the world is full of high-quality, ethical people; yet the real world also is inhabited by predators, crooks, sharks, frauds, and imposters. It is paradoxical that an entrepreneur cannot succeed without trust, but he or she probably cannot succeed with blind trust either. Trust is something that is earned, usually slowly, for it requires a lot of patience and a lot of testing in the real world. This is undoubtedly a major reason why investors prefer to see teams that have worked closely together. In the area of trust, a little cynicism goes a long way, and teams that do not pay attention to detail, such as performing due diligence with respect to a person or firm, fall into this pit.

REWARDS AND INCENTIVES

The Reward System

John L. Hayes and the late Brian Haslett of Venture Founders Corporation have made a major contribution in the area of reward systems, and the following is based on their work.

The reward system of a new venture includes both the financial rewards of a venture—such as stock, salary, and fringe benefits—*and* the chance to realize personal growth and goals, exercise autonomy, and develop skills in particular venture roles. Also, what is perceived as a reward by any single team member will vary. This perception will depend very much upon personal values, goals, and aspirations. Some may seek long-range capital gains while others desire more short-term security and income.

The reward system established for a new venture team should facilitate the interface of the venture opportunity and the management team. It needs to flow from team formation and enhance the entrepreneurial climate of the venture and the building of an effective team. For example, being able to attract and keep high-quality team members depends, to a great extent, on financial and psychological rewards given. The skills, experience, commitment, risk, concern, and so forth of these team members are secured through these rewards.

The rewards available to an entrepreneurial team vary somewhat over the life of a venture. While intangible rewards, such as opportunity for self-development and realization, may be available throughout, some of the financial rewards are more or less appropriate at different stages of the venture's development.

---

[13] The seminar, held at Babson College, was called "Raising Venture Capital," and was cosponsored by *Venture Capital Journal* and Coopers & Lybrand.

Because these rewards are so important and because, in its early stages, a venture is limited in the rewards it can offer, the *total* reward system over the life of the venture needs to be thought through very carefully and efforts be made to assure that the venture's capacity to reward is not limited as levels of contribution change or as new personnel are added.

External issues also have an impact on the reward system created for a new venture. It is important to realize that the division of equity between the venture and external investors will affect how much of the equity is available to the team members. Further, the way a venture deals with these questions also will determine its credibility with investors and others, because these people will look to the reward system for signs of commitment by the venture team.

Critical Issues

It is an early critical task for the lead entrepreneur to lead, based on the philosophy and vision discussed earlier, in dividing ownership among the founding team. Investors may provide advice but will, more often than not, dump the issue squarely back in the lap of the lead entrepreneur, since whether and how these delicate ownership decisions are resolved often is seen by investors as an important litmus test.

Also, the process by which a reward system is decided and the commitment of each team member to deal with problems in a way which will assure that rewards continue to reflect performance is of utmost importance. Each key team member needs to be committed to working out solutions that reflect the commitments, risks, and anticipated relative contributions of team members as fairly as possible.

A good reward system reflects the goals of the particular venture and is in tune with valuations. If a venture is not seeking outside capital, outside owners need not be considered; but the same issues need to be resolved. For example, if a goal is to realize a substantial capital gain from the venture in the next 5 to 10 years, then the reward system needs to be aimed at reinforcing this goal and encouraging the long-term commitment required for its attainment.

There are no time-tested formulas or simple answers to questions of how distributions should be made. However, the following issues should be considered:

- *Differentiation.* The democracy approach can work, but it involves higher risk and more pitfalls than a system that differentiates based on the value of contributions by team members. As a rule, different team members rarely contribute the same amount to the venture, and the reward system needs to recognize these differences.
- *Performance.* Reward needs to be a function of performance (as opposed to effort) during the early life of the venture and not during only one part of this period. Many ventures have been torn apart when the relative contributions of the team members changed dramatically several years after start-up without a significant change in rewards. (Vesting goes a long way toward dealing with this issue.)
- *Flexibility.* Regardless of the contribution of any team member at any given time, the probability is high that this will change over time. The performance of a team member may be substantially more or less than anticipated. Further, a team member may have to be replaced and someone may have to be recruited and added to the existing team. Flexibility in the reward system, including such mechanisms as vesting and setting aside a portion of stock for future adjustments, can help to provide a sense of justice.

Considerations of Timing

Again, division of rewards, such as the split of stock between the members of the entrepreneurial team, will most likely be made very early in the life of the venture. Rewards may be a way of attracting significant early contribution; however, it is performance over the life of the venture that needs to be rewarded.

For example, regarding equity, once the allocation of stock is decided, changes in the relative stock positions of team members will be infrequent. New team members or external investors may dilute each member's position, but the relative positions will probably remain unchanged.

However, one or more events may occur during the early years of a venture. First, a team member who has a substantial portion of stock may not perform and need to be replaced early in the venture. Or, a key team member may find a better opportunity and quit. Or, a key team member could die in an accident. In each of the above cases, the team will then be faced with the question of what will happen to the stock held by the team member. In each case, stock was intended as a reward for performance by the team member during the first several years of the venture, but the team member will not perform over this time period.

In the case of equity, several mechanisms are available to a venture when initial stock split is so made that the loss or freezing of equity can be avoided. To illustrate, a venture can retain an option of returning to its treasury stock at the price at which it was purchased in certain cases, such as when a team member needs to be replaced. A buy-back agreement is a mechanism to achieve this purpose.

To guard against the event that some portion of the stock has been earned and some portion will remain unearned, as when a team member quits or when one dies, the venture can place stock purchased by team members in escrow to be released over a two- or three-year period. Such a mechanism is called a "stock-vesting agreement," and such an agreement can foster longer-term commitment to the success of the venture, while, at the same time, providing a method for a civilized "no-fault" corporate divorce if things do not work out. Such a stock-vesting agreement is attached as a restriction on the stock certificate. Typically, the vesting agreement establishes a period of years, often four or more. During this period, the founding stockholders can "earn out" their shares. If a founder decides to leave the company prior to completion of the four-year vesting period, he or she may be required to sell the stock back to the company for the price that was originally paid for it, usually nothing. The departing shareholder, in this instance, would not own any stock after the departure. Nor would any capital gain windfall be realized by the departing founder. In other cases, founders may vest a certain portion each year, so they have some shares even if they leave. Such vesting can be weighted toward the last year or two of the vesting period. Other restrictions can give management and the board control over the disposition of stock, whether or not the stockholder stays or leaves the company. In essence, a mechanism such as a stock-vesting agreement confronts team members with the reality that "this is not a get-rich-quick exercise."

Other rewards, such as salary, stock options, bonuses, and fringe benefits, can be manipulated more readily to reflect changes in performance. But the ability to manipulate these, too, is somewhat dependent upon the stage of development of the venture. In the case of cash rewards, there is a trade-off between giving cash and the growth of the venture. Thus, in the early months of a venture, salaries will necessarily be low or nonexistent, and bonuses and other fringe benefits usually will be out of the question. Salaries, bonuses, and fringe benefits all drain cash, and, until profitability is achieved, cash can always be put to use for operations. After profitability is achieved, cash payments will still limit growth. Salaries can become competitive once the venture has passed breakeven, but bonuses and fringe benefits should probably be kept at a minimum until several years of profitability have been demonstrated.

Considerations of Value

Of course, the contributions of team members will vary in nature, extent, and timing. In developing the reward system, and particularly the distribution of stock, contributions in certain areas are of particular value to a venture, as follows:

- *Idea.*   In this area, the originator of the idea, particularly if trade secrets or special technology if a prototype was developed, or if product or market research was done, needs to be considered.
- *Business plan preparation.*   Preparing an acceptable business plan, in terms of dollars and hours expended, needs to be considered.
- *Commitment and risk.*   A team member may invest a large percentage of his or her net worth in the company, be at risk if the company fails, have to make personal sacrifices, put in long hours and major effort, risk his or her reputation, accept reduced salary, or already have spent a large amount of time on behalf of the venture. This commitment and risk need to be considered.
- *Skills, experience, track record, or contacts.*   A team member may bring to the venture skills, experience, track record, or contacts in such areas as marketing, finance, and technology. If these are of critical importance to the new venture and are not readily available, these need to be considered.
- *Responsibility.*   The importance of a team member's role to the success of the venture needs to be considered.

Being the originator of the idea or expending a great amount of time or money in preparing the business plan are frequently overvalued. Evaluated in terms of the real success of the venture down the road, it is difficult to justify much more than 15 percent to 20 percent of equity for these two items. Commitment and risk, skills, experience, and responsibility contribute more by far to producing success of a venture.

The above list is valuable in attempting to weigh fairly the relative contributions of each team member. Contributions in each of these areas have some value; it is up to a team to agree on how to assign value to contributions and, further, to leave enough flexibility to allow for changes.

CASE – BEANTOWN SEAFOODS, INC.

Preparation Questions

1. Contrast BSI's actual performance with the performance predicted in the original Halsey & Halsey, Inc., business plan (see the H & H case, Chapter 2). What impact does your analysis of BSI have on your earlier view of the opportunity?
2. After reviewing the chapters on opportunity analysis, what are the characteristics here of the opportunity and how "forgiving and rewarding" are the economics?
3. How does the opportunity compare with the one for Outdoor Scene, Inc. (see Chapter 1) and for Fibercom Applications, Inc. (see Chapter 3)?
4. What are the Halseys actually taking out of the business in total compensation and benefits? Have the Halseys made a good or a poor decision to go into business for themselves, and why do you think so?
5. First as a founder and then as a potential buyer of the business, determine what you believe the company is worth (i.e., the price that should be paid) at the end of the case.

BEANTOWN SEAFOODS, INC.

In early 1981, George Halsey, 27, was contemplating the next step in his entrepreneurial career. He had joined his father's company, Beantown Seafoods, in early 1978—at which point the 18-month-old venture had realized a profit of $13,000 on sales of $70,000. Over the next four years, George had played a key role in building the firm's sales dramatically, to nearly $5 million in 1980.

When George joined the firm, which—at his advice—was a corporation, rather than a sole proprietorship, his father, Daniel, agreed to give him 5 percent of the stock for every year that George was employed and the remainder of the shares when Daniel retired in 1984. Back in 1978, Daniel had been skeptical about why George wanted shares. "What is the value of all this? It's just you and I and a desk and a telephone and $70,000 in sales." "Dad," George replied, "I'm going to make it worth something. I'm going to build this business." On this note, both men informally agreed to the arrangement.

By 1981, however, with a projected $6 million in sales, Daniel had indicated that he wasn't sure he was going to keep the "gentleman's agreement"—and George wasn't sure how that would affect his future. After all, it was his original plan—see Halsey & Halsey, Inc., in Chapter 2—and the 90-hour weeks he had spent building the business that had been in great part responsible for the success of the company. Meanwhile, George had married and had a son. While acknowledging the personal growth and excitement of the past four years, George also realized that his father was a difficult man to work with and was set in his ways about certain aspects of doing business. To make things more difficult, George felt a sense of sadness because his father had never told him how much his efforts had been appreciated.

George was young and had an excellent track record in the industry. He loved the work, begrudging only the long hours that kept him from wife and son. His feelings toward his father were mixed. He felt that he had to do something about the situation soon—but what? And how would it change his future?

Company History: 1976–1978

Beantown Seafoods (BSI) was founded in 1976 by Daniel Halsey in Boston. Daniel intended to establish himself as a broker/wholesaler of fresh fish.[1] At age 55, Daniel had left his position as sales and marketing manager of a major frozen fish company in the wake of an internal corporate shakeup. Daniel, who had worked in the fish industry all his life, saw a niche for himself in the fresh fish area because of two major industry trends: The volume of fish caught was expected to increase after the 200-mile-limit law took effect, and the transportation of fresh fish to the Midwest and West had been greatly simplified by the introduction of wide-bodied jets.

BSI functioned as a service—a buyer and seller of processed (cleaned and filleted) fresh fish. Unlike a broker, however, BSI actually took possession of the fish, though it maintained no inventory. Its orders were received in three ways:

1. *Source initiated.* The supplier offered BSI a specific amount of fish at a specific price. BSI contacted its customers to determine need and then called the supplier to place an order.
2. *Customer initiated.* The request for an order came from the customer to BSI, which then checked with a number of suppliers to see whether the order could be filled within the

---

[1] See the case appendix for a note on the New England fishing industry.

customer's price range. BSI then contacted the customer with the findings and, at the customer's request, placed an order.

3. *BSI initiated.* Occasionally, BSI would recommend that a customer augment or diversify his product line. If the customer agreed, BSI checked with suppliers and placed the order.

The "hands-on" part of the operation occurred when BSI packaged individual customer orders from the bulk order. The packages would then be shipped by truck to the customer or to the airport.

Because of an agreement with two processors of perch, Beantown Seafoods opened operations with a single species — and targeted the Midwest and Southwest as the prime market area. The small amount of Atlantic fresh fish consumed there had been hauled by truck and was not all that fresh on arrival. In the early 1970s, airfreight cost 50 cents/pound; by 1976, the cost had dropped to 10 cents/pound and containers had been developed to hold 3,000 pounds of fish.

However, the airfreight concept had not worked smoothly. Unreliable route scheduling interfered with distribution on a regular basis. For example, wide-bodied jets flew to Florida only in winter months and were routed elsewhere during the summer. In the case of a newly-developed Phoenix market, the Boston–Phoenix route was suddenly dropped, and with it BSI's potential profits.

During 1976–77 George was attending Northeastern Business School in Boston. As part of a New Venture Strategy course, he wrote a business plan for Beantown Seafoods, with emphasis on redirecting the marketing strategy and increasing the product line. After graduation, he joined a large conglomerate in New York as a product manager; but before long he could no longer resist the challenge of joining his father's company and working to implement his new plans. He joined Beantown Seafoods in early 1978.

Company Operations: 1978–1981

Looking back over the years since he had joined the company, George gave his views of the company's growth and operations.

Market Repositioning

When George joined BSI, the company had a customer base of five; relied heavily on a single species of fish, perch; and shipped almost exclusively by airfreight to its major market, the Midwest. Beginning in 1978, George convinced his father to change the strategy radically. BSI began to compete in the traditional developed markets on the East Coast — supplying supermarkets with fresh fish via trucks. George believed that BSI could penetrate these markets by capitalizing on the chaos that customers felt in the highly fragmented industry and on the dissatisfaction that supermarkets experienced with the existing sources of supply, indicated by a lack of customer loyalty. BSI decided to stake its reputation and its ability to expand operations by providing quality and reliability to its customers; George intended to position BSI as "the buyer's buyer."

One important move on the supply side was to develop a strong chain of suppliers along the East Coast so as to be able to take advantage of the best prices. Since BSI began exclusively as a distributor of perch, George and Daniel had to develop new suppliers of other species. They also had to keep their present perch suppliers happy, and, in the main, this was accomplished by guaranteeing the perch suppliers year-round sales.

Exhibit A

Fresh haddock fillets	_____	Fresh ocean perch	_____
Fresh cod fillets	_____	Fresh ocean catfish	_____
Fresh pollock fillets	_____	Fresh sole fillets	_____
Fresh hake fillets	_____	Fresh grey sole	_____
Fresh cusk fillets	_____		
	_____		_____
Fresh swordfish	_____	Fresh black sea bass	_____
Fresh scup (porgies)	_____	Fresh striped bass	_____
Fresh butterfish	_____	Fresh shark	_____
Fresh mackerel	_____	Fresh whiting	_____
Fresh native bluefish	_____	Fresh halibut	_____
Fresh sea trout	_____	Fresh fluke	_____
	_____		_____
Sea scallops	_____	Littleneck clams	_____
Bay scallops	_____	Topnecks	_____
Cape scallops	_____	Cherrystones	_____
Lobster (chickens)	_____	Quahogs	_____
Lobster (1¼s)	_____	Steamers	_____
Lobster (1½s)	_____	Frying clams	_____
Lobster (2–3s)	_____	Mussels	_____
Lobster (3+)	_____	Crab	_____
	_____	Shrimp	_____
_____	_____	_____	_____

On the demand side, two major areas needed attention: BSI had to encourage its old customers (of which there were only five originals) to carry other fish than perch, and it had to find new customers who were receptive to carrying a variety of species. As George described it:

With the perch situation, we saw the kind of control we had. We didn't really understand it. It was kind of like the Arabs. They had all the oil for years and never knew what it really meant. Well, we did the same thing. We knew that we had the perch, and we didn't really twist their arms, but we certainly let it be known we wanted to sell other species. So, if you want the perch, you buy other things. We never came out and said it; we just positioned ourselves that way. That expanded our product line. So our objective now is to continue to try to build up species and downplay the perch.

Now we have maybe 100–150 customers. Our largest customer represents about 5 percent of the whole business. We did that purposely just to try to minimize the risk we'd have from any one customer accounting for a big percent of our sales.

My father had very hard perceptual problems understanding what we were trying to do. At times he tried to hold me back from growing too fast, but I felt the risk was too great if we didn't expand.

As of 1980, Beantown Seafoods sold more than 35 species of fish. *Exhibit A* is a partial listing. The species accounting for most of the 1980 sales were: ocean perch, 22 percent; sole fillets, 18 percent; scallops, 12.2 percent; and cod fillets, 11.4 percent. *Exhibit B* is a complete list of sales by product line.

Almost 100 percent of BSI's sales came from the Midwest in 1976, versus 40 percent in 1980. BSI distributed to markets in Chicago, Detroit, Rochester, Buffalo, Dallas, Houston, Fort Worth, and Los Angeles. *Exhibit C* gives BSI's sales by region for 1980.

George's marketing philosophy can be simply stated: He does not accept the idea that a buyer is ever perfectly content with his existing supplier or his existing business. In the face of resistance, George continues to try to establish new accounts because if he can make a *buyer's* business grow, BSI grows with it.

Exhibit B
Beantown Seafoods Sales by Product Line for Fiscal Year Ending October 31, 1980

Product	$ Sales	Percent of Total
Perch	$1,063,300	22.0%
Sole	867,300	17.9
Scallops	589,800	12.2
Cod	552,500	11.4
Haddock	322,700	6.7
Swordfish	303,300	6.3
Monk	219,300	4.5
Cat/cusk	193,400	4.0
Shellfish	189,800	3.9
Pollock	152,300	3.1
Wholefish	146,800	3.0
Lobster	80,700	1.7
Miscellaneous	68,100	1.4
Shrimp	55,300	1.1
Hake	20,500	0.4
Crab	9,600	0.2
Tuna	4,600	0.1
Frozen	1,300	0.1

Exhibit C
Beantown Seafoods Sales by Region for Fiscal Year Ending October 31, 1980

Region	$ Sales	Number of Customers	COGS
Chicago	$ 855,736	12	$ 781,000
Cleveland	1,735,148	13	1,601,035
Rochester/Buffalo	680,383	18	635,318
Detroit	240,944	4	222,403
Boston	147,476	9	134,247
Albany	7,004	2	6,242
Long Island	20,506	1	18,573
Denver	195,273	4	173,040
Los Angeles	234,220	4	211,921
Local Massachusetts	383,000	107	349,600
Miami	169,519	7	142,243
Omaha	19,038	2	18,144
Jackson	33,568	1	30,314
Oakland	4,322	1	3,924
Renn.	30,794	6	28,886
Miscellaneous	28,037	4	25,540
New air business	64,800	N.A.	N.A.
Total	$4,857,800		

Understanding the Marketplace: The Suppliers

Fish, like any other commodity, has its own unwritten code of operations, and George and Daniel were determined to learn the business carefully so as to establish trusting relationships and thereby ensure reliability. The three key variables are quality, quantity, and price. The two methods of doing business are at the pier and over the phone. The following anecdotes illustrate the difficult but successful job that BSI has done in establishing good relationships with its suppliers.

Since price varies daily and contracts must be signed days and weeks in advance, some suppliers will sell to the highest bidder regardless of previous arrangements.

You call up one fish plant and order 2,000 pounds of cod fillets. The truck is going to be there at 4 o'clock to pick it up. The supermarket and the supplier (processing plant or wholesaler) agree on a price of $1.40 per pound: a good price for that day. The supplier realizes it is a great price and has a chance to sell it for $1.60 per pound. So he sells it. He doesn't notify the supermarket buyer. He just sells it for $1.60 per pound. The supermarket truck is there at 10 minutes until four to pick it up. The supplier says, "I'm sorry. I didn't get the fish off the boat." So here's the supermarket truck with no product on it, and the ad is running in the paper the next day.

To avoid this pitfall, Daniel and George devised several strategies. First, they offered a premium per pound (5–10 cents) to those suppliers who they believed were reliable. Next, they established several groups of informal co-ops along the East Coast, groups of independent processors with unwritten agreements to trade with others—based on a bond of common trust. These co-ops guaranteed BSI a given supply of fish and set a minimum price; BSI pledged to resell it for at least that price and usually more. This arrangement allowed BSI to get the variety and volume of product it needed.

Another problem has been the relatively high turnover of new suppliers and the difficulty of monitoring the competition. New companies start up overnight; overhead costs are low. New companies disappear; one of BSI's suppliers went out of business overnight when three cutters quit and each went into business for himself.

A third problem hinges on a strategic decision: price versus volume. George's initial plan favored volume and the concomitant buying power that this strategy would bring to the company.

I would rather do a lot of volume for a low profit than a lot of profit with low volume just because of the buying power. Here's an example. There's a guy down on the pier who we've been with since day one of the corporation. But he's always been higher in price. Our sales with him have been pretty consistent. Through the grapevine he learned how significantly we'd grown. He really started to work on price. He originally quoted me $1.80 on cod. The same day he calls back and says, "If I got you $1.50 on cod, how many pounds would you be interested in?" I said, "How many could you get?" He says, "How many would you want? 500? 600? 700?" I said, "Well, how many could you get?" He says, "Maybe 3,000 pounds." I said, "Fine, I'll take them." He says, incredulously, "You want 3,000?" I said, "Yes. If you get more, give me a call." He called back and said, "I can get you another 500–600." I said, "OK. Give them to me." That's buying power.

However, George had to learn about pricing at the wholesale level the hard way, and also about the importance of keeping certain information private. Here is one of his early experiences:

I had to buy some perch from the pier. I was buying 200–300 pounds for two or three different clients. I was buying it at $1.50/pound. One supplier says, "My price is $1.80/pound." I said, "Come on, I'm buying it at $1.50 from everyone else. Why give you $1.80?" He said, "Who are you buying it from at $1.50?" Like a jerk, I said, "I'm buying it from him, him, and him." He said, "My price is $1.80. Take it or leave it." I had to have it, so I took it. Ten minutes later I get three phone calls from the other plants I named. They said, "What are you doing telling this guy what I'm selling to you for?" Like a fool, I got caught with my pants down. So, if you know something, keep it to yourself.

Quality is another problem. It is possible for a supplier to alter the decaying appearance of a less-than-fresh fish by passing it through salt water. "Brining" gives the fish a fresh sheen and is not easy to detect.

A supplier can also pass off one species for another. For instance, there are three sizes of cod fillets: market cod (average $1.50/pound), scrod cod (average $1.40/pound) and anything below scrod cod specifications, called snapper (average $1/pound). On one occasion, a supplier sold scrod to BSI with snapper mixed in. George got a call from the angry customer and confronted the supplier:

Bob, the scrod fillets look beautiful on the top, but when you look down in the box, there's a lot of snapper and broken, raggy fillets. What did you do, machine-cut these? What are you doing, hiring blind people? Bob, there's no way you could miss those raggy fillets. There are snapper in there, and that's really what the objection is. We pay $1.45 for scrod cod, and that's what we expect. Not snapper. I can buy snapper for $1. It's really a short-term gain on your part to do something like that.

Since the industry is small, information travels fast. Like all shrewd commodities traders, Daniel and George have had to learn when to blow the whistle and when to stay mum; whom to trust and whom to stay away from. The result of their experience and sensitivity is reflected on the bottom line — their ability to buy and sell fish.

Understanding the Marketplace: The Customers

The customers, for the most part, are supermarkets. Until recently, few supermarkets carried fresh fish, and those that did carried a limited selection. The supermarkets didn't understand how to market fish to the consumer, and the consumer was not in the habit of buying fresh fish from supermarkets. Thus, the first big job facing Daniel and George had been to help the supermarkets promote fresh fish.

First, the supermarkets had to be convinced of both the reliability and the quality of BSI's service. This meant fresh product, delivered when promised at a prearranged price. Next, the supermarkets had to be educated in how to display the fish, what temperature to hold them at, and how long their "shelf life" was, depending on species. Finally, the supermarkets needed to be educated in point-of-sale and media promotion. Luckily for BSI, the consumer demand for fresh fish had already begun, so the burden of education did not fall solely on Daniel and George. Still, remarked George, "it's been a long educational process for us to try to educate literally thousands of retail stores with only two guys."

The next best sources of customers are retail fish stores. Here, BSI must emphasize the importance of broadening their product line. Getting the customers is only part of the problem; customers can be a tricky lot. George requires the directness from his customers that he demands of himself, and sometimes he has to pressure them to develop this quality. For example, George quoted a customer a price of $1.35/pound for some product. When BSI received payment of $1.25/pound, George reminded the customer of the original quote. The customer's response was that he had recorded it for $1.25. George explained how he handled the situation.

There's nothing you can do about it. You don't know if he did it legitimately or not. But I have an old saying, "I don't get even, I get better." So when things are short and I know I can make more money, I do it. If I normally earn 5 cents a pound and a schmuck calls up, I'll put on 20 cents. If a customer takes advantage of me, I'm going to try to get even with him. On the other hand, if a good customer is in a bind, I'll bend over backwards to get him what he needs at the best price I can.

An unwritten rule in the industry, where the market changes every day, is: whatever you buy that day is at that price. If fish is bought one day but not shipped until the next, if the price dropped in 24 hours, the customer pays the quoted price on the day of sale. George talks about a customer who didn't want to play by the rules:

One customer had 3,000–4,000 pounds of product. When the market price dropped, he called up and said, "Lower your price." We said, "We can't. We're fixed at that price." He said, "Cancel my order." He did that three times, so I won't even talk to him any more. He still calls us because there are only so many kingpins that everything eventually has to come through, and we have slowly developed into one of those kingpins.

BSI makes most of its profit in the winter because it has access to an adequate fish supply. Nonregular customers come back to BSI in the winter. One of its customers wouldn't buy from BSI during the rest of the year because BSI was two cents higher. When supply was short in the winter, the customer came to BSI offering the two-cent difference. George refused his business because he had regular customers who never questioned his pricing.

This unwritten code of George's sometimes makes his customers mad. Some of his customers buy from the Canadians because of their lower prices. George told these customers that he could service them better if they bought from him on a regular basis. In the winter, when BSI carries a full product line, George doesn't sell to them.

George has learned to beat customers at their own games. In another transaction, BSI shipped product to a customer in Chicago. The customer called to say it was bad quality. George said, "OK, I'll take care of it." The customer responded, "How are you going to take care of it?" George said, "Watch." George called him back 10 minutes later and said, "I took care of it. I'm having it picked up by your competitor," another of BSI's accounts. The second account confirmed the shipment's high quality. The first customer never played the game again.

BSI's growth has come through its excellent reputation, not through market research. George believes that market research is not much help in this industry; "market research would probably help tell you a customer's perception of BSI," but George believes that the surest test of a customer's perception is the size and longevity of his account with the firm. "The researcher would have to be careful," he commented. "Otherwise, the customer would probably hang up."

Distribution

BSI ships 80 percent of its product by truck. Shipping costs are subject to fluctuation, since one or two of the trucking firms have a virtual monopoly over their routes.

BSI sells to supermarkets both directly and indirectly, since the company also wholesales to other buyers that resell to the supermarkets. Even though the supermarket pays another markup, it often will choose to do so if it is more convenient to deal with a local wholesaler. Yet, supermarkets often request a quote from BSI to confirm the price quoted by their supplier.

Physical Plant

BSI began operations in the immediate area of the Boston fish pier. In 1980, it relocated several miles inland, in Roxbury, Massachusetts. The area is a deteriorating, forbidding warehouse section of the city. Rent is artificially low. The plant is approximately 3,500 square feet in size. The fish-handling area, though dimly lit and crowded with waist-high tin fish containers, appears to be efficient. In addition to office space, there are a 600-foot freezer and 1,500 square feet of unused space.

Pricing Policies and Strategies

BSI's profit margins compare with those of supermarkets: 1 to 2 percent. Labor accounts for most of the fixed costs.

Daniel and George differ sharply over pricing strategy. Take this example: BSI commits to buy a given amount of fish from a processor at $1.60/pound. If it sells the fish for $1.70/pound, it makes a profit; if the price drops to $1.30/pound, it loses 30 cents/pound. However, the given amount is usually less than the entire volume needed that day, so BSI picks up the rest at the best price it can get.

Daniel expects to sell at a marked-up price in every transaction. Under Daniel's philosophy, BSI would sell the $1.60 cod for $1.70 and the $1.30 cod for $1.45. George, on the contrary, averages the cost of the two together and sells the entire lot for the average amount. He believes that the averaging system works well for his transactions.

George's guiding principle is to go for volume, not price. The lack of seasonality at BSI, which is not typical of the industry, allows it to avoid the shortsighted view of expecting to mark up every individual transaction. The same principle justifies his paying a premium (5 or 10 cents/pound) to reliable suppliers. He sees volume as a buffer if one or two deals go sour.

Suppose the customer starts playing games with you. For example, you sell first-quality codfish to a buyer in Chicago for $1.50/pound. When the product gets to Chicago, the customer calls to say that the quality is questionable and wants 20 cents per pound deducted from the price. There goes your profit. You have to sell a lot of fish to make up for that.

George also buys fish on speculation, that is, without a specific customer order. Historically, BSI bought fish by returning to the processing plants several times a day to purchase small quantities every time a customer called. This was a serious problem for the plants because they had to plan how much fish to buy. George started to give the plants a one-day advance on what his requirements would be. Daniel felt that this was speculation because George didn't know whether the fish would sell or not. He thought the next step was bankruptcy.

In 1979, George successfully gambled on a $15,000 investment in swordfish. In 1980, he speculated on $60,000 of swordfish. He is aware of the risk he is taking. "One of my competitors did the same thing when the FDA first banned swordfish. Well, even if I turned all my swordfish into cat food, I'd probably go bankrupt overnight, so I take two Excedrin every day and hope the FDA will go away."

George sees the greatest opportunity for expanding profit margins on sales in the undeveloped markets, where the concept of selling fresh fish is more unfamiliar and the market will bear the markup. Margins average between 5 and 10 cents/pound in the mature, traditional markets; George estimates that BSI can earn 25–30 cents/pound in the undeveloped markets, a few of which he has already explored. It takes time, however, to develop buyers in distant markets who (1) don't buy fresh fish in volume and (2) don't buy blind from East Coast suppliers whom they don't know and whom they would have to learn to trust. In BSI's experience, winning one influential buyer generally opens the door to other buyers. One supermarket chain feels compelled to carry the same product line as that carried by its competitors. However, George admits that several competitors are going after these markets, too.

Employee Relations

George works at being an effective manager. He tries to develop a team spirit among his 10 employees. When recruiting new employees, he tries to evaluate whether they will fit in with the others and he avoids hiring "superstars who I then have to squash." BSI employed a truck driver who believed it was his job just to drive the truck. George says, "In a small company you can't have a guy just to drive the truck. He's got to move boxes, run down to the store to get lunch; he's got to do everything."

George works side by side with his employees in the warehouse. He wears the smell of fish and a green uniform with everyone else. The rapport he's built with his employees conveys to them that he cares about what they're doing. "And every night before they go home, I make sure I say to them, 'Thank you very much for coming in. I appreciate your help.' Because I really do."

BSI has made mistakes and has worked to correct them. Most of them stem from George's implicit trust in the people he works with. At the outset, employee policies were liberal and informal, and began to be abused. Now there is a formal policy for sick leave and a no-personal-loan policy. George and Daniel feel that their casualness was an expensive lesson, but, as George remarked, "you never really know what's going to come up until it's come up."

George also has learned some lessons about whom to hire. Early on, in an effort to expand operations beyond the supermarket customer, George decided to try selling direct to the Boston-area restaurants. BSI hired an experienced restaurant salesman at $20,000 a year to develop this business. George believes in delegating authority, but at the time he did not realize the necessity of monitoring operations as well. Before long, BSI faced serious cash flow problems from the restaurant operation because customers were not paying their bills on time. Sensing imminent disaster, since BSI was a cash-intensive business, George fired the salesman and turned the project over to his brother Timothy, whom Daniel had hired as a supermarket salesman. Timothy hadn't shown much promise in this capacity; George described Timothy as "a social crusader, nonbusiness type with latent entrepreneurial qualities." Taking a chance, George set Timothy up as an independent contractor, while George maintained direct control over the restaurant payment schedule. The new arrangement suited Timothy's temperament well, and restaurant accounts rose to 5 percent of sales. "Timothy is getting kind of cocky now," laughed George. "Now he's thinking of buying from other sources."

George reluctantly admits that he is a victim of the old adage, "Never bring a friend into the business." George hired a friend to coordinate purchasing and distribution from the plants. He perceived his friend to be intelligent, with strong management ability. To his dismay, George discovered that his friend couldn't perform the task that he was hired for. He transferred the friend to the computer control operation and recently gave him a $2,000 raise; George feels that he can't fire him because he is a friend.

George hired another employee who was so good that BSI couldn't hold on to him. George taught Jerry the fish business. He was George's right-hand man for 1.5 years before he was hired away by one of BSI's competitors at twice his BSI salary.

Finances

The company was incorporated on November 1, 1977. The financial data on the operating history since 1977 are found in *Exhibits D* through *H*.

In 1980, George's objective was to stabilize fixed costs. He kept the number of his labor force stable. He increased volume, hoping that profits would skyrocket. They did. In 1980, net profits quadrupled (see *Exhibit G*).

Since trading fish is a cash business, theoretically, the account collection period is short. BSI did not finance receivables until eight months after it started business. Fishermen are paid in cash for their catch. BSI's suppliers have to have cash. BSI pays its processing plants within 14 days. In the early years, this was a hard goal. BSI, in turn, must be paid by its customers on time. Accounts over 30 days are bad accounts.

Daniel and George take very little money out of the business. They retain it for working capital, "to try to quicken the pace." Through inattention, BSI's checking account can contain $200,000 at any one time. George does not have the time or the extra personnel to attend to his cash flow right now. He realizes that he's neglecting the management of his working capital, but he sees no alternative at this time.

Because of its inexperience with credit, BSI had some bad accounts in the first few years. In 1976, it was selling product to a fresh fish distributor in LA whose sales to local restaurants ran about $86,000/week. The customer entered the restaurant business himself but neglected to tell BSI. Beantown Seafoods lost $15,000 because of the mail system. It takes five–seven

Exhibit D

BEANTOWN SEAFOODS, INC.
Balance Sheet
October 31, 1978
(Inception—November 1, 1977)

Assets

Current assets:		$ 12,103.26
Cash...		
Accounts receivable..............................		121,138.03
Prepaid items....................................		1,302.90
Total current assets..........................		134,544.19
Property and equipment (at cost):		
Office furniture and fixtures........................	$15,570.88	
Motor vehicle...................................	4,620.00	
	20,190.88	
Less: Accumulated depreciation...................	3,602.50	16,588.38
Security deposits.................................		945.42
Organization costs, unamortized....................		364.90
Notes and loans—officer...........................		875.42
		$153,318.31

Liabilities and Stockholders' Equity

Current liabilities:		
Accounts payable................................		$104,336.26
Salaries and wages payable.......................		18,000.00
Chattel mortgage payable—motor vehicle..........		1,361.16
Notes payable—bank (unsecured).................		6,644.76
Taxes withheld, accrued and payable..............		3,588.50
Total current liabilities........................		133,930.68
Long-term debt (net):		
Chattel mortgage payable—motor vehicle..........	$ 1,020.87	
Notes payable—bank (unsecured)................	3,876.11	4,896.98
Stockholders' equity:		
Capital stock—common—no par value:		
Authorized—12,500 shares		
Issued and outstanding—1,000 shares...........	2,000.00	
Investment tax credit............................	2,032.69	
Retained earnings *(Exhibit E)*......................	10,457.96	14,490.65
		$153,318.31

Accompanying accountants' report is an integral part of this unaudited statement.

---

days to receive a check in Boston from the West Coast. By the time the check is processed and mailed back to the customer's bank, marked "insufficient funds," 10–15 days have passed. Meanwhile, BSI was supplying the customer with fish. The original debt was $20,000 until Daniel flew to LA to collect payment. The customer gave Daniel a check for $5,000 as advance payment for more product. BSI never shipped the product.

After this experience, BSI tightened up its credit procedures. It established accounts in local banks in distant markets. The accounts deposit checks directly in the local banks. George calls the bank to confirm that the customer's check will clear. If it doesn't, BSI doesn't ship the product. It has been able to cut its losses on bad debts from $21,000 in 1979 to $9,800 in 1980 *(Exhibit G)*.

Another customer filed for Chapter 11 under the Bankruptcy Act with no warning. Both the customer and BSI started in business at the same time. When BSI did its second million,

Exhibit E

BEANTOWN SEAFOODS, INC.
Statement of Net Income
for the Year Ended October 31, 1978
(Inception—November 1, 1977)

Sales.		$2,110,593.17
Cost of sales:		
Purchases.	$1,925,244.33	
Freight.	14,273.81	
Outside services.	18,164.86	
Packaging.	2,899.11	
Salaries and wages.	19,733.17	1,980,315.28
Gross profit.		130,277.89
Operating and administrative expenses:		
Officer's salary.	36,000.00	
Bad debts.	12,560.16	
Depreciation.	5,602.50	
Dues and subscriptions.	119.00	
Group insurance.	1,891.94	
Insurance.	926.00	
Interest expense.	426.73	
Miscellaneous expense.	987.47	
Motor vehicle operating expense.	1,042.37	
Office and postage expense.	2,008.14	
Organization costs, amortized.	91.22	
Pension expense.	24,321.24	
Professional fees.	2,820.32	
Rent.	3,541.68	
Rental of motor vehicle.	3,843.00	
Repairs and maintenance.	823.17	
Taxes.	4,137.37	
Telephone.	11,314.43	
Travel, selling, and promotion.	5,630.15	
Utilities.	409.74	
Total operating and administrative expenses.		118,496.63
Net income from operations.		11,781.26
Interest income.	496.70	
Other income.	361.20	857.90
		12,639.16
Provision for federal income taxes.		2,181.20
Net income (transferred to Retained Earnings).		$ 10,457.96

Accompanying accountants' report is an integral part of this unaudited statement.

this customer did 12 million. Labor problems in the customer's plant were the beginning of his downfall. He was forced to sell his King Crab inventory that he had bought on speculation at a loss of $1/pound. He declared bankruptcy overnight. It cost BSI $10,000.

Summing up the present situation, George comments, "I know a lot about marketing but not much about money."

George's View—A Summary

George likes the freedom and independence of working for himself. The variety of functions he performs as a small business manager is exciting to George.

I am the chief executive officer, and I'm doing the same thing a CEO does at IBM or General Foods except on a smaller scale, and that is very exciting. I feel good that I have direct control over my success and my failures. I can determine my own fate.

Exhibit F

BEANTOWN SEAFOODS, INC.
Balance Sheet
October 31, 1980 and 1979

	1980	1979
Assets		
Current assets:		
Cash	$ 14,719.82	$ 5,766.03
Accounts receivable	610,166.90	271,407.86
Inventory	10,413.70	15,818.45
Prepaid items	1,580.85	2,948.27
Total current assets	636,881.27	295,971.11
Property and equipment (Note 1):		
Motor vehicles	34,506.30	27,799.01
Office furniture and fixtures	17,159.51	17,159.51
Machinery and equipment	480.03	3,109.47
	52,145.84	48,067.99
Less: Accumulated depreciation	16,821.85	10,440.15
Total property and equipment	35,323.99	37,627.84
Other assets:		
Security deposits	5,100.00	5,100.00
Organization costs, unamortized	–	273.70
Notes and loans—others	3,514.51	973.53
Total other assets	8,614.51	6,347.23
	$680,819.77	$339,946.18
Liabilities and Stockholders' Equity		
Current liabilities:		
Accounts payable	$452,752.65	$234,518.30
Chattel mortgages payable	7,724.68	6,148.08
Notes payable—bank	50,000.00	3,876.11
Accrued salaries payable	47,900.00	4,600.00
Accrued pension expense	–	20,000.00
Taxes withheld, accrued and payable	25,855.72	3,941.27
Total current liabilities	584,233.05	273,083.76
Long-term debt (net):		
Chattel mortgages payable	4,236.66	8,065.54
Notes and loans payable—officer	–	33,200.00
Total long-term debt		
Stockholders' equity:		
Capital stock—common—no par value:		
Authorized issue—12,500 shares		
Issued and outstanding—1,000 shares	2,000.00	2,000.00
Investment tax credits	2,996.81	2,286.89
Retained earnings (*Exhibit E*)	87,353.25	20,735.99
Total stockholders' equity	92,350.06	25,596.88
	$680,819.77	$339,946.18

See accountants' compilation report.

In addition to being the CEO, George was the bookkeeper in the first few years of BSI. With the first profits he bought a microcomputer for $18,000. It took nine months to get in operation, but it cut George's bookkeeping time from 30 hours a week to 3. George says the cash was hard to put out, but he knew the computer would allow him the time for selling and managing.

BEANTOWN SEAFOODS, INC.
Comparative Statement of Net Income and Retained Earnings
For the Years Ended October 31, 1980 and 1979

	1980	1979
Sales.	$4,856,970.08	$3,246,522.80
Cost of sales.	4,390,982.23	2,985,265.67
Gross profit.	465,987.85	261,257.13
Operating and administrative expenses:		
Officers' salaries (including bonuses).	90,187.00	39,270.00
Salaries and wages.	87,297.70	38,683.10
Advertising.	295.40	14.94
Bad debts.	9,838.35	21,103.85
Bank charges.	86.00	110.50
Bonuses.	8,700.00	8,100.00
Building—maintenance and security.	3,095.29	1,030.38
Collection expense.	308.96	—
Commissions.	12,000.27	163.43
Depreciation.	13,043.63	7,637.65
Dues and subscriptions.	440.50	143.00
Entertainment.	3,765.00	2,429.24
Freight—air.	5,265.53	3,051.71
Freight—ground.	22,733.33	16,258.32
Group insurance.	6,151.53	5,080.57
Insurance.	6,453.19	2,684.34
Life insurance expense—officers.	3,360.99	3,360.99
Miscellaneous expense.	1,991.74	1,267.01
Motor vehicle operating—automobiles.	4,795.53	2,235.80
Motor vehicle operating—trucks.	2,968.71	3,500.80
Motor vehicle operating—van.	1,621.15	—
Office supplies.	1,605.42	1,762.98
Outside services.	2,220.97	14,666.44
Packaging.	20,781.61	6,437.80
Pension fund expense.	700.00	20,000.00
Postage.	1,000.00	592.90
Professional and consulting fees.	6,649.70	3,732.80
Rent.	18,000.00	10,697.94
Rental of motor vehicle and equipment.	740.65	1,988.94
Repairs and maintenance—automobiles.	2,104.20	360.44
Repairs and maintenance—equipment.	1,242.42	—
Repairs and maintenance—trucks.	2,229.5	1,611.26
Salesmen's expenses.	543.78	60.04
Small tools expenses.	868.05	527.00
Stationery and printing.	1,384.11	2,024.16
Taxes.	21,927.56	7,978.05
Telephone.	17,948.09	15,015.91
Travel.	1,890.66	2,993.73
Utilities.	720.25	2,607.35
Total operating and administrative expenses	386,956.78	249,183.37
Net income from operations:		
Interest income.	1,536.11	780.96
Rental income.	2,300.00	2,045.42
Bad debt recovery.	600.00	—
WIN reimbursement.	9,112.50	—
	13,548.61	2,826.38
Less: Interest expense.	6,147.43	3,074.74
Amortization expense.	273.70	91.20
Loss on disposal of fixed assets.	2,764.26	320.00
	9,185.39	3,485.94
Net income before federal income taxes.	83,394.29	11,414.20
Provision for federal income taxes.	21,326.76	2,499.06
Less: New Job and WIN credits utilized.	4,549.73	1,362.89
	16,777.03	1,136.17
Net income for the year.	66,617.26	10,278.03
Retained earnings at beginning of year.	20,735.99	10,457.96
Retained earnings at end of year.	$ 87,353.25	$ 20,735.99

See accountants' compilation report.

Exhibit H

BEANTOWN SEAFOODS, INC.
Statement of Changes in Financial Position
For the Year Ended October 31, 1980

Source of funds:		
Operations:		
Net income for the year (net of loss on disposition of fixed assets—$2,764.26)		$ 69,381.52
Charges to net income not involving capital:		
Depreciation	$ 13,043.63	
Amortization of organization costs	273.70	13,317.33
Funds provided from operations		82,698.85
Investment tax credits acquired and utilized		765.12
Proceeds from sales of fixed assets		9,450.00
Total funds provided		92,913.97
Use of funds:		
Acquisition of motor vehicles	22,954.04	
Reduction of chattel mortgages payable	3,828.88	
Reduction of notes and loans payable—officer	33,200.00	
Investment tax credit recaptured	629.20	
Increase in notes and loans receivable	2,540.00	
Total funds used		63,153.10
Net increase in working capital		$ 29,760.87
Analysis of increase in working capital:		
Increase (decrease) in current assets:		
Cash		$ 8,953.29
Accounts receivable		338,759.04
Inventory		(5,434.75)
Prepaid items		(1,367.42)
Net increase in current assets		340,910.16
Decrease (increase) in current liabilities:		
Accounts payable	$(218,234.35)	
Accrued pension expense	20,000.00	
Chattel mortgages payable	(1,576.60)	
Notes payable—bank	(46,123.89)	
Accrued salaries payable	(43,300.00)	
Taxes withheld, accrued and payable	(21,914.45)	
Net increase in current liabilities		(311,149.20)
Net increase in working capital		$ 29,760.87

See accountants' compilation report.

A typical day for George might be as follows: George arrives at the plant by 5 A.M. He takes inventory in the warehouse. By 7 he is in the office talking to the processing plants to begin getting prices. He'll start selling what he knows he has coming in. He'll go back out onto the warehouse floor and begin loading the trucks, then back to selling on the phone again. In between, he may have talked to the insurance company about applying more benefits to the employees or called his bank to find out if he's overdrawn for the day.

Sales volume of BSI has effectively doubled every year since 1976. George believes that planning can be credited for this success. He feels that it is important to have a definite plan of where to concentrate your energy and resources to avoid pursuing routes to the wrong place. George says, "Dad doesn't understand the importance of planning. I guess he thinks we grow because God likes us and that's the way it runs. Well, to a certain degree that's true, but a lot of it is planned growth."

George regards marketing ability as the most important quality required to start your own business. He thinks his father's axiom "You don't *ever* lose money" is a shortsighted philosophy. Daniel would rather not make the transaction than lose money. George concludes that losing money occasionally is inevitable if your first priority is to service customers. He feels that if he doesn't make the transaction, the customer will go somewhere else. George thinks that if he can develop a customer's business, which may include taking a loss some days, revenues will increase in the long run.

LOOKING AHEAD

Strategic Planning for BSI

Sales in 1980 were $4.9 million: an increase of 50 percent over 1979 sales. Sales in 1979 increased 54 percent from 1978. George expects to continue to use his basic selling strategies that have gained them success. At the same time, he realizes the importance of planning for the future. He reports:

Beantown Seafoods will go out of business in 10 years unless we do something different, because the market matures and the markets we have developed are going to say "Why do we really need BSI? Why don't we go directly to the processing plant? We can save between 10 and 15 cents per pound." It's important that we do something different.

George plans to remove himself from the day-to-day operations so he can concentrate on ways the company can use its capital to expand. He wants to establish warehouses and sales offices offering full product lines and distribution services in markets on the East Coast, the Gulf, and the West Coast. He anticipates he needs 10 or 15 years, but it is a long-term goal he feels is realistic: "I would love to become the General Motors of the fresh fish industry, so that if a retailer thinks fresh fish, he says 'Beantown Seafoods.'" An immediate goal is to develop the extension markets. BSI is working to develop Minneapolis. Sales to Phoenix and Dallas have grown. BSI's sales report shows that their growth has come from the undeveloped markets. *Exhibit I* reports air business sales in 1980.

Another way to expand would be to buy a fish processing plant. By integrating backwards and cutting the fish themselves, BSI could realize another 30 to 40 cents per pound gross profit. This is attractive, since gross profits now average 5 cents per pound. However, commitments between processing plants and their suppliers are very private affairs. A processing plant may form an alliance with a fisherman where it buys equipment for the fisherman's boat. He knows that the plant bought it, and he knows that he owes the plant. If he tries to sell his fish elsewhere, the plant reminds him. George feels that these Mafia-like maneuvers are beyond the scope of BSI.

Another idea that captured George's interest was to make fresh fish a branded item. This would change the face of the industry. Fresh fish could be packaged under vacuum in tray packs. Hot dogs are packaged this way, as are fish in Europe. The shelf life of fish would

Exhibit I
Beantown Seafoods, Inc., Air Business Analysis (for fiscal year ending October 31, 1980)

Los Angeles	$224,400
Denver	194,800
Miami	167,900
New air business includes Jackson, Dallas–Fort Worth, Houston, St. Louis, Albuquerque	64,800
Total	$651,900

be extended to three or four weeks. The handling of fresh fish at the supermarket level would be eliminated. The risk of perishability would be dramatically reduced.

BSI can set up a tray-packing operation with no capital outlay. George can lease a packing machine from a packaging company that is anxious to use him as a guinea pig. BSI has the physical capacity. Its present plant has 1,500 square feet of unused space. Because BSI would assume the liability for the quality and safety of its packing, insurance rates would increase by $18,000–$20,000 per year.

There are risks involved. When vacuum-sealed packages are opened, a gassy smell leaks out. Whether the consumer would continue to purchase fish packaged in this way is a risk. Tray packing could be well received for a few months and then decline because of infrequent repeat purchases. Another risk is that supermarket butchers, some of whom are unionized, would be out of work. An additional risk: Since the packages cannot be packed in ice, the safe delivery of the fish would be determined by whether the trucker keeps his refrigerator unit working.

Daniel Halsey thinks that the risks outweigh the benefits, but George sees the potential of doubling profits in the long run. Daniel's concern is that the fish would be transported incorrectly. George says that BSI already takes this risk every day. George feels that it is a question of being willing to risk the reputation of the corporation.

Eventually, George would like to have a professional board of directors to act as arbitrators between him and his father. George's brother, Michael, a securities analyst in Chicago, has a lot of credibility with Daniel Halsey and often plays the part of arbitrator.

"One thing you have to learn if you start your own business is that your goal should be to get out," says George. "It's not going to last forever, nor are you going to last forever." By hiring and developing the right people now, George is planning for his future exit from the daily operations. "It's an investment," he says. "A union worker puts away wages in a pension fund much the same way I'm investing in people so it will be done the way I want it. When I'm ready to get out or do something else, they'll be there."

George sometimes longs for a life without hard work:

I'd love to be able to earn a lot of money and do nothing, but I don't know how to do it. It may be selling gold, but I don't know anything about gold. If God sent me a letter and told me how to do it, I'd do it. I'd like to be able to be out playing with my kid all day and go shopping with my wife. But I can't. I have to work for a living.

APPENDIX

The New England Fishing Industry

Descriptions of the New England fishing fleet in the last several years have varied according to the purpose of the speaker or writer. The fleet has been downgraded in order to attract financial support from government, upgraded to get lower interest and insurance rates from industry, romanticized as the "first industry," for Bicentennial purposes, praised for the independence of spirit and action it embodies for America's young men, and mourned for its precipitous decline.[1]

The U.S. consumption of fish has gradually increased in recent years (see *Exhibit 7A–1*).

Of the total amount of animal protein consumed by humans, fish and shellfish account for approximately 14 percent. Although Americans overwhelmingly prefer meat to fish, the Food and Agriculture Organization of the UN expects the consumption of fish to increase through 1990 at a growth rate higher than that of beef, pork, vegetables, cereal, or milk.

The U.S. coastal waters contain 20 percent of the world's fish resources. Overharvesting

---

[1] Susan Peterson and Leah Smith, *The New England Fishing Industry: A Basis for Management* (Woods Hole, Mass.: Woods Hole Oceanographic Institution, 1977), p. 10.

Exhibit 7A–1
U.S. per Capita Consumption of Fish (in pounds)

	1965	1970	1973	1974	1975	1976	1977	1978
Fish (edible weight)	10.8	11.8	12.9	12.2	12.1	13.0	12.8	12.9
Fresh and frozen	6.0	6.9	7.5	7.0	7.4	8.2	7.8	7.9
Canned	4.3	4.5	5.0	4.8	4.3	4.3	4.6	4.6
Cured	0.5	0.4	0.4	0.4	0.4	0.5	0.4	0.4

Source: U.S. Department of Agriculture, Economics, Statistics, and Cooperative Service.

and depletion had been allowed until recently. Marine resources are now considered exhaustible.

Groundfish, or bottom fish, caught on the seafloor, are abundant in New England waters. The varieties of New England groundfish consumed by Americans are haddock, cod, ocean perch, yellowtail flounder, whiting, pollock, cust, redfish, and hake.

The two main markets for the New England catch are fresh and frozen fish. There is a smaller market for nonfood fish (fishmeal). Fishing and distribution methods differ for each of these segments.

Because the retail price of fresh fish is higher than that of frozen, most of the groundfish landed by U.S. fishermen is not frozen.

The New England fishing fleet is a collection of diverse-sized fishing vessels that catch a variety of species. Each of the species is subject to different supply and demand conditions and price variations.

The Process

The fishing industry is made up of the producers (the fishermen), the processors (filleters and packagers), and wholesalers and distributors.

Boston, New Bedford, and Gloucester, Massachusetts, are the major New England ports where fresh fish is landed. Most of the boats are individually owned and operated by families. Fishermen are represented by organized labor in these ports, although they are not in other New England ports. With the exception of Boston, there is a strong tradition of fathers passing the trade to sons. The union data report that most of the fishermen are between 50 and 60 years of age. Some younger men work as deckhands.

The quantity of fish caught by any one vessel is a function of its type. Since groundfishing in New England is a labor-intensive industry, the ability and experience of the fishermen, which vary from boat to boat, are a major influence on the catch.

New England fishing vessels are small, aged wooden-hulled ships. In 1976, the average age of the boats was 20 years. Their length can range from 20 feet to 140 feet. The smaller boats are used for offshore fishing, and the larger boats for fishing longer distances. Most of the commercial market is supplied by fishermen who fish more than 12 miles off the coast in boats longer than 50 feet weighing 40 tons.

Neither the gear nor the fishing operation has changed signficantly in the last 100 years. Much of the operation is still conducted by hand. Electronic gear used to locate schools of fish was introduced after World War II. Otter trawls and purse seines are the more common means used to entrap fish. An otter trawl is a conical net dropped over the side of the boat and dragged along the sea bottom collecting fish. The mouth of the net is held open by otter or trawl boards. A purse seine is a large net that is laid around a school of fish. The ends are closed or pursed to contain the catch.

While at sea, the catch is stored on ice. The boats are not refrigerated.

On arrival in port, the fish is auctioned off before it is unloaded from the ship. Fish is sold for cash at auction on a per pound basis. The price received at auction changes daily, based on supply and demand. Although the quality of the catch will affect its price, the scarcity of the species for sale determines the final selling price. Even though the smaller auctions throughout New England account for most of the fish sold, the price received at the Boston auction sets the regional market price for fish. This is because prices can be artificially controlled at some of the smaller auctions. For example, in New Bedford there are four buyers who conspire to keep prices artificially low. Fishermen are paid on a share system. Until the fish has been auctioned off, the members of the crew don't know what their wages will be. From the gross revenues of the auction sale, the expenses of the trip are deducted. A percentage of the balance is awarded to the crew. Earnings vary from one trip to the next, one day to the next, one season to the next, and one boat to the next.

The fish is unloaded from the hold by a special crew, called "lumpers," who haul the fish with wire baskets. The fish is delivered to the processing plant of the purchaser.

The Economics of the Industry

The commercial fishing industry in the United States is characterized by a lack of technology and capital resources. It has been one of the last U.S. industries to resist technology. The lack of capital has prohibited modernization.

Small individually owned boats cannot compete with foreign fishing vessels that catch and process groundfish in one efficient operation in boats costing $15 million to $20 million to build.

Researchers from Woods Hole Oceanographic Institution offer a reason why fishermen don't favor new technology:

The fact that fishermen are paid by share rather than a fixed salary or hourly wage has several implications for the industry as a whole. For example, the crew may be resistant to changing fishing gear or fishing grounds because the cost of learning is absorbed by all of them rather than by the captain or owner interested in instituting a change. Also, since fewer men on a vessel receive a larger share of the total income, any plan to increase employment would have to consider individual losses of income. Plans to limit effort by requiring archaic gear and therefore requiring more men are also to the disadvantage of the crew. Share systems are usually advantageous to the owner because he assumes men will not be careless with gear or time for which they pay.[2]

Ex-vessel prices of fish are subject to seasonal fluctuations. During the spring and summer months, when the catch increases and demand decreases, prices drop.

The ex-vessel price of fish varies daily based on supply and demand. The retail prices of fish fluctuate far less than the ex-vessel price; therefore, it takes a long time for price increases to be passed on to the consumer.

Distribution and Marketing

After the fish has been landed, it must be filleted and packaged in quantities for sale to wholesalers. This is called "processing."

Fresh fish processors can obtain fish in several ways: (1) directly from the fishermen, (2) through auctions, (3) through sales controlled by fish co-ops, or (4) from wholesalers who buy on consignment.

[2] Ibid., p. 22.

Processing companies have a great deal of influence on the species caught because the fishermen bring to port only what they can sell. Fisherman direct their efforts toward landing species with higher values, rather than increasing the volume of fish they land. Many species of fish in New England coastal waters are not commercially fished because there is no market for them.

Most processing companies are also family controlled. Fishermen sellers and processor buyers have informal working alliances that have existed for generations.

Processing plants and fishermen often have formal co-op arrangements that aid in the production and marketing of fresh fish. Co-ops allow commercial fishermen to market their fish collectively. The unit cost of handling fish goes down, and the fishermen experience economies of scale. Other collective benefits are quantity purchases of gear and supplies. Co-ops also arrange financing and operate dock services. To gain higher ex-vessel prices for fishermen, co-op salesmen can spread the sale of a catch over more buyers. In this way, they give the illusion that the fish is scarce and they do not give volume discounts.

Fishermen catch whatever the co-op can sell. If the co-op deals in only a few species of fish, catching new species is discouraged.

In ports without co-ops, fishermen are subject to whatever price an auction dealer offers.

Both buyers and processors are affected by the seasonal fluctuations in the volume of fish landed in New England. Idle capacity and transportation arrangements to the markets are the main uncertainties.

Fresh fish is trucked to local markets. Most processors and buyers hire trucking services, rather than keeping their own fleet of trucks. Distant markets are supplied via air cargo.

In the last 20 years, there has been a shift in the source of supply in New England markets. There is less fish landed today in Boston than in New Bedford and Gloucester, Massachusetts, and in Maine. There has been an accompanying increase in the amount of fish processed outside Massachusetts.

Competition

Brian Veasy, general manager of the New Bedford Seafood Co-op, is quoted as follows:

Look at it this way. It costs me 90 cents a pound to buy fish from the local boats and fillet and pack them, where I can buy subsidized, duty-free, Canadian fish already filleted and packed for 75 cents. If we weren't a co-op, I wouldn't be buying from the boats here at all.[3]

The fishing industry in Canada is subsidized by the government. The Canadian government subsidizes fuel, makes loan guarantees for boats, and controls most of the fish landed in Canada by centralizing the processing of fresh fish in two plants. In July 1980, Canadian fishermen bought diesel fuel for 39 cents a gallon. Massachusetts fishermen paid 99 cents the same week. The subsidies allow Canadians to flood the U.S. market with fish prices below those for the U.S. catch. Eighty percent of the Canadian catch is exported to the United States. In the late 1960s, foreign fishing fleets subsidized by the East German, Russian, Japanese, and Polish governments fished in U.S. territorial waters. Factory boats the size of ocean liners cleaned out the ocean within three miles of the U.S. coastline. The Georges Bank fishery, an extension of Cape Cod, was almost totally depleted. Fish was processed, frozen, and stored on the foreign vessels. Typically, the factory boats landed 2,000–3,000 pounds of fish per hour versus the same quantity per day on a traditional U.S. vessel.

---

[3] "Plummeting Prices End New England's Fishing Boom," *New York Times,* July 6, 1980, p. 1.

Exhibit 7A–2
Aggregate Performance Data — Otter Trawl Fleet (Maine, New Hampshire, Massachusetts), 1974–1979

	1974	1975	1976	1977	1978	1979
Total landings (lbs.)	271,655,129	254,459,727	254,496,205	207,032,489	320,367,919	337,020,568
Total revenue ($)	49,093,988	57,860,618	65,348,495	75,055,295	93,416,891	107,572,789
Total vessels	586	597	599	602	652	780
Lbs./vessel	463,575	426,230	424,868	493,409	491,361	432,077
$ Nominal/vessel	83,778	96,918	109,095	124,676	143,277	137,914
$ 1976/vessel	96,344	100,795	109,095	117,195	126,083	104,814

They went through each square mile of rich ocean bottom like a combine going through a wheat field, reducing everything from fins and scales to lobster shells into a uniform fish flour which was later made into fish meal, fish cakes, and fertilizer.[4]

U.S. fishermen were clearly outstripped by foreign fishing methods.

In response to the loss of control over its fisheries, the U.S. government passed the Fishery Conservation and Management Act in 1976, which extended control over fish resources to within 200 miles of its coastline. The act is designed to ensure sufficient regeneration of the fish supply in the future. Americans and foreigners alike are subject to quotas. Fishery councils were established to allocate resources first to U.S. fishermen and the surplus to foreign fishermen.

The FCMA has effectively limited the large fleets of foreign factory boats. Prior to FCMA, as many as 2,500 occupied U.S. waters. Since 1977, less than 950 permits have been issued. The foreign catch has dropped by more than one third. The East Coast fishing fleet has increased 30 percent since the passage of the FCMA. In 1978, there was an 8 percent increase in the number of vessels, and in 1979 there was a 20 percent increase. Even though the amount of fish landed has dramatically increased in the last few years, the National Marine Fisheries Service estimates that the average landing per vessel has actually declined in many New England fisheries *(Exhibit 7A–2)*.

The Environment

Despite the 200-mile-limit law, observers of the fishing industry feel that it is in a period of decline. Fishermen are expected to incur serious losses because of insufficient government protection via subsidies.

In the late 1970s, the interest of the U.S. government in the fishing industry grew in response to a concern for the level of contaminants in fish, the possibility of drilling for oil in fishing grounds, and a fishing rights boundary dispute with Canada.

Because of high levels of mercury in swordfish in the 1970s, a ban resulted in all landed swordfish being seized.

Oil companies want to drill for oil in the Georges Bank area of the Gulf of Main *(Exhibit 7A–3)*. Georges Bank, one of the richest fishing grounds in the world, produces 17 percent of the fish consumed in the United States and 14 percent of world fish consumption. It has been estimated that Georges Bank would produce 900 million barrels of oil, enough to supply the needs of the United States for four to five days.

The oil companies claim that oil drilling and fishing are compatible. The U.S. Department of the Interior is reviewing bids from oil companies that want to drill in Georges Bank. Despite a court battle waged by the state of Massachusetts, the Department of the

---

[4] Ibid.

Exhibit 7A–3
New England Coastline

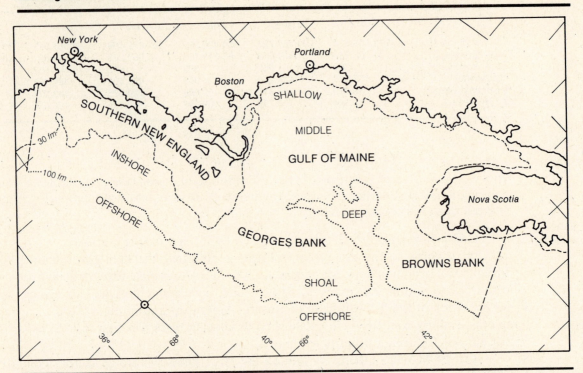

Source: *Sports Fishing Institute,* 1979, p. 387.

Interior has sold oil leases for rights to drill in Georges Bank. The lieutenant governor of Massachusetts, on behalf of the environmentalists, won the concession from the federal government that the oil companies must conduct biological studies of the area before development can begin. The oil companies have to use the "best available technology" with which to drill.

The danger of an oil spill poisoning the marine environment is great. Pipelines are preferable to tankers in transporting oil, but it is not economical for the oil industry to build a 150–200-mile pipeline to transport the marginal amount of oil estimated to be in Georges Bank. Loading oil into tankers in 30-foot seas increases the risk of an oil spill. Since the amount of oil is marginal, it is expected that developers will use cheaper technology to get to the oil. This may lead to a high risk of accidents and of oil discharges into the ocean.

Another environmental consideration is the boundary treaty for fishing rights between the United States and Canada. The dispute is over where and how the Gulf of Maine should be divided *(Exhibit 7A–3).* The United States claims that Georges Bank is a geographic extension of Cape Cod and, therefore, belongs to the United States. The Canadians claim that the northeastern corner of Georges Bank is closer to Canada and that the division should be made on the principle of equidistance. The other issue of the treaty is how to allocate the catch between the United States and Canada. The New England fishermen oppose Canada's claim. They feel that the Senate Foreign Relations Committee is trading away their traditional fishing grounds in return for unrelated natural gas and oil agreements with Canada.

EXERCISE – REWARDS

The following exercise can help an entrepreneur devise a reward system for a new venture. In proceeding with the exercise, it is helpful to pretend to look at these issues from an investor's point of view and to imagine that the venture is in the process of seeking capital from an investor group to which a presentation was made several weeks ago and which is favorably impressed by the team and its plan for the new venture. Imagine then that this investor group would like a brief presentation (of 10 to 15 minutes) about how the team plans to reward its members and other key contributors.

**EXERCISE
REWARDS**

NAME:

VENTURE:

DATE:

PART I

Part I is to be completed by each individual team member—*alone*.

STEP 1: INDICATE WHO WILL DO WHAT DURING THE FIRST YEAR OR TWO OF YOUR VENTURE, WHAT CONTRIBUTIONS EACH HAS MADE OR WILL MAKE TO CREATING A BUSINESS PLAN, THE COMMITMENT AND RISK INVOLVED FOR EACH, AND WHAT UNIQUE CRITICAL SKILLS, EXPERIENCE, CONTACTS, AND SO FORTH EACH BRINGS TO THE VENTURE.   Try to be as specific as possible, and be sure to include yourself.

Team Member	Responsibility	Title	Contribution to Business Plan	Commitment and Risk	Unique/Critical Skills, Etc.

STEP 2:   INDICATE BELOW THE APPROXIMATE SALARY AND SHARES OF STOCK (AS A PERCENT) EACH MEMBER SHOULD HAVE UPON CLOSING THE FINANCING OF YOUR NEW VENTURE.

Team Member	Salary	Shares of Stock (%)

STEP 3:   INDICATE BELOW WHAT YOU BELIEVE THE COMPANY SHOULD PROVIDE IN THE WAY OF FRINGE BENEFITS DURING THE FIRST YEAR OR TWO.

Team Member	Vacation	Holidays	Health/Life Insurance	Retirement Plan	Other

STEP 4: LIST OTHER KEY CONTRIBUTORS, SUCH AS MEMBERS OF THE BOARD OF DIRECTORS, AND INDICATE HOW THEY WILL BE REWARDED.

Name	Expertise/ Contribution	Salary	Shares of Stock (%)	Other

PART II

Part II involves meeting as a team to reach consensus on the responsibilities of each team member and how each will be rewarded. In addition to devising a reward system for the team and other key contributors, the team will examine how consensus was reached.

STEP 1: MEET AS A TEAM AND REACH CONSENSUS ON THE ABOVE TEAM ISSUES AND INDICATE THE CONSENSUS SOLUTION BELOW.

Responsibilities/Contributions

Team Member	Responsibility	Contribution to Business Plan	Commitment and Risk	Unique/Critical Skills, Etc.

Rewards

Team Member	Salary	Shares of Stock (%)

Rewards (cont'd)

Team Member	Title	Vacation	Holidays	Health/Life Insurance	Retirement Plan	Other

STEP 2: MEET AS A TEAM AND REACH CONSENSUS ON ISSUES INVOLVING OTHER KEY CONTRIBUTORS AND INDICATE THE CONSENSUS SOLUTION BELOW.

Name	Expertise/ Contribution	Salary	Shares of Stock (%)	Other

STEP 3: DISCUSS AS A TEAM THE FOLLOWING ISSUES AND INDICATE ANY IMPORTANT LESSONS AND IMPLICATIONS:

— What patterns emerged in the approaches taken by each team? What are the differences and similarities?

— How difficult or easy was it to reach agreement among team members? Did any issues bog down?

— If salaries or stock were equal for all team members, why was this so? What risks or problems might such an approach create?

— What criteria, either implicit or explicit, were used to arrive at a decision concerning salaries and stock? Why?

<table>
<tr><td>

The Family Venture

</td><td>

8 >

</td></tr>
</table>

Daring as it is to investigate the unknown, even more so it is to question the known.

Kaspar

RESULTS EXPECTED

Upon completion of the chapter, you will have:

1. Identified and examined the role and significance of the family in building a venture.
2. Analyzed some of the important problems associated with new venture teams that involve immediate family members.
3. Considered ways of managing problems of control, credibility, family dynamics, and succession.
4. Analyzed and developed courses of action to deal with a family business crisis.
5. Analyzed a case, Family Venture Partners, Inc.

POPULAR AND NUMEROUS

Family businesses are very popular today, and there has been an influx of young talent into family owned businesses for several reasons. As the editors of *Business Week* recently stated:

All over the country, the bright young types who formerly opted for management consulting or the fast track at blue-chip corporations are eagerly joining family businesses. . . . Changed attitudes and a changing economy account for this turnabout.[1]

It seems that people are tired of bureaucracy and have turned to family ventures in hopes of success, security, and humanistic work values.

Historically, involvement by families in business ventures has been the least understood aspect of new venture creation. Yet, of the more than 18 million businesses in the United States, 9 out of 10 are family dominated.[2] Family firms range in size from small local stores to such large multinational corporations as Mars, S. C. Johnson & Sons, and McDonnell Douglas. They employ half of the nation's work force and produce half the gross national product.

This chapter was written by Wendy C. Handler, D.B.A. Dr. Handler teaches family business management at Babson College and conducts research on succession in family firms from the perspective of next-generation family members.

[1] *Business Week,* July 1, 1985.

[2] R. Beckhard and W. G. Dyer, Jr., "Managing Continuity in the Family-Owned Business," *Organizational Dynamics,* Summer 1983, pp. 5–12.

Exhibit 8.1
Relationship of Goals in Three Types of Firms

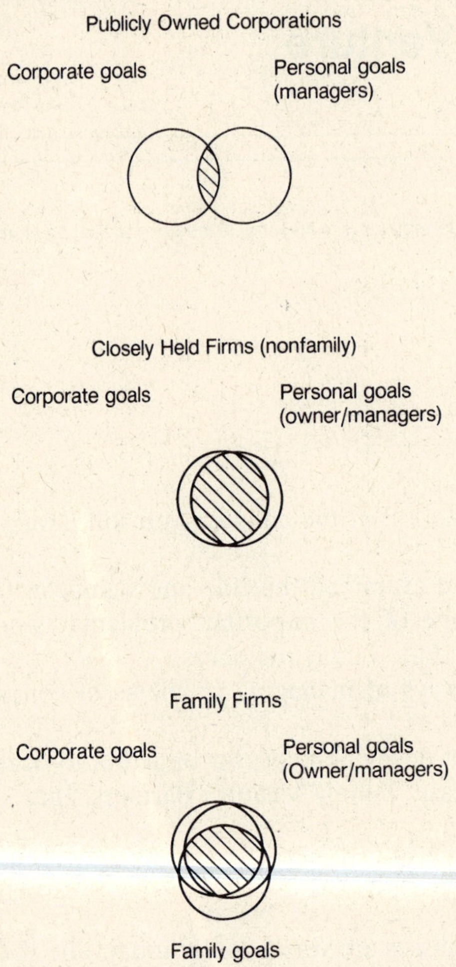

Publicly Owned Corporations

Corporate goals   Personal goals
                                   (managers)

Closely Held Firms (nonfamily)

Corporate goals   Personal goals
                                   (owner/managers)

Family Firms

Corporate goals   Personal goals
                                   (Owner/managers)

Family goals

THE IMPACT OF GOALS

Three Types of Firms

In successful businesses, the goals of the firm and the goals of the owners or managers, or both, overlap to some degree. Family businesses are unique in structure and purpose. They are unlike public corporations and closely held nonfamily firms, because of the existence of family members in business and the function of family goals. *Exhibit 8.1* shows how corporate goals and the goals of owners/managers, and for family firms, those of family members, overlap.

As can be seen in *Exhibit 8.1,* in *publicly owned corporations,* the overlap between corporate goals and the personal goals of managers is limited. Corporate and institutional goals supercede personal, especially nonbusiness, goals.

In *closely held corporations* that are nonfamily, this common area or area of overlap is usually greater, because the corporate goals are personally determined by those who own and operate the corporation, as shown in *Exhibit 8.1.*

Finally, in *family owned or controlled firms,* there is an additional set of goals or values determined by the family in charge. These values associated with the family influence the development of corporate goals. They also interact with the personal goals of managers in the determination of day-to-day business decisions and longer-term business strategy. Often, the overlap is much greater than in publicly owned or closely held corporations. One direct consequence is a much greater degree of potential conflicts and complications in balancing and achieving these goals. The interaction of the three sets of goals also is shown in *Exhibit 8.1.*

In family firms, the presence of the family can provide opportunities for collaboration, trust, and team effort. In these optimal cases, there is general agreement or synergy between the goals of the corporation, the family, and the owner/managers, who are typically family members. For example, the daughter of the founder of a successful New York-based real estate development firm talked about how working with her father and other family members was special because of the team spirit. She described one afternoon when three family members walked down Park Avenue. "We looked at buildings we have owned and pointed out different aspects of other buildings and . . . felt like the three of us were so in tune and learning from each other," she said.

In this case, values concerning *family togetherness, sharing, and closeness* were being met as were corporate values associated with *profit making and equity building,* and personal goals associated with *individual growth and learning.*

Convergent/Divergent Goals in Family Firms

On the other hand, personal goals or corporate goals may differ or clash with family goals, producing tension, conflict, and heated arguments in the context of the family firm. An example is in the Bingham family of Louisville, Kentucky, where personal goals concerning ownership conflicted with corporate and family goals leading to the downfall and sale of the $400 million media empire.

In other words, as is illustrated in *Exibit 8.2,* it is possible for the overlapping of goals to become greater, or for goals which overlapped, to begin to diverge at some time.

The implications are profound. There are more subtleties and complications, and there is a greater need for participants to pay attention to and devise strategies that take into account the nature of family relationships. For investors, lenders, suppliers, and customers, the additional family-ownership dimension introduces a dilemma beyond the normal exposure to risk in a nonfamily enterprise; and that is, will the family ownership enhance the

Exhibit 8.2
Shared or Divergent Goals in Family Firms

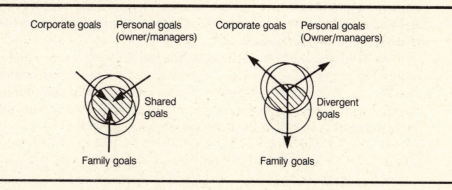

vigor and potential upside, or introduce a potential future risk through the eruption of conflicts, the development of problems in managing succession, and the resulting stagnation or demise of the firm? The same dilemma is faced also by anyone considering joining the family firm.

Timing

Family members may become involved in ventures at all stages of growth; each possibility has its own advantages and risks.

- *Start-up.* A family member may become involved from start-up (or buyout) as a partner or member of an entrepreneurial team. The advantages are that (1) initial costs and early losses may be more easily shared, (2) later success benefits the family as a whole, (3) the family can be together, and (4) trust. To illustrate, one of the major reasons married couples choose to go into business with one another is that they can be together, and this form of partnership has gained in popularity in the 1980s.[3] Family members also may trust one another more than they do people outside the family. For example, the issue of trust is paramount in the wholesale diamond business. As one member of a family firm in that industry explained, "Dealing with diamonds is basically a family business, because you're dealing with these small things that are very expensive, and you must have a lot of trust in whomever you work with. So you don't hire (nonfamily) salesmen."

- *Early growth.* A family member may join a recently launched family venture early in its operation. In this instance, the lead entrepreneur already has declared himself or herself and presumably has identified the areas in which the venture needs the help of potential family partners, employees, and backers. A family member may welcome the opportunity to help the business, because his or her working benefits the family and he or she may enjoy working together with other family members. Furthermore, a family member is typically seen as more trustworthy or responsible than outsiders and, thus, needs less close supervision resulting in less bureaucracy.

- *High growth/maturity.* A family member may join a family business at any time during the life of the organization as a second- or third-generation member. Advantages to joining the venture as a next-generation family member include opportunities to gain experience and to expand the venture or to find a niche in a rapidly expanding environment. In addition, a family member can help the family and experience personal job security, flexibility, and growth. For example, Thomas Watson, Jr., "got his job from his father, but built IBM into a colossus big enough to satisfy even the wildest of the old man's dreams."[4] Similarly, J. Willard Marriott, Jr., built the Marriott Corporation from a $750 million company in 1966 to a $7.5 billion company in 1989.

A significant number of the potential risks and problems associated with family ventures stem from the involvement of the family. They include problems of control, credibility, family dynamics, and succession. These issues as well as strategies for minimizing them are discussed later in the chapter.

As with other ventures, success within the family business will depend to a great extent on company growth and whether it's growing fast enough to accommodate new ideas or new divisions. Such questions as whether the company matured and stabilized at its present level of sales or if the management style permits latitude are also important. *Exhibit 8.3* shows characteristics of companies at various stages of growth.

---

[3] For more on couples in business, see Frank and Sharon Barnett, *Working Together: Entrepreneurial Couples* (Berkeley, Calif.: Ten Speed Press, 1988), and Sharon Nelton, *In Love and In Business* (New York: John Wiley & Sons, 1986).

[4] "The Greatest Capitalist in History," *Fortune,* August 31, 1987.

Exhibit 8.3
Characteristics of Company Growth

Organizational Characteristic	Patterns of the First Stage	Patterns of the Second Stage	Patterns of the Third Stage
Core problem	Survival	Management of growth	Managerial control and allocation of resources
Central function	Fusion of diverse talents and purposes into a unified company	Fission of general authority into specialized functions	Fusion of independent units into an interdependent union of companies
Control systems	Personal (inside); survival in marketplace (outside)	Cost centers and policy formulation (inside); growth potential (outside)	Profit centers and abstract performance criteria (inside); capital expansion potential (outside)
Reward and motivation	Ownership, membership in the family	Salary opportunities and problems of growth	Salary performance bonus, stock options, peer prestige
Management style	Individualistic; direct management	Integrating specialists; collaborative management	Integrating generalists; collection management
Organization:			
Structure	Informal	Functional specialists	Division organizations
CEO's primary task	Direct supervision of employees	Managing specialized managers	Managing generalist managers
Levels of management	Two	At least three	At least four

Source: L. B. Barnes and S. A. Hershon, "Transferring Power in the Family Business," *Harvard Business Review,* July–August 1976, p. 145.

Types of Involvement

Individuals join family businesses for many reasons. Research indicates that next-generation family members seek (1) to meet their *career interests,* (2) to develop their *personal identity,* and (3) to satisfy their needs associated with their *life stage* in the context of the family firm.[5]

In this regard, individuals in their early 20s are concerned with *exploration* of life's options, while *advancement* is critical in one's late 20s and 30s, and *balance* between work and other activities is the concern for individuals in their 40s. The degree to which each of these life-stage needs can be met in the context of the family firm is critical to the quality of the individual's experience.

The nature of involvement of family members can be distinguished in terms of three categories:

■ *Helper.* The helper is the individual who joins to help the family in the organization for an uncertain period of time. Often the helper joins at the early stages of the firm's development, when family members may need to be relied on for flexible work hours and pay. The helper may stay to learn the business "from the bottom up," in which case he or she usually does not have a regular title or position, but is expected to be a *factotum* — someone who does all kinds of work.

For the helper, the family firm can serve as a safety net and security blanket. If the helper is a son, daughter, or other relative, he or she may have one or more limitations: timidness; lack of confidence to seek work beyond the protective cover of the family; sheer lack of business power, creativity, and talent; or lack of ambition. The individual may choose to enter and remain in the family firm, because of the security it provides as well

---

[5] Research done by the author, Wendy C. Handler.

as a potential shelter from having to address his or her own apparent weaknesses. One of the hardest things for parents, sisters, brothers, aunts, and uncles to face up to is this harsh reality.

One well-known example of the timid and dutiful helper is Edsel Ford, only son of the original Henry Ford and father of Henry Ford II, who, even as president of Ford Motor Company, found himself overshadowed by his father, the real power in the company. For example, when his father told him to "shut up" when Edsel made a recommendation to a large group of executives, he "took it" because, "One, he was a loyal son. He loved his father. Two, he was a Ford, with that awful burden on his shoulders."[6]

- *Apprentice.* Some individuals use the family firm as a stepping stone on a career path. They are interested in it as a convenient career opportunity—a launching pad to other job choices. For example, two sons of restauranteur Anthony Anthanas, owner of Anthony's Pier 4 in Boston, set up a seafood supply company in Maine, with the intent of having their father be one of their most loyal customers. Another example: Ira Riklis, son of conglomerate Meshulam Riklis, of Rapid-American Corporation, worked for his father for one year, developing an ulcer and the conviction that the role was not for him. However, the contacts he made enabled him to start a successful company of his own.

- *Socialized successor.* This individual joins and becomes socialized into the family business, with the strong likelihood of becoming the next-generation president. One notable example is the Bechtel Corporation, begun by Warren Bechtel to build railroads. His son, Steve, Sr., directed the firm in construction of pipelines and nuclear power plants. Today, Steve, Jr., heads the $3 billion company, which has further diversified.

THE FAMILY VENTURE TEAM

Everything that has been said about choosing entrepreneurial teams and practicing teamwork applies to new family ventures.

Family partnerships can work well, particularly when the partners have abilities and responsibilities that complement each other, like brothers Ernest and Julio Gallo of Gallo Vineyards. Ernest, 77, is chairman and in charge of marketing, sales, and distribution. Julio, 76, is president and oversees production. Julio describes himself as a farmer at heart, who likes to "walk in the fields with the old-timers." Ernest's office, on the other hand, is cluttered with mementos from selling. The brothers mesh well: Julio's goal is to make more wine than Ernest can sell. Ernest's goal is to sell more wine than Julio can make.[7]

Critical Issues

Many individuals find that the complexities of putting together a venture team are compounded when immediate family members or other relatives, or both, become involved. Often family members fail to realize that they are entering a business relationship, and they make the assumption that these issues are "understood" because "it's all in the family."

As with other entrepreneurial teams, or even more so, it is important to have a clear understanding about the following issues:

- Who (if anyone) is the lead entrepreneur.
- What the backgrounds of each member of the team in business are.

---

[6] B. Herndon, *Ford: An Unconventional Biography of the Men and Their Times.*

[7] J. Fierman, "How Gallo Crushes the Competition," *Fortune,* September 1, 1986.

- What the specific strengths and weaknesses of each member of the team are; what and how each will contribute to the building of the business; and what skills and talents does the venture really need to succeed during its next phase.
- What the specific responsibilities of each will be.
- How much money will each put up, and how will equity be divided.
- Under what circumstances and on what terms nonfamily will be brought into the venture.
- What compensation each will receive — that is, what salary, bonuses, equity shares, or mixture of the above each will receive.
- What will be done in the event of a disagreement, or if one family member is not pulling his or her weight, and what mechanisms exist to facilitate and structure a graceful divorce.
- What the ante is, and whether it can be redeemed if the joining family member changes his or her mind.

Unique Problems

Members of family ventures can experience problems of control, credibility, family dynamics, and succession during the course of the firm's operation.

- *Control, fairness, and equity.* Problems of control, fairness, and equity are common. Conflicts over control result when each partner has a different idea of how to run the business, and both are unwilling to compromise. Issues of fairness and equity arise over division of work and how much each partner is contributing to profit. Also, while keeping a venture strictly in the family ensures complete control, this approach also may limit growth by discouraging able and potential partners from joining, if the inner circle is closed to them. It also may discourage potential investors, lenders, vendors, and customers who may question the growth potential of a tightly held operation.
- *Credibility.* A second related issue is establishing credibility. Founding parents often have difficulty believing that their children ever grow up. They may push their children to enter the business but then fail to give them responsibility or encouragement. Few next-generation family members appear to be given direct positive feedback about their performance. Often, they must find out from others if the parent thinks they are doing a good job.

  Gaining credibility is typically a slow, gradual dance between parent and child. Generally, the parent (particularly the founder) has worked hard and expects the child to do the same. Family often have higher expectations of family members in the firm, with one implication being that, *because* they are family, they do not have to praise their work.

  Alternatively, it also is possible for there to be "credibility inflation" or overkill. This occurs when there is a "pet child" or other family member who can "do no wrong." A family or parental myopia contributes to a grossly exaggerated level of credit and praise for the family member, which can be demoralizing to other high-performing family members as well as to nonfamily members.
- *Family dynamics.* A third complication of entering a family business is family dynamics. When there are no boundaries between family life and the business, tensions from one may spill over into the other. *Family strains* occur when the issues concerning the business pervade family discussions and interactions outside the business. *Business strains* occur due to excessive family emotionality, conflict, unrealistic expectations, and arbitrary policies for family members within the context of the business.

  For example, in the case of siblings and relatives — especially if they are close in age and of the same gender — rivalry and jealousy may crop up if the relationship is not carefully managed. In addition, the relationship between predecessor and next-generation family member can have a critical effect within the business. In one extreme case, the leadership of the organization was "in limbo" because of the relationship between father and heir apparent. Despite the father's alcoholism, the family auto dealership had been very successful under his control. However, he had never given his son adequate recognition, because he sought attention for himself. The son, who is now in charge, doubts his own abilities, because his father has given him and continues to give so many bad messages. His father will not give up control or the presidency, even though he no longer has any real responsibilities in the organization.

Furthermore, an entrepreneur employing a parent may experience role reversal, which can be awkward. In addition, the parent may be resentful, if the work is unrewarding, tedious, or difficult.

Even more extreme are cases of outright hostilities, such as family businesses that have been nearly destroyed by family feuds. Cesare Mondavi, founder of Mondavi Vineyards, before he died, mediated disputes between his two sons over running the family's Charles Krug Winery. The sons, Robert and Peter, had been known for fistfights at their grape-shipping plant. By 1972, Robert was suing Peter for his investment in Krug and being countersued for trying to monopolize the Napa Valley wine industry. In 1978, a California Superior Court judge ordered that Krug be sold. One month before the sale, Peter bought out Robert's share and saved the business from the auction block.[8]

And, in a business run by a couple, difficulties in the personal relationship may undermine the business. For example, Esprit, the billion-dollar international clothing company, has experienced plummeting sales, largely blamed on founder-owners Doug and Susie Tompkins being "at each other's throat," according to *Newsweek* magazine (May 23, 1988). They have moved into separate buildings on their estate overlooking San Francisco Bay. They disagree as well about the future direction of the company. She wants to produce more mature clothes for the aging baby boomers, while he insists on sticking with the youth market. In May of 1988, to placate concerned stockholders, the couple agreed to reorganize the company and have given up some of their personal control of it.

Succession.   *Exhibit 8.4* indicates the evolution of the relationship between the owner of a family firm and a next-generation family member in succession. This evolution is typically a slow, subtle process of transition.[9]

As the exhibit shows, the roles of both individuals evolve over time and also interact with one another. Central to succession is the disengagement of the owner and the

Exhibit 8.4
Evolution of Relationship between the Owner/Manager and Next-Generation in Succession

Owner/Manager

Sole operator → Monarch → Overseer/Delegator → Consultant

Interacts with

Next-Generation Family Member

Ambiguous role → Helper → Manager → Leader/Chief decision maker

[8] E. Topolnicki, "Family Firms Can Leave the Feuds Behind,"*Money,* July 1983.

[9] Wendy C. Handler, "Managing the Family Firm Succession Process: The Next-Generation Family Member's Experience," Doctoral dissertation, Boston University School of Management, Department of Organizational Behavior, 1989.

corresponding increased level of responsibility of the next-generation family member. However, often the owner has difficulty moving beyond his or her role as *monarch* with preeminent power over other family members. This is the classic problem of the owner who cannot let go. To many founders, the company is child and lover. The founder cannot stand to relinquish any part of it and will often deny the successor the training necessary to qualify to take it over.

For the next-generation family member to gain leadership responsibilities, the founder or owner must become first the *overseer and delegator* of management tasks, and then the *consultant* to the next generation. This involves giving up some control; otherwise the next-generation family member can become a permanent person-in-waiting.

This was the case for Stanley Marcus, who was son of Herbert Marcus, the founder of the Dallas-based retail store Neiman-Marcus. He described the greatest single disappointment in his life as his father's failure to name him president before his 40th birthday.

He had completed high school at 16 and college at 20 so that assuming a business presidency while still in his 30s would have completed his track record. Even when his health began to fail, Herbert Marcus remained in control; to promote his son at that time would have been recognition of his declining physical capacity, something to which no founder-father wants to admit.[10]

A seasoned observer has summarized the dilemma facing such owner/managers:

Dad's successor is an entrepreneur in training. He's expected to be the trail blazer when Dad passes on his machete. He's expected to be independent, yet he is forced to work for one of the most domineering bosses in existence, a successful business owner. To make it worse, this 'boss' is also the successor's father.[11]

Furthermore, as a well-known family business consultant has explained, the practice of choosing a successor is "an organizationally hazardous activity that might better be abolished."[12] Unconsciously, owner/managers may want to prove no one can fill their shoes. Successors appear to be aware of this dynamic. One, for example, is still trying to come to grips with his father's words, "if anything happens to me, don't think for one minute that you could ever run this business without me."

STRATEGIES FOR SUCCESS

Managing the family in the family venture means dealing with problems of control, credibility, dynamics, and succession. While there are no absolute prescriptions, problems of control, fairness, and equity can be mitigated by the following four strategies:

■ *Expression of interest.*   As a next-generation family member, it is important to express interest in the family business and to discuss goals if one is interested. It should not be assumed that family members know of them. Next-generation family members should be direct and forthright about the responsibility they want and what they are capable of. Research clearly indicates that they are more likely to achieve for themselves and the business when they are clear about their needs and communicate them directly to the owner in charge.

---

[10] P. Alcorn, *Success and Survival in the Family-Owned Business* (New York: McGraw-Hill, 1982), p. 152.

[11] L. Danco, *Inside the Family Business* (Cleveland: Center for Family Business, 1980), p. 131.

[12] H. Levinson, "Don't Choose Your Own Successor," *Harvard Business Review,* March–April 1971.

■ *Acquisition of experience.* It is recommended that a family member acquire practical business experience outside the family business, particularly if one is uncertain about a career in the family business. This helps increase knowledge, experience, and confidence. It is also the single most effective way to enhance credibility with employees in a family business, who may be skeptical about the qualifications of family members.

A son of the founder of a software marketing and consulting company in New York was adamant about gaining experience elsewhere. He said:

I think it gives you a very narrow perspective on life to go at age 21 into your family business and be there for the rest of your life. I think it limits your exposure; I don't think you can become as broad and as developed an individual if you're involved in one thing for your entire life. . . ."

■ *Acceptance of responsibility.* Family members should take responsibility for their own development and consider how—or if—personal goals are to be met by the family business. They should ask themselves:

— Am I cultivating an "entrepreneurial mind" (i.e., attitudes and behaviors discussed in Chapter 6)?
— What are the critical skills and know-how required in the business now and in the immediate future?
— In what ways will my personal needs be satisfied through the family venture?
— If we plan to double the size of the business in the next 3, 5, or 10 years, what are the likely requirements?
— What do I bring to the team now, and later?
— What are my strengths, and what do I need to work on?
— What additional relevant "chunks" of experience do I need, and how can I get them?
— What other aspects of the business do I need to learn?
— Do I have the qualities to be a leader?
— Am I happy working in the business, and does it "give me energy"?
— Is there anything else I need to be doing to meet my goals?

As part of one's responsibility, individuals who hope to become head of the business should learn as much about the business as they can. A leading family business expert suggests an initial learning stage to understand the business better, followed by a specialization stage to acquire a specific skill. He then suggests becoming a generalist and learning to manage.[13] How appropriate these steps are, however, depends on the nature, complexity, and size of the business.

■ *Establishment of networks.* It is recommended that individuals cultivate relationships with mentors, peers, and family members who can act as coaches, protectors, role models, counselors, or friends. Next-generation family members often try to manage their own development without seeking help or advice. They desire a sense of independence and tend to be ambivalent about having their parents serve as mentors, Actually, it may be unwise to turn to parents for mentoring, because of the possible inherent conflict of interest. Parents play many roles with children; for example, as has been mentioned, they may not want them to grow up and may have subconscious difficulty accepting this reality. Looking to respected individuals outside the family for counseling and long-term development support is a good strategy.

---

[13] S. Nelton, "Making Sure the Business Outlasts You," *Nation's Business,* January 1986.

Becoming involved in a peer network is also highly recommended for family entrepreneurs. There are a variety of national and regional organizations for individuals involved in family ventures. Through the Family Firm Institute, the Small Business Association, the American Management Association, or the National Family Business Council, one can become affiliated with local professionals and personal support groups. In addition, the Young Presidents Association is geared to presidents of entrepreneurial and family businesses.

Whatever issues a member of a family new venture team might be struggling with, it is likely that others have confronted them, or know someone who has. Sharing experiences can be useful and therapeutic for people involved in family ventures.

In addition, there are three ways to minimize problems of family dynamics:

- *Definition of responsibility.*   One is to define different responsibilities clearly and with minimum overlap and assign them according to personal capabilities and interests. In most well-managed family businesses, this approach is used. On the other hand, in family businesses plagued with conflict, siblings typically perform similar jobs, competing with each other and vying for attention from parents and other family members.
- *Emphasis on issues.*   Family members, if they fight, should fight over issues, not emotions. As a woman whose husband entered and then quit her father's business explained:

Two years ago, my husband was determined to make my father see the importance of expanding. After plotting and pushing, he got the ok. But this was the beginning of almost daily confrontations. He and my father began to fight over people hired and money being spent. If they had discussed plans for company expansion rationally, before my husband began working for my father, much of this could have been resolved.[14]

- *Establishment of mechanisms.*   Establishing various mechanisms to enhance communication (both informal sessions for sharing and formal means for family planning and exchange) is advised. The development of a family council also is advised, one composed of all family members key to the future of the business, such as the founder, spouse, and children, as well as other relatives who have a significant interest in the business.[15] Having regular family meetings allows the airing of problems or differences that might otherwise be ignored—but that will not go away. A family council helps establish open communication, understanding, and trust. It also serves as a forum for planning the future of the family and the business.

Since it is entirely possible that the "chemistry of the family" simply does not work and family history involves deep scars, resentment, hostility, and other complex emotional feelings that may not be easily mended, family members should realize it is all right, if not preferable, to recognize that reality and seek their fortunes elsewhere.

CASE—FAMILY VENTURE PARTNERS, INC.

Preparation Questions

1. If you were George, how would you respond to Dan? Be prepared to do some in-class role-playing of their conversation.
2. What is going on here, and how critical is the situation? How have they gotten to this point? How would you advise each man?

---

[14] M. Crane, "How to Keep Families from Feuding," *INC.*, February 1982.

[15] I. Lansberg, "The Succession Conspiracy," *Family Business Review,* Summer 1988.

3. What might have been done to avoid this situation and to allow for a mutually acceptable resolution?

4. What are the implications of the current situation for the Halseys, for would-be family venture participants, and for their backers?

FAMILY VENTURE PARTNERS, INC.

George and Daniel Halsey had come a long way on virtually nothing by early 1981 (see Halsey & Halsey, Inc., in Chapter 2 and Beantown Seafoods, Inc., in Chapter 7). The venture begun five years previously had substantially exceeded the start-up business plan projections. Yet, the extremely tight margins in the business left little cash in the bank and even less margin for error. Compounding these financial and business pressures were the extremely long hours put in by both George and Dan, often 90 to 100 hours a week or more over six days, and occasional Sundays.

The Ownership Issue

The future ownership of the company is a frequent argument between George and his father. George has been waiting five years for his father to agree to a shared ownership plan. He trusts his father to be fair. Up until 1980, Daniel believed that the company could go bankrupt at any time. They debate two issues: (1) whether Daniel will share ownership with George and (2) if he does, how they will place a value on BSI.

George says that problems arise when families work together. "There's no question about it. Ordinarily, when faced with a problem, there's a black-and-white answer. Should you do it? Yes or no, and why?" When a family is involved in decisions, there are other considerations that affect the outcome, "things like mothers who don't think the president of a corporation should be doing things the solution might call for." George continues:

I've gotten to the point with this stock redemption thing with my dad where I've said, "Look, I've had it with you, and I've had it with your waffling on these issues. Either you do it and you do it my way, or else forget it. I'll go out on my own. If I end up competing with you, then I end up competing with you. I'm not going to be subject to any more of this frustration."

As a result, George's brothers and sisters see him as ruthless. They expect him to steal their father's business and start his own company. George feels hurt by their misinterpretation of his intentions. He is desperate to resolve the issue. He wonders whether he's worked five years for nothing. He uses one of his previous jobs to describe his conflict. George was the manager of a radio station at the time Boston was experiencing racial tension over school busing. Most of his employees were black. Witnessing the tension and conflict that his employees felt "ripped my stomach apart." George says, "I have felt as bad in this job at BSI as I did at the radio station."

George has offered his father retirement at a $50,000 salary plus traveling expenses. Daniel is tempted but is not ready to leave the business. He thinks that the business can't run without him. George has offered him 10 percent of the worth of the company and a plan to buy the balance of shares over 10 years.

A BSI customer relates a similar incident: "George, I had exactly the same problem. I finally went to my father and said, 'Dad, I don't want to say this, but I'm hoping you're going to die.' My father said, 'I don't want you to think I'm going to die, so here, take the business.'"

In December 1980, Daniel signed over 20 percent ownership to George but retained the stock certificate. George legally owns 20 percent of the company but wonders whether he really does. By January George expects the issue to be concluded: "I'm not going to give him a lot of time to think about this offer. We've been negotiating for five years. There's no room for negotiating any more. If I allow him time, he'll drag it out for years."

George feels that his father doesn't listen to him. He has told Daniel that he's prepared to start his own company. Daniel's response was that George could not get the money. George's bank has offered financial backing. Daniel also does not believe that George is considering this alternative. George hopes his father realizes that he is serious and that he has his father's interests as well as the company's interests at heart. He wants his father to recognize the offer for its fairness.

If George started his own company, it would cause a rift between him and his brothers and sisters. Timothy knows something about the industry and about the value of BSI. He knows that he can get a share of the company by siding with his father. George feels that his family perceives him as an ogre.

If I buy out my father, it's going to be a real threat to Timothy's future goals. It's a problem for me not to be liked anymore by my brothers and sisters, but I can't live my life for them. Dad got really upset when I told him I wasn't living my life for him anymore. I have my own family.

My brothers and sisters see their own financial gains. My brother Michael, the MBA wizard, told my father that if he and I left the business, it would run by itself. Look around. Who would run the business? He had Dad believing that. Dad said we'd get someone in here to run it.

My family doesn't acknowledge that I raised this business from scratch. Our accountant, a mild-mannered fellow, was upset with Dad because he was being so callous about what was transpiring. Frank stood up in a meeting we had together and said, "(Expletive deleted), Daniel, what do you think made the business grow—fertilizer?"

So the time has come. As young as I am, fate has a way of being good to me in the long run. For example, on my first co-op job at college, I was working for an ad agency. I got fired because they thought I was looking for a job with another agency. At the time I thought, "How traumatic!" But from there, I went to New York, which was the best thing in the world for me. So I'm looking at this optimistically. I see it, not as a problem, but as a real opportunity. Whatever happens, happens. I'll roll with the punches. If it doesn't work out, I'll just go somewhere else and try something else.

Showdown

It was a pleasant Sunday morning in the spring of 1981. George had the day off, after another 100-hour week, including late Saturday. The phone rang, and George answered. It was Dan Halsey. "George, I want you to come in to the office right now," Dan insisted. (It was an hour's drive.)

"Dad, it's Sunday; it's my first day off in three weeks and I promised to be with Mary Jane and the kids. Why do I have to be there?" George said.

"Be here in an hour and a half. I'm still the boss here. Either get your butt in here or you are fired!" was Dan's reply.

Personal Ethics and the Entrepreneur

If you gain financial success at the expense of your integrity, you are not a success at all.

John Cullinane
Founder of Cullinet, Inc., and 1984 Inductee,
Babson Academy of Distinguished Entrepreneurs

RESULTS EXPECTED

Upon completion of this chapter, you will have:

1. Made decisions involving ethical issues and identified and analyzed your reasons for deciding as you did.
2. Discussed the ethical implications of the decisions you made with others and identified how they might affect you, your partners, your customers, and your competitors in the contexts described.
3. Acquired a background, based on history, philosophy, and research, about the nature of business ethics and a context for thinking about ethical behavior.
4. Gained an awareness of the importance of ethical awareness and high standards in an entrepreneurial career.

EXERCISE — ETHICS

In the Ethics Exercise, decisions will be made in ethically ambiguous situations and then analyzed. As in the real world, all the background information on each situation will not be available, and assumptions will need to be made in order to decide.

It is recommended that the Ethics Exercise be completed first — before reading the following material.

**EXERCISE
ETHICS**

Name:

Date:

PART I

STEP 1:   MAKE DECISIONS IN THE FOLLOWING SITUATIONS.   You will not have all the background information on each situation, and, instead, you should make whatever assumptions you feel you would make if you were actually confronted with the decision choices described. Select the decision choice that most closely represents the decision you feel you would make personally. You should choose decision choices even though you can envision other creative solutions that were not included in the exercise.

Situation 1.   You are taking a very difficult chemistry course, which you must pass to maintain your scholarship and to avoid damaging your application for graduate school. Chemistry is not your strong suit, and, because of a just-below failing average in the course, you will have to receive a grade of 90 or better on the final exam, which is two days away. A janitor, who is aware of your plight, informs you that he found the master stencil for the chemistry final in a trash barrel and saved it. He will make it available to you for a price, which is high but which you could afford. What would you do?

_____ *(a)*   I would tell the janitor thanks, but no thanks.
_____ *(b)*   I would report the janitor to the proper officials.
_____ *(c)*   I would buy the exam and keep it to myself.
_____ *(d)*   I would not buy the exam myself, but I would let some of my friends, who are also flunking the course, know that it is available.

Situation 2.   You have been working on some financial projections manually for two days now. It seems that each time you think you have them completed your boss shows up with a new assumption or another "what-if" question. If you only had a copy of a spreadsheet software program for your personal computer, you could plug in the new assumptions and revise the estimates with ease. Then, a colleague offers to let you make a copy of some software which is copyrighted. What would you do?

_____ *(a)*   I would readily accept my friend's generous offer and make a copy of the software.
_____ *(b)*   I would decline to copy it and plug away manually on the numbers.
_____ *(c)*   I would decide to go buy a copy of the software myself, for $300, and hope I would be reimbursed by the company in a month or two.
_____ *(d)*   I would request another extension on an already overdue project date.

Situation 3.   Your small manufacturing company is in serious financial difficulty. A large order of your products is ready to be delivered to a key customer when you discover that the product is simply not right. It will not meet all performance specifications, will cause problems for your customer, and will require rework in the field; but this, you know, will not become evident until after the customer has received and paid for the order. If you do not ship the order and receive the payment as expected your business may be forced into bankruptcy. And if you delay the shipment or inform the customer of these problems you may lose the order and also go bankrupt. What would you do?

_____ *(a)* I would not ship the order and place my firm in voluntary bankruptcy.
_____ *(b)* I would inform the customer and declare voluntary bankruptcy.
_____ *(c)* I would ship the order and inform the customer, after I received payment.
_____ *(d)* I would ship the order and not inform the customer.

Situation 4.   You are the cofounder and president of a new venture, manufacturing products for the recreational market. Five months after launching the business, one of your suppliers informs you it can no longer supply you with a critical raw material since you are not a large-quantity user. Without the raw material the business cannot continue. What would you do?

_____ *(a)* I would grossly overstate my requirements to another supplier to make the supplier think I am a much larger potential customer in order to secure the raw material from that supplier, even though this would mean the supplier will no longer be able to supply another, noncompeting small manufacturer who may thus be forced out of business.
_____ *(b)* I would steal raw material from another firm (noncompeting) where I am aware of a sizable stockpile.
_____ *(c)* I would pay off the supplier, since I have reason to believe that the supplier could be "persuaded" to meet my needs with a sizable "under the table" payoff that my company could afford.
_____ *(d)* I would declare voluntary bankruptcy.

Situation 5.   You are on a marketing trip for your new venture for the purpose of calling on the purchasing agent of a major prospective client. Your company is manufacturing an electronic system that you hope the purchasing agent will buy. During the course of your conversation, you notice on the cluttered desk of the purchasing agent several copies of a cost proposal for a system from one of your direct competitors. This purchasing agent has previously reported mislaying several of your own company's proposals and has asked for additional copies. The purchasing agent leaves the room momentarily to get you a cup of coffee, leaving you alone with your competitor's proposals less than an arm's length away. What would you do?

_____ *(a)* I do nothing but await the man's return.
_____ *(b)* I would sneak a quick peek at the proposal, looking for bottom-line numbers.
_____ *(c)* I would put the copy of the proposal in my briefcase.
_____ *(d)* I would wait until the man returns and ask his permission to see the copy.

Part II

STEP 1: BASED ON THE CRITERIA YOU USED, PLACE YOUR ANSWERS TO EACH OF THE ABOVE SITUATIONS ALONG THE CONTINUUM OF BEHAVIOR SHOWN BELOW:

	Duty	Contractual	Utilitarian	Situational
Situation 1				
Situation 2				
Situation 3				
Situation 4				
Situation 5				

STEP 2: AFTER SEPARATING INTO TEAMS OF FIVE TO SIX PEOPLE, RECORD THE ANSWERS MADE BY EACH INDIVIDUAL MEMBER OF YOUR TEAM ON THE FORM BELOW.   Record the answer of each team member in each box and the team's solution in the column on the far right.

Member Name   Team Answer

Situation 1					
Situation 2					
Situation 3					
Situation 4					
Situation 5					

STEP 3: REACH A CONSENSUS DECISION IN EACH SITUATION, IF POSSIBLE, AND RECORD THE CONSENSUS WHICH YOUR TEAM HAS REACHED ABOVE.   Allow 20 to 30 minutes.

STEP 4: REPORT TO AND DISCUSS WITH THE ENTIRE GROUP YOUR TEAM'S CONCLUSIONS AND HOW THE CONSENSUS, IF ANY, WAS REACHED. The discussion should focus on the following questions:
— Was a consensus reached by each group?
— Was this consensus difficult or easy to achieve and why?
— What kinds of ethical issues emerged?
— How were conflicts, if any, resolved, or were they left unresolved?

STEP 5: DISCUSS WITH THE GROUP THE FOLLOWING ISSUES:
- What role do ethical issues play and how important are they in the formation of a new venture management team?
- What role do ethical issues play and how important are they in obtaining venture capital—that is, how do investors feel about ethics and how important are they to them?
- What feelings bother participants most about the discussion and consensus reached—for example, if a participant believes that his or her own conduct was considered ethically less than perfect, does he or she feel a loss of self-respect or a sense of inferiority; does he or she fear others' judgment, etc.?

STEP 6: DEFINE EACH GROUP MEMBER'S GENERAL ETHICAL POSITION AND NOTE WHETHER HIS OR HER ETHICAL POSITION IS SIMILAR TO OR DIFFERENT FROM YOURS:

Member	Position	Different/ Similar

STEP 7: DECIDE WHOM YOU WOULD AND WOULD NOT WANT AS A BUSINESS PARTNER BASED ON THEIR ETHICAL POSITIONS:

Would Want	Would Not Want

OVERVIEW OF ETHICS

A good number of successful entrepreneurs believe that high ethical standards and integrity are exceptionally important to long-term success.

For example, the author and his colleague, Howard H. Stevenson, conducted a study among 128 presidents/founders attending the Harvard Business School's Owner/President Management Program (OPM) in 1983.[1] Their firms typically had sales of $40 million, and sales ranged from $5 million to $200 million. These entrepreneurs were also very experienced, with the average age in the mid-40s, and about half had founded their current companies. They were asked what the most critical concepts, skills, and know-how for success at their companies were at the time and what they would be in five years. The answer to this question was startling enough that even the Sunday *New York Times* reported the findings: 72 percent of the presidents responding stated that high ethical standards was the single most important factor in long-term success.

Conventional ethical disciplines have been accused of dealing with the business mode by narrowing and defining the scope of inquiry so as to avoid floundering. One author, for instance, *assumed* that "competitors are ethical and engaged in business, rather than jungle warfare."[2]

However, what is ethical and what is not often is not obvious; rather, situations involving ethical issues are often ambiguous. Today, as throughout much of this century, students, business people, and others have received many conflicting signals, as ". . . first artists and intellectuals, then broader segments of the society, challenged every convention, every prohibition, every regulation that cramped the human spirit or blocked its appetites and ambitions."[3]

This discussion has generated also a lot of controversy. As an example, a provocative and controversial article[4] published in the *Harvard Business Review* asserted that the ethics of business were not those of society but rather those of the poker game. The author of the article argued:

That most businessmen are not indifferent to ethics in their private lives, everyone will agree. My point is that in their office lives they cease to be private citizens; they become game players who must be guided by a somewhat different set of ethical standards.

The author further argued that personal ethics and business ethics are often not in harmony, and, either by negotiation or compromise, a resolution must be reached. The article provoked a storm of response.

Even the law, which should seemingly be black and white, is full of thorny issues. Laws not only have authority but also limitations. In the first place, laws are made with forethought and with the deliberate purpose of ensuring justice. They are, therefore, ethical in intent and deserve respect. However, laws are manmade, not God-made. Laws do not anticipate new conditions; they do not always have the effect they were intended to have; they sometimes conflict with one another; and they are, as they stand, incapable of making judgments where multiple ethical considerations hang in the balance or seem actually to war with one another. Thus, from the beginnings of recorded history in Egypt and the Middle

[1] Jeffry A. Timmons and Howard H. Stevenson, "Entrepreneurship Education in the 1980s," presented at the 75th Anniversary Entrepreneurship Symposium, Harvard Business School, Boston, 1983. *Proceedings,* pp. 115–34.

[2] Thomas Garrett, *Business Ethics* (New York: Appleton-Century-Crofts, 1966), pp. 149–50.

[3] Derek Bok, "Ethics, the University, & Society," *Harvard Magazine,* May–June 1988, p. 39.

[4] Albert Z. Carr, "Is Business Bluffing Ethical?" *Harvard Business Review,* January–February 1968, pp. 145–52.

East, a "code of laws" was always accompanied by a human "interpreter of laws," a judge, to decide when breaking the letter of the law did not violate the spirit or situation that the law was intended to cover. Great moments in history, religion, philosophy, and literature focus on the legal/ethical dilemma, and debating teams would wither away if the dilemma were to disappear.

ETHICAL STEREOTYPES

The 1980s have become the "Decade of Entrepreneurship" in America and around the world. The United States, now as in the past, is seen as providing an inviting and nurturing climate for those wishing to start their own enterprises and reap the rewards. In part, this is because the federal government has encouraged, to a greater degree than in any other country, an atmosphere under which free market forces, private initiative, and individual responsibility and freedom can flourish. Even such legislation as antitrust laws, laws regulating labor, and the graduated income tax have not hampered the growth of entrepreneurship in America.

These laws, enacted in response to society's changing perceptions of what constitutes "ethical" business practices, have had the equally desirable effect of encouraging those in many industries to develop codes of ethics—in large part because they wished to have the freedom to set their own rules, rather than to have rules imposed on them by Congress.

As the ethical climate of business has changed, so has the image of the entrepreneur. The "good" stereotype is personified by Horatio Alger. The "ruthless" stereotype is represented by entrepreneurs doing business in the unfettered economic climate in the 19th century—the era of the Robber Barons, where acts of industrial sabotage which today we would not condone were common. The battles of James Hill and Edward Harriman over the rights of railroads, the alleged sabotage by John D. Rockefeller of his competitors' oil refineries, the exploitation of child labor in New England's textile mills and of black labor in the southern cotton plantations, and the promoting of "snake oil" and Lydia Pinkham's tonics leave an unsavory aftertaste in the minds of today's more ethically conscious entrepreneurs.

Yet, thoughtful historians of American entrepreneurship will also recall that, regardless of standards by which they are judged or of the motivations attributed to them, certain American entrepreneurs gave back to society such institutions as the Morgan Library and the Rockefeller Foundation. The extraordinary legacy of Andrew Carnegie is another example. (And, of course, these scholars are much more inclined to examine and dissect the ethical behavior of the business sector, rather than that of the clergy, or even of academia itself. In many comparisons, the behavior of the business sector would look quite pure.)

Carnegie's case is also interesting because he described the total change of attitude that came over him after he had amassed his fortune. Carnegie was the son of a Scots weaver and was able personally to amass $300 million in the production of crude steel between 1873 and 1901. As Carnegie himself described, he believed that competition "insures the survival of the fittest in every department," and Carnegie also felt, "The fact that this talent for organization and management is rare among men is proved by the fact that it invariably secures enormous rewards for its possessor."[5] So apparently satisfied was Carnegie with the correctness of his view, he did not try to reconcile it with the fact that effectively British steel rails[6] were excluded by a protective tariff comprising over half the production price of each ton of steel rails. That Carnegie's mind was not easy over his fortune, however, is evident

---

[5] "Introduction to Contemporary Civilization in the West," *The Gospel of Wealth* (New York: Century, 1900), p. 620.

[6] W. E. Woodward, *A New American History* (Garden City, N.Y.: Garden City Publishing, 1938), p. 704.

from his statement that, "I would as soon give my son a curse as the almighty dollar."[7] After 1901, when he sold Carnegie Steel to United States Steel under pressure from a combine headed by J. P. Morgan, Carnegie personally supervised the giving in the United States and Great Britain of more than $300 million—an amount which is equivalent to many billions in today's dollars. Among his gifts to humanity were over 2,800 libraries, an Endowment for International Peace, and the Carnegie Institute of Pittsburgh.

From today's perspective, the entrepreneurs above might be described as acting in enlightened self-interest. However, when the same sort of entrepreneurial generosity is demonstrated today by such people as Armand Hammer of Occidental Petroleum and An Wang of Wang Laboratories, we are more likely to speak of their acts as philanthropy than as fulfilling their social contract.

Yet, a touch of suspicion still tinges entrepreneurial activity, and the word *entrepreneur* may still connote to some a person who belongs to a ruthless, scheming group located a good deal lower than the angels. In 1975, *Time* suggested that a businessman might make the best-qualified candidate for President but noted the "deep-rooted American suspicion of businessmen's motives."[8] Quoting John T. Conner, chairman of Allied Chemical and former head of Merck and Company, *Time's* editors added, "Anyone with previous business experience becomes immediately suspect. Certain segments think he can't make a decision in the public interest."[9]

However, in 1988, the prophecy of *Time* was fulfilled when George Bush, an oil entrepreneur, was elected as president of the United States, a revealing conclusion to America's most entrepreneurial decade.

SHOULD ETHICS BE TAUGHT?

More Controversy

Another furor about ethics occurred when *The Wall Street Journal* reported on a course taught at the Harvard Business School by Howard Raiffa on competitive decision making. It was reported that, during simulated negotiating sessions, students in this course were encouraged to use any tactic at all, including lying or making "strategic misrepresentations," in order to "win." It was also reported that the professor teaching the course had stated that "in strategic negotiations . . . it is unfortunately not always true that complete, unadorned open honesty is the best policy."[10]

Again, the protest mail poured into Harvard. Another publication[11] elicited comments from several dozen chief executive officers and professors of business to the leaders of the Girl and Boy Scouts. Sloan K. Childers, vice president of Phillips Petroleum, wrote:

Even though lying may be categorized as "strategic misrepresentation" it is still lying, and Phillips Petroleum Company does not condone or permit such activity in its operations. The course instructor states that in strategic negotiations it is unfortunately not always true that complete honesty is the best policy. We neither agree with this statement nor permit its implications to be applied by our people. It is our opinion that in business, as in other situations, honesty is always the best policy. I recognize that there are many honest differences of view; however, we do not subscribe to that statement that lying is now an acceptable part of negotiations.[12]

---

[7] Ibid., p. 622.

[8] "Time Essay: New Places to Look for Presidents," *Time,* December 15, 1975, p. 19.

[9] Ibid., p. 19.

[10] *The Wall Street Journal,* January 15, 1979, p. 1.

[11] Leonard H. Orr, ed., "Is Dishonesty Good for Business?" *Business & Society Review,* Summer 1979, pp. 4–19.

[12] Ibid., p. 12.

However, to view such controversies in either/or terms of lying versus telling the truth is to skirt the discussion of the ethical issues which a business practice, such as negotiation, involves. A more thoughtful appreciation of the study of ethical issues in the course was presented by the dean of the University of Chicago Business School,[13] who wrote:

In bargaining there often are facts that even the most ethical negotiator will conceal; facts that bear on the strength or weakness of his own position are an example. For this reason, and others, sunshine has proved less attractive in practice than its promise. As to Professor Raiffa's course and the account of it that appeared in *The Wall Street Journal,* I can comment only that newspaper writing does not lend itself readily to expression of subtle or complex ideas. Slightly rearranged, the facts of the article are: in artificially simple, one-time negotiations, students learn that dishonesty may pay; in complicated, repeated negotiations of the sort Harvard graduates often engage in, they learn that honesty often pays better. That lesson would have excited little attention, and consequently would likely not have appeared in *The Wall Street Journal.*

One great advantage of competition is that it provides powerful incentives for ethical behavior even among individuals not so inclined. I have noticed that most businessmen are far less likely to arouse expectations and then not fulfill them than politicians, journalists, clergymen, or university professors.[14]

Ethics Can and Should Be Taught

In an article that examines the ancient tradition of moral education, the decline of moral instruction beginning in the 19th century, and the renaissance of interest in ethics in the 1960s, Derek Bok, president of Harvard University, argues that ethics can and should be taught by educational institutions and that this teaching is both necessary and of value. He states:

Precisely because its community is so diverse, set in a society so divided and confused over its values, a university that pays little attention to moral development may find that many of its students grow bewildered, convinced that ethical dilemmas are simply matters of personal opinion beyond external judgment or careful analysis.

Nothing could be more unfortunate or more unnecessary. Although moral issues sometimes lack convincing answers, that is often not the case. Besides, universities should be the last institutions to discourage belief in the value of reasoned argument and carefully considered evidence in analyzing even the hardest of human problems.[15]

It is noteworthy that a former chairman of the New York Stock Exchange gave over $20 million to the Harvard Business School to help develop a way to include ethics in the MBA curriculum. Beginning in the fall of 1988, first-year students at the Harvard Business School participated in a unit during the third week totally dedicated to ethics in decision making.

Most entrepreneurs also believe ethics should be taught. In the research project mentioned on page 291, entrepreneurs and chief executive officers attending the Owner/President Management Program (OPM) at the Harvard Business School were asked the question: "Is there a role for ethics in business education for entrepreneurs?" Of those responding, 72 percent said ethics can and should be taught as part of the curriculum. (Only 20 percent said it should not, and two respondents were not sure.)

The most prominently cited reason for including ethics was that ethical behavior is at the core of long-term business success, because it provides the glue that binds enduring successful business and personal relationships together. In addition, the responses reflected

[13] Richard N. Rosett.
[14] Orr, "Is Dishonesty Good for Business?" p. 12.
[15] Ibid., p. 50.

a serious and thoughtful awareness of the fragile but vital role of ethics in entrepreneurial attainment and of the long-term consequences of ethical behavior for a business. Typical comments were:

If the free enterprise system is to survive, the business schools better start paying attention to teaching ethics. They should know that business is built on trust, which depends upon honesty and sincerity. BS comes out quickly in a small company.

And:

If our society is going to move forward, it won't be based on how much money is accumulated in any one person or group. Our society will move forward when all people are treated fairly—that's my simple definition of ethics. I know of several managers, presidents, etc., who you would not want to get between them and their wallets or ambitions.

And:

In my experience the business world is by and large the most ethical and law-abiding part of our society.

And:

Ethics should be addressed, considered and thoroughly examined; it should be an inherent part of each class and course . . .; instead of crusading with ethics, it is much more effective to make high ethics an inherent part of business—and it is.

However, these views were not universally held. One entrepreneur who helped to found a large company with international operations warned: "For God's sake, don't forget that 90 percent of the businessman's efforts consist of just plain hard work."

And, there is some cynicism. The 40-year-old head of a real estate and construction firm in the Northeast with 300 employees and $75 million in annual sales said: "There is so much hypocrisy in today's world that even totally ethical behavior is questioned since many people think it is some new negotiating technique."

The Usefulness of Academic Ethics

The study of ethics does seem to have the advantage of making students more aware of the pervasiveness of ethical situations in business settings, of bringing perspective to ethical situations from a distance, and of providing a framework for understanding ethical problems when they arise. Further, the study of ethics has been shown to affect, to some degree, both beliefs and behavior. For example, in a study of whether ethics courses affect student values, value changes in business school students who had taken a course in business ethics and those who did not were examined closely and were plotted across the multiple stages.[16]

The study used a sequence of stages, called the "Kohlberg construct," developed by Kohlberg in 1967. These stages are presented in *Exhibit 9.1*. In the Kohlberg construct, "being moral" in *stage 1* is synonymous with "being obedient," and the motivation is to avoid condemnation. In *stage 2,* the individual seeks advantage. Gain is the primary purpose, and interaction does not result in binding personal relationships. The orientation of *stage 3* is toward pleasing others and winning approval. Proper roles are defined by stereotyped images of majority behavior. Such reciprocity is confined to primary group relations. In *stage 4,* cooperation is viewed in the context of society as a whole. External laws serve to coordinate

---

[16] David P. Boyd, "Enhancing Ethical Development by an Intervention Program," unpublished manuscript, Boston, Northeastern University, 1980.

Exhibit 9.1
Classification of Moral Judgment into Stages of Development

Stage	Orientation	Theme
1	Punishment and obedience.	Morality of obedience.
2	Instrumental relativism.	Simple exchange.
3	Interpersonal concordance.	Reciprocal role taking.
4	Law and order.	Formal justice.
5	Legitimate social contract.	Procedural justice.
6	Universal ethical principle.	Individual conscience.

Source: Adapted from Kohlberg (1967).

moral schemes, and the individual feels committed to the social order. One thus subscribes to formal punishment by police or the courts. In *stage 5,* there is acknowledgement that reciprocity can be inequitable. New laws and social arrangements now may be invoked as corrective mechanisms. All citizens are assured of fundamental safety and equality. Cognitive structures at the *stage 6* level automatically reject credos and actions that the individual considers morally reprehensible, and the referent is a person's own moral framework, rather than stereotyped group behavior. Because most of one's fellows endorse a law does not guarantee its moral validity. When confronting social dilemmas, the individual is guided by internal principles that may transcend the legal system. Although these convictions are personal, they are also universal since they have worth and utility apart from the individual espousing them. Kohlberg's final stage thus represents more than mere conformity with state, teacher, or institutional criteria. Rather it indicates one's capacity for decision making and problem solving in the context of personal ethical standards.

In the study, those who took a course in business ethics showed a progression up the ethical scale, while those who had not taken a course did not progress.

A Framework for Analysis

It would be unfortunate if the entrepreneur did not realize his or her potential for combining action with ethical purpose because of the suspicion that the two are unrelated or inimical. There is no reason why they need be considered generically opposed. Nevertheless, the individual can expect no substitute in analyzing ethics for his or her own effort and intelligence.

A good framework for analyzing decisions involving ethical issues is the basis of a course that has been taught at the Harvard Business School by Kenneth E. Goodpaster.[17]

Goodpaster sees ethics for the manager as having dual aspects: that of the internal environment of the organization and that of the external environment of the organization, and he relates ethical transactions to these dual aspects. Thus, in this view, the corporation acts as the moral agent in its external environment in formulating business policy and in implementing that policy. Regarding the second aspect, the corporation is viewed as the moral environment to be managed. Transactions in this environment also involve issues of policy formulation and implementation.

In the course, Goodpaster considers the moral reasoning involved in decision making

[17] Taught as a second-year elective course, "Ethical Aspects of Corporate Policy." The following description of course material is from a course module by Kenneth E. Goodpaster, *Ethics in Management* (Boston: Harvard Business School, 1984), pp. 3–9.

within the context of philosophical ethics. Philosophical ethics is divided into three branches of ethical thinking: descriptive ethics, normative ethics, and metaethics. *Descriptive ethics* describes the values of individuals and groups. *Metaethics* is concerned with the meaning and the ability of ethical judgments to be proved. *Normative ethics* is concerned with criteria for right and wrong.

Normative ethics is divided into two levels—the first being moral common sense, and the second, critical thinking. *Moral common sense* is defined as a set of ethical values, principles, or rules of thumb. These include such ethical values as avoiding harming others, respecting the rights of others, not lying or cheating, keeping promises and contracts, obeying the law, helping those in need, being fair, and so forth, that guide decision making.

It is when items on an individual's moral common sense list conflict or are unclear or when items on one person's list do not agree with those of another person that an individual is forced to a second level of reasoning called "critical thinking." The professor states:

At this level, the search is for *criteria* that will justify the inclusion or exclusion of common sense norms, clarify their applicability in certain circumstances, and resolve conflicts among them.[18]

Goodpaster presents some normative views of critical thinking. These are called "utilitarianism, contractarianism, and pluralism."

In *utilitarianism,* "moral common sense is to be governed by a single dominant goal: maximizing net expectable utility (or happiness or pleasure or preference or welfare) for all parties affected by a decision or action."[19]

In *contractarianism,* "The central idea is that moral common sense is to be governed not by utility maximization, but by fairness."[20] Fairness, in this view, is defined as "a condition that prevails when all individuals are accorded equal respect as participants in social arrangements."[21]

In what is called "pluralism," the third approach:

The governing ethical ideal . . . is *duty.* For the pluralists, critical thinking about the first-level duties suggested by our moral common sense leads not to some single outside umpire (such as utility or fairness) but to a more reflective examination of duty itself. One must try to economize on one's list of basic duties, subordinating some to others, relying in the end on one's faculty of moral perception (or intuition or conscience) for the resolution of hard cases.[22]

The professor then states that analysis can then be guided by:

- Deciding whether there are ethical issues involved in a particular set of circumstances.
- Deciding whether they involve the internal or external environment of the company.
- Deciding the best courses of action to: (1) maximize utility, (2) achieve fairness, and (3) agree with duty.
- Analyzing the conflicts that exist between the courses of action.
- Deciding which course of action should override the others.
- Deciding if all ethically relevant considerations have been considered.
- Making a decision or devising an action plan.

[18] Ibid., p. 7.
[19] Ibid., p. 7.
[20] Ibid., p. 7.
[21] Ibid., p. 7.
[22] Ibid., p. 7.

Ethical Quicksand

It is worth noting that the above goal of utilitarianism is stated as maximizing utility for *all parties* affected by a decision or action. It is not a goal of maximizing the utility of the agent only. Believing that it is the agent's utility alone that should be maximized is a "quicksand" for some entrepreneurs. Further, a related notion that "the ends justify the means" is, for some, an irresistible temptation to rationalize nearly any behavior. It is not hard to argue that the Wall Street insider trading scandals of the 1980s, involving Ivan Boesky and Drexel Burnham's Michael Milken, were anchored in a mistaken "situational" view toward ethics.

THORNY ISSUES FOR ENTREPRENEURS

Action under Pressure

During an entrepreneurial career, an entrepreneur will have to act on issues under pressure of time and when struggling for survival. In addition, the entrepreneur will most likely decide ethical questions that involve obligations on many sides—to customers, employees, stockholders, family, partners, himself, or a combination of these. Walking the tightrope and balancing common sense with an ethical framework is precarious.

As a way to cope with the inevitable conflicts an entrepreneur will encounter, a first step is developing an awareness of his or her own explicit and implicit ethical beliefs, those of his or her team and investors, and those of the milieu within which the company competes for survival.

And, as the successful entrepreneurs quoted above believe, in the long run, succumbing to the temptations of situational ethics will, in all likelihood, will result in a tumble into the quicksand, not a safety net—just ask Ivan Boesky.

An appreciation of this state of affairs is succinctly stated by Fred T. Allen, chairman and president of Pitney-Bowes:

> As businessmen we must learn to weigh short-term interests against long-term possibilities. We must learn to sacrifice what is immediate, what is expedient, if the moral price is too high. What we stand to gain is precious little compared to what we can ultimately lose.[23]

Different Views

Different reactions to what is "ethical" may explain why some aspects of venture creation go wrong, both during start-up and in the heat of the battle, for no apparent reason. Innumerable examples can be cited to illustrate that broken partnerships often can be traced to apparent differences in the personal ethics among the members of a management team. So, too, with investors. While the experienced venture capital investor seeks entrepreneurs with a reputation for integrity, honesty, and ethical behavior, the definition is necessarily subjective and depends in part on the beliefs of the investor himself and in part on the prevailing ethical climate in the industry sector in which the venture is involved.

Problems of Law

For entrepreneurs, there are increasingly frequent situations where one law directly conflicts with another. For example, a small-business investment company in New York City became involved in serious financial trouble. The Small Business Administration stated that the company should begin to liquidate its investments, because it would otherwise be in

---

[23] Letter to the Editor, *The Wall Street Journal,* October 17, 1975.

defiance of its agreement with the SBA. However, the Securities and Exchange Commission stated that this liquidation would constitute unfair treatment of stockholders, due to resulting imbalance in their portfolios. After a year and a half of agonizing negotiation, the company was able to satisfy all the parties, but compromises had to be made on both sides.

Another example of conflicting legal demands involves conflicts between procedures of the Civil Services and the Fair Employment Practice Acts. The code states that hiring will include adherence to certain standards, a principle that was introduced in the last century to curb the patronage abuses in public service. Recently, however, the problem of encouraging and aiding minorities has led to Fair Employement Practice Acts, which require the same public agencies that are guided by Civil Service standards to hire without prejudice, and the requirement that a given test shall serve as the criterion of selection. Both these laws are based on valid ethical intent, but the resolution of such conflicts is no simple matter.

Further, unlike the international laws governing commercial airline transportation, there is no "international code of business ethics." When doing business abroad, entrepreneurs may find that those with whom they wish to do business have little in common with them — no common language, no common historical context for conducting business, and no common set of ethical beliefs about right and wrong and everything in between. For example, in the United States, bribing a high official to obtain a favor is considered both ethically and legally unacceptable; in parts of the Middle East, it is the only way to get things done. What we see as a "bribe," those in parts of the Middle East see as a "tip," like what you might give the headwaiter at a fancy restaurant in New York for a good table.

"When in Rome . . ." is one approach to this problem. Consulting a lawyer with expertise in international business before doing anything is another. And, assuming that the object of an entrepreneur's international business venture is to make money, he or she needs to figure out some way that is legally tolerable under the codes of laws which do apply and which is ethically tolerable personally.

Examples of the Ends-and-Means Issue

A central question in any ethical discussion concerns the extent to which a noble end may justify ignoble means — or whether using unethical means for assumed ethical ends may not subvert the aim in some way. As an example of a noble end, consider the case of a university agricultural extension service whose goal was to aid small farmers to increase their crop productivity. The end was economically constructive and profit-oriented only in the sense that the farmers might prosper from better crop yields. However, to continue being funded, the extension service was required to provide predictions of the annual increase in crop yield it could achieve, estimates it could not provide at the required level of specificity. Further, unless it could show substantial increases in crop yields, its funding might be heavily reduced. In this case, the extension service decided, if need be, to fudge the figures since it was felt that, even though the presentation of overly optimistic predictions was unethical, the objectives of the persons running the organization were highly ethical and even the unethical aspects could be condoned within the context of the inability of the various groups involved to speak each other's language clearly. The fact that the funding source finally backed down in its demand ameliorated the immediate problem. But if it had not, certainly a danger existed that the individuals in this organization, altruistic though their intentions were, would begin to think that falsification was the norm and would forget that actions that run contrary to one's ethical feelings gradually would build a debilitating cynicism.

Another example is given in the case of a merger of a small rental-service business with a middle-sized conglomerate, where a law's intent was in direct opposition to what would occur if the law were literally enforced. In this case, a partner in the rental firm, shortly before the merger, had become involved in a severe automobile accident, suffered multiple injuries, and was seemingly unable to return to work. The partner also knew that the outlook for his health in the immediate future was unpredictable. Under these circumstances, he was eager, for the sake of his family, to seek some of the stock acquired in the merger and make a large portion of his assets liquid. However, federal law does not allow quick profit taking from mergers and, therefore, did not allow such a sale. The partner consulted the president and officers of the larger company, and they acquiesced in his plans to sell portions of his stock and stated their conviction that no adverse effect on the stock would result. Still unsure, the man then checked with his lawyer and found that the federal law in question had almost never been prosecuted. Having ascertained the risk and having probed the rationale of the law as it applied to his case, the man then sold some of the stock acquired in the merger, in order to provide security for his family in the possible event of his incapacitation or death. Although he subsequently recovered completely, this could not have been foreseen.

In this instance, the partner decided that a consideration of the intrinsic purpose of the law allowed him to act as he did. In addition, he made as thorough a check as possible of the risks involved in his action. He was not satisfied with the decision he made, but he felt that it was the best he could do at the time. One can see in this example the enormous ethical tug of wars that go with the territory of entrepreneurship.

An Example of Integrity

That entrepreneurial decisions are complicated also is illustrated in the following example. At just age 27, an entrepreneur joined a new computer software firm with sales of $1.5 million as vice president of international marketing of a new division. His principal goal was to establish profitable distribution for the company's products in the major industrialized nations. Stock incentives and a highly leveraged bonus plan placed clear emphasis on profitability, rather than on volume. In one European country, the choice of distributors was narrowed to 1, from a field of over 20. The potential distributor was a top firm, with an excellent track record and management, and the chemistry was right. In fact, the distributor was so anxious to do business with the entrepreneur's company that it was willing to accept a 10 percent commission, rather than the normal 15 percent royalty. The other terms of the deal were acceptable to both parties. In this actual case, the young vice president decided to give the distributor the full 15 percent commission, in spite of the fact that it would have settled for much less. This approach was apparently quite successful because, in five years, this international division grew from zero to $18 million in very profitable sales, and the venture was acquired by a large firm for $80 million. In describing his reasoning, the entrepreneur said his main goal was to create a sense of long-term integrity. He said further:

I knew what it would take for them to succeed in gaining the kind of market penetration we were after. I also knew that the economics of their business definitely needed the larger margins from the 15 percent, rather than the smaller royalty. So I figured that if I offered them the full royalty, they would realize I was on their side, and that would create such goodwill that when we did have some serious problems down the road—and you always have them—then we would be able to work together to solve them. And that's exactly what happened. If I had exploited their eagerness to be our distributor, then it only would have come back to haunt me later on.

ETHICS EXERCISE REVISITED

The following statements are often made, even by practicing entrepreneurs: "How can we think about ethics when we haven't enough time even to think about running our venture?" *And:* "Entrepreneurs are doers, not thinkers—and ethics is too abstract a concept to have any bearing on business realities." *And:* "When you're struggling to survive, you're not worried about the means you use—you're fighting for one thing: survival."

However, the author feels that the contemplation of ethical behavior is not unlike poetry—emotion recollected in tranquility. This chapter is intended to provide one such tranquil opportunity.

Through the decisions actually made, or not made, an individual could become more aware of his or her own value system and how making ethical decisions can be affected by the climate in which these decisions are made. However, in the exercise, participants were asked only to answer questions. They were not being asked to carry out an action. Between intent and action lies a large gap, which can only be filled by confronting and acting in a number of ambiguous situations.

RESOURCE REQUIREMENTS   PART III

Resources to the entrepreneur are like the paint and the brush to the artist. They remain inert until the creative flair engages them with the canvas. There are special attitudes, strategies, and techniques used by successful entrepreneurs in *gaining control over the minimal resources* necessary to pursue an opportunity. Ownersip of these resources is not the key. What is vital is control and influence over OPR (other people's resources)—both monetary and nonmonetary. Often the latter are far more important than is commonly thought.

Identifying the necessary financial requirements of a start-up or emerging firm is a primary task. This includes knowing how much cash the venture will need, when, and where to raise it. Developing the appropriate financial statements "without the pain" is something every entrepreneur would like to accomplish. An exercise in the resources chapter, 10, will help entrepreneurs get started. Another significant task is identifying and utilizing effectively various outside resources—directors, advisors, accountants, attorneys, bankers, and the like. It is important to know where and how the best outsiders can be found, and what needs to be known about selecting, compensating, and working with them.

If the resources are the paint and brush, then the concept of the business plan is the canvas. By itself, it is sterile and bland. Knowing why, whether, and how to turn one's idea, a team, and resources into an artistic feat in the form of a first-rate business plan that can be used to raise money and resources and to grow the business is critical.

Finally, what do entrepreneurs do when the pace is so quick that there is simply not enough time to prepare a complete business plan? This can happen to an entrepreneur seeking to acquire a business, a license, a franchise, or other rights in a "hot seller's market." Knowing what to do and how to develop quickly a "dehydrated" business plan can make the difference between success and disappointment.

<table>
<tr><td>

Resource Requirements

</td><td>

10 >

</td></tr>
</table>

When it comes to control of resources . . . all I need from a source is the ability to use [the resource]. There are people who describe the ideal business as a post office box to which people send cash.

Howard H. Stevenson
Harvard Business School

RESULTS EXPECTED

Upon completion of the chapter, you will have:

1. Examined the successful entrepreneurs' unique attitudes about and approaches to resources — people, capital, and other assets.
2. Identified the important issues in the selection and effective utilization of outside professionals, such as members of a board of directors, lawyers, accountants, and consultants.
3. Examined decisions about financial resources.
4. Created simple cash flow and income statements and a balance sheet.

THE ENTREPRENEURIAL APPROACH TO RESOURCES

Resources include (1) people, such as the management team discussed in the last chapter, the board of directors, lawyers, accountants, and consultants; (2) financial resources; (3) assets, such as plant and equipment; and (4) a business plan.

Successful entrepreneurs view the need for and the ownership and management of these resources in the pursuit of opportunities differently from managers in many large organizations. This different way of looking at resources is reflected in the definition of entrepreneurship given in Chapter 1 — the process of creating or seizing an opportunity and pursuing it *regardless of the resources currently controlled.*[1]

Howard H. Stevenson has contributed to understanding the unique approach to resources of successful entrepreneurs.[2] The decisions on what resources are needed, when they are needed, and how to acquire them are strategic decisions that fit with the other driving forces of entrepreneurship. Further, as Stevenson has pointed out, entrepreneurs seek to use the minimum possible amount of all types of resources at each stage in their ventures' growth, and, rather than own the resources they need, they seek to control them.

Entrepreneurs with this approach reduce some of the risk in pursuing opportunities:

- *Capital.* The amount of capital required is simply smaller, thereby reducing the financial exposure and the dilution of the founder's equity.
- *Flexibility.* Entrepreneurs who do not own a resource are in a better position to commit

---

[1] This definition was developed by Howard Stevenson and colleagues at the Harvard Business School (see Chapter 1).

[2] Howard H. Stevenson's work on a paradigm for entrepreneurial management has contributed greatly to this area of entrepreneurship. See Howard H. Stevenson, "A New Paradigm for Entrepreneurial Management," *Proceedings from the 7th Anniversary Symposium on Entrepreneurship, July 1983* (Boston: Harvard Business School, 1984).

and decommit quickly, according to Stevenson.[3] One price of ownership of resources is an inherent inflexibility. With the rapidly fluctuating conditions and uncertainty with which most entrepreneurial ventures have to contend, inflexibility can be a serious curse. Response times need to be short, if a firm is to be competitive. Decision windows are most of the time small and elusive. And it is extremely difficult to predict accurately the resources which will be necessary to execute the opportunity. In addition, the entrepreneurial approach to resources permits "iterations" or "strategic experiments" in the venture process—that is, ideas can be tried and tested without committing to the ownership of all assets and resources in the business, to markets and technology which change rapidly, and so forth. For example, Howard Head says that, if he had raised all the money he needed at the outset, he would have failed by spending it all too early on the wrong version of his metal ski. Consider also, for example, the inflexibility of a company that commits permanently to a certain technology, software, or management system.

- *Low sunk cost.* In addition, sunk costs are lower were the firm to exercise the option to abort the venture at any point. Consider, instead, the enormous up-front capital commitment of a nuclear power plant and the cost of abandoning such a project.
- *Costs.* Fixed costs are lowered, thus favorably affecting break-even. Of course, the other side of the coin is that variable costs may rise. If the entrepreneur has found an opportunity with forgiving and rewarding economics, then there still will most likely be ample gross margins in the venture to absorb this rise.
- *Reduced risk.* In addition to reducing total exposure, other risks, such as the risk of obsolescence of the resource, are also lower. For example, it is no wonder that computer leasing caught on early and has prevailed.

While some might scoff at the practice, assuming erroneously that the firm "cannot afford to buy" a resource, the truth of the matter is that not owning one provides advantages and options. This is not to say that these decisions are not extremely complex, involving consideration of such details as the tax implications of leasing versus buying, and so forth.

Marshalling and Minimizing Resources

Minimizing resources is referred to in colloquial terms as "bootstrapping it" or, more formally, as a lack of resource intensity. Howard H. Stevenson put it this way:

Another characteristic we observe in good entrepreneurs is a multistage commitment of resources with a minimum commitment at each stage or decision point—in other words, a lack of resources intensity.

Entrepreneurs ask at every step how they can accomplish a little more with a little less and pursue the opportunity.

As was outlined in *Exhibit 6.2,* just the opposite attitude is often evident in large institutions that usually are characterized by a trustee or custodial viewpoint. Managers in larger institutions seek to have not only enough committed resources for the task at hand but also a cushion against the tough times.

---

[3] Ibid. See also Howard H. Stevenson, Michael J. Roberts, and H. Irving Grousbeck, *New Business Ventures and the Entrepreneur* (Homewood, Ill.: Richard D. Irwin, 1985).

Using Other People's Resources (OPR)

Another very important characteristic of the entrepreneurial approach to resources is obtaining the use of other people's resources, particularly in the start-up and early growth stages of a venture. In contrast, in large firms, often it is assumed that virtually all resources have to be owned to control their use, and decisions center around how these resources will be acquired and financed.

Not so with entrepreneurs. What is key is having the use of the resource and being able to control or influence the deployment of the resource. The quote at the beginning of the chapter illustrates this mind-set in its extreme.

Other people's resources can include such resources as money invested or loaned by friends, relatives, business associates, or other investors. These resources can include people, space, equipment, or other material loaned, provided inexpensively or free by customers or suppliers, or secured by bartering future services, opportunities, and the like.[4] Or, using other people's resources can be as simple as benefiting from free booklets and pamphlets, such as those published by many of the Big Eight accounting firms, or making use of low-cost educational programs or of government-funded management assistance programs.

Many examples of controlling, rather than owning, people resources exist. In real estate, even the largest firms do not employ top architects full time but, rather, secure them on a project basis. Most smaller firms do not employ lawyers but obtain legal assistance as needed. Technical consultants, design engineers, and programmers are other examples.

An example of this approach is a company that grew to $20 million in sales in about 10 years with $7,500 cash, a liberal use of credit cards, reduced income for the founders, and hard work and long hours. This company has not had to raise any additional equity capital.

An example of the opposite point of view is a proposed new venture in the minicomputer software industry. The business plan called for about $300,000, an amount which would pay only for the development of the first products. The first priority in the deployment of the company's financial resources outlined in the business plan was to buy outright a computer costing approximately $150,000. The founders refused to consider other options, such as leasing the computer or leasing computer time. The company was unable to attract venture capital, even though, otherwise, it had an excellent business plan. The $150,000 raised from informal private investors was not enough money to execute the opportunity, and the founders decided to give it back and abandon the venture. Would not a more entrepreneurial team have figured out a way to keep going under these circumstances?

OUTSIDE PEOPLE RESOURCES

Board of Directors

Initial work in evaluating the need for people resources is done in the process of forming a new venture team (see Chapter 7).

Once resource needs have been determined and a team has been selected, it will usually be necessary to obtain additional resources outside of the venture, in the start-up stage and during other stages of growth as well.

---

[4] For a discussion on finding and managing these outsiders, see Howard H. Stevenson and William Sahlman, "How Small Companies Should Handle Advisors," *Harvard Business Review,* March–April 1988, pp. 28–34. See also a *Harvard Business Review* reprint series called "Boards of Directors: Part I" and "Board of Directors: Part II" (Boston, Mass.: Harvard Business Review, 1976).

The decision of whether to have a board of directors[5] and, if the answer is yes, the process of choosing and finding the people who will sit on the board are troublesome for new ventures.

The Decision

The decision of whether to have a board of directors is influenced first by the form of organization chosen for the firm. If the new venture is organized as a corporation, it must have a board of directors, which must be elected by the shareholders. There is flexibility with other forms of organization.

In addition, certain investors will require a board of directors. Venture capitalists almost always require boards of directors and that they be represented on the boards.

Beyond that, deciding to involve outsiders is worth careful thought. This decision starts with the identification of what relevant missing experience, know-how, and networks, and of what the venture needs at this stage of its development, can be provided by outside directors. Their probable contributions then can be balanced against the fact that having a board of directors will necessitate greater disclosure to outsiders of plans for operating and financing the business. It also is worth noting here that one of the responsibilities of a board of directors is to elect officers for the firm, so the decision also is tied to decisions about financing and the ownership of the voting shares in the company.

A recent survey of entrepreneurial firms showed that one fourth of the companies responding had no outside directors and 16 percent had only one.[6] Of those who did have outside directors, these companies valued them most for their objectivity. Among the respondents, 93 percent had sales under $25 million, while 58 percent had annual revenues of less than $2 million. Eighty-three percent reported they were profitable. Sixty-four percent said the lead entrepreneur owned a controlling equity interest. This might account for a somewhat more sanguine view in the survey results.

The expertise that members of a board can bring to a venture, at a price it can afford, can far outweigh any of the negative factors mentioned above. In one venture, for instance, a venture capitalist who first invested in the company sat on the board of directors through the first years of highly successful growth. He made vital contributions in helping to recruit key top management, in giving the firm credibility with potential customers, in being a sounding board and devil's advocate, and in stimulating strategic thinking at a critical time—two years earlier than would have been done otherwise. The director served until it was evident that another kind of contribution was needed—that is, someone who could be valuable in helping in a public offering.[7]

Selection

Once the decision to have a board of directors has been made, finding the appropriate people for the board is a challenge. It is important to select people who are known to be trustworthy and to be objective. Most ventures typically look to personal acquaintances of the lead entrepreneur or the team or to their lawyers, bankers, accountants, or consultants for their first outside directors. While such a choice might be the right one for a venture, the

---

[5] The author is indebted to Howard H. Stevenson of the Harvard Business School, to John Van Slyke of Alta Research, and to Leslie Charm and Karl Youngman of Doktor Pet Centers and Command Performance hair salons, respectively, for insights into and knowledge of board of directors.

[6] "The *Venture* Survey: Who Sits on Your Board?" *Venture,* April 1984, p. 32.

[7] See Jeffry A. Timmons, "Venture Capital: More Than Money?" in *Pratt's Guide to Venture Capital Sources,* 8th ed. (Wellesley Hills, Mass.: Venture Economics), pp. 39–43.

process also involves finding the right people to fill the gaps discovered in the process of forming the management team.

New ventures are finding that people who could be potential board members are increasingly cautious about getting involved for a variety of reasons:

- *Liability.* Directors of a company can be held personally liable for its actions and those of its officers, and, worse, a climate of litigation exists in many areas. For example, some specific grounds of liability of a director have included voting a dividend that renders the corporation insolvent, voting to authorize a loan out of corporate assets to a director or an officer that ultimately becomes in default, and signing a false corporate document or report. Courts have held that, if a director acts in good faith, he or she is excused for his or her involvement. The problem is, however, that, for a director to *prove* that he or she has acted in good faith, especially in a start-up situation, is no easy matter. This proof is complicated by several factors, including possibly an inexperienced management team, the financial weaknesses and cash crises that occur and demand solution, and the lack of good and complete information and records, which are necessary as the basis for action. In recent years, many states have passed what is known as the "Dumb Director Law." In effect, the law allows that directors are normal human beings who can make mistakes and misjudgments, and this law, therefore, goes a long way in taking the sting out of potential lawsuits that are urged by "ambulance chasers."

- *Harassment.* Outside stockholders, who may have acquired stock through a private placement or through the over-the-counter market, can have unrealistic expectations about the risk involved in a new venture, the speed at which a return can be realized, as well as the size of the return. Such stockholders are a source of continual aggravation for boards and for their companies.

- *Time and risk.* Experienced directors know that often it takes more time and intense involvement to work with an early stage venture with sales of $10 million or less than with one having sales of $25 million to $50 million or more, and the former is riskier.

One solution to liability concerns is for the firm to purchase indemnity insurance for its directors. But this insurance is expensive. Despite the liability problems noted above, the survey mentioned found that just 11 percent of the respondents reported difficulty in recruiting board members.[8] In dealing with this issue, new ventures will want to examine a possible director's attitude toward risk in general and evaluate whether this is the type of attitude the team needs to have represented.

A top-notch outside director usually spends *at least* 9 to 10 days per year on his or her responsibilities. Four days per year are spent for quarterly meetings, a day of preparation for each meeting, a day for another meeting to cope with an unanticipated issue, plus up to a day or more for various phone calls. Yearly fees are usually paid for such a commitment.

Quality directors become involved for the learning and professional development opportunities, and so forth, rather than for the money. Compensation to board members varies widely. Fees can range from as little as $500 to $1,000 for a half- or full-day meeting to $10,000 to $30,000 per year for four to six full-day to day-and-a-half meetings, plus accessibility on a continuous basis. Directors are also usually reimbursed for their expenses incurred in preparing for and attending meetings. Stock in a start-up company, often 2 percent to 5 percent, or options, for 5,000 to 50,000 shares, are common incentives to attract and reward directors.

---

[8] "The *Venture* Survey: Who Sits on Your Board?" p. 32.

Alternatives to a Formal Board

The use of advisors and quasi boards can be a useful alternative to having a formal board of directors.[9] A firm can solicit objective observations and feedback for these advisors. Such informal boards can bring needed expertise to bear, without the legal entanglements and formalities of a regular board. Also, the possible embarrassment of having to remove someone who is not serving a useful role can be avoided. Informal advisors are usually much less expensive, with honorariums of $500 to $1000 per meeting common. It should perhaps be noted that the level of involvement of these advisors probably will be less than members of a formal board. The firm also does not enjoy the protection of law, which defines the obligations and responsibilities of board members of a formal board.

An informal group of advisors can also be a good mechanism through which a new venture can observe a number of people in action and select one or two as regular directors. The entrepreneur gains the advantages of counsel and advice from outsiders without being legally bound by their decisions.

Attorneys

The Decision

Almost all companies need and use the services of attorneys, and entrepreneurial ventures perhaps more so.[10] *INC.* magazine recently conducted a readership poll of approximately 5,000 subscribers and 5,000 lawyers. The typical subscribing company reported it had sales of $5.1 million, with 62 employees. Of these companies, 94 percent reported that they regularly relied on outside legal counsel. In addition, 88 percent of the attorneys who responded considered small business clients important to their practices.[11]

Indeed, it may be necessary for entrepreneurs to possess extensive knowledge of the law in addition to selecting good attorneys. John Van Slyke, a consultant who has also taught at Harvard Business School, has questioned whether entrepreneurs would be wise to pursue a law degree, either instead of or in addition to an MBA.[12] He believes that students of entrepreneurship have remained novices about the law and are not aware they are vulnerable. He says:

While lawyers are currently in abundant supply, quality in the profession is so thinly spread that our students are told repeatedly by guest speakers in class that it is vital to *find a good lawyer.* Yet experienced businessmen and women know that legal advice is in fact another form of outside expertise which must be managed effectively. To manage relationships with lawyers effectively, entrepreneurs must know what lawyers do and how they think. Prudent businessmen and women do not delegate wholesale all important legal matters to their lawyers, nor do they allow their lawyers to make many decisions for them. After all, the important signatures on contracts, tax forms, and other legal documents are those of the principals, not the lawyers.[13]

Just how attorneys are used by entrepreneurial ventures depends on the needs of the venture at its particular stage. Size is also a factor. *Exhibit 10.1* summarizes the findings of a survey by *INC.* magazine. Apparently, firms with sales under $1 million use attorneys mostly

[9] See the article by Harold W. Fox, "Quasi Boards: Useful Small Business Confidants," in *Growing Concerns,* ed. David E. Gumpert (New York: John Wiley & Sons and *Harvard Business Review,* 1984), pp. 307–16.

[10] The author wishes to acknowledge the input provided by Gerald Feigen of the Center for Entrepreneurial Studies, University of Maryland, from a course on entrepreneurship and the law he has developed and teaches at George Washington University Law School; also John Van Slyke of Alta Research.

[11] Bradford W. Ketchum, Jr., "You and Your Attorney," *INC.,* June 1982, pp. 51–56.

[12] John R. Van Slyke, "What Should We Teach Entrepreneurs about the Law," *Entrepreneurship: What It Is and How to Teach It* (Boston, Mass.: Harvard Business School, 1985), p. 135.

[13] Ibid., p. 139.

Exhibit 10.1
How Attorneys Are Used

Legal Service Used (ranked by total mentions)	Annual Company Sales				
	Under $1 Million	$1–2.9 Million	$3–4.9 Million	$5–24.9 Million	$25 Million or More
	Percent of Respondents				
Contracts and agreements	70%	74%	69%	84%	85%
Personal needs of top management	46	58	56	53	38
Formal litigation	34	50	63	61	91
Real estate and insurance matters	32	35	50	51	56
Incorporation	45	34	39	33	24
Estate planning	23	42	48	44	17
Delinquent accounts	20	33	39	34	21
Liability protection	20	17	22	33	41
Copyrights, trademarks, patents	21	19	24	28	38
Mergers and acquisitions	12	14	29	32	47
Employee benefit plans	10	26	19	27	27
Tax planning and review	13	17	22	17	12
Employee stock ownership plans	9	15	10	18	21
Franchising and licensing	13	11	14	14	12
Government-required reports	8	6	6	10	12
Prospectus for public offering	2	1	5	2	18
Labor relations	1	2	2	3	3

The need for legal counsel is obvious when it comes to contracts and lawsuits. But the *INC.* survey shows that small business managers also rely on company attorneys for personal problems ranging from tax matters to divorce and estate probate. As company size increases, so does the need for advice in such areas as liability, mergers, and benefit plans.

Reprinted with permission, *INC.* magazine (June 1982). Copyright ©1982 by Inc. Publishing Corporation, Boston.

for contracts and agreements. These companies also use a substantial amount of their attorneys' time for the personal needs of top management, matters surrounding incorporation, and formal litigation. As company size increases, so does the need for advice in such areas as liability, mergers, and benefit plans. It is also noteworthy that contracts and agreements were almost uniformly the predominant use, regardless of the size of the venture.

The following are areas of the law that entrepreneurs will most likely need to get assistance with:

- *Incorporation.* Issues, such as the forgivable and nonforgivable liabilities of founders, officers, and directors or the form of organization chosen for a new venture are important. As tax laws and other circumstances change, they are important for more-established firms as well. How important this area can be is illustrated by the case of a founder who nearly lost control of his company as a result of the legal maneuvering of the clerk and another shareholder. The clerk and the shareholder controlled votes on the board of directors, while the founder had controlling interest in the stock of the company. The shareholder tried to call a directors' meeting and not re-elect the founder president. The founder found out about the plot and adroitly managed to call a stockholders' meeting to remove the directors first.
- *Franchising and licensing.* Innumerable issues concerning future rights, obligations, and what happens in the event of nonperformance by either a franchisee or lessee or a franchisor or lessor require specialized legal advice.
- *Contracts and agreements.* Firms need assistance with contracts, licenses, leases, and other such agreements as noncompete employment agreements and those governing the vesting rights of shareholders.
- *Formal litigation, liability protection, etc.* In today's litigious climate, sooner or later most entrepreneurs will find themselves as defendants in lawsuits and require counsel.

- *Real estate, insurance, and other matters.* It is hard to imagine an entrepreneur who, at one time or another, will not be involved in various kinds of real estate transactions, from rentals to the purchase and sale of property, and require the services of an attorney.
- *Copyrights, trademarks, patents, and intellectual property protection.* Products are hard to protect. But, pushing ahead with development of products, such as software, before ample protection from the law is provided can be expedient in the short term but disastrous in the long term. For example, an entrepreneur, facing the loss of a $2.5 million sale of his business and uncollected fees of over $200,000 if his software was not protected, obtained an expert on the sale, leasing, and licensing of software products. The lawyer devised subtle but powerful protections, such as internal clocks in the software that shut down the software if they were not changed.
- *Employee plans.* Benefit and stock ownership plans have become complicated to use effectively and to administer. They require the special know-how of lawyers so common pitfalls can be avoided.
- *Tax planning and review.* Here, a word of caution is in order. All too frequently the tail of the accountant's tax avoidance advice wags the dog of good business sense. Entrepreneurs who worry more about finding good opportunities to make money, rather than tax shelters, are infinitely better off.
- *Federal, state, and other regulations and reports.* Understanding the impact of and complying with regulations often is not easy. Violations of federal, state, and other regulations often can have serious consequences.
- *Mergers and acquisitions.* There is specialized legal know-how in buying or selling a company. Unless an entrepreneur is highly experienced and has highly qualified legal advisors in these transactions, he or she can either loose the deal or end up having to live with legal obligations that may be costly.
- *Bankruptcy law.* Many people have heard tales of entrepreneurs who did not make deposits to pay various federal and state taxes in order to use that cash in their business. It is likely that these entrepreneurs falsely assumed that, if their companies went bankrupt, the government was out of luck, just like the banks and other creditors. They were wrong. In fact, the owners, officers, and often the directors are held personally liable for those obligations.
- *Other matters.* These matters can range from assistance with collecting delinquent accounts to labor relations.
- *Personal needs.* As entrepreneurs accumulate net worth (i.e., property and other assets), legal advice in estate, tax, and financial planning is important.

Selection

In a survey of what factors enter into the selection of a law firm or an attorney, 54 percent of the respondents said personal contact with a member of the firm was the main factor.[14] Reputation was a factor for 40 percent, and a prior relationship with the firm, 26 percent. Equally revealing was the fact that fees were mentioned by only 3 percent.

In many areas of the country are attorneys who specialize in new ventures and in firms with higher growth potential. The best place to start is with acquaintances of the lead entrepreneur, of members of the management team, or of directors. Recommendations from accountants, bankers, and associates also are useful. Other sources are partners in venture capital firms, partners of a Big Eight accounting firm (those who have privately owned and emerging company groups), a bar association, or the *Martindale-Hubbell Law Directory* (a listing of lawyers).

---

[14] Ketchum, "You and Your Attorney," p. 52.

An attorney, to be effective, needs to have the experience and expertise to deal with specific issues facing a venture. For example, one entrepreneur who relocated his business to new office space—in a renovated historical building that was being converted into office condominiums—did not use the two attorneys who handled his other business and personal affairs because neither had specific experience in office condominium deals involving historical properties and the complicated tax and multiple ownership issues involved.

As with members of the management team, directors, and investors, the chemistry is important.

Finally, advice to be highly selective and to expect to get what you pay for is sound. It is also important to realize that lawyers are not business people and that they do not usually make *business* judgments. Rather, they seek to provide "perfect" or "fail-safe" protection.

Most attorneys are paid on an hourly basis. Retainers and flat fees are sometimes paid, usually by larger ventures. The amount a venture pays for legal services expectedly rises as the firm grows. Many law firms will agree to defer charges or initially to provide services at a lower than normal rate in order to obtain a firm's business.

Bankers and Other Lenders

The Decision

The decision of whether to have a banker, or another lender, usually involves decisions about how to finance certain needs (see Part IV). It appears that most companies will need the services of a banker or other lender at some time in this respect. The decision also can involve how a banker or other lender can serve as an advisor.

As with other advisors, the banker or other lender needs to be a partner—not a difficult minority shareholder. First and foremost, therefore, an entrepreneur will be well advised to pick the *right banker or lender,* rather than to pick just a bank or a financial institution, although picking the bank or institution is also important. Different bankers and lenders have reputations ranging from "excellent" to "just OK" to "not OK" in how they work with entrepreneurial companies. Their institutions also have reputations for how well they work with entrepreneurial companies. Ideally, an entrepreneur needs an "excellent" banker or lender with an "excellent" bank or financial institution, although an "excellent" banker or lender with a "just OK" bank or institution is preferable to a "just OK" banker or lender with an "excellent" bank or financial institution.

For an entrepreneur to know clearly what he or she needs from a lender is an important starting point. Some will have needs that are asset-based, such as money for equipment, facilities, or inventory. Others may need working capital to fund short-term operating needs.

Having a business plan is invaluable preparation for selecting and working with a lender. Also, since a banker or other lender is a "partner," it is important to invite him or her to see the company in operation, to avoid late financial statements (as well as late payments and overdrafts), and to be honest and straightforward in sharing information.

Selection

Other entrepreneurs, lawyers, accountants that provide general business advisory services, and venture capitalists know bankers and other lenders. Starting with their recommendations is ideal. From among four to seven or so possibilities, an entrepreneur will find the right lender and the right institution.

Since today's banking and financial services marketplace is much more competitive than in the past, there are more choices, and it is worth the time and effort to shop around.

Key issues on which entrepreneurs focus in selecting a lender are the lender's knowledge of the industry and competition, his or her experience, his or her reputation for being creative and willing to take reasonable risk, his or her authority to make loans, and his or her ability to be an advocate. Chemistry also needs to be right. (See additional discussion in Chapter 16.)

Accountants

The Decision

The accounting profession has come a long way from the "green eyeshades" stereotype one hears reference to occasionally. Today, virtually all of the larger accounting firms have discovered the enormous client potential of new and entrepreneurial ventures, and a significant part of their business strategy is to cater specifically to these firms. In the Boston area, for instance, leading Big Eight accounting firms have located new offices for their small business groups on Route 128 in the heart of entrepreneurs' country.

Accountants often are unfairly maligned. As one author put it:

It is hard for entrepreneurs to fully appreciate accounting and what it can do for them. In fact, many tend to view the accountant as a bean counter, a sort of scorekeeper sitting on the sidelines, rather than as a player on the first team. This is a great mistake.[15]

Accountants who are experienced as advisors to emerging companies can provide, in addition to audits and taxation, other valuable services. An experienced general business advisor can be invaluable in helping to think through strategy, in helping to find and raise debt and equity capital, in mergers and acquisitions, in locating directors, and in helping to balance business decisions with important personal needs and goals.

Selection

In selecting accountants, the first step is for the venture to decide whether to go with a smaller local firm, a regional firm, or one of the Big Eight accounting firms. In making this decision, several factors come into play:[16]

- *Service.* Levels of service offered and the attention likely to be provided need to be evaluated. Chances are, for most start-ups, both will be higher in a small firm than a large one. But, if an entrepreneur of a higher-potential firm seeking venture capital or a strategic partner has aspirations to go public, a Big Eight firm is a good place to start.
- *Needs.* Needs, both current and future, have to be weighed against the capabilities of the firm. Larger firms are more equipped to handle highly complex or technical problems; while smaller firms may be preferable for general management advice and assistance, because the principals are more likely to be involved in handling the account. However, if the goal of the firm is to go public, a series of audits from one of the larger firms is preferable.
- *Cost.* Most Big Eight firms will offer very cost-competitive services to start-ups with significant growth and profit potential. If a venture needs the attention of a partner in a larger firm, services of the larger firm are more expensive. However, if the firm requires extensive technical knowledge, a larger firm may have more experience and, therefore, be cheaper.
- *Chemistry.* Always, chemistry is an important consideration.

---

[15] Gordon Baty, *Entrepreneurship for the 80s* (Reston, Va.: Reston Publishing, 1982), p. 107.

[16] Neil C. Churchill and Louis A. Werbaneth, Jr., "Choosing and Evaluating Your Accountant," in *Growing Concerns,* ed. David E. Gumpert (New York: John Wiley & Sons and *Harvard Business Review,* 1984), p. 265.

Of course, the right accountant is competent, as evidenced by the fact that he or she does not always adopt the government's point of view on tax matters, does not need to look up information often, and seems interested and informed on managerial issues.[17]

Sources of reference for good attorneys are also sources of reference for accountants. Other sources include trade groups.

Once a firm has reached any significant size, it will have many choices. The founders of one firm, which had grown to about $5 million in sales and had a strong potential to reach $20 million in sales in the next five years and eventually go public, put together a brief summary of the firm, including its background and track record, and a statement of needs for both banking and accounting services. The founders were quite startled at the time at the aggressive response they received from several banks and Big Eight accounting firms.

The accounting profession is straightforward enough. Whether the firm is small or large, they sell time, usually by the hour.

Consultants

The Decision

Consultants[18] are hired to solve particular problems and to fill gaps not filled by the management team. There are many skilled consultants who can be of invaluable assistance and a great source of "other people's resources."

Advice needed can be quite technical and specific or quite general or far ranging. Problems and needs also vary widely, depending upon whether the venture is just starting up or is an existing business.

Start-ups usually require help with critical one-time tasks and decisions that will have lasting impact on the business, such as assessing business sites, evaluating lease and rental agreements, setting up record and bookkeeping systems, finding business partners, obtaining start-up capital, and formulating initial marketing plans.

Existing businesses face ongoing issues resulting from growth. Many of these issues are of such a specialized nature that rarely is this expertise available on the management team. Issues of obtaining market research, evaluating when and how to go about computerizing business tasks, whether to lease or buy major pieces of equipment, and whether to change inventory valuation methods can be involved.

While it is not always possible to pinpoint the exact nature of a problem and sometimes simply an unbiased and fresh view is needed, a new venture is usually well advised to try to determine the broad nature of its concern, such as whether it involves a personnel problem, manufacturing problem, or marketing problem, for example. Observations in the *Harvard Business Review* by a consultant are revealing:

Management consultants are generally hired for the wrong reasons. Once hired, they are generally poorly employed and loosely supervised. The result is, more often than not, a final report that decorates an executive's bookshelf with as much usefulness as "The Life and Mores of the Pluvius Aegiptus" would decorate his coffee table—and at considerably more expense.[19]

Selection

Unfortunately, nowhere are the options so numerous, the quality so variable, and the costs so unpredictable as in the area of consulting. The number of people calling themselves management consultants alone is large and growing steadily. By 1989, there were an

[17] Ibid., p. 263.

[18] The following is excerpted in part from David E. Gumpert and Jeffry A. Timmons, *The Encyclopedia of Small Business Resources* (New York: Harper & Row, 1984), pp. 48–51.

[19] Jean Pierre Frankenhuis, "How to Get a Good Consultant," *Harvard Business Review,* November–December 1977, p. 133.

estimated 50,000 to 60,000 private management consultants around the country. It is estimated that approximately 2,000 or more are added annually. Further, somewhat more than half the consultants were found to work on their own, while the remainder work for firms. In addition, government agencies (primarily the Small Business Administration) employ consultants to work with businesses; various private and nonprofit organizations provide management assistance to help entrepreneurs; and others, such as professors, engineers, and so forth, provide consulting services part time. Such assistance also may be provided by other professionals, such as accountants and bankers.

Again, the right chemistry is critical. One company president who was asked what he had learned from talking to clients of the consultant he finally hired said, "They couldn't really pinpoint one thing, but they all said they would not consider starting and growing a company without him!"

As unwieldy and risky as the consulting situation might appear, there are ways of limiting the choices. For one thing, consultants tend to have specialties, and, while some consultants claim wide expertise, most will at least indicate the kinds of situations they feel most comfortable with and skillful in handling. Further, some of the desirable qualities in a consulting firm are summarized below:[20]

- A shirtsleeve approach to the problems.
- An understanding attitude toward the feelings of managers and their subordinates.
- A modest and truthful offer of services and an ability to produce results.
- A reasonable and realistic charge for services.
- A willingness to maintan a continuous relationship.

Three or more potential consultants can be interviewed about their expertise and approach and their references checked. Candidates who pass this initial screening then can be asked to prepare specific proposals.

A written agreement, specifying the consultant's responsibilities and objectives of the assignment, the length of time the project will take, and the type and amount of compensation, is highly recommended. Some consultants work on an hourly basis, some on a fixed-fee basis, and some on a retainer-fee basis. Huge variations in consulting costs for the same services exist. At one end of the spectrum is the Small Business Administration, which provides consultants to small businesses without charge. At the other end of the spectrum are well-known consulting firms that may charge large amounts for minimal marketing or technical feasibility studies.

While the quality of most products roughly correlates with their price, not so with consulting services. The point is that it is difficult to judge consultants solely on the basis of the fees they charge.

FINANCIAL RESOURCES

Analyzing Financial Requirements

Once the opportunity has been assessed, once a new venture team has been formed, and once all resources needs have been identified, *then* is the time for a new venture to evaluate what financial resources are required and when. (Sources of financing and how to obtain funding are covered in detail in Part IV.)

As has been noted before, there is a temptation, in this area particularly, to place the cart before the horse. Entrepreneurs are tempted to begin their evaluation of business

---

[20] Harvey C. Krentzman and John N. Samaras, "Can Small Business Use Consultants," in *Growing Concerns,* ed. David E. Gumpert (New York: John Wiley & Sons and *Harvard Business Review,* 1984), pp. 243–62.

opportunities, and particularly their thinking about formal business plans, with analyzing spreadsheets, rather than focusing first on defining the opportunity, deciding how to seize it, and then preparing the financial estimates of what is required.

However, when the time comes to analyze financial requirements, it is important to realize that cash is the life's blood of a venture. As James Stancill, professor of finance at the University of Southern California's business school, has said: "Any company, no matter how big or small, moves on cash, not profits. You can't pay bills with profits, only cash. You can't pay employees with profits, only cash."[21]

Financial resources are almost always limited, and important and significant trade-offs need to be made in evaluating a company's needs and the timing of those needs.

Spreadsheets

The computer, and spreadsheet programs, are tools that save time and increase productivity and creativity enormously. Spreadsheets are nothing more than pieces of accounting paper adapted for use with a computer. *Exhibit 10.2* shows a sample spreadsheet analysis done using Lotus 1-2-3 and Robert Morris Associates data. (See Appendix I for information on using RMA data.)

The origins of the first spreadsheet program, VisiCalc, reveal its potential relevance for entrepreneurs. It was devised by an MBA student[22] while he was attending Harvard Business School. The student was faced with analyzing pro forma income statements and balance sheets, cash flows, and breakeven for his cases. The question—"*What if* you assumed such and such?"—was inevitably asked.

The major advantage of using spreadsheets to analyze capital requirements is having the ability to answer questions of "what if." This takes on particular relevance also when one considers, as James Stancill points out:

Usual measures of cash flow—net income plus depreciation (NIPD) or earnings before interest and taxes (EBIT)—give a realistic indication of a company's cash position only during a period of steady sales.[23]

Take cash flow projections. For example, an entrepreneur could answer a question, such as, "What if sales grow at just 5 percent, instead of 15 percent, and what if only 50 percent, instead of 65 percent, of amounts billed are paid in 30 days?" The impact on cash flow of changes in these projections can be seen.

The same what-if process also can be applied to pro forma income statements and balance sheets, budgeting, and break-even calculations. To illustrate, by so altering assumptions about revenues and costs that cash reaches zero, breakeven can be analyzed. Thus, for example, Robert Morris Associates assumptions could be used as comparative boundaries for testing assumptions about a venture.

An example of how computer-based analysis can be of enormous value is the experience of a colleague who was seriously considering starting a new publishing venture. His analysis of the opportunity was encouraging, and important factors, such as relevant experience and commitment by the lead entrepreneur, were there. Assumptions about fixed and variable costs, market estimates, and probable start-up resource requirements had been assembled. What needed to be done next was to generate detailed monthly cash flows to determine more precisely the economic character of the venture, including the impact of the quite seasonal nature of the business, and to determine the amount of money needed to launch the business and the amount and timing of potential rewards. In less than three hours, the assumptions

[21] James M. Stancill, "When Is There Cash in Cash Flow?" *Harvard Business Review,* March–April 1987, p. 38.

[22] Dan Bricklin.

[23] Stancill, "When Is There Cash in Cash Flow?" p. 38.

Exhibit 10.2
Sample Spreadsheet Analysis

OUTPUT GENERATED:

```
***********************
*    Cash Budget      *
***********************
```

	Months 1	2	3	4	5	6	7	8	9	10	11	12
CASH BALANCE (Opening)	$50,000	$31,235	$9,073	($18,917)	($50,811)	($85,583)	($122,252)	($173,852)	($228,743)	($293,067)	($359,823)	($431,361)
Plus RECEIPTS: Sales Collections	$2,725	$6,000	$9,675	$13,350	$17,025	$20,700	$24,375	$28,050	$34,350	$38,775	$42,750	$46,425
Other Proceeds	$0	$0	$2,000	$0	$2,000	$5,000	$0	$4,000	$0	$0	$0	$0
Total	$2,725	$6,000	$11,675	$13,350	$19,025	$25,700	$24,375	$32,050	$34,350	$38,775	$42,750	$46,425
Less DISBURSEMENTS: Raw Material Payables	$16,875	$20,625	$26,250	$31,875	$37,500	$43,125	$50,625	$60,000	$67,500	$71,250	$76,875	$82,500
Other Expenses (Accruals)	$4,494	$6,806	$9,169	$11,531	$13,894	$16,256	$19,313	$22,369	$25,706	$28,069	$30,431	$32,794
Fixed Asset Additions	$0	$0	$3,000	$0	$0	$0	$2,400	$0	$0	$0	$0	$0
Lease Expense	$0	$80	$80	$80	$80	$80	$80	$80	$80	$80	$80	$80
Long Term Debt Payments	$5	$5	$5	$5	$5	$5	$5	$5	$5	$5	$5	$5
Other Expenses (Itemized)	$0	$30	$0	$60	$20	$0	$0	$500	$0	$0	$0	$0
"Other Asset" Additions	$0	$0	$10	$0	$0	$0	$0	$0	$0	$0	$0	$0
Federal Taxes (Operations)	$238	$645	$1,048	$1,430	$1,863	$2,285	$2,678	$2,840	$3,915	$4,328	$4,740	$5,153
Total	$21,611	$28,191	$39,561	$44,981	$53,381	$61,751	$75,100	$85,794	$97,206	$103,731	$112,131	$120,531
Net Cash Gain (Loss)	($18,886)	($22,911)	($27,886)	($31,631)	($34,336)	($36,051)	($50,725)	($53,744)	($62,856)	($64,956)	($69,381)	($74,106)
Cumulative Cash Balance	$31,114	$9,044	($18,813)	($50,548)	($85,147)	($121,634)	($172,977)	($227,595)	($291,599)	($358,023)	($429,205)	($505,467)
Financial Income (Expense), net of tax	$121	$29	($104)	($263)	($436)	($618)	($875)	($1,148)	($1,468)	($1,800)	($2,156)	($2,537)
ENDING CASH BALANCE	$31,235	$9,073	($18,917)	($50,811)	($85,583)	($122,252)	($173,852)	($228,743)	($293,067)	($359,823)	($431,361)	($508,004)
Desired Cash Level	$2,000	$2,000	$2,000	$2,000	$2,000	$2,000	$2,000	$2,000	$2,000	$2,000	$2,000	$2,000
Loan Required to Maintain Minimum Cash Level	$0	$0	$20,813	$52,548	$87,147	$123,634	$174,977	$229,595	$293,599	$360,023	$431,205	$507,467
Cash Surplus	$29,114	$7,044	$0	$0	$0	$0	$0	$0	$0	$0	$0	$0

Exhibit 10.2 *(continued)*

OUTPUT GENERATED :

```
*********************
*  Income Statement  *
*********************
```

	Months											
	1	2	3	4	5	6	7	8	9	10	11	12
NET SALES	$5,000	$10,000	$15,000	$20,000	$25,000	$30,000	$35,000	$40,000	$50,000	$55,000	$60,000	$65,000
Allowance for Slippage of Sales Forecast	$1,250	$2,500	$3,750	$5,000	$6,250	$7,500	$8,750	$10,000	$12,500	$13,750	$15,000	$16,250
GROSS SALES	$3,750	$7,500	$11,250	$15,000	$18,750	$22,500	$26,250	$30,000	$37,500	$41,250	$45,000	$48,750
Less: Materials Used	$1,875	$3,750	$5,625	$7,500	$9,375	$11,250	$13,125	$15,000	$18,750	$20,625	$22,500	$24,375
Direct Labor	$375	$750	$1,125	$1,500	$1,875	$2,250	$2,625	$3,000	$3,750	$4,125	$4,500	$4,875
Other Manufacturing Expense	$159	$319	$478	$638	$797	$956	$1,116	$1,275	$1,594	$1,753	$1,913	$2,072
Indirect Labor	$159	$319	$479	$638	$797	$956	$1,116	$1,275	$1,594	$1,753	$1,913	$2,072
COST OF GOODS SOLD	$2,569	$5,138	$7,706	$10,275	$12,844	$15,413	$17,981	$20,550	$25,688	$28,256	$30,825	$33,394
GROSS PROFIT	$1,181	$2,363	$3,544	$4,725	$5,906	$7,088	$8,269	$9,450	$11,813	$12,994	$14,175	$15,356
Less: Sales Expense	$188	$375	$563	$750	$938	$1,125	$1,313	$1,500	$1,875	$2,063	$2,250	$2,438
General and Administrative Expense	$94	$188	$281	$375	$469	$563	$656	$750	$938	$1,031	$1,125	$1,219
Bad Debt Expense	$75	$150	$225	$300	$375	$450	$525	$600	$750	$825	$900	$975
Depreciation Expense, Fixed Assets	$250	$250	$300	$300	$300	$300	$340	$340	$340	$340	$340	$340
Lease Expense	$0	$80	$80	$80	$80	$80	$80	$80	$80	$80	$80	$80
Other Expenses (Itemized Above)	$0	$30	$0	$60	$20	$0	$0	$500	$0	$0	$0	$0
OPERATING PROFIT	$575	$1,290	$2,095	$2,860	$3,725	$4,570	$5,355	$5,680	$7,830	$8,655	$9,480	$10,305
Income Taxes on Operations	$238	$645	$1,048	$1,430	$1,863	$2,285	$2,678	$2,840	$3,915	$4,328	$4,740	$5,153
OTHER FINANCIAL REVENUE (EXPENSE)	$243	$59	($208)	($525)	($871)	($1,236)	($1,750)	($2,296)	($2,936)	($3,600)	($4,312)	($5,075)
Income Tax Provision	$121	$29	($104)	($263)	($436)	($618)	($875)	($1,148)	($1,468)	($1,800)	($2,156)	($2,537)
NET PROFIT	$459	$674	$944	$1,167	$1,427	$1,667	$1,803	$1,692	$2,447	$2,528	$2,584	$2,615

Exhibit 10.2 *(continued)*

LIST OF ASSUMPTIONS:

Schedule A - Sales and Cost of Sales

	Months										
	1	2	3	4	5	6	7	8	9	10	11
Net Sales $	$5,000	$10,000	$15,000	$20,000	$25,000	$30,000	$35,000	$40,000	$50,000	$55,000	$60,000
Projected Sales, net of slippage	$3,750	$7,500	$11,250	$15,000	$18,750	$22,500	$26,250	$30,000	$37,500	$41,250	$45,000

	YEAR				
	1984	1985	1986	1987	1988
Slippage of Sales Forecast, % of sales.. What if?	25.0%	15.0%	10.0%	10.0%	5.0%
Material Costs, as % of sales	50.0%	48.0%	46.0%	45.0%	45.0%
Direct Labor, as % of sales	10.0%	10.0%	9.0%	9.0%	9.0%
Other m'fg expense (overhead, etc., but exclude depreciation), as % of sales	4.3%	4.3%	4.3%	4.3%	4.3%
Indirect Labor, as % of sales	4.3%	4.3%	4.3%	4.3%	4.3%
Sales expense, as % of sales	5.0%	4.0%	4.0%	4.0%	4.0%
General and Administrative, $	2.5%	2.5%	2.5%	2.5%	2.5%
Federal income tax rate, % of Profit before Tax	50.0%				
What month does this analysis begin? (1-12)	1				
What is the present year?	1984				

Schedule B - Accounts Receivable Aging

	1984	1985	1986	1987	1988
% Collections 0-30 Days	70%	70%	70%	80%	80%
% Collections 30-60 Days	20%	20%	20%	19%	19%
% Collections 60-90 Days	8%	8%	8%	0%	0%
% Uncollectable - Bad Debts	2%	2%	2%	1%	1%

Schedule C - Accounts Payable Aging (Raw Materials)

	1984	1985	1986	1987	1988
% Payments 0-30 Days	100%	100%	80%	80%	80%
% Payments 30-60 Days	0%	0%	20%	20%	20%
% Payments 60-90 Days	0%	0%	0%	0%	0%

Schedule E - Direct Labor, Indirect Labor, M'fg Expense, Selling and G & A Expense, Accruals Aging

	1984	1985	1986	1987	1988
% Payments 0-30 Days	100%	100%	90%	90%	90%
% Payments 30-60 Days	0%	0%	10%	10%	10%

Schedule F - Inventory Assumptions

	1984	1985	1986	1987	1988
What is desired cash level? ($)	$2,000	$5,000	$7,000	$10,000	$10,000
How many months of finished goods inventory on hand?	2	2	3	3	3
How many months of raw materials inventory on hand?	3	3	4	4	4

Schedule G - Financial Revenue and Term Debt Assumptions

	1984	1985	1986	1987	1988
What interest is payed on outstanding loans to maintain desired cash level?	12%	12%	12%	15%	15%
What is your return on a cash surplus?	10%	10%	10%	11%	11%

LIST OF ASSUMPTIONS (PAGE 2):

Schedule H - Beginning Balances, period one

ASSETS:

Cash Balance	$50,000
Accounts Receivable	$100
Raw Materials Inventory	$100
Finished Goods Inventory	$300
Fixed Assets, Depreciable	$3,000
Accumulated Depreciation	$50
Other Assets, net	$200
Total Assets	$53,650

LIABILITIES:

Raw Materials Payable	$100
Accruals Payable	$50
Notes Payable - Banks	$100
Long Term Debt	$100
Contributed Capital	$500
Retained Earnings	$52,800
Total Liabilities + Equity	$53,650

Other - Present Loss Carryforward (-)   ($100)

Schedule I - Cash Budget, Income Statement Monthly Changes $$

Months	1	2	3	4	5	6	7	8	9	10	11	12
Receipts (Cash Basis):												
Other Proceeds (LTD)	$0	$0	$2,000	$0	$2,000	$0	$0	$4,000	$0	$0	$0	$0
Contributed Capital Additions	$0	$0	$0	$0	$0	$5,000	$0	$0	$0	$0	$0	$0
Disbursements (Cash Basis):												
Long Term Debt Payments	$5	$5	$5	$5	$5	$5	$5	$5	$5	$5	$5	$5
Other Expenses	$0	$30	$0	$60	$20	$0	$0	$500	$0	$0	$0	$0
"Other Asset" Additions, non-depreciable	$0	$0	$10	$0	$0	$0	$0	$0	$0	$0	$0	$0

Schedule J - Fixed Asset Additions

	Asset 1	Asset 2	Asset 3
CURRENT ASSETS:			
Amount	$3,000		
Depreciation Period	1		
YEAR 1:			
Amount	$2,400	$3,000	$2,400
Month Bought (1-12)	2	3	7
Depreciation Period or Lease Term	3	5	5
Cash Basis = 1 / Lease = 2	2	1	1
YEAR 2:			
Amount	$3,600	$3,600	$3,600
Month Bought (1-12)	1	6	6
Depreciation Period or Lease Term	5	5	5
Cash Basis = 1 / Lease = 2	1	1	1
YEAR 3:			
Amount	$4,000	$4,000	$5,000
Date Bought	2	3	3
Depreciation Period or Lease Term	3	3	3
Cash Basis = 1 / Lease = 2	2	2	1

NOTE : YEARS FOUR AND FIVE ASSUMPTIONS SAME AS ABOVE

Exhibit 10.2 *(concluded)*

OUTPUT GENERATED :

```
*****************
*  Balance Sheet  *
*****************
  (End of Month)
```

	Months											
	1	2	3	4	5	6	7	8	9	10	11	12
ASSETS: Cash	$31,135	$8,973	$0	$0	$0	$0	$0	$0	$0	$0	$0	$0
Receivables	$1,125	$2,625	$4,200	$5,850	$7,575	$9,375	$11,250	$13,200	$16,350	$18,825	$21,075	$23,400
Less : Allowance for doubtful accts.	($75)	($225)	($450)	($750)	($1,125)	($1,575)	($2,100)	($2,700)	($3,450)	($4,275)	($5,175)	($6,150)
Net Receivables	$1,200	$2,850	$4,650	$6,600	$8,700	$10,950	$13,350	$15,900	$19,800	$23,100	$26,250	$29,550
Finished Goods Inventory (Net)	$13,144	$31,125	$54,244	$82,500	$115,894	$154,425	$200,663	$254,606	$313,688	$377,906	$447,263	$521,756
Raw Materials Inventory (Net)	$5,625	$9,375	$13,125	$16,875	$20,625	$24,375	$28,125	$33,750	$39,375	$43,125	$46,875	$50,625
CURRENT ASSETS	$50,954	$51,873	$71,119	$104,475	$142,968	$186,600	$237,938	$298,856	$365,963	$435,581	$510,038	$589,631
Fixed Assets	$3,000	$3,000	$6,000	$6,000	$6,000	$6,000	$8,400	$8,400	$8,400	$8,400	$8,400	$8,400
Accumulated Depreciation	$300	$550	$850	$1,150	$1,450	$1,750	$2,090	$2,430	$2,770	$3,110	$3,450	$3,790
Net Fixed Assets	$2,700	$2,450	$5,150	$4,850	$4,550	$4,250	$6,310	$5,970	$5,630	$5,290	$4,950	$4,610
Other Assets	$200	$200	$210	$210	$210	$210	$210	$210	$210	$210	$210	$210
TOTAL ASSETS	$53,854	$54,523	$76,479	$109,535	$147,729	$191,060	$244,458	$305,036	$371,803	$441,081	$515,198	$594,451
LIABILITIES: Notes Payable – Banks	$0	$0	$19,017	$50,911	$85,683	$122,352	$173,952	$228,843	$293,167	$359,923	$431,461	$508,104
Raw Materials Payable	$0	$0	$0	$0	$0	$0	$0	$0	$0	$0	$0	$0
Accruals Payable	$0	$0	$0	$0	$0	$0	$0	$0	$0	$0	$0	$0
Income Tax Payable	$0	$0	$0	$0	$0	$0	$0	$0	$0	$0	$0	$0
Total Current Liabilities	$0	$0	$19,017	$50,911	$85,683	$122,352	$173,952	$228,843	$293,167	$359,923	$431,461	$508,104
Total Long Term Debt	$95	$90	$85	$2,080	$2,075	$4,070	$4,065	$4,060	$8,055	$8,050	$8,045	$8,040
TOTAL LIABILITIES	$95	$90	$19,102	$52,991	$87,758	$126,422	$178,017	$232,903	$301,222	$367,973	$439,506	$516,144
CAPITAL STOCK: Contributed Capital	$500	$500	$500	$500	$500	$5,500	$5,500	$5,500	$5,500	$5,500	$5,500	$5,500
Retained Earnings	$53,259	$53,933	$54,877	$56,044	$57,471	$59,138	$60,941	$62,633	$65,080	$67,608	$70,192	$72,807
TOTAL LIABILITIES AND NET WORTH	$53,854	$54,523	$74,479	$109,535	$145,729	$191,060	$244,458	$301,036	$371,803	$441,081	$515,198	$594,451

about revenues and expenditures associated with the start-up were entered into a computer model. Within another two hours, he had been able to see what the venture would look like financially over the first 18 months and then to see the impact of several different what-if scenarios. The net result was that the new venture idea was abandoned, since the amount of money required appeared to outweigh the potential.

The strength of computer-based analysis is also a source of problems for entrepreneurs who place the "druther" before the fact. With so many moving parts, analysis that is not grounded in sound perceptions about an opportunity is most likely to be confused.

GENERAL SOURCES OF INFORMATION

There are *many* sources of information in the area of resources, including magazines such as *INC.* and *Venture.* Online database services mentioned in Chapter 3 are good sources of information. A book written by the author with David Gumpert puts together, under one cover, basic sources of information. It is called *The Encyclopedia of Small Business Resources* (Harper & Row, 1984). See the Annotated Bibliography for a summary of "best selections" of interest to entrepreneurs.

EXERCISE — FINANCIAL STATEMENTS

For most entrepreneurs, preparing financial statements is a pain. To help make the preparation of financial statements, William D. Bygrave, professor in entrepreneurial studies at Babson College, prepared a guide for students at Babson College. The Financial Statements Exercise is based on this guide and will help you get *started.* See also information in Appendices I and II.

The basic financial statements entrepreneurs use are the following:

- Income statements, monthly for the first two years and then quarterly for the next three years.
- Cash flow statements, monthly for the first two years and then quarterly for the next three years.
- Balance sheets, yearly for five years.

The Financial Statements Exercise will help you generate financial statements like those shown in *Exhibit 10.3* through *Exhibit 10.5.* These financial statements were created for a fictional company, Bygrave & Schuman, Inc., a start-up business that manufactures alternative lifestyle bicycles. In the exercise, the fiscal year is the calendar year.

While the Financial Statements Exercise is a guide to get you started, it is based on a very simple example. Accounting in your venture will most likely be more complicated. For example, you could use LIFO (last in/first out) or FIFO (first in/first out) in accounting for inventory; you may have fixed assets and need to choose from different methods of depreciation; etc. There are excellent texts available. It also is recommended that you consult an accountant.

Exhibit 10.3
Balance Sheet

BYGRAVE & SCHUMAN, INC.
Balance Sheet
Years Ending December 31
($1,000)

	1989	1990	1991	1992	1993
ASSETS					
Current:					
Cash	$255				
A/R*	100				
Inventory	49				
Rent deposit	9				
Utilities dep.	2				
Total	$415				
LIABILITIES					
Current:					
A/P†	$ 15				
Bank loan	60				
Long-term:					
Bank loan	240				
Equity pd.-in	20				
Ret. earnings	80				
Total	$415				

* A/R means Accounts Receivable.
† A/P means Accounts Payable.

Exhibit 10.4
Assumptions for Financial Statements

(1) Wages and salaries are paid in month they are earned (i.e., no accruals).
(2) Material is paid for one month after purchase.
(3) Finished goods are shipped and booked as sales in the month after they were manufactured.
(4) Payment terms are net 30 days; so A/R equals revenue in the prior month.
(5) There are prepaid deposits for rent and utilities.
(6) Insurance is paid quarterly.
(7) Income tax is paid in the current month (i.e., no accruals or deferrals). (It is a crude approximation.)
(8) Loan is to be repaid in years 2 through 6.
(9) Ending inventory is the CGS in the following month (i.e., the goods manufactured in the current month are sold next month).

Exhibit 10.5
Income and Cash Flow Statements

BYGRAVE & SCHUMAN, INC.
Income Statement
($1,000)

	1989 Jan.	Feb.	Mar.	Apr.	May	June	July	Aug.	Sept.	Oct.	Nov.	Dec.	1989 Total Year
Revenues	$ 0	$100	$150	$200	$200	$150	$100	$ 50	$100	$100	$200	$100	$1,450
Material	0	15	23	30	30	23	15	8	15	15	30	15	218
Labor	0	30	45	60	60	45	30	15	30	30	60	30	435
Bldg. rent	0	2	2	2	2	2	2	2	2	2	2	2	22
Equip. rent	0	2	2	2	2	2	2	2	2	2	2	2	22
Total CGS	0	49	72	94	94	72	49	27	49	49	94	49	697
Gross income	$ 0	$ 51	$ 79	$106	$106	$ 79	$ 51	$ 24	$ 51	$ 51	$106	$ 51	$ 754
Salaries	20	20	20	20	20	20	20	20	20	20	20	20	240
Marketing	20	20	20	20	20	20	5	5	20	20	20	20	210
Utilities	5	5	5	5	5	5	5	5	5	5	5	5	60
Insurance	4	4	4	4	4	4	4	4	4	4	4	4	48
Office rent	1	1	1	1	1	1	1	1	1	1	1	1	12
Automobiles	1	1	1	1	1	1	1	1	1	1	1	1	12
Travel	2	2	2	2	2	2	2	2	2	2	2	2	24
Entertainment	1	1	1	1	1	1	1	1	1	1	1	1	12
Total GA&S	54	54	54	54	54	54	39	39	54	54	54	54	618
Interest	3	3	3	3	3	3	3	3	3	3	3	3	36
Income tax	0	0	0	0	8	5	2	0	0	0	5	0	$ 20
Net income	($ 57)	($ 6)	$ 22	$ 49	$ 41	$ 17	$ 7	($ 19)	($ 6)	($ 6)	$ 44	($ 6)	$ 80

Cash flow
($1,000)

	Jan.	Feb.	Mar.	Apr.	May	June	July	Aug.	Sept.	Oct.	Nov.	Dec.
Begin cash	$ 0	$210	$ 93	$ 54	$ 45	$105	$190	$254	$275	$223	$179	$157
Bank loan	300											
Equity pd. in	20											
Revenue	0	0	100	150	200	200	150	100	50	100	100	200
Total cash in	$320	$ 0	$100	$150	$200	$200	$150	$100	$ 50	$100	$100	$200
Material	0	15	23	30	30	23	15	8	15	15	30	15
Labor	30	45	60	60	45	30	15	30	30	60	30	30
Bldg. rent	8	2	2	2	2	2	2	2	2	2	2	2
Equip. rent	2	2	2	2	2	2	2	2	2	2	2	2
Salaries	20	20	20	20	20	20	20	20	20	20	20	20
Marketing	20	20	20	20	20	20	5	5	20	20	20	20
Utilities	7	5	5	5	5	5	5	5	5	5	5	5
Insurance	12			12			12			12		
Office rent	4	1	1	1	1	1	1	1	1	1	1	1
Automobiles	1	1	1	1	1	1	1	1	1	1	1	1
Travel	2	2	2	2	2	2	2	2	2	2	2	2
Entertainment	1	1	1	1	1	1	1	1	1	1	1	1
Interest	3	3	3	3	3	3	3	3	3	3	3	3
Income tax	0	0	0	0	8	5	2	0	0	0	5	0
Tot. cash out	100	177	140	159	140	115	86	80	102	144	122	102
Ending cash	$210	$ 93	$ 54	$ 45	$105	$190	$254	$275	$223	$179	$157	$255

EXERCISE
FINANCIAL STATEMENTS

STEP 1:   CREATE YOUR INCOME STATEMENT, EXCEPT FOR INTEREST, PROFIT BEFORE TAXES, TAXES, AND PROFIT AFTER TAXES.   Use a cash basis, rather than an accrual basis.
- Determine your sales revenue on a monthly basis. Remember this is actual revenue received.
- Determine cost of goods sold. Remember that the cost of goods sold in any period is the cost of the goods that actually were sold in the period, not the cost of goods that were manufactured but not sold.
- Determine overhead costs. Do not include interest at this point because, until you have made cash flow projections, you do not know how much money you will need. And, do not fool with income tax at this point.

STEP 2:   CREATE A CASH FLOW STATEMENT, EXCEPT FOR INTEREST AND TAXES.   You will be creating a "real-time" cash flow statement, not a sources and uses of funds statement (although you can do that later), so use a cash basis, rather than an accrual basis, in accounting for income and expenses.
- Start with beginning cash of $0 and add to it any equity paid in at the start of the company. Do not include any loans at this point, since any debt will be determined from the initial cash flow projections.
- Determine, month by month, when the company will receive payments for goods and/or services; and when the company will pay wages, bills, interest, taxes, etc., as follows:
  a. Add any revenue that the company expects to receive in that month. Remember, this is actual cash received, not accounts receivable.
  b. Subtract cash that flows out. Remember, this is not accounts payable or wages payable; rather, payments are recognized when the cash leaves the company. Recognize payroll taxes and corporate income taxes in the month they become due (a conservative approach). Do not include interest and income taxes at this point, because you do not yet know how much money you need to borrow.
  c. Use ending cash for the period as beginning cash for the next period.

STEP 3:   DETERMINE HOW MUCH MONEY YOU NEED TO BORROW, THE INTEREST, AND THE INCOME TAXES.
- Determine, by looking at when the maximum cash shortfall and estimating the amount needed for contingencies, the amount you need to borrow.
- Determine interest and income taxes. Be sure to carry forward losses from period to period.
- Since interest and income taxes will change the amount of the maximum shortfall, adjust, as needed, the amount you need to borrow.
- Go through as many iterations of the income and cash flow statements as necessary to determine the amounts.

STEP 4:   COMPLETE YOUR INCOME STATEMENT.
- Determine monthly interest payments.
- Determine profit before taxes.
- Determine corporate income taxes.
- Determine profit after taxes.

STEP 5:   COMPLETE YOUR CASH FLOW STATEMENT.
- Determine interest and income tax payments.

STEP 6:   CREATE YOUR BALANCE SHEET.
- Determine current assets. It is assumed there are no fixed assets.

   a. Determine cash, the ending cash balance on December 31.
   b. Determine accounts receivable on December 31.
   c. Determine inventory on December 31.
   d. Determine other assets, such as a rent deposit or a deposit with the telephone company.
 — Determine current liabilities:
   a. Determine accounts payable on December 31.
   b. Determine the amount of your bank loan that is due in the next 12 months.
 — Determine long-term liabilities:
   a. Determine the amount of the bank loan that is due after the next 12 months.
   b. Determine paid-in equity (i.e., total equity paid in by the stockholders).
   c. Determine retained earnings (or losses) — that is, accumulated earnings (or losses) from the inception of the company through the date of the balance sheet.

STEP 7:   WRITE FOOTNOTES DETAILING IMPORTANT ASSUMPTIONS USED.

The What, Whether, and Why of the Business Plan

11

*Madame, enclosed please find the novel you commissioned. It is in two volumes.
If I had more time I could have written it in one.*

Voltaire

RESULTS EXPECTED

Upon completion of this chapter, you will have:

1. Identified what a business plan is, whether a business plan needs to be prepared, who needs to prepare it, and why.
2. Examined requirements of effective business plans.
3. Looked at common pitfalls of planning.
4. Studied how to write a business plan, including learning the difference between opportunity screening and writing a business plan, who develops the business plan, how to develop the action steps necessary, and some dos and don'ts in planning.
5. Analyzed a classic business plan written by entrepreneurs to raise venture capital for an actual company.

PLANNING AND THE BUSINESS PLAN

The What

Planning is a way of thinking about the future of a venture; that is, of deciding where a firm needs to go and how fast, how to get there, and what to do along the way to reduce the uncertainty and to manage risk and change.

Effective planning is a *process* of setting goals and deciding how to attain them. Planning occurs in start-up situations, in growing enterprises, and in very large firms.

In some sense, most successful ventures plan. One author writing in the *Harvard Business Review* observed that:

The smaller companies weathering the current difficult economic times seem to be those following an idea—call it a no-frills, down-to-earth, but clear plan—of how to take advantage of the environment and how to allocate resources.[1]

A business plan is one type of planning document, which results from the process of planning. A business plan is a written document that (1) summarizes a business opportunity (i.e., why the opportunity exists and why the management team has what it takes to execute the plan) and (2) defines and articulates how the management team expects to seize and execute the opportunity identified.[2]

---

[1] Phillip Thurston, "Should Smaller Companies Make Formal Plans?" *Harvard Business Review,* September–October 1983, p. 184.

[2] See an article by J. A. Timmons, "A Business Plan Is More Than a Financing Device," *Harvard Business Review,* March–April 1980.

A complete business plan usually is of considerable length. In recent years, however—particularly in business based on certain technologies, products, or services, where there is turbulence, greater-than-usual unpredictability, and rapid change—an alternative to a complete full-blown business plan has become acceptable. This can be called a "dehydrated" business plan. Dehydrated business plans serve most often as trial balloons for prospective investors and are launched before a decision is made to undertake a complete business plan.

In any case, creating a business plan is more a process than simply a product, and the resulting plan is not immutable. By the same token, the business plan for a business is not "the business." A business plan is analogous to a pilot's cross-country flight plan, in that it defines the most desired, most timely, and least-hazardous route to a given destination. Yet, innumerable factors, such as unexpected weather and traffic, can significantly alter the course of the actual flight. Similarly, for new companies, it is common for the actual course of the business to diverge from that originally developed in a business plan. For as was said in the first century, B.C., "It is a bad plan that admits of no modification."[3]

The Why

Business plans are used primarily (1) for raising capital and (2) as a means of guiding growth.

The decision whether to plan, and ultimately to write a business plan, then involves the following:

- Whether the venture needs to raise capital, and whether a business plan is valuable for this purpose.
- Whether the planning process itself will be valuable enough in terms of defining and anticipating potential risks, problems, and trade-offs in a venture to justify the time spent.

For ventures seeking to raise venture capital or other equity in today's highly competitive environment, a quality business plan is a must. As William Egan, founding partner of one of the nation's largest and most successful venture capital funds, Burr, Egan & Deleage, put it:

Ten to fifteen years ago, a high-quality business plan really stood out and gave the entrepreneur a competitive edge in getting our attention. Today, you have to have a high-quality plan as a given—without it you're dead—but since everyone coming to us for money has a highly professional plan, the plan won't give you much of an edge by itself.

As a vehicle for raising capital, a business plan convinces investors that the new venture has identified an opportunity, has the entrepreneurial and management talent to exploit that opportunity, and has a rational, coherent, and believable program for achieving revenue and expense targets on time. If the business plan passes the initial screening, the plan will be given a more detailed evaluation, and it will become a prime measure of the abilities of those involved to define and analyze opportunities and problems and to identify and plan actions to deal with them.

A business plan can be particularly helpful after start-up as a tool to understand and as a means of guiding growth. One can think of developing a business plan as using a flight simulator. The consequences of different strategies and tactics and the human and financial requirements for launching and building the venture can be determined and worked through

[3] Said by Publilius Syrus.

4 percent decrease in total manufacturing cost. For subsequent financial analysis these productivity improvements were assumed to be achieved by Rapidrill over a three-year period, utilizing a 90 percent "learning curve" on assembly operations.

Rapidrill's manufacturing operations will also seek further efficiencies through the use of modern production, inventory control, and purchasing systems that will be focused on reducing the costs of buying, storing, and handling the large content of purchased components used in rotary drills. The implementation of these systems will be significantly aided by employing "parts grouping" techniques (see Section 5) in the product line design. Parts grouping will allow flexibility in assembly scheduling and will minimize inventory requirements.

The total result of such manufacturing operations will be minimum capital equipment and inventory investment and manufacturing costs (after sufficient "learning curve" improvement) from 6 percent to 8 percent below those of present competition. This manufacturing cost reduction, together with the anticipated 3 percent to 4 percent reduction in Rapidrill's selling expenses, as compared to those of its competitors, means that Rapidrill's manufacturing and selling costs should be from 9 percent to 12 percent less than those of its competitors. Cost advantages of this order in products with a high purchased content could give Rapidrill a strong competitive advantage.

7. Schedule

Figure F

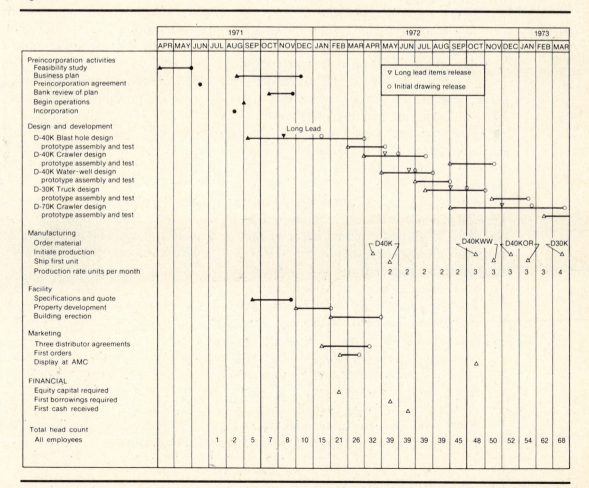

8. Risks

As with any new venture, there are risks in Rapidrill's plans. Recognition of these risks, evaluation of their severity, and proper contingency planning for their possible occurrences have been considered in Rapidrill's planning.

While the following discussion of specific risks is not intended to be all-inclusive, it is felt to cover those of significant possible impact. Risks are *not* listed in order of probability of occurrence or of degree of possible impact.

1. *Risk:* Legal action by Indiana Tool, Inc. (ITI).

   Evaluation: While the departure of its key team members has jeopardized ITI's rotary drill market dominance, it is the opinion of Rapidrill's counsel that no cause for action by ITI has been created. Letters between legal counsel for ITI and Rapidrill have been exchanged, and the prognosis is that the likelihood of further action by ITI is slim.

   Contingency: Rapidrill has had policy guidelines prepared by counsel and plans no actions that could be construed as unfair competition or breach of ITI's legal rights.

2. *Risk:* Price cutting by competitors.

   Evaluation: Market will absorb everyone's capacity for the next few years. At that time Rapidrill will have sufficient volume to be price competitive with any of its competitors. Historically, existing manufacturers have not responded to new competition with price cuts.

   Contingency: Financial planning included generous contingencies in unit costs. If costs are close to present estimates, Rapidrill has immediate ability to reduce its prices and remain profitable.

3. *Risk:* Cost estimates exceeded by engineering and/or manufacturing.

   Evaluation: Design has progressed sufficiently so 60 percent of purchased components are firmly priced. Rapidrill's principals have extensive experience with design and manufacturing start-up phases, so estimates should be accurate.

   Contingency: In financials, 10 percent was added to material cost estimates and 100 percent excess assembly time was added to year 1 estimates, and 80 percent to year 2, giving Rapidrill leeway on meeting actual costs.

4. *Risk:* Machine doesn't meet specification performance.

   Evaluation: This is considered a low-risk item. Engineering track record of F. T. Samuels is excellent; however, rapid acceptance of Rapidrill units will depend on immediate support of unit in the field.

   Contingency: In addition to $25,000 allocated to development testing (2.5 times normal), financial planning includes expenditure of $10,000 per unit in field support of first eight units (about five times past experience levels), then progressively less but allowance for significant warranty expenditures. Additional $20,000 allocated for a demonstration program could be directed to development.

5. *Risk:* Sales forecasts not achieved.

   Evaluation: Analysis shows a low breakeven level (less than 50 percent of year 2 forecasts), and some fixed costs can be delayed to reduce further the breakeven if sales are falling well below forecasts.

   Contingency: Procurements will be committed for lower-level production than forecast but at forecast rate, allowing time for additional procurements within lead time if sales trend to forecast levels or higher.

6. *Risk:* Delays in design and/or manufacturing.

   Evaluation: Delays in design unlikely for first unit since most design work now complete. Delays in either can be minimized to about $20,000 additional cash requirement per month delay. Financial plan shows cash balance of $64,000 for first year-end, allowing, in worst case, a two- to three-month delay.

Contingency: Watch design and manufacturing schedule closely, and expedite procurements closely. An additional $60,000 borrowing is available to Rapidrill in year 2 within debt-equity guidelines; so another three-month contingency could be available.

7. *Risk:* Long lead-time procurements encountered.

Evaluation: Trucks, diesel engines, compressors, and hydraulic components are on order, with satisfactory shipments promised. Rapidrill's early requirements, two per month, can be met with minor disturbance even if vendors have major problems. Vendors have confirmed this.

Contingency: Closely follow procurements—some purchased components have four- to five-month lead times—and we cannot afford to order backup from other vendors.

8. *Risk:* Economy downturn or fuel shortage affecting sales.

Evaluation: Energy shortages should enhance the sale of drills to mining markets and accelerate, rather than deter, Rapidrill's growth.

Contingency: Watch signals closely; trend should be apparent before manufacturing is started.

9. *Risk:* Tight money affecting Rapidrill's ability to obtain the required line of credit.

Evaluation: Plan has been reviewed by three largest banks in Nashville, which supported financial assumptions regarding borrowing. Money supply has eased somewhat since those commitments.

Contingency: Secure committed lines of credit in excess of forecast requirements to the limit of reasonable debt-equity ratios.

10. *Risk:* Legislation to curtail strip mining.

Evaluation: In light of the forecast energy shortage and the fact that 10 percent of the nation's energy presently comes from surface-mined coal, this eventuality is considered small.

Contingency: Diversion of initial selling efforts to other market segments. Planned sales of first two years could be achieved in several other market segments.

9. Financial Plan

Introduction

Using the sales levels and rotary drill prices developed by the marketing forecast, detailed estimates of material, labor, and burden generated by engineering and manufacturing, and estimates of design, development, and general sales and administrative expenses, detailed financial statements were drawn up depicting the forecast results of Rapidrill's operations for the five years from 1972 to 1976, inclusive. The following assumptions were used in arriving at the results:

1. All operations are performed in a leased facility in Nashville, Tennessee. Labor rates, shipping costs, lease rates, etc., used are consistent with the area.
2. All projections are in 1971 dollars.
3. Interest payments are computed at 15 percent on borrowings. Borrowings will be provided by bank lines of credit.
4. Balance sheet assumptions are:
   a. Accounts receivable: 30-day collection through mid-1975; 45 days thereafter.
   b. Notes receivable: Average 36-month repayment schedule at 10 percent simple interest. Financing by Rapidrill will commence in the fourth quarter of 1975. Earlier

Exhibit A

RAPIDRILL CORPORATION
Sales and Earnings Forecasts
Fiscal Years Ended September 30, 1972–1976
(000s omitted)

	1972	1973	1974	1975	1976
Sales:					
Units	$ 730	$3,827	$6,596	$ 9,067	$11,400
Spares	51	383	989	1,813	2,280
Total	781	4,210	7,585	10,880	13,680
Cost of sales:					
Material	434	2,204	3,722	5,269	6,620
Labor	16	98	201	258	323
Burden	98	387	500	589	631
Total	548	2,689	4,423	6,116	7,574
Gross margin	233	1,521	3,162	4,764	6,106
Percent	29.8	36.1	41.7	43.8	44.6
Selling and marketing	77	430	648	991	1,246
Engineering	74	134	273	425	534
Administration and general	306	483	705	1,103	1,387
Total	457	1,047	1,626	2,519	3,167
Earnings before interest and taxes	(224)	474	1,536	2,245	2,939
Interest expense (income)	5	48	52	(3)	(64)
Earnings before federal and state taxes	(229)	426	1,484	2,248	3,003
Federal and state taxes		214	751	1,347	1,519
Net earnings before extraordinary item	(229)	212	733	1,111	1,484
Extraordinary item—reduction in federal income taxes resulting from carryover of prior years' operating losses		114			
Net earnings	$(229)	$ 326	$ 733	$ 1,111	$ 1,484
Percent sales before extraordinary item		5.0	9.7	10.2	10.8
Percent sales after extraordinary item		7.7	9.7	10.2	10.8

financing to be accomplished utilizing an independent financial institution. Cavanagh Leasing Corporation has expressed interest.

c. Inventories: Four turns per year.

d. Accounts payable: 60-day average through 1975; 36–40 days thereafter.

Income taxes include state and federal.

Loss for 1972 carried forward and deducted from 1973 income in accordance with IRS Code Section 172.

Organizational expenses and initial design cost, estimated to be $14,000 and $240,000, respectively, have been expensed.

Pro forma financial statements are presented as *Exhibits A* through *I,* and *Exhibit J* is a breakeven chart.

Financial Performance

1. *Sales and Earnings Forecasts* (see *Exhibits A* through *C*): Sales of Rapidrill are projected to increase from $730,000 in 1972 to $13,680,000 in 1976. After a projected loss of $229,000 in the first year, after-tax profits are expected to increase from $326,000 in 1973 to $1,484,000 in 1976 (see *Exhibit A*). After-tax profit as a percentage of sales is 7.7 percent in the second year of Rapidrill's operation and increases to 10.8 percent in the fifth year. Even

Exhibit B

RAPIDRILL CORPORATION
Monthly Sales and Earnings Forecasts
Fiscal Year Ended September 30, 1972
(000s omitted)

	Oct.	Nov.	Dec.	Jan.	Feb.	Mar.	Apr.	May	June	July	Aug.	Sept.	Total
Sales:													
Units..............								$ 92	$ 182	$ 92	$ 182	$ 182	$ 730
Spares.............								6	13	6	13	13	51
								98	195	98	195	195	781
Cost of sales:													
Material..............								54	109	54	109	108	434
Labor...............								2	4	2	4	4	16
Burden.............								12	24	12	25	25	98
								68	137	68	138	137	548
Gross margin..........								30	58	30	57	58	232
Percent..............								30.6	29.7	30.6	29.2	29.7	29.8
Selling and marketing....						$ 2	$ 13	13	13	14	14	15	84
Engineering............	$ 5	$ 2	$ 3	$ 6	$ 4	7	7	7	8	9	9	10	77
Administration and													
general.............	45*	15	14	16	16	17	28	39	29	29	29	29	296
	50	17	17	22	20	26	48	59	50	52	52	54	457
Earnings before interest and taxes............	(50)	(17)	(17)	(22)	(20)	(26)	(48)	(20)	8	(22)	5	5	(224)
Interest expense (income).............										1	2	2	5
Earnings before federal and state taxes.........	(50)	(17)	(17)	(22)	(20)	(26)	(48)	(20)	8	(23)	3	3	(229)
Federal and state taxes													
Net earnings...........	$(50)	$(17)	$(17)	$(22)	$(20)	$(26)	$(48)	$ (20)	$ 8	$ (23)	$ 3	$ 3	$(229)

* Note: Includes expenses during five months prior to incorporation.

if actual sales are one half of those forecast, Rapidrill will be profitable in its second year of operation (see breakeven chart, *Exhibit J*, and *Exhibit A*).

2. *Cash Flow* (see *Exhibits D* through *F*):   The equity capital raised in this offering, together with the investment of the principals and lines of credit of $250,000 in 1972, $350,000 in 1973, and $475,000 in 1974, should be enough to finance Rapidrill's operations. Ideally, a slightly larger line of credit should be sought to increase Rapidrill's cash in the third and fourth quarters of 1973. Note that the cash flow provided by operations becomes positive in the third year. In the first two years, cash is being used to finance Rapidrill's start-up and working capital. Because bank borrowings are used principally to finance working capital, sales volumes less than forecast will require that less of the line of credit be drawn down.

3. *Balance sheets* (see *Exhibits G* through *I*): Rapidrill's proposed financial plan provides financial strength and liquidity. The lowest ratio of current assets to current liabilities plus bank loans payable is not projected to be less than about 1:2. And much of Rapidrill's inventory consists of standard components and materials that should be readily salable. After the investment of this offering (assumed to be in February 1972), Rapidrill's working capital is estimated not to fall below about $140,000.

Rapidrill's liquidity should hold up reasonably well if sales are somewhat less than forecast. This is because Rapidrill has little invested in fixed assets and bank borrowings are primarily used for working capital. If sales fall from forecasts, current assets, current liabilities, and bank borrowings should tend to drop proportionately and the effect of the

Exhibit C

RAPIDRILL CORPORATION
Quarterly Sales and Earnings Forecasts
Fiscal Years Ended September 30, 1973–1974
(000s omitted)

	1973					1974				
	1Q	2Q	3Q	4Q	Total	1Q	2Q	3Q	4Q	Total
Sales:										
Units.........	$ 764	$ 874	$1,126	$1,063	$3,827	$1,382	$1,657	$2,086	$1,471	$6,596
Spares.......	76	88	113	106	383	207	249	313	220	989
	840	962	1,239	1,169	4,210	1,589	1,906	2,399	1,691	7,585
Cost of sales:										
Material......	464	516	641	583	2,204	775	937	1,175	834	3,722
Labor........	13	20	32	33	98	42	51	61	47	201
Burden.......	83	88	113	103	387	103	126	152	119	500
	560	624	786	719	2,689	921	1,114	1,388	1,000	4,423
Gross margin....	280	338	453	450	1,521	668	792	1,011	691	3,162
Percent......	33.3	35.1	36.6	38.5	36.1	42.0	41.6	42.1	40.9	41.7
Selling and marketing.....	97	98	127	108	430	136	163	205	144	648
Engineering.....	33	33	33	35	134	68	68	69	68	273
Administration and general ...	115	117	124	127	483	176	177	176	176	705
	245	248	284	270	1,047	380	408	450	388	1,626
	1973	1974								
Earnings before interest and taxes.........	35	90	169	180	474	288	384	561	303	1,536
Interest expense (income)......	11	13	13	11	48	13	18	14	7	52
Earnings before federal and state taxes.........	24	77	156	169	426	275	366	547	296	1,484
Federal and state taxes.........	12	39	78	85	214	139	185	277	150	751
Net earnings before extraordinary item......	12	38	78	84	212	136	181	270	146	733
Extraordinary item — reduction in federal income taxes resulting from carryover of prior years' operating losses.........	6	21	42	45	114					
Net earnings.....	$ 18	$ 59	$ 120	$ 129	$ 326	$ 136	$ 181	$ 270	$ 146	$ 733
Percent sales before extraordinary item......	1.4	4.0	6.3	7.2	5.0	8.6	9.5	11.2	8.6	9.7
Percent sales after extraordinary item......	2.1	6.1	9.7	11.0	7.7	8.6	9.5	11.2	8.6	9.7

Exhibit D

RAPIDRILL CORPORATION
Pro Forma Cash Flows
Fiscal Years Ended September 30, 1972–1976
(000s omitted)

	1972	1973	1974	1975	1976
Cash receipts:					
Accounts receivable.	$ 586	$3,824	$7,320	$10,379	$13,330
Notes receivable.					200
Interest.				5	64
Total.	586	3,824	7,320	10,384	13,594
Cash disbursements:					
Purchases of materials.	504	2,178	4,015	5,587	6,698
Manufacturing labor.	56	224	418	552	617
Manufacturing overhead.	76	183	185	222	225
Warranty expense.	20	60	100	100	100
Administration, general, selling, and					
engineering.	453	1,044	1,624	2,518	3,166
Equipment.	28	12	12	10	10
Federal and state taxes.		100	751	1,137	1,519
Interest.	5	48	52	2	
Total.	1,140	3,849	7,157	10,128	12,335
Cash provided (drained) by operations.	(554)	(25)	163	256	1,259
Investment in long-term notes receivable. . . .				163	1,275
Bank borrowing (repayment).	250	(25)	(150)	(75)	
Sale of common stock.	280				
Net increase (decrease) in cash balance.	$1 (24)	$ (50)	$ 13	$ 18	$ (16)

sales drop on liquidity or the ratio of current assets to current liabilities plus bank debt should tend to be small.

4. *Breakeven Analysis* (see *Exhibit J*):   At its currently proposed sales prices and costs, Rapidrill's breakeven sales are about 19 units and $1,900,000. Rapidrill recognizes that this may be somewhat high. It is also apparent that a 10 percent increase in Rapidrill's prices would lower the breakeven to 12 units and $1,300,000 in sales. Accordingly, Rapidrill will closely watch its competitors' pricing behavior and, if appropriate, consider the possibility of increasing its prices. In any case, if sales volume should drop, it should be possible to lower Rapidrill's fixed cost by cutting back on some of its general and administrative expenses.

Cost Control

Achievement of the financial plan delineated above will depend in significant measure on Rapidrill's ability to control its costs. To do this, Rapidrill's principals will draw on their experience in designing and implementing systems to control the costs of design, development, and manufacturing programs.

Design and development programs will use a job cost reporting system. Each equipment development project will be broken down into subtasks, and labor, overhead, purchased materials, and subcontracting costs will be separately reported for each subtask. Cost reports will be issued every two weeks and the cost and progress to date monitored and compared to budgets. These reports will be monitored by Messrs. Miller, Price, and MacMillan, and

Exhibit E

RAPIDRILL CORPORATION
Pro Forma Monthly Cash Flows
Fiscal Year Ended September 30, 1972
(000s omitted)

	Oct.	Nov.	Dec.	Jan.	Feb.	Mar.	Apr.	May	June	July	Aug.	Sept.	Total
Cash receipts:													
Accounts and notes received..........									$ 98	$195	$ 98	$195	$ 586
Interest..............													
Total...........									98	195	98	195	586
Cash disbursements:													
Purchases of materials.............							$ 52		113	115	113	111	504
Manufacturing labor. . .					$ 1	$ 4	8	$ 8	8	9	9	9	56
Manufacturing overhead..............					11	13	9	9	9	9	7	7	74
Warranty expense.....							2	3	4	3	4	4	20
Administration, general, selling, and engineering.............	$ 44	$ 22	$ 17	$ 22	19	26	48	49	48	55	50	53	453
Equipment............	2			1		10	10			5			28
Federal and state taxes Interest..............										1	2	2	5
Total............	46	22	17	23	31	53	129	69	182	197	185	186	1,140
Cash provided (drained) by operations.........	(46)	(22)	(17)	(23)	(31)	(53)	(129)	(69)	(84)	(2)	(87)	9	(554)
Investment in long-term notes receivable.......													
Bank borrowing (repayment)................								50	100		100		250
Sale of common stock. . .		40			240								280
Net increase (decrease) in cash balance.......	$(46)	$ 18	$(17)	$(23)	$209	$ (53)	$(129)	$(19)	$ 16	$ (2)	$ 13	$ 9	$ 24
Opening cash balance. . .	88*	42	60	43	20	229	176	47	28	44	42	55	
Closing cash balance 88*.............	42	60	43	20	229	176	47	28	44	42	55		

* Initial cash balance from investments of principals made prior to October 1, 1971. No corporate expenditures prior to October 1, 1971.

weekly meetings will be held to discuss and determine solutions to actual or potential cost problems.

When a drill model (e.g., D–40K) is released for production, a set of standard costs for assembly labor, purchased components, overhead, etc., will be established. Actual costs will be accumulated by subtask and cost category and compared to the standards. Significant differences between actual and standard costs will be evaluated to see if these are due to inefficiencies or are real cost increases. If the former, corrective actions will be identified and taken; if the latter, the standards may need revision. Warranty and field service costs will also be carefully monitored to ensure that Rapidrill's allowance for these is adequate.

Finally, ratio analysis of costs to sale price will be used to identify any cost element that may be deviating significantly from the norms and be cause for concern.

Exhibit F

RAPIDRILL CORPORATION
Pro Forma Quarterly Cash Flows
Fiscal Years Ended September 30, 1973–1974
(000s omitted)

	1973					1974				
	1Q	2Q	3Q	4Q	Total	1Q	2Q	3Q	4Q	Total
Cash receipts:										
Accounts and notes received........	$719	$890	$1,008	$1,207	$3,824	$1,375	$1,848	$2,052	$2,045	$7,320
Interest...........										
Total.........	719	890	1,008	1,207	3,824	1,375	1,848	2,052	2,045	7,320
Cash disbursements:										
Purchases of materials........	453	531	561	633	2,178	852	1,034	1,028	1,101	4,015
Manufacturing labor...........	31	45	74	74	224	82	111	112	113	418
Manufacturing overhead...........	38	52	50	43	183	45	45	48	47	185
Warranty expense..	12	14	17	17	60	22	25	26	27	100
Administration, general, selling, and engineering......	243	248	283	270	1,044	379	408	449	388	1,624
Equipment.........	5	3	2	2	12	5	2	5		12
Federal and state taxes...........	25	25	25	25	100	191	191	191	178	751
Interest...........	11	13	13	11	48	13	18	14	7	52
Total.........	818	931	1,025	1,075	3,849	1,589	1,834	1,873	1,861	7,157
Cash provided (drained) by operations......	(99)	(41)	(17)	132	(25)	(214)	14	179	184	163
Investment in long-term notes receivable..........										
Bank borrowing (repayment)..........	100			(125)	(25)	250		(200)	(200)	(150)
Sale of common stock.............										
Net increase (decrease) in cash balance...........	$ 1	$ (41)	$ (17)	$ 7	$ (50)	$ 36	$ 14	$ (21)	$ (16)	$ 13
Opening cash balance...........	$ 64	$ 65	$ 24	$ 7		$ 14	$ 50	$ 64	$ 43	
Closing cash balance...........	65	24	7	14		50	64	43	27	

10. Proposed Rapidrill Offering

Financing

Rapidrill Corporation is incorporated in the state of Delaware and currently has 720,000 shares of 10 cents par value common voting stock authorized, with 451,000 shares issued as of November 30, 1971.

Rapidrill now intends to raise $240,000 through the sale of 240,000 shares of its common voting stock at $1 per share. The common stock sold in this financing will represent about 35 percent of Rapidrill's outstanding common stock after the offering is completed.

Exhibit G

RAPIDRILL CORPORATION
Pro Forma Balance Sheets
Fiscal Years Ended September 30, 1971–1976
(000s omitted)

	1971	1972	1973	1974	1975	1976
Current assets:						
Cash.........................	$88	$ 64	$ 14	$ 27	$ 45	$ 29
Accounts receivable...................		195	581	846	1,360	1,710
Notes receivable.....................					150	1,225
Inventory...........................		393	563	824	1,315	1,502
Total..........................		652	1,158	1,697	2,870	4,466
Property, plant, and equipment cost.........		28	40	52	62	72
Less: Depreciation.......................		5	13	23	33	43
		23	27	29	29	29
Total assets...........................	$88	$ 675	$1,185	$1,726	$2,899	$4,495
Current liabilities:						
Accounts payable and accrued expenses...........................		$ 286	$ 495	$ 453	$ 590	$ 702
Bank loans payable......................		250	225	75		
Equity:						
Capital stock—common 10¢ par value, 720,000 authorized shares.............	$37	69	69	69	69	69
Paid-in surplus........................	51	299	299	299	299	299
Retained earnings......................		(229)	97	830	1,941	3,425
	88	139	465	1,198	2,309	3,793
Total liabilities and equity................	$88	$ 675	$1,185	$1,726	$2,899	$4,495

Capitalization

Exhibit K shows the capitalization of Rapidrill before and after the proposed offering.

Use and Sources of Funds

The money raised in this offering ($240,000), together with the money raised ($128,460) earlier from the sale of stock to Rapidrill's principals and key employees, will be used primarily to design, fabricate, and test the first D–40K truck-mounted rotary drill and to set up a marketing and distribution system. These $368,000 of equity funds will be supplemented by bank borrowings that will be used to finance inventories and receivables. The bank borrowings reach maximums of $250,000 in 1972, $350,000 in 1973, and $475,000 in 1974 (see Pro Forma Cash Flows and Balance Sheets). Rapidrill expects to have a $600,000 to $700,000 revolving line of credit with Nashville banks and has obtained preliminary approval of such a line of credit. Final approval will be contingent on raising the $240,000 of this offering.

Notes to Balance Sheet

Accounts Receivable

Thirty days. Considered to be 100 percent collectible due to financial strength of customers. These customers have demonstrated prompt and consistent payment of invoices in past associations with Rapidrill's principals. The few drills that have been

Exhibit H

RAPIDRILL CORPORATION
Pro Forma Monthly Balance Sheets
Fiscal Year Ended September 30, 1972
(000s omitted)

	Oct.	Nov.	Dec.	Jan.	Feb.	Mar.	Apr.	May	June	July	Aug.	Sept.
Current assets:												
Cash.............	$ 40	$ 18	$ 43	$ 20	$ 229	$ 176	$ 47	$ 28	$ 44	$ 42	$ 55	$ 64
Accounts receivable............								98	195	98	195	195
Notes receivable												
Inventory					13	83	216	283	282	347	337	393
	40	18	43	20	242	259	263	409	521	487	587	652
Property, plant, and equipment—at cost.............	2	2	2	3	3	13	23	23	23	28	28	28
Less: Depreciation....						1	2	2	3	4	4	5
	2	2	2	3	3	12	21	21	20	24	24	23
Total assets.........	$ 42	$ 20	$ 45	$ 23	$ 245	$ 271	$ 284	$ 430	$ 541	$ 511	$ 611	$ 675
Current liabilities:												
Accounts payable and accrued expenses........	$ 6	$ 1	$ 1	$ 1	$ 3	$ 55	$ 116	$ 232	$ 235	$ 228	$ 225	$ 286
Bank loans payable...								50	150	150	250	250
Equity:												
Capital stock— common 10¢ par value, 720,000 shares authorized............	37	45	45	45	69	69	69	69	69	69	69	69
Paid-in surplus.....	51	83	83	83	299	299	299	299	299	299	299	299
Retained earnings ..	(50)	(67)	(84)	(106)	(126)	(152)	(200)	(220)	(212)	(235)	(232)	(229)
	36	19	44	22	242	216	168	148	156	133	136	139
Total liabilities and equity.............	$ 42	$ 20	$ 45	$ 23	$ 245	$ 271	$ 284	$ 430	$ 541	$ 511	$ 611	$ 675

repossessed have repeatedly been sold in the used market for up to 90 percent of their original selling price, thus limiting the loss from an uncollected receivable. Experience of Rapidrill's principals indicates that with proper credit control, industrywide losses are insignificant.

Notes Receivable

Range from 12 to 60 months in duration. Usually secured by the equipment. Loss expectancy extremely low.

Inventory

Approximately 80 percent value in off-the-shelf, standard, stock items easily returnable; therefore, more liquid than custom-specified items.

Accounts Payable

Sixty days, 1972 through second quarter of 1973. Vendors have indicated a willingness to work on these terms during Rapidrill's start-up period.

Exhibit I

RAPIDRILL CORPORATION
Pro Forma Quarterly Balance Sheets
Fiscal Years Ended September 30, 1973–1974
(000s omitted)

	1973 1Q	1973 2Q	1973 3Q	1973 4Q	1974 1Q	1974 2Q	1974 3Q	1974 4Q
Current assets:								
Cash	$ 65	$ 24	$ 7	$ 14	$ 50	$ 64	$ 43	$ 27
Accounts receivable................	316	388	619	581	795	853	1,200	846
Notes receivable...................								
Inventory.........................	439	477	424	563	651	630	538	824
	820	889	1,050	1,158	1,496	1,547	1,781	1,697
Property, plant, and equipment— at cost...........................	33	36	38	40	45	47	52	52
Less: Depreciation...................	7	9	11	13	15	18	20	23
	26	27	27	27	30	29	32	29
Total assets	$ 846	$ 916	$1,077	$1,185	$1,526	$1,576	$1,813	$1,726
Current liabilities:								
Accounts payable and accrued expenses	$ 339	$ 350	$ 391	$ 495	$ 450	$ 319	$ 486	$ 453
Bank loans payable..................	350	350	350	225	475	475	275	75
Equity:								
Capital stock—common 10¢ par value, 720,000 shares authorized.........	69	69	69	69	69	69	69	69
Paid-in surplus	299	299	299	299	299	299	299	299
Retained earnings	(211)	(152)	(32)	97	233	414	684	830
	157	215	336	465	601	782	1,052	1,198
Total liabilities and equity..............	$ 846	$ 916	$1,077	$1,185	$1,526	$1,576	$1,813	$1,726

Exhibit J
Rapidrill Corporation—1972–1973 Breakeven Analysis

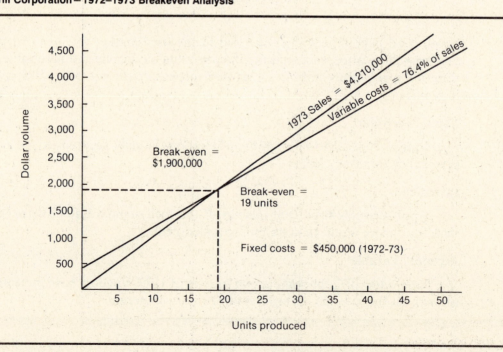

Exhibit K
Rapidrill Corporation — Present and Proposed Capitalization

	Shares Owned		Percent Ownership Post-Offering	Investment	Cost per Share
Stockholders	Pre-Offering	Post-Offering			
S. A. Price	135,000	135,000	19.6%	$ 20,400	$0.15
M. F. Einman	78,000	78,000	11.3	20,280	0.26
F. T. Samuels	78,000	78,000	11.3	20,280	0.26
G. A. Miller	42,000	42,000	6.1	12,600	0.30
W. D. MacMillan	36,000	36,000	5.2	14,400	0.40
J. Jones*	27,000	27,000	3.9	13,500	0.50
D. Mead*	27,000	27,000	3.9	13,500	0.50
S. Ross*	27,000	27,000	3.9	13,500	0.50
Investors of this offering		240,000	34.8	240,000	1.00
	451,000	691,000	100.0%	$368,460	

* These are the three distributor representatives mentioned in Section 2.

Loans

Currently negotiating with local banks for a $600,000–$700,000 revolving line of credit. Already have had preliminary approvals of loans and now preparing a package to be presented to the credit committees. Final approval contingent on raising $240,000 of this offer.

Retained Earnings

No dividend payments are planned during program.

Rapidrill has 29,000 shares of common stock authorized but unissued. These shares will be used to attract additional management personnel or reserved for future use as stock options to key employees.

The Business Plan Guide

12 >

Never promise more than you can perform.

Publilius Syrus
1st Century, B.C.

RESULTS EXPECTED

Upon completion of the chapter, you will have:

1. Looked at the difference between thinking about and screening opportunities and writing a business plan.
2. Written a business plan for a new venture.

PREPARING A BUSINESS PLAN

A Complete Business Plan

It may seem to an entrepreneur who has completed the Opportunity Screening Guide in Chapter 4 and who has spent hours of thinking and planning informally that all that now needs to be done is to jot down a few things. *But, there is a great difference between screening an opportunity and developing a business plan.*

There are two important differences in the way these issues need to be addressed. First, a business plan can have two uses: (1) inducing someone to part with maybe $500,000 to $2 million, or even more, and (2) guiding the policies and actions of the firm over a number of years. Therefore, strategies and statements made need to be well thought out, unambiguous, and capable of being supported.

Another difference is that more detail is needed. (The exception to this is the "Dehydrated Business Plan" discussed later in this chapter.) This means that the team needs to spend more time in gathering detailed data, in interpreting it, and in presenting it clearly. For example, for the purpose of screening an opportunity, it may be all right to note (if one cannot do any better) that the target market for a product is in the $30- to $60-million range and the market is growing over 10 percent per year. For purposes of planning to launch an actual new enterprise, determine strategy, and so forth, this level of detail would not get by. The size range would need to be narrowed considerably; if not, those reading or using the plan will have little confidence in this critical number. And saying the target market is growing at over 10 percent is too vague. Does that mean the market grew at the stated rate between last year and the year before, or does it mean that the market grew on average by this amount over the past three years? Also, a statement phrased in terms of "over 10 percent" smacks of imprecision. The actual growth rate needs to be known and needs to be stated. Whether the rate will or will not remain the same, and why, needs to be explained also.

Preparing an effective business plan for a start-up can easily take 200 to 300 hours. Squeezing that amount of time into evenings and weekends can make the process stretch over 3 to 12 months.

A business plan for a business planning expansion or for a situation, such as a leveraged buyout, typically can take half this effort. The reason is that the "knowns" about the business, including the market, its competition, financial and accounting information, etc., at this point are greater.

Exhibit 12.1 is a sample table of contents for a business plan. Included in most effective business plans is the information shown. The way information is presented in this exhibit is a good framework to follow. First, organizing the material into "sections" makes dealing with the information more manageable. Second, while the amount of detail and the order of presentation may vary for a particular venture according to its particular circumstances, most effective business plans contain this information in some form. (Note that the amount of detail and the order in which information is presented is important. These can vary for each particular situation, and will depend upon, among other factors, the purpose of the plan and the age and stage of the venture.)

The Dehydrated Business Plan

A dehydrated business plan usually runs in length from 4 to 10 pages, but rarely more. It covers key points, such as those suggested for the executive summary in the Business Planning Guide, which follows. Essentially, such a plan documents the analysis of and information about the heart of the business opportunity, competitive advantages the company will enjoy, and *creative insights* that an entrepreneur often has in his or her head.

Since it can be prepared in usually a few hours, it is preferred by entrepreneurs who find it difficult to find enough slack time while operating a business to write a complete plan. In many instances investors prefer a dehydrated plan in the initial screening phase.

It is important to note that such a plan is not intended to be used exclusively in the process of raising or borrowing money, and it is not useful in guiding the operations of a business over time.

EXERCISE — THE BUSINESS PLAN GUIDE

The Business Plan Guide follows the order of *presentation* outlined in *Exhibit 12.1.* Based on a guide originally developed at Venture Founders Corporation by Leonard E. Smollen and the late Brian Haslett, and over 20 years of observing and working with entrepreneurs and actually preparing and evaluating hundreds of plans, it is intended to make this challenging task easier.

Certainly, there is no single "best way" to write a business plan, and there are many ways to approach the preparation for and writing of a business plan. It is recommended that you begin with the market research and analysis sections. In the final analysis, the task will evolve in a way that suits you and your situation.

In writing your plan it is helpful to keep in mind that, while one of the important functions of a business plan is to influence investors, you and your team need to prove to yourselves and others that your opportunity is worth pursuing and to construct how you will do it, rather than to prepare a fancy presentation. Gathering information, making hard decisions, and developing plans comes first.

Writing the business plan follows at this point, and the plan guide that follows shows how to present information succinctly and in a format acceptable to investors. While it is useful to keep in mind who your audience is, and that information not clearly presented will most likley not be used, it also is important not to be concerned *just* with format.

In the Business Plan Guide, issues are indicated. The intent is to show you what needs to be included in a business plan and why.

Table 12.1
Business Plan

Table of Contents

  I.   EXECUTIVE SUMMARY
       A.   Description of the Business Concept and the Business.
       B.   The Opportunity and Strategy.
       C.   The Target Market and Projections.
       D.   The Competitive Advantages.
       E.   The Economics, Profitability, and Harvest Potential.
       F.   The Team.
       G.   The Offering.
 II.   THE INDUSTRY AND THE COMPANY AND ITS PRODUCT(S) OR SERVICE(S)
       A.   The Industry.
       B.   The Company and the Concept.
       C.   The Product(s) or Service(s).
       D.   Entry and Growth Strategy.
III.   MARKET RESEARCH AND ANALYSIS
       A.   Customers.
       B.   Market Size and Trends.
       C.   Competition and Competitive Edges.
       D.   Estimated Market Share and Sales.
       E.   Ongoing Market Evaluation.
 IV.   THE ECONOMICS OF THE BUSINESS
       A.   Gross and Operating Margins.
       B.   Profit Potential and Durability.
       C.   Fixed, Variable, and Semivariable Costs.
       D.   Months to Breakeven.
       E.   Months to Reach Positive Cash Flow.
  V.   MARKETING PLAN
       A.   Overall Marketing Strategy.
       B.   Pricing.
       C.   Sales Tactics.
       D.   Service and Warranty Policies.
       E.   Advertising and Promotion.
       F.   Distribution.
 VI.   DESIGN AND DEVELOPMENT PLANS
       A.   Development Status and Tasks.
       B.   Difficulties and Risks.
       C.   Product Improvement and New Products.
       D.   Costs.
       E.   Proprietary Issues.
VII.   MANUFACTURING AND OPERATIONS PLAN
       A.   Operating Cycle.
       B.   Geographical Location.
       C.   Facilities and Improvements.
       D.   Strategy and Plans.
       E.   Regulatory and Legal Issues.
VIII. MANAGEMENT TEAM
       A.   Organization.
       B.   Key Management Personnel.
       C.   Management Compensation and Ownership.
       D.   Other Investors.
       E.   Employment and Other Agreements and Stock Option and Bonus Plans.
       F.   Board of Directors.
       G.   Other Shareholders, Rights, and Restrictions.
       H.   Supporting Professional Advisors and Services.
 IX.   OVERALL SCHEDULE
  X.   CRITICAL RISKS, PROBLEMS, AND ASSUMPTIONS
 XI.   THE FINANCIAL PLAN
       A.   Actual Income Statements and Balance Sheets.
       B.   Pro Forma Income Statements.
       C.   Pro Forma Balance Sheets.
       D.   Pro Forma Cash Flow Analysis.
       E.   Breakeven Chart and Calculation.
       F.   Cost Control.
       G.   Highlights.
XII.   PROPOSED COMPANY OFFERING
       A.   Desired Financing.
       B.   Offering.
       C.   Capitalization.
       D.   Use of Funds.
       E.   Investors' Return.
XIII. APPENDICES

Further, you may feel as though you have seen much of this before. You should. The guide is based on the analytical framework described in the book and builds upon the Opportunity Screening Guide in Chapter 4. If you have not completed the Opportunity Screening Guide, it will help you to do so before proceeding. It is assumed in the Business Plan Guide that you will be able to draw on data and analysis developed in the Opportunity Screening Guide to help you prepare your business plan.

As you proceed through the Business Plan Guide, remember that statements need to be supported with data where possible. Note also that it is sometimes easier to present data in tabular form. Include the source of all data, the methods and/or assumptions used, and the credentials of people doing research. If data on which a statement is based is available elsewhere in the plan, be sure to indicate where it can be found.

Finally, it is important to remember that the Business Plan Guide is just that—a guide. It is intended to be applicable to a wide range of product and service businesses. For any particular industry or market, there are certain to be critical issues which are unique to that industry or market. In the chemical industry, for example, some special issues of significance, such as increasingly strict regulations at all levels of government covering the use of chemical products and the operation of processes; diminishing viability of the high capital cost, special-purpose chemical processing plants serving a narrow market; and long delivery times of processing equipment, currently exist. In the electronics industry, the special issues may be the future availability and price of new kinds of large-scale integrated circuits.

Common sense should rule in applying the guide to your specific venture.

EXERCISE
THE BUSINESS PLAN GUIDE

NAME:

VENTURE:

DATA:

STEP 1: SEGMENT INFORMATION INTO KEY SECTIONS AND SET PRIORITIES FOR EACH SECTION, WHO IS RESPONSIBLE, AND DUE DATES FOR DRAFTS AND FINAL VERSIONS.   When you segment your information, it is vital to keep in mind that the plan needs to be integrated in logic and that information be consistent. Note that, since the market opportunity section is the heart and soul of the plan and, most likely, the most difficult, it is best to assign it a high priority and to begin work there first. Remember to include such tasks as printing in the list.

Section or Task	Priority	Person(s) Responsible	Date to Begin	1st Draft Due Date	Date Completed or Final Version Due Date

STEP 2: DEVISE AN OVERALL SCHEDULE FOR PREPARING THE PLAN AND LIST TASKS THAT NEED TO BE COMPLETED, PRIORITIES, WHO IS RESPONSIBLE, WHEN THE TASK IS TO BE STARTED, AND WHEN IT IS TO BE COMPLETED.   It is helpful to break larger items (such as field work to gather customer and competitor intelligence, trade show visits, etc.) into the small possible components (such as phone calls required before a trip can be taken) and to include the components as a "task." Be as specific as possible.

Task	Priority	Person Responsible	Date to Begin	Date of Completion

STEP 3: COMBINE THE LIST OF SEGMENTS AND THE LIST OF TASKS AND CREATE A CALENDAR.   In combining your list, consider if anything has been omitted and whether you have been realistic in what people can do, when they can do it, what needs to be done, and so forth. To create your calendar, place an *X* in the week when the task is to be started and an *X* in the week it is to be completed and then connect the *X*s. When you have placed all tasks on the calendar, look carefully again for conflicts or lack of realism. In particular, evaluate if team members are "overscheduled."

Task	Week														
	1	2	3	4	5	6	7	8	9	10	11	12	13	14	15

STEP 4:   DEVELOP AND WRITE A BUSINESS PLAN USING THE FOLLOWING AS A FRAMEWORK.   As has been discussed, the framework follows the format of the table of contents shown in *Exhibit 12.1* — that is, the order of presentation. While preparing your own plan, you will most likely want to consider sections in an order other than the one in which they are presented. (Also, when you integrate your sections into your final plan, you may choose to present material somewhat differently.)

Cover

The cover page includes the name of company, its address, its telephone number, the date, and the securities offered. Usually, the name, address, telephone number, and the date are centered at the top of the page and the securities offered are listed at the bottom. Also suggested on the cover page at the bottom are the words:

> This business plan has been submitted on a confidential basis solely for the benefit of selected, highly qualified investors in connection with the private placement of the above securities and is not for use by any other persons nor may it be reproduced, stored, or copied in any form. By accepting delivery of this plan, the recipient agrees to return this copy to the corporation at the address listed above if the recipient does not undertake to subscribe to the offering. Do not copy, fax, reproduce, or distribute without permission.

Table of Contents

Included in the table of contents is a list of the sections, any appendices, and any other information and the pages on which they can be found. (See *Exhibit 12.1*.)

I.   Executive Summary

The first section in the body of the business plan is usually an executive summary. The summary is usually short and concise (one or two pages). The summary articulates what the opportunity conditions are and why they exist, who will execute the opportunity and why they are capable of doing so, how the firm will gain entry and market penetration, and so on. Essentially, the summary for your venture needs to mirror the criteria shown in *Exhibit 3.3* and the Venture Opportunity Screening Guide.

The summary is usually prepared after the other sections of the business plan are completed. It, therefore, is helpful, as the other sections are drafted, to note one or two key sentences, and some key facts and numbers, from each.

The summary is important for those ventures trying to raise or borrow money. Many investors, bankers, managers, and other readers use the summary to determine quickly whether the venture the plan describes is of interest. Therefore, unless the summary is appealing and compelling, it may be the only section read, and you may never get the chance to make a presentation or discuss your business in person.

Therefore, leave plenty of time to prepare the summary. (Successful public speakers have been known to spend an hour of preparation for each minute of their speech.)

The executive summary usually contains a paragraph or two covering each of the following:

> *A.   Description of the Business Concept and the Business.*   Describe the business concept for the business you are or will be in. For example, Outdoor Scene, Inc. (see Chapter 1), wanted to produce tents, but the concept was "to become a leader in providing quality, service, and on-time delivery in outdoor leisure products." Be sure the description of your concept explains how your product or service will fundamentally change the way customers currently do certain things. For example, Arthur Rock, the lead investor in Apple Computer and Intel, has stated that he focuses on concepts that will change the way people live and/or work. When the

company was formed, what it will do, what is special or proprietary about its product, service, or technology, and so forth, needs to be identified. Include summary information about any proprietary technology, trade secrets, or unique capabilities that give you an edge in the marketplace. If the company has existed for a few years, a brief summary of its size and progress is in order. Try to make your description 25 words or less, and mention the specific product or service.

B. *The Opportunity and Strategy.* Summarize what the opportunity is, why it is compelling, and the entry strategy planned to exploit it. This information may be presented as an outline of the key facts, conditions, competitors' vulnerabilities (such as sleepiness, sluggishness, poor service, etc.), industry trends, and other evidence and logic that define the opportunity. Note plans for growth and expansion beyond the entry products or services and into other market segments (such as international markets) as appropriate.

C. *The Target Market and Projections.* Identify and briefly explain the industry and market, who the primary customer groups are, how the product(s) or service(s) will be positioned, and how you plan to reach and service these groups. Include information about the structure of the market, the size and growth rate for the market segments or niches you are seeking, your unit and dollar sales estimates, your anticipated market share, the payback period for your customers, and your pricing strategy (including price versus performance/value/benefits considerations).

D. *The Competitive Advantages.* Indicate the significant competitive edges you enjoy, or can create, as a result of your innovative product, service, and strategy; advantages in lead time; competitors' weaknesses and vulnerabilities; and other industry conditions.

E. *The Economics, Profitability, and Harvest Potential.* Summarize the nature of the "forgiving and rewarding" economics of the venture (e.g., gross and operating margins, expected profitability and durability of those profits); the relevant time frames to attain breakeven and positive cash flow; key financial projections; the expected return on investment; etc. Be sure to include a brief discussion of your contribution analysis and the underlying operating and cash conversion cycle. Use key numbers whenever possible.

F. *The Team.* Summarize the relevant knowledge, experience, know-how, and skills of the lead entrepreneur and any team members, noting previous accomplishments, especially those involving profit and loss responsibility, and general management and people management experience. Include significant information, such as the size of a division, project, or prior business with which the lead entrepreneur or a team member was the driving force.

G. *The Offering.* Briefly indicate the dollar amount of equity and/or debt financing needed, how much of the company you are prepared to offer for that financing, what principal use will be made of the capital, and how the targeted investor, lender, or strategic partner will achieve its desired rate of return.

II. The Industry and the Company and Its Product(s) or Service(s)

A major area of consideration is the company, its concept for its product(s) and service(s), and its interface with the industry in which it will be competing. This is the context into which the marketing information, for example, fits. Information needs to include a description of the industry; a description of the concept; a description of your company; and a description of the product(s) or service(s) you will offer, the proprietary position of these product(s) or service(s), their potential advantages, and entry and growth strategy for the product(s) or service(s).

A. *The Industry*
- Present the current status and prospects for the industry in which the proposed business will operate. Be sure to consider industry structure.
- Discuss briefly market size, growth trends, and competitors.
- Discuss any new products or developments, new markets and customers, new requirements, new entrants and exits, and any other national or economic trends and factors that could affect the venture's business positively or negatively.

B. *The Company and the Concept*
- Describe generally the concept of the business; what business your company is in, or intends to enter; what product(s) or service(s) it will offer; and who are or will be its principal customers.
- By way of background, give the date your venture was incorporated and describe the identification and development of its products and the involvement of the company's principals in that development.
- If your company has been in business for several years and is seeking expansion financing, review its history and cite its prior sales and profit performance; and if your company has had setbacks or losses in prior years, discuss these and emphasize what has and will be done to prevent a recurrence of these difficulties and improve your company's performance.

C. *The Product(s) or Service(s)*
- Describe in some detail each product or service to be sold.
- Discuss the application of the product or service and describe the primary end use as well as any significant secondary applications.
- Emphasize any unique features of the product or service and how these will create or add significant value; also, highlight any differences between what is currently on the market and what you will offer that will account for your market penetration. Be sure to describe how value will be added and the payback period to the customer—that is, discuss how many months it will take for the customer to cover the initial purchase price of the product or service as a result of its time, cost, or productivity improvements.
- Include a description of any possible drawbacks (including problems with obsolescence) of the product or service.
- Define the present state of development of the product or service and how much time and money will be required to complete development, test, and introduce the product or service. Provide a summary of the functional specifications, and photographs if available, of the product.
- Discuss any head start you might have that would enable you to achieve a favored or entrenched position in the industry.
- Describe any features of the product or service that give it an "unfair" advantage over the competition. Describe any patents, trade secrets, or other proprietary features of the product or service.
- Discuss any opportunities for the expansion of the product line or the development of related products or services. (Emphasize opportunities and explain how you will take advantage of them.)

D. *Entry and Growth Strategy*
- Indicate key success variables in your marketing plan (e.g., an innovative product, timing advantage, or marketing approach) and your pricing, distribution, advertising, and promotion plans.
- Summarize how fast you intend to grow and to what size during the first five years and your plans for growth beyond your initial product or service.
- Show how the entry and growth strategy is derived from the opportunity and value-added or other competitive advantages, such as the weakness of competitors.

III. Market Research and Analysis

Because of the importance of market analysis and the critical dependence of other parts of the plan on this information, you are advised to prepare this section of the business plan before any other. Take enough time to do this section very well and to check alternate sources of market data.

Information in this section needs to support the assertion that the venture can capture a substantial market in a growing industry in the face of competition.

This section of the business plan is one of the most difficult to prepare and, yet, it is one of the most important. Other sections of the business plan depend on the market research and analysis presented here. For example, the predicted sales levels directly influence such factors as the size of the manufacturing operation, the marketing plan, and the amount of debt and equity capital you will require. Yet most entrepreneurs seem to have great difficulty preparing and presenting market research and analyses that show their ventures' sales estimates are sound and attainable.

A. *Customers*
  — Discuss who the customers for the product(s) or service(s) are or will be. Note that potential customers need to be classified by relatively homogeneous groups having common, identifiable characteristics (e.g., by major market segment). For example, an automotive part might be sold to manufacturers and to parts distributors supplying the replacement market, so the discussion needs to reflect two market segments.
  — Show who and where are the major purchasers for the product(s) or service(s) in each market segment. Include regional and foreign countries, as appropriate.
  — Indicate whether customers are easily reached and receptive, how customers buy (e.g., wholesale, through manufacturers' representatives, etc.), where in their organizations such buying decisions are made, and how long such decisions take. Describe customers' purchasing processes, including the bases on which they make purchase decisions (e.g., price, quality, timing, delivery, training, service, personal contacts, or political pressures) and why they might change current purchasing decisions.
  — List any orders, contracts, or letters of commitment that you have in hand. These are far and away *the most powerful data* you can provide. List also any potential customers who have expressed an interest in the product(s) or service(s) and indicate why, also any potential customers who have shown no interest in the proposed product or service. Explain why they are not interested and explain what you will do to overcome negative customer reaction. Indicate how fast you believe your product or service will be accepted in the market.
  — If you have an existing business, list your principal current customers and discuss the trends in your sales to them.
B. *Market Size and Trends*
  — Show for five years the size of the current total market and the share you will have, by market segment and/or by region and/or country, for the product or service you will offer, in units, dollars, and potential profitability.
  — Describe also the potential annual growth for at least three years of the total market for your product(s) or service(s) for each major customer group, region, or country, as appropriate.
  — Discuss the major factors affecting market growth (e.g., industry trends, socioeconomic trends, government policy, and population shifts) and review previous trends in the market. Any differences between past and projected annual growth rates need to be explained.
C. *Competition and Competitive Edges*
  — Make a realistic assessment of the strengths and weaknesses of competitors. Assess the substitute and/or alternative products and services and list the companies that supply them, both domestic and foreign, as appropriate.
  — Compare competing and substitute products or services on the basis of market share, quality, price, performance, delivery, timing, service, warranties, and other pertinent features.
  — Compare the fundamental value that is added or created by your product or service, in terms of economic benefits to the customer and to your competitors.
  — Discuss the current advantages and disadvantages of these products and services and say why they are not meeting customer needs.
  — Indicate any knowledge of competitors' actions that could lead you to new or improved products and an advantageous position. For example, discuss whether competitors are simply sluggish or nonresponsive or are asleep at the switch.

- Review the strengths and weaknesses of the competing companies and determine and discuss the share of the market of each competitor, its sales, its distribution methods, and its production capabilities.
- Review also the financial position, resources, costs, and profitability of the competition and their profit trend. Note you can utilize Robert Morris Associates data for comparison (see Appendix I).
- Indicate who are the service, pricing, performance, cost, and quality leaders. Discuss why any companies have entered or dropped out of the market in recent years.
- Discuss the three or four key competitors and why customers buy from them, and determine and discuss why customers *leave* them.
- From what you know about the competitors' operations, explain why you think that they are vulnerable and you can capture a share of their business. Discuss what makes you think it will be easy or difficult to compete with them. Discuss, in particular, your competitive advantages gained through such "unfair" advantage as patents.

D. *Estimated Market Share and Sales*
- Summarize what it is about your product(s) or service(s) that will make it saleable in the face of current and potential competition. Mention, especially, the fundamental value added or created by the product(s) or service(s).
- Identify any major customers (including international customers) who are willing to make, or who have already made, purchase commitments, and indicate the extent of those commitments and why they were made, and discuss which customers could be major purchasers in future years and why.
- Based on your assessment of the advantages of your product or service, the market size and trends, customers, the competition and their products, and the trends of sales in prior years, estimate the share of the market and the sales in units and dollars that you will acquire in each of the next three years. Remember to show assumptions used.
- Show how the growth of the company sales in units and its estimated market share are related to the growth of its industry and customers and the strengths and weaknesses of competitors. Remember, the assumptions used to estimate market share and sales need to be clearly stated.
- If yours is an existing business, also indicate the total market, your market share, and sales for two prior years.

E. *Ongoing Market Evaluation*
- Explain how you will continue to evaluate your target markets so as to assess customer needs and service and to guide product-improvement programs and new-product programs, plan for expansions of your production facility, and guide product/service pricing.

IV.   The Economics of the Business

The economic and financial characteristics, including the apparent magnitude and durability of margins and profits generated, need to support the fundamental attractiveness of the opportunity. The underlying operating and cash conversion cycle of the business, the value chain, and so forth, need to make sense in terms of the opportunity and strategies planned.

A. *Gross and Operating Margins*
- Describe the magnitude of the gross margins (i.e., selling price less variable costs) and the operating margins for each of the product(s) and/or service(s) you are selling in the market niche(s) you plan to attack. Include results of your contribution analysis.

B. *Profit Potential and Durability*
- Describe the magnitude and expected durability of the profit stream the business will generate—before and after taxes—and reference appropriate industry benchmarks, other competitive intelligence, or your own relevant experience.
- Address the issue of how perishable or durable the profit stream appears to be, and why, such as barriers to entry you can create, your technological and market lead time, and so on.

C. *Fixed, Variable, and Semivariable Costs*
- Provide a detailed summary of fixed, variable, and semivariable costs, in dollars and as percentages of total cost as appropriate, for the product or service you offer and the volume of purchases and sales upon which these are based.
- Show relevant industry benchmarks.

D. *Months to Breakeven*
- Show, given your entry strategy, marketing plan, and proposed financing, how long will it take to reach a unit breakeven sales level.
- Note any significant stepwise changes in your breakeven that will occur as you grow and add substantial capacity.

E. *Months to Reach Positive Cash Flow*
- Show, given the above strategy and assumptions, when the venture will attain a positive cash flow.
- Show if and when you will run out of cash. Note where the detailed assumptions can be found (see pp. 324–25 and 369–74).
- Note any significant stepwise changes in cash flow that will occur as you grow and add capacity.

V. Marketing Plan

The marketing plan describes how the sales projections will be attained. The marketing plan needs to detail the overall marketing strategy that will exploit the opportunity and your competitive advantages. Include a discussion of sales and service policies; pricing, distribution, promotion, and advertising strategies; and sales projections. The marketing plan needs to describe *what* is to be done, *how* it will be done, *when* it will be done, and *who* will do it.

A. *Overall Marketing Strategy*
- Describe the specific marketing philosophy and strategy of the company, given the value chain and channels of distribution in the market niche(s) you are pursuing. Include, for example, a discussion of the kinds of customer groups that you already have orders from or that will be targeted for initial intensive selling effort and those targeted for later selling efforts; how specific potential customers in these groups will be identified and how will they be contacted; what features of the product or service, such as service, quality, price, delivery, warranty, or training, will be emphasized to generate sales; if there are any innovative or unusual marketing concepts that will enhance customer acceptance, such as leasing where only sales were previously attempted; and so forth.
- Indicate whether the product(s) or service(s) will initially be introduced internationally, nationally, or regionally; explain why; and, if appropriate, indicate any plans for extending sales at a later date.
- Discuss any seasonal trends that underlie the cash conversion cycle in the industry and what can be done to promote sales out of season.
- Describe any plans to obtain government contracts as a means of supporting product development costs and overhead.

B. *Pricing*
- Discuss pricing strategy, including the prices to be charged for your product and service, and compare your pricing policy with those of your major competitors, including a brief discussion of payback (in months) to the customer.
- Discuss the gross profit margin between manufacturing and ultimate sales costs and indicate whether this margin is large enough to allow for distribution and sales, warranty, training, service, amortization of development and equipment costs, price competition, and so forth—and still allow a profit.
- Explain how the price you set will enable you to (1) get the product or service accepted, (2) maintain and increase your market share in the face of competition, and (3) produce profits.
- Justify your pricing strategy and differences between your prices and those for competitive or substitute products or services in terms of economic payback to the customer and value added through newness, quality, warranty, timing, performance, service, cost savings, efficiency, and the like.

- If your product is to be priced lower than those of the competition, explain how you will do this and maintain profitability (e.g., through greater value added via effectiveness in manufacturing and distribution, lower labor costs, lower material costs, lower overhead, or other component of cost).
- Discuss your pricing policy, including a discussion of the relationship of price, market share, and profits. For example, a higher price may reduce volume but result in a higher gross profit.
- Describe any discount allowance for prompt payment or volume purchases.

C. *Sales Tactics*
- Describe the methods (e.g., own sales force, sales representatives, ready-made manufacturers' sales organizations, direct mail, or distributors) that will be used to make sales and distribute the product or service and both the initial plans and longer-range plans for a sales force. Include a discussion of any special requirements (e.g., refrigeration).
- Discuss the value chain and the resulting margins to be given to retailers, distributors, wholesalers, and salespeople and any special policies regarding discounts, exclusive distribution rights, etc., given to distributors or sales representatives and compare these to those given by your competition. (See the Venture Opportunity Screening Guide.)
- Describe how distributors or sales representatives, if they are used, will be selected, when they will start to represent you, the areas they will cover and the build-up (a head count) of dealers and representatives by month, and the expected sales to be made by each.
- If a direct sales force is to be used, indicate how it will be structured and at what rate (a head count) it will be built up; indicate if it is to replace a dealer or representative organization and, if so, when and how.
- If direct mail, magazine, newspaper, or other media, telemarketing, or catalog sales are to be used, indicate the specific channels or vehicles, costs (per 1,000), and expected response rates and yield (as percentage) from the various media, etc., used. Discuss how these will be built up.
- Show the sales expected per salesperson per year and what commission, incentive, and/or salary they are slated to receive, and compare these figures to the average for your industry.
- Present a selling schedule and a sales budget that includes all marketing promotion and service costs.

D. *Service and Warranty Policies*
- If your company will offer a product that will require service, warranties, or training, indicate the importance of these to the customers' purchasing decisions and discuss your method of handling service problems.
- Describe the kind and term of any warranties to be offered, whether service will be handled by company servicepeople, agencies, dealers and distributors, or returns to the factory.
- Indicate the proposed charge for service calls and whether service will be a profitable or breakeven operation.
- Compare your service, warranty, and customer training policies and practices to those of your principal competitors.

E. *Advertising and Promotion*
- Describe the approaches the company will use to bring its product or service to the attention of prospective purchasers.
- For original equipment manufacturers and for manufacturers of industrial products, indicate the plans for trade show participation, trade magazine advertisements, direct mailings, the preparation of product sheets and promotional literature, and use of advertising agencies.
- For consumer products, indicate what kind of advertising and promotional campaign is contemplated to introduce the product and what kind of sales aids will be provided to dealers, what trade shows, and so forth, are required.
- Present a schedule and approximate costs of promotion and advertising (including direct mail, telemarketing, catalogs, etc.), and discuss how these costs will be incurred.

F. *Distribution*
- Describe the methods and channels of distribution you will employ.
- Indicate how sensitive shipping cost is as a percent of the selling price.

      — Note any special issues or problems that need to be resolved, or present potential vulnerabilities.

      — If international sales are involved, note how these sales will be handled, including distribution, shipping, insurance, credit, and collections.

VI. Design and Development Plans

The nature and extent of any design and development work and the time and money required before a product or service is marketable needs to be considered in detail. (Note that design and development costs are often underestimated.) Such design and development might be the engineering work necessary to convert a laboratory prototype to a finished product; the design of special tooling; the work of an industrial designer to make a product more attractive and salable; or the identification and organization of employees, equipment, and special techniques, such as the equipment, new computer software, and skills required for computerized credit checking, to implement a service business.

    A. Development Status and Tasks
      — Describe the current status of each product or service and explain what remains to be done to make it marketable.
      — Describe briefly the competence or expertise that your company has or will require to complete this development.
      — List any customers or end users who are participating in the development, design, and/or testing of the product or service. Indicate results to date or when results are expected.

    B. Difficulties and Risks
      — Identify any major anticipated design and development problems and approaches to their solution.
      — Discuss the possible effect on the cost of design and development, on the time to market introduction, and so forth, of such problems.

    C. Product Improvement and New Products. In addition to describing the development of the initial products, discuss any ongoing design and development work that is planned to keep product(s) or service(s) competitive and to develop new related product(s) or service(s) that can be sold to the same group of customers. Discuss customers who have participated in these efforts and their reactions, and include any evidence that you may have.

    D. Costs
      — Present and discuss the design and development budget, including costs of labor, materials, consulting fees, etc.
      — Discuss the impact on cash flow projections of underestimating this budget, including the impact of a 15 to 30 percent contingency.

    E. Proprietary Issues
      — Describe any patent, trademark, copyright, or intellectual property rights you own or are seeking.
      — Describe any contractual rights or agreements that give you exclusivity or proprietary rights.
      — Discuss the impact of any unresolved issues or existing or possible actions pending, such as disputed rights of ownership, relating to proprietary rights on timing and on any competitive edge you have assumed.

VII. Manufacturing and Operations Plan

The manufacturing and operations plan needs to include such factors as plant location, the type of facilities needed, space requirements, capital equipment requirements, and labor force (both full- and part-time) requirements. For a manufacturing business, included in the manufacturing and operations plan need to be policies on inventory control, purchasing, production control, and which parts of the product will be purchased and which operations will be performed by your work force (called make-or-buy decisions). A service business may require particular attention to location (proximity to customers being generally a "must"), minimizing overhead, and obtaining competitive productivity from a labor force.

A. Operating Cycle
- Describe the lead/lag times that characterize the fundamental operating cycle in your business. (Include a graph similar to the one found in the Venture Opportunity Screening Guide.)
- Explain how any seasonal production loads will be handled without severe dislocation (e.g., by building to inventory or using part-time help in peak periods).

B. Geographical Location
- Describe the planned geographical location of the business. Include any location analysis, etc., that you have done.
- Discuss any advantages or disadvantages of the site location in terms of such factors as labor (including labor availability, whether workers are unionized, and wage rates), closeness to customers and/or suppliers, access to transportation, state and local taxes and laws (including zoning regulations), access to utilities, and so forth.

C. Facilities and Improvements
- For an existing business, describe the facilities, including plant and office space, storage and land areas, special tooling, machinery, and other capital equipment currently used to conduct the company's business, and discuss whether these facilities are adequate. Discuss any economies to scale.
- For a start-up, describe how and when the necessary facilities to start production will be acquired.
- Discuss whether equipment and space will be leased or acquired (new or used) and indicate the costs and timing of such actions and how much of the proposed financing will be devoted to plant and equipment.
- Explain future equipment needs in the next three years.
- Discuss how and when, in the next three years, plant space and equipment will be expanded to the capacities required by future sales projections and any plans to improve or add to existing plant space or move the facility; and indicate the timing and cost of such acquisitions.

D. Strategy and Plans
- Describe the manufacturing processes involved in production of your product(s) and any decisions with respect to subcontracting of component parts, rather than complete in-house manufacture.
- Justify your proposed make-or-buy policy in terms of inventory financing, available labor skills, and other nontechnical questions, as well as production, cost, and capability issues.
- Discuss who potential subcontractors and/or suppliers are likely to be and any information about or any surveys which have been made of these subcontractors and suppliers.
- Present a production plan that shows cost/volume information at various sales levels of operation with breakdowns of applicable material, labor, purchased components, and factory overhead and that shows the inventory required at various sales levels.
- Describe your approach to quality control, production control, inventory control, and explain what quality control and inspection procedures the company will use to minimize service problems and associated customer dissatisfaction.

E. Regulatory and Legal Issues
- Discuss here any relevent state, federal, or foreign regulatory requirements unique to your product, process, or service, such as laws or other regulatory compliance unique to your business and any licenses, zoning permits, health permits, environmental approvals, and the like, necessary to begin operation.
- Note any pending regulatory changes that can affect the nature of and timing for your opportunity.
- Discuss any legal or contractual obligations that are pertinent as well.

VIII. Management Team

This section of the business plan includes a description of the functions that will need to be filled, a description of the key management personnel and their primary duties, an outline of the organizational structure for the venture, a description of the board of directors, a description of the ownership position of any other investors, and so forth. Indications of commitment, such as the willingness of team members to initially accept modest salaries, and of the existence of the proper balance of technical, managerial, and business skills and experience in doing what is proposed, need to be presented.

A. *Organization*
- Present the key management roles in the company and the individuals who will fill each position. (If the company is established and of sufficient size, an organization chart needs to be appended.)
- If it is not possible to fill each executive role with a full-time person without adding excessive overhead, indicate how these functions will be performed (e.g., using part-time specialists or consultants to perform some functions), who will perform them, and when they will be replaced by a full-time staff member.
- If any key individuals will not be on board at the start of the venture, indicate when they will join the company.
- Discuss any current or past situations where key management people have worked together that could indicate how their skills complement each other and result in an effective management team.

B. *Key Management Personnel*
- For each key person, describe in detail career highlights, particularly relevant know-how, skills, and track record of accomplishments, that demonstrate his or her ability to perform the assigned role. Include in your description sales and profitability achievements (budget size, numbers of subordinates, new product introductions, etc.) and other prior entrepreneurial or general management results.
- Describe the exact duties and responsibilities of each of the key members of the management team.
- Complete resumes for each key management member need to be included here or as an exhibit and need to stress relevant training, experience, and concrete accomplishments, such as profit and sales improvement; labor management success; manufacturing or technical achievements; and meeting of budgets and schedules.

C. *Management Compensation and Ownership*
- State the salary to be paid, the stock ownership planned, and the amount of their equity investment (if any) of each key member of the management team.
- Compare the compensation of each key member to the salary he or she received at his or her last independent job.

D. *Other Investors*
- Describe here any other investors in your venture, the number and percent of outstanding shares they own, when they were acquired, and at what price.

E. *Employment and Other Agreements and Stock Option and Bonus Plans*
- Describe any existing or contemplated employment or other agreements with key members.
- Indicate any restrictions on stock and vesting that affect ownership and disposition of stock.
- Describe any performance-dependent stock option or bonus plans that are contemplated.
- Summarize any incentive stock option or other stock ownership plans planned or in effect for key people and employees.

F. *Board of Directors*
- Discuss the company's philosophy about the size and composition of the board.
- Identify any proposed board members and include a one- or two-sentence statement of the member's background that shows what he or she can bring to the company.

G. *Other Shareholders, Rights, and Restrictions*
- Indicate any other shareholders in your company and any rights and restrictions or obligations, such as notes, guarantees, associated with these. (If they have all been accounted for above, simply note that there are no others.)

H. *Supporting Professional Advisors and Services*
- Indicate the supporting services that will be required.
- Indicate the names and affiliations of the legal, accounting, advertising, consulting, and banking advisors selected for your venture and the services each will provide.

IX.   Overall Schedule

A schedule that shows the timing and interrelationship of the major events necessary to launch the venture and realize its objectives is an essential part of a business plan. The underlying cash conversion and operating cycle of the business will provide key inputs for the schedule. In addition to being a planning aid, by showing deadlines critical to a venture's success, a well-presented schedule can be extremely valuable in convincing potential investors that the management team is able to plan for venture growth in a way that recognizes obstacles and minimizes investor risk. Since the time to do things tends to be underestimated in most business plans, it is important to demonstrate that you have correctly estimated these amounts in determining the schedule. Create your schedule as follows:

Step 1:   Lay out (use a bar chart) the cash conversion cycle in the business to capture for each product or service expected the lead and elapsed times from an order to the purchase of raw materials or inventory to shipping and collection.

Step 2:   Prepare a month-by-month schedule that shows the timing of such activities as product development, market planning, sales programs, production, and operations, and that includes sufficient detail to show the timing of the primary tasks required to accomplish an activity.

Step 3:   Show on the schedule the deadlines or milestones critical to the venture's success, such as:
— Incorporation of the venture.
— Completion of design and development.
— Completion of prototypes.
— Obtaining of sales representatives.
— Obtaining product display at trade shows.
— Signing up of distributors and dealers.
— Ordering of materials in production quantities.
— Starting of production or operation.
— Receipt of first orders.
— Delivery on first sale.
— Receiving the first payment on accounts receivable.

Step 4:   Show on the schedule the "ramp up" of the number of management personnel, the number of production and operations personnel, and plant or equipment and their relation to the development of the business.

Step 5:   Discuss in a general way the activities most likely to cause a schedule slippage, what steps will be taken to correct such slippages, and the impact of schedule slippages on the venture's operation, especially its potential viability and capital needs.

X.   Critical Risks, Problems, and Assumptions

The development of a business has risks and problems, and the business plan invariably contains some implicit assumptions about them. This needs to include a description of the risks and the consequences of adverse outcomes relating to your industry, your company and its personnel, your product's market appeal, and the timing and financing of your start-up. Be sure to discuss assumptions about and behind sales projections, customer orders, and so forth. If the venture has anything that could be considered a fatal flaw, discuss why it is not. The discovery of any unstated negative factors by potential investors can undermine the credibility of the venture and endanger its financing. Be aware that most investors will read the section describing the management team first and then this section.

It is recommended that you *not omit* this section. If you do, the reader will most likely come to one or more of the following conclusions:

1.   You think he or she is incredibly naive or stupid, or both.
2.   You hope to pull, deliberately, the wool over his or her eyes.
3.   You do not have enough objectivity to recognize and deal with assumptions and problems.

Identifying and discussing the risks in your venture demonstrates your skills as a manager and increases the credibility of you and your venture with a venture capital or a private investor. Taking the initiative on the identification and discussion of risks helps you to demonstrate to the investor that you have thought about them and can handle them. Risks then tend not to loom as large black clouds in the investor's thinking about your venture.

1. Discuss assumptions and risks implicit in your plan.
2. Identify and discuss any major problems and other risks, such as:
   — Running out of cash *before* orders are secured.
   — Potential price cutting by competitors.
   — Any potentially unfavorable industrywide trends.
   — Design or manufacturing costs in excess of estimates.
   — Sales projections not achieved.
   — An unmet product development schedule.
   — Difficulties or long lead times encountered in the procurement of parts or raw materials.
   — Difficulties encountered in obtaining needed bank credit.
   — Larger-then-expected innovation and development costs.
   — Running out of cash *after* orders pour in.
3. Indicate what assumptions or potential problems and risks are most critical to the success of the venture, and describe your plans for minimizing the impact of unfavorable developments in each.

XI. The Financial Plan

The financial plan is basic to the evaluation of an investment opportunity and needs to represent your best estimates of financial requirements. The purpose of the financial plan is to indicate the venture's potential and to present a timetable for financial viability. It also can serve as an operating plan for financial management using financial benchmarks. In preparing the financial plan, you need to look creatively at your venture and consider alternative ways of launching or financing it.

As part of the financial plan, financial exhibits need to be prepared. To estimate *cash flow needs,* use cash-based, rather than an accrual-based, accounting (i.e., use a "real-time" cash flow analysis of expected receipts and disbursements). This analysis needs to cover three years. Included also are current- and prior-year income statements and balance sheets, if applicable; profit and loss forecasts for three years; pro forma income statements and balance sheets; and a breakeven chart. On the appropriate exhibits, or in an attachment, assumptions behind such items as sales levels and growth, collections and payables periods, inventory requirements, cash balances, cost of goods, and so forth need to be specified. Your analysis of the operating and cash conversion cycle in the business will enable you to identify these critical assumptions.

Pro forma income statements are the plan-for-profit part of financial management and can indicate the potential financial feasibility of a new venture. Since usually the level of profits, particularly during the start-up years of a venture, will not be sufficient to finance operating asset needs, and since actual cash inflows do not always match the actual cash outflows on a short-term basis, a cash flow forecast that will indicate these conditions and enable management to plan cash needs is recommended. Further, pro forma balance sheets are used to detail the assets required to support the projected level of operations and, through liabilities, to show how these assets are to be financed. The projected balance sheets can indicate if debt-to-equity ratios, working capital, current ratios, inventory turnover, and the like are within the acceptable limits required to justify future financings that are projected for the venture. Finally, a breakeven chart showing the level of sales and production that will cover all costs, including those costs that vary with production level and those that do not, is very useful.

A. Actual Income Statements and Balance Sheets
   — For an existing business, prepare income statements and balance sheets for the current year and for the prior two years.
B. Pro Forma Income Statements
   — Using sales forecasts and the accompanying production or operations costs, prepare pro forma income statements for at least the first three years.

- Fully discuss assumptions (e.g., the amount allowed for bad debts and discounts, or any assumptions made with respect to sales expenses or general and administrative costs being a fixed percentage of costs or sales) made in preparing the pro forma income statement and document them.
- Draw on Section X of the business plan and highlight any major risks, such as the effect of a 20 percent reduction in sales from those projected or the adverse impact of having to climb a learning curve on the level of productivity over time, that could prevent the venture's sales and profit goals from being attained, plus the sensitivity of profits to these risks.

C. *Pro Forma Balance Sheets*
- Prepare pro forma balance sheets semiannually in the first year and at the end of each of the first three years of operation.

D. *Pro Forma Cash Flow Analysis*
- Project cash flows monthly for the first year of operation and quarterly for at least the next two years, detailing the amount and timing of expected cash inflows and outflows; determine the need for and timing of additional financing and indicate peak requirements for working capital; and indicate how needed additional financing is to be obtained, such as through the equity financing, through bank loans, or through short-term lines of credit from banks, on what terms, and how it is to be repaid. Remember they are based on cash and not accrual accounting.
- Discuss assumptions, such as those made on the timing of collection of receivables, trade discounts given, terms of payments to vendors, planned salary and wage increases, anticipated increases in any operating expenses, seasonality characteristics of the business as they affect inventory requirements, inventory turnovers per year, capital equipment purchases, and so forth. Again, these are real time (i.e., cash), not accrual.
- Discuss cash flow sensitivity to a variety of assumptions about business factors (e.g., possible changes in such crucial assumptions as an increase in the receivable collection period or a sales level lower than that forecasted).

E. *Breakeven Chart*
- Calculate breakeven and prepare a chart that shows when breakeven will be reached and any stepwise changes in breakeven which may occur.
- Discuss the breakeven shown for your venture and whether it will be easy or difficult to attain breakeven, including a discussion of the size of breakeven sales volume relative to projected total sales, the size of gross margins and price sensitivity, and how the breakeven point might be lowered in case the venture falls short of sales projections.

F. *Cost Control*
- Describe how you will obtain information about report costs and how often, who will be responsible for the control of various cost elements, and how you will take action on budget overruns.

G. *Highlights*
- Highlight the important conclusions, such as what the maximum amount of cash required is and when it will be required, the amount of debt and equity needed, how fast any debts can be repaid, etc., that can be drawn.

XII. Proposed Company Offering

The purpose of this section of the plan is to indicate the amount of any money that is being sought, the nature and amount of the securities offered to the investor, a brief description of the uses that will be made of the capital raised, and a summary of how the investor is expected to achieve its targeted rate of return. It is recommended that you read the discussion about financing in Part IV.

It is important to realize the terms for financing your company that you propose here are the *first step* in the negotiation process with those interested in investing, and it is very possible that your financing will involve different kinds of securities than originally proposed.

A. *Desired Financing*
   — Based on your real-time cash flow projections and your estimate of how much money is required over the next three years to carry out the development and/or expansion of your business as described, indicate how much of this capital requirement will be obtained by this offering and how much will be obtained via term loans and lines of credit.

B. *Offering*
   — Describe the type (e.g., common stock, convertible debentures, debt with warrants, debt plus stock), unit price, and total amount of securities to be sold in this offering. If securities are not just common stock, indicate by type, interest, maturity, and conversion conditions.
   — Show the percentage of the company that the investors of this offering will hold after it is completed or after exercise of any stock conversion or purchase rights in the case of convertible debentures or warrants.
   — Securities sold through a "private placement" and that, therefore, are exempt from SEC registration should include the following statement in this part of the plan:
     The shares being sold pursuant to this offering are restricted securities and may not be resold readily. The prospective investor should recognize that such securities might be restricted as to resale for an indefinite period of time. Each purchaser will be required to execute a Non-Distribution Agreement satisfactory in form to corporate counsel.

C. *Capitalization*
   — Present in tabular form the current and proposed (postoffering) number of outstanding shares of common stock. Indicate any shares offered by key management people and show the number of shares that they will hold after completion of the proposed financing.
   — Indicate how many shares of your company's common stock will remain authorized but unissued after the offering and how many of these will be reserved for stock options for future key employees.

D. *Use of Funds*
   — Investors like to know how their money is going to be spent. Provide a brief description of how the capital raised will be used. Summarize as specifically as possible what amount will be used for such things as product design and development, capital equipment, marketing, and general working capital needs.

E. *Investors' Return*
   — Indicate how your valuation and proposed ownership shares will result in the desired rate of return for the investors you have targeted and what the likely harvest or exit mechanism (e.g., IPO, outright sale, merger, MBO, etc.) will be.

XIII. Appendices

Include pertinent information here that is too extensive for the body of the business plan but which is necessary (e.g., product specs or photos; lists of references; suppliers of critical components; special location factors, facilities, or technical analyses; reports from consultants or technical experts; and copies of any critical regulatory approval, licenses, and so forth).

STEP 5: INTEGRATE YOUR DISCRETE SECTIONS INTO A COHERENT AND LOGICAL BUSINESS PLAN, WHICH CAN BE USED FOR THE PURPOSE FOR WHICH IT IS CREATED.

STEP 6: GET FEEDBACK, AND, IF YOUR PLAN IS TO BE SUBMITTED TO OUTSIDE INVESTORS, HAVE YOUR PLAN REVIEWED BY YOUR ATTORNEY.   Once written, it is recommended that you get the plan reviewed. No matter how good you and your team are, you will most likely overlook issues and treat aspects of your venture in a manner that is less than clear. A good reviewer can give you the benefit of an outside objective evaluation. Your attorney can make sure that there are no misleading statements in your plan and that it contains all the caveats and the like.

FINANCING ENTREPRENEURIAL VENTURES

PART IV

A financing strategy should be driven by corporate and personal goals, by resulting financial requirements, and ultimately by the available alternatives. In the final analysis, these alternatives are governed by the entrepreneur's relative bargaining power. In turn, that bargaining power is governed to a large extent by the cruelty of *real time*. It is governed by when the company will run out of cash given its current cash burn rate.

There are more numerous alternatives for financing a company than ever before. Many contend that money remains plentiful for well-managed emerging firms with the promise of profitable growth. Yet, savvy entrepreneurs remain vigilant for the warnings noted here to avoid the myopic temptation to "take the money and run."

While some of these alternatives look distinct and separate, a financing strategy probably will encompass a combination of both debt and equity capital.

In considering which financial alternatives are best for a venture at any particular growth stage, it is important to draw on the experience of others who have already been there. This includes other entrepreneurs, professional investors, lenders, accountants, and other professionals.

In their search for either debt or equity capital, it is important that entrepreneurs take a professional approach to selecting and presenting their ventures to investors and lenders.

Entrepreneurial Finance

Happiness to an entrepreneur is a positive cash flow.

Fred Adler
Venture Capitalist

RESULTS EXPECTED

Upon completion of this chapter, you will have:

1. Examined critical issues in financing new ventures.
2. Studied the difference between entrepreneurial finance and conventional administrative or corporate finance.
3. Examined the process of crafting financial and fund-raising strategies and the critical variables involved, including identifying the financial life cycles of new ventures, a financial strategy framework, and investor preferences.
4. Analyzed the issues and approaches utilized by a nontechnology service-oriented company, Hindman & Company, to fund its start-up and early rapid growth.

VENTURE FINANCING

Navigating Uncharted Waters

Earlier chapters in Parts I, II, and III focused on the lead entrepreneur and the opportunity—what constitutes an attractive venture opportunity and how, when, and what kind of management team, entry strategy, and business plan can be developed to seize it. This chapter focuses on the financing of new and existing ventures.

Imagine the following: It has taken you over 10 years, a lot of sweat equity, many sleepless nights, and personal guarantees on company bank loans to build your software firm to $5 million in sales. Profits have been up and down as a result of your spending current income to grow, but you are confident the firm can exceed $11 million in quite profitable sales by 1992. But, growing a company requires cash. By early 1988, your banker—and 10 other banks you have approached—say "no" to your request to extend your line of credit from $500,000 to $1.5 million to help fund your growth plans. Unless you can raise more equity, which you do not personally have, the banks are going to pass. You meet a lawyer at a seminar for entrepreneurs who insists he can take you public in Vancouver or London and raise $2.5 million. That sounds like good news. After all, that would dramatically improve your balance sheet and provide the cash you sorely need for expansion. Then you figure out the cost: The lawyers, underwriters, accountants, printers, and regulators will require 35 percent of the total offering off the top! You wonder if this is your only alternative. And you are out of cash.

Or imagine: After nearly 10 years of acquiring the "50,000 chunks" of relevant know-how, experience, and track-record, you sense an opportunity to launch a new firm in the fiberoptics industry. You and your partners bet $100,000 of your own hard-earned cash to provide the seed money to so develop a business plan that another $750,000 can be raised. Eight months later you have exhausted your seed money and have had rejections from every possible source of funding you can think of, including over 40 venture capital firms and some investment bankers. Your worst fears seem to be becoming reality, and quitting your good job, investing too much of your nest egg, and working without time off may all be for naught. You ask what has gone wrong and wonder if there are any viable financing alternatives left. Is there a strategy to find and secure desperately needed capital?

These stories above have at least one thing in common: in them, you are sailing in unfamiliar waters, and you may not have a compass or the right chart.

Even in good times, the financial domain for most entrepreneurs and smaller company presidents — by their own admission — is the least-familiar, most-feared territory. Lack of any technical education or first-hand knowledge and experience with financing is common. And, many entrepreneurs in small companies may subscribe to the leading entrepreneurial publications but do not have working relationships with venture capitalists, investment bankers, "angels," or even advisors they can rely on as impartial friendly advocates.

For an entrepreneur to know what he or she is getting into, what risks to accept or not, and what trade-offs to look for and to look out for is often every bit as important as how much money is obtained and from whom. And, for the entrepreneur, these issues and risks are not generally "advertised" or visible in advance.

Critical Financing Issues

Exhibit 13.1 illustrates the central issues in entrepreneurial finance. These include the creation of value, how the value pie is sliced and divided among those who have a stake or have participated in the venture, and the handling of the risks inherent in the venture. Developing financing and fund-raising strategies, knowing what alternatives are available, and obtaining funding are tasks vital to the survival and success of most higher-potential ventures.

As a result, entrepreneurs face certain critical issues and problems, which bear on the financing of entrepreneurial ventures, such as:

- *Creating Value*
  - Who are the constituencies for whom value must created or added to achieve a positive cash flow and to develop harvest options?
- *Slicing the Value Pie*
  - How are deals, both for start-ups and for the purchases of existing ventures, structured and valued, and what are the critical tax consequences of different venture structures?
  - What is the legal process and what are the key issues involved in raising outside risk capital?
  - How do entrepreneurs make effective presentations of their business plans to financing and other sources?
  - How can entrepreneurs apply the microcomputer and applications software to the financial analysis and evaluation inherent in the above questions?
  - What are some of the nastier pitfalls, minefields, and hazards that need to be anticipated, prepared for, and responded to?
  - How critical and sensitive is timing in each of these areas?

Exhibit 13.1
Central Issues in Entrepreneurial Finance

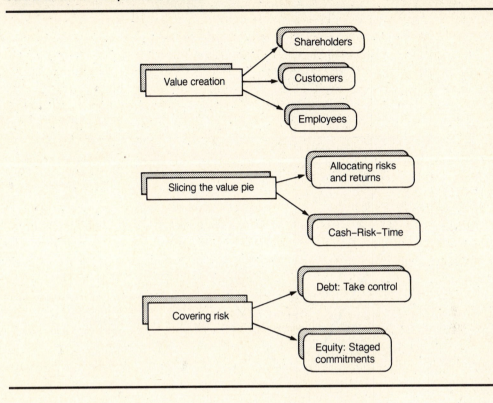

■ *Covering Risk*
— How much money is needed to start, acquire, or expand the business, and when, where, and how can it be obtained on acceptable terms?
— What are the sources of risk and venture capital financing—equity, debt, and other innovative "types"—available, and how is appropriate financing negotiated and obtained?
— Who are the financial contacts and networks that need to be accessed and developed?
— How do successful entrepreneurs marshall the necessary financial resources and other financial equivalents to seize and execute opportunities, and what pitfalls do they manage to avoid, and how?

A clear understanding of the financing requirements is especially vital for new and emerging companies, because new ventures go through "financial hell" compared to existing ongoing firms, both smaller and larger, which have a customer base and revenue stream. In the early going, new firms are gluttons for capital and, yet, are usually not very debt-worthy. To make matters worse, the faster they grow, the more gluttonous is their appetite for cash.

This phenomenon is best illustrated in *Exhibit 13.2,* where loss as a percent of initial equity is plotted against time.[1] The shaded area represents the cumulative cash flow of 157

---

[1] Special appreciation is due to Bert Twaalfhoven, founder and chairman of Indivers, the Dutch firm that compiled this summary and that owns the firm on which the chart is based. Mr. Twaalfhoven was also a leader in the Class of 1954 at Harvard Business School and has been active in supporting the Entrepreneurial Management Interest Group and research efforts there.

Exhibit 13.2
Initial Losses by Small New Ventures

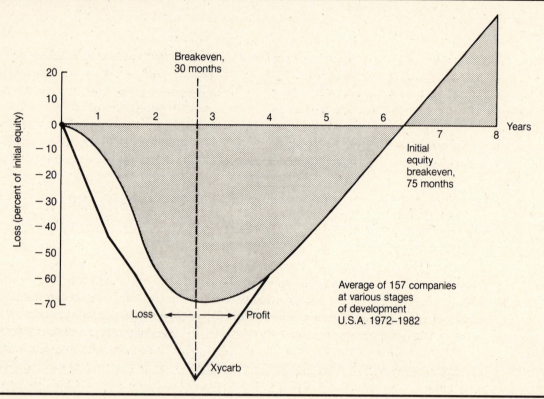

Source: Indivers.

companies from their inception. For these firms, it took 30 months to achieve operating breakeven and 75 months (or, going into the *seventh* year) to recover the initial equity. As can be seen from the illustration, *cash goes out for a long time before it starts to come in.* And it is this phenomenon that is at the heart of the financing challenges facing new and emerging companies.

Entrepreneurial Finance

If an entrepreneur who has had responsibility for financing in a large established company and also in a private emerging firm is asked whether there are differences between the two, the person asking will get quite an earful.

While there is, of course, some common ground, there are both stark and subtle differences, both in theory and in practice, between entrepreneurial finance as practiced in higher potential ventures and corporate or administrative finance, which usually occurs in larger publicly traded companies. Further, there are important limits to some financial theories as applied to new ventures.

Knowledge of the limits of financial theories, of differences in the domain of entrepreneurial finance, and of understanding the implications is a core task for entrepreneurs. In order to begin to appreciate the character and flavor of these limits and differences, consider the following sampling:

- *Cash flow and cash.*   Cash flow and cash are king and queen in entrepreneurial finance. Accrual-based accounting, earnings per share, or creative and aggressive use of the tax codes and rules of the Securities and Exchange Commission are not.

- *Time and timing.* Financing alternatives for the financial health of an enterprise are often more sensitive to, or vulnerable to, the time dimension. In entrepreneurial finance, time for critical financing moves often is shorter and more compressed, the optimum timing of these moves changes more rapidly, and financing moves are subject to wider, more volatile swings from lows to highs and back.

- *Capital markets.* Capital markets for over 95 percent of the financing of private entrepreneurial ventures are relatively imperfect, in that they are frequently inaccessible, unorganized, and often invisible. Virtually all the underlying characteristics and assumptions that dominate such popular financial theories and models as the capital asset pricing model simply do not apply, even up to the point of a public offering for a small company. In reality, there are so many and such significant information, knowledege, and market gaps and asymmetries that the rational, perfect market models suffer enormous limitations.

- *Emphasis.* Capital is one of the least important factors in the success of higher potential ventures. Rather, higher potential entrepreneurs seek not only the best deal but also the backer who will provide the most value in terms of know-how, wisdom, counsel, and help. In addition, higher potential entrepreneurs invariably opt for the value added (beyond money), rather than just the best deal or share price.

- *Strategies for raising capital.* Strategies that optimize or maximize the amount of money raised can actually serve to increase risk in new and emerging companies, rather than lower it. Thus, the concept of "staged capital commitments," whereby money is committed for a 3- to 18-month phase and is followed by subsequent commitments based on results and promise, is a prevalent practice among venture capitalists and other investors in higher potential ventures. Similarly, wise entrepreneurs may refuse excess capital when the valuation is less attractive and when they believe that valuation will rise substantially.

- *Downside consequences.* Consequences of financial strategies and decisions are imminently more personal and emotional for the owners of new and emerging ventures than for the managements of large companies. The downside consequences for such entrepreneurs of running out of cash or failing are monumental and relatively catastrophic, since personal guarantees of bank or other loans are common. Contrast these situations with that of the new president of RJR Nabisco. His bonus for signing and his five-year employment package guarantees him a total of $25 million, and he could earn substantially more based on his performance. However, even if he does a mediocre or lousy job, his downside is $25 million.

- *Risk/reward relationships.* While the high-risk/high-reward and low-risk/low-reward relationship (a so-called law of economics and finance) works, by and large, in efficient, mature, and relatively perfect capital markets (e.g., those with money market accounts, deposits in savings and loan institutions, widely held and traded stocks and bonds, certificates of deposit, and so on), just the opposite occurs all too often in entrepreneurial finance to permit much comfort with this "law." Time and again, some of the most profitable, highest return venture investments have been quite *low-risk* propositions from the outset. Many leveraged buyouts using extreme leverage are probably much more risky than many start-ups. Yet, the way the capital markets price these deals is just the reverse. The reasons are anchored in the second and third points noted above—timing and the asymmetries and imperfections of the capital markets for deals. Entrepreneurs or investors who create or recognize lower-risk/very high yield business propositions, before others jump on the Brink's truck, will defy the "law" of economics and finance.

- *Valuation methods.* Established company valuation methods, such as those based on discounted cash flow models used in Wall Street megadeals, seem to favor the seller, rather than the buyer, of private emerging entrepreneurial companies. A seller loves to see a recent MBA or investment banking firm alumnus or alumna show up with an HP-12C calculator or the latest laptop personal computer and then proceed to develop "the 10-year discounted cash flow stream." The assumptions normally made and the mind-set behind them are irrelevant or grossly misleading for valuation of smaller private firms.

- *Conventional financial ratios.*   Current financial ratios are misleading when applied to most private entrepreneurial companies. For one thing, entrepreneurs often own more than one company at once and move cash and assets from one to another. For example, an entrepreneur may own real estate and equipment in one entity and lease it to another company. Use of different fiscal years compounds the difficulty of interpreting what the balance sheet really means and the possibilities for aggressive tax-avoidance. Further, many of the most important value and equity builders in the business are off-balance-sheet or hidden assets: the excellent management team; the best scientist, technician, or designer; or know-how and business relationships that cannot be bought or sold, let alone valued for the balance sheet.
- *Goals.*   Creating value over the long term, rather than maximizing quarterly earnings, is a prevalent mind-set and strategy among highly successful entrepreneurs. Since profit is more than just the bottom line, financial strategies are geared to build value, often at the expense of short-term earnings. The growth required to build value often is heavily self-financed, thereby eroding possible "accounting earnings."

CRAFTING FINANCIAL AND FUND-RAISING STRATEGIES

Critical Variables

When financing is needed, whether financing is available, what the alternatives are, what alternatives are most suitable, and what various alternatives will cost all depend on a number of factors:

- Investor's perceived risk.
- Industry and technology.
- Venture upside potential.
- Venture anticipated growth rate.
- Venture age and stage of development.
- Amount of capital required.
- Founders' goals regarding growth, control, liquidity, and harvesting.
- Relative bargaining positions.

Certainly, numerous other factors, especially an investor's or lender's view of the quality of a business opportunity and the management team, will also play a part in a decision to invest in or lend to a firm.

Generally speaking, a company's operations can be financed through debt and through some form of equity financing.[2] Moreover, it is generally believed that a new or existing business needs to obtain both equity and debt financing if it is to have a sound financial foundation for growth without excessive dilution of the entrepreneur's equity.

Usually, short-term debt (i.e., debt incurred for one year or less) is used by a business for working capital and is repaid out of the proceeds of its sales. Longer-term borrowings

---

[2] In addition to the purchase of common stock, equity financing is meant to include the purchase of both stock and subordinated debt, or subordinated debt with stock conversion features, or warrants to purchase stock.

(i.e., term loans of one to five years or long-term loans maturing in more than five years) are used for working capital and/or to finance the purchase of property or equipment that serve as collateral for the loan. Equity financing is used to fill the nonbankable gaps, preserve ownership, and lower the risk of loan defaults.

However, a new venture just starting operations will have difficulty obtaining either short-term or longer-term bank debt without a substantial cushion of equity financing or long-term debt that is subordinated or junior to all bank debt.[3] As far as a lender is concerned, a start-up has little proven capability to generate sales, profits, and cash to pay off short-term debt and even less ability to sustain profitable operations over a number of years and retire long-term debt. Even the underlying protection provided by a venture's assets used as loan collateral may be insufficient to obtain bank loans. Asset values can erode with time and, in the absence of adequate equity capital and good management, may provide little real loan security to a bank.[4]

A bank may loan money to a start-up to some maximum debt-to-equity ratio. As a rough rule of thumb, a start-up *may* be able to obtain debt for working capital purposes that is equal to its equity and subordinated debt. A start-up can also obtain loans through such avenues as the Small Business Administration, manufacturers and suppliers, or through leasing.

An existing business seeking expansion capital or funds for a temporary use has a much easier job obtaining both debt and equity. Sources like banks, professional investors, and leasing and finance companies often will seek out such companies and regard them as important customers for secured and unsecured short and term loans or as good investment prospects. Furthermore, an existing and expanding business will find it easier to raise equity capital from private or institutional sources and to raise it on better terms than the start-up.

A key message from the above is that awareness of criteria used by various sources of financing—whether for debt, equity, or some combination—that are available for a particular situation is central to devise a time-effective and cost-effective search for capital.

Financial Life Cycles

One useful way to begin the process of identifying equity financing alternatives, and when and if certain alternatives are available, is to consider what can be called "the financial life cycle of firms." *Exhibit 13.3* shows the types of capital available over time for different types of firms at different stages of development (i.e., as indicated by different sales levels).[5] It also summarizes, at different stages of development (i.e., research and development, start-up, early growth, rapid growth, and exit), the principal sources of risk capital and costs of risk capital.

As can be seen in the exhibit, sources have different preferences and practices, including how much money they will provide, when in a company's life cycle they will invest, and the cost of the capital or expected annual rate of return they are seeking. The available sources of capital change dramatically for companies at different stages and rates of growth, and there will be variations in different parts of the country.

---

[3] For lending purposes, commercial banks regard such subordinated debt as equity. Venture capital investors normally subordinate their business loans to the loans provided by the bank or other financial institutions.

[4] The bank loan defaults by the real estate investment trusts (REITs) in 1975 are examples of the failure of assets to provide protection in the absence of sound management and adequate equity capital.

[5] William H. Wetzel, Jr., of the University of New Hampshire, originally showed different types of equity capital that are available to three types of companies. The exhibit is based on a chart by Wetzel, which the author has taken the liberty of updating and modifying. See Wetzel's 1979 paper: William H. Wetzel, Jr., "The Cost of Availability of Credit and Risk Capital in New England," in *A Region's Struggling Savior: Small Business in New England,* ed. J. A. Timmons and D. E. Gumpert (Waltham, Mass.: Small Business Foundation of America, 1979).

Exhibit 13.3
Financing Life Cycles

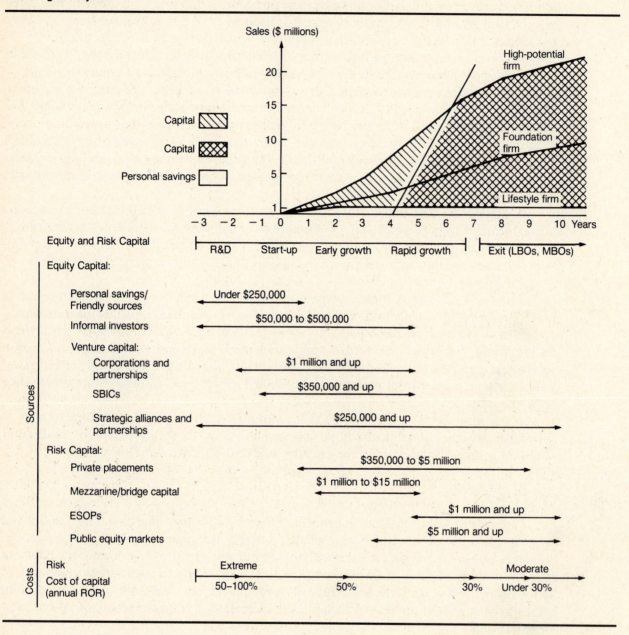

Thus, one can see that many of the sources of equity are not available until a company progresses beyond the earlier stages of its growth. Conversely, some of the sources available to early-stage companies, especially personal sources, friends, and other informal investors or angels, will be insufficient to meet the financing requirements generated in later stages, if the company continues to grow successfully.

One also can see that another key factor affecting the availability of financing is the upside potential of a company. Recall that, of the 1.3 million new businesses of all kinds expected to be launched in the United States in 1989, for example, probably 5 percent or less of these will achieve the growth and sales levels of high potential firms. Foundation firms will comprise around 8 percent to 12 percent of all new firms, which will grow more slowly but exceed $1 million in sales and may grow to $5 million to $15 million. The remaining are the traditional, stable lifestyle firms. What have been called high potential firms (i.e., those that grow rapidly and are likely to exceed $20 million to $25 million or more in sales) are strong prospects for a public offering and have the widest array of financing alternatives, including combinations of debt and equity and other alternatives (which are noted later on), while foundation firms have fewer, and lifestyle firms are limited to the personal resources of their founders and whatever net worth or collateral they can accumulate.

In general, investors believe the younger the company, the more risky the investment. This is a variation of the old saying in the venture capital business that has been seen before: The lemons ripen in two and a half years, but the plums take seven or eight.

While the time line and dollar limits shown are only guidelines, they do reflect how these money sources view the riskiness, and thus the required rate of return, of companies at various stages of development.

Financial Strategy Framework

The financial strategy framework shown in *Exhibit 13.4* is a way to begin the crafting of financial and fund raising strategies.[6] The exhibit provides a flow and logic with which an otherwise confusing, if not befuddling task, can be attacked. *The opportunity, and the business, leads and drives the business strategy and, thus, the financial requirements, the sources and deal structures, and the financial strategy.* (Again, unless and until this part of the exercise is well defined, developing spreadsheets and "playing with the numbers" is just that—playing.)

Once the core of the market opportunity and the strategy for seizing it are well defined (as best can be done since these may well change, even dramatically), an entrepreneur can then begin to examine the financial requirements in terms of (1) operating needs (i.e., working capital for operations) and (2) asset needs (for start-up or for expansion facilities, equipment, research and development, and other one-time—for now—expenditures). This framework leaves ample room for crafting a financial strategy, for creatively identifying sources, for devising a fund-raising plan, and for structuring deals.

Each *fund-raising strategy,* and accompanying deal structure, commit the company to actions that incur actual costs and costs in terms of real time and may enhance or inhibit future financing options. Similarly, each *source* has particular requirements and costs—both apparent and hidden—that carry implications for both financial strategy and financial requirements. The premise is that successful entrepreneurs are aware of potentially punishing situations, and, further, they are careful to "sweat the details" and proceed with a certain degree of wariness as they evaluate, select, negotiate, and craft business relationships with potential funding sources. In doing so, they are more likely to find the right sources, at the right time, and on the right terms and conditions. They are also more likely to avoid potential mismatches, costly sidetracking for the wrong sources, and the disastrous marriage to these sources that might follow.

Certain changes in the financial climate, such as the aftershocks felt after October 1987, can cause repercussions across financial markets and institutions serving smaller

---

[6] This framework was developed for the course, Financing Entrepreneurial Ventures, at Babson College and is used in the course, Entrepreneurial Finance, at the Harvard Business School.

Exhibit 13.4
Financial Strategy Framework

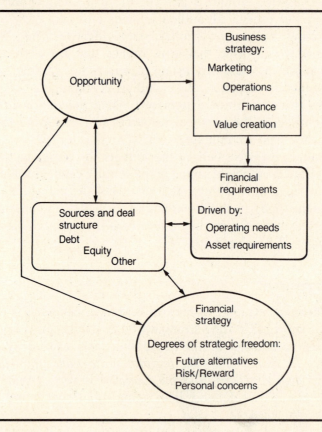

companies. These take the form of greater caution by lenders and investors alike as they seek to increase their protection against risk. When the financial climate becomes harsher, an entrepreneur's capacity to devise financing strategies and to effectively deal with financing sources can be stretched to the limit and beyond. Also, certain lures of cash that come in unsuspecting ways turn out to be a punch in the wallet. (What some of these potentially fatal lures are and what some of the issues and considerations are in recognizing and avoiding these traps, while devising a fund-raising strategy, evaluating, and negotiating with different sources, are covered in the next chapter.)

Investor Preferences

It is important to realize that precise practices of investors or lenders may vary between individual investors or lenders in a given category, may change with the current market conditions, and may vary in different areas of the country from time to time.

Identifying realistic sources, and a fund-raising strategy to tap them, depend upon knowing what kinds of investments investors or lenders are seeking. While the stage, amount, and return guidelines noted in *Exhibit 13.3* can help, doing the appropriate homework in advance on specific investor or lender preferences can save months of wild goose chases and personal cash, while significantly increasing the odds of successfully raising funds on acceptable terms.

CASE—HINDMAN & COMPANY

Preparation Questions

1. Evaluate the business opportunity for the franchisee and the franchisor. How do they make money in this business?
2. Evaluate the company's growth and financial strategy. What have been the consequences?
3. Evaluate the current strategy, both for growth and for financing. How much money is needed and when?
4. What should Hindman do?

HINDMAN & COMPANY

Black Friday

It is March 10, 1983, another "Black Friday" for Jiffy Lube, Inc., and Jim Hindman, president and founder. Today's layoffs are the latest in a series of cutbacks that have reduced Jiffy Lube's payroll by over 40 percent since the beginning of February. The layoffs and other cost reductions are painful, but Hindman realizes that things can still get worse.

Jim Hindman founded Jiffy Lube in 1979. Now, in March 1983, it is the largest franchisor of quick oil change and lubrication service centers in the United States. Jiffy Lube service centers perform a "14 point fluid maintenance program" on automobiles in approximately 10 minutes. Customers pay $18–$20 for the basic service (optional services also are provided for an additional charge).

Background

After graduating from the University of Minnesota with a master's degree in health care administration, Hindman worked 10 years as a hospital administrator. In 1967, he started his own health-care business, Hindman & Associates. The company built 32 nursing homes and eventually diversified into several unrelated businesses. By the mid-1970s, Hindman's ownership interests in these ventures were worth several million dollars, and he was bored and looking for new challenges.

In the early 1970s, Hindman began coaching football in his free time, eventually taking over as head coach of Western Maryland College in 1977. By 1979, Hindman was again restless and looking for new business opportunities. One of the factors that prompted Hindman to start another business was a comment made by one of his students, who claimed that: "There are no opportunities left. You couldn't make a million dollars in America today."

"I was really perplexed at how in the hell he could come away from college believing that," recalls Hindman. "That really was a major, triggering, emotional event that caused me to start looking around for a new business." Joining him were Ed Kelley and Steve Spinelli. Kelley had worked for Hindman in the health-care business and was an assistant coach at Western Maryland.

The fast oil change business quickly caught Hindman's attention. Research revealed that, in the prior 10 years, the number of full-service gas stations had been reduced by almost half. Most had been replaced by self-service stations, which didn't do oil changes or other minor maintenance. Hindman's brother-in-law knew a man who operated a "Jiffy Lube" franchise (part of a chain of oil change centers headquartered in Utah). After several meetings with Jiffy Lube's owner in Utah, Hindman purchased the Jiffy Lube trademark and the rights to seven franchises.

Exhibit A
Business Plan

Over 100 Jiffy Lube Service centers will be in operation by the end of 1982. Expansion will be accomplished through:

1. Sales of new franchises
2. Acquisition of existing service centers or small franchise chains which meet the company's specifications

Franchising will be used as the primary means of expanding the Jiffy Lube network. Franchising will attract qualified managers to each individual center because of the ownership opportunity offered them. Franchising will also accelerate growth because it eliminates many of the managerial and financial requirements that would be necessary to develop and maintain a large network of company-operated centers.

Franchises will be positioned to create blocks of service centers in targeted cities. "Clustering" these centers in large blocks will build name recognition and make advertising cost-effective.

The overall image of Jiffy Lube is not yet at the point where all franchisees will be willing to pay up front the $250–$300K required to purchase land and develop a new center. In many situations it may be necessary for Jiffy Lube to provide the real estate development financing.

Reaching 100 units by the end of 1982 will require the sale of 40 to 60 new franchises (depending on the number of units acquired from existing chains). The company may find it necessary to provide real estate financing for half, or 20 to 30, of these units. Based on a cost of $300K per unit, Jiffy Lube will need to obtain real estate financing of $6 to $9 million to achieve the projected level of new franchise sales.

Early Strategy

Jim Hindman describes Jiffy Lube's early progress after acquiring the first seven units in May 1979:

We spent most of the first year putting together a formal policy and procedure manual for the franchises and developing a standard design for the service centers. E&W assisted us in the development of our franchise audit program and in setting up our accounting system. We also did a complete market study; we were trying to develop a system that would be responsive to the customer.

Jiffy Lube's early strategy is summarized in excerpts from a business plan prepared in the first year of operation (see *Exhibit A*).

Ed Kelley sums up their early strategy:

Our goal was to get to 100 units as quickly as possible. We were trying to reach a level of respectability. That would allow us to go out and do some of the things we needed to do, which was primarily to attract capital, and attract people to buy our franchises.

Expansion . . . and Losses

The Jiffy Lube "network" of service centers has grown rapidly from its original seven units *(Exhibit B)*. The growth has come from the acquisition of four small chains of service centers (approximately 30 units in total), the acquisition of individual centers, and the sale of new franchises.

Jiffy Lube has successfully expanded its network of service centers, but it has incurred cumulative losses of more than $5 million since inception *(Exhibit C)*. The entire network of

Exhibit B
Jiffy Lube Service Center Network (includes statistics for both franchised and company-owned centers)

	Year Ending March 31			
	1980	*1981*	*1982*	*1983 (projected)*
Total gross sales for network (millions)	$1.5	$2.5	$7.1	$15.6
Total centers in operation:				
Franchised	7	19	40	96
Company owned	1	10	30	0

Exhibit C
Jiffy Lube, Inc., Operating Results

	Year Ended March 31 *(in millions)*			
	1980	*1981*	*1982*	*1983 (projected)*
Revenues	$ .2	$ 2.0	$ 3.5	$ 5.5
Net loss	$(0.4)	$(0.7)	$(1.4)	$(2.6)

See *Exhibit G* for projected 1983 financial statements.

service centers is projected to generate over $15 million in sales for fiscal 1983. However, as the franchisor, Jiffy Lube shares in only a portion of this total. Jiffy Lube's revenues are made up of the following:

Royalty fees from franchisees (approximately 5 percent of each franchisee's gross sales).

Rental income on property leased or subleased to franchisees.

Initial fees from new franchises (approximately $20,000 per new service center).

Sales by company-owned centers (however, as described in a later section, all company-owned centers were disposed of in fiscal 1983).

The majority of franchisees are individuals who operate one or two franchises.

Early Financing

Jiffy Lube was financed during its start-up and first several years of growth largely through Jim Hindman's personal resources. During the first three years of operation Hindman contributed over $1.5 million in the form of cash, assumptions of debt, and forgiveness of personal loans made to Jiffy Lube. Hindman also personally guaranteed certain transactions Jiffy Lube entered into, including lines of credit with banks, loans relating to the purchase or development of service centers, and real estate lease obligations. Ernst & Whinney provided introductions to several banks, and, at Hindman's request, participated in key meetings with the bankers.

Financing also was obtained through the sale of stock to directors, officers, employees, and other investors. The most significant sale was a private placement of $530K in preferred stock, the majority of which was sold to a small group of Midwest investors. In addition, Jiffy Lube used its common stock in several acquisitions, the largest being the purchase of Speedy Lube, a franchisor and operator of seven oil change centers.

In addition to the above, the need for real estate financing outlined in Jiffy Lube's business plan resulted in the company's most significant financing transaction to date, its 1981 agreement with Pennzoil.

Exhibit D
Pennzoil Agreement

Pennzoil will purchase 10,000 shares of Jiffy Lube Convertible Preferred Stock for $1,000,000.

Cumulative dividends of $12 per Preferred share are payable quarterly. Any deficiency must be paid or declared before setting aside any funds for any junior stock. These shares are redeemable by Jiffy Lube at any time after November 17, 1985, upon payment in cash of $110 per share plus an amount equal to all accrued dividends. They can be converted at the option of Pennzoil into common stock at a conversion price of $0.553 per share of each $1.00 Preferred Stock value.

Pennzoil shall have the option of electing the greater of 3 or 30 percent of the members of the board of directors of Jiffy Lube.

Jiffy Lube agrees to furnish Pennzoil certain financial information, including audited financial statements within 150 days after the close of each fiscal year, and unaudited statements within 45 days after the close of the first three fiscal quarters.

Jim Hindman, and then Jiffy Lube, shall have the right of first refusal should Pennzoil desire to sell any of its shares of Jiffy Lube stock. Pennzoil has the right of first refusal should Jim Hindman decide to sell any of his shares of Jiffy Lube stock.

Pennzoil agrees to issue a commitment to guarantee $6,250,000 worth of indebtedness to be incurred in connection with the financing of real estate site acquisition and construction cost in connection with the erection of Jiffy Lube centers. These units are to be built east of the Mississippi River and generally along the eastern seaboard.

Pennzoil agrees to guarantee an additional $1,000,000 in order to finance Jiffy Lube's purchase from Pennzoil of four units which Pennzoil has financed under its "Build to Suit" program.

Any units built using financing guaranteed by Pennzoil will be required to enter into a Lube Center Sales Agreement and to execute a Pennzoil Sign Agreement. Pennzoil will have the right to approve the selection of new sites to be financed under this agreement.

Pennzoil Agreement

In December 1980, Hindman and Kelley attended a trade meeting put on by Pennzoil for its regional sales people and major distributors. Pennzoil was the oil supplier for the majority of Jiffy Lube centers and believed that the quick oil change business could become a new major distribution channel for oil products. Pennzoil saw the quick change industry as an opportunity to gain market share from Quaker State, the leading oil distributor in the eastern United States. Pennzoil's national sales manager told Hindman that the oil company planned on building 100 quick oil change centers in the East.

Hindman spent the night writing a proposal to convince Pennzoil to work with Jiffy Lube, rather than compete against it. In October 1981, the two companies signed an agreement *(Exhibit D)*. For $1 million Jiffy Lube sold convertible preferred stock representing 29 percent of the company to Pennzoil. The agreement allowed Pennzoil to place four members on Jiffy Lube's board of directors. Pennzoil agreed to guarantee $6.3 million of real estate financing. Service centers developed with the financing guaranteed by Pennzoil were required to purchase the majority of their oil products from Pennzoil.

Pennzoil's financing allowed Jiffy Lube to initiate its aggressive expansion plan. The agreement also strengthened Jiffy Lube's financial credibility, and enabled it to increase its bank line of credit from $300K to over $1.2 million.

The relationship with Pennzoil was far from perfect, however. The two companies apparently had different objectives, which resulted in different strategies for Jiffy Lube's expansion. Jiffy Lube's business plan emphasized "clustering" and "franchising"; Pennzoil advocated "wide coverage" and "assured distribution channel" (company-owned service centers).

Jiffy Lube quickly discovered that Pennzoil's "right to approve the selection of new sites" as outlined in the agreement really meant that the oil company would select the new sites. Pennzoil used a "scattergun" approach to site selection. To create maximum exposure for the Pennzoil name, the oil company wanted one service center to be developed in as many markets as possible. "It seemed like we had one center in every major city from Miami to Boston," recalls Hindman.

In addition, Pennzoil did not believe that franchising should be relied on to provide all of the growth. Jim Hindman: "As soon as we signed the agreement and walked out of their corporate offices, they took me by the hand and got us involved in the acquisition of service centers which we were to operate. This was despite the fact that our business plan specifically stated that we were going to go out and franchise."

Under Pennzoil's direction, Jiffy Lube acquired three chains of oil change centers (23 units in total) in late 1981 and early 1982. Hindman felt that Pennzoil's strategy ran counter to Jiffy Lube's own strategy and that "our business plan had been trashed. We were not capitalized to operate these centers, and we didn't have the management team." Why did Jiffy Lube go along? "They were supplying the money. I felt that we just got married to these guys; we've got to go along to get along."

The acquired stores quickly became a burden to Jiffy Lube. By the end of fiscal 1982, 30 of the 70 Jiffy Lube centers were owned and operated by the company. These required a large commitment of Jiffy Lube's managerial and financial resources and resulted in significant overhead costs. And sales at many of the new centers were not growing as fast as expected. "Every market where we had just one unit we were dying," recalls Hindman. Jiffy Lube lost $1.4 million in the year ended March 31, 1982, and is expected to lose $2.6 million for fiscal 1983.

By April 1982 Hindman made three major decisions:

1. All company-owned centers would be sold to franchisees.
2. Hindman was going to buy Pennzoil's Jiffy Lube stock.
3. Jiffy Lube would have to find other sources of financing to continue its growth plans.

Between May 1982 and February 1983, Jiffy Lube sold all of its company-owned centers to franchisees. In most cases, to expedite the sale, Jiffy Lube retained ownership of the service center's real estate and sold only the rights to operate the franchise. The real estate was then leased to the franchisee.

Hindman had also tried to resolve the conflict with Pennzoil:

We tried to convince Pennzoil that: (1) we had to cluster and (2) we had to have a different relationship. They were a giant and they took too long. They had 10 committees, and everything required 10 sign offs. We needed to move fast to get back to our original strategy. Our only solution was to buy them out. We had to move carefully, though. We wanted to end up with a good relationship with Pennzoil. Even if they sold us the stock back, they were still our largest supplier, and had guaranteed over $5 million in real estate financing for us.

From October 1982 to February 1983, I didn't put any money into the company even though we were hurting. I knew that if I started putting money in, it would just give Pennzoil an incentive to want to keep their stock. So we let our payables build up and let a large part of our staff go.

In February 1983, Pennzoil agreed to sell Hindman its stock for $435K. Jiffy Lube's worsening financial status during fiscal 1983 made it easier for Hindman to buy out Pennzoil:

Exhibit E
Financial Characteristics of Typical Jiffy Lube Franchise

Real estate requirements	15,000 square feet of land (building interior covers 2,500 square feet)
Cost of land and building	$300,000
Start-up costs (equipment, etc.)	$100,000
Monthly fixed costs	$8,000
Variable costs	57% of sales
Breakeven car count/day	28–35 cars
Typical months to breakeven	7–8 months

A "typical" mature unit (approximately two years old) will service between 60–70 cars per day, producing annual revenues of about $400,000–$500,000 and $75,000–$100,000 of pretax income.

Depending on whether the franchisee owns or leases the real estate, the monthly fixed costs include a charge for either:

1. Rent ($3,000–$4,000) paid to Jiffy Lube or to a 3rd party lessor, or
2. A similar charge for mortgage interest.

The 96 franchises currently in operation have the following real estate arrangements:

Real estate owned by Jiffy Lube and rented to the franchisee	20
Real estate leased by Jiffy Lube and subleased to the franchisee	4
Real estate owned or leased by the franchisee (approximately 30 of these were part of chains to which Jiffy Lube acquired the franchise rights. In these cases the franchisees already had their own real estate arrangements before Jiffy Lube became involved.)	72

"They wanted out. Maybe they thought we were going bankrupt, and they could pick up the service centers after we went under."

The split with Pennzoil was reasonably amicable. Hindman:

They recognized that the arrangement wasn't working. Pennzoil still believed in the concept of quick oil change centers, though. They believed that, regardless of whether we survived or not, a large amount of oil was going to be sold through the quick change centers. Pennzoil kept their real estate guarantees in place.

Current Situation: 1983

Now, in 1983, Jiffy Lube feels that it is well positioned for the future, despite the past losses and current cash crises. Jiffy Lube has 96 units and is the largest franchisor of quick oil change centers in the United States. The company has reached a respectable size and feels it can take advantage of the name recognition being generated in some areas.

In addition, the company has gotten back to its original strategy of franchising, rather than operating service centers. The sale of all company-owned stores has cut costs and freed management to spend more time selecting and selling new franchise sites. The company expects to open at least 25 new franchises in the coming year. Jiffy Lube also expects improvements in the units it recently sold, as franchised centers have historically outperformed the company-owned centers. *Exhibit E* summarizes the financial characteristics of the typical franchise.

Fiscal 1983 is coming to a close, and projected financial statements have been prepared based on the first 11 months of operation (*Exhibits G, H, I,* and *J*). Jiffy Lube is now dependent on franchise royalties and rental income, because of the sale of the company stores. Management's analysis of future operations is included below (*Exhibit F*).

Exhibit F
Management's Analysis of Future Operations

Management has made the following projections of future operations:

	Service Centers in Operation		
Fiscal Year	At Year End	On Average during the Year	Total Gross Sales for Network
1983	96	83	$16 million
	(based on 11 months of actual operations)		
1984	125	111	$28 million
1985	200	163	$49 million
1986	300	250	$75 million

In addition to projecting the future revenues, management has reviewed current expenditures and made the following prognosis for the upcoming year:

1. All expenses relating to the company-operated centers have been eliminated.
2. Management believes that, because of the recent restructuring, selling, general, and administrative expenses can be held to approximately $2.1 million during fiscal 1984. To achieve the growth projected for fiscal 1985 and 1986, it is anticipated that S, G, & A expenses will have to increase to $2.6 million and $3.1 million respectively.
3. The only other significant expenses expected are interest on the outstanding debt and real estate lease commitments.

Exhibit G
Projected Statement of Operations

Projected Statement of Operations

	Year Ended March 31, 1983
	(projected)
Revenues:	
Sales by company-operated units	$ 3,877,000
Initial franchise fees	685,000
Franchise royalties	542,000
Rental income from franchisees	276,000
Net gain on sales of company-operated units	40,000
Miscellaneous	41,000
Total revenues	5,461,000
Expenses:	
Company-operated units:	
Cost of products sold	1,300,000
Salaries and wages	1,090,000
Depreciation and amortization	180,000
Interest	258,000
Rent	308,000
Other	1,250,000
Total units expenses	4,386,000
Commissions	136,000
Selling, general, and administrative expenses	2,749,000
Interest expense	762,000
Total expenses	8,033,000
Net loss	$(2,572,000)

continued

Exhibit G *(continued)*
Projected Balance Sheet

Projected Balance Sheet

March 31, 1983

(projected)

Assets

Current assets:	
Cash	$ 139,000
Accounts receivable	962,000
Prepaid expenses	23,000
Total current assets	1,124,000
Accounts receivable from future franchises	636,000
Property and equipment:	
Land	2,372,000
Buildings and improvements	3,913,000
Automobiles, furniture, and equipment	255,000
Construction in progress	682,000
	7,222,000
Less allowances for depreciation	203,000
	7,019,000
Intangible assets—trademarks, franchise rights, and deferred finance costs	815,000
Deferred franchise costs	199,000
Other assets	103,000
	$ 9,896,000

Liabilities and Stockholders' Equity

Current liabilities:	
Accounts payable and accrued expenses	$ 1,252,000
Due to officers, directors, and employees	696,000
Notes payable	2,211,000
Current portion of long-term debt	86,000
Current portion of capital lease obligations	4,000
Total current liabilities	4,249,000
Long-term debt, less current portion	6,577,000
Capital lease obligations, less current portion	359,000
Deferred franchise fees	1,143,000
Stockholders' equity:	
Series A 12% cumulative convertible preferred stock	1,307,000
$12.00 cumulative convertible preferred stock	1,000,000
Common stock	166,000
Capital in excess of par value	880,000
Retained-earnings deficit	(5,238,000)
	(1,885,000)
Less cost of common stock held in treasury	(547,000)
Total stockholders' equity	(2,432,000)
Total liabilities and stockholders' equity	$ 9,896,000

Because of its dependence franchise royalties, Jiffy Lube needs to quickly increase the number of franchises. Much of the growth to date has come through the acquisition of existing chains. Franchise agreements for new units are typically made with individuals for one or two service centers. Experience to date has proven that the sale and development of new franchises can be accelerated when Jiffy Lube offers to provide or arrange for real estate and construction financing.

Exhibit H
Long-term Debt/Rent Commitments at March 1983

Description	March 1983 Balance	Interest Rate	Payment Terms/Comments
Construction loans:			
INA mortgage	$5,372,000	16.5%	Monthly payments of approximately $75,000 are required in fiscal 1984. Requires increasing monthly payments for interest and maturity through February 1994. Guaranteed by Pennzoil.
Maryland National Bank	524,000	Prime	Monthly payments of approximately $7,000, varying based on the prime interest rate.
Notes relating to acquisitions of service center chains:			
Benchmark/Archeo	250,000	Prime + 1%	Due 6/85
Browns Quick Lube	117,000	13%	Due 2/87
Joe Wilkerson	117,000	13%	Due 2/87
Stock repurchase—John Lindholm	104,000	Prime	Annual payments of approximately $50,000.
Others	179,000	Vary from 12% to 18%	Mature at various times through 1987.
	$6,663,000		
Rent commitments:			
Fiscal 1984 commitments *payable* under capital and operating leases ($150K represents real estate subleased to franchisees; the remainder is office building, etc., included in S, G, & A)	$ 230,000		
Rentals *receivable* in fiscal 1984 from franchises already in operation, land, buildings, and improvements rented to franchisees	$ 775,000		

Exhibit I
Notes Payable and Amounts Due to Officers, Directors and Employees at March 1983

Description	March 1983 Balance	Interest Rate	Payment Terms/Comments
Notes payable:			
Bank lines of credit:			
Maryland National Bank	$ 499,000	Prime + 1%	Minimum interest rate of 12%. The notes become payable at various times between 6/83 and 3/84. Jiffy Lube has drawn the full amount of each line.
Savings Bank	500,000	Prime + 1%	
1st National	250,000	Prime + 1%	
Jiffy Lube International Partnership #1	675,000	Prime + ½%	Due on demand. Hindman owns 27% of partnership. Another 56% is owned by 4 individuals who are directors (or former directors) of Jiffy Lube.
Notes to 4 accounts payable vendors	287,000	0–10%	All due by 6/83.
	$2,211,000		
Due to officers, directors, and employees:			
Jim Hindman	$ 550,000	Prime +1%	Due on demand.
Others	146,000		Majority are noninterest-bearing demand notes to J. Hindman.
	$ 696,000		

Exhibit J
Ownership at March 1983

	Shares	Percent
Common stock:		
Jim Hindman, president/CEO	2,133,333	69%
Gilbert Campbell, director	285,710	9
Others (less than 5%)	675,775	22
	3,094,818	100%
Series A 12% cumulative preferred stock:		
Jim Hindman	7,255	66%
Others (less than 5%)	5,815	44
	13,070	100%

(Convertible at the option of the holders into approximately 1,568,000 shares of common stock)

$12.00 cumulative convertible preferred stock:		
Jim Hindman	10,000	100%

(Convertible at the option of the holders into approximately 1,808,000 shares of common stock)

Possible Alternatives

Hindman has already used the majority of his liquid assets in his prior contributions to Jiffy Lube and in the purchase of the Pennzoil stock. His major remaining assets are his interests in W. James Hindman, Ltd. (75 percent ownership), and several other nursing home partnerships (these might be worth as much as $3 million).

Hindman has considered disposing of his partnership interests to provide cash for Jiffy Lube. However, Hindman's tax basis in these (approximately $200K) is far less than the current market value, and he views the outright sale of them as a last resort because of the tax consequences. Several other investors in W. James Hindman, Ltd., are also shareholders in Jiffy Lube and seem willing to use their investments to raise cash for Jiffy Lube.

Another source Jiffy Lube has considered is a second private placement with existing shareholders. Specific terms haven't been discussed, and it is unknown how much these investors would be willing to contribute.

Risk Capital

14 >

Money is like a sixth sense without which you cannot make a complete use of the other five.

W. Somerset Maugham
Of Human Bondage

RESULTS EXPECTED

At the conclusion of the chapter, you will have:

1. Discussed the process of obtaining risk capital, including considerations of timing and what an investor can add to a venture.
2. Identified how to find and contact principal sources of equity capital.
3. Discovered how equity capital investors make decisions.
4. Examined types of risk investment.
5. Analyzed a case about a proposed financing for a rapidly expanding venture, Bridge Capital Investors, Inc.

OBTAINING RISK CAPITAL

Timing

First and foremost, timing is critical. It is important that a venture not delay looking for capital until it has a serious cash shortage and not seek equity capital before it is needed. For a start-up, especially one with no experience or success in raising money, it is unwise to delay looking for capital since it is likely to take six months or more to raise capital. In addition to the problems with cash flow, the lack of planning implicit in waiting until there is a cash shortage can undermine the credibility of a venture's management team and negatively impact its ability to negotiate with investors.

On the other hand, if a venture tries to obtain equity capital too early, the equity position of the founders may be unnecessarily diluted and the discipline instilled by financial leanness may be eroded inadvertently.

The Ideal Investor

When looking for investors, entrepreneurs need to seek those who (1) are considering new financing proposals and can provide the required level of capital; (2) are interested in companies at the particular stage of growth; (3) understand and have a preference for investments in the particular industry (i.e., market, product, technology, or service focus); (4) can provide good business advice, moral support, and contacts in the business and financial community, as well as just venture capital; (5) are reputable and ethical and with whom the entrepreneur gets along with; and (6) have successful track records of 10 years or more advising and building smaller companies.

The right investor can add value in a number of ways, such as:[1]

- Identifying and helping recruit key management team members and providing key industry and professional contacts.
- Serving as a mentor, confidant, and sounding board for ideas and plans to solve problems or quicken growth.
- Helping to establish relationships with key customers or suppliers, or both.
- Having "deep pockets" to participate in and syndicate subsequent rounds of financing.

THE ENTREPRENEUR AND FRIENDLY INVESTORS

One source of equity capital is from the founding entrepreneur or entrepreneurs themselves.

"Friendly" sources are sources which invest on the basis of personal or business relationships with the principals of new ventures and which will generally invest in an "opportunistic" way (i.e., without too much study or investigation).[2] These sources include the personal and professional contacts of the founding entrepreneur(s), such as:

- Family and friends.
- Professional advisers and business acquaintances.
- Past employers.
- Potential customers and suppliers.
- Prospective employees.

Friendly sources are used by all types of firms in the R&D phase. They can also invest at a later stage of development, but the capital then required usually will exceed what they alone can supply.

INFORMAL INVESTORS

Who They Are

Wealthy individuals are probably the single most important source of capital for start-up and emerging businesses in America today.[3] According to an article by William Wetzel, there are 250,000 or more such wealthy individuals, known as angels, in the United States, 100,000 of whom are active.[4] In total, Wetzel believes angels invest $5 billion to $10 billion annually in 20,000 to 30,000 companies, an amount which is staggering in comparison to the 3,500 to 3,000 investments made each year by the United States venture capital industry. Typical

---

[1] Harry A. Sapienza and Jeffry A. Timmons, "Launching and Building Entrepreneurial Companies: Do the Venture Capitalists Build Value?" *Proceedings,* Babson Entrepreneurship Research Conference, May 1989 (St. Louis, Mo.: St. Louis University, 1989). See also Jeffry A. Timmons, "Venture Capital: More Than Money," in *Pratt's Guide to Venture Capital Sources,* 13th ed., ed. Jane Morris (Needham, Mass.: Venture Economics, 1989), p. 71.

[2] The late Patrick R. Liles pointed out it is worth insuring that such sources are not unethical or just interested in fast profits with no concern for the entrepreneurs or their ventures. See Patrick R. Liles, *New Business Ventures and the Entrepreneur* (Homewood, Ill.: Richard D. Irwin, 1974), p. 467.

[3] G. Baty, *Initial Financing of the New Research Based Enterprise in New England,* Federal Reserve Bank of Boston Research Report no. 25 (Boston, Mass., 1964); and G. Baty, *Entrepreneurship: Play to Win* (Reston, Va.: Reston Publishing, 1974), p. 97. See also William E. Wetzel, "Informal Investors—When and Where to Look," *Pratt's Guide to Venture Capital Sources,* 6th ed., ed. Stanley E. Pratt (Wellesley Hills, Mass.: Capital Publishing, 1982). p. 22.

[4] William H. Wetzel, Jr., calls wealthy investors "angels." The information in the text about angels is based on his work. See his informative article "Angels and Risk Capital," *Sloan Management Review* 24, no. 4, (Summer 1984), pp. 23–34.

investments are in the $20,000 to $50,000 range, with 36 percent involving less than $10,000 and 24 percent over $50,000. These amounts are usually too small for professional venture capital sources.

Wetzel has found that these angels are mainly America's self-made entrepreneur millionaires—nearly two million of them. They have made it on their own, have substantial business and financial experience, and are likely to be in their 40s or 50s. They are also well educated; 95 percent hold college degrees from four-year colleges, and 51 percent have graduate degrees. Of the graduate degrees, 44 percent are in a technical field and 35 percent are in business or economics.

Since the typical informal investor will invest from $10,000 to $50,000 in any one venture, informal investors are particularly appropriate for the following:[5]

- Ventures with capital requirements of between $50,000 and $500,000.
- Ventures with sales potential of between $2 million and $20 million within 5 to 10 years.
- Small, established, privately held ventures with sales and profit growth of 10 percent to 20 percent per year, a rate which is not rapid enough to be attractive to a professional investor, such as a venture capital firm.
- Special situations, such as very early financing of high-technology inventors who have not developed a prototype.

These investors may invest alone or in syndication with other wealthy individuals, may demand considerable equity for their interests, or may try to dominate ventures. They also can get very impatient when sales and profits do not grow as they expected.

Usually, these informal investors will be knowledgeable and experienced in the market and technology areas they invest in. If the right angel is found, he or she will add a lot more to a business then just money. As an advisor or director, his or her savvy, know-how, and contacts that come from having "made it" can be far more valuable than the $20,000 to $50,000 invested. Generally, the evaluations of potential investments by such wealthy investors tends to be less thorough than those undertaken by organized venture capital groups, and such noneconomic factors as the desire to be involved with entrepreneurship may be important to their investment decisions. For example, a successful entrepreneur may want to help other entrepreneurs get started, or a wealthy individual may want to help build new businesses in his or her community.

Finding Informal Investors

Finding these backers is not easy. One expert noted:

Informal investors, essentially individuals of means and successful entrepreneurs, are a diverse and dispersed group with a preference for anonymity. Creative techniques are required to identify and reach them.[6]

Invariably, they are found by tapping an entrepreneur's own network of business associates and other contacts. Other successful entrepreneurs know them, as do many tax attorneys, accountants, bankers, and other professionals. Apart from serendipity, the best way to find informal investors is to seek referrals from attorneys, accountants, business associates, university faculty, and entrepreneurs who deal with new ventures and are likely

---

[5] Wetzel, "Informal Investors—When and Where to Look," p. 22.

[6] Ibid., p. 22.

to know such people. Since such investors learn of investment opportunities from their business associates, fellow entrepreneurs, and friends, and since many informal investors invest together, more or less regularly, in a number of new venture situations, one informal investor contact can lead the entrepreneur to contacts with others.

In most larger cities, there are law firms and private placement firms who syndicate investment packages as Regulation D offerings to networks of private investors. They may raise from several hundred thousand dollars to several million. Directories of these firms are published annually by *Venture* magazine and are written about in magazines such as *INC*.

Contacting Investors

If an entrepreneur has obtained a referral, he or she needs to get permission to use the name of the person making a referral when the investor is contacted. A meeting with the potential investor then can be arranged. At this meeting, the entrepreneur needs to make a concise presentation of the key features of the proposed venture.

However, entrepreneurs need to avoid meeting with more than one informal investor at the same time. Meeting with more than one investor often results in any negative viewpoints raised by one investor being reinforced by another. It is also easier to deal with negative reactions and questions from only one investor at a time. Like a wolf on the hunt, if an entrepreneur isolates one target "prey" and then concentrates on closure, he or she will increase the odds of success.

Whether or not the outcome of such a meeting is continued investment interest, the entrepreneur needs to try to obtain the names of other potential investors from this meeting. If this can be done, the entrepreneur will develop a growing list of potential investors and will find his or her way into one or more networks of informal investors.

If the outcome is positive, often the participation of one investor who is knowledgeable about the product and its market will trigger the participation of other investors.

Evaluation Process

An informal investor will want to review a business plan, meet the full management team, and see any product prototype or design that may exist, and so forth. The investor will conduct background checks on the venture team and its product potential, usually through someone he or she knows who knows the entrepreneur and the product. The process is not dissimilar to the due diligence of the professional investors (see below) but may be less formal and structured.

On the part of the new venture, if given a choice, it is wise to select an informal investor who can be a useful advisor and whose objectives are consistent with those of the entrepreneur.

The Decision

If he or she decides to invest, the investor will have some sort of investment agreement drafted by an attorney. This agreement may be somewhat simpler than those used by professional investors, such as venture capital firms (see Chapter 15). All the cautions and advice about investors and investment agreements that are discussed later on in the chapter apply here as well.

Most likely, the investment agreement with an informal investor will include some form of a "put," whereby the investor has the right to require the venture to repurchase his or her stock after a specified number of years at a specified price. If the venture is not harvested, this put will provide an investor with a cash return.

PROFESSIONAL INVESTORS

Venture Capital Investors

The 1980s saw a metamorphosis of the venture capital industry, and, at present, the organized venture capital community is operating in the most favorable environment in its short history.[7]

The reduction in capital gains and the revision of the ERISA "prudent man" rules led to an explosion of new money in 1979, and, by 1984, there was 80 times as much new venture capital available as there had been 8 to 10 years earlier. As shown in *Exhibit 14.1,* a staggering $4.1 billion of new money flowed into venture capital funds in 1987.[8] The outflow, in the form of investments in companies, amounted to $2.6 billion, $2.9 billion, and $3.9 billion in 1985, 1986, and 1987, respectively. In 1988, $2.81 billion of new capital was committed to private independent venture funds. Estimates for 1988 were not complete at this writing but should be greater than $3 billion.[9]

This exhibit does not tell the whole story, however. The 1980s have been somewhat of a roller coaster ride for venture capital financing of start-ups. Investments of this type peaked in 1983. This peak year has been called "the great binge of 1983." According to *Venture Capital Journal,* fully 42 percent of the deals done that year were start-ups, but, by 1985 to 1986, the number had fallen dramatically to 14 percent. For the most part, this was due to high valuations and the reality that many of the start-up investments of 1982, 1983, and 1984 were ripening as "lemons." By 1988 and 1989, start-up activity had rebounded with about 25 percent of the deals being seed and start-up investments.

The exhibit also shows some of the internationalizing of the venture capital markets. The United Kingdom has experienced the birth of a venture capital industry during the 1980s. In 1988, about $1.3 billion of new capital was committed to funds in the United Kingdom.

At the end of 1988, organized venture capital groups consisted of about 700 organizations with a total capital base of over $30 billion, according to *Venture Capital Journal.* This new structure of the United States venture capital industry is summarized in *Exhibit 14.2.* The sources are becoming increasingly specialized and focused. This has very important implications for entrepreneurs seeking money and for those investing it.

Capital from a professional venture capitalist can be very attractive to a new venture, in that the venture capitalist brings, in addition to money, the experience of having done it before. Some venture capital firms become actively involved financially and managerially at the seed/start-up stage of new ventures. Moreover, a venture capital firm has "deep pockets" and contacts with other groups that can facilitate the raising of money as the venture develops.

However, professional venture capital investors have stringent criteria for their investments, and the equity cost to a new venture of venture capital can be substantial. Venture capital investors look for ventures with very high growth potential, where they can quintuple their investment in five years; they place a very high premium on the quality of the management in a venture; and they like to see a management team with complementary business skills headed by someone who has previous entrepreneurial or profit-and-loss management experience. In fact, these investors are searching for the "superdeal." Superdeals meet all the investment criteria outlined in *Exhibit 14.3.*[10] Because of these

---

[7] Stanley E. Pratt, *Pratt's Guide to Venture Capital Sources,* 13th ed., ed. Jane Morris (Wellesley, Mass.: Capital Publishing Corp., 1989).

[8] *Venture Capital Journal,* February 1989, p. 13. Note that these are gross figures, including all growth stages and all rounds of financing.

[9] *1987 Yearbook, Venture Capital Journal,* 1987.

[10] *Exhibit 14.3* shows the cream of the venture crop and criteria used to screen such ventures are an extension of the criteria in *Exhibit 3.3* in Chapter 3.

Exhibit 14.1
Commitments to Venture Capital Funds in the United States and United Kingdom, 1981–1988

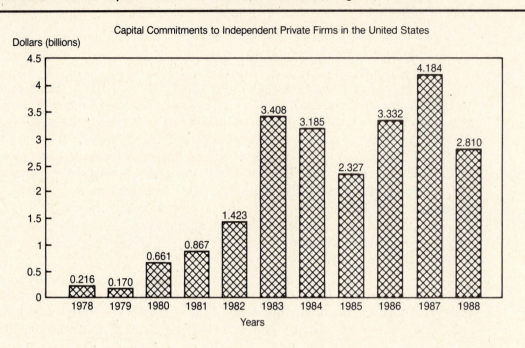

Capital Commitments to Independent Private Firms in the United States

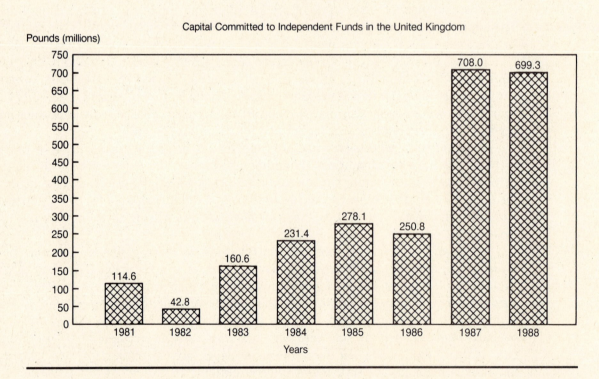

Capital Committed to Independent Funds in the United Kingdom

stringent criteria, no more than 2 percent to 4 percent of the ventures contacting venture capital firms receive financing from them. Further, as was discussed above, an entrepreneur may give up 25 percent to 75 percent of his or her equity for seed/start-up financing, and, after several rounds of venture financing have been completed, an entrepreneur may own no more than 10 percent to 20 percent of the venture.

Exhibit 14.2
New Heterogeneous Structure of the Venture Capital Industry*

	"Megafunds"	"Mainstream"	"Second Tier"	Specialists and "Niche" Funds	Corporate Financial & Corporate Industrial
Estimated no. and type (1988)	89 Predominately private, independent funds	100–125 + Predominately private & independent; some large institutional SBICs and corporate funds	150–175 Mostly SBICs; some private independent funds	40–50 Private, independent	85 & 84, respectively
Size of funds under management	$100M +	$25–$99M	Below $25M	$3–$15M	$25–$50M +
Typical invest. (1st rd)	$1–$3M +	$750K–$1M	$500K–$750K	$50K–$200K	Larger $10–$15M deals possible
Stage of investment	Later expansion, LBOs, start-ups	Later expansion, LBOs, some starts; mezzanine	Later stages; few starts; specialized areas	Seed and start-up Technology or market focus	Later
Strategic focus	Technology; national & international markets; capital gains; broad focus	Technology & manufacturing; national & regional markets; capital gains; more specialized focus	Eclectic—more regional than national; capital gains, current income; service business	Hi-technology national & international links; "feeder funds" capital gains	Windows on technology direct investment in new markets and suppliers; diversification; strategic partners; capital gain
Balance of equity & debt	Predominately equity	Predominately equity; convertible preferred	Predominately debt; about 91 SBICs do equity principally	Predominately equity	Mixed
Principal sources of capital	Mature national and international institutions; own funds; and insurance company and pension funds; institutions and wealthy individuals; foreign corporation and pension funds; universities		Wealthy ind., some smaller Institutions	Institutions & foreign co.; & insts. wealthy individuals	Internal funds
Main investing role	Active lead or co-lead; frequent syndications; board seat		Less co-investing with some solo investing	Initial or lead investor; outreach; shirt-sleeves involvement	Later stages, rarely start-ups; direct investor in funds and portfolio companies

Note: Target rates of return vary considerably; depend on stage and market conditions. Seed and start-up investors may seek compounded after-tax rates of return in excess of 50–100 percent; in mature, later stage investments they seek returns in the 30–40 percent range. The rule of thumb of realizing gains of 5–10 times the original investment in 5–10 years is a common investor expectation.

* The author is most appreciative of the assistance of Jane Morris, editor, *Venture Capital Journal,* in providing some of the data for this table.

© Jeffry A. Timmons, 1990

Venture capital sources fall into three main categories:

■ *Venture capital corporations or partnerships.* These corporations have an established capital base and professional management. Their investment policies cover a range of preferences in investment size and the maturity, location, and industry of a venture. Capital for these can be provided by one or more wealthy families; one or more financial institutions (e.g., insurance companies or pension funds); and wealthy individuals. Most are organized as limited partnerships, in which the fund managers are the general

Exhibit 14.3
Characteristics of the "Superdeal" from an Investor's Perspective

Mission
- Build a highly profitable and industry-dominant company.
- Go public or merge within four to seven years at a high price-earnings (P/E) multiple.

Complete Management
- Led by industry "superstar."
- Possess proven entrepreneurial, general management, and P&L experience in the business.
- Have leading innovator or technologies & marketing head.
- Possess complementary & compatible skills.
- Have unusual tenacity, imagination, and commitment.
- Possess reputation for high integrity.

Proprietary Product
- Has significant competitive lead and "unfair" advantages.
- Has product or service with high value-added properties resulting in early payback to user.
- Has or can gain exclusive contractual or legal rights.

Large and Rapidly Growing Market
- Will accommodate $50 million entrant in five years.
- Has sales currently at $100 million, and more, and growing at 25 percent per year.
- Has no dominant competitor now.
- Has clearly identified customers and distribution channels.
- Possesses forgiving and rewarding economics, such as:
  - Gross margins of 40 percent to 50 percent, or more.
  - Ten percent or more profit after tax.
  - Early positive cash flow and breakeven sales.

Deal Valuation and ROR
- Has "digestible" first-round capital requirements (i.e., greater than $1 million and less than $10 million).
- Able to return 10 times original investment in five years at P/E of 15 times or more.
- Has possibility of additional rounds of financing at substantial markup.
- Has antidilution and IPO subscription rights.

© Jeffry A. Timmons, 1990

---

partners and the investors, the limited partners. Today, most of these funds prefer to invest from $500,000 to $1 million or more, although some of the smaller funds will invest less. Most of their investments are in the range of $500,000 to $1.5 million. Some of the so-called megafunds, with upwards of $100 million to invest, do not like to consider investments of less than $1 million to $2 million. The investigation and evaluation of potential investments by venture capital corporations and partnerships are thorough and professional. Most of their investments are in high-technology businesses, but a good number will consider investments in other areas except construction and real estate.

- *Small business investment companies.* SBICs are licensed by the Small Business Administration and can obtain debt capital from the Small Business Administration. Some have active venture capital programs in addition to loan programs. An SBIC's equity capital generally is supplied by commercial banks, wealthy individuals, and the investing public. SBICs are limited by law to taking minority shareholder positions and can invest no more than 20 percent of their equity capital in any one situation. A typical financing is in the range of $200,000 to $400,000. Because SBICs borrow much of their capital from the SBA and most service this debt, they prefer to make some form of interest-bearing investments. Four common forms of financing are long-term loans with options to buy stock, convertible debentures, straight loans, and preferred stock. Also, because of their SBA debt, SBICs tend not to finance start-ups and early-stage companies but rather make investments in more mature companies. (A directory of SBICs is available from the Investment Division of the SBA, Washington, D.C.)

■ *Strategic alliances or partnerships.*   Corporate venture capital investors include nonfinancial corporations, such as Exxon, that have set up their own venture capital groups. In the 1980s, there was a significant increase in the number of direct investments by larger United States and foreign corporations in emerging United States companies. One estimate by Venture Economics is that this activity has grown from around 60 investments in 1980 to over 300 by 1987.

Most of these investors are primarily interested in growing their own acquisition candidates and, at the time of their initial investment, make arrangements under which they can acquire equity at a future time. Other reasons given for this type of venture activity are to obtain a "window onto new technologies," such as Digital Equipment's investment in Trilogy, and to obtain licenses to manufacture and sell new products. The latter objective was the reason some of the major pharmaceutical companies invested in such biotechnology start-ups as Cetus. Cetus raised $36 million from corporate investors, including Dekalb Agrisearch and National Distillers, in return for rights to use some of the technology from the Cetus genetics research. Notwithstanding this, some corporations have venture capital groups whose principal objectives are capital gains.

In exchange for an investment, a small firm may receive any or all of the following: capital, market access, equipment, facilities, technology base, and the organizational skills it may not have. What a firm gives up may include: equity, additions to the partner's product line, new opportunities, and identification of new applications of technology. For example, an innovator/entrepreneur raised a small amount of seed capital to develop a prototype for a highly innovative printer head to compete with existing dot matrix printers. He struck a deal for $1.5 million with a major Japanese company as a strategic partner. The Japanese partner hoped both to utilize the new product in its line of printers and develop a marketing agreement with this tiny American firm.

Advantages for entrepreneurs of obtaining money from corporate venture capital groups are that these investors have a tendency to overinvest, they are very patient investors with a time horizon of 10 to 20 years for returns, and they have been known to supply capital in the range of $10 million to $20 million. There are two potential advantages in consummating a strategic alliance. First, the return on investment threshold may be lower than those of other investment bankers and venture capitalists. Second, the corporate partner can contribute more than money to the fledgling firm. To illustrate this, one former student managed to convince a larger firm to become a strategic partner. The larger partner provided $250,000 in advance payments, space in one of its buildings, computers, and other equipment – in total, an equivalent of $600,000 to $700,000 in start-up capital. The student gave up rights for 10 percent of his company and maintained the proprietary rights to the products he sought to develop. Venture capitalists, on the other hand, had been suggesting he give up 40 percent to 45 percent of his start-up for a similar amount.

The disadvantages tend to center on four issues. First, the possibility of incompatible and changing goals (particularly if management changes). Loss of control and the effect on the entrepreneur's desire for independence is a second area. Third, often it is difficult to define or measure success. Last, it often is unclear how the relationship will be resolved and a harvest realized. (Often this is not given enough attention up front.)

Finding Professional Investors

It is relatively easier to find professional investors. And, sometimes, professional investors find entrepreneurs. Rather than wait for a deal to come to them, a venture capital investor may decide on a product or technology it wishes to commercialize and then put its own deal together. Kleiner Perkins used this approach to get Genentech and Tandem Computer Corporation launched, as did Greylock and J. H. Whitney in starting MassComp.

Entrepreneurs will be well advised to screen prospective investors to determine the appetites of such investors for ventures of the age and industry, technology, and capital requirements proposed. For example, in 1988 to 1989, many venture capital firms were once again seeking start-up and early-stage investments; but the bulk of the financing continued to be in expansion financings, bridge and mezzanine deals, and leveraged and management buyouts.

It also is useful to determine which investors have money to invest, which are actively seeking deals, and which have the time and people to investigate new deals. Depending on its size and investment strategy, a fund which is a year or two old will generally be in an active investing mode.

There are also some things to be wary of in finding investors. These warning signs are worth avoiding unless an entrepreneur is so desperate that he or she has no real alternatives:

- *Attitude.* Entrepreneurs need to be wary if they cannot get through to a general partner in an investment firm and keep getting handed off to a junior associate, or if the investor thinks he or she can run the business better than the lead entrepreneur or the management team.
- *Overcommitment.* Entrepreneurs need to be wary of lead investors who indicate they will be active directors and yet also sit on the boards of six to eight other start-up and early-stage companies or who are in the midst of raising money for a new fund.
- *Inexperience.* Entrepreneurs need to be wary of dealing with partners who have an MBA from a top business school; are under 30 years of age; have worked only on Wall Street or as a consultant; have no operating, hands-on experience in new and growing companies; *and* have a predominantly financial focus.
- *Unfavorable reputation.* Entrepreneurs need to be wary of funds that have a reputation for early and frequent replacement of the founders, or those where over one fourth of the portfolio companies are in trouble or failing to meet projections in their business plans.

If an entrepreneur is searching for a venture capital investor, a good place to start is with *Pratt's Guide to Venture Capital Sources,* 13th edition, published by Venture Economics of Needham, Massachusetts, one of several directories of venture capital firms. (A computerized data base of venture capital firms also is available from Venture Economics.) Entrepreneurs also can seek referrals from accountants, lawyers, investment and commercial bankers, and businesspeople who are knowledgeable about professional investors. Especially good sources of information are other entrepreneurs who have recently tried, successfully or unsuccessfully, to raise money for a venture.

Contacting Investors

The best way to proceed is to contact a *small* number of desirable investors (perhaps 5 to 10) that have a reasonable probability of being interested. Contacting too many investors and, especially, mass mailing a business plan to a large number of venture capital investors are not the things to do.

An entrepreneur wants to avoid having his or her venture classified as "shopworn" (i.e., a venture that has been seen and turned down by a number of investors). Classification of a venture as shopworn will discourage an investor from making an investment. Since, typically, venture capitalists reject in a few hours about 80 percent to 90 percent of the venture deals to which they are exposed, it is thus inevitable that, if a large number of investors are exposed to a venture deal, there will be enough rejections to classify the deal as shopworn, regardless of the merits of the particular venture.

To receive the proper attention from a potential investor, it is desirable that an entrepreneur be properly introduced to him or her. This can be done by the person who suggested the particular investor or by someone else who knows him or her. This referral need not be much more than a telephone call to the investor to say that a particular entrepreneur and his or her venture are worthy of consideration.

Entrepreneurs who are having difficulty obtaining such introductions often consider employing a finder, or intermediary, who will introduce them to potential investors for a fee. This fee can be up to 5 percent of larger deals, and as much as 10 percent of smaller ones. Most entrepreneurs find, however, that they can obtain introductions to investors on their own. There are also the problems of (1) knowing who the good finders are and (2) dislike of finders and paying finders fees on the part of some investors.

With or without a referral, an entrepreneur's initial contact with a potential investor usually will be via telephone. During this first contact, the entrepreneur needs to describe his or her venture, its product(s) or service(s), the backgrounds of the management team, the amount of capital sought, and the expected performance of the venture for two or three years after the investment is made. The entrepreneur needs to convey enough of the potential of the venture to persuade the investor to find out more about it.

An entrepreneur need not be discouraged by a rejection at this point. For example, somewhere between 60 percent to 80 percent of all ventures presented to venture capitalists are rejected during this first telephone contact. Yet, a recent study found that 70 percent of the "rejects" managed to carry on and were in business three years later.[11]

The rejection may very well be unrelated to the quality of the entrepreneur and the venture. For example, the investor may not like the industry of the venture or may have too many investments in that industry. It is also possible that the entrepreneur may have done a poor job presenting the venture.

Meetings and Presentations

If the venture passes the initial telephone contact, the founding entrepreneur will be asked to meet the potential investors, discuss the proposal, and submit a business plan.

An investor will typically read the plan, spending usually one hour or less, and, on this basis, decide whether the venture will receive further consideration. If the investor likes the business plan, the venture team will be asked to make a presentation.

No more than 10 percent to 20 percent of all the entrepreneurs who originally contacted an investor will be asked to make a presentation. The presentation is usually the first, and if handled improperly is the only face-to-face opportunity an entrepreneur will have to convince an investor that his or her venture and management team have substantial potential and are worthy of an investment.

In the case of start-ups and early-stage ventures, the presentation usually is made at the investor's office. In the case of an existing venture, the meeting is more likely to occur at the venture's facilities. Anywhere from two or three days to two weeks can elapse from the time of telephone contact to this meeting.

---

[11] A. Bruno and T. Tyebjee, "The One That Got Away," in *Frontiers of Entrepreneurship Research: 1983,* ed. J. A. Hornaday, J. A. Timmons, and K. H. Vesper (Babson Park, Mass.: Babson College, 1983), pp. 289–306.

The entrepreneur and up to three key members of his or her management team are the best people to prepare for and make the presentation.

A good rule of thumb in getting prepared, especially with venture capital investors, is called the "20/20 Rule," which says that, if an entrepreneur cannot get his or her story across in 20 pages and 20 minutes, he or she probably never will. (However, a good presentation will most likely get more time.)

In the presentation, each individual needs to describe and discuss that part of the business for which he or she will be responsible. The presentation needs to highlight the key material in the business plan. The use of flip charts, slides, or overhead transparencies for presenting key materials is a good idea. Prototypes, demo disks, drafts of product brochures, and the like are useful. Giving the impression that the firm is creating a market, instead of responding to a customer-anchored need, needs to be avoided. A well-rehearsed presentation and command of key facts, rather than having to dive for a briefcase, is important. Most of all fancy dog-and-pony shows that are more fluff than substance are to be avoided.

An investor will be interested in the presentation not only for what he or she will learn about the venture but also for the opportunity to meet the entrepreneur and management team and to judge their individual capabilities and their ability to function as an effective team. Some or all of the investor's representatives present will have read the entrepreneur's business proposal, and they will have some hard questions. And, they will be interested in not only the answers but who answers them and how they are answered. They will be looking for evidence of business knowledge and experience in specific areas that are of concern to them. If a venture's marketing manager is unable to provide answers that indicate an understanding of the size and growth of the market and the competition, or cannot explain the rationale for a particular sales strategy, the investor may have serious questions about that manager's capability and the venture itself. Similarly, a tendency for the entrepreneur to bypass his management team and answer all questions can raise doubts about the capabilities of the management team and the entrepreneur's ability to be an effective president. Any attempt by the entrepreneur to dodge tough questions, ignore or be ignorant of risks and problems, or know all the answers will be viewed unfavorably by the investors.

The Process of Evaluation

Recall that *Exhibit 14.3* in this chapter and *Exhibit 3.3* in Chapter 3 showed criteria used by investors to evaluate superdeals and to screen for higher potential ventures, respectively. Recall that studies of this investor screening process have shown investors *focus* upon these factors.[12]

Investors consider the above criteria and other factors as follows:

- *Business plan.* Investors look for realistic and "do-able" business plans that give an analysis of the opportunity and how it is unique and has durable and rewarding growth and profit potential; that show the unique skills and backgrounds of the key members of the management team that qualify them for their role in the venture; that discuss the history of the venture; that show projected sales and profits and key assumptions; that recognize and discuss potential risks and problems; and so forth.
- *Management team.* Investors look for management teams of high caliber that function effectively.

[12] Jeffry A. Timmons et al., "Opportunity Recognition: The Core of Entrepreneurship" in *Frontiers of Entrepreneurship Research 1987,* ed. N. C. Churchill, J. A. Hornaday, O. J. Krasner et al., Babson College, Center for Entrepreneurial Studies, Babson Park, MA.

- *Industry/market niche.* Investors will consider whether ventures are in growth or glamor industries and whether they have previously invested in the industry successfully.
- *Competitive advantages.* Investors will consider if a venture has a unique or really superior product or service based on a technology, skill, and the like that can give it significant competitive advantages.
- *Potential.* That there is profit potential that a venture can be harvested is important to investors. If a venture is an existing venture, investors will consider (1) if it has a positive net worth and working capital and (2) if the venture is borrowed to capacity. Investors will look to see if there are any questionable or troublesome assets (such as over-capitalized patents) or liabilities (such as unpaid and deferred withholding taxes). Investors also will look to see if the magnitudes of current and projected sales and profits are high enough to be interesting.
- *Investor preference.* Preferences and practices of investors, including rate-of-return goals, company stage, and deal dollar size and structure are important. Investors will also consider timing and conditions in capital markets.
- *Compatibility.* Compatibility of goals and in personal chemistry is often a crucial factor for investors in their decisions to make investments.

An investor then will make a decision on whether to proceed. At this stage, a decision to go ahead with a serious investigation of the venture and its management indicates the absence of a negative decision, not a positive decision.

Due Diligence Investigation

The next step is a due diligence investigation. The investigation and analysis of a business by professional investors, such as venture capitalists, are extensive. The process includes checks on management, the markets for the product(s) or service(s), technical feasibility, and detailed financial analysis. (While a venture capitalist is checking out a venture, the entrepreneur also can check out the investor.)

Since an important factor to investors is the quality of the entrepreneur and the management team, much of the evaluation of a business involves getting to know the entrepreneur and the team in depth and observing how they perform in a variety of situations and under stress. These situations can involve requests for more data regarding a venture's market or competitors, or meetings and discussions with the entrepreneurial team in which various aspects of the business, as well as the skills, attitudes, motivations, and commitment of the entrepreneur and the team, are probed. The investor also will have conversations with former employers, business associates, bankers, and technical references to check the business records and competencies of the entrepreneur and his or her key associates. Credit checks often are conducted to make sure there is nothing dishonest or disreputable about the entrepreneur and the other venture principals.

The investor will verify claims and data about the venture's technology, products, markets, and industry trends. This may be done by talking to such people as the venture's suppliers, customers, competitors, and customers of competitors, and to knowledgeable business and technical acquaintances of the investor. In many cases, an investor will use a technical consultant for a market appraisal or to evaluate the technical feasibility of a venture's product. Trade association and industry statistics will be examined to verify market trends, and competitors' track records may be studied to obtain an indication of the venture's growth, profitability, and harvest potential.

While the decision to proceed to this step is merely the absence of a negative decision, how much time an investor allocates to the process can be indicative of his or her interest. As one author has noted, "One of the best ways to judge a venture capitalist's interest is in the time allocated for substantive investigation."[13] However, on the whole, investigating a start-up takes longer than investigating ventures in later stages.

Typically, an investigation takes from 6 to 10 weeks, and, if a positive decision is not made by then, it is very unlikely that such a decision will ever be forthcoming.

During the due diligence process, it is recommended that the entrepreneur discreetly and selectively make presentations to a limited number of other venture capitalists, some of whom may be suggested by the interested investor. There are several reasons for doing this. First, if an entrepreneur does not do it, he or she may find himself or herself with a negative decision after two to three months of investigation by the venture capitalist, short on cash, and in a poor bargaining position with other potential investors. Second, the exposure to more than one venture capitalist is desirable if an entrepreneur is to know the attractiveness and worth of his or her venture. Last, if the venture requires financing that exceeds the investment limit of one venture firm, other investors will have to be brought into the deal. Further, many times venture firms like to involve other venture investors so there are enough "deep pockets" to provide some or all of the capital for subsequent financings.

However, once a venture capitalist *commits* to finance a venture and the offer is accepted, through execution of an agreement called a *terms sheet,* the entrepreneur should not contact other investors without the advice and consent of the lead investor.

The "Decision"

An investor will make a reasoned judgment using the information he or she has obtained. If the investor feels uncomfortable in any way about the venture, he or she will probably reject the investment. Most entrepreneurs will get more than one rejection in seeking such financing. While most investors will use polite ways to say no, with such comments as: "Interesting venture, but it does not meet our investment criteria," or "Interesting deal and good management. But we are not lead investors. If you find a strong lead investor, we might be very interested in investing."[14]

A "No" Decision

To avoid repeating this sort of experience an entrepreneur can try to determine the true reason for a rejection and either correct the flaw or decide the venture has basic limitations that make obtaining venture capital improbable if not impossible. However, note that only about 1 to 3 percent of all ventures seen by venture capital investors make it past the final evaluation to a positive decision and the investment of capital.[15]

Some of the most common things that turn off the investor include:

■ *Mousetrap myopia.*   Founders who are madly in love with the inventions, products, or elegant technologies they have devised, rather than with the customer, market, and building a business, turn off investors.

■ *Secrecy.*   Investors are turned off by founders who will not describe or reveal anything unless the investors first sign onerous nondisclosure agreements.

[13] Stanley E. Pratt, "Guidelines for Dealing with Venture Capitalists" in *Pratt's Guide to Venture Capital Sources,* 9th ed., ed. Stanley E. Pratt (Wellesley, Mass.: Venture Economics, 1985), pp. 51–53.

[14] Burton J. McMurtry and Donald M. Dible, "Objectives of the Venture Capitalist," in *Winning the Money Game* (Santa Clara, Calif.: Entrepreneur Press, 1975), pp. 211–26.

[15] There have been many studies of the screening process. See A. Bruno and T. Tyebjee, "The Entrepreneur's Search for Capital," *Frontiers of Entrepreneurship Research: 1984,* ed. J. Hornaday et al. (Babson Park, Mass.: Babson College, 1984), pp. 18–31; J. A. Timmons, N. Fast, and W. D. Bygrave, "Seed and Start-up Venture Capital Investment in Technological Companies," *Frontiers of Entrepreneurship Research: 1984,* ed. J. Hornaday et al. (Babson Park, Mass.: Babson College, 1984), pp. 1–17; and E. Roberts, "Business Planning and Start-up in High Technology Enterprises," *Frontiers in Entrepreneurship Research: 1983,* ed. J. Hornaday et al. (Babson Park, Mass.: Babson College, 1983), pp. 107–17.

- *Unrealistic assumptions.*   Investors are turned off by unrealistic assumptions. Examples would be a founder who is an engineer and who has a product which he or she believes is 95 percent complete but needs another $1 million (only!) and 12 to 15 months to perfect; a founder who unequivocally insists that his or her firm has "no competition"; or a founder who insists that the firm will get off the ground and sell out at a huge gain in two years.
- *Unsuitable investments.*   Businesses that are unsuitable (e.g., basically a jobshop or custom-engineering or design house) turn investors off.
- *Management problems.*   Management problems turn investors off (e.g., a new venture which was not planned well and needs the investment in the bank in 30 days or less) or the existence of a lead entrepreneur who is a "nondelegator" and who wants total control.

A "Yes" Decision

A "yes" decision means only that investors and entrepreneurs will attempt to negotiate a deal (i.e., the percentage of ownership of the venture that will be given to an investor in exchange for his or her invested capital). This process of negotiation is the subject of the next chapter.

Investment Agreements

Once a deal is negotiated, the parties will document it with several investment agreements. These also are discussed in the following chapter. Suffice it to say here that a deal is not "done" until all the agreements have been signed by all parties.

TYPES OF RISK INVESTMENT

Private Placements

Private placements[16] involve selling securities to a spectrum of sources. Certain federal and state laws regulate these fund-raising activities and how such offerings are made. Because private placements are complex, it is unwise for a new venture to undertake such offerings of securities without the advice of an attorney who is skilled in these matters.

Most important, a venture undertaking a private placement will want to avoid having its sale of securities accidentally classified as a public offering. Unintentional public offerings are potentially very damaging, in that disgruntled, unsophisticated stockholders can seek recision of the deal and the return of their invested capital. This, in turn, can result in personal liabilities on the part of a company's management and directors.

A private placement is subject to instrastate registration and private placement, and certain conditions need to be met to effect the sale of securities to friendly sources, wealthy individuals, or venture capital firms via a private placement. As outlined below, purchasers may be accredited, nonaccredited, and sophisticated investors. Accredited investors include:

- Institutional investors, such as banks, insurance companies, venture capital firms, registered investment companies, and SBICs.
- Any person who buys at least $150,000 of the offered security and whose net worth, including that of his or her spouse, is at least five times the purchase price.
- Any person who, together with his or her spouse, has a net worth in excess of $1 million at the time of purchase.

---

[16] Sources for this section were M. M. Coleman and I. P. Seldie, *A Businessman's Guide to Capital Raising under the Securities Law* (Philadelphia: Packard Press, 1982); and R. H. Kessel, *High Technology Financing in the 80s* (Boston: Pandick Press, 1984).

- Any person whose individual income is in excess of $200,000 in each of the last two years and who expects the same income for the current year.
- Directors, executive officers, or general partners of the company or partnership selling the securities.
- Certain tax-exempt organizations with more than $500,000 in assets.

If an investor is not an accredited investor, he or she is a nonaccredited investor. Broadly defined, sophisticated investors are wealthy individuals who invest more or less regularly in new and/or early-stage and late-stage ventures. They are knowledgeable about the technical and commercial opportunities and risks of the businesses in which they invest. They know what kind of information they want about their prospective investment and have the experience and ability to obtain and analyze the data provided to them.

Private placements can be for any amount and involve an offering of stock, subordinated debt, convertible debt, and the like. Most private placements for young companies are subject to Regulation D adopted by the Securities and Exchange Commission in April 1982. Regulation D simplifies the raising of capital by small businesses by simplifying and expanding how securities offerings can be exempted from the regulations governing public offerings. There are three separate exemption criteria that are based on the amount of money being raised, as follows:

- For placements up to $500,000, there are no specific disclosure/information requirements, and no limit on the kind or type of purchasers.
- For placements up to $5 million, the criteria for a public offering exemption get somewhat more difficult. Sales of securities can be made to not more than 35 nonaccredited purchasers and an unlimited number of accredited purchasers. There are no limits on the number or qualifications of the offerees. There are no special information requirements for accredited purchasers. If there are nonaccredited as well as accredited purchasers, there are specified information-disclosure requirements. Investors also must have the opportunity to obtain additional information about the company from its management.
- For securities sales in excess of $5 million, the criteria for purchasers is not more than 35 nonaccredited and an unlimited number of accredited purchasers. However, the nonaccredited purchasers must be "sophisticated" in investment matters. There are also specific disclosure requirements, which are more detailed than for offerings between $500,000 and $5 million. And investors must have the opportunity to obtain any additional information from the company and its management.

In addition to meeting the federal regulations described above, private placements need to comply also with state securities laws, called *blue sky* regulations, in each of the states where the securities will be sold.

ESOP Financing

Used by existing companies that have high confidence in the stability of their future earnings and cash flow, employee stock option plans (ESOPs) are another potential source of funding for growth, leveraged or partner buyouts, or acquisition. ESOPs have become highly popular, with several hundred thousand firms electing to utilize this vehicle in the 1980s.

While the various entities, flow of funds, and obligations are not simple, they can be readily understood. However, this is another area where experienced legal counsel and accounting advice is essential.

In essence, an ESOP borrows money, usually from a bank or insurance company, and uses these cash proceeds to buy the company's stock (usually from the owners or the treasury). The stock then becomes collateral for the bank note, while the owners or the treasury have cash that can be used for a variety of purposes. For the lender, usually a bank or insurance company, 50 percent of the interest earned on the loan to an ESOP is tax exempt. The company makes annual tax-deductible contributions—of *both* interest and principal—to the ESOP in an amount needed to service the bank loan. Compared to normal equity, there is a tax advantage for the company. In addition, there is the motivating impact of having employees who are owners.

Primary sources of funds for ESOP loans are commercial banks or insurance companies. The credit analysis and criteria are the same as for other medium or long-term loans.

Mezzanine Capital

This is the layer of junior debt, behind the senior debt, in financing for expansion and MBOs and LBOs.

This alternative is not feasible for start-ups, since fluctuation in earnings and cash flow present risks that neither the lenders nor the company owners are likely to accept.

Bridge Capital

This alternative is used by growing firms, typically those with sales in the $5 million to $100 million range, which anticipate a public offering or private sale of the firm in the next 6 to 36 months.

Public Stock Offerings

A public stock offering (called an *IPO* if it is an initial public offering) raises capital through federally registered and underwritten sales of the company's shares. A full gamut of federal and state securities laws and regulations govern such offerings.

In the past, such as during the strong bull market for new issues that occurred in 1980, 1981, and 1983, it was possible to raise money for an early-growth venture or even for a start-up through IPOs. Forty percent to 50 percent of these IPOs were for "glamorous" high-technology companies. Thus, the number of new issues jumped from 281 in 1980 to an astounding 888 in 1983, representing a jump from $1.4 billion in 1980 to about three times that figure in 1983.[17] Again, in 1986, the new issues market heated up.

In other more difficult financial environments, such as that of 1973 to 1975 or, even more dramatically, following the stock market "crash" of October 19, 1987, the new issues market became very quiet for entrepreneurial companies, compared to times of hot markets, such as 1983 and 1986. As a result, exit opportunities have been limited. In addition, it has been very difficult to raise money for early-growth or even more mature companies from the public market. The following example is typical: An entrepreneur spent a dozen years building a firm in the industrial mowing equipment business from scratch to $50 million in sales. The firm had a solid record of profitable growth in recent years. Although the firm was still "small" by Fortune 500 standards, it was the dominant firm in the business in mid-1987. Given the firm's plans for continued growth, the entrepreneur, his backers, and the directors decided the timing was right for an IPO, and the underwriters agreed. By early October 1987, everything was on schedule and the "road show," which was to present the company to the

[17] *INC.*, August 1984.

various offices of the underwriter, was scheduled to begin in November. The rest is history. Nearly two years later (when there had been only 39 new issues in the first quarter), the IPO was still "on hold."

The more mature a company is when it makes a public offering, the better the terms of the offering—that is, a higher valuation can be placed on the company and less equity will be given up by the founders for the required capital.

There are two main reasons why a new or young company might want to go public. First, in the right times, the company will get a higher stock price from an IPO than from a venture capital investor. Second, an IPO establishes a public price for the stock and gives a company a sense of wealth, at least on paper. (However, the sale of the stock will have certain restrictions on it.)

Notwithstanding the above, there are a number of reasons why IPOs can be disadvantageous. Principal among these are:

- The legal, accounting, and administrative costs of raising money via a public offering are more disadvantageous than other ways of raising money.
- A large amount of effort, time, and expense on the part of management are required to comply with SEC regulations and reporting requirements and to maintain the status of a public company. This diversion of management's time and energy from the tasks of running the company can adversely affect its performance and growth.
- The required disclosures to stockholders and, through them, to outsiders can make known information about a company's products, performance, and financial condition that would be better kept secret.
- Management can become more interested in maintaining the price of the company's stock and computing capital gains than in running the company. Short-term activities to maintain or increase a current year's earnings can take precedence over longer-term programs to build the company and increase its earnings.
- The liquidity of a company's stock achieved through a public offering may be more apparent than real. Without a sufficient number of shares outstanding and a strong "market maker," there may be no real market for the stock and, thus, no liquidity.
- The investment banking firms willing to take a new or unseasoned company public may not be the ones with whom the company would like to do business and establish a long-term relationship.

These disadvantages appear to be real. A survey of 494 companies out of 3,000 that had underwritten public offerings over a 10-year period ending in 1971 reported the following: 40 percent said that they would not go public if they had the opportunity to make the decision again, and 45 percent said that they had severed their relationship with the underwriter that took them public.[18] In a survey of companies that had filed initial registration statements in 1971 and that successfully concluded a public offering, 91 percent of the 107 survey respondents said that the amount of key management time consumed in the underwriting was a moderate to severe problem; 58 percent said that unanticipated costs of the underwriting was a moderate to severe problem; 51 percent said that the amount of disclosure required in the offering prospectus was a moderate to severe problem; and 52 percent said that the pricing of the issue had been a moderate to severe problem.[19] This earlier pattern persisted right through the late 1980s.

---

[18] Graeme K. Howard, Jr., "Going Public When It Makes Sense," in *Guide to Venture Capital Sources,* 3d ed. (Chicago: Capital Publishing, 1974), pp. 77–78.

[19] Ibid., pp. 77–78. Further information about the number of 1971 survey respondents was obtained from a private conversation with Mr. Howard.

CASE—BRIDGE CAPITAL INVESTORS, INC.

Preparation Questions

1. Evaluate the situation and financing alternatives Hindman is now facing. What is his strategy?
2. Is the $10 million Bridge investment enough money? How long will it last? What is Hindman's relative bargaining position? BCIs? Be prepared to represent both the company and BCI in a meeting to negotiate the proposed financing.
3. What are the consequences for JLI of the proposed financing? Calculate the consequences of the "put."
4. What should Hindman do? What should Bridge do?

BRIDGE CAPITAL INVESTORS, INC.*

"Local Savings & Loan Collapses, State Takes Over."

The morning headline on May 6, 1985, highlighted what was more than just a local interest story to Jiffy Lube. Old Court Savings & Loan was the company's primary real estate lender, and its collapse left the development of 37 new service centers, and Jiffy Lube's future, at risk.

Throughout the summer of 1985, the Jiffy Lube team battled the crises through short-term borrowings and other stopgap measures. It is now November 1985, and time is running out. Construction costs have depleted the company's finances, and Jim Hindman's personal resources are running out. Serious competition has also appeared. In August, Quaker State Oil bought Minit Lube, the number two company in the quick change industry, for $35 million. As Jim Hindman notes, "This puts us up against the big boys for the first time."

However, not all is bleak. Since March 1983, Jiffy Lube has rapidly expanded and recorded its first operating profits *(Exhibit A)*. Despite the current problems, Jiffy Lube's number one position in the industry creates a number of alternatives. Last month, Shearson Lehman Brothers proposed a $10 million private debt placement. Also, five major oil companies are showing varying degrees of interest in Jiffy Lube, ranging from outright purchases to strategic partnerships.

Jiffy Lube's recent growth (and survival) were made possible by creative financing obtained in early 1983 and a major change in strategy.

1983 Financing

In March 1983, Jim Hindman and a group of other investors contributed their interests in W. James Hindman, Ltd., and two other nursing home partnerships to Jiffy Lube in an exchange for common stock. These interests had a combined fair market value of over $3.4 million. For some time Hindman had considered the idea of using the value of his partnership interests to help finance Jiffy Lube. Selling the partnership interests to raise cash represented a second-rate alternative. Hindman had almost no tax basis in his interests, and income taxes would have consumed a significant portion of the proceeds from a sale.

After reviewing the available options, Ernst & Whinney helped Hindman and a small group of investors structure the transaction as a tax-free exchange under Internal Revenue

*Copyright © 1987 Curtis-Palmer & Co., Inc., Harvard, Mass. This case was prepared by Dale Sander of Ernst & Whinney's national office, Privately Owned Emerging Business Services Group, Cleveland, Ohio, and Jeffry A. Timmons. No part of this publication may be reproduced, stored in a retrieval system, or transmitted in any form or by any means without permission.

Exhibit A
Jiffy Lube, Inc., Operating Results (year ended March 31; dollars in millions)

	1983	1984	1985	1986 (projected)
Revenue	$ 5.5	$6.0	$14.5	$29.8
Net income	$(2.6)	$.3	$.6	$1.9
Service centers (franchised/ company owned)	96/0	120/1	208/23	361/23

See *Exhibit H* for 1984 and 1985 financial statements.

Code Section 351. The group transferring the assets represented a controlling group (i.e., they owned over 80 percent of Jiffy Lube's stock after the transfer). As a controlling group they were able to transfer their interests to the company at the existing tax basis without realizing any gain for tax purposes.

The partnership interests were sold by Jiffy Lube to third parties during the following year and raised much needed cash. A tax gain of over $3 million was recognized from the sales but was offset by the massive net operating loss carry forwards from prior years.

Also part of the "351 transaction" was the contribution of an additional $1.9 million in cash from the Midwest individuals and other shareholders in exchange for common stock.

New Corporate Strategy

During its first several years of operation, the majority of Jiffy Lube's franchises had been sold one unit at a time. But individual sales of franchises did not saturate areas quickly enough to achieve name recognition and make advertising cost effective. In early 1983, Neal O'Shea, vice president for franchise sales, suggested that Jiffy Lube stop selling franchises on a unit-by-unit basis.

Instead, Jiffy Lube began selling "area development rights" to investors and entrepreneurs. In return for an up-front nonrefundable fee, Jiffy Lube gives investors the exclusive right to build a certain number of franchises within a specified geographical location. Fees have varied depending on the potential of the market (e.g., Tampa—$150K; San Francisco—$250K). As Jiffy Lube continues to grow, management expects the rights to become more valuable, eventually selling for as much as $1 million in some larger markets (such as Los Angeles).

In addition to the up-front fee, Jiffy Lube also collects an initial franchise fee ($20–$25,000) for each individual franchise developed. If investors fail to complete the required number of units within the agreed-upon time, they forfeit their exclusive rights to the area.

The area development concept increased growth, advanced the clustering concept, and attracted more sophisticated franchisees. The up-front fees also were a significant source of cash for Jiffy Lube. Earnings also dramatically improved as the development fees went straight to the bottom line. In fiscal 1984, Jiffy Lube was in the black for the first time.

At the same time, management recognized that the area development fees are going to decline and eventually fade away as the rights to all of the major metropolitan areas are sold. Royalty fees collected from franchisees (originally 5 percent of gross franchise sales) will progressively become a more important source of revenue and key determinant of profitability.

In 1984, Jiffy Lube took advantage of its growing leadership position in the industry to enhance its royalty agreement with new franchisees. Under these newer agreements, Jiffy Lube collects a 6 percent royalty after the franchise has been operating for one year. Jiffy Lube also achieved some vertical integration in its business by acquiring its major supplier of automotive supplies, Heritage Merchandising.

Jiffy Lube's goals and strategy for the future are summarized in this excerpt from its business plan prepared in the late sumer of 1985:

The company's goal is to become the nation's dominant supplier of fast oil changes, with approximately 1,300 service centers by 1990. Its strategy for achieving this goal is to cluster centers in the 30 major metropolitan markets, thereby realizing economies of scale in operations, advertising, and the distribution of auto supplies. As the company becomes a nationwide firm and undertakes national advertising and promotional campaigns, it should be able to capture an increasingly large market share.

Jim Hindman summarized Jiffy Lube's plan with the following comparison: "We will become the 'McDonald's' of the quick oil change business." With approximately 270 service centers currently open in late 1985, these goals require the opening of over 1,000 new centers by 1990.

Construction Financing

Jiffy Lube's growth and the sale of the large area development rights increased the need for real estate financing. Purchasing real estate today for a new center generally costs between $100K and $275K, while construction typically costs an additional $225K. Even with more sophisticated investors, it is often necessary to provide real estate and construction financing to speed the development of the new franchises (approximately 50 percent of the franchisees have required assistance with their real estate and construction financing). Jiffy Lube funds real estate purchases and construction costs through two main sources.

"Permanent real estate financing" consists of mortgages on properties owned by the company and rented to franchisees. The mortgage payments are offset by rental income received from the franchisees. The other source is "construction financing," used to develop centers to be sold to franchisees. Upon sale of the centers, Jiffy Lube uses the proceeds to retire the debt, while the franchisees obtain their own permanent financing.

In 1983, Jiffy Lube signed an agreement with Old Court Savings & Loan to provide $16 million in construction financing for the purchase and development of 37 new centers (*Exhibit B*). In addition, Old Court agreed to supply permanent financing to a partnership purchasing these centers from Jiffy Lube.

By May 1985, other projects were also in process, and the company had 60 new service centers in various stages of development. Jiffy Lube determined that its growth pace would require additional capital, and it researched the possibility of a private placement. Management hoped to raise up to $10 million and began working with Shearson Lehman Brothers in April 1985 to organize a deal.

May 1985: Crisis

In May 1985, as the morning headlines announced, the state declared Old Court Savings & Loan insolvent and appointed a conservator. The state had been investigating the S&L since early in the year, but there had been no warning that the situation was this serious and Jiffy Lube's management was caught off guard. All loan activity was halted, including the funding on Jiffy Lube's development projects. Before the collapse, partial financing (approximately $6.3 million) on only 25 of the 37 service centers had been provided.

Exhibit B
Old Court Savings & Loan Master Commitment

OLD COURT SAVINGS AND LOAN

May 24, 1983

Jiffy Lube, Inc.

RE: Various Sites—Jiffy Lube—Master Commitment

Gentlemen:

Please be advised that Old Court Savings & Loan, Inc., will provide construction funds, on various sites, for buildings to be built by your company. As your request draws on specific sites Old Court will issue individual commitments to you. The following is a general outline of our understanding of your request and Old Court's commitment to you:

BORROWER:	Jiffy Lube, Inc.
TOTAL COMMITMENT AMOUNT:	Not to exceed Sixteen Million ($16,000,000) Dollars.
INTEREST RATE:	Two (2%) percent over Union Trust Prime.
TERM OF EACH INDIVIDUAL LOAN:	Six (6) months after closing, with one six month extension.
LOAN FEES:	One and one-half (1½) points for first (1st) six (6) months, one (1%) percent additional if additional six month extension is used.

SPECIAL CONDITIONS:

1. Subject to satisfactory appraisal on each site.
2. Subject to satisfactory financial statements, to be up-dated from time to time.
3. Review and approval of all loan documents by Old Court's attorney.
4. Subject to availability of funds for loan.

Please indicate your acceptance of this general outline of terms and conditions by signing the bottom of this letter and returning it to me.

Sincerely,

David Falco
Executive Vice-President

Jiffy Lube quickly found that obtaining substitute financing from another lender was unlikely. Old Court had liens on the partially funded properties; because of the existing liens, no lenders were willing to fund the completion of these units.

As Jim Hindman describes:

Whatever could go wrong, did go wrong. We had one bank lined up who seemed ready to continue the financing. On Monday, we went down to Old Court to show the bank the records detailing the loans, property liens, etc. During the weekend, the state had moved some of Old Court's records to another location, and lost all the Jiffy Lube documents! The bank we had lined up got nervous and said "see you later." (The records were eventually located.)

In late May, Shearson Lehman also backed away and progress on the private placement stopped. "It was a case of guilt by association," notes Hindman. The state's investigation had turned up allegations of improprieties at Old Court, including charges of falsified appraisals on certain loans. Although Jiffy Lube was not involved or implicated in any of the allegations, the shadow of Old Court appeared to scare off potential backers.

Another investment banker, Alex. Brown & Sons, proposed raising $10 million in equity for a real estate partnership. The partnership would then obtain $40 million in debt from a savings and loan. The money would be used to replace Old Court and fund the development of Jiffy Lube centers.

Hindman was confident that the deal would go through, but Alex. Brown's final review committee turned down the proposal. The Ernst & Whinney CSE phoned a contact at Alex. Brown and determined that the deal had been rejected because of the Old Court situation. Old Court's key officers were under investigation for improper activities and "no one wanted to touch anything Old Court had been involved with."

Short-Term Solutions

Management decided immediately after the May 6 announcement of Old Court's collapse that Jiffy Lube could not wait for funding from the S&L to resume (particularly since this did not appear to be a likely possibility). Development of the service centers involved a series of events which could not be put on hold. Jiffy Lube would default on a number of real estate purchases if cash payments were not made by specified dates. Contractors were lined up, and individuals expecting to earn their livelihood operating franchises were depending on the service centers being completed.

In addition, significant delays would damage the company's strategy. Jim Hindman:

I really believe that the guy that gets his distribution system in place first is going to have the chance of being the "McDonald's" of the industry. Speed is the most critical element; we have to get out there before anyone else does. It's like Patton's rush across Europe in World War II; go until you run out of fuel. Once you take territory, you never have to give it back.

There have been many times when we could have pulled back and been just a regional company. A couple of our directors have always pushed for us to slow down and concentrate more on short-term profits. Look at what is happening now, though. The small firms are being snapped up—like all of the local chains we've bought. And now Minit Lube has been acquired by Quaker State. If we maintain our growth, we will be the only independent company in the industry with the ability to go on national television, and the smaller chains will see their car counts go down.

Jiffy Lube decided to proceed with construction of the centers and to fund the costs itself out of its limited operating capital. Construction draws required approximately $150–$200K per week, and Jiffy Lube's cash reserves were quickly used up. Hindman lent Jiffy Lube $865K.

Franchisees also rallied behind Jiffy Lube. Jiffy Lube had recognized from the start that the franchisees were the parties responsible for actually selling and providing the quick lube service to consumers. They were the key link to the success or failure of Jiffy Lube. Acknowledging their importance, Jiffy Lube had worked hard to create a "partnership" relationship between it and the franchisees. Shortly after the crises began, franchisees combined with employees to make $1.2 million in short-term unsecured loans to Jiffy Lube.

The cash drain continued, however, and, by July, Jiffy Lube was again out of cash. John Sasser, the CFO, walked into Hindman's office on a Wednesday and told him that they needed a million dollars by Monday if Jiffy Lube was to meet its commitments. With no apparent sources of cash immediately available, Hindman consulted with his attorney, Jacques Schlenger, about the options available, including the potential benefits of filing Chapter 11.

Schlenger happened to represent two entrepreneurs who had recently cashed out of a business. Schlenger set up a 45-minute meeting between Hindman and one of the men on Thursday. By Monday, Jiffy Lube had a loan for the $1 million it needed.

In the late summer of 1985, the state of Maryland determined that Old Court was not salvageable and placed the S&L in receivership for the purpose of liquidation. Ed Kelley, senior vice president, describes the decision Jiffy Lube had to make:

We didn't know if we should join the bandwagon and threaten suits against Old Court and the state, or try diplomacy. We decided that the best approach was to be nice guys, and told them "Look, we understand you've got a problem and we want to cooperate with you to work it out. We want to pay you back everything that we've borrowed, but we can't do that until these units are completed."

In September, the receiver of Old Court agreed to allow the S&L to extend a $4 million line of credit to Jiffy Lube for temporary construction financing on the units Jiffy Lube could not complete on its own (16 units). The key points of this agreement are summarized in *Exhibit I.*

Decision-Making Time: Long-Term Alternatives

By late summer, Shearson Lehman became convinced that Jiffy Lube was not going to suffer any more fallout as a result of the Old Court disaster, and again became interested in putting together a private placement. At the same time a number of major oil companies demonstrated an interest in Jiffy Lube.

The environment Jiffy Lube faced in late 1985 is summarized in the following excerpts *(Exhibit C)* from the company's business plan:

Exhibit C
Industry Trends and Current Developments

Fast oil change specialists currently perform approximately 3.5 percent of the 367 million oil changes estimated annually for automobiles and light trucks. The company believes the market share should grow rapidly due to the decline in the number of full-service gas stations. According to the 1985 National Petroleum News Factbook Annual Issue, the number of gas stations offering oil changes decreased to less than 137,000 in 1985 from 226,000 in 1973. A recent Pennzoil study concluded that quick oil change centers would become one of the major distribution channels for oil lubrication products by the early 1990s.

The company currently has approximately 270 service centers operating, and estimates that the other major fast oil change operators have the following numbers of centers:

Minit Lube	90
Grease Monkey	45
Rapid Oil Change	26
Kwik Change	19
McQuick Oilube	16
Lube Pit Stop	14

On August 1, 1985, Quaker State Oil Refining Corporation announced that it had signed a letter of intent to acquire Arctic Circle, Inc., for $35 million in stock. Arctic Circle, Inc., is the parent company of Minit Lube, and holds over 100 Arctic Circle restaurants in addition to the oil change centers.

Since the Old Court collapse, Jiffy Lube has followed through on its business strategy by using a variety of the short-term financing sources available to it. The new agreement with Old Court, though, requires Jiffy Lube to quickly pay off $2.5 million of the $6.3 million construction loans outstanding. Jiffy Lube has committed to paying this amount with the proceeds from the private placement proposed by Shearson or through other means.

Exhibit D
Debt Outstanding at September 30, 1985

Description	September 30, 1985, Balance (000's)	Interest Rate	Payment Terms/Comments
Financing for centers under construction:			
Old Court Savings & Loan	$ 6,300	Prime + 2%	See "Amended Master Commitment" (Exhibit J).
James McDonagh and Robert Vogel	1,000	11%	Due 8/86.
Jim Hindman	865	15%	Five notes, maturing between 9/85 and 1/86.
Other directors, employees, and franchisees	1,185	15%	Due 3/86.
	9,350		
Permanent real estate financing:			
INA Mortgage	5,250	16.5%	Requires increasing monthly payment through 2/94. Current payments are approximately $80,000.
Other mortgages	2,052	Prime + 1 to 2%	Monthly payments of approximately $40,000. All mature by 1993.
	7,302		
Funds borrowed to acquire companies or assets:			
Pennzoil	1,800	14.25%	Due 2/86.
Maryland National Bank	1,300	Prime + 1%	Borrowed under line of credit agreement and due on demand. Under an oral agreement with the bank, the loan can be paid over 5 years, beginning in 12/85, if necessary.
Others (included notes payable to selling shareholders of chains acquired, and debts assumed in acquisitions)	2,900	8–18%	Mature over the next 4 years.
	6,000		
Total at September 30, 1985	$22,652		

Personal loans and other short-term borrowings are also coming due (see *Exhibit D* for a summary of the outstanding debt). And, additional financing is needed if the company is to execute its long-term growth plan. Jiffy Lube, with the assistance of Ernst & Whinney, prepared a projection of its operations for fiscal 1986 and for the five years following. A summary of the projections is included in *Exhibit E*.

November 1985 Alternatives

Bridge Capital Investors

As the Old Court episode cooled down toward the end of August, Shearson Lehman again proposed putting together a private placement. Shearson worked through the rest of August and September searching for parties interested in a $10 million private debt placement. By early October 1985, Shearson had identified four interested parties, and key management from Jiffy Lube flew to New York to meet with each of them.

One of the four, Bridge Capital Investors, expressed an immediate interest in Jiffy Lube. Bridge Capital Investors, a mezzanine capital partnership, proposed providing financing through the purchase of $10 million in subordinated notes with warrants attached to purchase 10 percent of Jiffy Lube. The proposed terms are summarized in *Exhibit F*.

Exhibit E
Jiffy Lube, Inc., Projected Operations

	1986	1987	1988	1989	1990	1991
Revenue:						
Sales by company-operated units	$ 7,683	$10,169	$14,218	$18,840	$ 22,210	$ 23,954
Initial franchise fees	3,630	4,527	4,735	5,048	5,215	2,706
Area development fees	2,000	500				
Franchise royalties	5,280	9,946	16,062	23,405	32,162	41,014
Sales of automotive products	8,880	15,789	24,489	34,623	46,169	56,561
Rental income from franchisees	2,328	3,010	3,701	4,440	5,137	5,442
Total revenues	29,801	43,941	63,205	86,356	110,893	129,677
Costs and expenses:						
Company-operated units	6,377	8,440	11,801	15,637	18,434	19,882
Cost of sales of automotive products	7,548	13,420	20,816	29,429	39,243	48,077
Expenses related to rental properties, including interest	1,711	1,546	1,502	1,433	1,341	1,332
Selling, general, and administrative expenses	8,880	14,399	20,341	26,163	31,694	35,221
Total costs and expenses	24,516	37,805	54,460	72,662	90,712	104,512
Income from operations	5,285	6,136	8,745	13,694	20,181	25,165
Other income (expense):						
Interest expense	(2,798)	(3,423)	(2,650)	(2,827)	(2,883)	(2,259)
Other	315	324	97	68	439	1,286
Income before income taxes	2,802	3,037	6,192	10,935	17,737	24,192
Income tax expense	951	1,518	3,096	5,465	8,868	12,096
Net income	$ 1,851	$ 1,518	$ 3,096	$ 5,467	$ 8,868	$ 12,096
Service centers in operation:						
Franchised	361	578	805	1,047	1,297	1,427
Company-operated	23	31	39	47	47	47

These projections were prepared assuming that Jiffy Lube obtains $10 million in debt financing.

Don Remey, general partner, described Bridge Capital as a "$50 million partnership financed by pension funds and insurance companies. We specialize in financing growing companies, using debt with equity kickers." Remey also indicated that "unlike venture capital, we do not seek control or a major share of ownership." The personal chemistry between Hindman and Remey was positive from the first meeting on.

Quaker State

The president of Quaker State called in August and said, "Look, we just bought Minit Lube and I think we should talk." After some preliminary meetings, Jiffy Lube agreed to let Quaker State perform "due diligence" on the company as a prelude to a possible purchase offer. In September, Quaker State made an offer to purchase Jiffy Lube. The purchase price is contingent on future earnings as described in the purchase offer summarized in *Exhibit G.*

Details of Quaker State's Arctic Circle/Minit Lube acquisition are now available (these were outlined in the S-14 filing related to the transaction and in the company's September 30, 1985, 10-Q). The shareholders of Arctic Circle received 1,425,000 shares of Quaker State common stock; the stock was trading at $24⅞ at the time of the transaction; Arctic Circle had sales and net income of $31 million and $1.4 million, respectively, for the year ended March 31, 1985. Minit Lube accounted for 47 percent and 57 percent of the sales and net income, respectively.

Financial details of debt and operations are in *Exhibits H* and *I;* Jiffy Lube's master agreement for real estate and construction is in *Exhibit J.*

Exhibit F
Bridge Capital Investors: Proposed Private Placement

12% Senior Subordinated Notes Due 1992 with Warrants

NOTES

Amount	$10,000,000
Issue price	97.254%
Maturity	December 15, 1992 (7 years)
Interest rate	12%, payable quarterly

Mandatory sinking fund

Beginning during the fourth year, the Company will make eight equal semiannual payments of $1,250,000.

In the event of an initial public offering of $20 million or more, the Company shall prepay at par 50% of the Notes from the proceeds of the offering.

Subordination

The Notes will be subordinate in payment of principal and interest to senior debt, and senior to all subsequent subordinated debt.

WARRANTS

Amount

549,218 warrants to purchase 10% of the fully diluted, pro forma shares of Common Stock. After six months there will be an adjustment for any new shares or warrants issued to maintain 10%.

Issue price	$0.50 per warrant
Exercise price	$6 per share
Term	Seven years

Put Provision

If during five years from issuance, the Company's Common Stock has not traded publicly at levels set forth in the table that follows, the Purchasers may put the warrants and/or underlying stock to the Company. The price will be determined by the calculation of the amount necessary to result in a 30% per annum internal rate of return to the Purchasers on that proportion of warrants not previously sold, taking into account all interest premium and principal repayment on the proportionately related Notes.

If (i) the Company completes one or more public offerings of Common Stock with aggregate proceeds to the Company of at least $15 million and (ii) the average closing price for 60 consecutive trading days exceeds:

6 months ending 6/88 – $17.50
6 months ending 12/88 – $20.00
6 months ending 6/89 – $25.00
6 months ending 12/89 – $30.00
6 months ending 6/90 – $35.00
6 months ending 12/90 – $40.00

then the put provision will expire.

In the event the Company is unable to pay the amount due, the Purchasers have the right to nominate a majority of the Board of Directors.

Merger/Sale

If prior to December 21, 1987, the Company is sold or merged into another company the Purchasers shall be entitled to not less than $15 per warrant share.

BOARD OF DIRECTORS

Donald P. Remey to be elected as Director.

Pennzoil

Jiffy Lube had maintained a good relationship with Pennzoil despite Hindman's repurchase of the oil company's investment. Pennzoil was Jiffy Lube's largest supplier of oil products, and it had arranged financing for the development and acquisition of some Jiffy Lube centers. Jiffy Lube was a major channel of distribution, and Pennzoil had much to lose if Jiffy Lube was acquired by another oil company.

Exhibit G
Quaker State Purchase Offer

PURCHASE PRICE

Quaker State will purchase the outstanding shares of Jiffy Lube for $13 per share, contingent on Jiffy Lube meeting the earnings requirements detailed below. The total potential purchase price is as follows:

Total shares (shares outstanding, warrants, and options)	4,144,681
Purchase price per share	× $13
Total	$53,880,853

$5 million will be paid in cash at closing, the remainder is payable June 30, 1989, based on Jiffy Lube's net income for the three years ending March 31, 1989 (in aggregate):

Aggregate Net Income for 3 Years Ending March 31, 1989	Purchase Price Per Share	Total
Exceeding $10 million	$13.0	$53,880,853
8	10.4	43,104,682
6	7.8	32,328,512
4	5.2	21,552,341
2	2.6	10,776,171
$2 million or less	1.2	5,000,000

An additional $25 million will be paid to management as bonuses based on Jiffy Lube's net income for the 5 years ending March 31, 1991 (in aggregate):

Aggregate Net Income for 5 Years Ending March 31, 1991	Total Bonus
Exceeding $25 million	$25 million
20	20
15	15
10	10
5	5
$5 million or less	0

TRANSACTIONS PRIOR TO CLOSE OF SALE

Upon signing of a contract of sales, Quaker State will loan Jiffy Lube $10 million. If negotiations break down or are stopped for antitrust reasons, Jiffy Lube will repay the debt one year after the formal break off of negotiations.

Jiffy Lube management will be independent of Quaker State from signing until closing except that no new stock, warrants, or options shall be issued until the deal is closed, cancelled, or one year passes.

ORGANIZATION AND CONTINUING OPERATIONS

Jiffy Lube will operate as a separate subsidiary, reporting directly to the President or CEO of Quaker State. Jiffy Lube will have a separate board composed of Jiffy Lube and Quaker State management.

The name "Jiffy Lube" shall be maintained on all units in the system.

In any market where Jiffy Lube has sold the exclusive area rights or where Jiffy Lube units and Minit Lube units have conflicting franchise or territorial rights, the Minit Lube system must be kept separate until an agreement is reached between the Jiffy Lube and Minit Lube franchisees.

REAL ESTATE FINANCING

Quaker State commits to provide at least $50 million of real estate financing to Jiffy Lube per year for the next four (4) years at competitive rates. Such debt will be used to build quick lubrication centers, all of which will, as a condition of the lease, use at least 80 percent of their motor oil from Quaker State.

INA debt guaranteed by Pennzoil is to be repaid or assumed.

Pennzoil told Hindman, "We don't think we should buy you. You don't want to be owned by a large oil company. Your biggest need is for real estate financing. Let's cut a deal whereby we can arrange a financing vehicle that will allow you to grow. With enough money for real estate development you can attract equity on your own." The two parties agreed to continue to discuss this possibility.

Exhibit H
Consolidated Balance Sheet

	March 31	
	1985	1984
Assets		
Current assets:		
Cash	$ 1,476,889	$ 510,282
Accounts receivable, less allowance of $164,800 in 1985 and $47,000 in 1984	1,933,576	1,181,396
Current portion of fees receivable from franchises in development	1,311,000	143,500
Current portion of loans and notes receivable and net investment in direct financing leases	1,215,825	628,824
Current portion of loans and notes receivable from related parties	411,221	219,177
Inventory	985,554	467,351
Real estate held for resale	6,510,781	1,516,492
Prepaid expenses	122,178	181,449
Total current assets	13,967,024	4,848,471
Fees receivable from franchises in development	1,232,500	975,000
Loans and notes receivable, less current portion	898,805	642,876
Loans and notes receivable from related parties, less current portion		261,000
Net investment in direct financing leases	1,006,057	
Investments in and advances to affiliates	306,204	
Property and equipment:		
Land	2,854,344	2,371,679
Buildings and improvements	6,868,768	3,998,741
Automobiles, furniture, and equipment	1,205,801	335,600
	10,928,913	6,706,020
Less allowances for depreciation	761,455	433,686
Intangible assets, less accumulated amortization:		
Franchise rights	5,246,583	461,918
Other	913,628	549,185
	6,160,211	1,011,103
Deferred franchise costs	335,050	144,780
Other assets	206,870	23,374
Total assets	$34,280,179	$14,178,938
Liabilities and Stockholders' Equity		
Current liabilities:		
Accounts payable and accrued expenses	$ 5,129,510	$ 1,387,460
Notes payable	1,679,470	300,000
Construction advances for real estate held for resale	5,936,682	1,506,015
Current portion of long-term debt and capital lease obligations	864,312	165,506
Total current liabilities	13,609,974	3,358,981
Long-term debt, less current portion	10,196,905	5,639,701
Capital lease obligations, less current portion	2,341,217	417,353
Deferred franchise fees	3,595,250	1,302,500
Minority interest	36,498	
Stockholders' equity:		
Common stock, par value $0.05:		
Authorized—5,000,000 shares		
Issued —3,499,521 shares in 1985		
—3,243,996 shares in 1984	174,974	162,198
Capital in excess of par value	9,648,965	8,875,764
Retained-earnings deficit	(4,427,524)	(5,030,730)
Less: Cost of common stock held in treasury—22,808 shares	546,829	546,829
Due from officers for purchase of common stock	349,251	
Total stockholders' equity	4,500,335	3,460,403
Total liabilities and stockholders' equity	$34,280,179	$14,178,938

Exhibit I
Consolidated Statement of Operations

	Year Ended March 31	
	1985	1984
Revenue:		
Sales by company-operated units	$ 2,037,325	$ 80,118
Initial franchise fees	1,177,875	672,500
Area development fees	2,208,125	1,219,500
Franchise royalties	2,141,600	1,294,617
Sales of automotive products	5,811,421	1,839,270
Rental income from franchisees	1,108,852	909,597
Total revenues	14,485,198	6,015,602
Costs and expenses:		
Company-operated units	1,714,645	59,585
Cost of sales of automotive production	4,985,386	1,779,658
Costs and expenses related to rental properties, including interest of $966,894 in 1985 and $928,974 in 1984	1,413,794	1,250,485
Selling, general, and administrative expenses	5,908,195	2,821,181
Total costs and expenses	14,022,020	5,910,909
Income (loss) from operations	463,178	104,693
Other income (expense):		
Other income	339,663	203,810
Interest expense	(212,702)	(304,062)
Minority interest in loss of subsidiary	13,067	
Income (loss) before income taxes	603,206	4,441
Income tax expense	301,603	
Income (loss) before disposal of partnership interests and extraordinary item	301,603	4,441
Income from operations and disposition of partnership interests, net of tax of $115,906		190,933
Income (loss) before extraordinary item	301,603	195,374
Extraordinary reduction of income tax expense arising from the utilization of prior year's net operating losses	301,603	115,906
Net income (loss)	$ 603,206	$ 311,280

Other Options

In the summer, Ashland Oil (the makers of Valvoline) contacted Jiffy Lube to see if the two companies had any interest in each other (e.g., investment, joint venture, purchase). A team of Ashland executives and attorneys came out to do their own due diligence on Jiffy Lube, but the talks have not yet moved beyond the conceptual stage.

Exxon also expressed an interest because of surplus properties it was holding. No serious discussions have been held.

Working for Amoco, Boston Consulting Group had tried to put together a deal whereby Amoco would acquire both Jiffy Lube and Minit Lube. Now, after Quaker State's purchase of Minit Lube, Boston Consulting was working on a proposal for Amoco to purchase Jiffy Lube. No serious discussions have been held yet.

Opportunities or "Vultures"?

In Ed Kelley's words, Jiffy Lube is in the middle of a "feeding frenzy." Management has little time to do anything other than contend with the parties interested in arranging a deal with the company.

Exhibit J
Old Court Savings & Loan: Amended Master Commitment

On September 12, 1985, Jiffy Lube signed an agreement with Old Court Savings and Loan:

Amended Master Commitment for Real Estate Acquisition and Construction Financing on Sixteen (16) Jiffy Lube Locations

The agreement is summarized in the excerpts below:

Financing shall consist of no more than sixteen (16) loans (collectively the "Loan," and individually, the "Individual Loan"). Proceeds of each loan to be used to defray a portion of the acquisition and construction costs for the purchase of each individual property.

Terms and conditions:

Loan Amount.   *On each Individual Loan the amount of the total advance shall be equal to eighty percent (80%) of the appraised fair market value of the real estate, including the improvements to be constructed thereon. In no event, however, shall the amount of the loan exceed the sum of Four Million Dollars ($4,000,000).*

Interest Rate.   *A floating rate two percent (2%) over the prime rate charged by the Union Trust Company of Maryland, but in no event shall the rate be less than thirteen percent (13%) per annum.*

Interest Payments.   *Interest only is payable on the first (1st) day of each month following closing and upon payment in full of each Individual Loan.*

Maturity.   *Each Individual Loan shall mature on the first (1st) day of the seventh (7th) calendar month following closing. Borrower shall have the option to extend the maturity of each Individual Loan to the first (1st) day of the tenth (10th) calendar month following closing.*

Special Conditions:

This commitment letter supersedes the May 24, 1983, Master Commitment. Borrower releases and holds harmless the Bank for any claims arising out of the Master agreement or any alleged defaults by the bank thereunder.

All existing notes and mortgages will be modified to provide for payment in full on the first (1st) day of the seventh (7th) month following execution of this commitment letter. Borrower will have the right, upon payment of an extension fee equal to one (1%) percent of the loan amount, to extend the maturity date of the loans to first day of the thirteenth (13th) month following the date of the commitment.

Bank's obligation to perform hereunder is expressly conditioned upon:

(i) the delivery by Borrower to Bank a letter from Shearson Lehman Brothers wherein Shearson agrees that it will use its best efforts to market not less than Nine Million dollars ($9,000,000) of subordinated notes with warrants of Jiffy Lube International, Inc., of which Two and One-half Million Dollars ($2,500,000) will be paid to Bank within five days of Borrower's closing under its agreement with Shearson.

(ii) the delivery by Borrower to Bank a letter from Reality Income Corporation (RIC) wherein RIC agrees that it will purchase eighteen (18) Jiffy Lube locations which are secured by mortgages to Bank.

(Note: Both letters referred to above were delivered to the bank at the time the agreement was signed.)

Jiffy Lube is an enigma; it is the largest quick lube franchisor in the United States but is continually fighting for survival. Hindman feels that the oil companies, especially Quaker State, are "playing hardball" because they don't expect Jiffy Lube to last much longer on its own. Sometimes it seems like Jiffy Lube is surrounded by vultures waiting to pick up the pieces.

Valuing, Negotiating, and Structuring the Deal

Always assume the deal will not close and keep several alternatives alive.

James Hindman
Founder, Chief Executive Officer,
and Chairman
Jiffy Lube International

RESULTS EXPECTED

Upon completion of the chapter, you will have:

1. Identified how to find and contact principal sources of equity and debt capital.
2. Examined the criteria and evaluation process involved in obtaining capital, and "sand traps" in venture financing.
3. Discussed how investors think about pricing a venture and their approach to negotiating and structuring a deal.[1]
4. Studied the investment documents which result from financing decisions.

STRUCTURING THE DEAL

What is meant by "deal structure"? The structure of the deal gets at the heart of legally defining what has been negotiated and agreed upon—who gets what, what rights and obligations will be incurred, and what governing documents will define all of the above.

Deal structure defines:

- Ownership share.
- Cost of the capital obtained.
- Legal and financial control of the company.
- Instruments and their terms and conditions, which define the rights and obligations of the various investors and the entrepreneur.

In today's risk capital markets, most deals provide the outside investor with a safety valve as follows: If current management cannot achieve the aggressive sales and earnings objectives, then the outside owners who have a minority position will have a mechanism in the deal structure to gain a majority of the board of directors and, thereby, the votes necessary to replace what they believe is inadequate management.

---

[1] While Chapter 15 discusses valuing, negotiating, and structuring equity deals, the principals discussed here are also applicable to debt financing discussed in Chapter 16.

NEGOTIATING

It is highly recommended that entrepreneurs negotiate with people who have authority.[2] Negotiations with professional investors normally are handled by a senior member of the investing firm and the president of the venture. In the case of an investment by a syndicate of investors, one firm will usually serve as the "lead investor" and conduct negotiations for the investor group.

In these negotiations, entrepreneurs are usually at a considerable disadvantage. As one experienced venture capital attorney, Sandy Taylor, put it:

I've been on both sides of the table, and I'd rather be on the side of the venture capitalist any day of the week. It does not matter what the entrepreneur's attorney argues, I know I hold all the trump cards.[3]

Yet, what Herb Cohen says about the other side having deadlines in negotiations also applies to the fact of negotiation in general:

Take it from me, as an article of faith, that the other side — *every* "other side" — *always* has a deadline. If they didn't have some pressure to negotiate, you would not be able to find them.[4]

Far more is negotiable than entrepreneurs think.[5] A normal ploy of the attorney representing the investors is to insist, matter of factly, that "this is our boilerplate" and that the entrepreneur should take it or leave it. Yet, it is possible for an entrepreneur, in a number of cases, to negotiate and craft an agreement that is responsive to his or her needs and requirements.

During the negotiation, the investors will be evaluating the negotiating skills, intelligence, and maturity of the entrepreneur. The entrepreneur has precisely the same opportunity to size up his or her investor.

If investors see anything that shakes their confidence or trust, they probably will withdraw from the deal. Similarly, if an investor turns out to be arrogant, hot-tempered, unwilling to see the other side's needs and to compromise, and seems bent on getting every last ounce out of the deal by locking an entrepreneur into as many of the "burdensome clauses" as is possible, the entrepreneur might well want to withdraw.

Throughout the negotiations, entrepreneurs need to bear in mind that a successful negotiation is one in which both they and the investor believe that they have made a fair deal. The best deals are those in which neither party wins and neither loses, and such deals are possible to negotiate. Further, more important than exact ownership shares is a constructive working relationship between the new venture and the investor.

VALUATION

The starting point of such a negotiation usually will be an analytic consideration of the current and projected value of the venture.

Valuation is based on the earnings expected to be generated over a certain time period — which are reasoned hopes. Thus, especially for start-ups and early-stage ventures that have little or no record of sales or earnings, valuation is highly subjective and largely dependent on the valuation assigned to ventures of similar age, technology, and potential by the marketplace. Also a factor in determining valuation are the return objectives of the investor, which will include considerations of risk and so forth.

---

[2] Herb Cohen, *You Can Negotiate Anything* (New York: Bantam, 1980), p. 126. This paperback gives you very valuable practical examples and advice about negotiating.

[3] Mr. Taylor's firm, Testa, Thibeault and Hurwitz of Boston, represents about two dozen venture capital firms and a large number of early stage and emerging high-technology ventures, including Lotus Development.

[4] Cohen, *You Can Negotiate Anything,* p. 96.

[5] See for example, H. M. Hoffman and J. Blakey, "You Can Negotiate with Venture Capitalists," *Harvard Business Review,* March – April 1987, pp. 16–24.

If an entrepreneur has not yet done so, he or she would do well to determine how a professional investor would value the venture and be able to reconcile this with his or her desired valuation.

Investors determine the value of a company using various methods. The steps involved in one common method (called *residual value*) are as follows:

- *Determination of earnings potential.* — An investor will usually consider after-tax profits at a point in time. For example, suppose a company being considered is making a believable projection of after-tax profits in three years of $550,000:

$$\text{After-tax profits} = \$550,000$$

- *Determination of industry valuations.* — An investor then will consider how other companies in the industry are being valued. Assume, for example, that investors investing in the above company's industry value companies of similar age, etc., at a conservative six to eight times after-tax profits. Therefore, the value in *three years* of the company being considered would range between $3.3 million to $4.4 million, as follows:

$$\$550,000 \times 6 = \$3,300,000$$

and

$$\$550,000 \times 8 = \$4,400,000$$

- *Determination of future value.* — An investor will then discount this future value to the present, using its return criteria to determine the present value of the company. The following present value formula underlies this determination, where PV = present value, FV = future value, i = investment rate of return, and n = number of years the investment is held:

$$PV = \frac{FV}{(1 + i)^n}$$

For example, assume (1) the investor is considering a $1,500,000 investment for three years and (2) the investor feels that a 40 percent per year growth rate of the original investment would justify the level of risk in the venture. Future value would be determined as follows:

$$\$1,500,000 = \frac{FV}{(1 + 0.40)^3} = \frac{FV}{2.744}$$

$$FV = \$4,116,000$$

Thus, the $1,500,000 invested today, if it grew at 40 percent per year, would be worth approximately $4,116,000 at the end of three years. Note this was the investor's return objective.

- *Determination of amount of equity.* — For the investor to receive its return objective, it needs to receive for its investment a portion of the company. For example, if the venture is worth $3,300,000 to $4,400,000 at the end of year three, the $1,500,000 put into the venture by the investor today should buy from 34 percent to 45 percent of the company:

$$\frac{\$1,500,000}{\$4,400,000} = 34\%$$

or:

$$\frac{\$1,500,000}{\$3,300,000} = 45\%$$

Exhibit 15.1
Investor's Required Share of Ownership Given ROR Objectives

Price/ Earnings Ratio	Investor's Return Objective Percent/Year Compounded			
	30%	40%	50%	60%
10×	30%	43%	61%	84%
15×	20	29	41	56
20×	15	22	30	42
25×	12	17	24	34

© Jeffry A. Timmons, 1990

A number of critical variables influence valuation, and variation in any variable can change the valuation. The following critical variables can vary significantly:

■ Investor's required rate of return.
■ Amount invested.
■ Number of years the investment is held.
■ Actual after-tax profits in the year of the expected harvest.
■ Price-earnings multiple (called the *P-E ratio*) at the time the company is harvested.

For example, predicting the price-earnings ratio in advance is guesswork at best.

Exhibit 15.1 shows, for a given investment for three years of $1 million and a rate-of-return objective of 40 percent, the effect on ownership share of changes in the price-earnings ratio. Further, if other assumptions, such as the after-tax profits, the rate-of-return objective, or the holding period were to change, the ownership share would change accordingly.[6] One can quickly see how critical assumptions can be on any determination of how much of a company an entrepreneur has to give up.

THE DEAL

Amount of Investment

The amount and timing of investment is, of course, subject to negotiation. In the case of a venture in the early stages, financing usually will be staged. Initial financing will be provided to allow the company to achieve one or more specified objectives (e.g., development of a prototype or sales and profits of a certain amount). The investment will be made with the expectation that additional funds then will be available from current and new investors to take the company to the next stage of development. If a venture has achieved its objectives, this next round of financing can usually command a higher price than the earlier one.

Staged financing has advantages for the investor and the new venture. The investor minimizes its financial risk in an early-stage investment, and a new venture can wind up selling less equity than it would in a single, large early-stage financing.

Ownership Share

The actual percentage of equity purchased by an investor is usually the result of negotiation. First, while the starting point may be an analysis of the current and projected value of the venture and the return on investment objectives of the investor, ultimately the issue of venture valuation is a subjective one, because valuations depend as much as anything

---

[6] Students who are interested are encouraged to try their own assumptions to see the effect on ownership share.

Exhibit 15.2
Rates of Return Sought by Venture Capital Investors

Stage	Annual ROR %	Typical Expected Holding Period
Seed & start-up	50–100+%	~10+ years
First stage	40–60	5–10
Second stage	30–40	4–7
Expansion	20–30	3–5
Bridge & mezzanine	20–30	1–3
LBOs	30–50	3–5
Turnarounds	50+	3–5

© Jeffry A. Timmons, 1990

else on valuations of ventures of similar age, technology, and potential in the marketplace at that time. In addition, the type of investor and the track record of the management team are considerations.

Various investors will require different rates of return for investments in different stages of development and will expect holding periods of various lengths. For example, *Exhibit 15.2* summarizes, as ranges, the annual rates of return that venture capital investors seek on investments in firms by stage of development and how long they expect to hold these investments. Of course, these can be expected to vary regionally and from time to time as market conditions change, because these investments are in what are decidedly imperfect capital market niches to begin with.

Ranges of ownership given to venture capitalists in the late 1980s, for example, can be seen in the following:

- Twenty-five percent to 75 percent for investing all the required funds in the start-up stage.
- Ten percent to 40 percent in ventures beyond the start-up stage — the percentage depending on the amount invested and the maturity and track record of the venture.
- Ten percent to 30 percent in a seasoned venture, which is likely to have had earlier investments of significant size, which has demonstrated successful performance, and which needs additional funds to sustain its growth.
- Up to 70 percent to 80 percent of a leveraged buyout or a management buyout is likely to go to the outside money sources in stock, warrants, or other equity kickers.

Inevitably, entrepreneurs will receive investment offers that place lower valuations on their ventures than they think they merit. How far entrepreneurs need to compromise on valuations depends partially on the attractiveness of the venture and heavily on the availability of venture capital for similar ventures. During "raging bull markets," such as in 1983 and 1986 to 1987, for example, the percentage of equity taken by the investors was less.

Directly related to the rate of return investors look for in determining ownership shares is the value of the company when it is harvested. Since the price-earnings ratio of the company is viewed as driving the valuation of the company when it is harvested, investors also consider price-earnings ratios. For example, *Exhibit 15.3* shows for given return objectives of investors and a company's price-earnings ratio, the ownership share the investor will require.

It is important to recognize that the actual rates of return of venture capital funds organized during the 1980s have been low by historical standards. Single-digit returns

Exhibit 15.3
Effect of Changes in P-E Ratios on Ownership Share

P-E Ratio	PAT	FV	PV	Investor's Ownership Share
10	$1 million	$10 million	$3.61 million	27%
12	$1 million	$12 million	$4.33 million	23%

Assumptions:
$1 million investment.
ROR objective of 40 percent.
Three-year holding period.
© Jeffry A. Timmons, 1990

(i.e., less than 10 percent) and losses by a significant portion of the funds have been the pattern.[7]

Other factors that influence the negotiation of ownership share are an investor's or lender's view of the quality of a business opportunity, including the venture's upside potential, anticipated growth rate, industry and technology, and so forth; previous profit responsibility and/or above-average profit or harvest performance by the lead entrepreneur; the presence of a complete management team with in-depth and up-to-date knowledge of the target market and substantial previous experience in selling to, and getting orders from, the venture's prospective customers; a demonstrably strong position for the venture's product or service in terms of patent protection, know-how, exclusive market, lead time, and so forth; etc.

Ownership share also depends on conditions in capital markets, such as the market for IPOs (initial public offerings). A highly favorable IPO market tends to be accompanied by frenzied venture capital investing, such as occurred in mid-1983.

The incentive value of an entrepreneur's and team's equity position also can influence ownership share. Most investors, even those investing at very early stages, recognize the incentive value of the entrepreneurial team's equity position. Thus, most investors will leave the team with an attractive share of the venture or options or warrants to buy that share. What "attractive" means is negotiable; but few investors would dilute the ownership position of an entrepreneurial team below 20 percent to 25 percent of their venture at the start-up stage for fear of diluting their commitment to the venture. This includes considerations of whether substantial additional equity funding will be needed within the next 18 to 24 months, and whether such funding would dilute the entrepreneurial team's percentage ownership below the level at which they feel they have a real stake in the business.

Risk is also important. If a venture is a start-up with no record of sales or profits, the investor is likely to be taking the vast majority of the financial risk — unless the entrepreneurs are putting up some cash themselves. If a management team is investing capital at the same time as an investor, that money should buy stock on the same terms, and the purchased stock usually is added to that received by members of the team for their skill, and so on. Of course, as is reflected in the different return requirements for ventures at various stages of development shown in *Exhibit 15.2,* a successful track record of sales and profits demonstrates that a team can work effectively together and quantifies one of the key risks in the venture. Other risks, such as market acceptability of the product and the ability of the venture to sell the product at a profit, are also more quantifiable after some sales and profits are achieved.

---

[7] William D. Bygrave, "Rates of Return of Venture Capital Investing: A Study of 131 Funds," in *Frontiers of Entrepreneurship Research: 1988,* ed. B. Kirchhoff et al. (Babson Park, Mass.: Babson College), pp. 275–89.

Other Elements*

While a primary focus of negotiation will be on how much the entrepreneur's equity is worth and how much is to be purchased by the investor's investment, there are numerous other issues involving legal and financial control of the company and the rights and obligations of various investors and the entrepreneur that, in various situations, may be as important as valuation and ownership share. (And not the least of these other elements is the value beyond money—such as contacts and helpful expertise, additional financing when and if required, and patience and interest in the long-term development of the company—that a particular investor can bring to the venture.)

Some of the most critical aspects of a "deal" going beyond "just the money" include:

- Number, type, and mix of stock (and perhaps of stock and debt) and various features that may go with them, such as puts, and thus the investor's rate of return.
- The amounts and timing of take-downs and conversions, etc.
- Interest rate on debt or preferred shares.
- The number of seats and who actually will represent investors on the board of directors.
- Possible changes in the management team and in the composition of the board.
- Registration rights for investor's stock (in the case of a registered public offering).
- Right of first refusal granted to the investor on subsequent private or initial public stock offerings.
- Stock vesting schedule and agreements.
- Employment, noncompete, and proprietary rights agreements.
- The payment of legal, accounting, consulting, or other fees connected with putting the deal together.

Entrepreneurs may find some subtle but highly significant issues negotiated. If they, or their attorneys, are not familiar with these, they may be missed as "just more boilerplate" when, in fact, they have crucial future implications for the ownership, control, and financing of the business.

Some issues that can prove burdensome for entrepreneurs are:

- *Cosale provision.* This is a provision by which investors can tender their shares of their stock before an IPO. It protects the first-round investors but can cause conflicts with investors in later rounds and can inhibit an entrepreneur's ability to cash out.
- *Ratchet antidilution protection.* This enables the lead investors to get for free additional common stock if subsequent shares are ever sold at a price lower than that originally paid. This protection can create a "dog-in-the-manger syndrome," whereby first-round investors can prevent the company from raising additional necessary funds during a period of adversity for the company. While nice from the investors' perspective, it ignores the reality that, in distress situations, the last money in calls the shots on price and deal structure.
- *Washout financing.* This is a strategy of last resort, which wipes out all previously issued stock when existing preferred shareholders will not commit additional funds, thus diluting everyone.
- *Forced buyout.* Under this provision, if management does not find a buyer or cannot take the company public by a certain date, then the investors can proceed to find a buyer at terms they agree upon.
- *Demand registration rights.* Here, investors can demand at least one IPO in three to five years. In reality, such clauses are hard to invoke since the market for new public stock issues ultimately governs the timing of such events, rather than the terms of an agreement.
- *Piggyback registration rights.* These grant to the investors (and to the entrepreneur, if he or she insists) rights to sell stock at the IPO. Since the underwriters usually make this decision, the clause normally is not enforceable.

*© Jeffry A. Timmons, 1990

■ *Mandatory redemption of preferred stock.* Under mandatory redemption, the company is required to buy out investors if an IPO fails to occur. However, if a company is not attractive enough to go public, it will most likely not be attractive enough to raise other cash for a buyout.

■ *Key-person insurance.* This requires the company to obtain life insurance on key people. The named beneficiary of the insurance can be either the company or the preferred shareholders.

COMMON DEAL DOCUMENTS

Once the investor and the entrepreneur reach agreement on the amount of equity to be sold for the required investment and on the other terms of the investment, formal investment documents will be drafted. These agreements cover critical details of the relationship between the entrepreneur, investors, and key employees.

While no document can make a good deal out of a bad one, the opposite can be true if agreements are not properly drawn. An entrepreneur needs to make sure that the attorney he or she consults is experienced in preparing investment documents. Since these documents are complex, it is unlikely that the lawyer who drew up a venture's incorporation papers is best suited to counsel an entrepreneur on the venture's investment documents. See Appendix III for a discussion of the legal process of investment.

Formal investment documents normally will include:

■ Terms sheet.
■ Purchase agreement or investment agreement.
■ Stock restriction agreements.
■ Employee stock purchase or option agreements.
■ Employee confidentiality and proprietary rights agreements.
■ Escrow agreement for the invested funds.
■ Officers' compliance certificate.
■ Legal audit opinions.

When completed and ready for execution for all parties, the number of documents may be several inches thick and can take an hour for all parties around a table to actually sign. *A deal is not closed until the formal investment agreement is signed by both parties.*

Terms Sheet

The terms sheet defines the "handshake agreement" that has been reached. It specifies the terms agreed upon and subsequently will be used to prepare a formal investment agreement. See Appendix IV for a sample terms sheet.

Purchase or Investment Agreement

The purchase or investment agreement defines the terms and conditions upon which an investor will invest in a venture.

If prepared properly, an investment agreement will accomplish the following objectives:

■ Define the specific terms of the transaction (i.e., amount, type, and terms of the investment).
■ Provide terms that motivate and retain the entrepreneurial team if they perform as planned.

- Provide "downside protection" to investors by giving them control of the venture if it is in danger of failing.
- Provide and protect opportunities for the investor to realize capital gains and liquidity.

To meet these objectives, the investment agreement needs to anticipate and consider a number of future contingent events. The resultant document can be lengthy and contain issues that may not have been explicitly discussed during negotiations.

To accomplish the above objectives, there are normally seven basic categories of terms, conditions, and representations in an investment agreement:

- *Description of the investment.* This part of the agreement defines the basic terms of the investment, including naming the parties to the agreement; the kind, amount, and price of securities to be issued; and the description of the collateral, guarantees, or subordination associated with debt. If the investment involves warrants for stock or debt conversion privileges, the terms (such as time limits, price, and the like) will be completely described.
- *Preconditions to closing.* Preconditions are things the venture must do, or supplementary data and agreements it must submit to the investor, before the investment can be closed. Examples of such preconditions are the execution of employment contracts or the venture's securing a line of credit.
- *Representations and warranties.* Representations and warranties are legally binding statements made by the venture's officers that describe its condition on or before the closing date. For example, the venture will warrant that it is a duly organized corporation in good standing with assets as represented on financial statements. Although most warranties and representations are made by the venture, there are some that must be made by the investor. For example, if the securities are sold via a private placement, the investor will warrant that the stock is being acquired solely for investment and not with a view to resale or distribution.
- *Affirmative covenants.* These define what the venture must do to run its business in a manner that is acceptable to the investor. Requirements to have investors on the venture's board of directors are examples of affirmative covenants.
- *Negative covenants.* These define what the venture must not do, or must not do without the prior approval of the investor. Restrictions on loans and management salaries are typical negative covenants.
- *Conditions of default.* These describe those events that constitute a breach of the investment agreement if not corrected within a specified time. One condition of default is a failure to comply with the affirmative or negative covenants.
- *Remedies.* Remedies are the actions that an investor may take in the event a condition of default has occurred. Remedies can include acceleration of debt repayment, forfeiture of escrowed stock, or temporary voting rights to control the company's board of directors.

See Appendix V for an outline of an investment agreement.

Other Agreements

In addition to executing the investment agreement, the closing of a deal generally involves the execution of a number of ancillary agreements. These can include noncompete agreements, employee stock purchase or option agreements,[8] employee confidentiality and

---

[8] Stock vesting agreements define how much of an entrepreneur's stock is subject to repurchase at cost if the entrepreneur leaves the employ of the venture for any reason. Generally, an entrepreneur's stock in an early-stage venture will not be fully vested (subject to repurchase) until three to five years after the closing of an investment.

proprietary rights agreements, legal audit opinions, and so forth. As discussed above, agreements giving an investor preemptive rights are so used that he or she can maintain his or her percentage ownership of the venture. Stock vesting agreements define how much of an entrepreneur's stock is subject to repurchase at what cost if the entrepreneur leaves the employ of the venture for any reason. Appendix VI contains a sample vesting agreement.

COMMON INVESTMENT INSTRUMENTS

There are three investment instruments generally used by investors, such as venture capitalists:

- *Common stock.* Holders of common stock have the right to vote on such issues as the composition of the board of directors. They also have the right to the earnings and assets of the firm only after all other expenses, debt, and obligations have been met. Thus, in most venture situations, the investor with common stock has little chance to recoup any of the investment if the business moves sideways or fails. On the positive side, the purchase of common stock gives the investor the most equity for the invested dollar and a large potential for capital gain.
- *Convertible preferred stock.* Convertible preferred stock is convertible into a number of common stock shares at the option of the investor. Generally, the number of common shares received per share of preferred stock is adjusted upward if stock is subsequently sold at a lower per-share price than that of the preferred stock. This instrument can include gaining voting control over the majority of common shares if performance expectations are not met. The preferred shareholders have a preference over common stockholders, but not debtors, in the event of liquidation of the company. Sometimes, 5 to 10 years after the investment date, the company may be required to redeem at an appreciated value shares of preferred that have not been converted. Currently, convertible preferred stock is the favored form of investment for start-ups and early-stage deals.
- *Subordinated debt with conversion privileges or warrants.* Subordinated debt provides an investor with the advantages of a debt instrument without retricting a venture's ability to obtain senior debt from banks. An investor generally will issue subordinated debt with a stock-convertible feature or warrants to purchase stock.[9] Either of these arrangements provides the venture capital investor with a future option to obtain common stock and realize the greater-than-normal return that accrues to equity owners in a successful company. At the same time, the investor can receive interest payments on the debt and has a higher call than common or preferred stock on the assets of a company in the event of liquidation. Subordinated debt usually will be considered as equity by lenders as long as it does not dominate the balance sheet. Subordinated debt also gives an investor greater protection than that provided to common or preferred stockholders if things do not go well. One way investors obtain this protection is through an accelerated payment clause in the indenture (debt) agreement that makes the full amount of the loan payable within a specified time of a venture's failure to comply with certain agreed-upon conditions. These conditions might include the venture's agreeing to maintain minimum

---

[9] The difference between convertible subordinated debt and subordinated debt with warrants should be noted. If the warrants are nondetachable, they are equivalent to a conversion feature, and the stock must be purchased before the debt has been repaid. However, if the warrants are detachable, then the stock purchase can be made before or after the debt has been repaid, providing that the exercise time of the warrants has not run out.

working capital or agreeing not to merge or sell certain assets. Because a young venture is not likely to be able to retire the debt, the investor has the power to bankrupt the venture if it does not change its operations to meet the terms of the debt agreement. However, investors usually do not want to run ventures in which they invest and resort to this only to protect their investments.

Whenever possible, stock that is issued should be so-called 1244 stock. This stock has a significant tax advantage to investors. Losses from investing in 1244 stock of up to $25,000 (or $50,000 in the case of a joint tax return) can be deducted from ordinary income in any one year, while gains are taxed at the capital gains rate.

To be able to issue 1244 stock, a company must have less than $500,000 of capital and paid-in surplus prior to the issue and no more than $1 million in equity after the 1244 offering. Further, a company must have only one class of stock and receive more than one half its income from other sources than rents and royalties. A 1244 stock-issue plan is adopted by vote of the directors of a company.

SAND TRAPS*

Strategic Circumference

Each fund-raising strategy sets in motion some actions and commitments by management that will eventually *scribe a strategic circumference* around the company in terms of its current and future financing choices. These future choices will permit varying degrees of freedom as a result of the previous actions. Those who fail to think through the consequences of a fund-raising strategy and the effect on their degrees of freedom fall into this trap.

While it is impossible to avoid strategic circumference completely, and while in some cases scribing a strategic circumference is clearly intentional, others may be unintended and, unfortunately, unexpected. For example, a company that plans to remain private or plans to maintain a 1.5 to 1.0 debt-to-equity ratio has intentionally created a strategic circumference.

Legal Circumference

Many have an aversion to becoming involved in the minutia of the legal or accounting details. Many believe that, since they pay sizeable professional fees, their advisors should and will pay attention to the details.

Legal documentation spells out the terms, conditions, responsibilities, and rights of the parties to a transaction. Since different sources have different ways of structuring deals, and since these legal and contractual details come at the *end* of the fund-raising process, an entrepreneur may find himself or herself at a point of no return facing some very onerous conditions and covenants that are not only very difficult to live with but also create tight limitations and constraints—legal circumference—on future choices that are potentially disastrous. Entrepreneurs cannot rely on attorneys and advisors to protect them in this vital matter.

To avoid this trap, entrepreneurs need to have as a fundamental precept that the "devil is in the details." It is very risky for an entrepreneur *not* to read carefully final documents and very risky to use a lawyer who is *not* experienced and competent. It also is helpful to keep a few options alive and to conserve cash. This also can keep the other side of the table more conciliatory and flexible.

*© Jeffry A. Timmons, 1990

Attraction to Status and Size

It seems there is a cultural attraction to higher status and larger size, even when it comes to raising capital. Simply targeting the largest or the most well-known or prestigious firms is a trap entrepreneurs often fall in.

These are often the most visible because of their size and investing activity and because they have been around a longer time. Yet, as the venture capital industry has become more heterogeneous and for other reasons, such firms may or may not be a good fit.

Take, for example, an entrepreneur with a patented, innovative device that was ready for use by manufacturers of semiconductors. He was running out of cash from an earlier round of venture capital investment and needed more money for his device to be placed in test sites and then, presumably, into production. Although lab tests had been successful, his prior backers would not invest further, since he was nearly two years behind the schedule in his business plan. For a year, he concentrated his efforts on many of the largest and most well-known firms and celebrities in the venture capital business, but to no avail. With the help of outside advice, he then decided to pursue an alternative fund-raising strategy. First, he listed those firms that were mostly likely prospects as customers for the device. Next, he sought to identify investors who already had investments in this potential customer base, because it was thought that these would be the most likely potential backers, since they would be the most informed about his technology, its potential value-added properties, and any potential competitive advantages the company could achieve. Less than a dozen venture capital firms were identified (from among a pool of over 700), and none had been contacted previously by this entrepreneur. In fact, many were virtually unknown to him, even though they were very active investors in the industry. In less than three months, offers were on the table from three of them and the financing was closed.

It is best to avoid this trap by looking for financial backers, whether debt or equity, who have intimate knowledge and first hand experience with the technology, marketplace, and networks of expertise and intelligence in the competitive arena and to focus on the relevant know-how that would characterize a good match.

Unknown Territory

Venturing into unknown territory is another problem. Entrepreneurs need to know the terrain in sufficient detail, particularly the requirements of and alternatives from various equity sources. If they do not, they may make critical strategic blunders and waste time.

For example, a venture that is not a "mainstream venture capital deal" may be overvalued and directed to investors who are not a realistic match, rather than being realistically valued and directed to small and more specialized funds, private investors, or potential strategic partners. The example is a real one. The founders went through nearly $100,000 of their own funds, strained their relationship to the limit, and nearly had to abandon the project.

Another illustration of a fund-raising strategy that was ill conceived and, effectively, a lottery—rather than a well thought-out focused search—is a company in the fiberoptics industry called Opti-Com.[10] Opti-Com was a spin-off as a start-up from a well-known public company in the industry. The management team was entirely credible but was not considered superstars. The business plan suggested the company could achieve the magical $50 million in sales in five years, which the entrepreneurs were told by an outside advisor was the minimum size that venture capital investors would consider. The plan proposed to raise $750,000 for about 10 percent of the common stock of the company. Realistically, since the firm was a custom supplier for special applications, rather than a provider of a new

---

[10] This is a fictional name for an actual company.

technology advance with a significant proprietary advantage, a sales estimate of $10 million to $15 million in five years would have been more plausible. The same advisor urged that their business plan be submitted to 16 blue-ribbon mainstream venture capital firms in the Boston area. Four months later they had received 16 rejections. The entrepreneurs then were told to "go see the same quality venture capital firms in New York." A year later, the founders were nearly out of money and had been unsuccessful in their search for capital. When redirected away from mainstream venture capitalists to a more suitable source, a small fund specifically created in Massachusetts—to provide risk capital for emerging firms that might not be robust enough to attract conventional venture capital but would be a welcome addition to the economic renewal of the state—the fit was right. Opti-Com raised the necessary capital, but at a valuation much more in line with the market for start-up deals.

Opportunity Cost

The lure of money often leads to a most common trap—the opportunity cost trap.

After all, an entrepreneur's optimism leads him or her to the conclusion that, with good people and products (or services), there has to be a lot of money out there with "our name on it!" In the process, entrepreneurs tend to underestimate grossly the real costs of getting the cash in the bank. Further, and perhaps the least appreciated aspect in raising capital, entrepreneurs also underestimate the real time, effort, and creative energy required. In both these cases, there are opportunity costs in expending these resources in a particular direction when both the clock and the calendar are moving.

For a start-up company, for instance, founders can devote nearly all of their available time for months seeking out investors and telling their story. It may take six months or more to get a "yes" and up to a year for a "no." In the meantime, a considerable amount of cash and human capital has been flowing out, rather than in, and this cash and capital might have been better spent elsewhere.

One such start-up began its search for venture capital in 1984. A year later the founders had exhausted $100,000 of their own seed money and had quit their jobs to devote full time to the effort. Yet, they were unsuccessful after approaching over 35 sources of capital. The opportunity costs are clear.

There are opportunity costs, too, in existing emerging companies. In terms of human capital, it is common for top management to devote as much as half of its time trying to raise a major amount of outside capital. Again, this requires a tremendous amount of emotional and physical energy as well, of which there is a finite amount to devote to the daily operating demands of the enterprise. The effect on near-term performance is invariably negative. In addition, if expectations of a successful fund-raising effort are followed by a failure to raise the money, morale can deteriorate and key people can be lost.

There are also significant opportunity costs incurred in foregone business and market opportunities that could have been pursued. Take, for example, the start-up firm just noted. When asked what level of sales the company would have achieved in this past year had it spent the $100,000 of the founders' own seed money on generating customers and business, the founder answered without hesitation, "We'd be at $1 million sales by now, and would probably be making a small profit."

Underestimation of Other Costs

Entrepreneurs tend to underestimate the out-of-pocket costs associated both with raising the money and living with it. For instance, there are incremental costs after a firm becomes a public company. The Securities and Exchange Commission requires regular audited financial statements and various reports; there are outside directors' fees and liability insurance premiums; there are legal fees associated with more extensive reporting requirements; and so on. These can add up quickly, often to $100,000 or more annually.

Another "cost" that can be easily overlooked is of the disclosure that may be necessary to convince a financial backer to part with his or her money. An entrepreneur may have to reveal much more about the company and his or her personal finances than he or she ever imagined. Thus, company weaknesses, ownership and compensation arrangements, personal and corporate financial statements, marketing plans and competitive strategies, and so forth may need to be revealed to people whom the entrepreneur does not really know and trust and with whom he or she may eventually not do business. In addition, the ability to control access to the information is lost.

Greed

The entrepreneur—especially one who is out of cash, or nearly so—may find the money irresistible. One of the most exhilarating experiences for an entrepreneur is the prospect of raising that first major slug of outside capital, or obtaining that substantial bank line needed for expansion. If the fundamentals of the company are sound, however, then there is money out there.

Being Too Anxious

Usually, after months of hard work finding the right source and negotiating the deal, another trap awaits the hungry but unwary entrepreneur. And, all too often, the temptation is overwhelming. It is the trap of believing the deal is done and terminating discussions with others too soon. Entrepreneurs fall into this trap because they want to believe the deal is done with a handshake (or perhaps with an accompanying letter of intent or an executed terms sheet).

The following is a good illustration of a masterful handling of such a situation. An entrepreneur and a key vice president of a company with $30 million sales had been negotiating with several venture capitalists, three major strategic partners, and a mezzanine source for nearly six months. The company was down to 60 days' worth of cash, and the mezzanine investors knew it. The offer from the mezzanine investors of $10 million was a take-it-or-leave-it proposition. The vice president, in summarizing the company's relative bargaining position, said, "It was the only alternative we had left; everything else had come to rest by late last month; and the negotiations with (the three major companies) had not reached serious stages. We felt like they were asking too much, but we needed the money." Yet the two had managed to keep this weakness from being apparent to the mezzanine investors. Each time negotiations had been scheduled, the entrepreneur had made sure he also had scheduled a meeting with one of the other larger companies for later that afternoon (a good two-hour plane ride away). In effect, he was able to create the illusion that these discussions with other investors were far more serious than they actually were. The deal was closed on terms agreeable to both. The company then went public in six months and is highly successful today.

Impatience

Yet another trap is being impatient when an investor does not understand quickly and because each deal has velocity and momentum.

Take, as an example, the effort of one group to acquire a firm in the cellular car phone business for whom they were employed. As the management team, they became the first to know in May that the company was going to be sold by its owners. By early July, the investment bankers representing the sellers were expected to have the offering memorandum ready for the open market. To attempt to buy the company privately would necessitate the management team raising commitments for about $150 million in three to four weeks, hardly enough time to put together even a crude business plan let alone raise such a substantial sum. The train was moving at 140 miles per hour and gaining speed each day. The founders identified five top-notch and interested venture capital and leveraged buy-out firms and sat down with representatives of each to walk through the summary of the business plan and the proposed financing. One excellent firm sent an otherwise very experienced and capable partner. One of his main questions about how the company prevented its phones from being stolen revealed that he knew little about the business. Car phones are not stolen like CB radios, because they cannot be used without an authorized installation and activation of service. The group looked elsewhere.

Had the group fallen into this trap of being impatient because the train was moving quickly, it would have exposed itself to risk. The investor had a serious lack of elementary knowledge of the industry and the business and had not done his homework in advance. By the time this investor became knowledgeable about the business, it would be too late.

Take-the-Money-and-Run Myopia

A final trap in raising money for a company is a take-the-money-and-run myopia that invariably prevents an entrepreneur from evaluating one of the most critical longer-term issues — that is, to what extent can the investor add value to the company beyond the money? An entrepreneur falls into this trap who does not get a clear sense that his or her prospective financial partner possesses the relevant experience and know-how in the market and industry area, the contacts he or she needs but does not have, the savvy and the reputation that adds to his or her association with the investor, and yet takes the money.

As has been said before, the successful development of a company can be critically impacted by the interaction of the management team and the financial partners. If an effective relationship can be established, the value-added synergy can be a powerful stimulant for success. Many founders overlook the high value-added contributions that some investors are accustomed to making and erroneously opt for a "better deal."

```
┌─────────────────────────────────────────────────────────┐  ╲
│  ┌───────────────────────────────────────────────────┐  │   ╲
│  │                                                   │  │    ╲
│  │   Obtaining Debt Capital                          │  │  16  ╲
│  │                                                   │  │    ╱
│  │                                                   │  │   ╱
│  └───────────────────────────────────────────────────┘  │  ╱
└─────────────────────────────────────────────────────────┘
```

Obtaining Debt Capital   16

Neither a Lender, nor a Borrower Be.

Inscribed in granite on
Garrison Keillor's
Bank of Lake Wobegon, Minnesota
From the Prairie Home Companion

RESULTS EXPECTED

Upon completion of the chapter, you will have:

1. Discussed issues involved in borrowing debt capital, including timing, what lenders can add to a venture, how lenders think about making loans and how they approach risk coverage, and what is "bankable."
2. Identified how to find and contact principal sources of debt capital.
3. Examined the evaluation process involved in obtaining such debt capital.
4. Studied how to negotiate a loan agreement.
5. Identified other sources of capital.
6. Analyzed a case involving bank financing of the purchase of a company, Michigan Lighting, Inc.

BORROWING DEBT CAPITAL

Timing

As is the case with the search for equity capital and equity investors, it is important not to wait until there is a dire need for funds to try to establish a lending relationship. When an entrepreneur faces a near-term financial crisis, the venture's financial statements are at their worst, and lenders have good cause to wonder about his or her financial and planning skills.

The Ideal Lender

In addition, as was discussed in Chapter 10, a lender can bring more to a venture than just money. In fact, choosing a lender is critically important. A good relationship with a banker or other lender sometimes can mean the difference between the life and death of a business during difficult times. For example, there have been cases where, other things being equal, one bank has called its loans to a struggling business, causing its demise, and another bank has stayed with its loans and helped a business to survive and prosper.

Exhibit 16.1
What Is "Bankable"?

Security	Credit Capacity
Accounts receivable	70–80% of < 90 days. 60–80% of invoice for factoring.
Inventory	40–60%, depending on obsolescence risk.
Equipment	70–80% of market value (less if specialized).
Chattel mortgage	100–150%+ of auction appraisal value.
Conditional sales contract	60–70%+ of purchase price.
Plant improvement loan	60–80% of appraised value or cost.

© Jeffry A. Timmons, 1990

Understanding a Lender's Perspective

With lenders, three critical motivations are pervasive. First, lenders are motivated to *earn money,* and lenders have income goals associated with lending decisions. What might come as a surprise is how narrow the profit margins are for banks. Banks typically earn a 0.5 percent to 1.0 percent return on total assets, and a return of 1.5 percent would be excellent. Thus, a bank would earn $500,000 to $1 million on a $100 million loan, or $5,000 to $10,000 on a $1 million loan. Further, as with other lenders, approximately *half* of a bank's income comes from points and origination fees (i.e., fees for agreeing to make the loan in the first place) and the other half from the interest on the loan.

The second motivation is unabashed *fear,* fear of the bad loan. Since profit margins are so low, bad loans have to be made up for by a lot of good loans. For example, for a bank, one bad loan of $1 million would typically require a good loan of $100 million to recover the loss.

The first two motivations therefore lead rapidly to the third—*risk avoidance.* Given the punishing consequences to the profitability of a loan portfolio of bad loans, lenders, and particularly bankers, take great care to avoid such risks of loss.

Given these realities, it may be easier to appreciate why banks generally do not make loans to start-up companies that have no equity and little or no collateral.

What Is "Bankable"?

An enduring question from entrepreneurs is the question of what is "bankable"—that is, the question of how much money can be borrowed based on specifics in a firm's balance sheet. *Exhibit 16.1* summarizes general lending criteria for certain security. While these criteria may vary from region to region and from bank to bank, they do provide a good picture of what is commonly used. In addition, apprehension about the future of the economy may cause a tightening of these criteria.

TRADITIONAL DEBT SOURCES

Who They Are

Obtaining debt capital most often involves dealing with banks and other institutional lenders.

Exhibit 16.2 summarizes the leading sources of debt by type of business financed and by term of financing for new and existing firms.[1] A detailed description of each type of

---

[1] *Exhibit 16.2* is an updated and revised chart originally prepared by D. E. Gumpert and J. A. Timmons. See D. E. Gumpert and J. A. Timmons, *The Encyclopedia of Small Business Resources* (New York, N.Y.: Harper & Row, 1982), p. 160.

Exhibit 16.2
General Lending Criteria by Type of Business and Term of Financing

Source	Type of Business Financed		Term of Financing		
	Start-up	Existing	Short	Medium	Long
Trade credit	Yes	Yes	Yes	Yes	Possible
Commercial banks	Occasionally, with strong equity	Yes	Most frequently	Some	Rare
Finance companies	Rare (if assets are available)	Yes	Most frequently	Yes (asset based)	Rare (depends on asset)
Factors	Rare	Yes	Most frequently	Rare	No
Leasing companies	Difficult except for start-ups with VC	Yes	No	Most frequently	Some
Mutual savings banks, S&Ls	Rare	Real estate and other asset-based	No	No	Real estate and other asset-based
Insurance co.	Rare, except along-side venture capital	Yes	Rare	More frequent	Yes

© Jeffry A. Timmons, 1990

financing and their advantages and disadvantages could well be the subject of a separate book.[2] Suffice it to say that advantages and disadvantages of each are basically determined by such obvious dimensions as the interest rate or cost of capital; key terms, conditions, and covenants; and fit with the entrepreneur's situation and the company's needs at the time. The above, in turn, depend on the firm's relative bargaining position and the competitiveness among the alternatives.

Finding a Lender

Because of the importance of a banking or other lending relationship, an entrepreneur needs to "shop around" before making a choice.

Finding a lender is best accomplished through references from other entrepreneurs, lawyers, accountants, and others. For example, professional investors will refer ventures in their portfolios to the lenders for debt financing. A complete listing of banks can be found, arranged by state, in the *American Bank Directory* published by McFadden Business Publications. In centers of high-technology and venture capital activity, the main offices of major banks will have one or more lending officers who specialize in making loans to early-stage high-tech ventures. Through much experience, such bankers have come to understand the market and operating idiosyncrasies, problems, and opportunities of such ventures. (In addition, they generally have close ties to venture capital firms and will refer entrepreneurs to such firms for possible equity financing.)

Choosing the Lender

Selection of a lender needs to be based on more than just loan interest rates. Just how particular an entrepreneur can be in choosing a lender will depend upon the particular situation and the market. But with the increase in competition in recent years, there has been an increased interest among banks in attracting entrepreneurial companies as customers, and far more options exist now for entrepreneurs.

---

[2] A source on obtaining financing from the SBA is Richard Rubin and Philip Goldberg, *The Small Business Guide to Borrowing Money* (New York: McGraw-Hill, 1982), p. 115.

Other factors that are especially important to an entrepreneur in selecting a lender are the following:[3]

- *Size.* The lender selected needs to be big enough to service a venture's foreseeable needs but not so large as to be relatively indifferent to its business.
- *Desire and capacity.* Lenders differ greatly in both the desire and capacity to work with small firms. Some lenders have people who specialize in small businesses and regard new and early-stage ventures as the seeds of very large future accounts. Other lenders see loans to such new ventures merely as bad risks.
- *Approach to problems.* Lenders differ also on how they handle problems. Some lenders tend to call or reduce loans to small businesses that have problems, and, when they have less capital to lend, some banks cut back on small business loans and favor older, more solid customers. Some are imaginative, creative, and helpful when a venture has a problem. For example, to quote one author, one way to select a bank is to ask, "Do they [the bank] just look at your balance sheet and faint or do they try to suggest constructive financial alternatives?"[4]
- *Industry experience.* Lenders differ in their experience in particular industries, and especially with young developing companies in an industry. Lenders who have had such experience will be quicker to lend, will be more tolerant of problems, and will be able to help in exploiting the opportunities.

Given that a deal with a debt source is at or above an acceptable threshold, the person a firm will be dealing with is more critical than the institution, the amount, or the terms. In other words, a firm will be better off seeking the right banker or other provider of capital than the right bank or institution. Unfortunately, these often are not the same.

In finding the right lender several important questions need to be addressed:[5]

- *Experience.* Lenders, as do their lending institutions, differ in their experience with a specific industry, with competitors in the industry, and with new ventures.
- *Authority.* Different lenders may have different authority to make loans of a given size. The lending authority of the lender needs to exceed the company's needs now and in the future if things are to work smoothly.
- *Champion.* Whether the lender can be an advocate (i.e., whether he or she can explain the company's business, technology, or other unique aspects competently to other loan officers) is important.
- *Reputation.* Different lenders have different reputations. A reputation for being reasonable, creative, and willing to take sound risks is important and whether the lender's track record indicates that he or she can be counted on needs to be considered.
- *Value.* What the lender brings to the table besides the money that will add value to the business is important.
- *Personal chemistry.* The chemistry is critical.

Consulting with accountants, attorneys, and other entrepreneurs who have had dealings with lenders being considered can be helpful in determining which lenders are good prospects. Meetings with lenders at several lending institutions also can indicate their attitudes and approaches to their business borrowers. For example, who attends a meeting

---

[3] These factors for selecting banks were described by Gordon Baty and James Stancill. They apply equally well to other lenders. See G. B. Baty, *Entrepreneurship, Playing to Win* (Reston, Va.: Reston Publishing, 1974), p. 157; and J. M. Stancill, "Getting the Most from Your Banking Relationship," *Harvard Business Review,* March–April 1980.

[4] Baty, *Entrepreneurship: Playing to Win,* p. 158.

[5] Jeffry A. Timmons, *Planning and Financing a New Business* (Acton, Mass.: Brick House Publishing, 1989), Chap. 15.

and for how long and with how many interruptions can be a useful measure of a lender's interest in such an account. Finally, contacting references from a lender's base of borrowers can be particularly useful.

Contacting a Lender

A referral from a venture capital firm or from a businessperson who knows the lender will be very helpful.

The initial contact with a lender will likely be by telephone. The entrepreneur needs to be prepared to describe quickly the nature, age, and prospects of the venture; the amount of equity financing and who provided it; the prior financial performance of the business; the experience and background of the entrepreneur and team members; and the sort of bank financing desired.

Meetings and Submitting Business Plans

If the banker agrees to a meeting, he or she may well request that a business plan and financial statements be sent prior to any further contact. For a start-up, a well-prepared business plan is vital. For an existing business, the lender will want much of the information that is in a business plan, if not a plan itself.

One of the best ways for an entrepreneur to answer the questions bankers have is by providing the banker with a well-prepared business plan containing projections of cash flows and profits (and losses) and balance sheets that demonstrate the need for a loan and how it can be repaid. Lenders will also most likely want from existing businesses such items as financial statements from prior years prepared or audited by a certified public accountant, a list of aged receivables and payables, the turnover of inventory, and key customers and creditors. The lender also will want to know that all taxes are paid. Finally, he or she will need to know details of fixed assets and any liens on receivables, inventory, or fixed assets.

Obtaining debt is a sales job, a fact many borrowers tend to forget. Entrepreneurs with early-stage ventures need to sell themselves, as well as the viability and potential of their businesses, to bankers. Entrepreneurs need to convey an air of self-confidence and an optimistic but realistic views of their ventures' prospects. It is advantageous that they appear on top of things and that required data are provided promptly and in a form that can be readily understood. The better the material entrepreneurs can supply to demonstrate their business's credibility, the easier and faster it will be for them to obtain a positive lending decision. Further, a well-prepared business plan (and a reasonable amount of equity financing) can pique a lender's interest—even for a start-up or a very young venture, for example.

The first meeting with a lender will likely be at the venture's place of business, and the lender will use this meeting to evaluate the integrity and business acumen of those who will ultimately be responsible for the repayment of the loan. The lender will be interested in meeting the management team, in seeing how different members relate to the lead entrepreneur, in getting a sense of what sorts of financial controls and reporting are used, and in seeing how well things seem to run. He or she also may want to meet one or more of the venture's equity investors.

There are four key questions that a banker or other lender will want answered satisfactorily:

- What is the venture going to do with the money?
- How much does it need?
- When and how will the money be paid back?
- When does it need the money?

Exhibit 16.3
Summary Loan Proposal

Date of Request:	May 13, 1987	
Borrower:	Hanson Ski Products	
Amount:	$4,200,000	
Use of Proceeds:	For increased A/R: up to	$1,600,000
	For increased inventory: up to	824,000
	For increased WIP: up to	525,000
	For new marketing: up to	255,000
	For ski show specials	105,000
	For contingencies	50,000
	For officer loans due	841,000
	Total	$4,200,000

Type of Loan:	Seasonal revolving line of credit
Closing Date:	June 15, 1987
Term:	One year
Rate:	Prime + 1, no compensating balances, no points or origination fees
Take Down:	$ 500,000 at closing
	$1,500,000 on Aug. 1, 1987
	$1,500,000 on Oct. 1, 1987
	$ 700,000 on Nov. 1, 1987
Collateral:	70% of A/Rs
	50% of inventory
Guarantees:	None
Repayment Schedule:	$4,200,000 or balance on anniversary of note
Source of Funds for Repayment:	(a) Excess cash from operations (see cash flow)
	(b) Renewal and increase of line if growth is profitable
	(c) Conversion to three year note
Contingency Source:	(a) Sale & leaseback of equipment
	(b) Officer's loans

© Jeffry A. Timmons, 1990

In other words, the lender will want to know if the use to which the money will be put makes business sense. He or she will require justification of the amount requested and a description of how the debt fits into an overall plan for financing and developing the business. Further, an entrepreneur will be expected to show that the amount requested has enough "cushion" to allow for unexpected developments. The lender will want to know if some or all of the money required should be equity capital, rather than debt. For new and young businesses, lenders do not like to see total debt to equity ratios greater than one.

When and how the loan will be paid back is an important question. For this reason, short-term loans, such as for seasonal inventory buildup or for financing receivables, are preferred by lenders and easier to obtain than term loans, especially for early-stage businesses. In this regard, also, since presumably a venture will be borrowing money to finance an activity that will throw off enough cash to repay the loan, the lender will be interested in the risks involved in the activity and how these will be dealt with and in contingency plans. For example, a banker may be interested if there is a secondary source of repayment (e.g., a guarantor of means).

If the loan is needed "tomorrow," lenders will be skeptical. This type of a request indicates poor planning by a poor manager. If on the other hand the money is needed next month or the month after, the lender will have time to investigate and process the loan application (and an ability to plan ahead is demonstrated).

Answers to the above questions will also determine the type of loan (e.g., line of credit or a term loan).

Exhibit 16.3 shows an example of a summary loan proposal for a company with current sales of $11 million that is seeking an extension on its line of credit of $4.2 million. A one-page document such as the one shown helps to pull together information and focus the lender's attention on the key features of the loan. Notice how, in the exhibit, the "sources for repayment" and "contingency source" address the motivations and fears noted above. Actual examples of commercial and SBA loan applications and specific guidelines for obtaining bank loans are given in *The Encyclopedia of Small Business Resources.*[6]

Reference and Other Checks

Data for evaluation will come from meetings with the entrepreneur and his or her management team and conversations with customers and creditors of the business. Reference checks also will be made with former employers and business associates of the entrepreneur and his or her team. The banker will check references suggested by the entrepreneur and some which he or she chooses.

Special attention will be paid to past and projected financial statements and to such financial ratios as current assets to current liabilities; gross margins and net worth to debt; and accounts receivable and payable periods, inventory turns, and net profit to sales. These financial statements and financial ratios will be compared to financial statements and to average ratios for competitive firms to see how the potential borrower measures up as well as to uncover potential problems.

The Evaluation Process

As has been noted, some lenders will make loans to start-ups and early-stage ventures, and other will not. Lenders that do usually make these loans (1) to previously successful entrepreneurs or (2) to start-ups that have a significant infusion of initial equity from an investor with whom they have had prior relationships and whose judgment they trust or from its founder (i.e., from his or her personal net worth or personal guarantee). For example, banks lend almost exclusively to existing businesses with identifiable cash flows and collateral. And, as was shown in *Exhibit 16.1,* it is difficult to find sources of debt financing for more than one year.

And again, the industry and market characteristics, venture age and stage of development, venture upside potential, anticipated growth rate, amount of capital required, founder's goals, and perceived risk are central to the evaluation process. With debt, the health of the firm in terms of cash flow, debt coverage, and collateral is particularly important.

Conventional banking wisdom is that, regardless of the size and nature of a business, lending decisions are based on what are called the *Five Cs of Credit:*

- *Character.* Above all else, the lender will loan money only to people he or she trusts and who impress him or her as men or women of integrity. More specifically, character means that, when the borrower promises to repay a loan, he or she means it. Further, the borrower has the ability and will do everything he or she can to conserve business assets and repay the loan.
- *Capacity.* This "C" addresses whether the borrower has the capacity to repay the loan (i.e., whether management has the capacity to use the loan and create the business growth it projects). These are the capacity issues.
- *Capital.* A lender will want to see an adequate amount of equity capital from insiders or outsiders or both, who invested in the business. First, cash investments by the lead entrepreneur or other founders are evidence of their faith in the future of the business. Second, a lender will look for sufficient equity capital (e.g., that giving a debt-to-equity

---

[6] Gumpert and Timmons, 1982.

ratio of no more than one to two) so the lender can safely retain his or her position. Without sufficient equity capital, the lender can essentially become a very unwilling shareholder, a position he or she does not want to be in.

- *Conditions.* According to experts and old credit hands, conditions "are what change for the worse after you extend the credit."[7] Primarily, consideration of conditions involves whether general business conditions and those within the specific industry of the borrower are such to give the lender cause for concern or optimism. Included in these considerations are the nature of the borrower's product and its competitive position in the marketplace.
- *Collateral.* This "C" involves the decision about whether or not the loan is to be collateralized and, if so, with what. The lender will consider if he or she forecloses on the collateral, to whom can it can be sold, and for how much or will its sale at auction cover the loan. Established businesses with high credit ratings do most of their short-term borrowings on an unsecured basis. Entrepreneurs with new or early-stage businesses generally will be required to back their loans with all of the assets of their business, key-man life insurance payable to the bank, and personal guarantees. Also, the larger the loan compared to net worth, the more important is the issue of collateral and the value of the collateral.

The Lending "Decision"

If a lender is favorably impressed by what he or she has seen, heard, and read, he or she will ask for further information and references and begin to discuss the amount and timing of funds that the bank might lend to the business.

Typically, a lending decision can be made in one to three weeks. Again, such a "decision" is a decision to negotiate.

Negotiating the Loan Agreement

A loan agreement is a document that defines the terms and conditions under which a lender provides capital. A sample loan agreement is included as Appendix VII.

For the lender, the purpose of the loan agreement is (1) to protect its position as creditor and (2) to try to assure repayment of the loan as agreed. To achieve these purposes there are negative and positive covenants in the agreement.

Positive covenants define what the borrower must do and usually include the following:

- Repayment of the loan and interest according to the terms of the agreement.
- Maintenance of a minimum net worth or working capital.
- Prompt payment of all federal and state taxes.
- Maintenance of adequate insurance on key people and property.
- Provision to the lender of periodic financial statements and reports.

Whether or not a loan is collateralized, a lender will usually place certain limitations and restrictions in the agreement to protect itself if things do not go well and/or against poor management practices that might endanger the repayment of a loan. These limitations and restrictions depend to a great extent on the lender's perception of the risk involved. For example, if a company is thought to be a good risk, it should be subject to minimum

[7] R. C. Belew, *How to Negotiate Business Loans* (New York: Van Nostrand Reinhold, 1974), p. 167.

limitations. On the other hand, a loan to an early-stage venture would probably be viewed as somewhat risky and be subject to more restrictions.

Such restrictions are called *negative covenants* and are things that the borrower must not do without prior approval of the lender. Ones to watch out for include:

- No further additions to the borrower's total debt.
- No pledge to others of assets of the borrower.
- No payment of dividends.
- No additions to, or changes in, management or directors.
- No acquisition or sale of assets, including equipment and facilities.
- No development of new products or changes in corporate direction.

Some restrictions can hinder a company's growth. For example, a flat restriction against further borrowing often is based on the value of the borrower's assets at the time of the loan. However, as a business grows, its total assets and net worth increase, and it will need and be able to carry the additional debt required to sustain its growth. Similarly, covenants that require certain minimums on working capital or current ratios may be very difficult for some businesses, particularly a highly seasonable business, to maintain at all times of the year.

Generally, terms are negotiable to some extent. (This is similar to the negotiations invovled in obtaining equity discussed in Chapter 15.)

For example, because of a lender's small profit margins, it is sometimes a good negotiating tactic to offer a lender extra incentives up front to enhance the loan's profitability (without increasing the interest rate paid) to gain concessions elsewhere.

Most important, however, an entrepreneur needs to negotiate terms that his or her venture can live with next year as well as today, and it is highly recommended that attorneys and accountants of the company be consulted before any loan papers are signed. Once loan terms are agreed upon and the loan is made, the entrepreneur and his or her venture will be bound by them. Failure to comply with the terms of a loan agreement and to correct such failure within a specified time can put the loan in default.

Consider a small public company called CommnaComp.[8] After over two months of very tough negotiations with its bank to convert an unsecured demand bank note of over $1.5 million to a one-year term note, the final documentation arrived. Among the numerous convenants and conditions was one clause buried deep in the agreement that stated, "Said loan will be due and payable on demand in the event there are any material events of any kind that could affect adversely the performance of the company." Such a clause is so open to interpretation that it gave, as a practical matter, to a bank that already had been adversarial a loaded gun with a hair trigger. Even the slightest miscue or unexpected event could be used to call the loan, thereby throwing an already troubled company into such turmoil and so restict business options that the company, in all likelihood, would be forced into bankruptcy. An acceptable agreement eventually was worked out, which excluded this and other potentially punitive details. Since the company could continue to function normally without the daily threat that the bank could "pull the plug," management was able to regain momentum and calm frayed nerves and morale among employees, customers, and suppliers and attract new key people. Equally important, this new agreement gave the company enough breathing room to begin to arrange alternative financing.

[8] A fictional name.

When the Lender Says No

As unpleasant as this news is, an entrepreneur needs to be prepared to respond. One question is whether the company needs a new lender or a new lending institution. One direct approach is to reassess key issues, and, if the proposal is sound and realistic, a call can be made to the head of the commercial lending section to ask for a meeting. Presenting a case well here will either get things back on track or indicate that it is wise to go elsewhere.

Issues to be reassessed include the following:

- *Need.*   Here, questions of (1) whether expenditures are necessary and (2) whether cash can be generated from other sources, on and off the balance sheet, and within or without the company, can be asked, and answered, again.
- *Realism.*   Often, a lender may be nervous because it perceives growth which is too rapid or uncontrolled. Questions about what the company's balance sheet really says and whether a comparison with industry norms has been made (using Robert Morris Associates data) to see if the company's projections are in line or differences can be clearly explained can be addressed.
- *Clarity.*   Lenders are often busy and cannot do extensive homework. For example, bank loan officers often have from 50 to 200 accounts to look after. In addition, it is good practice to submit a written loan proposal, rather than a verbal request with no backup. To illustrate, it is not a good policy to request a loan or an increase in credit casually (e.g., at lunch or during a golf game). Whether the loan was presented and supported well can be reassessed.

A Word about Personal Guarantees

It is not too hard to envision why a lender will want personal guarantees. Lenders will ask for personal guarantees when a loan will be undercollateralized; when a company has a history of poor or erratic performance; when there are management problems; when the lending relationship is strained; when a new lender, such as a new loan officer, takes over; when there is turbulence in the credit markets; when there has been a wave of bad loans and crackdowns; and so on.

Such guarantees expose an entrepreneur to the risk of personal bankruptcy if things do not work out. It is best to avoid them like the plague. The best single way to avoid personal guarantees is performance, performance, and performance. In addition, developing a detailed financial plan, with performance targets and a timetable, is critical. Managing the balance sheet with conservative financial management pays off. And, of course, there is no substitute for collateral and risk coverage.

Another challenge is eliminating personal guarantees which have already been given. In addition to negotiating with the lender, it is a good idea for an entrepreneur in this situation to keep up an active search for alternatives.

After the Loan

Cultivating a close working relationship with a lender is important. Too many businessmen and women do not see their lending officers until they need another loan. They thus do not benefit from advice from such advisors. Also, by paying close attention to this relationship and keeping his or her lender informed about the business, an entrepreneur can improve the chances of obtaining larger loans for expansion and of cooperation from the lender in troubled times.

Exhibit 16.4
Additional Sources of Debt Financing

Advance payments and deposits from customers	Prospective employees
Family and friends	SBIR program
Professional advisors and acquaintances	Strategic alliances
"Angels"	Various state and federal programs
Private placement finders/packagers	ESOPs
Present or potential customers, suppliers	Franchisees, licensees
Past employers	Barter arrangements

This has been aptly described by an expert in the field as the quid pro quo in a banker/entrepreneur relationship.[9] In such a relationship, quid pro quo means that the banker has the right to expect the entrepreneur to continue to use the bank as his or her business grows and prospers and not to go shopping for a better interest rate. In return, the entrepreneur has the right to expect that the bank will continue to provide him or her with needed loans, particularly during difficult times.

Some of the things that can be done to build such a relationship are fairly simple:[10]

- Establishment of a track record of borrowing before it is needed and then repaying the loan.
- Provision of product news releases and any trade articles about the business or its products.
- Invitations to the venture's facility to review product development plans, prospects for the business, and any foreseeable loan needs.
- Provision of monthly and annual financial statements.
- Sincere efforts, even if the business is growing, to meet the financial targets that have been set and discussed with the banker.
- Sincere efforts never to surprise the banker with bad news. Such surprises are interpreted as a sign that the entrepreneur is not being candid or that management does not have the business under proper control. For example, if a future loan payment cannot be met, the entrepreneur needs to visit the banker before the payment due date and explain why the loan payment cannot be made and when it will be made, rather than panic and avoid his or her banker.

OTHER CREATIVE AND OFF-BALANCE-SHEET SOURCES

Other creative possibilities exist. For example, debt can be combined with equity.

Exhibit 16.4 highlights sources that can be tapped. Most of these sources were described in Chapter 14. In addition to those already described, customers are sources of debt to the extent that they can be persuaded to pay deposits or full amounts in advance. Suppliers can be sources in that people, equipment, and facilities can be obtained from them through barter and similar arrangements.

---

[9] Stancill, "Getting the Most from Your Banking Relationship," p. 20.
[10] Baty, *Entrepreneurship,* p. 159.

CASE—MICHIGAN LIGHTING, INC.*

Preparation Questions

1. Evaluate the company. How much do you believe the company is worth? Bring to class a written bid of how much you would pay for it if you were Scott and Peterson.
2. What should they do to resolve the ownership situation?
3. How would you finance the purchase of the company?
4. Assume you do purchase the company: What specific actions would you plan to take on the first day? By the end of the first week? By the end of six months? Explain how and why.

MICHIGAN LIGHTING, INC.

Jack Peterson was discouraged by the continuing conflicts with his partner, David Scott, and had sought advice on how to remedy the situation from friends and associates as early as 1976. In 1984, Jack was beginning to believe that he and David had just grown too far apart to continue together. Jack had to find a mutually agreeable way to accomplish a separation. One alternative was for one partner to buy the other out, but they would first have to agree on this and find an acceptable method. David seemed to have no interest in such an arrangement.

During 1984, the differences between the partners grew. The vacillations in leadership were disruptive to the operation and made the employees very uncomfortable.

By early 1985, the situation was growing unbearable. Jack recalled the executive committee's annual planning meeting in January:

It was a total disaster. There were loud arguments and violent disagreements. It was so bad that no one wanted to ever participate in another meeting. We were all miserable.

What was so difficult was that each of us truly thought he was right. On various occasions other people in the company would support each of our positions. These were normally honest differences of opinion, but politics also started to enter in.

Company Description

Michigan Lighting, Inc. (MLI), manufactures custom-engineered fluorescent lighting fixtures used for commercial and institutional applications. Sales in 1985 were approximately $4.4 million with profits of $115,000.

Most sales are for standard items within the nine major lines of products designed and offered by the company. Ten percent of sales are completely custom designed or custom built fixtures, and 15 percent of orders are for slightly modified versions of a standard product. In 1985, CFI shipped 66,000 fixtures. Although individual orders range from one unit to over 2,000 units, the average order size is approximately 15–20 fixtures. Modified and custom designed fixtures average about 25 per order. Jack Peterson, MLI president, describes their market position:

Our product marketing strategy is to try to solve lighting problems for architects and engineers. We design products which are architecturally styled for specific types of building constructions. If an architect has an unusual lighting problem, we design a special fixture to fit his needs. Or if he designs a lighting fixture, we build it to his specifications. We try to find products that satisfy particular lighting needs that are not filled by the giant fixture manufacturers. We look for niches in the marketplace.

Having the right product to fit the architect's particular needs is the most important thing to our customer. Second is the relationship that the architect, the consulting engineer, or the lighting designer has with the people who are representing us. The construction business is such that the

*© Jeffry A. Timmons, 1990

Exhibit A
Historical Performance

Year	Net Sales	Profit after Tax	No. of Fixtures Shipped	Total Employees	Hourly Employees
1985	$4,412,191	$115,209	66,000	104	70
1984	3,573,579	101,013	58,000	94	58
1983	2,973,780	106,528	52,000	82	52
1982	2,935,721	63,416	54,000	82	50

architect, engineer, contractor, distributor, and manufacturer all have to work as a team together on a specified project to ensure its successful completion. The architect makes a lot of mistakes in every building he designs, unless he just designs the same one over and over. Consequently, there's a lot of trading that goes on during the construction of a building, and everybody's got to give and take a little to get the job done. Then the owner usually gets a satisfactory job and the contractors and manufacturers make a fair profit. It requires a cooperative effort.

Most of our bids for orders are probably compared with bids from half a dozen other firms across the country. Since a higher percentage of our orders are for premium priced products, we are not as price sensitive as producers of more commonplace lighting fixtures. It is difficult for a small firm to compete in that market. As many as 30 companies might bid on one standard fixture job.

MLI owns its own modern manufacturing facility located outside Pontiac, Michigan. Production consists of stamping, cutting, and forming sheet metal, painting, and assembly of the fixture with the electrical components which are purchased from outside suppliers. The company employs a total of 104 workers, with 34 sales, engineering, and administrative employees and another 70 in production and assembly.

The company sells nationwide through regional distributors to contractors and architects for new buildings and renovations. Prior to 1983, MLI sold primarily to a regional market. At that time, marketing activities were broadened geographically. This is the primary reason that sales have been increasing over the last few years even during a weak construction market. (See *Exhibit A* for historical sales, earnings, unit sales, and employment.)

Background

Michigan Lighting, Inc., was formed in Flint, Michigan, in 1936 by Daniel Peterson and Julian Walters. Each owned one half of the company. Peterson was responsible for finance and engineering and Walters for sales and design. They subcontracted all manufacturing for the lighting systems they sold.

After several years, differences in personal work habits led Peterson to buy out Walters' interest. Daniel Peterson then brought in Richard Scott as his new partner. Scott had been one of his sheet metal subcontractors. Richard Scott became president and Daniel Peterson the treasurer. Ownership was split so that Peterson retained a few shares more than half and all voting control because of his prior experience with the company.

In 1940, MLI began manufacturing and moved its operations to a multifloor 50,000 square foot plant also located in Flint. The company grew and was quite profitable during the war years and during the following boom in construction of the early 1950s. Peterson and Scott were quite satisfied with the earnings they had amassed during this period and were content to let the company remain at a steady level of about $1 million in sales and about $15,000 in profit after taxes.

Daniel Peterson's son, Jack, joined MLI as a saleman in 1963 after graduating from MIT and then Colorado Business School. Richard Scott's son, David, who was a graduate of Trinity College, also became a MLI salesman in 1964 when he was discharged from the service. The two sons were acquaintances from occasional gatherings as they were growing up but had not been close friends.

In 1966, Daniel Peterson had a heart attack and withdrew from management of the business. Although he remained an interested observer and sometimes advisor to his son, Daniel was inactive in company affairs after this time. Richard Scott assumed overall responsibility for the management of the company.

Jack Peterson moved inside to learn about other parts of the company in 1967. His first work assignments were in manufacturing and sales service. David Scott joined his father in the manufacturing area a year later. Jack Peterson became sales manager, David Scott became manufacturing manager, and, at Richard Scott's suggestion, another person was added as financial manager. These three shared responsibility for running the company and worked well together, but major decisions were still reserved for Richard Scott, who spent less and less time in the office.

As the new group began revitalizing the company, a number of employees who had not been productive and were not responding to change were given early retirement or asked to leave. When the man who had been Richard Scott's chief aide could not work with the three younger managers, they ultimately decided he had to be discharged. Richard Scott became so angry that he rarely entered the plant again.

For several years the three managers guided the company as a team. However, there were some spirited discussions over the basic strategic view of the company. As sales manager, Jack Peterson pressed for responding to special customer needs. This, he felt, would be their strongest market niche. David Scott argued for smooth production flows and less disruption. He felt they could compete well in the "semistandard" market.

In 1968, Jack Peterson began to work with an individual in forming a company in the computer field. The company rented extra space from MLI, and MLI provided management and administrative support, helping the new company with bidding and keeping track of contracts. Although David Scott was not active in this company, Jack split his partial ownership in this new company with David because they were partners, and because Jack was spending time away from MLI with the computer company.

In 1969, the fathers moved to restructure the company's ownership to reflect the de facto changes in management. The fathers converted their ownership to nonvoting class A stock, and then each transferred 44 percent of their nonvoting stock to their sons. Daniel Peterson decided to relinquish his voting control at this time in an effort to help things work as the new generation took over. Accordingly, Jack Peterson and David Scott were each issued 50 percent of the class B voting shares.

Due to the demands associated with the start-up of the computer company, this new effort began to weaken the relationship between Jack and David. At the same time, David and the financial manager began to have strong disagreements. These seemed to arise primarily from errors in cost analysis, which led the financial manager to question some of David's decisions. There were also differences of opinion over relations with the workforce and consistency of policy. David preferred to control the manufacturing operation in his own way. Jack felt David could be more consistent, less arbitrary, and more supportive of the workforce. When the computer company was sold in 1975, the financial manager joined it as treasurer and resigned from MLI.

Growing Conflict

The departure of the financial manager led to a worsening of the relationship between Jack and David. Jack had been made company president in 1970. Jack recalled the decision:

Richard Scott had resigned as president and the three of us were sitting around talking about who should be president. David Scott finally said, "I think you should be it." And I said, "Okay."

Yet even after Jack was made president, the three managers had really operated together as a team for major decisions. Now, Jack was upset that they had lost an excellent financial manager, someone critical to the operation (partially due, in his opinion, to the disagreements with David). Also there was no longer a third opinion to help resolve conflicts. Although the financial manager was replaced with an old classmate of David's, the new manager became one of several middle-level managers who had been hired as the company grew.

The pressure of growth created more strains between Jack and David. Sales had reached $1.8 million and had begun to tax MLI's manufacturing capacity. Jack felt that some of the problems could be alleviated if David would change methods that had been acceptable during slacker periods but hindered intense production efforts. David had different views. Both, however, agreed to look for additional space.

The transition to a new factory outside Pontiac, Michigan, in 1977 eased the stresses between the partners. A major corporation had purchased an indirect competitor to obtain its product lines and sold MLI the 135,000 square foot plant. MLI also entered into an agreement to manufacture some of the other company's light fixtures as a subcontractor. The plant was in poor condition and David Scott took over the project of renovating it and continuing production of the other company's lines.

Jack Peterson remained in Flint running the MLI operation alone until such time that it became possible to consolidate the entire operation in Pontiac. Jack described this interlude:

The next year was a sort of cooling off period. David was immersed in the project with the new factory and I was busy with the continuing operation. David had always enjoyed projects of this sort and was quite satisfied with this arrangement.

Then, in 1978, we hired a plant manager to run the Pontiac plant and David came back to work in Flint. By that time, of course, a lot of things had changed. All of Flint had been reporting to me. I had somewhat reshaped the operation and the people had gotten used to my management style, which was different from David's.

David's reaction was to work primarily with the design and engineering people, but he really wasn't involved very much with the daily manufacturing any more. He developed a lot of outside interests, business and recreation, that took up much of his time.

I was very happy with the arrangement because it lessened the number of conflicts. But when he did come back, the disagreements that did arise would be worse. I guess I resented his attempts to change things when he only spent a small amount of time in the company.

Then, in 1980, we made the decision to sell the Flint plant and put the whole company in Pontiac. We were both involved in that. Most of the key people went with us. David and I were very active in pulling together the two groups, and in integrating the operations.

That began a fairly good time. I was spending my time with the sales manager trying to change the company from a regional company to a national one and was helping to find new representatives all over the country. David Scott spent his time in the engineering, design, and manufacturing areas. There was plenty of extra capacity in the new plant, so things went quite smoothly. In particular, David did an excellent job in upgrading the quality standards of the production force we had acquired with the plant. This was critical for our line of products and our quality reputation.

This move really absorbed us for almost two years. It just took us a long time to get people working together and to produce at the quality level and rate we wanted. We had purchased the plant for an excellent price with a lot of new equipment and had started deleting marginal product lines as we expanded nationally. The company became much more profitable.

During the company's expansion, a group of six people formed the operating team. David Scott concentrated on applications engineering for custom fixtures and new product design. In addition, there was a sales manager, financial manager, engineering manager, the plant manufacturing manager, and Jack Peterson. Disagreements began again. Jack recounted the problems:

Our operating group would meet on a weekly or bi-weekly basis, whatever was necessary. Then we would have monthly executive committee meetings for broader planning issues. These became a disaster. David had reached the point where he didn't like much of anything that was going on in the company and was becoming very critical. I disagreed with him, as did the other managers on most occasions. Tempers often flared and David became more and more isolated.

He and I also began to disagree over which topics we should discuss with the group. I felt that some areas were best discussed between the two of us, particularly matters concerning personnel, and that other matters should be left for stockholders meetings. The committee meetings were becoming real battles.

In 1977, Richard Scott died. Although he had remained chairman of the board, he had generally been inactive in the company since 1968. Daniel and Jack Peterson and David Scott remained as the only directors.

Search for a Solution

When Jack Peterson returned from a summer vacation in August 1985, he was greeted by a string of complaints from several MLI's sales agents and also from some managers. Jack decided that the problem had to be resolved. Jack sought an intermediary:

I knew that David and I weren't communicating and that I had to find a mediator David trusted. I had discussed this before with Allen Burke, our accountant. He was actually far more than our accountant. Allen is a partner with a Big 8 accounting firm and is active in working with smaller companies. Allen was a boyhood friend who had grown up with David. I felt he had very high integrity and was very smart. David trusted him totally and Allen was probably one of David's major advisors about things.

When I first talked to Burke in March, he basically said, "Well, you have problems in a marriage and you make it work. Go make it work, Jack." He wasn't going to listen much.

Then, in early September, I went back to say that it wasn't going to work any more. I asked him for his help. Allen said that David had also seen him to complain about the problems, so Allen knew that the situation had become intolerable.

Both directly and through Burke, Jack pressured David to agree to a meeting to resolve the situation. Although David was also unhappy about their conflicts, he was hesitant to meet until he had thought through his options.

Jack felt that there were several principal reasons for David's reluctance to meet. Since they couldn't seem to solve their differences, the alternative of one of them leaving the company, or becoming a silent partner, glared as a possibility. Jack knew that David's only work experience was with MLI and was limited primarily to managing manufacturing operations he had known for years. Second, Jack thought that David was very uncertain about and had little training in financial analysis. Because he had not been directly involved in the financial operations, he was not aware of all the financial implications for his decision. Jack felt that this made David's task of weighing the pros and cons of alternative courses of action much more difficult. Finally, there was the emotional tie to the company and the desire to avoid such a momentous decision.

As discussion began to result in the possibility of both partners selling the company, David's reluctance waxed and waned. Just before Thanksgiving, David called Jack, who was

Exhibit B
Statement of Earnings

	Year Ended December 31		
	1985	1984	1983
Net sales	$4,412,191	$3,573,579	$2,973,780
Costs of goods sold:			
Inventories at beginning of year	742,907	593,185	416,512
Purchases	1,599,426	1,275,665	1,109,781
Freight in	19,520	26,595	20,966
Direct labor	430,154	360,568	328,487
Manufacturing expenses	977,229	802,172	673,643
	3,769,236	3,058,185	2,549,389
Inventories at end of year	826,228	742,907	593,185
	2,943,008	2,315,278	1,956,204
Gross profit	1,469,183	1,285,301	1,017,576
Product development expenses	131,746	128,809	102,299
Selling and administrative expenses	1,112,542	915,140	740,801
	1,244,288	1,043,949	843,100
Operating income	224,895	214,352	174,476
Other expense (income):			
Interest expense	56,259	37,790	32,416
Payments to retired employee	10,000	10,000	20,000
Miscellaneous	(923)	(1,551)	(6,193)
	65,336	46,239	46,223
Earnings before income taxes	159,559	168,113	128,253
Provision for income taxes	44,350	67,100	49,000
Earnings before extraordinary income	115,209	101,013	79,253
Extraordinary income – life insurance proceeds in excess of cash surrender value			27,275
Net earnings	$ 115,209	$ 101,013	$ 106,528
Earnings per share of common stock	$19.15	$16.79	$13.17

sick at home, and said he decided to fire the financial manager and become the treasurer of the company. David wanted to look at the figures for a year or so, and then he would be able to make a better decision. Jack felt that the financial manager was essential and could not be discharged. He thought that this was really more of an attempt to buy time. After some discussion, Jack convinced David that the financial manager should be retained.

After another month of give and take, Jack and David realized that they had no estimate of the value of the company if it were to be sold. Both felt that this might alter the attractiveness of the alternatives that each were considering.

Valuing the Company

Before making his decision, Jack reviewed the thinking he had done since first considering the idea of buying or selling the company. He began with the company's current position. With the serious discussions going on about the buyout agreement, preparation of the financial statements for 1985 had been accelerated and they were already completed. (These are shown together with the results for 1984 and 1983 as *Exhibits B* and *C.*)

Jack had also begun developing the bank support he might need to fund a buyout. The company's banker indicated that he would loan Jack funds secured by his other personal assets if Jack was the buyer, but that, since he had not worked with David, the bank would

Exhibit B *(continued)*
Balance Sheet

	December 31		
	1985	1984	1983
Assets			
Current assets:			
Cash	$ 51,248	$ 3,778	$ 70,520
Accounts receivable:			
Customers	600,361	430,750	318,356
Refundable income taxes	23,001		
Other		2,276	5,289
	623,362	433,026	323,645
Less allowance for doubtful receivables	3,500	3,500	3,500
	619,862	429,526	320,145
Inventories:			
Raw materials	291,790	259,550	277,072
Work in progress	534,438	483,357	316,113
	826,228	742,907	593,185
Prepaid insurance and other	14,028	20,134	26,070
Total current assets	1,511,366	1,196,345	1,009,920
Property, plant, and equipment:			
Buildings and improvements	341,426	325,686	295,130
Machinery and equipment	210,493	173,073	135,419
Motor vehicles	32,578	32,578	29,421
Office equipment	42,866	43,905	36,949
	627,363	575,242	496,919
Less accumulated depreciation	273,284	233,444	185,215
	354,079	341,798	311,704
Land	11,101	11,101	11,101
	365,180	352,899	322,805
Other assets:			
Cash surrender value of life insurance policies (less loans of $19,748 in 1985, $19,590 in 1984, and $19,432 in 1983)	81,978	77,215	72,569
Total assets	$1,958,524	$1,626,459	$1,405,294

decline to finance an acquisition with David as the buyer. In addition, the bank would continue the company's existing line of credit, which was secured by MLI's cash and accounts receivable. The maximum which could be borrowed with this line was an amount equal to 100 percent of cash plus 75 percent of receivables. Both types of borrowing would be at one percent over the prime rate (then about 9 percent).

Jack worked with the financial manager to develop financial projections and valuation assessments. To be conservative, Jack had made the sales projections about 10 percent lower each year than he really thought they would achieve. Because fixed costs would not rise appreciably with modest increases in sales, any improvements in sales volume would directly increase profits. He felt he should consider how these various changes would impact his financing requirements and his assessment.

Jack also had sought out common valuation techniques. By looking through business periodicals and talking to friends, he found that these methods were not necessarily precise. Private manufacturing companies were most often valued at between 5 and 10 times after tax earnings. Book net asset value also helped establish business worth, but was often

Exhibit B *(continued)*
Balance Sheet *(continued)*

	December 31		
	1985	1984	1983
Liabilities and Stockholders' Equity			
Current liabilities:			
Current maturities of long-term debt	$ 12,184	$ 10,558	$ 9,000
Note payable—bank	325,000	200,000	
Note payable—officer		30,000	39,000
Accounts payable	389,582	295,208	313,203
Amount due for purchase of treasury stock			75,000
Accrued liabilities	154,590	116,134	88,957
Total current liabilities	881,356	651,900	525,160
Long-term debt	176,522	189,122	195,710
Stockholders' Equity			
Contributed capital:			
6% cumulative preferred stock— authorized 10,000 shares of $10 par value; issued 2,000 shares	20,000	20,000	20,000
Common stock:			
Class A (nonvoting): Authorized 15,000 shares of $10 par value; issued 8,305 shares	83,050	83,050	83,050
Class B (voting): Authorized 5,000 shares of $10 par value; issued and outstanding 20 shares	200	200	200
	103,250	103,250	103,250
Retained earnings	892,396	777,187	676,174
	995,646	880,437	779,424
Less shares reacquired and held in treasury—at cost:			
2,000 shares 6% cumulative preferred stock	20,000	20,000	20,000
2,308 shares Class A common stock	75,000	75,000	75,000
	95,000	95,000	95,000
	900,646	785,437	684,424
Total liabilities and stockholders' equity	$1,958,524	$1,626459	$1,405,294

adjusted to reflect differences between the market value of assets and the carrying values shown on balance sheets. For MLI, this was significant because they had obtained their new plant at an excellent price. Jack felt that it alone was probably worth $200,000 more than the stated book value.

To Jack, the variations in worth suggested by these different methods not only reflected the uncertainty of financial valuation techniques but also showed that a business had different values to different people. His estimate would have to incorporate other more personal and subjective elements.

Personal Financial Considerations

One important consideration was what amount of personal resource each could and should put at risk. Both Jack and David were financially very conservative. Neither of them had ever had any personal long-term debt—even for a house. Jack could gather a maximum of $650,000 of assets outside of MLI that could be pledged to secure borrowing. His bank

Exhibit B *(continued)*
Statement of Changes in Financial Position

	Year Ended December 31		
	1985	1984	1983
Working capital provided:			
From operations:			
Earnings before extraordinary income	$115,209	$101,013	$ 79,253
Add depreciation not requiring outlay of working capital	55,978	50,658	44,267
Working capital provided from operations	171,187	151,671	123,520
Extraordinary income from life insurance proceeds			27,275
Capitalized equipment lease obligation		5,295	
Proceeds from cash surrender value of life insurance policies			51,877
Total working capital provided	171,187	156,966	202,672
Working capital applied:			
Additions to property, plant, and equipment	68,259	80,752	47,107
Increase in cash surrender value of life insurance policies—net of loans	4,763	4,646	5,954
Reduction of long-term debt	12,600	11,883	8,995
Purchase of 2,308 shares of nonvoting Class A stock			75,000
Total working capital applied	85,622	97,281	137,057
Increase in working capital	$ 85,565	$ 59,685	$ 65,615
Net change in working capital consists of:			
Increase (decrease) in current assets:			
Cash	$ 47,470	$ (66,742)	$ 64,854
Accounts receivable—net	190,336	109,381	(3,548)
Inventories	83,321	149,722	176,673
Prepaid expenses	(6,106)	(5,936)	(4,980)
	315,021	186,425	232,999
Increase (decrease) in current liabilities:			
Current portion of long-term debt	1,626	1,558	500
Notes payable to bank	125,000	200,000	
Note payable to officer	(30,000)	(9,000)	
Accounts payable	94,374	(17,995)	104,083
Amount due for purchase of treasury stock		(75,000)	75,000
Contribution to profit-sharing trust			(20,000)
Accrued liabilities	38,456	27,177	7,801
Total	229,456	126,740	167,384
Increase in working capital	85,565	59,685	65,615
Working capital at beginning of year	544,445	484,760	419,145
Working capital at end of year	$630,010	$544,445	$484,760

had already confirmed that he could borrow against those assets. However, for him to put his entire worth at risk to purchase David's share of the company, he would want to be very comfortable that the price was a reasonable one. Jack described his feelings:

You get very protective about what you have outside the company. The problem you always have with a small company is that most of your worth is tied up in it and you may have very little to fall back on if something goes sour. We both have never been big leverage buyers or anything like that.

Besides the element of increased financial risk, there were several other considerations that tempered Jack's willingness to pay a very high price. Since they had moved to the plant

Exhibit C
Pro Forma Financial Statements

Income Statement Projections (prepared by Jack Peterson)

Historical Percentages			Projected Percentages				(Thousands of Dollars)		
1983	1984	1985	1986	1987	1988		1986	1987	1988
100.00	100.00	100.00	100.0	100.0	100.0	Net sales	$4,800	$5,100	$5,400
65.80	64.79	66.70	67.0	67.0	67.0	Cost of goods sold	3,216	3,417	3,618
34.22	35.21	33.30	33.0	33.0	33.0	Gross income	1,584	1,683	1,782
28.61	29.28	28.25	28.0*	28.0	28.0	Operating, general, & admin.	1,344	1,428	1,512
5.61	5.93	5.05	5.0	5.0	5.0	Profit before taxes	240	255	270
38.20	39.90	27.80	39.0†	39.0	39.0	Taxes	94	99	105
						Net earnings	$ 146	$ 156	$ 165

* Projected percentages reflect an assumption that one partner will leave the company, and include a $25,000 cost reduction for the reduced
   salary requirements of a replacement.
† Effective tax rate.

in Pontiac, the one hour commute to work had been a bit burdensome. It would be nice not to have that drive. Jack also felt that he had good experience in the overall management of a business and his engineering undergraduate degree and MBA gave him a certain amount of flexibility in the job market. This was important because, for both financial and personal reasons, he felt he would still have to work should he no longer be associated with MLI.

On the other hand, some factors encouraged Jack to be aggressive. His father cautioned him to be reasonable, but Jack knew his father would be very disappointed if he lost the company, and Jack himself had strong emotional ties to MLI. Jack also developed a point of view that in some ways he was buying the entire company, rather than just half:

I'm sitting here with a company that I have no control over because of our disagreements. If I buy the other half share, I'm buying the whole company — I'm buying peace of mind, I could do what I want, I wouldn't have to argue. So I'd buy a "whole peace of mind" if I bought the other half of the company.

Finally, Jack considered his competitive position versus David. Although David had not accumulated the personal resources that Jack had, he had a brother-in-law with a private company that Jack knew had the ability to match Jack's resources and might be willing to back David financially. The brother-in-law would also be giving David financial advice in evaluating his alternatives and setting a value for the company. David also probably had fewer job prospects if he sold out. His undergraduate study was in liberal arts and his entire experience was within MLI. Jack also thought David might have some doubts about his ability to manage the company on his own.

The Meeting

After another conversation with Allen Burke, David Scott called Jack Peterson at home one evening.

Jack, I realize that you're right — I can't live in this tense environment any longer. I've spoken with Allen, and he has agreed to meet with both of us to discuss our situation, and to attempt to identify some possible solutions. Would Friday at 9:00 be convenient for you?

START-UP AND AFTER

PART V

Under conditions of rapid growth, entrepreneurs face unusual paradoxes and challenges as their companies grow and the management modes required by these companies change.

Whether they have the adaptability and resiliency in the face of swift developments to grow fast enough as managers and whether they have enough courage, wisdom, and discipline to balance growing fast enough to keep pace with the competition and lightning-like industry movements and turbulence will become crystal clear.

There are enormous pressures and physical and emotional wear and tear that entrepreneurs will face during the rapid growth of their companies. It goes with the territory. Entrepreneurs after start-up find that "it" has to be done now, that there is no room to falter, and that there are no "runners up." It is clear that those with a personal entrepreneurial strategy, who are healthy, who have their lives in order, and who know what they are signing up for fare better than those who do not.

Among all the stimulating and exceedingly difficult challenges entrepreneurs face — and can meet successfully — none is more liberating and exhilarating than a harvest. Perhaps the point is made best in one of the final lines of the play *Oliver:* "In the end all that counts, is in the bank, in large amounts!"

Obviously, money is not the only thing, or everything. But money is the vehicle that can ensure both independence and autonomy to do what you want to do, mostly on your terms, and can significantly increase the options and opportunities at your discretion. In effect, for entrepreneurs, net worth is the final score card of the value creation process.

Entrepreneurs in Action 17 >

They say it can't be done. But that don't always work.

Casey Stengel
Legendary Manager,
New York Yankees

RESULTS EXPECTED

Upon completion of the chapter,[1] you will have, through a case example:

1. Examined the iterative process whereby entrepreneurs develop and organize operating philosophies.
2. Looked at how, in actuality, the three essentials of venture creation—the opportunity, the people, and the resources—can come together.
3. Looked briefly at the specifics of setting up a business.
4. Examined strategies for success and specific credibility-building components that need to be addressed during start-up.

ANATOMY OF THE ITERATIVE PROCESS

Starting a business is a complex process and is unique for each venture. To understand how complex an activity and how creative an act it truly is, it is useful to examine what actual entrepreneurs did to pursue and finally to seize two opportunities.

Five Goose Chases

Beginning

The lead entrepreneur, Charles, received his bachelor of science degree in business administration with a minor in engineering. At the time, he knew he wanted to start a business, but first he wanted to strengthen his engineering abilities. Consequently, he went to work as an engineer in the development laboratory of a chain belt manufacturer, CB Company. He thought he would be working on new product development, which would provide him with experience directly related to starting a new venture.

However, he spotted a need in CB for an automatic inspection machine for chain links, and he proposed to the laboratory director that he develop such a machine for CB's use. His proposal was accepted, and, while he was working on the machine, the laboratory director and he, who were graduates of the same school, discussed the possibility of Charles starting a company to manufacture a chain link testing instrument that had been developed by the director.

With little data, they decided that the market for the instrument was not large enough to be the basis for a small company. Further, they did not seriously consider developing an

---

[1] The author is most appreciative to Alexander L. M. Dingee for contributing the material for the chapter.

integrated line of chain testing instruments and handling tools to create the business volume necessary for a viable venture.

Charles also had discussions with Bill, a shop foreman who had worked his way up from a machine repair mechanic, about his desire to start a new business. Bill was very skilled at setting up grinding machines and special machine alterations. Charles and Bill spent many hours trying to identify a product that could capitalize on the skills of the foreman. However, the two were unable to define a product that would meet any generalized grinding machine need.

Charles also had discussions with Tom, a clever mechanical engineer at CB Company. Tom had a unique design capability, and they talked of possible products based upon mechanical technology. Charles' father, a physicist, was also asked about products. He said, "Tell me what the market needs, and I might be able to design a product to fit that need." Charles and Tom were unable to identify a potential product or need because they had no detailed knowledge of any market.

Charles, Tom, and an electrical engineer, Carl, then tried to come up with ideas. They decided they needed a place to work and began fixing Carl's chicken coop for this purpose. Nine to 10 months later, Charles had a nice chicken coop, but the team had no ideas for business. The work on the chicken coop had effectively drained 9 to 10 months of effort away from the more primary goal of finding an idea that met a market need.

Two years after his first attempt to identify a venture opportunity, Charles was drafted into the army. At this time, Tom suggested that he, Charles, and Carl design an electromechanical toy. Tom was an exacting craftsman, and one of his hobbies was working on model cars and planes. He was also very adept at home automobile repair.

After much discussion, they decided to develop powered model cars and planes. A car and a helicopter were picked first, and the car was given priority on the basis of Tom's love and knowledge of cars and the potential difficulty in making a working powered model helicopter. Charles and Tom agreed that there must be a market for a properly designed powered model car at the right price. This supposition was based only on knowledge that model cars and toy trains did sell in enough volume to support a fair-sized industry.

With no market data, they began to design a model car based upon their feelings about what was wanted by the consumer. Charles and Tom built a prototype of the car, and Carl made a significant contribution to the design of the electrical control.

Since Charles was stationed at an army base some distance away, he drove several hundred miles each weekend to work on the car model. About 10 months after conception of the idea, with the part-time effort of Charles and Tom, a prototype of a model car was completed. The car consisted of a single eight-inch-long model car powered on a restricted track and controllable in both speed and steering exterior to the car. The design appeared to be simple enough to allow low-cost manufacture.

Developing a Business Strategy

With a successful prototype completed, Charles and Tom decided they would either try to license it to an existing manufacturer or start a business to manufacture and sell it. Charles and Tom tried to find somebody with experience with whom they could discuss how to start a company in the toy field, but they failed to find any sources of good advice.

Charles then attended a large toy manufacturers' sales show in New York to size up the industry. The competitive rat-race image obtained from viewing two hotels full of toy exhibits and from two days of discussions with toy company representatives left Charles feeling that he wanted nothing to do with starting a business in the toy industry. Further, Charles and Tom both felt completely inadequate to start into large-scale production and consumer distribution of such a toy. It was obvious to them that only by licensing the car model to a toy manufacturer could they realize some return from their efforts.

Testing the Market

Charles made appointments to display the prototype car model to the Lionel and the A. C. Gilbert companies, both manufacturers of toy trains. The chief engineer of Lionel said the concept was interesting and that an excellent job had been done in reducing the concept to practice. However, a corporate policy decision had been made at Lionel to get out of the toy field and go into government contracting.

The meeting at A. C. Gilbert went better. The board of directors happened to be meeting that day and became interested in the model car. Several of its directors "drove" the car around the track and hugely enjoyed themselves. However, there was a powered model car project already started at Gilbert. Despite this, Charles and Tom were told that, if a second car could be added to the track, A. C. Gilbert would be interested in their product.

Reappraisal

At this point, there was a significant question in the minds of the team members about the merits of putting any more effort into the project. It was not obvious that a second car could be put on the track without significant complication and work. Further, it was not at all certain that A. C. Gilbert would really be interested in licensing the model car, or that any valid patent could be obtained to protect the idea from being used without compensation.

Three years had passed since Charles began trying to start a venture. Since Charles was now seriously considering a sixth idea, and although Tom agreed to go further in development of a two-car system, the priority set on this task was so low that no further developmental progress was made.

The "Chunks" Gained

The five goose chases described above were failures as far as directly starting a new venture was concerned. The goose chases were, however, crude venture action plans that Charles tried to follow.

The major lesson learned from the fifth goose chase was that, by taking step-by-step action toward meeting defined goals, two very inexperienced individuals could develop a workable product prototype. This prototype had attracted favorable attention from the top management of two leading companies in the chosen field. To Charles, this was coming within shooting distance of success and served to build his self-confidence.

After five goose chases, Charles had also learned that, for him, it was necessary to have a partner to provide a balance of abilities in a venture effort. In Charles's first venture, it became clear that the laboratory director was not a potential team member, and Charles first recognized the need for active partners who would provide complementary skills and who would reinforce each other in the quest for an attractive venture. He also had identified some of the complementary abilities he needed in a partner and was aware of the necessity for high quality in these abilities. In working with the shop foreman, it became apparent to Charles that a combination of abilities in analysis and innovation were necessary for development of a standard product. Charles, in his later venture attempts, did combine with Tom and Carl to obtain this innovation ability. Akin to team considerations were those of business contacts. Charles had learned that he had no business contacts from which to get advice. He was convinced that any future effort he made would include expanding his business horizons and contacts on a planned basis. A further conclusion was that of the importance of the choice of business field. The failure in the third venture effort to identify a potentially viable business led to the dead-end street in the fourth venture effort—that of developing a plant facility, the renovated chicken coop. The wasted time involved in this mistake finally brought home the absolute necessity for a clear definition of a product and a market in founding a venture. As can be seen, this lesson was still not learned because Charles and Tom, in the next venture effort, defined a product in a field too competitive for their taste. Further, the toy field required mass production and marketing techniques beyond their capabilities. An earlier examination of the toy industry would have shown the entrepreneurs that they were headed for failure. Charles now realized that an entrepreneur needs to pick a general field of business that (1) appeals to him or her on a personal basis, (2) he or she can make a significant contribution to, and (3) basically requires skills that the entrepreneurial team has.

Massey-Dickinson Is Caught

Plans for Action

Charles was convinced that he could use his remaining 10 months in the army to get a venture started. Charles was transferred, at his request, to a quiet quartermaster corps laboratory in Boston. He was assigned to a job that required a Ph.D. in mechanical engineering and that was completely beyond his ability.

Since he could neither learn the job nor design a meaningful research program in his final eight months of army time, Charles decided instead to use every available minute of his remaining time in the service to initiate a business. Through library research, Charles identified industrial instruments as a growing general field. Through thinking about what was around him, Charles identified the medical equipment and supply field as a second area of interest, and Boston, noted as a center for medical research, seemed an ideal place to base a venture dealing in new medical products. This idea quickly flowered and took precedence in Charles's mind because the thought of working in a field that would be helping humanity directly appealed to him.

Identification of General Field

Library research showed that the medical equipment and supply market was large and growing rapidly, compared to other markets, and that profit margins in the industry were above average. Charles visited various medical supply houses and determined that much of the instrumentation, equipment, and specialized medical furniture could be improved. From talking with the supply houses, Charles found that many of the companies manufacturing medical products were small. Therefore, Charles felt that he could start small and be successful. There were existing channels of distribution for medical products that a small company could use—again showing Charles that a new medical venture could establish itself through these channels. Charles and Tom agreed that an effort to develop some medically oriented business on a spare-time basis looked acceptable. Carl was not considered as a serious team member because of his previous lack of effort after an initial investment of a few hours.

Definition of the Business

However, neither Charles nor Tom had experience in starting a company. Each had only development engineering experience with CB Company and had no experience in marketing, production, or finance, or in the medical field that they wanted to enter. CB Company had sales of $110 million per year, so the experience they had was not small-company experience.[2]

Charles decided he had several assets: his ability to live on his wife's pay and his meager army pay for six months while getting a company started; the existence of personal savings of $12,000; Tom's willingness to work evenings at no cost to the venture; the ability of he and Tom to design mechanical and electromechanical devices; and their proximity to large

---

[2] Dollar figures have been corrected for inflation.

amounts of active medical records and to such technological resources of Boston as consultants, machine shops, and electronics manufacturing facilities.

Charles decided the proposed company should design special medical research instruments upon request. After completion of design, the company would subcontract the manufacture of the instruments to eliminate the capital cost of equipping a shop and to retain manufacturing flexibility. The design and manufacture of the instruments would be done for a fixed price agreed upon with the customer before work was begun. It was anticipated that many instruments would be built only once, but that occasionally there would be repeat orders. This approach of selling services appeared to Charles to be a low-risk and low-profile way of entering the medical field, using what experience the team had as advantageously as possible.

More Plans for Action

Charles developed an action plan. First he needed to establish contacts. He visited a well-known senior scientist at M.I.T., who had contacts in the medical research field. The scientist encouraged Charles to proceed with the medical instrument business and gave Charles the names of several medical researchers. He also mentioned that his son, who had just been through starting a successful company, might give Charles some useful tips. Charles visited the son, Jack, who gave Charles the name of a subcontract machine shop and the name of his corporate lawyer. Charles visited the corporate lawyer, who agreed to handle the new firm's legal needs, and who recommended that the new firm be a partnership to avoid incorporation costs until it was determined that there was a market, that significant sales were possible, and that a method of limiting personal liability was needed.

Charles visited two of the medical researchers recommended to him. The first doctor was affiliated with Massachusetts General Hospital and, upon hearing of Charles's design service, asked if he would be interested in designing and building a new muscle-fatigue measuring instrument based upon an old instrument. Charles agreed to return with a proposal. The doctor further encouraged Charles about the need for such service as he would provide. The second medical researcher also encouraged Charles about the need for special instrument service and recommended a machine shop that he might use.

The Goose Is Caught

Charles and Tom decided to go ahead with their proposed venture. They now needed a company name. They felt that the name must seem solid and established, because the medical field is a conservative one. After many hours of thinking, the name Massey-Dickinson Company was chosen. Massey was Charles's middle name and Dickinson was Tom's last name. The name sounded both like Becton Dickinson, a company in the medical field, and Massey Ferguson, a company in the machinery field, thereby giving on a subconscious level a feeling of substance and longevity. Using names that belonged to the partners seemed to them to give some personal substance to the company. Incidentally, the company initials were M.D., which also seemed appropriate.

More Plans for Action

With five months left in the army, Charles began accelerating his efforts. Business cards and a letterhead were designed and printed, a telephone answering machine was attached to Charles's telephone, contact was made with a local bank, potential subcontracting machine shops were visited, and quotes were obtained for subcontract construction of the muscle fatigue instrument. Then a large number of hours were poured into readying a proposal for that instrument.

Charles submitted the proposal for the muscle fatigue instrument, including a three-dimensional drawing of the proposed instrument. The cost of manufacture, exclusive of engineering, overhead, and profit, was estimated at $3,400, and the price quoted for the design and manufacture of the instrument was $4,500. (The entrepreneurs had decided to "buy" their first contract to give them some experience.) The doctor gave them a purchase order for the instrument, and Tom began making final drawings while Charles made a selection of the subcontractor and ordered parts.

The Business Becomes Real (and so does the work)

As Charles's time in the army came to an end, he was swamped with the details of supervising the construction of the machine and with visiting more researchers at Massachusetts General Hospital to obtain additional work. Charles made liberal use of army leave time, three-day weekend passes, evenings, and very extended lunch hours.

Upon separation from the army in July 1957, and almost four years after Charles initiated his first efforts to launch a venture, Massey-Dickinson Company was in business. Its first order was nearing completion, several additional proposals had been submitted, and many discussions with potential customers were under way.

Since, after a few months, Charles decided that he could not maintain a professional image operating out of his apartment, he arranged to rent office space from a subcontractor whose work he had found to be the most satisfactory. Charles felt that being next to his major manufacturing facility was efficient and would allow work in progress to be monitored closely. Massey-Dickinson now had an established air about it, with a telephone, office, calling cards, letterhead stationery, a full-time employee (Charles), customers, and a book of pictures showing the several completed and delivered instruments.

Charles was very enthusiastic and put in a large number of hours per week, handling everything from sweeping the floor to purchasing, managing subcontracts, engineering, bookkeeping, and selling.

Apart from the rush of productive work on medical equipment, Charles was achieving his venture action plan by meeting many other venture milestones at the same time: equipping office space, moving his offices, hiring a part-time bookkeeper, arranging for typing service, incorporating the partnership, choosing his board of directors, getting product liability insurance, making up a brochure describing the medical equipment development service, broadening his contacts with subcontracting shops and with engineers who could provide backup design services, hiring a mechanical engineer, strengthening his contacts with his bank, and developing a business plan preparatory to raising needed equity money.

Team Issues

At the end of one year, Charles was loaded with work on special medical instruments. He had hired a disabled mechanical engineer who was able to draw a small pay from the company. Tom continued to work evenings for no salary. He enjoyed the engineering work as a hobby, but it turned out he lacked the drive necessary for a going business. Tom enjoyed the security of a larger company, and Charles knew he needed to find team members for Massey-Dickinson. Charles felt, though, that until he had something to offer, his options were limited. In the meantime, Charles was extending his experience and range of contacts and Massey-Dickinson Company was becoming an experienced company in the medical instrument field.

A New Plan of Action

As Charles's reputation increased, he saw that the current business volume of about $20,000 per month could be increased within the next 12 months to support two or three professionals. He felt from his experience in the labs that the size of the market in which the company was competing would not allow the company to expand much beyond. To expand further would require a service or product with a larger market potential.

Accordingly, Charles decided to analyze the special medical products to learn if there were any for which a sizable market might be indicated. Eight types of medical products were identified: neurological tools, test-tube-handling equipment, cardiographs, medical pumps, medical furniture, programming equipment, data processing equipment, and animal cages. Charles invested significant attention to testing the market for each.

Charles's method was simple. He obtained an order for one item in the area of interest (e.g., a special data integrator). The product would be designed to meet the needs of a more general business, and the engineering design was done on a shoestring. The revenue obtained from sale of the product would generally defray the cost of manufacture. Products were then brought to the attention of the market by a variety of means—from new product releases in technical journals to papers presented by the involved and interested researchers who were buying the equipment. The proof of the market test would be interested potential customers and sales. After a year and a half, this product development effort had cost a considerable amount.

The fact that he faced a bank debt approaching $200,000, based on inventory, work in progress, receivables, and Charles's signature, forced Charles to pick the product that looked best and to push it into the marketplace.

Another Product Opportunity Defined

Charles picked behavioral programming equipment used to program psychological or physiological tests on humans and animals that was based on an advanced computer-type approach to an old product. The product Massey-Dickinson had developed and built in a laboratory had been market tested at a major scientific meeting with good results, and many scientists wanted to buy this equipment or see a catalog. Massey-Dickinson decided to design a standard product, and the design was completed at the same time that orders were being taken from local researchers and a catalog written. Charles selected an electronics subcontractor to build the equipment.

Charles, along with a medical research doctor, an electronics technician from a medical laboratory, and the engineering subcontractor became the entrepreneurial team. Charles was the general manager; Charles and the doctor did systems design; the doctor tested the equipment and made a list of potential buyers; the electronics technician did application engineering and became sales manager; and the subcontractor carried out engineering (on speculation) and manufacture. An immense effort was expended to bring the product to market in time to meet the demand.

The product was sold through display at four scientific meetings a year, through selected visits to customers, and by direct mail. Massey-Dickinson followed how other companies sold their equipment in this field. The market had a defined size, and some existing companies in the field had sales of up to $8 million per year. Charles felt able to cope with the size of the market and that he had a sales method he could control. Also, the market niche was not large enough to attract major competition.

The unique solid-state approach of the Massey-Dickinson product gave it a strong edge over existing equipment suppliers. It was possible to develop the market with a reasonable amount of capital by leaning on the subcontractor to carry inventory and conduct engineering on a speculative basis. Approximately 30 percent of Massey-Dickinson was sold to raise the equity capital necessary for this market development.

More "Chunks" Gained

Charles learned a considerable amount about how to start a business and make progress according to a venture action plan in the process of catching the first goose. He succeeded in transferring technology from a previous source of employment to another enterprise (called *spinning off*).

He also had gained a great deal of general knowledge:

- Knowledge of managing an entire business, including integrating many factors in management decisions.
- A broad range of specific knowlede of market study techniques; marketing techniques, such as using free new product releases, generation of data sheets, and exhibiting at trade shows; managing sales representatives and distributors; handling of customers; managing engineering; managing subcontractors; costing proposed products; establishing business contacts and banking relations, including using patent and corporate attorneys and consultants; using debt and equity financing; and so forth.
- Knowledge of how to maximize use of subcontractors' facilities and assets, how to select good subcontractors, and bid jobs accurately.
- How to identify the type of marketplace that fitted his psychological makeup and skills and in which customers could be defined and reached easily. For example, choosing a small niche within a large and growing field allowed him personal contact with major customers, direct sale to the end user, and reward for high technical performance.
- A sense of the dynamic, demanding, and interdependent nature of the goals in a venture action plan.
- Reinforcement and refinement of all his previous learning. For example, he had learned more about step-by-step action toward meeting a goal. In short, he learned that, during the early stages of a new venture, the entrepreneur need not set goals so rigid that they prevent him from responding to actual business feedback. But, on the other hand, the entrepreneur needs to find and identify his basic goal and put all his energy into its development—at least until a secure base of sales is obtained.

Geodyne Is also Caught

As Charles was busy developing the behavioral programming equipment, a small job he had done at Woods Hole Oceanographic Institute suddenly provided a new opportunity and had the allure of the ocean.

A scientist at the institute had purchased a single instrument from Charles and now wanted Charles to design a product based on this instrument in return for 12 orders. The scientist claimed there would also be a market for those instruments with other oceanographers. Conversations with other oceanographers at the institute and with two laboratories for fisheries indicated that there was some potential for the instrument and also a need for other instruments. Further, the staff at the institute said there were significantly increased funding levels indicated for oceanographic research using measuring instruments.

With two hours of work in the library, he discovered that the federal government also was a purchaser of large amounts of equipment for ocean research. In addition, Woods Hole represented a significant ocean research customer, and one which was actually asking him to develop and supply equipment. Charles felt a strong desire to create a business concerned with the ocean.

A Dilemma and Its Resolution

Charles was concerned that starting a second major business effort would dilute effort on the behavioral programming equipment. However, the behavioral programming equipment product was not sure to be a major success. Further, the product was well along in development, using the subcontractor, and the doctor who was the sales manager could make all the sales trips the company could afford. The rest of Massey-Dickinson's business could be tapered off faster than planned, and this would free a considerable amount of Charles's time and allow him to develop the oceanographic instrument business.

Another Business Defined

The major problem to be met if an oceanographic equipment business was to be started was the need for increased engineering capacity and instant shop facilities of impressive size, since Woods Hole would not buy major equipment from a cellar-type operation. If this problem could be solved, it was a potential advantage because it would keep all other cellar shops from competing. The subcontractor manufacturing the behavioral programming equipment had a facility that was electronically oriented and with no mechanical shop capability. Further, the facility was unimpressive. The five-man machine shop used for the rest of Massey-Dickinson's work was not up to producing a volume of electromechanical and electronic instruments and also had no engineering capability.

Resources Located

Charles picked a large machine shop he had used before on Route 128 around Boston. This shop was founded and run by a father and son, both of whom were engineers. The shop itself was in an inexpensive but modern and well-organized building. A proposal was made to the founders, and it was agreed that the instrument order would be taken under the name of Massey-Dickinson. It was decided how the work load would be shared, how development and use of capabilities and resources and potential ownership would be divided, and what the criteria for market evaluation were. The engineering work was to be provided free and split between the machine shop and the doctor from the behavioral programming equipment product. The shop would charge normal rates for its work, and any profit would be split equally between the two groups. The shop facility could be shown to the institute as available for meeting their needs, and the shop also would handle telephone calls about the project. It was further decided that, if a real market were identified and proven by sales to the institute and other groups, a separate company would be formed and the ownership would be divided equally between the two companies.

Developing the Product

A good reliable instrument was developed by Charles, his partner, and the shop facility and then produced by the shop. It was decided to make a component to perform a timing function, since this was not available commercially. Therefore, a special timing device was searched out, tested, and imported in volume from Switzerland, and this device was altered and calibrated in the machine shop.

In June of 1961, 10 months after receipt of a $35,000 purchase order, instruments were delivered to the Woods Hole Oceanographic Institute. The instruments were well received. There was particular interest in the unique timing component, which could be used on another instrument, and, after testing, the institute placed an order for 100 of the timing components at $240 each. A program manager at the institute suggested that Charles and his partner make the timer and other components for a new type of instrument that the institute had developed and was testing.

Legal Organization

In January of 1962, Charles and his partner decided to legally form a company. Manufacturing would still be done in the machine shop, but the company would have a name, letterhead, calling cards, and a symbol. This move kept the financial commitment low, while presenting a more integrated image to the customer.

Since the oceanographic equipment business was thought to be glamorous and fun by both Charles and his partner, they decided to create an image to go along with the glamor of dealing with the ocean.

The company was incorporated and the stock split equally between Charles and his partner, Fred. This was done according to their original agreement, since it was felt that Charles had identified a potential instrument business with live customers and had instrument-manufacturing experience and that Fred had a shop facility that provided instant credibility to those customers and also had some instrument experience. The two partners seemed equal in what they were contributing to the venture.

Company Image

After much effort, they had decided to call the company Geodyne Corporation. This name was specific enough to indicate the type of field but nonlimiting for the expansion that was visualized. Charles's partner designed a company symbol that placed the letters GEODYNE within a world globe. The design looked so good that an advertising artist did all the graphics necessary for the letterhead, business cards, labels, and data sheet format for a very small fee so he could carry them in his portfolio.

Geodyne developed a data sheet on the timing device, using a format drawn up by the advertising artist, and duplicated it on the copying machine. Later, it was printed as a two-color data sheet.

Other Orders

At this time, Woods Hole asked Geodyne to start supplying major components of the new instrument that it had developed and had been making itself. Now orders of these instruments and the first instrument designed by Geodyne began to flow in from other institutions. Oceanographers at these institutions had heard papers presented by institute scientists and had seen the instruments demonstrated at the institute.

Keeping the Best Customer

The staff of Woods Hole felt that Geodyne should be located near the institute to properly service its needs. Charles and Fred realized that instruments in use at the institute were Geodyne's best salespeople and that the institute was crucial to early venture success; however, Charles and Fred did not want to lose the many resources available to them in Boston. As a compromise, Geodyne, in the middle of 1962, with sales still under $500,000 (about $2 million in 1990 dollars), opened a small technical office next to the institute in the basement of the Woods Hole Inn. The office was artistically furnished at low cost and equipped with one of each of the instruments and mechanisms Geodyne was selling. Further, copies of data taken by Geodyne instruments and plotted by the scientists at the institute were displayed, along with photos of the instruments in use at sea and photos of the interior and exterior of the machine shop. In short, the office looked functional and businesslike and created an atmosphere of success and an image of a major operation existing in a main facility in Boston.

A Major Hire

To man the office, a third partner, Paul, who was personable, who was an oceanographer and electrical engineer, and who had been employed at the institute and lived in Woods Hole, was put on Geodyne's payroll at a small salary. The concept of a technical office manned by a professional oceanographer near the institute kept the institute as an excellent customer. Oceanographers visiting the institute could stop by the office and talk shop and business.

More Customers

The day the office was opened, a government official attending a technical meeting at the institute walked into the office and said that his agency, the United States Public Health Service, wanted to buy what amounted to $3 million worth of equipment. However, it was obvious to Fred and Charles that it would be necessary to prove that Geodyne was more than a paper company in order to close the sale.

More Resources

On the basis of the potential order, an entrepreneur, Jack, who had recently founded and built a major scientific product company, agreed to join the Geodyne board of directors. The seasoned Boston lawyer for this entrepreneur's business also agreed to be on the board.

At this time, a building only 500 feet away from the shop facility and belonging to a company that had gone bankrupt came up at auction. The building was located directly on Route 128 and, as a result, had significant visibility. Charles and Fred obtained the building for $600,000. In the summer of 1962, the team felt that this move would give substance to Geodyne as a company capable of producing $3 million worth of equipment. They also felt that the risk in buying the building was low, because the price was low, and a building directly on Route 128 was a reasonably liquid asset. Further, if the $3 million contract did not materialize, space within the building could be sublet until company sales volume grew to the size capable of supporting the full building.

The plant was equipped for a small capital investment using several pieces of equipment that had been developed to build other instruments in the shop facility. These were moved into the newly acquired building. The work to be moved from the machine shop was assembly, testing, packing, shipping, engineering, sales, and administrative. The Geodyne symbol was mounted on the Route 128 side of the building, and the exterior and interior were now assuming a going, businesslike image. A few individuals were shifted from the shop facility payroll to the Geodyne payroll, and several new people were hired. Since the work to be conducted in the building was low-skill assembly, it was not difficult to hire the people needed, and the idea of going to work for a company manufacturing oceanographic equipment had allure to many of those hired.

The bank that had serviced both the shop facility and Massey-Dickinson over a number of years had been kept up to date on the progress of Geodyne. It provided a mortgage for the full purchase price of the building, treating some small improvements that Geodyne had made in the building as the down payment. The bank also agreed to give references.

Since capital equipment and working capital were necessary to progress further, Charles, Fred, Fred's father, Paul, and Jack all invested varying amounts in Geodyne. Charles had to find $50,000 to hold his ownership in Geodyne at the level he desired. To do this, he went more heavily in debt to the bank. The bank allowed him to do this because it believed Geodyne had a tangible value.

Problems

The government agency official stated that Geodyne would have to prove the data from its instruments could be handled automatically, to justify the contract. This required developing a very complex automatic reader that the institute had been going to develop but had never started. The development of such a device was no minor undertaking, and Paul worked full time on finding a subcontractor to do the very specialized job, while Charles worked on development. To Charles, it rapidly became apparent that building a data-reading machine could never be accomplished in time to win the $3 million dollar contract. Paul found a contractor with a general-purpose computer with optical input that could be altered to read data. He convinced this young company of the excitement and promise of the field and the long-term future of Geodyne.

The machine alteration required a very expensive type of movie projector. Working furiously, the reading technique was demonstrated to the satisfaction of the government agency. For the demonstration, such a projector was rented, torn apart, and fitted into the system.

More Problems

When the government agency put out a request for a bid, Geodyne submitted the second-lowest bid. Since the lowest bid was rejected because there was no automatic reader, the contract was awarded to Geodyne.

However, the contract was taken away one month later because of political intervention caused by the low-bid competitor, since Geodyne had demonstrated only a crude prototype data-reading capability. However, the government agency fought hard to overcome political pressure. It was willing to fight this battle because the instruments were proven in use and because Geodyne projected a successful businesslike atmosphere that left the client feeling the delivery, quality, and performance promises would be met.

Resolution

The full $3 million contract was reinstated two months after it was canceled. Delivery was completed successfully over a period of 18 months, ending in the spring of 1964. This contract gave the company the resources to develop a series of new products and services.

Epilogue

Geodyne built a full team of entrepreneurs, managers, and skilled engineers. Production, at the outset, was managed by nonequity-owning employees, who later received stock options. The company became predominant in the manufacture of buoy-mounted oceanographic instruments. It also successfully provided data processing services based upon its instrument capabilities. In 1967, merger with a larger company expanded its services into environmental data collection. Prior to the merger, company sales were just under $7 million per year. Seven years after the merger, total sales of oceanographic instruments and environmental data collection services were approaching $25 million. In 1963, one year after Geodyne had moved into its building, a very conservative brokerage house offered to take Geodyne public at a valuation of $10 million. The venture components of marketplace, contact with customers, existing contracts, sales growth, profits, location, Woods Hole office, and quality of team undoubtedly entered into the evaluation. In any case, it is nice to be wanted, but the team refused the offer because they personally did not need liquidity and the company was financing its development and growth from profits and bank debt.

And More "Chunks"

Again, the process of spinning off technology was involved in catching the second goose. The original technology became commercialized and was spun off as a second-generation enterprise. This spin-off process demonstrates the learning through trial and error which occurs in entrepreneurship. A study of 24 technology-based ventures showed a marked difference in performance between 12 first-generation ventures and 12 second-generation ventures.[3] The second-generation ventures were far more product-oriented than their first-generation counterparts and also, on the whole, had more balanced teams, had higher initial financing, had higher sales in the first year, had reached profitability earlier, and had significantly higher profits in their most recent year of operation.

Another lesson learned was that decisions on many aspects of a new venture are interrelated and that keeping these interdependencies in balance is crucial to survival. In the

[3] Lawrence M. Lamont, "What Entrepreneurs Learn from Experience," *Journal of Small Business Management*, July 1972, pp. 35–41.

case of Geodyne, the machine shop became interested because of the product potential from the Woods Hole Oceanographic Institute, which became seriously interested in large volume production from Geodyne because of the involvement of the machine shop. The outside directors were interested in being involved with Geodyne because of its potential for success based on major orders. The largest of these orders was partially dependent upon the company's demonstration of corporate strengths, such as a good board of directors, and upon automatic data-reading ability. The data-reading contractor made a major effort to demonstrate an ability to read and process data because of the potential of the contract and the contractor's belief that Geodyne could successfully supply over $3 million worth of equipment, though the company's sales had been less than $500,000 the year before. The contractor's belief in Geodyne came from the customers' belief in Geodyne, which partly came from the contractor's capability.

The history of Geodyne displays a number of administrative issues that were utilitarian but created high value. By careful selection, Geodyne obtained attractive but pivotal items, such as the Geodyne name, the Route 128 building, the Woods Hole office, the entire product line, and so forth, at reasonable cost. Presenting a crisp, consistent image of a competent winner helped relations with customers, banks, suppliers, and stockholders. Fortunately, many high-image administrative components can have a low dollar cost.

For the shoestring start-up venture, time often can be used in place of capital. The team, relatives, and friends provide a resource for accomplishing design of a letterhead, choosing a company name, and so forth.

Also evident was the fact that entrepreneurs need to keep reexamining plans for action to make sure that milestones are being met, that new action steps are being phased in correctly, and that changing situations are taken into account. For example, timing, cost, and utility need to be evaluated in meeting particular milestones.

STRATEGIES FOR SUCCESS

A Business or Venture Action Plan

A great deal of planning precedes the start-up of a new venture, and this planning ideally generates a series of action steps and dates—a venture action plan—whether or not a formal business plan is drawn up.

Most entrepreneurs find a formal business plan to be helpful in guiding growth during and after start-up. Recall, however, that the process of planning is an iterative one, which needs to continue throughout the life of a venture.

Once a venture action plan is devised, be it a formal business plan or an informal venture action plan, successful entrepreneurs step mentally through their plans time and again to test sequence, timing, completeness, and so forth. Research has suggested that dart players can actually improve their accuracy by merely thinking about the process of throwing darts—by forming a mental image of hitting the right spot—and likewise, thinking about his or her action plan can improve the entrepreneur's accuracy.

Thus, when one looks back on a venture action or business plan after its execution, one will recognize steps that were defined beforehand and then carried out, those that were recognized as they were happening, and even some that were evident as action steps only after the fact.

Making step-by-step progress in carrying out a plan is probably the most powerful single method an entrepreneur can use to obtain success. A venture's success, particularly in its first year, is dependent upon the close-knit, well-balanced, and intelligent operation of the entrepreneurial team. A team needs to monitor a venture aggressively and revise the action plan as the venture grows and when changes in direction are indicated.

The Bandwagon Effect

In developing a successful business, most new ventures need a network of contacts and good rapport with outsiders, such as customers, suppliers, bankers, and professional support services. However, these individuals are taking some amount of risk in dealing with a fledgling company, and, to do so, they need to feel they are dealing with a winner.

For a team, the aura of being a winner comes from its ability to communicate many of the philosophies and considerations already discussed. The team's view of the ultimate goal provides a strong base to talk from, and a detailed knowledge of all aspects of the venture is essential so questions asked by outsiders get answered correctly and skillfully. Further, steady step-by-step progress toward defined goals, combined with meeting those goals on or ahead of schedule, all build credibility in the eyes of outsiders.

Thus, a bandwagon effect is created that, in itself, adds momentum to the new venture. Outside associates want the tangible benefits of doing business with a winner, and they enjoy associating with success early enough to prove their ability to discern it. This requires that they jump on the bandwagon, which means they supply the new venture with scarce resources, such as materials or money, or buy the venture's products.

The bandwagon sometimes will move faster than the venture, but sometimes it is necessary for the team to push it faster. For instance, when introducing a unique new product to the market, getting the first customer is often a major difficulty. If the venture team is talking with a number of potential customers, it certainly does not hurt for the most likely potential customer to hear about the other groups who are, in fact, considering purchase of the new product. With other customers considering jumping on the bandwagon, the bandwagon by definition is going faster, and, to become the first customer, one must now run faster to catch the bandwagon.

A Backdoor Policy

In all operational situations that have any significant risk, it is wise to keep alternate solutions or backdoors available. An obvious example is that of keeping available a second supplier of a unique crucial component used in a company's main product. Another example would be keeping good relations with a second banking source, even though the main bank is very happy with its relationship with the venture.

Keeping It Simple

Business needs to be kept as simple as possible, as George Naylor, a seasoned Boston lawyer for corporations and new ventures, has noted. The more complicated a relationship, the more unknowns, variables, and surprises lie in wait for the entrepreneurial team. For example, the cost of generating legal documents concerning complex relationships is high, and the later interpretation of such documents may, in itself, cause some surprises.

Communication

Two-way communication is difficult to achieve and maintain. Communication is essential with both external associates and internal. Just because something is said and someone responds does not mean communication has taken place. Particularly in crucial areas, understandings need to be tested repeatedly to make sure that communication has taken place.

Involvement

The life blood of a company is revenue and derived profit. Revenues come from sales in the marketplace, and the lead entrepreneur needs to understand the marketplace well and spend time in contact with it—regardless of who else on the team is involved with sales and marketing. Any other mode of operation for a new venture needs an overwhelming rationale for proper strategic justification.

SETTING UP A BUSINESS

What form of organization a company will select, what kinds of registrations a venture has to file, what kinds of records it has to keep, what insurance it should buy, what taxes it has to pay, and so forth are complex considerations. For example, there are issues of liability and tax to be considered. Regarding registration, federal, state, and local requirements and the requirements of the Securities and Exchange Commission, and the like, need to be considered.

Generally, taxes can include the following: federal and state income taxes to be withheld from employees, Social Security taxes, federal unemployment tax, federal corporation income tax, federal highway use tax, state sales taxes, state unemployment tax, state minimum corporate tax, state meals tax, state excise tax, and local taxes, including property taxes and so on.

Insurance coverages that might be considered include the following: worker's compensation, automobile insurance, liability insurance, fire insurance, business interruption insurance, crime insurance, life and disability insurance for key employees, health insurance for employees, and so forth.[4]

There is bountiful literature on setting up a business and on setting up procedures and systems, such as for bookkeeping, managing accounts receivable and payable, inventory control, order processing, and so on. (Some of the things entrepreneurs need to address, such as taxes and insurance, were discussed briefly in Chapter 15.) While it is beyond the scope of this book to discuss these systems and procedures in detail, entrepreneurs are encouraged to pay particular attention to this important area.

Other important start-up items are unique to particular businesses. For example, some businesses require product, user, and service documentation. Entrepreneurs will do well to consider these items.

A more complete description of these matters is outside the scope of this text. There are many books on these subjects, and it is recommended that entrepreneurs obtain expert legal advice about the form of organization for their business, registrations that need to be filed, and the like, before taking action in these matters.

CREDITABILITY BUILDERS

Creditability is important in business, and there are things that entrepreneurs can do to enhance the creditability of their companies that are not expensive. For example, the very brief history of Geodyne given above displays how a number of creditability builders that were utilitarian added value. This value was demonstrated when, one year after Geodyne moved into its building, a very conservative brokerage house offered to take it public at a valuation of $10 million (an offer that was refused, since the members did not need the liquidity and since the company was financing its development and growth from profits and through bank debt). The high valuation, however, undoubtedly reflected the addition of the creditability builders.

Exhibit 17.1 is a list of creditability builders that a new venture can use.

---

[4] A booklet is available from the Small Business Administration, called *Insurance Checklist for Small Businesses.*

Exhibit 17.1
Examples of Creditability Builders

Creditability Builder	Comment
Administrative item	
Company name	Can be developed by the entrepreneurial team.
Letterhead	Could be printed for less than $600.
Mailing label	Could be printed for less than $300.
Calling card	Could be printed for less than $300.
Address	Home address is free. A post office box or an office that accepts your mail can be arranged.
Brochure	A simple brochure can cost less than $1,000.
Microcomputer	Can cost under $2,000.
Business phone	Can cost less than $200 a year.
Answering of phone	Answering service can cost as little as $25–30 per month.
Office	Sometimes can be obtained free from an interested supplier.
Corporation	Legal and filing fees can cost less than $1,200.
Company vehicle	Can have name of corporation painted on your own car.
Fax machine	Can cost under $1,500.
Market and product	
Field the company is entering	The choice of an attractive field to enter often costs nothing, while greatly enhancing the image of the venture.
Access to major customers	Oceanographic instrument company specializes in selling services to Woods Hole Oceanographic Laboratory and has friendly contact there. Cost is often entrepreneurial time.
Product idea	Can sometimes be picked up from a purchasing agent, customer, or government laboratory at no cost.
Product development paid for by government laboratory or customer	Shows that you know how to use assets at hand. Also gives the feeling of venture getting something free that moves to pocket of investor.
Prototype of product	Can cost anything from a few dollars to six-figure numbers.
Production model	Can cost anything from a few dollars to six-figure numbers.
Production	The company can be producing the product for customers.
Proven market	Can come with the product idea free (e.g., the tent market is well defined).
Market test	Can be made by entrepreneurs, prospective customer, or carried out by independent group for a fee.
Business plan	Can be written by entrepreneurial team.
Access to potential customers	Documented by a letter of interest.
Articles or papers describing product, authored by company personnel or others	A powerful low-cost selling tool that establishes the credibility of the venture and the product.
New product release in trade publications	The cost is the time to write up and mail the release.
Product literature	Adds significantly to image of activity. Sometimes a Xerox sheet at first.
Testing of product	Can be conducted in company facility and documented at very low cost.
Validated testing of product	Sometimes a potential user will conduct tests at own expense.
Potential patent position	Inventory of ideas recorded, dated, and witnessed and, therefore, protected for what they are worth, at cost of time and a notebook.
Patent applications	Cost is a few hundred dollars to get started. Must be examined as to timing and cost effectiveness.

Exhibit 17.1 *(concluded)*

Creditability Builder	*Comment*
Personal and institutional resources	
The lead entrepreneur	Your ability to communicate, entrepreneurial drive, training, business skills, and ability to put the venture together are company assets that are of immense value. These assets do cost the company your incentive equity.
The team	Same comments as above. The team should demonstrate its ability to work together successfully at least on a part-time basis.
Board of directors	A good board can contribute significantly to credibility, general operating decisions, location of resources, and potential business. The cost is entrepreneurial time and perhaps a dinner meeting that you pay for. As the company gets stronger, the cost may go up.
Advisers and consultants	Setting up arrangements for future use of consultants establishes credibility for today. The arrangements define fee schedules but don't cost the venture dollars until they are put into action. Both parties benefit.
Good relations with several banks and an accounting firm	Adds to credibility and provides needed services. Again, only activated when needed.
Subcontractor	Can provide production credibility. Further, to win future business, subcontractor may provide aids, such as working capital for items subcontracted for, office space, telephone answering, or design at very nominal cost or free.
University contacts	In certain businesses, relevant contacts in a university can add credibility and real value to the venture, while giving the university more contact with the outside world.
Progress made to date in putting above pieces together into an integrated venture effort	This costs only the effort that you are making to put the venture together, but it demonstrates your entrepreneurial skill and value.

Managing Rapid Growth | 18 >

Bite off more than you can chew, and then chew it!

Roger Babson
Founder,
Babson College

RESULTS EXPECTED

Upon completion of the chapter, you will have:

1. Studied how higher potential firms "grow up big," including their stages of growth, the variables that determine the special management requirements of rapid growth, and special problems in rate of growth.
2. Examined the dimension of organizational culture and climate and approaches to management which foster this culture and climate.
3. Explored signals and clues that can alert management to impending crises and approaches for solving these.

GROWING UP BIG

Stages of Growth Revisited

Higher potential ventures do not stay small very long. While an entrepreneur may have done a good job of assessing an opportunity, forming a new venture team and marshalling resources, planning, and so forth, managing and growing such a venture is, simply put, a different managerial game.

Ventures in the high growth stage face the problems discussed in Chapter 6. These include forces that limit the creativity of founders and team; that cause confusion and resentment over roles, responsibilities, and goals; that call for specialization and, therefore, erode collaboration; that require operating mechanisms and controls; and the like.

Recall also that managers of rapidly growing ventures are usually relatively inexperienced in launching a new venture and yet face situations where time and change are compounded and where events are nonlinear and nonparametric. Usually, structures, procedures, and patterns are fluid, and decision making needs to follow counter-intuitive and unconventional patterns.

That companies experience stages or phases during their growth was discussed in Chapter 6. Recall that the first three years before start-up are called the *research-and-development* (R&D) *stage;* the first three years the *start-up stage;* years 4 through 10, the *early-growth stage;* the 10th year through the 15th or so, *maturity;* and after the 15th year, *stability stage.* Remember that these time estimates are approximate and may vary somewhat in particular cases.

Various life-cycle models, and our discussion before, depicted the life cycle of a growing firm as a smooth curve with rapidly ascending sales and profits and a leveling off toward the peak and then dipping toward decline.

511

In truth, however, very very few, if any, new and growing firms experience such smooth and linear phases of growth. By and large, if the actual growth curves of new companies are plotted over their first 10 years, the curves will look far more like the ups and downs of a roller coaster ride than the smooth progressions usually depicted. Over the life of a typical growing firm, there are periods of jerks, bumps, hiccups, indigestion, and renewal interspersed with periods of smooth sailing. Sometimes there is continual upward progress through all this; but, with others, there are periods of considerable peril, where the firms seem near collapse or at least in considerable peril.

Core Management Mode

As was noted earlier, changes in several critical variables determine just how frantic or easy transitions from one stage to the next will be. As a result, it is possible to make some generalizations about the main management challenges and transitions that will be encountered as the company grows. The core management mode is influenced by the number of employees a firm has, which is in turn related to its dollar sales.[1]

Recall that, in *Exhibit 6.3* in Chapter 6, until sales reach approximately $3 million and employees number 20 to 25, the core management mode is one of *"doing."* Between $2 million to $10 million in sales and 25 to 75 employees, the core management mode is *"managing."* When sales exceed $7.5 million and employees number over 75 to 100 and more, the core management mode is *"managing managers."*

The central issue facing entrepreneurs in all sorts of businesses is, that, as the size of the firm increases, the core management mode likewise *changes from doing to managing to managing managers.*

During each of the stages of growth of a firm, there are entrepreneurial crises, or hurdles, that most firms will confront. *Exhibit 18.1* and the following discussion considers by stage some indications of crisis.[2] As the exhibit shows, for each fundamental driving force of entrepreneurship, there are a number of "signals" that crises are imminent. While the list is long, these are not the only indicators of crises new ventures can and most likely will see—only the most common. Of course, each of these signals does not necessarily indicate that particular crises will happen to every company at each stage; but when the signals are there, serious difficulties cannot be too far behind.

The "Problem" in Rate of Growth

Difficulties in anticipating these shifts by recognizing signals and developing management approaches are compounded by rate of growth itself. The faster the rate of growth, the greater is the potential for difficulty, because of the various pressures, chaos and confusion, and loss of control. It is not an exaggeration to say that these pressures and demands increase geometrically, rather than in a linear way (see discussion in Chapter 6).

Growth rates affect all aspects of a business. Thus, as sales increase, as more people are hired, and as inventory increases, sales outpace manufacturing capacity. Facilities are then increased, people are moved between buildings, accounting systems and controls cannot keep up, and so on. The cash burn rate accelerates, and such acceleration continues. Learning curves do the same. Worst of all, cash collections lag behind, as shown in *Exhibit 18.2.*

---

[1] Harvey "Chet" Krentzman described this phenomenon to the author many years ago. The principal still applies.

[2] The crises discussed here are the ones the author considers particularly critical, and, usually, failure to overcome even a few can seriously imperil a venture at a given stage. There are, however, many more, and a complete treatment of all of them is outside the scope of this book.

Exhibit 18.1
Crises and Symptoms

Prestart-Up (years −3 to −1)

Entrepreneurs

- *Focus.*   Is the founder really an entrepreneur, bent on building a company, or an inventor, technical dilettante, or the like?
- *Selling.*   Does the team have the necessary selling and closing skills to bring in the business and make the plan—on time?
- *Management.*   Does the team have the necessary management skills and relevant experience, or is it overloaded in one or two areas (e.g., the financial or technical areas)?
- *Ownership.*   Have the critical decisions about ownership and equity splits been resolved, and are the members committed to these?

Opportunity

- *Focus.*   Is the business really user- , customer- , and market-driven (by a need), or is it driven by an invention of a desire to create?
- *Customers.*   Have customers been identified with specific names, addresses, and phone numbers, and have purchase levels been estimated, or is the business still only at the "concept stage"?
- *Supply.*   Are costs, margins, and lead times to acquire supplies, components, and key people known?
- *Strategy.*   Is the entry plan a shotgun and cherry-picking strategy, or is it a rifle shot at a well-focused niche?

Resources

- *Resources.*   Have the required capital resources been identified?
- *Cash.*   Are the founders already out of cash ("OOC") and their own resources?
- *Business plan.*   Is there a business plan, or is the team "hoofing it"?

Start-Up and Survival (years 0 to 3)

Entrepreneurs

- *Leadership.*   Has a top leader been accepted, or are founders vying for the decision role or insist on equality in all decisions?
- *Goals.*   Do the founders share and have compatible goals and work styles, or are these starting to be in conflict and diverge once the enterprise is underway and pressures mount?
- *Management.*   Are the founders anticipating and preparing for a shift from "doing" to "managing" and letting go—of decisions and control—that will be required to make the plan on time?

Opportunity

- *Economics.*   Are the economic benefits and payback to the customer actually being achieved, and on time?
- *Strategy.*   Is the company a one-product company with no encore in sight?
- *Competition.*   Have previously unknown competitors or substitutes appeared in the marketplace?
- *Distribution.*   Are there surprises and difficulties in actually achieving planned channels of distribution on time?

Resources

- *Cash.*   Is the company facing a cash crunch early as a result of not having a business plan (and a financial plan)—that is, is it facing a crunch because no one is asking: "When will we run out of cash?" Are the owners' pocketbooks exhausted?
- *Schedule.*   Is the company experiencing serious deviations from projections and time estimates in the business plan? Is the company able to marshall resources according to plan and on time?

Exhibit 18.1 *(continued)*

Early Growth (years 4–10)

Entrepreneurs
- *"Doing" or "managing."* Are the founders still just "doing," or are they managing for results by a plan? Have the founders begun to delegate and let go of critical decisions, or do they maintain veto power over all significant decisions?
- *Focus.* Is the mind-set of the founders operational only, or is there some serious strategic thinking going on as well?

Opportunity
- *Market.* Are repeat sales and sales to new customers being achieved on time, according to plan, and because of interaction with customers, or are these coming from the engineering, R&D, or planning group? Is the company shifting to a marketing orientation without losing its "killer instinct" for closing sales?
- *Competition.* Are price and quality being blamed for loss of customers or for an inability to achieve targets in the sales plan, while customer service is rarely mentioned?
- *Economics.* Are gross margins beginning to erode?

Resources
- *Financial control.* Are accounting and information systems and control (purchasing orders, inventory, billing, collections, cost and profit analysis, cash management, etc.) keeping pace with growth and being there when they are needed?
- *Cash.* Is the company always out of cash—or nearly OOC, and is no one asking when it will run out or is sure why or what to do about it?
- *Contacts.* Has the company developed the outside networks (directors, contacts, and so forth) it needs to continue growth?

Maturity (years 10–15 plus)

Entrepreneurs
- *Goals.* Are the partners in conflict over control, goals, or underlying ethics or values?
- *Health.* Are there signs that the founders' marriages, health, or emotional stability are coming apart (i.e., are there extramarital affairs, drug and/or alcohol abuse, or fights and temper tantrums with partners or spouses)?
- *Teamwork.* Is there a sense of team-building for a "greater purpose," with the founders now managing managers, or is there conflict over control of the company and disintegration?

Opportunity
- *Economics/competition.* Are the products and/or services that have gotten the company this far experiencing unforgiving economics as a result of perishability, competitor blind sides, new technology, or off-shore competition, and is there a plan to respond?
- *Product encore.* Has a major new product introduction been a failure?
- *Strategy.* Has the company continued to cherry-pick in fast-growth markets, with a resulting lack of strategic definition (which opportunities to say "no" to)?

Resources
- *Cash.* Is the firm OOC again?
- *Development/information.* Has growth gotten out of control, with systems, training, and development of new managers failing to keep pace?
- *Financial control.* Have systems continued to lag behind sales?

Exhibit 18.1 *(concluded)*

Harvest/Stability (years 15–20 plus)

Entrepreneurs

- *Succession/ownership.* Are there mechanisms in place to provide for management succession and the handling of very tricky ownership issues (especially family)?
- *Goals.* Have the partners' personal and financial goals and priorities begun to conflict and diverge? Are any of the founders simply bored or burned out, and are they seeking a change of view and activities?
- *Entrepreneurial passion.* Has there been an erosion of the passion for creating value through the recognition and pursuit of opportunity, or are turf-building, acquiring status and power symbols, and gaining control favored?

Opportunity

- *Strategy.* Is there a spirit of innovation and renewal in the firm (such as, a goal that half the company's sales come from products or services less than five years old), or has lethargy set in?
- *Economics.* Have the core economics and durability of the opportunity eroded so far that profitability and return on investment is nearly as low as that for the Fortune 500?

Resources

- *Cash.* Has OOC been solved by increasing bank debt and leverage because the founders do not want—or cannot agree—to give up equity?
- *Accounting.* Have accounting and legal issues, especially their relevance for wealth building and estate and tax planning, been anticipated and addressed? Has a "harvest concept" been part of the long-range planning process?

Exhibit 18.2
Spend-rate/Orders/Collection Leads and Lags

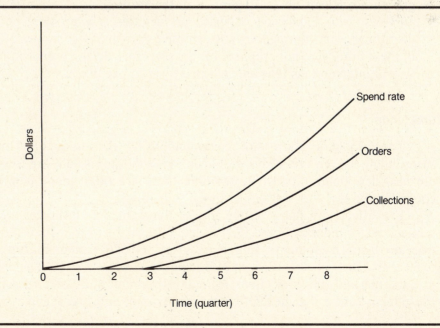

For example, distinctive issues caused by rapid growth were considered at seminars at Babson College with the founders and presidents of rapidly growing companies — companies with sales of at least $1 million and growing in excess of 30 percent per year.[3] These founders and presidents pointed to the following:

- *Abundance of opportunities.* Rather than lacking enough sales or new market opportunities, a classic concern in mature companies, these firms faced an abundance. Choosing from among these was a problem.
- *Abundance of capital.* While most stable or established smaller or medium-sized firms often have difficulties obtaining equity and debt financing, most of the rapidly growing firms were not constrained by this. The problem was, rather, how to evaluate investors as "partners" and the terms of the deals with which they were presented.
- *Misalignment of cash burn and collection rates.* These firms all pointed to problems of cash burn rates racing ahead of collections. They found that, unless effective integrated accounting, inventory, purchasing, shipping, and invoicing systems and controls are in place, this misalignment can lead to chaos and collapse. One firm, for example, had tripled its sales in three years from $5 million to $16 million. Suddenly, its president resigned, insisting that, with the systems which were in place, the company would be able to grow to $100 million. However, the computer system was disastrously inadequate and, thereby, compounded other management weaknesses. The generation of any believable financial and accounting information that could be relied upon was not possible for many months. Losses of more than $1 million annually mounted, and the company's lenders panicked. To make matters worse, the auditors failed to stay on top of the situation until it was too late and were replaced. While the company has survived, it has had to restructure its business and has shrunk to $6 million in sales, to pay off bank debt and to avoid bankruptcy. Fortunately, it is in the process of recovering.
- *Decision making.* Many of the firms succeeded because they executed functional day-to-day and week-to-week decisions, rather than strategizing. Strategy had to take a back seat. Many of the representatives of these firms argued that in conditions of rapid growth it was only about 10 percent of the story.
- *Surprises, etc.* Expansion of space or facilities is a problem and one of the most disrupting events during the early explosive growth of a company. Management of many of these firms were not prepared for the surprises, delays, organizational difficulties, and system interruptions that are spawned by such expansion.

Industry Turbulence

The problems above are compounded by the amount of industry turbulence surrounding the venture. Firms with higher growth rates usually are found in industries that are also developing rapidly. In addition, there are often many new entrants, both with competing products or services and with substitutes.

The effects are many: Often, prices fluctuate. For instance, the turbulence in the semiconductor industry in the 1980s is a good example. From June 1984 to June 1985, the price to original equipment manufacturers (OEMs) of 64K memory chips fell from $2.50 each to 50 cents. The price to OEMs of 256K chips fell from $15 to $3. The disruption this caused in marketing and sales projections, in financial planning and cash forecasting, etc., for firms in the industry can be imagined. Often, there are rapid shifts in cost and experience curves, also.

---

[3] These seminars were held at Babson College near Boston in 1985 and 1986. A good number of the firms represented had sales over $1 million, and a good number were growing at greater than 100 percent per year.

THE IMPORTANCE OF CULTURE AND ORGANIZATIONAL CLIMATE

Six Dimensions

The organizational culture and climate, either of a new venture or of an existing organization, are critical in how well the organization will deal with growth.

A number of studies of performance in large business organizations that used the concept of organizational climate (i.e., the perceptions of people about the kind of place it is to work in) have led to two general conclusions.[4] First, the climate of an organization can have significant impact on performance. Further, climate is created both by the expectations people bring to the organization and the practices and attitudes of the key managers.

The climate notion has relevance for new ventures, as well as for entrepreneurial efforts in large organizations. An entrepreneur's style and priorities—particularly, how he or she manages tasks and people—is well known by the people being managed and affects performance. Recall the entrepreneurial climate described by Enrico of Pepsi, where setting high performance standards by developing short-run objectives, which do not sacrifice long-run results; providing responsive personal leadership; encouraging individual initiative; helping others to succeed; developing individual networks for success; and so forth, were critical.

Evidence suggests that superior teams operate differently in terms of setting priorities, in resolving leadership issues, in what and how roles are performed by team members, in attitudes toward listening and participation, and in dealing with disagreements. Further, evidence suggests that specific approaches to management can impact the climate of a growing organization. For example, gains from the motivation, commitment, and team-work, which are anchored in a consensus approach to management, while not immediately apparent are striking later on. Here, there is swiftness and decisiveness in actions and in follow-through, since the negotiating, compromising, and accepting of priorities is history. Also, new disagreements that emerge generally do not bring progress to a halt, since there is both high clarity and broad acceptance of overall goals and underlying priorities. Without this consensus, each new problem or disagreement often necessitates a time-consuming and painful confrontation and renegotiation simply because it was not done initially.

Organizational climate can be described along six basic dimensions:

- *Clarity.* The degree of organizational clarity in terms of being well organized, concise, and efficient in the way that tasks, procedures, and assignments are made and accomplished.
- *Standards.* The degree to which management expects and puts pressure on employees for high standards and excellent performance.
- *Commitment.* The extent to which employees feel committed to the goals and objectives of the organization.
- *Responsibility.* The extent to which members of the organization feel individual responsibility for accomplishing their goals without being constantly monitored and second-guessed.
- *Recognition.* The extent to which employees feel they are recognized and rewarded (nonmonetarily) for a job well done, instead of only being punished for mistakes or errors.
- *Esprit de corps.* The extent to which employees feel a sense of cohesion and team spirit, of working well together.

---

[4] See Jeffry A. Timmons, "The Entrepreneurial Team: Formation and Development," a paper presented at the Academy of Management, annual meeting, Boston, August 1973.

Approaches to Management

In achieving the entrepreneurial culture and climate described above, certain approaches to management (also discussed in Chapter 6) are common across core management modes.

Leadership

No single leadership pattern seems to characterize successful ventures. Leadership may be shared, or informal, or a "natural leader" may guide a task. Common, however, is the pattern whereby a manager defines and gains agreements on who has what responsibility and authority and who does what with and to whom. Roles, tasks, responsibilities, accountabilities, and appropriate approvals are defined.

There is no competition for leadership in these organizations, and leadership is based on expertise, not authority. Emphasis is placed on performing task-oriented roles, but someone invariably provides for "maintenance" and group cohesion by good humor and wit. Further, the leader does not force his or her own solution on the team or exclude the involvement of potential resources. Instead, the leader understands the relationships among tasks and between the leader and followers and is able to lead in those situations where it is appropriate, including managing actively the activities of others through directions, suggestions, and so forth.

This approach is in direct contrast to the "commune approach," where two to four entrepreneurs, usually friends or work acquaintances, leave unanswered questions of who is in charge, who makes the final decisions, and how real differences of opinion are resolved. While some overlapping of roles and a sharing in and negotiating of decisions are desirable in a new venture, too much looseness is debilitating.

This approach is also in contrast to that where a self-appointed leader takes over, where there is competition for leadership, or where one task takes precedence over other tasks.

Consensus Building

Leaders of most successful new ventures define authority and responsibility in a way that builds motivation and commitment to cross-departmental and corporate goals. Using a consensus approach to management requires managing and working with peers and with the subordinates of others (or with superiors) outside formal chains of command and balancing multiple viewpoints and demands.

In the consensus approach, the manager is seen as willing to relinquish his or her priorities and power in the interests of an overall goal, and the appropriate people are included in setting cross-functional or cross-departmental goals and in making decisions. Participation and listening are emphasized.

The most effective managers, in addition, are committed to dealing with problems and working problems through to agreement by seeking a reconciliation of viewpoints, rather than emphasizing differences, and by blending ideas, rather than playing the role of hard-nose negotiator or devil's advocate to force their own solution. There is open confrontation of differences of opinion and a willingness to talk out differences, assumptions, reasons, and inferences. Logic and reason tend to prevail, and there is a willingness to change opinions based on consensus.

Communication

The most effective managers share information and are willing to alter individual views. Listening and participation are facilitated by such methods as circular seating arrangements, few interruptions or side conversations, and calm discussion versus many interruptions, loud or separate conversations, and so forth, in meetings.

Encouragement

Successful managers build confidence by encouraging innovation and calculated risk-taking, rather than by punishing or criticizing what is less than perfect, and by expecting and encouraging others to find and correct their own errors and to solve their own problems. They are perceived by their peers and others as accessible and willing to help when needed, and they provide the necessary resources to enable others to do the job. When it is appropriate, they go to bat for their peers and subordinates, even when they know they can't always win.

Further, differences are recognized and performance is rewarded.

Trust

The most effective managers are perceived as trustworthy and straightforward. They do what they say they are going to do; they are not the corporate rumor carriers; they are more open and spontaneous, rather than guarded and cautious with each word; and they are perceived as being honest and direct. They have a reputation of getting results and become known as the creative problem-solvers who have a knack for blending and balancing multiple views and demands.

Development

Effective managers have a reputation for developing human capital (i.e., they groom and grow other effective managers by their example and their mentoring). As noted in Chapter 6, Bradford and Cohen distinguish between the "heroic manager," whose need to be in control in many instances actually may stifle cooperation, and the "postheroic manager," a developer who actually brings about excellence in organizations by developing entrepreneurial middle management. If a company puts off developing middle management until price competition appears and its margins erode, the organization may come unraveled. Linking a plan to grow human capital at the middle management and the supervisory levels with the business strategy is an essential first step.

ANTICIPATING AND COPING WITH PROBLEMS

The existence of problems and severe time pressures can easily force an entrepreneurial team into a fire-fighting mode, where all their time is spent responding to crises.

Anticipating the major problems that may be encountered allows for standard operating procedures to cut down possible crises. Anticipation of likely operational problems provides an incentive to establish organized operational methods.

Anticipation also increases the team's sensitivity and ability to recognize a problem early so the proper response can be developed before the problem becomes a major crisis.

Beyond this, a team, when aware of what typical operating problems or incipient crises may confront their venture, will often, almost subconsciously, be preparing alternate strategic solutions or venture contingency plans. Therefore, the problems, when they occur, do not cause a major psychological shock.

Problem Areas

The management of new ventures often find themselves confronting problems that are impossible to anticipate, such as: a major potential customer who demands a far more detailed instruction and service manual than was expected; a shortage of telephone lines; a sales manager who quits; a major defect discovered in the function of a product; the need to attend immediately to important customers in different parts of the country; an increase in the price and delivery time of a product component, which cannot be obtained elsewhere; an illness in the family of a key team member; and so on.

Year in and year out, other problems facing new ventures seem to occur most often in certain areas of difficulty. In a 1983 questionnaire, the chief executive officers of businesses with sales under $1 million were asked to rank a number of problems according to how seriously they affected their businesses.[5] The 503 executives that answered ranked seven problem categories above the rest, as follows:

- Cash flow (20 percent).
- Inflation (20 percent).
- Controlling costs (15 percent).
- Finding qualified, motivated employees (12 percent).
- Excessive government regulation (9 percent).
- Inadequate demand (8 percent).
- High interest rates (8 percent).

Further, a report on the causes of business failure in 1980 indicated the apparent causes of failure were competitive weakness and heavy operating expenses. These were affected by the skills of the management team and their ability to develop basic strategy to cope with new situations.[6] Major apparent causes in business failure were, 60 percent of the time, inadequate sales; 30 percent, heavy operating expenses; and 23 percent, competitive weakness. A similar 1968 report lists inadequate sales, 40 percent, and heavy operating expenses, 14 percent.[7]

Monitoring Variables

The specific problems of any one particular company will certainly vary, and identifying these problems as early as possible is important.

Venture problems suddenly appear in varying states of maturity, ranging from a minor thorn in the side to a full-blown crisis. It may be difficult to see these problems in the forest of day-to-day operations. *Exhibit 18.3* shows actions or patterns that might be expected to cause operating problems. Note that these are only a few of the actions or patterns which signal problems.

One way to identify a problem early is to monitor certain critical variables. These variables may vary from company to company depending upon its stage.

One venture capitalist believes there are certain critical variables that can be monitored. He put it this way:

There are 8 or 10 critical variables in any new venture which will be different for each venture but need monitoring to allow management to properly anticipate operating problems. One of the entrepreneurial arts is developing simple ways to get a handle on these critical variables.

The venture capitalist above monitors the following key variables:

- Orders in hand.
- Potential orders being processed.
- Accounts receivable.

[5] James S. Howard, "Annual Survey of Small Business Presidents," *Dun & Bradstreet Reports* (New York: Dun & Bradstreet Credit Services, 1983), pp. 18–21.

[6] "Causes of 11,742 Business Failures in 1980," Dun & Bradstreet Credit Services, 99 Church Street, New York, New York.

[7] Report of the President's Task Force on improving the prospects of small business, *Improving the Prospects of Small Business* (Washington, D.C.: United States Government Printing Office, 1980).

Exhibit 18.3
Patterns and Actions

Area	*Pattern or Action*
Team	
Lead entrepreneur	• If the lead entrepreneur is overburdened with things that need never reach his or her desk, this may indicate either a lack of delegation in team and staff function or, worse, a reverse delegation from partners and subordinates who do not have a clear picture of company goals or policy or are not capable of handling their positions.
	• If the lead entrepreneur is uncomfortable doing things he or she does not know how to do, is not communicating effectively, or mistrusts the ethics, motivation, and so forth of any of the management team, he or she may not be functioning well with the team.
Team members	• Widely conflicting perceptions of the same event from different team and staff members may mean a lack of clarity and commitment to goals.
	• A repeated inability to come to a consensus may mean the company does not manage with a vision or the vision/harvest objective is unclear.
	• Lack of communication of critical information in timely fashion may mean a lack of collaboration and harmful rivalries.
	• Making of bad decisions by subordinates, and making of crucial decisions by subordinates that have not been checked out with their superiors, are indicative of problems.
	• Failing to permit subordinates to make decisions they are better positioned and prepared to make and to let them grow by making nonfatal mistakes may signal a perfectionist who greatly overcontrols subordinates.
	• Failure to settle up front equity splits among the team members or if these do not reflect true contributions over time may mean that mechanisms for adjustment are needed.
	• The phrase, "We need a system for . . . ," may indicate the need for a system—or it may indicate the need for a working team.
	• Formation of cliques which do not communicate with one another can signify the lack of a strong unifying belief in the venture's goals.
	• High employee turnover may be another indicator of low morale. Sometimes expectations are too high for employees working for pay with no equity incentive.
Other personnel	• Part-time employees usually do not take ultimate responsibility for success as a team member would, or some, such as lawyers, have not been hired to solve business problems. An entrepreneur can expect sound advice and a resource for the facts he or she needs, but not necessarily detailed creative solutions to problems.
Planning	• "Do" lists are powerful tools for moving a business step by step toward each of its goals. Lack of effective do lists on the part of any of a venture's managerial personnel is a warning light that needs to be heeded.

Exhibit 18.3 *(continued)*

Area	Pattern or Action
	• Absence of strategy meetings often indicates such problems as lack of communication, mistrust of partners, and no recognition of day-to-day problems. However, when this condition exists over a significant number of weeks, it clearly indicates a team preference for fire-fighting or action-oriented activity, rather than goal-oriented activity and planning.
	• The fact that no one knows for sure how the company is doing and how it is going to achieve a harvest may mean that the business plan has been abandoned and needs to be modified

Product(s) or service(s)

Area	Pattern or Action
Product diversification	• Dilution of resources must be watched closely, because it is one of the more insidious venture dilutions. A common product mistake is simply having too many. In starting into a new field, the venture often may rapidly develop products to meet customer needs. When it is not apparent what products are going to be crucial to success, this is a valid strategy to carry if development can be worked out on spare time or if the customer pays for it. However, at some point, there will be products that bring little in sales, customer good will, or image, while they dilute management, sales, engineering, service effort, and working capital. There will be many defenders of the broad product line, and objective analysis is necessary to keep a line in proper balance.
	• A team may be tempted to accept business for products or services in areas in which the team has little experience. It is important that the venture always build on what its team has already done. When the ratio of unknowns to knowns in a project gets high, the risk of failure increases greatly.
Testing	• Misunderstanding the extent or cause of failure in testing and in the field under real conditions may lead to large unexpected overruns in development cost and a lack of strategic options.
Service and user documentation	• An endemic problem in small companies is that of service or user manuals and documentation. A venture must remain alert to the real costs attached to providing sufficient user information over the long run and must expect to meet this need. As the field matures, there will often be standard requirements for documentation that must be met to compete effectively.
Production documentation	• Corollary to the user product information problem is documentation for production of the product. As the in-house manufacturing facility grows, documentation also becomes more crucial to facilitate individual and department communication and performance. Here, again, the problem will show up as one of quality control.
Product pricing	• Every start-up team is nervous about getting customers and marketing and salespeople who want to succeed, so there is a tendency for new venture teams to underprice their product(s) or service(s) and oversell performance capabilities.
	• Further, development engineers often are inclined to give too much product for a given sales price.

Exhibit 18.3 *(continued)*

Area	*Pattern or Action*
Performance specifications	• It is important not to "overspecify" performance. In a new field, the customer often does not know what he or she wants in the way of performance, and, further, unrealistic specifications can be costly to a new firm. This concept can be carried to many aspects of a new business. For example, when borrowing from the bank, a new venture should not promise more than necessary.
Nonstandard products	• There are often projects, such as delivery of a nonstandard system on a tight schedule to a fussy customer, that present considerable risk to the venture if they do not succeed. While the potential market opened by development of a new service or product may be large, failure to perform satisfactorily on the contract could jeopardize the financial stability of the company.

Sales

Orders	• Failure to close sales is a common problem in new ventures. It often is hard to believe that a customer will not buy what or when he or she said. A mistake that entrepreneurs continue to make is failing to realize that a customer may buy only a portion of what he or she promised, or may not buy anything at all in the end. Sometimes, too, a team believes its own sales story and forgets it has to perform to succeed.
Potential orders	• The life blood of the company is sales, collections, and repeat orders.
Customer satisfaction	• A company may have good sales but some irate customers. One irate customer can do a company a lot of sales damage, since he or she will "bad mouth" to a number of other customers.
Advance payments	• If the product or service is as spectacular as the business plan and sales brochures say, then a company can (and perhaps should) ask for advance payment.

Inventory and work in process

Inventory level	• No matter how effective the accounting system is believed to be, actual physical inventory shows where things actually stand. It is common for firms with goods having a high value per unit to take inventory monthly.
Work in process	• Management needs to know how work in process matches with the order rate and inventory requirements.
Purchase level	• Management needs to know how the purchase level matches the order rate and inventory requirements.

Financial

Accounts receivable	• A chief financial officer who gets indignant (when there is plenty of cash in the bank) at questions about when the company will run out of cash does not understand the implications of the question and is probably in over his or her head.

Exhibit 18.3 *(concluded)*

Area	Pattern or Action
	• A problem for new firms is that sometimes a team is too busy having fun developing new products to "waste time" doing the dirty work of pursuing accounts receivable. When the venture is unexpectedly short of cash, the firm increases its bank loan instead of collecting accounts due.
Profitability	• Value building includes the bottom line—and much more.
Cash in the bank	• Cash shortages can come from many causes, and questions need to be asked about when the company will run out of cash, how the company knows this, and why it will run out.
Expenses	• When expenses run higher than predicted, a team should get nervous. The underlying causes may take time to solve.
Product costs	• Rarely does the company know the real variable and other costs of each of its products. Yet, only knowing accounting costs and total costs will not do it.
Environment	
Awareness	• A venture exists in the marketplace and the world. If the economy is going down, the effect will eventually get to a venture no matter how insulated it thinks its business is. Watch out for interest rates going up, loans getting scarce, and accounts receivable stretching out as a result.
Arrogance	• A team needs to remain alert to the problem of arrogance. The business arrogance of believing you have the key to a successful operating mode for your field may be disastrous if conditions should change. Technical arrogance may lead to development of products that are too narrow and become obsolete; sales arrogance may leave a firm with new competitors; and personal arrogance may add a spin-off from the company to the list of competitors.

- Cash in the bank.
- Inventory level.
- Work in process.
- Level of purchases.
- Production efficiency.
- Engineering load.

In addition to the variables monitored, the need for monitoring, the methods used to monitor, and the frequency of monitoring will vary with the venture, its stage of development, its core management mode, its business and cultural environment, and the team and its management style.

For example, the following two companies, in radically different fields, monitored variables they felt were key. A manufacturer of textile-related recreational equipment believed that the way to beat competition in his market niche depended on attracting and holding an increasing number of end-users who looked for high-quality products and on-time delivery. The list of key variables to be monitored, therefore, looked like this: production schedule, work load of key people, orders in hand, materials cost, materials delivery, quality, cash flow, and market feedback.

In contrast, a manufacturer of complex oceanographic instruments and systems recognized that his success was dependent less on the number of end-users (which were relatively few) but rather on the number of major orders being considered or processed. He believed that, because the processing time for a major order could run 6 to 18 months, many orders would have to be in process to ensure a steady and growing business. Further, he believed the ratio of orders won to orders lost was crucial because, if a bid was lost to the competition, most of the 6- to 18-month lead time would be gone and, since the cost to bid on a large job was high, a loss of a bid meant an increase in overhead. Consequently, the company developed a list of key variables it needed to monitor, as follows: backlog of orders; orders being processed or considered by customers; orders predicted versus orders closed; awareness by team of internal and external events; knowledge of manufacturing costs for a wide variety of subassemblies; competitors' pricing; competitors' political action; customer satisfaction; instrument reliability; ability of management to process data quickly; state of the art in oceanographic instruments and other fields that could be applied to products; and management and technical team balance.

SOLVING PROBLEMS

Attitudes

Venture problems or crises sometimes require only a quick and commonsense response on the telephone. Not always. In difficult cases, more involved processes may be required.

In solving problems, a positive mental attitude, a vision of the future in perspective, and a total dedication, combined with an understanding of vulnerabilities, will allow for a faster recovery when undesirable events hit. Even in the cases where massive data gathering and analytical effort is required, the actual solution to the problem is synthesized in an entrepreneur's mind through creative cognitive processes.

■ *Positive mental attitude.* Having a positive mental attitude and being aware of problem areas are illustrated in the following example. Some years ago, the head of Inetron was told in July of the year by the director of a federal government office that, with heavy fiscal pressures on the office's budget, it was extremely likely that Inetron's service would not receive additional funding after January of the following year. Since the government office was Inetron's only significant customer and since the service being supplied was of such a specialized nature that it would have almost no market other than to this one agency, the news was disastrous. It looked as if over two years of intensive work on a unique service would be halted, with grave implications for survival of the venture. Rather than give up, Inetron's lead entrepreneur called the director to outline six ways to ease the government's funding problem for that service and to voice concern that the government would stop funding a project which had had initial success and had met significant needs of the government agency. The director laughed at the persistence of the entrepreneur and invited Inetron back for further discussions. A specific list of results that Inetron had to obtain to retain its government funding was hammered out. The venture achieved these results, was funded, and has continued to provide a unique successful service since that time.

■ *Vision of the future.* A vision of the future can help an entrepreneur through present-day details and problems that need to be dealt with. The ultimate goals of the venture need to become as real or more real to the entrepreneur than present-day life. This vision of the future can take the form of one or more models of the future in the entrepreneur's mind. Factual data will eliminate, confirm, or strengthen features of the model, and each mental walk through the future will make the entrepreneur more aware of priorities and relationships. For instance, recently an entrepreneurial team was trying to establish a price for a new financial management service. Normally, the fee charged would be a percentage (usually 3 percent to 4 percent) of the capital being handled. However, the costs involved in supplying this proposed new service were too high to allow a fee of only 3 percent to 4 percent. In viewing the new venture being proposed, not as a management service but as a development operation with a subsidiary management function involved, past management fee precedents did not bear on setting the proposed fee.

■ *Total immersion and dedication.* Knowledge of the essential details of an entire business and field (e.g., the company's operation, the product, marketplace, venture environment, competition, current literature, and innovations) requires that enough intelligent hours be applied. A larger company can use more people to attack problems. Yet, adding more people to a decision and to the action process often means more complication, more time required to move, more reasons not to move, more chances for things to fall through the cracks, and, ultimately, higher overhead and prices. Thus, the dedicated, totally immersed new venture team can carve itself a place in the market based on its ability to make rapid, integrated decisions and to take positive action in a timely cost-effective way. Many ventures continue to operate on this principle long after reaching a solid market position. Digital Equipment Corporation is now the second largest computer company in the world, and several of its founding entrepreneurs and some new first- and second-level management are still totally immersed in its operation nearly 30 years after its start-up.

Problem-Solving Steps

The following steps suggest a possible approach to responding to venture problems:

■ *Define the problem.* The first step in solving a problem is to separate the problem from its symptoms and to define it in detail. Correctly defining a problem, as correctly defining a goal in planning, is a key factor in problem solving. In the financial services example mentioned earlier in the chapter, the symptom of the problem was the inability to sell a financial management service. If the symptom were defined as the problem, the solution might be to look for a new set of customers. However, the problem was that product cost was too high to allow selling in competition with financial management services viewed by the customers as similar to those proposed. Thus, the answer to the correctly stated venture problem was to sell a new package, a development service, and at a new price to the same customers, rather than to look for new customers.

■ *Break the problem into pieces.* When confronting a seemingly insoluble problem, breaking the problem into pieces sometimes helps. Then it may be possible to solve each piece separately.

■ *Establish goals.* Goals that are: specific and concrete, measurable, related to time, realistic and attainable, capable of being modified and adapted, and certain to make a significant difference (see Chapter 11).
  Collect and analyze data. These data and analyses might include cash flow, breakeven investment requirements, returns on investment, risks-reward ratios, market directions, patent positions, competitive strengths, and so forth.

■ *Log peripheral factors.* Noting peripheral factors (those which are outside the core problem and not central to its resolution) is helpful so these factors will not be a distraction.

- *Catalog available resources.*   Many problems need a spectrum of resources to allow solution, and cataloging these resources needs to take account of time. Time is involved when a new venture uses time as capital, much in the same way that real-dollar capital allows a wealthy venture to buy resources all at one time when needed. To illustrate, in the financial management service example mentioned above, several specialized and talented individuals became available over the period of three years, and they were put on the venture's payroll to accomplish very productive and valuable consulting tasks. When the time came to place the full development and services product in the marketplace, these individuals were there, tested and trained in new techniques and adding greatly to the credibility of the venture in the eyes of customers and potential investors, and in reality.

  Time is involved in the need to gauge carefully when resources need to be committed to the solution of a problem. Often an entrepreneur, when confronted with a problem, will fall into the good manager syndrome (i.e., the syndrome where it is felt that a problem to be solved should be solved quickly and dispatched). However, it can sometimes be advantageous to put off final decisions so the venture has flexibility. Further, specific problems change over time, thus opening potential new solutions. For example, Inetron tried continually to market to a second government agency, initially with little success. Finally, a new director of the second agency was appointed, who was somewhat more responsive to the potential of the service; but, even with this change in the agency, it was difficult to come to agreement. A change in circumstances over time, combined with the technique of tossing a discouraging job back and forth among close-knit team members, broke this most difficult marketing problem. With each shift, new energy was brought to the problem and a better fit in skills and personality was provided at different stages. Time is involved in the need to gauge carefully when resources need to be committed to the solution of a problem.

  Solving a problem by using time is, in effect, stringing out the problem over time or treating the problem serially, which is, in turn, a form of breaking a problem into pieces — a most powerful problem-solving tool.

- *Brainstorm.*   This step allows management to consider solutions to similar problems and bring to bear the experience and training of the team and its backup advisers. A highly productive venture problem-solving tool is that of role-playing, where an entrepreneur can imagine himself or herself in the role of a major or critical component of the problem. For example, by having one of its team members play the role of a competitor, a company was able to become the lowest bidder on a $500,000 contract. Another technique is to take the worst thing that could happen and turn it into an advantage. In the case of Massey-Dickinson, the lead entrepreneur took being drafted into the army and turned this to his advantage. Business progress often consists of taking two steps forward and sliding back one. If some of the major slides back can be turned to major steps forward, a venture's business progress can be smoothed and improved.

- *Choose the best solution.*   Alternate solutions need to be developed. These solutions can be ordered according to their desirability and the best can be chosen.

- *Reassemble.*   Reassemble the problem's pieces and their solutions and examine the interrelationships of the parts for dysfunctions. If these dysfunctions can be balanced with additional solutions, an integrated solution to the entire problem will have been devised.

The Entrepreneur and the Troubled Company

Yes, I did run out of time on a few occasions, but I never lost a ball game!

Bobby Lane, great quarterback
in the 1950s and 1960s
of the Detroit Lions and the
Pittsburgh Steelers

RESULTS EXPECTED

Upon completion of this chapter,[1] you will have:

1. Examined the principal causes and danger signals of impending trouble.
2. Discussed both quantitative and qualitative symptoms of trouble.
3. Examined the principal diagnostic methods to devise intervention and turnaround plans.
4. Identified remedial actions used for dealing with lenders, creditors, and employees.

WHEN THE BLOOM IS OFF THE ROSE

This chapter is about the entrepreneur and the troubled company. It traces the firm's route into and out of crisis and provides some insight into how a troubled company can be rescued by a turnaround specialist.

As was seen in Chapter 1, sooner or later the competitive dynamics of the free enterprise system catch up with many smaller companies. This is a natural process of birth, growth, and death of firms. Even firms in the Fortune 500 are not immune to such forces. Today, over one third of the Fortune 500 companies of 1970 no longer exist. Some have failed and gone bankrupt, others have been absorbed by larger firms, and still others have been acquired and dismantled.

Although there are similarities between the experiences of new and emerging companies and large companies that experience trouble, there are important differences. New and emerging firms need to approach crises more quickly and have less in the way of financial resources to help them. New and emerging firms deal with simpler strategic and organizational issues. Yet, these firms are more likely to commit errors in the area of financial planning and policy, commonly manage working capital poorly, underutilize assets, and have weak information systems. Finally, these firms are often too insignificant in the eyes of government to qualify for the kind of help Chrysler received.

There is a saying among horsemen and women that the rider who has never been thrown from a horse probably has never ridden one! This insight captures the essence of the ups and downs that can occur during the growth and development of a new venture.

[1] Special credit is due to Robert Bateman, Scott Douglas, and Ann Morgan for the material in this chapter. The material is the result of research and interviews wih turnaround specialists and was submitted in a paper as a requirement for the author's Financing Entrepreneurial Ventures course in the MBA program at Babson College.

The author is especially grateful to two specialists, Leslie B. Charm, chairman of Doktor Pet Centers, and Leland Goldberg, of Coopers & Lybrand, Boston, who contributed enormously to the efforts of Bateman, Douglas, and Morgan and to the material.

Getting Into and Out of Trouble

Troubled companies face a situation similar to that described by Winston Churchill in *While England Slept:*

. . . descending inconstantly, fecklessly, the stairway which leads to dark gulf. It is a fine broad stairway at the beginning, but after a bit the carpet ends, a little farther on there are only flagstones, and a little farther on still these break beneath your feet.

If a firm has in sight a good opportunity, crisis for such a firm is usually the result of management error, although external uncontrollable factors (such as the oil embrago of 1973) can precipitate crisis.

In these management errors are found part of the solution to problems of the troubled company. It is pleasing to see that many companies—even companies that are insolvent or have negative net worth or both—can be rescued and restored to profitability.

The causes and signals of trouble described below, and the process of developing an action plan for turnaround, are usually more readily recognized by outsiders than those insiders who are immersed as part of the problem. However, the best single insurance policy to avoid such trouble, or at least to minimize the painful consequences, is to keep the company entrepreneurial in mind-set, culture, and management action.

Causes of Trouble

Trouble can be caused by external forces not under the control of management. Among the most frequently mentioned are: recession, interest rate changes, changes in government policy, inflation, the entry of new competition, and industry/product obsolescence.

However, those who manage turnarounds find that, while such circumstances define the environment to which a troubled company needs to adjust, they rarely account for an individual company failure by themselves. External shocks impact all companies in an industry, and only some of them fail. Others can survive and prosper.

Most causes of failure can be found within company management. Although there are many causes of trouble, the most frequently cited fall into three broad areas: inattention to strategic issues, general management problems, and poor financial/accounting systems and practices. There is striking similarity between these causes of trouble and the causes of start-up failure given in Chapter 1.

- *Strategic issues*
  - *Misunderstood market niche.*   The first of these issues is a failure to understand the company's market niche and to focus on growth without considering profitability. Instead of developing a strategy, these firms take on low-margin business and add capacity in an effort to grow. They then can find they run out of cash.
  - *Mismanaged relationships with suppliers and customers.*   Related to the issue of not understanding market niche is the failure to understand the economics of relationships with suppliers and customers. Some firms allow practices in the industry to dictate payment terms, and so forth, when in fact they may be in a position to dictate their own terms.
  - *Diversification into an unrelated business area.*   A common failing of cash-rich firms that suffer from the growth syndrome is diversification into unrelated business areas. These firms use the cash flow generated in one business to start another without good reason. As one turnaround consultant said, "I couldn't believe it. There was no synergy at all. They added to their overhead but not to their contribution. No common sense!"

- *Mousetrap myopia.* Related to the problem of starting a firm around an idea, rather than an opportunity, is the problem of firms that have "great products" looking for other markets where they can be sold. This is done without analyzing opportunities.
- *The big project.* This cause is discussed here because it relates to start-up strategy. The company gears up for a "big project" without looking at the cash flow implications. Cash is expended by adding capacity and hiring personnel. When sales do not materialize, or take longer than expected to materialize, there is trouble. Sometimes the "big project" is required by the nature of the business opportunity. An example of this would be the high-technology start-up that needs to capitalize on a "first-mover" advantage. The company needs to prove the product's "right to life" and grow quickly to the point where it can achieve a public market or become an attractive acquisition candidate for a larger company so a larger company cannot copy the technology and use its advantages in scale and existing distribution channels to achieve dominance over the start-up.
- *Lack of contingency planning.* As has been stated over and over, the path to growth is not a smooth curve heading up. Firms need to be geared to think about what happens if things go sour — if sales fall or if collections slow. There need to be plans in place for lay-offs and capacity reduction.

- ■ *Management issues*
  - *Lack of management skills, experience, and know-how.* As was mentioned in Chapter 6, while companies grow, managers need to change their management mode from "doing" to "managing" to "managing managers."
  - *Weak finance function.* Often, in a new and emerging company, the finance function is nothing more than a bookkeeper. One company was five years old, with $20 million in sales, before the founders hired a financial professional.
  - *Turnover in key management personnel.* Although a critical concern in businesses that deal in specialized or proprietary knowledge, turnover of key management personnel can be difficult in any firm. For example, one firm lost a bookkeeper who was the only one who really understood what was happening in the business.
  - *Big-company influence in accounting.* A mistake that some companies often make is to focus on accruals, rather than cash.

- ■ *Poor planning, financial/accounting systems, practices, and controls*
  - *Poor pricing, overextension of credit, and excessive leverage.* These causes of trouble are not surprising and need not be elaborated. Some of the reasons for excess use of leverage are interesting. Use of excess leverage can result when growth outstrips the company's internal financing capability. The company then relies increasingly on short-term notes until a cash flow problem develops. Another reason is the use of guaranteed loans in place of equity for either start-up or expansion financing. As one entrepreneur remarked, "It [the guaranteed loan] looked just like equity when we started, but when trouble came it looked more and more like debt."
  - *Lack of cash budgets/projections.* This is a most frequently cited cause of trouble. In small companies cash budgets/projections are often not done.
  - *Poor management reporting.* While some firms have good financial reporting, they suffer from poor management reporting. As one turnaround consultant stated, the general ledger system "just tells where the company has been. It doesn't help *manage* the business. If you look at the important management reports — inventory analysis, receivables agings, sales analysis — they're usually late or not produced at all. The same goes for billing procedures. Lots of emerging companies don't get their bills out on time."

— *Lack of standard costing.*   Poor management reporting extends to issues of costing, too. Many emerging businesses have no standard costs against which they can compare the actual costs of manufacturing products. The result is they have no variance reporting. The company cannot identify problems in process and take corrective action. The company will know only after the fact how profitable a product is.

Even when standard costs are used it is not uncommon to find that engineering, manufacturing, and accounting each has its own version of the bill of material. The product is designed one way, manufactured a second way, and costed a third.

— *Poorly understood cost behavior.*   Companies often do not understand the relationship between fixed and variable costs. For example, one manufacturing company thought it was saving money by closing on Saturday. In this way, management felt it would save paying overtime. It had to be pointed out to the lead entrepreneur by a turnaround consultant that "he had a lot of high-margin product in his manufacturing backlog that more than justified the overtime."

It is also important for entrepreneurs to understand the difference between theory and practice in this area. The turnaround consultant mentioned above said, "Accounting theory says that all costs are variable in the long run. In practice, almost all costs are fixed. The only truly variable cost is a sales commission."

THE GESTATION PERIOD OF CRISIS

Crisis rarely develops overnight. The time between the initial cause of trouble and the point of intervention can run from 18 months to five years. Rarely does intervention occur in less than a year.

What happens to a company during the gestation period has implications for the later turnaround of the company. Thus, how management reacts to crisis and what happens to morale determine what will need to happen in the intervention. A situation that usually develops is a demoralized and unproductive organization whose members think only of survival, not turnaround, and an entrepreneur who has lost credibility. Further, the company has lost valuable time.

The Paradox of Optimism

A typical scenario for a troubled company is as follows: The first signs of trouble (such as declining margins, customer returns, or falling liquidity) go unnoticed or are written off as teething problems of the new project or as the ordinary vicissitudes of business. For example, one entrepreneur saw increases in inventory and receivables as a good sign, since sales were up and the current ratio had improved. However, although sales were up, margins were down, and he did not realize he had a liquidity problem until cash shortages developed.

Although management may miss the first signs, outsiders usually do not. Banks, board members, suppliers, and customers see trouble brewing. They wonder why management does not respond. Credibility begins to erode.

Soon management has to admit that trouble exists, but valuable time has been lost. Furthermore, any of the requisite actions to meet the situation is anathema. The lead entrepreneur is emotionally committed to people, to projects, or to business areas. Further, to cut back in any of these areas goes against instinct, because the company will need these resources when the good times return.

The company continues its downward fall, and the situation becomes stressful. Turnaround specialists mention that stress can cause avoidance on the part of an entrepreneur. Others have likened the entrepreneur in a troubled company to a rabbit caught in a car's headlights: The entrepreneur is frozen and can take no action. Avoidance has a basis in human psychology. One organizational behavior consultant who has worked on turnarounds said that, when a person under stress does not understand the problem and does not have the skills to deal with it, the person will tend to replace the unpleasant reality with fantasy. The consultant went on to say that the outward manifestation of this fantasy is avoidance. This consultant noted it is common for an entrepreneur to deal with pleasant and well-understood tasks, such as selling to customers, rather than dealing with the trouble. The result is that credibility is lost with bankers, creditors, and so forth. (However, these are the very people whose cooperation needs to be secured if the company is to be turned around.)

Often, what decisions the entrepreneur does make during this time are poor and accelerate the company on its downward course. To illustrate, the accountant or the controller may be fired with the result that the company is then "flying blind." One entrepreneur, for example, running a company that manufactured a high-margin product, announced across-the-board cuts in expenditures, including advertising, without stopping to think that cutting advertising on such a product only added to the cash flow problem.

Finally, the entrepreneur may make statements that are not true or may make promises he or she cannot keep. This is the death knell of his or her credibility.

Decline in Organizational Morale

Among those who notice trouble developing are the employees. They deal with customer returns, calls from creditors, and the like, and they wonder why management does not respond. They begin to lose confidence in management.

Despite troubled times, the lead entrepreneur talks and behaves optimistically. Employees hear of trouble from each other and from other outsiders. They lose confidence in the formal communications of the company. The grapevine, which is always exaggerated, takes on increased credibility. Company turnover starts to increase. Morale is eroding.

It is obvious there is a problem and that it is not being dealt with. Employees wonder what will happen, whether they will be laid off, and whether the firm will go into bankruptcy. With their security threatened, employees lapse into "survival mode." As an organizational behavior consultant explains:

The human organism can tolerate anything except uncertainty. It causes so much stress that people are no longer capable of thinking in a cognitive, creative manner. They focus on survival. That's why in turnarounds you see so much uncooperative, finger-pointing behavior. The only issue people understand is directing the blame elsewhere.

As last, crisis can force intervention. The occasion is usually forced by the board of directors or a lender. For example, the bank may call a loan, or the firm may be put on cash terms by its suppliers. Perhaps creditors try to put the firm into involuntary bankruptcy.

PREDICTING TROUBLE

Since crises develop over time and typically result from an accumulation of fundamental errors, the question can be asked whether crisis can be predicted. The obvious benefit of being able to predict crisis is that the entrepreneur, employees, and significant outsiders, such as investors, lenders, trade creditors, and even customers, could see trouble brewing in time to take corrective actions.

There have been several attempts to develop predictive models. Two are presented below and have been selected, because each is easy to calculate and uses information available in common financial reports. Since management reporting in emerging companies is often inadequate, the predictive model needs to use information available in common financial reports.

Exhibit 19.1
Z-Scores

Public Z-Score	0.012×1	0.014×2	0.033×3	0.006×4	0.999×5
< 1.81 = Danger	WC	RE	EBIT	MVE	SALES
> 2.99 = Safe	TA	TA	TA	TL	TA
Private Z-Score	0.717×1	0.847×2	3.107×3	0.420×4	0.998×5
< 1.23 = Danger	WC	RE	EBIT	NW	SALES
> 2.90 = Safe	TA	TA	TA	TL	TA

Where:
WC	=	Working capital
RE	=	Retained earnings
EBIT	=	Earnings before interest & taxes
MVE	=	Market value equity
SALES	=	Sales
NW	=	Net worth
TL	=	Total liabilities
TA	=	Total assets

Each of the two approaches below uses easily obtained financial data to predict the onset of crisis as much as two years in advance. For the smaller public company, these models can be used by all interested observers. With private companies, they are useful only to those privy to the information and are probably only of benefit to such nonmanagement outsiders as lenders and boards of directors.

In considering the two models, it is important to note that the most frequently used denominator in all these ratios is the figure for total assets. This figure often is distorted by "creative accounting," with expenses occasionally improperly capitalized and carried on the balance sheet or by substantial differences between tangible book value and book value (i.e., overvalued or undervalued assets).

Z-Score

The first model, shown in *Exhibit 19.1,* was developed by Edward Altman, who set out to predict bankruptcy in publicly held companies.[2] He used multiple-discriminate analysis to produce an equation of five weighted ratios. These ratios then are summed to produce a Z-Score. He found that the Z-Score can predict bankruptcy with significant reliability as much as two years in advance.

Altman also had a version for predicting bankruptcy in private companies. Again, multiple-discriminate analysis is used to produce an equation of five weighted ratios. The only difference between the two equations is in one of the numerators, with a measure of book value of the private company replacing the market value of common stock of the public company.

Net-Liquid-Balance-to-Total-Assets Ratio

The second model, shown in *Exhibit 19.2,* was developed by Joel Shulman, formerly a Babson College professor, to predict loan defaults.[3] Shulman also found that his ratio can predict loan defaults with significant reliability as much as two years in advance. In fact, the reliability of Shulman's approach is slightly higher than the reliability associated with Altman's Z-Score.

[2] E. I. Altman, R. G. Haldeman, and P. Narayanan, "ZETA Analysis: A New Model to Identify Bankruptcy Risk," *Journal of Banking and Finance,* June 1977, pp. 29–54.

[3] A working paper by Joel Shulman, Wayne State University, Detroit, Michigan.

Exhibit 19.2
Net-Liquid-Balance-to-Total-Assets Ratio

Net-Liquid-Balance-to-Total-Assets Ratio = NLB/Total assets
Where:
NLB = (Cash + Marketable securities) − (Notes payable + Contractual obligations)

Shulman's approach is noteworthy, because it explicitly recognizes the importance of cash. Among current accounts, Shulman distinguishes between operating assets (such as inventory and accounts receivable) and financial assets (such as cash and marketable securities). The same distinction is made among liabilities, where notes payable and contractual obligations are financial liabilities and accounts payable are operating liabilities.

Shulman then subtracts financial liabilities from financial assets to obtain a figure known as the *New Liquid Balance* (NLB). NLB can be thought of as "uncommitted cash," cash the firm has available to meet contingencies. Because it is the short-term margin for error should sales change, collections slow, or interest rates change, it is a true measure of liquidity.

The NLB is then divided by total assets to form the predictive ratio.

Nonquantitative Signals

Discussed in Chapter 18 were patterns and actions that could lead to trouble, indications of common trouble by growth stage, and critical variables that can be monitored.

There are also some nonquantitative signals that turnaround specialists use as indicators of the possibility of trouble. As with the signals discussed in Chapter 18, the presence of a single one of these does not necessarily imply an immediate crisis. However, once any of these does surface and if the others follow over the ensuing days and weeks, then trouble is likely to mount.

- Change in management or advisors, such as directors, accountants, or other professional advisors.
- Inability to produce financial statements on time.
- Accountant's opinion that is qualified and not certified.
- Changes in behavior of the lead entrepreneur (such as avoidance of phone calls or coming in later than usual).
- New competition.
- Launching of a "big project."
- Lower research and development expenditures.
- Writing off of assets.
- Lowering of credit line.

THE THREAT OF BANKRUPTCY

It is unfortunate that the heads of most troubled companies usually do not understand the benefits of bankruptcy law. To them, bankruptcy carries the stigma of failure, and the law merely defines the priority of creditors' claims when the firm is liquidated.

Although bankruptcy can provide for the liquidation of the business, it also can provide for its reorganization. Since bankruptcy is not an attractive prospect for creditors, because they stand to lose at least some of their money, they often are willing to negotiate. The prospect of bankruptcy also can be a foundation for bargaining in a turnaround.

Voluntary Bankruptcy

When bankruptcy is granted under bankruptcy law (called *Chapter 11*), a firm is given immediate protection from creditors. Interest payments are suspended, and creditors must wait for their money. A trustee is appointed (who is sometimes the entrepreneur himself), and creditor committees are formed.

The great benefit of Chapter 11 is that it buys time for the firm. The firm has 120 days to come up with a reorganization plan and 60 days to obtain acceptance of the plan by creditors.

Under the reorganization plan, debt can be extended. Debt also can be restructured (composed). Interest rates can be increased, and convertible provisions can be introduced to compensate debt holders for any increase in their risk as a result of the restructuring. Occasionally, debt holders need to take part of their claim in the form of equity. Trade creditors can be asked to take equity as payment, and they occasionally need to accept partial payment. If liquidation is the result of the reorganization plan, partial payment is the rule, with the typical payment ranging from zero to 30 cents on the dollar, depending on the priority of the claim.

Involuntary Bankruptcy

In involuntary bankruptcy, creditors force a troubled company into bankruptcy. Although this is regarded as a rare occurrence, it is important for an entrepreneur to know the conditions under which creditors can force a firm into bankruptcy.

A firm can be forced into bankruptcy by any three creditors whose total claim exceeds the value of assets held as security by $5,000 and by any single creditor who meets the above standard when the total number of creditors is less than 12.

Bargaining Power

For creditors, having a firm go into bankruptcy is not particularly attractive. *Bankruptcy, therefore, is a tremendous source of bargaining power for the troubled company.*

The reasons bankruptcy is not attractive to creditors are the following: Once protection is granted to a firm, creditors must wait for their money. Further, they are no longer dealing with the troubled company but with a trustee, as well as with other creditors. Even if creditors are willing to wait for their money, they may not get full payment and may have to accept payment in some unattractive form. Last, the legal and administrative costs of bankruptcy, which can be substantial, are paid before any payments are made to creditors.

Faced with these prospects, many creditors conclude that their interests are better served by negotiating with the firm. Since the law defines the priority of creditors' claims, an entrepreneur can use it to determine who might be willing to negotiate.

Since the trade has the lowest claim (except for owners), it is often the most willing to negotiate. In fact, the worse the situation, the more willing it may be. If the firm has negative net worth but is generating some cash flow, the trade should be willing to negotiate extended terms or partial payment, or both.

However, the secured creditors, with their higher priority claims, may be less willing to negotiate. Many factors affect the willingness of secured creditors to negotiate. Two are the strength of their collateral and their confidence in management. Yet, bankruptcy is still something they wish to avoid for the reasons cited above.

Bankruptcy can free a firm from obligations under executory contracts. This has caused some firms to file for bankruptcy as a way out of union contracts. Since bankruptcy law in this case conflicts with the National Labor Relations Act, the law has been updated and a good-faith test has been added. The firm must be able to demonstrate that a contract prevents it from carrying on its business. While most lawyers say that using bankruptcy law in this way is a questionable practice, some entrepreneurs have used it.

INTERVENTION

A company in trouble usually will want to use the services of an outside advisor who specializes in turnarounds.

The situation the outsider advisor usually finds at intervention is not encouraging. The company is often technically insolvent or has a negative net worth. It already may have been put on a cash basis by its suppliers. It may be in default on loans, or, if not, it is probably in violation of loan covenants. Call provisions may be exercised. Creditors may be trying to force the company into bankruptcy, and the organization is demoralized.

The critical task is to quickly diagnose the situation, develop an understanding of the company's bargaining position with its many creditors, and produce a detailed cash flow business plan for the turnaround of the organization.

To this end, a turnaround advisor usually quickly signals that change is coming. He or she will elevate the finance function, putting the "cash person" (often the consultant himself) in charge of the business. All payments are put on hold until problems can be diagnosed and remedial actions decided upon. Creditors are called and informed that the company is experiencing difficulties.

Diagnosis

The task of diagnosis can be complicated by the mixture of strategic and financial errors. For example, for a company with large receivables, questions need to be answered about whether receivables are bloated because of poor credit policy or because the company is in a business where liberal credit terms are required to compete.

Diagnosis takes place in three areas: the appropriate strategic posture of the business, analysis of management, and "the numbers."

Strategic Analysis

The purpose of this analysis in a turnaround is to identify the markets in which the company is capable of competing and deciding on a competitive strategy. With small companies, turnaround experts state that most strategic errors relate to the involvement of firms in unprofitable product lines, customers, and geographic areas.

It is outside the scope of this book to cover strategic analysis in detail. (See the many texts in the area.)

Analysis of Management

Analysis of management consists of interviewing members of the management team and coming to a subjective judgment of who belongs and who does not. Turnaround consultants can give no formula for how this is done except that it is the result of judgment that only comes from experience.

The Numbers

Involved in "the numbers" is a detailed cash flow analysis, which will reveal areas for remedial action. The task is to identify and quantify the "profitable core" of the business.

- *Determine available cash.* The first task is to determine how much cash the firm has available in the near term. This is accomplished by looking at bank balances, receivables (those not being used as security), and the confirmed order backlog.
- *Determine where money is going.* This is a more complex task than it appears to be on the surface. A common technique is called *subaccount analysis,* where every account that posts to cash is found and accounts are arranged in descending order of cash outlays. Accounts then are scrutinized for patterns. These patterns can indicate the functional areas where problems exist. For example, it was noticed that one company had its corporate address on its bills, rather than the lock box address at which checks were processed. The result was that the practice was adding two days to its dollar days outstanding.
- Another technique is to calculate percent-of-sales ratios for different areas of a business and then analyze trends in costs. Typically, several of the trends will show "flex points," where relative costs have changed. For example, for one company that had undertaken a big project, an increase in cost of sales, which coincided with an increase in capacity and in the advertising budget, was noticed. Further analysis revealed this project was not producing enough in dollar contribution to justify its existence. Once the project was eliminated, excess capacity could be reduced to lower the firm's breakeven point.
- *Reconstruct the business.* After determining where the cash is coming from and where it is going, the next step is to compare the business as it should be to the business as it is. This involves reconstructing the business "from the ground up." For example, a cash budgeting exercise can be undertaken and collections, payments, and so forth determined for a given sales volume. Or, the problem can be approached by determining labor, materials, and other direct costs and the overhead required to drive a given sales volume. What is essentially a cash flow business plan is created.
- *Determine differences.* Finally, the cash flow business plan is "tied into" pro forma balance sheets and income statements. The "ideal" cash flow plan and financial statements are compared to the business's current financial statements. For example, the pro forma income statements can be compared to existing statements to see where expenses can be reduced. The differences between the projected and actual financial statements form the basis of the turnaround plan and remedial actions.

The most commonly found areas for potential cuts/improvements are: (1) working capital management, from ordering processing and billing to receivables, inventory control, and, of course, cash management; (2) payroll; and (3) overcapacity and underutilized assets. It is interesting to note that over 80 percent of potential reduction in expenses can usually be found in work-force reduction.

The Turnaround Plan

The turnaround plan not only defines remedial actions but, because it is a detailed set of projections, provides a means to monitor and control turnaround activity. Further, by varying the assumptions about unit sales volume, prices, collections, and negotiating success, it can provide a means by which worst-case scenarios—complete with contingency plans—can be constructed.

Since short-term measures may not solve the cash crunch, a turnaround plan gives a firm enough credibility to buy time to put other remedial actions in place. For example, one firm's consultant approached its bank to buy time with the following:

By reducing payroll and discounting receivables, we can improve cash flow to the point where the firm can be current in five months. If we are successful in negotiating extended terms with trade creditors, then the firm can be current in three months. If the firm can sell some underutilized assets at 50 percent off, it can become current immediately.

The turnaround plan helps address organizational issues. The plan replaces uncertainty with a clearly defined set of actions and responsibilities. Since it signals to the organization that action is being taken, it is of great help in getting employees out of their "survival mode." An effective plan breaks tasks into the smallest achievable unit, so successful completion of these simple tasks soon follows and the organization begins to experience success. Soon the downward spiral of organizational morale is broken.

Finally, the turnaround plan is an important source of bargaining power. By identifying problems and providing for remedial actions, the turnaround plan enables the firm's advisors to approach creditors and tell them in a very detailed fashion how and when they will be paid. If the turnaround plan proves that creditors are better off working with the company as a going concern, rather than in liquidation, they will most likely be willing to negotiate their claims and terms of payment. Payment schedules can then be worked out that can keep the company afloat until the crisis is over.

Quick Cash

Ideally, the turnaround plan has established enough creditor confidence to buy the turnaround consultant time to raise additional capital and turn underutilized assets into cash. It is imperative, however, to raise cash quickly. The result of the actions described below should be an improvement in cash flow. The solution is far from complete, however, because suppliers need to be satisfied.

For the purpose of quick cash, the working capital accounts hold the most promise.

Accounts receivable is the most liquid noncash asset. Receivables can be factored, but negotiating such arrangements take time. The best route to cash is discounting receivables. How much receivables can be discounted depends on whether they are securing a loan. For example, a typical bank will loan up to 80 percent of the value of receivables that are under 90 days. As receivables age past the 90 days, the bank needs to be paid. New funds are advanced as new receivables are established as long as the 80 percent and under-90-day criteria are met. Receivables under 90 days can be discounted no more than 20 percent, if the bank obligation is to be met. Receivables over 90 days can be discounted as much as is needed to collect them, since they are not securing bank financing. One needs to use judgment in deciding exactly how large a discount to offer. A common method is to offer a generous discount with a time limit on it, after which the discount is no longer valid. This provides an incentive for the customer to pay immediately. Consultants agree it is better to offer too large a discount than too small a one. If the discount is too small and needs to be followed by further discounts, customers may hold off paying in the hope that another round of discounts will follow.

Inventory is not as liquid as receivables but still can be liquidated to generate quick cash. An inventory "fire sale" gets mixed reviews from turnaround experts. The most common objection is that excess inventory is often obsolete. The second objection is that since, for the small manufacturer, much inventory is work in process, therefore it is not in salable form and requires money to put in salable form. The third is that discounting finished-goods inventory may generate cash but is liable to create customer resistance to restored margins after the company is turned around. The sale of raw materials inventory to *competitors* is generally considered the best route.

One interesting option to the company with a lot of work-in-process inventory is to ease credit terms. It often is possible to borrow more against receivables than against inventory. By easing credit terms, the company can increase its borrowing capacity to perhaps enough to get cash to finish work in process. This option may be difficult to work out, because, by the time of intervention, the firm's lenders are following the company very closely and may veto the arrangements.

Also relevant to generating quick cash is the policy regarding current sales activity. Increasing the total dollar value of margin, generating cash quickly, and keeping working capital in its most liquid form need to be guiding criteria. Prices and cash discounts need to be increased and credit terms eased. Easing credit terms, however, can conflict with the receivables policy described above. Obviously, care needs to be taken to maintain consistency of policy. Easing credit is really an "excess inventory" policy. The overall idea is to leverage policy in favor of cash first, receivables second, and inventory third.

Putting all accounts payable on hold is the next option. Clearly, this eases the cash flow burden in the near term. Although some arrangement to pay suppliers needs to be made, the most important uses of cash at this stage are meeting payroll and paying lenders. Suppliers may not like this solution, but a company with negative cash flow simply needs to "prioritize" its use of cash. Suppliers are the least likely to force the company into bankruptcy because, under the law, they have a low priority claim.

Dealing with Lenders

The next step in the turnaround is to negotiate with lenders. Lenders need to be satisfied that there is a workable long-term solution, if they are to continue to do business with the company.

However, at the point of intervention, the company is most likely in default on its payments. Or, if payments are current, the financial situation has probably deteriorated to the point where the company is in violation of loan covenants. It also is likely that many of the firm's assets have been pledged as collateral. To make matters worse, it is likely that the troubled entrepreneur has been avoiding his or her lenders during the gestation period and has demonstrated that he or she is not in control of the situation. Credibility has been lost.

It is important for a firm to know that it is not the first ever to default on a loan, that the lender is usually willing to work things out, and that it is still in a position to bargain.

Strategically, there are two sources of bargaining power. The first is that, to a lender, despite its senior claims, bankruptcy is an unattractive result. A low-margin business cannot absorb large losses easily. (Recall that banks typically earn 0.5 percent to 1.0 percent total return on assets.)

The second is credibility. The firm that, through its turnaround specialist, has diagnosed the problem and produced a detailed turnaround plan with best case/worst case scenarios, the aim of which is to prove to the lender that the company is capable of paying, is in a better bargaining position. The plan details specific actions (e.g., layoffs, assets plays, changes in credit policy, etc.) which will be taken.

There are also two tactical sources of bargaining power. First, there is the strength of the lender's collateral. The second is the bank's inferior knowledge of aftermarkets — and the entrepreneur's superior ability to sell.

The following example illustrates that, when the lender's collateral is poor, it has little choice but to look to the entrepreneur for a way out without incurring a loss. It also shows that the entrepreneur's superior knowledge of his business and ability to sell got himself and the lender out of trouble. One turnaround company in the leather business overbought inventory one year, and, at the same time, a competitor announced a new product that made his inventory almost obsolete. Since the entrepreneur went to the lender with the problem, it was willing to work with him. The entrepreneur had plans to sell the inventory at reduced prices and also to enter a new market that looked attractive. The only trouble was he needed more money to do it, and he was already over his credit limit. The lender was faced with the certainty of losing 80 percent of its money and putting its customer out of business or the possibility of losing money by throwing good money after bad. The lender decided to work with the entrepreneur. It got a higher interest rate and put the entrepreneur on a "full following mechanism," which meant that all payments were sent to a lock box. The lender processed the checks and reduced its exposure before it put money in his account.

Another example illustrates the existence of bargaining power with a lender who is undercollateralized and stands to take a large loss. A company was importing look-alike Cabbage Patch dolls from Europe. This was financed with a letter of credit. However, when the dolls arrived in this country, the company could not sell the dolls because the Cabbage Patch doll craze was over. The dolls, and the bank's collateral, were worthless. The company found that the doll heads could be replaced, and with the new heads, the dolls did not look like Cabbage Patch dolls. It found also that one buyer of dolls would buy all the inventory. The company needed $30,000 to buy the new heads and have them put on, so it went back to the bank. The bank said that, if the company wanted the money, key management had to give liens on their houses. When this was refused, the banker was astounded. But what was he going to do? The company had found a way for him to get his money out, so it got the $30,000.

In addition, lenders are often willing to advance money for a company to meet its payroll. This is largely a public relations consideration. The other reason is that, if a company does not meet its payroll, a crisis may be precipitated before the lender can consider its options.

However, it is important to be aware that, when the situation starts to improve, a lender then may call the loan. Such a move will solve the lender's problem but may put the company under. While many bankers will deny this ever happens, some will concede that such an occurrence "depends on the loan officer."

Dealing with Trade Creditors

In dealing with trade creditors, the first step is to understand the strength of the company's bargaining position. Trade creditors have the lowest priority claims should a company file for bankruptcy and, therefore, are often the most willing to deal. In bankruptcy, trade creditors often are left with just a few cents on the dollar.

Another aspect of the bargaining power a firm has with trade creditors is the existence of a turnaround plan. As long as a company demonstrates that it can offer a trade creditor a better result as a going concern than it can in bankruptcy proceedings, the trade creditor should be willing to negotiate.

Also, trade creditors have to deal with the customer relations issue. Trade creditors will work with a troubled company if they see it as a way to preserve a market.

The relative weakness in the position of trade creditors has allowed some turnaround consultants to negotiate impressive deals. For example, one company got trade creditors to agree to a 24-month payment schedule for all outstanding accounts. In return, the firm pledged to keep all new payables current. The entrepreneur was able to keep the company from dealing on a cash basis with many of its creditors and to convert short-term payables into what amounted to long-term debt. The effect on current cash flow was very favorable.

The second step is to prioritize trade creditors according to their importance to the turnaround. The company then needs to take care of those creditors that are most important. For example, one entrepreneur told his controller never to make a commitment he could not keep. The controller was told that, if the company was going to miss a commitment, he was to get on the phone and call. The most important suppliers were told that if something happened and they really needed payment sooner than had been agreed, they were to let the company know and it would do its best to come up with the cash.

The third step in dealing with trade creditors is to switch vendors if necessary. Inevitably, the lower priority suppliers will put the company on cash terms or refuse to do business at all. The troubled company needs to be able to switch suppliers, and its relationship with its priority suppliers will help it to do this, because they can give credit references. One firm said, "We asked our best suppliers to be as liberal with credit references as possible. I don't know if we could have established new relationships without them."

The fourth step in dealing with trade creditors is to communicate effectively. "Dealing with the trade is as simple as telling the truth," said one consultant. If a company is honest, there is not much a creditor can do, and at least it can plan.

Work-Force Reductions

With work-force reduction representing 80 percent of the potential expense reduction, layoffs are inevitable in a turnaround situation.

A number of turnaround consultants use the following guidelines: Turnaround specialists recommend that layoffs be announced to an organization as a one-time reduction in the work force and be done all at one time. They recommend further that layoffs be accomplished as soon as possible, since employees will never regain their productivity until they feel some measure of security. Finally, they recommend that a firm cut deeper than seems necessary. The reason for this is that, if other remedial actions turn out to be difficult to implement, the difference may have to be made up in further reductions in the work force. For example, it is one thing to set out to reduce capacity by half and quite another thing to sell or sublet half a plant.

Longer-term Remedial Actions

If the turnaround plan has created enough credibility and has bought the firm time, longer-term remedial actions can be implemented.

These actions will usually fall in three categories:

- *Systems and procedures.*   Systems and procedures that contributed to the problem in the first place can be improved, or they can be implemented.
- *Asset plays.*   Assets that could not be liquidated in a shorter time frame can be liquidated. For example, real estate could be sold. Many smaller companies, particularly older ones, carry real estate on their balance sheet at far below market value. This could be sold and leased back or could be borrowed against to generate cash.
- *Creative solutions.*   Creative solutions that depend, of course, on the situation need to be found. For example, one firm had a large amount of inventory that was useless in its current business. However, it found that, if the inventory could be assembled into parts, there would be a market for it. The company shipped the inventory to Jamaica, where labor rates were low, for assembly, and it was able to sell very profitably the entire inventory.

As was stated at the beginning of the chapter, many companies—even companies that are insolvent or have negative net worth or both—can be rescued and restored to profitability. It is perhaps helpful to recall another quote from Winston Churchill, "I have nothing to offer but blood, toil, tears, and sweat."

The Harvest and Beyond

And don't forget: Shrouds have no pockets.

The late Sidney Rabb
Chairman,
Stop & Shop, Boston

RESULTS EXPECTED

After completing the chapter, you will have:

1. Examined the importance of a harvest goal and of crafting a harvest strategy.
2. Identified and examined the principal harvest options.
3. Looked beyond the harvest.

THE JOURNEY

A Look Back

What is the journey really like? Entrepreneurs, more often than not, describe the exhilarations and pain, uncertainties and surprises, and the joy and terror. They use the analogies mentioned in Chapter 1 and others, such as riding a bucking bronco, white water canoeing on a new stretch of river, or a roller coaster ride.

These entrepreneurs also talk of the venture's incredibly insatiable appetite for not only cash but also time, attention, and energy. Some say it is an addiction. Most say it is far more demanding and difficult than they ever imagined. Most, however, plan not to retire and would do it again.

For the vast majority of entrepreneurs it takes 10, 15, even 20 years or more to build a significant net worth. According to the popular press and government statistics, there are more millionaires than ever in America. In 1990, as many as 2 million persons in the United States (or nearly 1 percent of the population) will be millionaires—their net worth exceeding $1 million. While these numbers may be true, a million dollars, sadly, is not really all that much money today, as a result of high inflation, and, while lottery and sweepstakes winners become instant millionaires, entrepreneurs do not. The number of years it usually takes to accumulate such a net worth is a far cry from the instant millionaire, the get-rich-quick impression associated with lottery winners or in fantasy TV shows.

In Sight of the Destination

In addition, the total immersion required, the huge workload, the many sacrifices for a family, and the burnout often experienced by an entrepreneur is real. Maintaining the energy, enthusiasm, and drive to get across the finish line, to achieve a harvest, may be, when the time comes, exceptionally difficult. For instance, one entrepreneur in the computer software business, after working alone for several years, developed highly sophisticated software. Yet, he was the first one to insist that he could not stand the computer business for another day. Imagine trying to position a company for sale effectively and to negotiate a deal for a premium price after such a long battle.

And some entrepreneurs, even with what most of us would agree has been raging success, wonder if the price of victory is too high. One very successful entrepreneur put it this way: "What difference does it make if you win, have $20 million in the bank — I know several who do — and you are a basket case, your family has been washed out, and your kids are a wreck?"

The opening quote of the chapter is a sobering reminder and its message is clear: Unless an entrepreneur enjoys the journey and thinks it is worthy, he or she may find oneself ending up on the wrong train to the wrong destination.

GETTING TO THE FINAL DESTINATION

A Harvest Goal

A harvest goal, and crafting a strategy to achieve it, is indeed what separates successful entrepreneurs from the rest of the pack. Many entrepreneurs seek only to create a job and a living for themselves. But, it is quite another thing to grow a business that creates a living for many others, including employees and investors, by creating value — value that can result in a capital gain.

Setting a harvest goal achieves many purposes, not the least of which is helping an entrepreneur get after-tax cash out of an enterprise and enhancing substantially his or her net worth.

Such a goal also can create high standards and a serious commitment to excellence over the course of developing the business. It can provide, in addition, a motivating force and a strategic focus that does not sacrifice customers, employees, and value-added products and services just to maximize quarterly earnings.

There are other good reasons as well. The workload demanded by a harvest-oriented venture versus one in a venture that cannot achieve a harvest may actually be less and is probably no greater. Such a business, in fact, may be less stressful than managing a business that is not oriented to harvest. Imagine the plight of the 46-year-old entrepreneur, with three children in college, whose business is overleveraged and on the brink of collapse. Contrast that frightful pressure with the position of the founder and major stockholder of another venture who, at the same age, sold his venture for $15 million. Further, the options open to the harvest-oriented entrepreneur seem to rise geometrically in that investors, other entrepreneurs, bankers, and the marketplace respond. There is great truth in the old cliche that "success breeds success."

There is a very significant societal reason as well for seeking and building a venture worthy of a harvest. These are the ventures that provide enormous impact and value added in a variety of ways. These are the companies that contribute most disproportionately to technological and other innovations, to new jobs, to returns for investors, and to economic vibrancy.

Also, within the process of harvest, the seeds of renewal and reinvestment are sown. Such a recycling of entrepreneurial talent and capital is at the very heart of our system of private responsibility for economic renewal and individual initiative. Entrepreneurial companies organize and manage for the long haul in ways to perpetuate the opportunity creation and recognition process and, thereby, insure the process of economic regeneration, innovation, and renewal.

Thus, a harvest goal is not just a goal of selling and leaving the company. Rather, it is a long-term goal to create real value added in a business. (It is true, however, if real value added is not created, the business simply will not be worth very much in the marketplace.)

Crafting a Harvest Strategy

Consistently, entrepreneurs avoid thinking about harvest issues. When a company is first launched, then struggles for survival, and finally begins its ascent, the farthest thing from its founder's mind usually is selling out. Selling out is often viewed by the entrepreneur as the equivalent to complete abandonment of his or her very own "baby."

Thus, time and again, a founder does not consider selling out until terror, in the form of the possibility of losing the whole company, is experienced. Usually, this possibility comes unexpectedly: new technology threatens to leapfrog over the current product line, a large competitor suddenly appears in a small market, or a major account is lost. A sense of panic then grips the founders and shareholders of the closely held firm, and the company is suddenly for sale — for sale at the wrong time, for the wrong reasons, and, thus, for the wrong price.

Selling at the right time, willingly, involves hitting a strategic window, one of the many strategic windows that entrepreneurs face.

Entrepreneurs find that harvesting is clearly a nonissue until something begins to sprout, and again there is a vast distance between creating an existing revenue stream of an ongoing business and ground zero. Most entrepreneurs agree that securing customers and generating continuing sales revenue is much harder and takes much longer than even they could have imagined. Further, the ease with which those revenue estimates can be cast and manipulated on a spreadsheet belie the time and effort necessary to turn those projections into cash.

At some point with a higher potential venture, it becomes possible to realize the harvest. In terms of the strategic window, it is wiser to be selling as it is opening, rather than as it is closing. Bernard Baruch's wisdom is as good as it gets on this matter. He has said, "I made all my money by selling too early."

Time and again, this has worked. For example, in 1986, a private candy company with $150 million in sales was not considering selling. After contemplating advice to sell early, the founders recognized a unique opportunity to harvest and sold the firm for 19 times earnings, an extremely high valuation. Another example is that of a cellular phone company that was launched and built from scratch and began operations in late 1987. Only 18 months after purchasing the original rights to build and operate the system, the founders decided to sell the company, even though the future looked extremely bright. They sold because the sellers' market they faced at the time had resulted in a premium valuation — 30 percent higher on a per capital basis (the industry valuation norm) than that for any previous cellular transaction to date. The harvest returned over 25 times the original capital in a year and a half. (Interestingly, the founders had not invested a dime of their own money.)

If the window is missed, disaster can strike. For example, at the same time as the harvests described above were unfolding, another entrepreneur saw his real estate holdings rapidly appreciate to nearly $20 million, resulting in a personal net worth, *on paper,* of nearly $7 million. The entrepreneur used this equity to refinance and leverage existing properties (to more than 100 percent in some cases) to seize what he perceived as further prime opportunities. Unfortunately, following changes in the federal tax law in 1986 and the 1987 stock market "crash" was a major softening of the real estate market in 1988. As a result, in early 1989, half of the entrepreneur's holdings were in bankruptcy, and the rest were in a highly precarious and vulnerable position, because prior equity in the properties had evaporated, leaving no collateral as increasing vacancies and lower rents per square foot turned a positive cash flow into a negative one.

Shaping a harvest strategy is an enormously complicated and difficult area. Thus, crafting such a strategy cannot begin too early. For example, HTC, Inc., a company that became a leading innovator in developing vapor-phase technology for soldering printed circuit boards, began crafting its harvest strategy in 1977, when it was basically a one-person garage-shop venture with no marketable product, and when it had been able to raise venture capital of just $10,000 for 10 percent of the venture from a firm that was very reluctant to invest a dime. An advisor worked closely with the lead entrepreneur from the beginning, and he thus knew the intricacies of the market, the industry, the competitors, the customers, and the internal management capabilities of the firm intimately. In 1984, the company had grown to nearly $7 million in sales and was subsequently sold for $15 million cash to a larger firm.

In shaping a harvest strategy, some guidelines and cautions can help:

- *Patience.*   As has been shown, most successful companies require several years to launch and build, and, therefore, patience can be invaluable. A harvest strategy is more sensible if it allows for a time frame of at least 3 to 5 years and as long as 7 to 10.
- *Vision.*   The other side of the patience coin is not to panic as a result of precipitate events. Selling under duress is usually the worst of all worlds.
- *Realistic valuation.*   If impatience is the enemy of an attractive harvest, then greed is its executioner. For example, an excellent small firm in New England, which was nearly 80 years old and run by the third generation of a line of successful family leaders, had attracted a number of prospective buyers and had obtained a bona fide offer for over $25 million. The owners, however, had become convinced that this "great little company" was worth considerably more, and they held out. Before long, there were no buyers, and market circumstances changed unfavorably. In addition, interest rates skyrocketed. Soon thereafter, the company collapsed financially, ending up in bankruptcy. Greed was the executioner.
- *Outside advice.*   Finding an advisor who can help craft a harvest strategy while the business is growing and, at the same time, maintain objectivity about its value and have the patience and skill to maximize it is difficult but worthwhile. A major problem seems to be that people who sell businesses, such as investment bankers or business brokers, are performing the same economic role and function as real estate brokers and, in essence, their incentive is their commissions during a quite short time frame, usually a matter of months. However, an advisor who works with a lead entrepreneur for as much as five years or more can help shape and implement a strategy for the whole business so it is positioned to spot and to respond to harvest opportunities when they appear.

HARVEST OPTIONS

There are seven principal avenues by which a company can realize a harvest from the value it has created. Described below, these most commonly seem to occur in the order in which they are listed. No attempt is made here to do more than briefly describe each avenue, since there are entire books written on each of these, including their legal, tax, and accounting intricacies.

Capital Cow

A "capital cow" is to the entrepreneur what a "cash cow" is to a large corporation. In essence, the high-margin profitable venture (the cow) throws off more cash for personal use (the milk) than most entrepreneurs have the time and uses or inclinations to spend it on.

The result is a capital-rich and cash-rich company with enormous capacity for debt and reinvestment. Take, for instance, a health-care-related venture that was started in the early 1970s, that realized early success, and that went public. Several years later, the founders decided to buy the company back from the public shareholders and to return it to its closely held status. Today the company has sales in excess of $100 million and generates extra capital of several million each year. This capital cow has enabled its entrepreneurs to form investing entities to invest in several other higher-potential ventures, which included participation in the leveraged buy out of a $150 million sales division of a larger firm and in some venture capital deals.

Employee Stock Ownership Plan

Employee stock ownership plans (ESOPs) have become very popular among closely held companies as a valuation mechanism for stock for which there is no formal market. They are also vehicles through which founders can realize some liquidity from their stock by sales to the plan and other employees. And, since an ESOP usually creates widespread ownership of stock among employees, it is viewed as a positive motivational device as well.

Management Buy Out

Another avenue, called a *management buy out* (MBO), is one by which a founder can realize a gain from a business by selling it to existing partners or to other key managers in the business. If the business has both assets and a healthy cash flow, the financing can be arranged via banks, insurance companies, and financial institutions that do leveraged buy outs (LBOs) and MBOs. Even if assets are thin, a healthy cash flow that can service the debt to fund the purchase price can convince lenders to do the MBO.

Usually, the problem is that the managers who want to buy out the owners and remain to run the company do not have the capital. Unless the buyer has the cash up front—and this is rarely the case—such a sale can be very fragile, and full realization of a gain is questionable. MBOs typically require the seller to take a limited amount of cash up front and a note for the balance of the purchase price over several years. If the purchase price is linked to the future profitability of the business, the seller is totally dependent on the ability and integrity of the buyer. Further, the management, under such an arrangement, can lower the price by growing the business as fast as possible, spending on new products and people, and showing very little profit along the way. In these cases, it is often seen that, after the marginally profitable business is sold at a bargain price, it is well positioned with excellent earnings in the next two or three years. As can be seen, the seller will end up on the short end of this type of deal.

Merger and Strategic Alliance

Merging with another firm is still another way for a founder to realize a gain. For example, two founders who had developed high-quality training programs for the rapidly emerging personal computer industry consummated a merger with another company. These entrepreneurs had backgrounds in computers, rather than in marketing or general management, and the results of the company's first five years reflected this gap. Sales were under $500,000, based on custom programs and no marketing, and they had been unable to attract venture capital, even during the market of 1982 to 1983. The firm with which they merged was a $15 million company that had an excellent reputation for its management training programs, had a Fortune-1000 customer base, had repeat sales of 70 percent, and had requests from the field sales force for programs to train managers in the use of personal computers. The buyer obtained 80 percent of the shares of the smaller firm, to consolidate the revenues and earnings from the merged company into its own financial statements, and the two founders of the smaller firm retained a 20 percent ownership in their firm. The two founders also obtained employment contracts, and the buyer provided nearly $1.5 million of capital advances during the first year of the new business. Under a "put" arrangement, the founders will be able to realize a gain on their 20 percent of the company, depending upon performance of the venture over the next few years.[1] The two founders now are reporting to the president of the parent firm, and one founder of the parent firm has taken a key executive position with the smaller company, an approach common for mergers between closely held firms.

In a strategic alliance, founders can attract badly needed capital, in substantial amounts, from a large company interested in their technologies. Such arrangements often can lead to complete buy outs of the founders downstream.

Outright Sale

Outright sale[2] is viewed by most advisors as the ideal route to go. This is because cash, up front, is preferred over most stock, even though the latter can result in a tax-free exchange. In a stock-for-stock exchange, the problem is the volatility and unpredictability of the stock price of the purchasing company. Many an entrepreneur has been left with a fraction of the original purchase price when the stock price of the buyer's company declined steadily. Often the acquiring company wants to lock key management into employment contracts for up to several years. Whether this makes sense depends on the goals and circumstances of the individual entrepreneur.

Public Offering

Probably the most sacred "business school cow" of all—other than the capital cow—is that of taking a company public.[3] The vision or fantasy of having one's venture listed on one of the stock exchanges, even over-the-counter, arouses passions of greed, glory, and greatness. For many would-be entrepreneurs, this aspiration is unquestioned and enormously appealing. Yet, for all but a chosen few, taking a company public, and then living with it, may be far more time and trouble—and expense—than it is worth.

After the stock market crash of October 1987, the market for new issues of stock shrank to a fraction of the robust IPO market of 1986, as is shown in *Exhibit 20.1,* and a fraction of those of 1983 and 1985, as well. By the first quarter of 1989, there had been just 39 new issues, compared to over 200 per quarter in 1983 and 1986. At this writing, despite a rebound of the Dow Jones Industrial Average to a postcrash high of over 2,400, the IPO market remains dormant, with no signs of an early revival.

Also, a fraction of the companies that go public are new or very young ventures. (Companies such as Lotus, Compaq, and Apple Computer of the world do get unprecedented attention and fanfare, but these firms are truly exceptions to the rule.)

Finally, just because stock is listed does not mean its owners can realize a liquid gain. SEC restrictions on the timing and amount of stock that officers, directors, and insiders can dispose of in the public market are increasingly severe. As a result, it can take several years after an initial public offering before a liquid gain is possible.

---

[1] This is an arrangement whereby the two founders can force (the "put") the acquirer to purchase their 20 percent at a predetermined and negotiated price.

[2] See several relevant articles on selling a company in *Growing Concerns,* ed. David E. Gumpert (New York: John Wiley & Sons, 1984), pp. 332–98.

[3] The Big Eight accounting firms, such as Ernst & Whinney, publish information on deciding to take a firm public. See also an article by Richard Salomon, "Second Thoughts on Going Public," in *Trials and Rewards of the Entrepreneur,* ed. David E. Gumpert (Boston: Harvard Business Review, 1983).

Exhibit 20.1
Initial Public Offerings

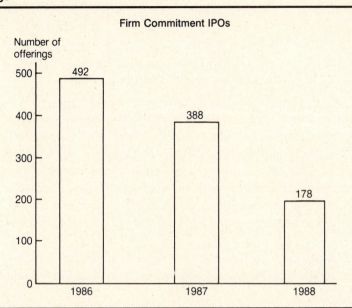

Firm Commitment IPOs

Number of
offerings

Wealth-building Vehicles

The 1986 Tax Reform Act has severely limited the generous options previously available to build wealth within a private company through large deductible contributions to a retirement plan. To make matters worse, the administrative costs and paperwork necessary to comply with federal laws have become a nightmare. Nonetheless, there are still mechanisms that can enable an owner to contribute up to 25 percent of his or her salary to a retirement plan each year, an amount which is deductible to the company and grows tax free. Entrepreneurs who can contribute such amounts for just a short time will, having Uncle Sam as a financial partner, build significant wealth. For example, if an individual contributed 15 percent of a $200,000 salary per year and invested it in the money market at 9 percent (rates at this writing), he or she could have over $1.5 million in 15 years.

BEYOND THE HARVEST

A majority of highly successful entrepreneurs seem to accept a responsibility to renew and perpetuate the system that has treated them so well. Somehow they are keenly aware that our unique American system of opportunity and mobility depends in large part upon a self-renewal process.

There are many ways in which this happens. Some of the following data often surprise people:

■ *College endowments.*   It was shown a few years ago that over half of the endowment at M.I.T. has come from gifts of stock and other assets made by the founders of companies. A recent study of Babson College alumni showed that up to eight times as many entrepreneurs, compared to other graduates, made large gifts to the college.[4] Among

---

[4] John A. Hornaday, "Patterns of Alumni Giving," in *Frontiers of Entrepreneurship Research: 1984,* ed. J. Hornaday et al. (Babson Park, Mass.: Babson College, 1984).

the most generous and enthusiastic contributors to the Harvard Business School are the graduates of the Smaller Company Management Program, a short nondegree course for the heads of smaller firms. Among Harvard Business School alumni, entrepreneurs lead the way.

■ *Community activities.*   Entrepreneurs who have harvested their ventures very often reinvest their leadership skills and money in such community activities as symphony orchestras, museums, and local colleges and universities. These entrepreneurs lead fund-raising campaigns, serve on boards of directors, and devote many hours to other voluntary work. One Swedish couple, after spending six months working with venture capital firms in Silicon Valley and New York, was "astounded at the extent to which these entrepreneurs and venture capitalists engage in such voluntary, civic activities." This couple found this pattern in sharp contrast to the Swedish pattern, where paid government bureaucrats perform many of the same services.

■ *Investing in new companies.*   Postharvest entrepreneurs also reinvest their efforts and resources in the next generation of entrepreneurs and their opportunities.

Successful entrepreneurs behave this way since they seem to know that perpetuating the system is far too important, and too fragile, to be left to anyone else. They have learned the hard lessons.

The innovation, the job creation, and the economic renewal and vibrancy are all results of the entrepreneurial process. The complicated and little understood process is *not caused* by government, though it can certainly be impeded or facilitated by it. Nor is it caused by the stroke of a legislative pen, though it can be ended by such a stroke. Rather, it is created by entrepreneurs, investors, and hard-working people in pursuit of opportunities.

Fortunately, entrepreneurs seem to accept a disproportionate share of the responsibility to make sure the process is renewed. And, judging by the new wave of entrepreneurship in the United States, both the marketplace and society once again are prepared to allocate the rewards to entrepreneurs that are commensurate with their acceptance of responsibility and delivery of results.

SEVEN SECRETS OF SUCCESS

The following seven secrets of success are included for your contemplation and amusement:

■ There are no secrets. Understanding and practicing the fundamentals discussed here, along with hard work, will get results.

■ As soon as there is a secret, everyone else knows about it, too. Searching for secrets is a mindless exercise.

■ Happiness is a positive cash flow.

■ If you teach a person to work for others, you feed him or her for a year; but, if you teach a person to be an entrepreneur, you feed him or her, and others, for a lifetime.

■ Do not run out of cash.

■ Entrepreneurship is fundamentally a human, rather than a financial or technological process. *You* can make an enormous difference.

■ Happiness is a positive cash flow.

CRAFTING A PERSONAL ENTREPRENEURIAL STRATEGY

PART VI

Acknowledging the extreme complexity in predicting or aligning people to careers, especially when both are constantly changing, and the difficulty in accurately measuring enough of the relevant variables to do so, principal tasks for an entrepreneur are to determine what kind of an entrepreneur he or she wants to become, based on his or her attitudes, behaviors, management competencies, experience, and so forth, and whether these fit with the requirements and demands of a specific opportunity.

At a practial and personal level, then, an aim of this book is to help you (1) evaluate thoroughly your *attraction* to entrepreneurship and (2) the *fit* between you and the demands of a particular opportunity. Seen frequently in business is the old adage, "What is one person's jam is another person's poison." Different people will investigate the same venture and come to opposite conclusions.

If there is a fit, then you can shape a strategy, including an action plan. It is fair to say that an entrepreneur's first 10 years out of school can make or break him or her in terms of how well prepared he or she is for serious entrepreneuring. While it may never be too late, evidence suggests that the most durable entrepreneurial careers, those found to last 25 years or more, were begun across a broad age spectrum but after the person selected prior work or a career to prepare for an entrepreneurial career.

Why leave it to chance when you don't have to? Isn't taking charge of your own life and career a part of the thrill and exhilaration of entrepreneuring in the first place? To help you in this, Chapter 21 provides an integrated self-assessment exercise.

As an entrepreneur who founded a rapidly growing database and information firm in the medical field put it, "Self-assessment is the hardest thing for entrepreneurs to do, but if you don't do it, you will really get into trouble." The reason is that, if you do not do it, who will?

Crafting a Personal Entrepreneurial Strategy

If you don't know where you're going, any path will take you there.

The Koran

RESULTS EXPECTED

Upon completion of this chapter, you will have:

1. Looked at the self-assessment process.
2. Examined a framework for self-assessment and developed a personal entrepreneurial strategy.
3. Identified data to be collected in the self-assessment process.
4. Learned about receiving feedback and setting goals.

PLANNING REVISITED

A Personal "Business Plan"

Crafting a personal entrepreneurial strategy can be viewed as the personal equivalent of developing a business plan. As with planning in other situations, the process itself is more important than the plan.

The process and discipline that puts an individual in charge of evaluating and shaping the choices and initiating action that makes sense for him or for her, rather than letting things just happen, is key. Having such a longer-term sense of direction can be highly motivating. It also can be extremely helpful in determining to what to say no (which is much harder than saying yes) and can temper impulsive hunches with a more thoughtful strategic purpose. This is important because today's choices, whether or not they are thought out, become tomorrow's track record. They may end up shaping an entrepreneur in ways that he or she may not find so attractive 10 years hence and, worse, may also result in failure to obtain just those experiences needed in order to have high-quality opportunities later on.

A personal strategy, therefore, can be invaluable, but it need not be a prison sentence. It is a point of departure, rather than a contract of indenture, and can and will change over time.

This process of developing a personal strategy for an entrepreneurial career is a very individual one and, in a sense, one of self-selection. One experienced venture capital investor in small ventures, Louis L. Allen, shares this view of the importance of the role of self-selection:

Unlike the giant firm which has recruiting and selection *experts* to screen the wheat from the chaff, the small business firm, which comprises the most common economic unit in our business systems, cannot afford to employ a personnel manager. . . . More than that, there's something very special about the selection of the owners: they have selected themselves. . . . As I face self-selected top managers across my desk or visit them in their plants or offices I have become more and more impressed with the fact that this self-selection process is far more important to the *success or failure* of the company the man is starting than the monetary aspects of our negotiations.

553

Reasons for planning are similar to those for developing a business plan (see Chapter 11). Reasons for planning are that they help an entrepreneur to manage the risks and uncertainties of the future; that they help him or her to work "smarter," rather than simply "harder"; that they keep him or her in a *future-oriented* frame of mind; that they help him or her to develop and update a keener strategy by testing the sensibility of his or her ideas and approaches with others; that they help motivate; that they give him or her a "results orientation"; that they can be effective in managing and coping with what is by nature a stressful role; and so forth.

Rationalizations and reasons given for not planning, like those mentioned in Chapter 11, are that plans become out of date as soon as they are finished and that no one knows what tomorrow will bring and, therefore, it is dangerous to commit to uncertainty. Further, the cautious, anxious person may find that setting personal goals creates a further source of tension and pressure and a heightened fear of failure. There is also the possibility that future or yet unknown options, which actually might be more attractive than the one chosen, may become lost or exclude opportunities.

Commitment to a career-oriented goal, particularly for an entrepreneur who is younger and lacks much real-world experience, can be premature. For the person who is inclined to be a compulsive and obsessive competitor and achiever, goal setting may have the effect of adding gasoline to the fire. And, invariably, some events and environmental factors entirely beyond one's control may boost or sink the best-laid plans.

Personal plans fail for the same reasons as business plans, including frustration when the plan appears not to work immediately and problems of changing behavior from an activity-oriented routine to one that is goal-oriented. Other problems are developing plans that are based on admirable missions, such as improving performance, rather than goals; those that fail to anticipate obstacles; those that lack of progress milestones and reviews; and so forth.

A Conceptual Scheme for Self-assessment

Exhibit 21.1 shows one conceptual scheme for thinking about the self-assessment process, called the *Johari Window.* According to this scheme, there are two sources of information about the self: the individual himself and others. According to the Johari Window, there are three areas in which individuals can learn about themselves.

There are two potential obstacles to self-assessment efforts. First, it is hard to obtain feedback, and, second, it is hard to receive and benefit from it. Everyone possesses a personal frame of reference, values, and so forth, which influence his or her first impressions of each other. It is, therefore, almost impossible for an individual to obtain an unbiased view of himself or herself from someone else. Further, in most social situations, people usually present self-images that they want to preserve, protect, and defend, and behavioral norms usually exist that prohibit people from telling a person that he or she is presenting a face or impression that differs from what the person thinks is being presented. For example, most people will not point out to a stranger during a conversation that a piece of spinach is prominently dangling from between his or her front teeth.

The first step for an individual in self-assessment is to generate data through observation of his or her thoughts and actions and by getting feedback from others for the purposes of (1) becoming aware of "blind spots" and (2) reinforcing or changing existing perceptions of both strengths and weaknesses.

Once an individual has generated the necessary data, the next steps in the self-assessment process are to study the data generated, develop insights, and then to establish apprenticeship goals to gain any learning, experience, and so forth. Finally, choices can be made in terms of goals and opportunities to be created or seized.

Exhibit 21.1
Peeling the Onion

	Known to Entrepreneur and Team	Not Known to Entrepreneur and Team
Known to prospective investors and stakeholders	**Area 1** *Known* area (what you see is what you get)	**Area 2** *Blind* area (we do not know what we do not know, but you do)
Not known to prospective investors and stakeholders	**Area 3** *Hidden* area (unshared—you do not know what we do, but the deal does not get done until we find out)	**Area 4** *Unknown* area (no venture is certain or risk free)

Source: Derived from an original concept called the "Johari Window" in D. A. Kolb, I. M. Rubin, and J. M. McIntyre, *Organizational Psychology: An Experiential Approach,* 2nd ed. (Englewood Cliffs, N.J.: Prentice-Hall, 1974).

CRAFTING AN ENTREPRENEURIAL STRATEGY

Profiling the Past

One useful way to begin the process of self-assessment and planning is for an individual to think about his or her entrepreneurial "roots" (i.e., what he or she has done, his or her preferences in terms of lifestyle and work style, and so forth) and couple this with a look into the future and what he or she would like most to be doing and how he or she would like to live.

In this regard, everyone has a personal history that has played and will continue to play a significant role in influencing his or her values, motivations, attitudes, and behaviors. Some of this history may provide some useful insight into prior entrepreneurial inclinations, as well as into his or her future potential "fit" with an entrepreneurial role. It is safe to say that, unless an entrepreneur is enjoying what he or she is doing for work most of the time, when he or she is in his or her 30s, 40s, or 50s, having a great deal of money without enjoying the journey will be a very hollow success.

Profiling the Present

It then is useful to "profile the present." Possession of certain personal entrepreneurial attitudes and behaviors (i.e., an "entrepreneurial mind") have been linked to successful careers in entrepreneurship. These attitudes and behaviors deal with such factors as commitment, determination, and perseverance; the drive to achieve and grow; an orientation toward goals; the taking of initiative and personal responsibility; and so forth.

In addition, various "role demands" result from the pursuit of opportunities. These role demands are external in the sense that they are imposed upon every entrepreneur by the nature of entrepreneurship. Discussed in Chapter 6, the external business environment is given, the demands of a higher potential business in terms of stress and commitment are given, and the ethical values and integrity of key actors are given. Required as a result of the demands, pressures, and realities of starting, owning, and operating a substantial business are such factors as accommodation to the venture, toleration of stress, and so forth. A realistic appraisal of entrepreneurial attitudes and behaviors in light of the requirements of the entrepreneurial "role" is useful as part of the self-assessment process.

And, part of any self-assessment is an assessment of management competencies and what "chunks" of experience, know-how, and contacts need to be developed.

Getting Constructive Feedback

A Scottish proverb says, "The greatest gift that God hath given us is to see ourselves as others see us." One common denominator among successful entrepreneurs is a desire to know how they are doing and where they stand. They have an uncanny knack for asking the right questions about their performance at the right time. This thirst to know is driven by a keen awareness that such feedback is vital to improve their performance and their odds for success.

Receiving feedback from others can be a most demanding experience. The following guidelines in receiving feedback can help:

- Feedback needs to be solicited ideally from those who know the individual well (e.g., someone he or she has worked with or for) and who can be trusted.
- The context in which the person is known needs to be considered. For example, a business colleague may be better able to comment upon an individual's managerial skills than a friend. Or, a personal friend may be able to comment on motivation or on the possible effects on the family situation.
- It is helpful to chat with the person *before* asking him or her to provide any specific written impressions and to indicate the specific areas he or she can best comment upon. One way to do this is to formulate questions first. For example, the person could be told, "I've been asking myself the following question . . . and I would really like your impressions in that regard."
- Specific comments in areas that are particularly important either personally or to the success of the venture need to be solicited and more detail probed, if what the person giving feedback intended to say is not clear. A good way to check if a statement is being understood correctly is to paraphrase a statement.
- The person needs to be encouraged to describe and give examples of specific situations or behaviors that have influenced the impressions he or she has developed.
- Feedback is most helpful if it is neither all positive nor all negative.
- Feedback needs to be obtained in writing so that person can take some time to think about the issues, and so feedback from various sources can be pulled together.
- The person asking for feedback needs to be honest and straightforward with himself or herself and with others. Time is too precious and the road to new venture success too treacherous to clutter this activity with game playing or hidden agendas.
- The person receiving feedback needs to avoid becoming defensive and taking negative comments personally.
- It is important to listen carefully to what is being said and think about it. "Answering," "debating," or "rationalizing" should be avoided.
- An assessment of whether the person soliciting feedback has considered all important information and has been realistic in his or her inferences and conclusions needs to be made.
- Help needs to be asked in identifying common threads or patterns; possible implications of self-assessment data and certain weaknesses, including alternative inferences or conclusions; and other relevant information that is missing.

Exhibit 21.2
Fit of Entrepreneur and Venture Opportunity

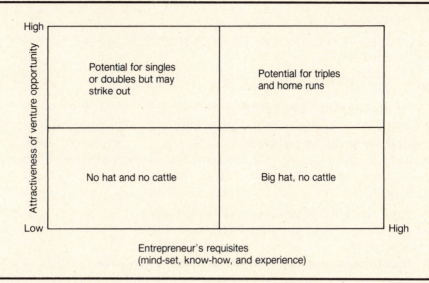

- Additional feedback from others needs to be sought to verify feedback and to supplement the data.
- Reaching final conclusions or decisions needs to be left until a later time.

Putting It All Together

Exhibit 21.2 shows the relative fit of an entrepreneur with a venture opportunity, given his or her relevant attitudes and behaviors and relevant general management skills, experience, know-how, and contacts, and given the role demands of the venture opportunity. Again, although a considerable amount of research about the entrepreneurial mind and the role demands of entrepreneurship has been conducted in recent years, the precise identification of these remains elusive. Further, the need for specific "chunks" (i.e., managerial competencies, experience, know-how, and contacts) varies with each situation.

A "clean" appraisal is almost impossible. Self-assessment just is not that simple. The process is cumulative, and what an entrepreneur does about weaknesses, for example, is far more important than what the particular weaknesses might be. After all, everyone has weaknesses.

Thinking Ahead

As it is in developing business plans, goal setting is important in personal planning. Yet, few people are effective goal setters. Perhaps fewer than 5 percent have ever committed their goals to writing, and perhaps fewer than 25 percent of adults even engage in setting goals mentally.

Again, goal setting is a process, a way of dealing with the world. Effective goal setting demands time, self-discipline, commitment and dedication, and practice. Goals, once set, do not become static targets.

A number of distinct steps are involved in the goal setting process, steps that are repeated over and over as conditions change:

- Establishment of goals which are:
  - Specific and concrete (rather than abstract and out of focus).
  - Measurable.
  - Related to time (i.e., specific about what will be accomplished over a certain time period).
  - Realistic and attainable.
- Establishment of priorities, including the identification of conflicts and trade-offs and how these can be resolved.
- Identification of potential problems and obstacles that could prevent goals from being attained.
- Specification of action steps that are to be performed to accomplish the goal.
- Indication of how results will be measured.
- Establishment of milestones for reviewing progress and tying these to specific dates on a calendar.
- Identification of risks involved in meeting the goals.
- Identification of help and other resources that may be needed to obtain goals.
- Periodic review of progress and revision of goals.

EXERCISE – PERSONAL ENTREPRENEURIAL STRATEGY

The exercise that follows will help you in gathering data, both from yourself and from others, in evaluating the data you have collected, and in crafting a personal entrepreneurial strategy.

The exercise requires *active* participation on your part. The estimated time to complete the entire exercise is 1.5 to 3.0 hours. Those who have completed the exercise – students, practicing entrepreneurs, and others – report that the self-assessment process was most worthwhile. They hasten to add that completing the exercises was also a most demanding task. Issues addressed will require a great deal of thought, and there are, of course, no "right" answers.

Although this is a self-assessment exercise, it is useful to receive feedback. Whether you choose to solicit feedback and how much, if any, of the data you have collected you choose to share with others is your decision. Of course, the exercise will be of value only to the extent that you are honest and realistic in your approach.

And, again, a complex set of factors clearly goes into making someone a successful entrepreneur. No individual has all of the personal qualities, managerial skills, and the like indicated in the exercise. And, even if an individual did possess most of these, his or her values, preferences, and such may make him or her a very poor risk to succeed as an entrepreneur. It is worth repeating that the presence or absence of any single factor does not guarantee success or failure as an entrepreneur. Before proceeding, remember, "It is no embarrassment to reach for the stars and fail to reach them. It is a failure not to reach for the stars."

EXERCISE
PERSONAL ENTREPRENEURIAL STRATEGY

NAME:

DATE:

PART I – PROFILE OF THE PAST

STEP 1: EXAMINE YOUR PERSONAL PREFERENCES:
   — What gives you energy, and why? These are things from either work or leisure, or both, that give you the greatest amount of personal satisfaction, sense of enjoyment, and energy.

Source of Energy	Reason

   — What takes away your energy, and why? These create for you the greatest amount of personal dissatisfaction, anxiety, or discontent and take away your energy and motivation.

Source of Depletion	Reason

— Rank (from the most to the least) the items you have listed above:

Gives Energy	Takes Energy

— In 20 to 30 years, how would you like to spend an "ideal" month? Include in your description your desired lifestyle, work style, income, friends, and so forth, and a comment about what attracts you to and what repels you about this ideal existence.

— Review the Idea Generation Guide you completed in Chapter 2 and list the common attributes of the 10 businesses you wanted to enter and the 10 businesses you did not:

Attributes	
Would Energize	Would Turn Off

— Which of these attributes would give you energy and which would take it away, and why?

Attribute	Give or Take Energy	Reason

— Complete the sentence "I would/would not like to start/acquire my own business someday because . . ."

— Discuss any patterns, issues, insights, and conclusions which have emerged:

— Rank the following in terms of importance to you:

Important ⟵⟶ Irrelevant

	5	4	3	2	1
Location Geography (particular area)					
Community size and nature					
Community involvement					
Commuting distance (one way): 20 minutes or less					
30 minutes or less					
60 minutes or less					
More than 60 minutes					

Lifestyle and Work Style
 Size of business:
  Less than $1 million sales or under 20 employees

  More than $1 million sales or 20 employees

  More than $10 million sales and 200 employees

Rate of real growth:
 Fast (over 25%/year)

 Moderate (10% to 15%/year)

 Slow (less than 10%/year)

Work load (weekly):
 Over 70 hours

 55 to 60 hours

 40 hours or less

Marriage

Family

Travel away from home:
 More than 60%

30% to 60%

Less than 30%

None

Standard of Living
  Tight belt/later capital gains

Average/limited capital gains

High/no capital gains

Become very rich

Personal Development
  Utilization of skill & education

Opportunity for personal growth

Contribution to society

Positioning for opportunities

Generation of significant contacts, experience, and know-how

Status and Prestige

Impact on Ecology and Environment

Capital Required
From you

From others

Other Considerations

— Imagine you had $1,000 with which to "buy" the items you ranked above. Indicate below how you would allocate the money. For example, the item that is most important should receive the greatest amount. You may spend nothing on some items; you may spend equal amounts on some; and so forth. Once you have allocated the $1,000, rank the items in order of importance, the most important being number 1.

Item	Share of $1,000	Rank
Location		
Lifestyle and work style		
Standard of living		
Personal development		
Status and prestige		
Ecology and environment		
Capital required		
Other considerations		

STEP 2: EXAMINE YOUR PERSONAL HISTORY:
- List activities (1) that have provided you financial support in the past (e.g., a part-time or full-time business, a paper route, etc.), (2) that have contributed to your well-being (e.g., financing your education or a hobby), and (3) that you have done on your own (e.g., building something).

- Discuss why you became involved in each of the activities above and what specifically influenced each of your decisions.

- Discuss what you learned about yourself, about self-employment, about managing people, and about making money.

— List and discuss your full-time work experience, including descriptions of specific tasks for which you had responsibility, specific skills you used, the number of people you supervised, whether you were successful, and so forth.

— Discuss why you became involved in each of the employment situations above and what specifically influenced each of your decisions.

— Discuss what you learned about yourself, about employment, about managing people, and about making money.

— List and discuss other activities, such as sports, in which you have participated and indicate whether each activity was individual (e.g., chess or tennis) or team (e.g., football).

— What lessons and insights emerged, and how will these apply to life as an entrepreneur?

— If you have ever been fired from or quit either a full-time or part-time job, indicate the job, why you were fired or quit, the circumstances, and what you have learned and what difference this has made.

— If you have ever changed jobs or relocated, indicate the job, why the change, the circumstances, and what you have learned from those experiences.

— Among those individuals who have influenced you most, do any own and operate their own businesses or engage independently in a profession (e.g., certified public accountant)?

— How have the people above influenced you, how do you view them and their roles, and what have you learned from them about self-employment? Include a discussion of the things that attract or repel you, the trade-offs they have had to consider, the risks they have faced and rewards they have enjoyed, and entry strategies that have worked for them.

— If you have ever started a business of any kind or worked in a small company, list the things you liked most and those you liked least, and why.

Liked Most	Reason

Liked Least	Reason

— If you have ever worked for a larger company (over 500 employees or about $50 million to $60 million in sales), list the things you liked most and those you liked least about your work, and why.

Liked Most	Reason

Liked Least	Reason

— Summarize those factors in your history that you believe are entrepreneurial strengths or weaknesses.

Strengths	Weaknesses

PART II—PROFILE OF THE PRESENT: WHERE YOU ARE

STEP 1:   EXAMINE YOUR "ENTREPRENEURIAL MIND."   That is, examine your attitudes, behaviors, and know-how:
  — Rank yourself below. (See Chapter 5 for a discussion of these attitudes and behaviors.)

Strongest ←⎯⎯⎯⎯⎯⎯⎯⎯→ Weakest

	5	4	3	2	1
Commitment and Determination					
Decisiveness					
Tenacity					
Discipline					
Persistence in solving problems					
Willingness to sacrifice					
Total immersion					
Opportunity Obsession					
Having knowledge of customers' needs					
Being market driven					
Obsession with value-creation and enhancement					

Tolerance of Risk, Ambiguity, and Uncertainty
Calculated risk-taker

Risk minimizer

Risk sharer

Tolerance of uncertainty and lack of structure

Tolerance of stress and conflict

Ability to resolve problems and integrate solutions

Creativity, Self-reliance, and Ability to Adapt
Nonconventional, open-minded, lateral thinker

Restlessness with status quo

Ability to adapt

Lack of fear of failure

Ability to conceptualize and to "sweat details" (helicopter mind)

Motivation to Excel
Goal and results orientation

Drive to achieve and grow (self-imposed standards)

Low need for status and power

Ability to be interpersonally supporting (vs. competitive)

Awareness of weaknesses (and strengths)

Having perspective and sense of humor

Leadership
Being self-starter

Having internal locus of control

Having integrity and reliability

Having patience

Being team builder and hero maker

— Summarize your entrepreneurial strengths.

— Summarize your entrepreneurial weaknesses.

STEP 2: EXAMINE ENTREPRENEURIAL ROLE REQUIREMENTS:
— Rank where you "fit" in the following roles. (See Chapter 5.)

Strongest ⟵——————————⟶ Weakest

5	4	3	2	1

Accommodation to Venture
Extent to which career and venture are
No. 1 priority

Stress
The cost of accommodation

Values
Extent to which conventional values are
held

Ethics and Integrity

— Summarize your strengths and weaknesses.

STEP 3: EXAMINE YOUR MANAGEMENT COMPETENCIES:
— Rank your skills and competencies below. (See Management Competency Inventory in Chapter 6.)

	Strongest ←				→ Weakest
	5	4	3	2	1
Marketing Market research and evaluation					
Marketing planning					
Product pricing					
Sales management					
Direct mail/catalog selling					
Telemarketing					
Customer service					
Distribution management					

Product management

New product planning

Operations/Production
Manufacturing management

Inventory control

Cost analysis and control

Quality control

Production scheduling and flow

Purchasing

Job evaluation

Finance
Accounting

Capital budgeting

Cash flow management

Credit and collection management

Managing relations with financial sources

Short-term financing

Public and private offerings

Administration
Problem solving

Communications

Planning

Decision making

Project management

Negotiating

Personnel administration

Management information systems

Computer

Interpersonal/Team
Leadership/vision/influence

Helping and coaching

Feedback

Conflict management

Teamwork and people management

Law
Corporations

Contracts

Taxes

Securities

Patents and proprietary rights

Real estate law

Bankruptcy

Unique Skills

STEP 4: BASED ON AN ANALYSIS OF THE INFORMATION GIVEN IN STEPS 1–3, INDICATE THE ITEMS YOU WOULD ADD TO A "DO" LIST.

PART III—GETTING CONSTRUCTIVE FEEDBACK

Part III is an organized way for you to gather some constructive feedback. (If you choose not to get constructive feedback at this time, proceed to Part IV.)

STEP 1: (OPTIONAL) GIVE A COPY OF YOUR ANSWERS TO PARTS I AND II TO THE PERSON DESIGNATED TO EVALUATE YOUR RESPONSES. ASK HIM OR HER TO ANSWER THE FOLLOWING:

— Have you been honest, objective, hard-nosed, and complete in evaluating your skills?

— Are there any strengths and weaknesses you have inventoried incorrectly?

— Are there other events or past actions that might affect this analysis and that have not been addressed?

STEP 2: SOLICIT FEEDBACK. Give one copy of the Feedback Form to each person who has been asked to evaluate your responses.

Feedback Form

Feedback for:

Prepared by:

STEP 1: PLEASE CHECK THE APPROPRIATE COLUMN NEXT TO THE STATE-MENTS ABOUT MY ENTREPRENEURIAL ATTRIBUTES, AND ADD ANY ADDITIONAL COMMENTS YOU MAY HAVE:

	Strong	Adequate	Weakness	No Comment
Commitment and Determination				
Decisiveness				
Tenacity				
Discipline				
Persistence in solving problems				
Willingness to sacrifice				
Total immersion				
Opportunity Obsession				
Having knowledge of customers' needs				
Being market-driven				
Obsession with value creation and enhancement				

Tolerance of Risk, Ambiguity, and Uncertainty			
Calculated risk taker			
Risk minimizer			
Risk sharer			
Tolerance of uncertainty and lack of structure			
Tolerance of stress and conflict			
Ability to resolve problems and integrate solutions			
Creativity, Self-reliance, and Ability to Adapt			
Nonconventional, open-minded, lateral thinker			
Restlessness with status quo			
Ability to adapt			
Lack of fear of failure			
Ability to conceptualize and to "sweat details" (helicopter mind)			

Motivation to Excel				
Goal and results orientation				
Drive to achieve and grow (self-imposed standards)				
Low need for status and power				
Ability to be interpersonally supporting (vs. competitive)				
Awareness of weaknesses (and strengths)				
Having perspective and sense of humor				
Leadership				
Being self-starter				
Having internal locus of control				
Having integrity and reliability				
Having patience				
Being team builder and hero maker				

Additional Comments

(Please make any comments you can on such matters as my energy, health, and emotional stability; my creativity and innovativeness; my intelligence; my capacity to inspire; my values; and so forth.)

STEP 2:   PLEASE CHECK THE APPROPRIATE COLUMN NEXT TO THE STATE-MENTS ABOUT ENTREPRENEURIAL ROLE REQUIREMENTS TO INDI-CATE MY "FIT" AND ADD ANY ADDITIONAL COMMENTS YOU MAY HAVE:

	Strong	Adequate	Weakness	No Comment
Accommodation to Venture				
Stress (cost of accommodation)				
Values (conventional economic and professional values of free enterprise system)				
Ethics and Integrity				
Additional Comments				

STEP 3: PLEASE CHECK THE APPROPRIATE COLUMN NEXT TO THE STATE-
MENTS ABOUT MANAGEMENT COMPETENCIES, AND ADD ANY AD-
DITIONAL COMMENTS YOU MAY HAVE:

	Strong	Adequate	Weakness	No Comment
Marketing				
Market research and evaluation				
Marketing planning				
Product pricing				
Sales management				
Direct mail/catalog selling				
Telemarketing				

Customer service				
Distribution management				
Product management				
New product planning				
Operations/Production Manufacturing management				
Inventory control				
Cost analysis and control				

Quality control

Production scheduling and flow

Purchasing

Job evaluation

Finance
Accounting

Capital budgeting

Cash flow management

Credit and collection management				
Managing lender relations				
Short-term financing				
Public and private offerings				
Administration Problem solving				
Communications				
Planning				

Decision making

Project management

Negotiating

Personnel administration

Management information systems

Computer

Interpersonal/Team
Leadership/vision/influence

Helping and coaching				
Feedback				
Conflict management				
Teamwork and people management				
Law Corporations				
Contracts				
Taxes				

Securities

Patents and proprietary rights

Real estate law

Bankruptcy

Unique Skills

Additional Comments

STEP 4:   PLEASE EVALUATE MY STRENGTHS AND WEAKNESSES:
- In what area or areas do you see my greatest potential or existing strengths in terms of the venture opportunity we have discussed, and why?

Area of Strength	Reason

- In what area or areas do you see my greatest potential or existing weaknesses in terms of the venture opportunity we have discussed, and why?

Area of Weakness	Reason

— If you know my partners and given the venture opportunity, what is your evaluation of their "fit" with me and the "fit" among them?

— Given the venture opportunity, what you know of my partners, and your evaluation of my weaknesses, should I consider any additional members for my management team, and, if so, what should be their strengths and relevant experience?

— Please make any other suggestions that would be helpful for me to consider (e.g., comments about what you see that I like to do, my lifestyle, work style, patterns evident in my skills inventory, the implications of my particular constellation of management strengths and weaknesses and background, the time implications of an apprenticeship, and so forth).

STEP 3: DECIDE IF ANY FEEDBACK IS PERTINENT AND HOW IT CHANGES YOUR ASSESSMENT.

PART IV – PUTTING IT ALL TOGETHER

STEP 1: REFLECT ON YOUR PREVIOUS RESPONSES AND FEEDBACK YOU HAVE SOLICITED OR HAVE RECEIVED INFORMALLY (SUCH AS FROM CLASS DISCUSSION OR FROM DISCUSSIONS WITH FRIENDS, PARENTS, AND SO FORTH).

STEP 2: ASSESS YOUR ENTREPRENEURIAL STRATEGY:
— What have you concluded at this point about entrepreneurship and you?

— How do the requirements of entrepreneurship—especially the sacrifices, total immersion, heavy work load, and long-term commitment—fit with your own aims, values, and motivations?

— What specific conflicts do you anticipate between your aims and values and the demands of entrepreneurship?

— How would you compare your entrepreneurial mind, your fit with entrepreneurial role demands, your management competencies, and so forth, with those of other people you know who have pursued or are pursuing an entrepreneurial career?

— Thinking ahead 5 to 10 years, or more, and assuming that you would want to launch or acquire a higher potential venture, what "chunks" of experience and know-how do you need to accumulate?

— What are the implications of this assessment of your entrepreneurial strategy in terms of whether you should proceed with your current venture opportunity?

— What is it about the specific opportunity you want to pursue that will provide you with sustained energy and motivation? How do you know this?

— At this time, given your major entrepreneurial strengths and weaknesses and your specific venture opportunity, are there other "chunks" of experience and know-how you need to acquire or attract to your team? (Be specific!)

— What other issues or questions have been raised for you at this point that you would like answered?

PART V—THINKING AHEAD

Part V considers the crafting of your personal entrepreneurial strategy.   REMEMBER, GOALS SHOULD BE SPECIFIC AND CONCRETE, MEASURABLE, AND, EXCEPT WHERE INDICATED BELOW, REALISTIC AND ATTAINABLE.

STEP 1:   LIST, IN *THREE* MINUTES, YOUR GOALS TO BE ACCOMPLISHED BY THE TIME YOU ARE 70.

STEP 2: LIST, IN *THREE* MINUTES, YOUR GOALS TO BE ACCOMPLISHED OVER THE NEXT SEVEN YEARS.   (If you are an undergraduate, use the next four years.)

STEP 3: LIST, IN *THREE* MINUTES, THE GOALS YOU WOULD LIKE TO ACCOMPLISH IF YOU HAVE EXACTLY ONE YEAR FROM TODAY TO LIVE.   Assume you would enjoy good health in the interim but would not be able to acquire any more life insurance or borrow an additional large sum of money for a "final fling." Assume further that you could spend that last year of your life doing whatever you want to do.

STEP 4: LIST, IN *SIX* MINUTES, YOUR REAL GOALS AND THE GOALS YOU WOULD LIKE TO ACCOMPLISH OVER YOUR LIFETIME.

STEP 5:   DISCUSS THE LIST FROM *STEP 4* WITH ANOTHER PERSON AND THEN REFINE AND CLARIFY YOUR GOAL STATEMENTS.

STEP 6:   RANK YOUR GOALS ACCORDING TO PRIORITY.

STEP 7:   CONCENTRATING ON THE TOP THREE GOALS, MAKE A LIST OF PROBLEMS, OBSTACLES, INCONSISTENCIES, AND SO FORTH THAT YOU WILL ENCOUNTER IN TRYING TO REACH EACH OF THESE GOALS.

STEP 8: DECIDE AND STATE HOW YOU WILL ELIMINATE ANY IMPORTANT PROBLEMS, OBSTACLES, INCONSISTENCIES, AND SO FORTH.

STEP 9: FOR YOUR TOP THREE GOALS, WRITE DOWN ALL THE TASKS OR ACTION STEPS YOU NEED TO TAKE TO HELP YOU ATTAIN EACH GOAL AND INDICATE HOW RESULTS WILL BE MEASURED.   It is helpful to organize the goals in order of priority.

Goal	Task/Action Step	Measurement	Rank

STEP 10:   RANK TASKS/ACTION STEPS IN TERMS OF PRIORITY.   To identify high-priority items, it is helpful to make a copy of your list and cross off any activities or task that cannot be completed in the next seven days, or at least begun, and then identify the single most important goal, the next most important, and so forth.

STEP 11:   ESTABLISH DATES AND DURATIONS (AND, IF POSSIBLE, A PLACE) FOR TASKS/ACTION STEPS TO BEGIN.   Organize tasks/action steps according to priority. If possible, the date should be during the next seven days.

Task/Action	Date Begin	Duration	Place

STEP 12: MAKE A LIST OF PROBLEMS, OBSTACLES, INCONSISTENCIES, AND SO FORTH.

STEP 13: DECIDE HOW YOU WILL ELIMINATE ANY IMPORTANT PROBLEMS, OBSTACLES, INCONSISTENCIES, AND SO FORTH, AND ADJUST THE LIST IN **STEP 11.**

STEP 14: IDENTIFY RISKS INVOLVED AND RESOURCES AND OTHER HELP NEEDED.

APPENDIXES

I   INFORMATION ABOUT RMA "PROJECTION OF FINANCIAL STATE-
        MENTS" AND RMA STATEMENT STUDIES

II   INFORMATION ABOUT *INDUSTRY NORMS AND KEY BUSINESS RATIOS*,
        PUBLISHED BY DUN & BRADSTREET

III   "THE LEGAL PROCESS OF VENTURE CAPITAL INVESTMENT" BY
        RICHARD J. TESTA

IV   SAMPLE TERMS SHEET

V   OUTLINE OF AN INVESTMENT AGREEMENT

VI   SAMPLE VESTING AND STOCK RESTRICTION AGREEMENT

VII   SAMPLE LOAN AGREEMENT

VIII   VASES AND FACES EXERCISE

APPENDIX I—INFORMATION ABOUT RMA "PROJECTION OF FINANCIAL STATEMENTS" AND RMA STATEMENT STUDIES

The following is part of an article* about preparing and using "worksheet schedules" in completing an RMA form, "Projection of Financial Statements," and information from RMA Statement Studies.

Projection of Financial Statements—and the Preparatory Use of Worksheet Schedules for Budgets†

I don't know about other credit men, but without exception, all the budgets that I have seen were submitted without supporting schedules showing the source of the figures being used. Without this source, the budgets left me with an uneasy feeling of nebulous value and questionable accuracy, because it was impossible to check back any figures used.

I will be the first one to admit that I am not an expert in the preparation of "Projection of Financial Statements" (RMA Form C–117), but I'd say that it is impossible to complete these forms with any consistent degree of accuracy without the prior preparation of supporting schedules. In fact, the easiest, quickest—and possibly the only—way to complete the budget form is to sit down beforehand and gather up all the necessary information in a logical, concise, and intelligent manner in the form of "worksheet schedules." This article is directed primarily to the preparation and use of such schedules.

For purposes of illustration, I am going to deal with a hypothetical company, Sample Company, Inc. Starting out with (1) a 12/31/59 balance sheet and income statement (which the reader can find in the first column of the accompanying completed C–117) and (2) with certain additional pertinent financial facts (given below for the reader), my goal was to project Sample Company's financial statements monthly for 1960—i.e., to complete C–117. Each of the five schedules I had to prepare before tackling C–117 are reproduced in the article, and, following the schedules, there is presented a line-by-line explanation of the entries made on C–117.

Here are the necessary pertinent facts about Sample Company, established by competent management opinions:

---

* Reprinted with permission. The Robert Morris Associates, 1616 Philadelphia National Bank Building, Philadelphia, Pennsylvania 19107.

† By Chester G. Zimmerman, Director of Loan Review, American National Bank and Trust Company of Chicago, Chicago, Illinois. Reprinted from the April 1961 issue of the *Bulletin* (now *The Journal of Commercial Bank Lending*) published by Robert Morris Associates, The National Association of Bank Loan and Credit Officers, 1432 Philadelphia National Bank Bldg., Philadelphia, Pa. 19107. (Copyright 1961, Robert Morris Associates.)

Sales Proposed (see Schedule A for detail by month)	$12,000,000
Cost Figures—1959 percentages to be used	
Inventory supply on hand—45 days' supply, based upon next month's material costs with December inventory the same as at the beginning.	
Accounts Receivable Collections:	
January through April	15 days
May and June	30 days
July and August 50% in 30 days, 25% in 60 days, 25% in 90 days	
September 75% in 30 days, 25% in 60 days	
October through November	30 days
December	20 days
Trade payments every 15 days	
Additions to fixed assets (equally over the year)	$120,000 per annum
Depreciation (equally over the year)	$ 72,000 per annum
Direct Labor, Indirect Labor, and Manufacturing Expenses Paid Every 15 Days	
Sales Expense—5% of sales—Paid by End of Month	
General and Administrative Expense—2.5% of Sales—Paid by End of Month	
Minimum Cash Balances to Be Carried	$250,000
Monthly Payments on Long-term Obligations	$ 5,000
Borrowing Will Be in Multiples of	$ 50,000

The first logical schedule to be prepared ("A") would be the proposed sales, cost of sales, and other expenses making up the profit and loss figures for the coming year. These data complete the upper third of the form, and, because of the segregation of expenses, some details are brought forward to additional schedules to support cash projections and balance sheet data.

Schedule "A" projects by month:
  Cost of Sales (85% based upon 1959 percentages)
  Material Costs (80% of cost of sales based upon 1959 percentages)
  Direct Labor Costs (10% of cost of sales—1959 percentages)
  Indirect Labor Costs (5% of cost of sales—1959 percentages)
  Manufacturing Overhead (5% of cost of sales—exclusive of depreciation—1959 percentages)
  Sales Expense (5% of sales)
  General and Administrative Expense (2.5% of sales)

WORK SHEET SCHEDULES TO SUPPORT PROJECTION OF FINANCIAL STATEMENTS —

SAMPLE COMPANY, INC.

SCHEDULE "A" — SALES AND COST OF SALES PROJECTED FOR 1960 (000) Omitted

Details	January	February	March	April	May	June	July	August	September	October	November	December	Totals
Net Sales	$ 800	$ 800	$1,500	$1,200	$ 800	$ 600	$ 400	$ 700	$ 1,000	$ 1,500	$ 1,500	$ 1,200	$12,000
Material Costs—80% of Cost of Sales	544	544	1,020	816	544	408	272	476	680	1,020	1,020	816	$ 8,160
Direct Labor—10% of Cost of Sales	68	68	128	102	68	50	34	60	84	128	126	102	1,018
Mfg. Overhead (Excl. Deprec.) 5% of Cost of Sales	34	34	64	51	34	25	17	30	42	64	63	51	509
Indirect Labor—5% of Cost of Sales	34	34	64	51	34	25	17	30	42	64	63	51	509
Cost of Sales—85% of Sales	$ 680	$ 680	$1,276	$1,020	$ 680	$ 508	$ 340	$ 596	$ 848	$1,276	$1,272	$1,020	$10,196
Gross Profit	120	120	224	180	120	92	60	104	152	224	228	180	$ 1,804
Sales Expense—5% of Sales	$ 40	$ 40	$ 75	$ 60	$ 40	$ 30	$ 20	$ 35	$ 50	$ 75	$ 75	$ 60	$ 600
General & Admin. Expense—2½% of Sales	20	20	37	30	20	15	10	17	25	38	37	30	299
Operating Profit before Deprec. & Taxes	$ 60	$ 60	$ 112	$ 90	$ 60	$ 47	$ 30	$ 52	$ 77	$ 111	$ 116	$ 90	$ 905

Material Costs are brought into Schedule "C"

Direct Labor and Manufacturing Overhead are brought into Schedule "E"

Sales Expenses and General & Administrative Expenses are combined for Line 25

Depreciation is set forth on Line 12. Income Tax is provided at 50% (for ease in computation) and added to total of Line 48 less payments made on Line 27

Line 15 is net profit which is added to previous month balance of Line 56 for current month total for Line 56

SCHEDULE "B" — ACCOUNTS RECEIVABLE OUTSTANDINGS AND COLLECTIONS (000) Omitted

Details	January	February	March	April	May	June	July	August	September	October	November	December	Totals
Balance — Beginning of Month	$ 366	$ 400	$ 400	$ 750	$ 600	$ 800	$ 600	$ 400	$ 900	$1,450	$1,925	$1,500	
Add: Sales	800	800	1,500	1,200	800	600	400	700	1,000	1,500	1,500	1,200	$12,000
Total	$1,166	$1,200	$1,900	$1,950	$1,400	$1,400	$1,000	$1,100	$1,900	$2,950	$3,425	$2,700	
Balance — End of Month — Based on Collection Terms	400	400	750	600	800	600	400	900	1,450	1,925	1,500	800	
Cash Collections	$ 766	$ 800	$1,150	$1,350	$ 600	$ 800	$ 600	$ 200	$ 450	$1,025	$1,925	$1,900	$11,566
Collection Terms — in Days	15	15	15	15	30	30	30	30 50% -60 & 90 25% -60 & 90	75% -30 25% -60	30	30	20	

Balance — End of Month — listed on Line 36

Monthly Cash Collections listed on Line 17

SCHEDULE "C" — MATERIAL FLOW AND PURCHASES (000) Omitted

Details	January	February	March	April	May	June	July	August	September	October	November	December	Totals
Beginning Inventory	$ 788	$ 816	$1,530	$1,224	$ 816	$ 612	$ 408	$ 711	$1,020	$1,530	$1,530	$1,224	
Less: Materials Used from Schedule "A"	544	544	1,020	816	544	408	272	476	680	1,020	1,020	816	$ 8,160
Net Remaining before Required Purchases	$ 244	$ 272	$ 510	$ 408	$ 272	$ 204	$ 136	$ 238	$ 340	$ 510	$ 510	$ 408	
Add: Purchases Required	572	1,258	714	408	340	204	578	782	1,190	1,020	714	380	$ 8,160
Ending Inventory — 45 Days' Supply	$ 816	$1,530	$1,224	$ 816	$ 612	$ 408	$ 714	$1,020	$1,530	$1,530	$1,224	$ 788	

"Purchases Required" are brought forward to Schedule "D" to obtain cash disbursements and accounts payable at end of month

"Purchase Required" is always an amount which when added to the "net inventory" results in the pre-computed ending inventory

Ending inventories are set forth on Line 37

SCHEDULE "D" — ACCOUNTS PAYABLE — CASH FLOW — 15 DAY TERMS (000) Omitted

Details	January	February	March	April	May	June	July	August	September	October	November	December	Totals
Accounts Payable — Beginning of Month	$ 341	$ 286	$ 629	$ 357	$ 204	$ 170	$ 102	$ 289	$ 391	$ 595	$ 510	$ 357	
Add: Monthly Purchases Required — Schedule "B"	572	1,258	714	408	340	204	578	782	1,190	1,020	714	380	$ 8,160
Total	913	1,544	1,343	765	544	374	680	1,071	1,581	1,615	1,224	737	
Less Accounts Payable — End of Month	286	629	357	204	170	102	289	391	595	510	357	190	
Cash Disbursed on Trade Payables	$ 627	$ 915	$ 986	$ 561	$ 374	$ 272	$ 391	$ 680	$ 986	$1,105	$ 867	$ 517	$ 8,311

Accounts Payable — End of month are listed on Line 22

Cash Disbursed is listed on Line 22

SCHEDULE "E" — DIRECT LABOR, MANUFACTURING EXPENSES AND INDIRECT LABOR — ACCRUALS AND CASH DISBURSED (000) Omitted

Details	January	February	March	April	May	June	July	August	September	October	November	December	Totals
Accruals — Beginning of Month	$ 95	$ 68	$ 68	$ 128	$ 102	$ 68	$ 50	$ 34	$ 60	$ 84	$ 128	$ 126	
Add: Monthly Expense from Schedule "A" of 3 totals	136	136	256	204	136	100	68	120	168	256	252	204	$ 2,036
Total	231	204	324	332	238	168	118	154	228	340	380	330	
Less: Accruals — End of Month — Paid 15 days	68	68	128	102	68	50	34	60	84	128	126	102	
Cash Disbursed	$ 163	$ 136	$ 196	$ 230	$ 170	$ 118	$ 84	$ 94	$ 144	$ 212	$ 254	$ 228	$ 2,029

Accruals — End of Month listed on Line 51

Cash Disbursed listed on Lines 23 and 24

Sample Company, Inc.: Source of Figures for Budget Form

Line No.	Source
1	Sales from Schedule A
2	Material Costs from Schedule A
3	DIrect Labor from Schedule A
4	Manufacturing Overhead from Schedule A
5	Indirect Labor from Schedule A
6	Cost of Goods Sold from Schedule A
7	Gross Profit—Line 1 less Line 6
8	Sales Expense—Schedule A
9	General and Administrative Expenses—Schedule A
11	Line 7 less totals of Lines 8, 9, and 10
12	Depreciation—from Preliminary Facts
13	50% for purposes of illustration (or current tax rate) or Difference between Line 11 less Line 12
14	
15	Line 11 less total of Lines 12, 13, and 14
16	Balance of Line 33 (from previous month)
17	Monthly Cash Collections from Schedule B
20	Bank Loan Proceeds—an amount to be added (Line 20) to the difference of Line 21 less Line 32 to equal cash balances (Line 33) of not less than $250,000. Borrowings to be made in multiples of $50,000.
21	Totals of Lines 16 through 20
22	Cash Disbursed on Trade Payables from Schedule D
23 24	Cash Disbursed from Schedule E
25	Total of Lines 8 and 9 above
26	Monthly amounts of fixed-asset additions from preliminary facts
27	Balance on Line 48 (from actual balance sheet) distributed in March and June, with 25% of the amount in excess of $100,000 of estimated income taxes payable in September and December
30	Balance on Line 49 (actual) distributed in accordance with terms of payment
31	When bank loans are outstanding if Line 21 exceeds Line 32 (without Line 31 added in), any amount which reduces cash balances (Line 33) to not less than $250,000 should be placed in Line 31
32	Totals of Lines 22 to 31
33	The difference between Line 21 less Line 32—at no time to be less than $250,000
34	From Line 33
36	Balance—End of Month—from Schedule B
37	Ending Inventory—from Schedule C
39	Totals of Lines 34 through 38
40	Line 26 less Line 12 added to outstanding of previous month
41	No change—brought across from actual
44	No change—brought across from actual
45	Total of Lines 39 through 44
46	Total of Line 20 less total of Line 31 added to previous month balance
47	Accounts Payable end of month from Schedule D
48	Previous month's balance plus Line 13 less Line 27
49	(Current Maturities—Term Debt) year-end actual total less payments on Line 30, plus maturities of Line 53 becoming current obligations
51	Accruals end of month from Schedule E
52	Total of Lines 46 through 51
53	(Term Debt) Outstanding balance (from actual) less maturities becoming current obligations
54	(Total Liabilities) Total of Lines 52 and 53
56 57	Previous month's outstanding balance plus Line 15
58	Total of Lines 54 and 56
59	Line 39 less Line 52

rma

'77 annual statement studies

fiscal year-ends 6/30/76 through 3/31/77

with other sources of composite
financial data

Published by Robert Morris Associates, Philadelphia, Pa.

CHEMICALS & ALLIED PRODUCTS — SIC# 5161 | WHOLESALERS | DRUGS, DRUG PROPRIETARIES & DRUGGISTS' SUNDRIES — SIC# 5122

60(6/30-9/30/76) 0-250M **23**	250M-1MM **65**	105(10/1/76-3/31/77) 1-10MM **72**	10-50MM **5**	ALL **165**	ASSET SIZE NUMBER OF STATEMENTS	48(6/30-9/30/76) 0-250M **16**	250M-1MM **26**	67(10/1/76-3/31/77) 1-10MM **58**	10-50MM **15**	ALL **115**
%	%	%	%	%	**ASSETS**	%	%	%	%	%
7.9	7.7	8.9		10.9	Cash & Equivalents	9.6	5.5	3.6	8.9	8.6
34.3	35.0	33.6		30.4	Accts. & Notes Rec - Trade(net)	30.3	28.4	32.3	26.8	29.1
32.2	28.8	24.6		28.5	Inventory	39.9	44.6	44.6	41.2	42.7
1.0	2.3	2.5		1.8	All Other Current	.7	1.2	2.0	.9	1.9
75.4	73.9	67.7		71.6	Total Current	80.6	79.6	82.4	78.7	80.3
14.8	19.4	25.5		21.9	Fixed Assets (net)	8.3	12.2	11.8	16.4	14.3
.3	.7	.8		.6	Intangibles (net)	.0	1.0	.6	1.1	.9
9.5	5.9	6.0		6.0	All Other Non-Current	11.1	7.2	5.1	3.8	4.5
100.0	100.0	100.0		100.0	Total	100.0	100.0	100.0	100.0	100.0
					LIABILITIES					
12.6	10.2	9.5		7.6	Notes Payable-Short Term	10.9	10.6	13.3	3.6	7.9
4.0	2.8	3.5		2.5	Cur. Mat.-L/T/D	2.2	2.7	1.2	.9	1.1
22.2	26.0	28.4		29.5	Accts. & Notes Payable - Trade	30.4	31.2	29.2	26.9	28.0
10.2	5.4	5.4		4.6	Accrued Expenses	3.8	6.1	4.3	5.1	4.8
2.8	3.9	5.1		7.4	All Other Current	1.0	2.8	.8	1.5	1.7
51.7	48.3	51.9		51.6	Total Current	48.3	53.4	49.8	38.0	43.4
15.8	12.1	10.2		9.3	Long Term Debt	16.1	7.4	9.5	8.2	8.7
2.2	2.0	2.4		2.5	All Other Non-Current	.0	7.2	1.3	3.2	2.5
30.4	37.7	35.5		36.6	Net Worth	35.6	32.0	39.4	50.6	45.3
100.0	100.0	100.0		100.0	Total Liabilities & Net Worth	100.0	100.0	100.0	100.0	100.0
					INCOME DATA					
100.0	100.0	100.0		100.0	Net Sales	100.0	100.0	100.0	100.0	100.0
64.9	75.6	80.5		79.5	Cost Of Sales	73.5	71.7	82.1	79.7	80.5
35.1	24.4	19.5		20.5	Gross Profit	26.5	28.3	17.9	20.3	19.5
29.1	21.3	16.2		16.3	Operating Expenses	23.3	25.3	15.0	16.2	16.0
6.0	3.0	3.2		4.2	Operating Profit	3.2	3.0	2.9	4.1	3.5
1.1	.6	.2		.3	All Other Expenses (net)	-.3	.4	.7	.3	.5
4.9	2.4	3.1		3.9	Profit Before Taxes	3.5	2.6	2.2	3.8	3.1
					RATIOS					
2.1 / 1.6 / 1.1	2.0 / 1.5 / 1.2	1.7 / 1.4 / 1.1		1.9 / 1.4 / 1.1	Current	1.9 / 1.7 / 1.5	2.3 / 1.6 / 1.2	2.0 / 1.7 / 1.3	2.9 / 2.1 / 1.8	2.1 / 1.7 / 1.4
1.2 / .9 / .6	1.1 / .9 / .6	1.1 / .8 / .6		1.1 / .8 / .6	Quick	1.5 / 1.0 / .4	1.1 / .7 / .3	.9 / .7 / .6	1.4 / .9 / .8	1.1 / .8 / .5
26 14.3 / 41 8.8 / 72 5.1	28 13.1 / 36 10.1 / 54 6.8	33 10.9 / 46 7.9 / 60 6.1		31 11.7 / 42 8.6 / 57 6.4	Sales/Receivables	23 16.1 / 30 12.2 / 47 7.8	22 16.9 / 42 8.7 / 52 7.0	28 13.1 / 39 9.4 / 54 6.7	29 12.6 / 38 9.7 / 44 8.3	27 13.5 / 38 9.6 / 49 7.4
42 8.6 / 60 6.1 / 87 4.2	26 13.8 / 44 8.3 / 73 5.0	24 15.0 / 42 8.6 / 64 5.7		28 13.2 / 46 7.9 / 70 5.2	Cost of Sales/Inventory	50 7.3 / 74 4.9 / 104 3.5	56 6.5 / 79 4.6 / 118 3.1	49 7.4 / 62 5.9 / 87 4.2	60 6.1 / 63 5.8 / 69 5.3	54 6.8 / 68 5.4 / 87 4.2
7.9 / 8.9 / 44.4	7.6 / 13.9 / 34.3	10.4 / 14.9 / 38.9		8.3 / 13.9 / 36.9	Sales/Working Capital	7.7 / 9.2 / 20.0	6.1 / 8.6 / 21.0	6.9 / 10.7 / 16.4	5.0 / 7.5 / 9.4	6.6 / 9.3 / 15.1
(19) 13.0 / 6.0 / 3.3	(50) 11.8 / 3.2 / 1.7	(51) 12.1 / 4.7 / 2.0		(123) 12.1 / 4.7 / 1.9	EBIT/Interest	(12) 7.4 / 4.6 / 2.1	(23) 13.8 / 4.6 / 1.3	(43) 10.1 / 5.2 / 1.8	(12) 29.4 / 12.3 / 4.3	(90) 11.3 / 5.1 / 2.0
	(32) 4.1 / 2.1 / 1.0	(41) 5.6 / 3.7 / 1.6		(83) 4.9 / 2.9 / 1.1	Cash Flow/Cur. Mat. L/T/D		(12) 4.7 / 2.9 / 1.2	(28) 11.2 / 2.8 / 1.3	(10) 27.4 / 8.4 / 2.5	(55) 8.9 / 2.9 / 1.3
.1 / .3 / 1.6	.2 / .5 / 1.2	.3 / .6 / 1.0		.2 / .5 / 1.1	Fixed/Worth	.1 / .2 / .5	.1 / .3 / .9	.1 / .2 / .4	.1 / .2 / .5	.1 / .2 / .5
.8 / 1.9 / 7.3	.9 / 2.2 / 3.5	1.1 / 1.9 / 3.6		1.0 / 2.0 / 3.6	Debt/Worth	1.3 / 1.7 / 2.4	1.0 / 1.7 / 5.0	1.1 / 1.7 / 2.9	.6 / 1.0 / 1.4	1.0 / 1.6 / 2.9
(20) 88.5 / 45.0 / 15.3	(71) 35.1 / 17.1 / 10.8	36.0 / 23.3 / 10.3		(161) 37.5 / 22.4 / 10.8	% Profit Before Taxes/Tangible Net Worth	(15) 52.2 / 31.1 / 8.2	(22) 37.8 / 16.2 / 9.2	28.9 / 17.5 / 10.1	(110) 29.0 / 19.7 / 7.5	34.2 / 18.1 / 9.8
21.1 / 10.7 / 4.4	10.8 / 5.4 / 3.0	13.9 / 8.3 / 3.2		14.1 / 7.4 / 3.2	% Profit Before Taxes/Total Assets	19.0 / 10.9 / 3.7	13.7 / 6.7 / 3.0	11.0 / 7.3 / 2.7	14.0 / 10.0 / 2.0	13.8 / 7.8 / 3.3
65.2 / 29.2 / 11.7	60.8 / 20.5 / 9.6	41.9 / 14.9 / 9.3		53.3 / 17.8 / 9.7	Sales/Net Fixed Assets	113.6 / 48.0 / 14.5	85.9 / 26.8 / 16.0	81.8 / 42.6 / 22.3	51.6 / 33.4 / 23.1	81.2 / 36.3 / 17.7
3.9 / 2.7 / 1.9	4.0 / 3.2 / 2.3	3.8 / 2.8 / 2.3		3.8 / 2.9 / 2.2	Sales/Total Assets	3.8 / 3.1 / 2.6	3.8 / 2.7 / 1.9	4.0 / 3.2 / 2.4	3.5 / 3.0 / 2.8	3.9 / 3.1 / 2.4
(19) .7 / 1.1 / 1.9	(61) .4 / .9 / 1.7	(70) .6 / 1.0 / 2.1		(155) .5 / 1.0 / 1.8	% Depr., Dep., Amort./Sales	(13) .3 / .5 / 1.0	(23) .4 / .7 / 1.3	(51) .2 / .4 / .7	(14) .3 / .5 / .9	(101) .3 / .5 / .9
(18) .9 / 1.6 / 2.9	(36) .2 / 1.0 / 1.2	(43) .2 / .7 / 1.4		(100) .3 / .9 / 1.5	% Lease & Rental Exp/Sales	(13) .7 / 1.4 / 4.7	(18) .6 / 1.0 / 2.2	(36) .4 / .6 / 1.3	(74)	.5 / .9 / 1.5
(15) 3.7 / 6.5 / 8.8	(35) 2.2 / 3.4 / 6.4	(33) 1.2 / 1.7 / 3.1		(84) 1.6 / 3.1 / 5.2	% Officers' Comp/Sales	(13) 3.9 / 5.9 / 8.7	(14) 2.4 / 3.6 / 5.0	(25) .9 / 1.5 / 2.2	(54)	1.3 / 2.4 / 4.9
96612M	117496M	603504M	196173M	926785M	Net Sales ($)	8699M	43413M	662937M	800390M	1515439M
33486M	37519M	216024M	106577M	393486M	Total Assets ($)	2504M	14802M	206362M	267752M	491420M

©Robert M...s Assoc... 1977

M = $thousand   MM = $million

DEFINITION OF RATIOS
INTRODUCTION

Below the common size balance sheet and income statement presented on each data page are series of ratios which have been computed from the financial statement data. Each ratio has three values: the upper quartile, median, and lower quartile. For any given ratio, these figures are calculated by first computing the value of the ratio for *each* financial statement in the sample. These values are then arrayed—"listed"—in an order from the strongest to the weakest. (We acknowledge that, for certain ratios, there may be differences of opinion concerning what is a strong or a weak value. RMA has resolved this problem by following general banking guidelines consistent with sound credit practice in its presentation of data.)

In such an array of ratio values, the figure which falls in the middle between the strongest and the weakest ratios is the *median*. The figure that falls halfway between the median and the strongest ratio is the *upper quartile*. The figure that falls halfway between the median and the weakest ratio is the *lower quartile*. The median and quartile values will always be shown on the data pages in the order indicated below:

Upper Quartile
Median
Lower Quartile

There are several reasons for using medians and quartiles instead of an average. One is to eliminate the influence which values in an "unusual" statement would have on an average. The method used more accurately reflects the ranges of ratio values than would a straight averaging method.

It is important to understand that the spread (range) between the upper and lower quartiles represents the middle 50% of all the companies in a sample. Ratio values greater than the upper or less than the lower quartiles, therefore, begin to approach "unusual" values.

For some ratio values, you will occasionally see an entry that is other than a conventional number. These unusual entries are defined as follows:

(1) *INF*—This stands for infinity, a value so large as to be beyond any practical value. It is the result of the denominator having the value of zero in a ratio calculation. With respect to the ratios sales/working capital, debt/worth, and fixed/worth, the value ± *INF* may occasionally appear as a quartile or median. This is the result of interpolation between positive and negative values in the nonlinear arrays typical of these ratios.

(2) *999.8*—When a ratio value equals 1,000 or more, it also becomes an "unusual" value and is given the "999.8" designation. This is considered to be a close enough approximation to the actual atypically large value.

(3) *−.0*—In a few places in this book, we encounter a negative value so minute that, when rounded, it becomes zero. We have used the symbol "−.0" to reflect this, but it is important to recognize that it is the result of rounding a *negative* number.

Throughout the *Statement Studies*, the ratio values have been omitted whenever there were less than ten statements in a sample. Occasionally, the number of statements used in a ratio array will differ from the number of statements in a sample because certain elements of data may not be present in all financial statements. In these cases, the number of statements used is shown in parentheses to the left of the array.

In interpreting ratios, the "strongest" or "best" value is not always the largest numerical value, nor is the "weakest" always the lowest numerical value. The following description of each of the ratios appearing in the *Statement Studies* will provide details regarding the arraying of the values.

The ratios in the *Statement Studies* are grouped into five principal categories: liquidity, coverage, leverage, operating, and specific expense items.

LIQUIDITY RATIOS

Liquidity is a measure of the quality and adequacy of current assets to meet current obligations as they come due.

CURRENT RATIO

Computation: Total current assets divided by total current liabilities.

$$\frac{\text{total current assets}}{\text{total current liabilities}}$$

Interpretation: This ratio is a rough indication of a firm's ability to service its current obligations. Generally, the higher the current ratio, the greater the "cushion" between current obligations and a firm's ability to pay them. The stronger ratio reflects a numerical superiority of current assets over current liabilities. However, the composition and quality of current assets is a critical factor in the analysis of an individual firm's liquidity.

The ratio values are arrayed from the highest positive to the lowest positive.

QUICK RATIO

Computation: Cash and equivalents plus accounts and notes receivable (trade) divided by total current liabilities.

$$\frac{\text{cash \& equivalents} + \text{accounts \& notes receivable (trade)}}{\text{total current liabilities}}$$

Interpretation: Also known as the "ACID TEST" ratio, it is a refinement of the current ratio and is a more conservative measure of liquidity. The ratio expresses the degree to which a company's current liabilities are covered by the most liquid current assets. Generally, any value of less than 1 to 1 implies a reciprocal "dependency" on inventory or other current assets to liquidate short-term debt.

The ratio values are arrayed from the highest positive to the lowest positive.

If the number of statements used in the calculation of this ratio differs from the sample size used in the asset category column, the sample size for each ratio will be printed in parentheses to the left of the array.

SALES/RECEIVABLES

Computation: Net sales divided by accounts and notes receivable (trade) .

$$\frac{\text{net sales}}{\text{accounts \& notes receivable (trade)}}$$

Interpretation: This ratio measures the number of times accounts and notes receivable (trade) turn over during the year. The higher the turnover of receivables, the shorter the time between sale and cash collection. For example, a company with sales of $720,000 and receivables of $120,000 would have a sales/receivables ratio of 6.0, which means receivables turn over six times a year. If a company's receivables appear to be turning slower than the rest of the industry, further research is needed and the quality of the receivables should be examined closely.

A problem with this ratio is that it compares one day's receivables, shown at statement date, to total annual sales and does not take into consideration seasonal fluctuations. An additional problem in interpretation may arise when there is a large proportion of cash sales to total sales.

When the receivables figure is zero, the quotient will be infinity (INF) and represents the best possible ratio. The ratio values are therefore arrayed starting with infinity (INF) and then from the numerically highest to the numerically lowest value. The only time a zero will appear in the array is when the sales figure is low and the quotient rounds off to zero. By definition, this ratio cannot be negative.

Days' Receivables: The sales/receivables ratio will have a figure printed in bold type directly to the left of the array. This figure is the days' receivables.

Computation: The sales/receivables ratio divided into 365 (the number of days in one year).

$$\frac{365}{\text{sales/receivable ratio}}$$

Interpretation: This figure expresses the average time in days that receivables are outstanding. Generally, the greater number of days outstanding, the greater the probability of delinquencies in accounts receivable. A comparison of a company's daily receivables may indicate the extent of a company's control over credit and collections. The terms offered by a company to its customers, however, may differ from terms within the industry and should be taken into consideration.

In the example above, 365 : 6 = 61—i.e., the average receivable is collected in 61 days.

COST OF SALES/INVENTORY

Computation: Cost of sales divided by inventory.

$$\frac{\text{Cost of Sales}}{\text{Inventory}}$$

Interpretation: This ratio measures the number of times inventory is turned over during the year. High inventory turnover can indicate better liquidity or superior merchandising. Conversely it can indicate a shortage of needed inventory for sales. Low inventory turnover can indicate poor liquidity, possible overstocking, obsolescence, or in contrast to these negative interpretations a planned inventory buildup in the case of material shortages. A problem with this ratio is that it compares one day's inventory to cost of goods sold and does not take seasonal fluctuations into account. When the inventory figure is zero, the quotient will be infinity (INF) and represents the best possible ratio. The ratio values are arrayed starting with infinity (INF) and then from the numerically highest to the numerically lowest value. The only time a zero will appear in the array is when the cost of sales figure is very low and the quotient rounds off to zero.

Days' Inventory
The cost of sales inventory ratio will have a figure printed in bold type directly to the left of the array. This figure is the days' inventory.

Computation: The cost of sales/inventory ratio divided into 365 (the number of days in one year).

$$\frac{365}{\text{cost of sales/inventory ratio}}$$

Interpretation: Division of the inventory turnover ratio into 365 days yields the average length of time units are in inventory.

SALES/WORKING CAPITAL

Computation: Net sales divided by net working capital (current assets less current liabilities equals net working capital).

$$\frac{\text{Net Sales}}{\text{Net Working Capital}}$$

Interpretation: Working capital is a measure of the margin of protection for current creditors. It reflects the ability to finance current operations. Relating the level of sales arising from operations to the underlying working capital measures how efficiently working capital is employed. A low ratio may indicate an inefficient use of working capital while a very high ratio often signifies overtrading —a vulnerable position for creditors.

If working capital is zero, the quotient is infinity (INF). If working capital is negative, the quotient is negative. The ratio values are arrayed from the lowest positive to the highest positive, to infinity, and then from the highest negative to the lowest negative.

The value ± INF may occasionally appear as a quartile or median. This is the result of interpolation between positive and negative values in the nonlinear array typical of this ratio.

COVERAGE RATIOS

Coverage ratios measure a firm's ability to service debt.

EARNINGS BEFORE INTEREST AND TAXES (EBIT)/INTEREST

Computation: Earnings (profit) before annual interest expense and taxes divided by annual interest expense.

$$\frac{\text{Earnings Before Interest \& Taxes}}{\text{Annual Interest Expense}}$$

Interpretation: This ratio is a measure of a firm's ability to meet interest payments. A high ratio may indicate that a borrower would have little difficulty in meeting the interest obligations of a loan. This ratio also serves as an indicator of a firm's capacity to take on additional debt.

Only those statements which reported annual interest expense were used in the calculation of this ratio. If the number of statements used in the calculation of these ratios differed from the sample size used in the asset category column, the sample size for each ratio will be printed in parentheses to the left of the array. If there were less than 10 ratios in an array, no entry will be shown. The ratio values are arrayed from the highest positive to the lowest positive and then from the lowest negative to the highest negative.

CASH FLOW/CURRENT MATURITIES LONG-TERM DEBT

Computation: Net profit plus depreciation, depletion, and amortization expenses, divided by the current portion of long-term debt.

$$\frac{\text{Net Profit} + \text{Depreciation, Depletion, Amortization Expenses}}{\text{Current Portion of Long-Term Debt}}$$

Interpretation: This ratio expresses the coverage of current maturities by cash flow from operations. Since cash flow is the primary source of debt retirement, this ratio measures the ability of a firm to service principal repayment and is an indicator of additional debt capacity. Although it is misleading to think that all cash flow is available for debt service, the ratio is a valid measure of the ability to service long-term debt.

Only data for *corporations* which have the following items were used;

    (1)   Profit or loss after taxes (positive, negative, or zero)
    (2)   A positive figure for Depreciation/Depletion/Amortization expenses
    (3)   A positive figure for current maturities of long-term debt

If the number of ratios used differed with the total number of firms reported in a column, the sample size is printed to the left of the array. If less than 10 ratios were available, the array was not printed. Ratio values are arrayed from the highest to lowest positive and then from the lowest to the highest negative.

LEVERAGE RATIOS

Highly leveraged firms (those with heavy debt in relation to net worth) are more vulnerable to business downturns than those with lower debt to worth positions. While leverage ratios help to measure this vulnerability, it must be remembered that they vary greatly depending on the requirements of particular industry groups.

FIXED/WORTH

Computation: Fixed assets (net of accumulated depreciation) divided by tangible net worth.

$$\frac{\text{Net Fixed Assets}}{\text{Tangible Net Worth}}$$

Interpretation: This ratio measures the extent to which owner's equity (capital) has been invested in plant and equipment (fixed assets). A lower ratio indicates a proportionately smaller investment in fixed assets in relation to net worth, and a better "cushion" for creditors in case of liquidation. Similarly, a higher ratio would indicate the opposite situation. The presence of substantial leased fixed assets (not shown on the balance sheet) may deceptively lower this ratio.

Fixed assets may be zero, in which case the quotient is zero. If tangible net worth is zero, the quotient is infinity (INF). If tangible net worth is negative, the quotient is negative. The ratio values are arrayed from the lowest positive to the highest positive, infinity, and then from the highest negative to the lowest negative.

The value $\pm$ INF may occasionally appear as a quartile or median. This is the result of interpolation between positive and negative values in the nonlinear array typical of this ratio.

DEBT/WORTH

Computation: Total liabilities divided by tangible net worth.

$$\frac{\text{Total Liabilities}}{\text{Tangible Net Worth}}$$

Interpretation: This ratio expresses the relationship between capital contributed by creditors and that contributed by owners. It expresses the degree of protection provided by the owners for the creditors. The higher the ratio, the greater the risk being assumed by creditors. A lower ratio generally indicates greater long-term financial safety. A firm with a low debt/worth ratio usually has greater flexibility to borrow in the future. A more highly leveraged company has a more limited debt capacity.

Tangible net worth may be zero, in which case the ratio is infinity (INF). Tangible net worth may also be negative which results in the quotient being negative. The ratio values are arrayed from the lowest to highest positive, infinity, and then from the highest to lowest negative.

The value $\pm$ INF may occasionally appear as a quartile or median. This is the result of interpolation between positive and negative values in the nonlinear array typical of this ratio.

OPERATING RATIOS

Operating ratios are designed to assist in the evaluation of management performance.

% PROFITS BEFORE TAXES/TANGIBLE NET WORTH

Computation: Profit before taxes divided by tangible net worth and multiplied by 100.

$$\frac{\text{Profit Before Taxes}}{\text{Tangible Net Worth}} \times 100$$

Interpretation: This ratio expresses the rate of return on tangible capital employed. While it can serve as an indicator of management performance, the analyst is cautioned to use it in conjunction with other ratios. A high return, normally associated with effective management, could indicate an under-capitalized firm. Whereas, a low return, usually an indicator of inefficient management performance, could reflect a highly capitalized, conservatively operated business.

This ratio has been multiplied by 100 since it is shown as a percentage.

Profit before taxes may be zero, in which case the ratio is zero. Profits before taxes may be negative resulting in negative quotients. Firms with negative tangible net worth have been omitted from the ratio arrays. Negative ratios will therefore only result in the case of negative profit before taxes. If the tangible net worth is zero, the quotient is infinity (INF). If there are less than 10 ratios for a particular size class, the result is not shown. The ratio values are arrayed starting with infinity (INF), and then from the highest to the lowest positive values, and from the lowest to the highest negative values.

% PROFIT BEFORE TAXES/TOTAL ASSETS

Computation: Profit before taxes divided by total assets and multiplied by 100.

$$\frac{\text{Profit Before Taxes}}{\text{Total Assets}} \text{ x } 100$$

Interpretation: This ratio expresses the pre-tax return on total assets and measures the effectiveness of management in employing the resources available to it. If a specific ratio varies considerably from the ranges found in this book, the analyst will need to examine the makeup of the assets and take a closer look at the earnings figure. A heavily depreciated plant and a large amount of intangible assets or unusual income or expense items will cause distortions of this ratio.

This ratio has been multiplied by 100 since it is shown as a percentage. If profit before taxes is zero, the quotient is zero. If profit before taxes is negative, the quotient is negative. These ratio values are arrayed from the highest to the lowest positive and then from the lowest to the highest negative.

SALES/NET FIXED ASSETS

Computation: Net sales divided by net fixed assets (net of accumulated depreciation).

$$\frac{\text{Net Sales}}{\text{Net Fixed Assets}}$$

Interpretation: This ratio is a measure of the productive use of a firm's fixed assets. Largely depreciated fixed assets or a labor intensive operation may cause a distortion of this ratio.

If the net fixed asset figure is zero, the quotient is infinity (INF). The only time a zero will appear in the array will be when the net sales figure is low and the quotient rounds off to zero. These ratio values cannot be negative.

They are arrayed from infinity (INF) and then from the highest to the lowest positive values.

SALES/TOTAL ASSETS

Computation: Net sales divided by total assets.

$$\frac{\text{Net Sales}}{\text{Total Assets}}$$

Interpretation: This ratio is a general measure of a firm's ability to generate sales in relation to total assets. It should be used only to compare firms within specific industry groups and in conjunction with other operating ratios to determine the effective employment of assets.

The only time a zero will appear in the array will be when the net sales figure is low and the quotient rounds off to zero. The ratio values cannot be negative. They are arrayed from the highest to the lowest positive values.

EXPENSE TO SALES RATIOS

The following three ratios relate specific expense items to net sales and express this relationship as a percentage. Comparisons are convenient because the item, net sales, is used as a constant. Variations in these ratios are most pronounced between capital and labor intensive industries.

% DEPRECIATION, DEPLETION, AMORTIZATION/SALES

Computation: Annual depreciation, amortization, and depletion expenses divided by net sales and multiplied by 100.

$$\frac{\text{Depreciation, Amortization, Depletion Expenses}}{\text{Net Sales}} \quad \text{x 100}$$

% LEASE AND RENTAL EXPENSES/SALES

Computation: Annual lease and rental expenses divided by net sales and multiplied by 100.

$$\frac{\text{Lease \& Rental Expenses}}{\text{Net Sales}} \quad \text{x 100}$$

% OFFICERS' COMPENSATION/SALES

Computation: Annual officers' compensation divided by net sales and multiplied by 100.

$$\frac{\text{Officers' Compensation}}{\text{Net Sales}} \quad \text{x 100}$$

Only statements showing a positive figure for each of the expense categories shown above were used. If the number of statements used in an array differs from the sample population for an asset size category, the number of statements used is shown in parentheses to the left of the array. When there are less than 10 ratios, the array is not printed. The ratios are arrayed from the lowest to highest positive values.

SIC NUMBERS APPEARING IN THE STATEMENT STUDIES

SIC No.	Page	SIC No.	Page	SIC No.	Page
0161	186	2065	51	2512	59
0181	185	2074	56	2514	57
0211	182	2075	56	2515	56
0212	181	2076	56	2522	57
0251	183	2082	45	2541	58
0781	185	2084	46	2542	58
0782	185	2085	46	2621	85
0783	185	2086	183	2631	85
1211	182	2087	45	2642	84
1311	184	2091	51	2643	84
1381	193 & 200	2211	94	2648	84
1442	184	2221	94	2651	85
1521	191 & 199	2231	94	2652	85
1522	191 & 199	2241	97	2653	85
1541	191 & 199	2252	95 & 96	2654	85
1542	191 & 199	2253	96	2655	85
1611	192 & 199	2254	96	2711	89
1622	192 & 199	2257	96	2721	89
1623	197 & 202	2258	96	2731	87
1711	195 & 201	2261	95	2732	86
1721	194 & 200	2262	95	2751	87
1731	189 & 198	2272	97	2752	88
1741	193 & 200	2282	98	2761	88
1742	195 & 201	2311	42	2789	86
1743	197 & 202	2321	42	2791	90
1752	190 & 198	2327	41	2821	49
1761	196 & 201	2328	41	2831	47
1771	189 & 198	2335	43	2833	47
1791	196 & 201	2337	44	2834	47
1794	190 & 198	2341	44	2841	50
2011	54	2342	43	2844	49
2013	55	2351	39	2851	48
2016	54	2352	39	2861	48
2021	52	2371	39	2865	48
2022	52	2391	38	2873	47
2023	52	2392	40	2874	47
2024	52	2394	37	3021	91
2026	52	2421	63	3111	61
2033	52	2431	62	3143	60
2034	52	2435	61	3144	60
2037	53	2441	63	3161	60
2041	53	2451	100	3171	60
2048	55	2452	62	3172	60
2051	50	2511	58	3251	91

APPENDIX II – INFORMATION ABOUT *INDUSTRY NORMS AND KEY BUSINESS RATIOS,* PUBLISHED BY DUN & BRADSTREET

The following is summary information and a table of contents from the Library Edition, *Industry Norms and Key Business Ratios,* produced for libraries by Dun & Bradstreet as a reference tool.

Contents

	Page
Preface	
Background	i
Industry Norms for Financial Analysis	iii
Applications by Functional Area	iv
Calculations of the 14 Key Business Ratios	v
Special Bank Data	vii
Industry Overview	x
Industry Norms and Key Business Ratios	
Special Bank Data	
(SIC #s 6020, 6030, and 6710)	1
Agriculture, Forestry, and Fishing	
(SIC #s 0111–0913)	3
Mining	
(SIC #s 1041–1499)	14
Construction	
(SIC #s 1521–1799)	18
Transportation, Communication, Electric, Gas, and Sanitary Services	
(SIC #s 4011–4071)	24
Manufacturing	
(SIC #s 2011–3999)	37
Wholesale Trade	
(SIC #s 5012–5199)	126
Retail Trade	
(SIC #s 5211–5999)	141
Finance other than Banks, Insurance, and Real Estate	
(SIC #s 6121–6799)	157
Services	
(SIC #s 7011–8999)	167
Appendix – U.S. Standard Industrial Classifications	

Source: Dun & Bradstreet, 1983 Edition. Reprinted with permission.

Background

The Library Edition, *Industry Norms and Key Business Ratios,* hereafter referred to as *Industry Norms,* is specifically produced for libraries only as a reference tool. This book is made possible through the over 1 million financial statements in the Dun's Financial Profiles computerized database. This file consists of U.S. corporations, partnerships, and proprietorships, both public and privately owned, in all size ranges, and includes over 800 different lines of business as defined by the U.S. Standard Industrial Classification (SIC) code numbers. Our data are collected weekly, maintained daily, and constantly edited and updated by the Dun's Financial Profiles Department. All of these factors combine to make this financial information unequaled anywhere for scope and timeliness.[1]

---

[1] To provide the most current information available, fiscal years July 1–June 30 were utilized to calculate the Norms.

It should be noted that only general data are supplied in the Library Edition; however, for more detailed asset/geographical breakdowns of these data, a set of industry norm books are also published by Dun & Bradstreet for the corporate marketplace in the following five industry volumes:

1. *Agriculture/Mining/Construction/Transportation/Communication/Utilities*
2. *Manufacturing*
3. *Wholesaling*
4. *Retailing*
5. *Banking/Finance/Insurance/Real Estate/Services*

All five segments are available in three different formats (for a total of 15 books). The three formats are as follows:

1. *Industry Norms* for last three years ("Full File").
2. *Industry Norms* for the most recent year ("Partial File").
3. *Key Business Ratios* (only) for the most recent year.

Note that the *Industry Norms* books contain "typical" balance sheets and income statements, and "common-size" financial figures, as well as key business ratios. The *Key Business Ratios* books contain 14 indicators of performance.

Industry Norm Format

At the top of each industry norm will be identifying information: SIC code number and short title. Beside the year date, in parentheses, is the number of companies in the sample. The "typical" balance sheet figures are in the first column and the "common-size" balance sheet figures are in the second. The respective income statements begin with the item "Net Sales," and the respective key business ratios begin with the item "Ratios." The latter are further broken down, or refined, into the median and the upper quartile and lower quartile.

The Common-Size Financial Statement

The common-size balance sheet and income statement present each item of the financial statement as a percentage of its respective aggregate total. Common-size percentages are computed for all statement items of all the individual companies used in the industry sample. An average for each statement item is then determined and presented as the industry norm.

This enables the analyst to examine the current composition of assets, liabilities, and sales of a particular industry.

The Typical Financial Statement

The typical balance sheet figures are the result of translating the common-size percentages into dollar figures. They permit, for example, a quick check of the relative size of assets and liabilities between one's own company and that company's own line of business.

After the common-size percentages have been computed for the particular sample, the actual financial statements are then sequenced by both total *assets* and total *sales,* with the median, or midpoint, figure in both these groups serving as the "typical" amount. We then compute the typical balance sheet and income statement dollar figures by multiplying the common-size percentages for each statement item by their respective total amounts.

(For example, if the median total assets for an SIC category are $669,599, and the common-size figure for cash is 9.2 percent, then by multiplying the two we derive a cash figure of $61,603 for the typical balance sheet.)

Key Business Ratios

The 14 key business ratios are broken down into median figures, with upper and lower quartiles, giving the analyst an even more refined set of figures to work with. These ratios cover all those critical areas of business performance, with indicators of solvency, efficiency, and profitability. They provide a profound and well-documented insight into all aspects for everyone interested in the financial workings of business—business executives and managers, credit executives, bankers, lenders, investors, academicians, students.

In the ratio tables appearing in this book, the figures are broken down into the median—which is the midpoint of all companies in the sample—and the upper quartile and lower quartile—which are midpoints of the upper and lower halves.

Upper-quartile figures are not always the highest numerical value, nor are lower-quartile figures always the lowest numerical value. The quartile listings reflect judgmental ranking; thus, the upper quartile represents the best condition in any given ratio and is not necessarily the highest numerical value. (For example, see the items Total Liabilities-to-Net Worth or Collection Period, where a lower numerical value represents a better condition.)

Each of the 14 ratios is calculated individually for every concern in the sample. These individual figures are then sequenced for each ratio according to condition (best to worst), and the figure that falls in the middle of this series becomes the median (or midpoint) for that ratio in that line of business. The figure halfway between the median and the best condition of the series becomes the upper quartile; and the number halfway between the median and the least favorable condition of the series is the lower quartile.

In a statistical sense, each median is considered the *typical* ratio figure for a concern in a given category.

APPENDIX III—"THE LEGAL PROCESS OF VENTURE CAPITAL INVESTMENT" BY RICHARD J. TESTA

The following article is about the legal process of venture capital investment. It was written by Richard J. Testa, a partner in the Boston law firm of Testa, Hurwitz & Thibeault. He and his firm have served as counsel for several professional venture capital companies as well as for a large number of businesses that have been financed by venture capital sources, including Lotus Development.*

Section I. General Considerations Relating to Legal Documentation

A key element in the attainment of a successful relationship between a young business enterprise and its venture capital investors is the careful crafting of the legal structure of the investment transaction. Venture capital investing is a long-term commitment of support to a company. As such, the parties involved in structuring and implementing the investment transaction must bring to the process a sensitivity to the changing and different objectives and requirements (financial, legal, personal, etc.) of the business and its principal participants. The legal documents must foresee the evolution of the enterprise from a development stage start-up to a publicly held company or viable acquisition candidate. Not only do the investment documents represent a charter of the legal rights of the parties spanning the growth cycle of the business, but they also set the tone of the relationships between the management/entrepreneurs and the financial backers of the enterprise, serving as a model for resolution of their often differing interests.

* Reprinted from the 8th edition of *Pratt's Guide to Venture Capital Sources,* 1984, with the permission of the author and publisher. Venture Economics, Wellesley Hills, Massachusetts.

Despite increasing standardization of the venture capital process, it remains, fundamentally, highly idiosyncratic, with each transaction reflecting the particular chemistry between entrepreneur and investor. Accordingly, there exists no such thing as the "perfect model" of legal documentation for the investment transaction. Each deal should be tailored to reflect the unique combination of styles and interests involved. Generally, however, each transaction will encompass the following common set of documents:

1. *The term sheet,* summarizing in broad stroke the principal financial and other terms of the investment.
2. *The investment agreement,* detailing the terms of purchase and provisions of the securities (equity or debt) being acquired.
3. *The stockholders agreement,* containing restrictions upon the transfer and voting of securities by management and (occasionally) investors.
4. *Employee stock purchase or stock option agreements,* governing the current and future allocation of equity in the business to key employees.
5. *Employee confidentiality and proprietary rights agreements,* assuring the retention by the business of its valuable trade secrets and business rights.
6. *Legal opinion* of company counsel.

Section II.   The Term Sheet

The handshake "agreement" between investor and entrepreneur is often set forth in a written term sheet or letter of intent. Although the term sheet may take a variety of forms, from a cursory and informal letter to a more detailed and formal memorandum, it is intended to accomplish the following purposes:

1. To reflect the agreed-upon valuation of the business and to quantify the proposed allocation of that value between the entrepreneurs and investors.
2. To summarize key financial and legal terms of the transaction which will serve as the basis for preparing definitive legal documents.
3. On occasion, to impose enforceable legal obligations upon the parties, such as requiring payment of expenses in the event the investment does not close or prohibiting negotiations with other parties pending the completion of the transaction.

Above all, the term sheet should be used by the venture capitalist to elicit those concerns of the entrepreneurs which, if unaddressed and unresolved, might later develop into "deal killers." For example, if the venture capitalist intends to require that the entrepreneurs submit their stock ownership in the enterprise to buy-back or forfeiture restrictions in the event they sever employment, such a condition should be covered in the term sheet since it encroaches in an area in which the entrepreneur will be especially sensitive. Similarly sensitive topics are the composition of the board of directors and matters relating to the terms of employment of the entrepreneurs.

Section III.   The Investment Agreement

A.   Principal Purposes and Legal Consequences

The long-form investment agreement has four principal business objectives:

1. Most importantly, it sets forth the detailed substantive terms of the investment.
2. It serves as the basic disclosure document in which the relevant historical, business, financial, and legal data relating to the enterprise are set forth or referenced.

3. It presents, through the use of conditions precedent to closing, a "stop-action" photograph or image of the issuer that must exist at the time of closing. The level of detail of this photograph will vary depending upon the round of financing involved in the transaction and the simplicity or complexity of the company's operations.

4. It defines the several business parameters within which the enterprise must operate in the future. The several commandments to management range from relatively simple "thou shall not's" to complex "thou shalt's."

The legal effect of the investment agreement is similar to that of many commercial contracts. The most common consequence of a breach of agreement in the capital investment context is the ability of the investor to refuse to close the transaction because of the company's failure to satisfy a condition precedent or the existence of a significant misrepresentation by the company. Once the closing has occurred, remedies in the nature of recision are rare. Moreover, while claims for damages do arise, they are uncommon in the high-risk venture area. Common remedies available for breach of covenant are specific performance and injunctive relief. As a practical matter, however, remedies that are self-executing, such as ratchet-down provisions in an antidilution formula or extraordinary voting rights granted to a class of preferred stock, are more formidable than those remedies which frequently amount to waving a stick in the air, such as accelerated repayment of debt securities.

B. Description of the Transaction

The investment agreement memorializes the terms of the transaction. Consequently, the agreement should include a description of the securities being purchased, the purchase price, and a requirement that the securities be properly authorized.

If the investor acquires a note (whether or not convertible) or a stock purchase warrant, the form of the security should be attached as an exhibit to the investment agreement. If the investor acquires a class of stock other than conventional common stock, the terms of the class of stock as set forth in the corporate charter should be attached to the investment agreement as an exhibit.

If more than one investor participates in the financing, they may be listed or referenced in an exhibit to the agreement. In some cases, the company will execute separate but identical investment agreements with the other investors. A condition of each investor's obligation to purchase may be that identical investment agreements have been executed simultaneously with each investor, such agreements have not been amended and are in full force on the closing date, and a specified minimum number of dollars has been raised by the company.

In some transactions, the entire investment will not be made available to the company at a single closing. The purchase may be made in two or more installments over fixed periods of time, in which event the major condition precedent to closing each successive installment is the absence of any material adverse changes affecting the company since the initial closing. In a "staged" investment, the purchase of additional securities at subsequent closings is conditioned upon the accomplishment of certain financial or operational goals, such as the attainment of specified revenue levels or completion of development work on a new product, as well as the absence of adverse changes. A stage investment serves as an incentive to management to proceed diligently with the development of its product as outlined in its business plan and enables the venture capitalist to target his investment with a maximum impact on the development of the business.

C. Representations and Warranties of the Company

It is a rare issuer company that is totally "clean," that is, a company which has no stated exceptions to the several business, financial, and legal topics addressed by the representation and warranty section of the investment agreement. Only a new start-up company with neither employees nor sales is likely to fall into this category. Since the venture capitalist has already conducted a thorough factual review of the company's business prior to issuing his term sheet or letter of intent, the representations and warranties are not intended to "screen" the company for suitability as an investment (although the disclosure of significant adverse information not previously known to the investor may scuttle the investment) but rather to provide full disclosure of the fine details of the company's operations which may be relevant in advising management with regard to the future conduct of the business.

The following list of specific representations and warranties are common in most venture capital investment agreements. Each category is prefaced by an affirmative declaration or affirmation of compliance, subject to stated exceptions which are normally appended as an exhibit.

1. *Organization and authority:* The company is properly organized, in good standing, and has legal authority to conduct its business.
2. *Corporate action:* All necessary actions under state corporate law, and the company's corporate charter and bylaws, have been taken to authorize and perform the transaction.
3. *Governmental approvals:* All consents and approvals of governmental agencies necessary to complete the transaction have been obtained. In particular, this covers compliance with federal and state securities laws.
4. *Absence of litigation:* No litigation or other proceedings exist, or are threatened, which would adversely affect the company's business or the financing transaction.
5. *Employment of key personnel:* No restrictions exist relating to employment of key personnel or use of business information, particularly as a result of prior employment of such personnel by another enterprise.
6. *Compliance with other agreements:* No violations of the company's corporate charter, bylaws, or other valid agreements exist, or will exist as a result of the financing.
7. *Ownership of properties and assets:* The company possesses sufficient ownership rights in its business assets, particularly its proprietary rights and other intangible assets, to conduct its business.
8. *Financial information:* Audited and internal unaudited financial statements have been prepared in accordance with generally accepted accounting principles and fairly present the financial position and operating results of the company. Statements as to specific categories of items, such as inventory valuation and status of accounts receivables, may be included. No adverse changes have occurred since the date of the most recent financial statements furnished.
9. *Transactions with insiders:* Disclosure is made of any direct or indirect transactions between the company and its directors, officers, and stockholders.
10. *Third-party guaranties or investments:* Absence of continuing financial involvements with third parties.
11. *Compliance with federal securities laws:* Certification that the transaction complies with federal and state securities laws, including the possibility that the transaction may be integrated with other securities sales.
12. *Disclosure:* The business plan used to seek financing is accurate and complete, and all material disclosures have been made to investors either in the business plan or in legal documents relating to the transaction.
13. *Brokerage:* Disclosure of any finder's or broker's fees or commissions payable in connection with the transaction.
14. *Capitalization:* Description of the company's authorized capitalization and status of outstanding securities, including warrants, options, and convertible securities. Any transfer restrictions, repurchase rights, or preemptive rights are also described, as well as registration rights.

D. Covenants and Undertakings of the Company

The covenants section of the investment agreement contains several affirmative and negative undertakings of the company relating to the future conduct of its affairs. Affirmative covenants are actions, positions, or results that the company promises to achieve or undertake. Negative covenants are actions, positions, or results that the company promises to avoid.

If, under the terms of the investment agreement, the board of directors is to be controlled by inside management, the covenants are frequently extensive. In an equity-oriented venture capital investment, however, where the investors will frequently control the board of directors, the covenants are often kept to a minimum. In such a situation, the affirmative covenants might merely provide that the investor will receive periodic financial information and will be represented on the board. The negative covenants might limit only the company's ability to amend its corporate charter or merge or sell its assets without the investor's consent. A venture capital firm with board control will generally rely upon this control to influence the development of a company and will not, as a rule, find it necessary to impose extensive contractual restrictions on the conduct of the business by insisting on strict affirmative and negative covenants.

Both affirmative and negative covenants may remain in effect as long as the investors hold any of the investment securities or, alternatively, may terminate upon the occurrence of certain events, such as the completion of an initial public offering, conversion of debt-oriented convertible securities into equity, or mere passage of time.

Among the customary *affirmative* covenants which are found in venture capital investment agreements are the following:

1. *Payment of taxes and claims:* The company will pay all lawful taxes, assessments, and levies upon it or its income or property before they become in default. This covenant sometimes provides that all trade debt and principal and interest on debt securities acquired by the investor will be paid when due.
2. *Property and liability insurance:* The company will maintain insurance against hazards and risks and liability to persons and property to the extent customary for companies engaged in the same or similar businesses.
3. *Maintenance of corporate existence:* The company will maintain its corporate existence and all rights, licenses, patents, copyrights, trademarks, etc. useful in its business, and will engage only in the type of business described in the business plan.
4. *Legal compliance:* The company will comply with all applicable laws and regulations in the conduct of its business.
5. *Access to premises:* The investor or his representative will generally be permitted to inspect the company's facilities, books, and records. To the extent that confidentiality of corporate business information may be compromised by such rights of access, investors generally agree to confidentiality restrictions or to limiting access to lead or other major investors.
6. *Accounts and reports:* The company may be asked by the investor to agree to maintain a standard system of accounting in accordance with generally accepted accounting principles consistently applied, and to keep full and complete financial records.
7. *Repair and maintenance:* The company will keep all necessary equipment and property in good repair and condition, as required to permit the business to be properly conducted.
8. *Approval of budgets:* The investor will frequently require management to produce comprehensive annual budgets for approval by the investor or by the board of directors. Revisions of the budget during the year may also require advance approval.

9. *Protection of proprietary rights:* The company will agree to take all necessary steps to protect proprietary developments made in the future, including causing all key employees to sign confidentiality and proprietary rights and agreements.

10. *Compliance with key agreements:* The company will enforce its rights under key agreements, such as the stockholders agreement, and will cause future stockholders to join the agreement.

11. *Life insurance:* The investor will often require the company to maintain insurance on the lives of key officers and employees. The face amount in some cases may be as much as the purchase price of the securities, and the insurance proceeds are often payable directly to the investor, particularly if the investor holds debt securities.

12. *Board of directors:* Venture capital firms will generally seek assurances that they will be represented on the company's board of directors. The right to be represented on the board may be backed up by voting agreements with the principal stockholders. If the investor is not to be represented on the board, the company may be required to notify the investor of the time and place of board meetings and to permit the investor or his representative to attend such meetings. Frequency of board meetings and financial arrangements may also be covered.

13. *Financial and operating statements:* The company will invariably agree to provide the investor with detailed financial and operating information. The information to be provided may include annual, quarterly, and sometimes monthly reports of sales, production, shipments, profits, cash balances, receivables, payables, and backlog; all statements filed with the Securities and Exchange Commission or other agencies; notification of significant lawsuits or other legal proceedings; and any other information that the investor may need for his own voluntary or involuntary filing requirements. Particularly where an investor is acquiring debt securities or preferred stock containing extensive financial and other covenants, financial statements are required to be accompanied by a certificate from the company's chief executive or financial officer and, in the case of audited financial statements, its auditors, to the effect that the company is in compliance with all provisions of the investment agreement. The right to receive financial information is often terminated when the company goes public in order to avoid dissemination of "inside" information. Although companies generally concede the legitimate interests of investors to receive business information, negotiation over the scope and form of this information may be considerable in view of the operational burden and potential liabilities it can impose upon management.

14. *Current ratio, working capital, or net worth:* These covenants normally are included only in debt financings and are agreements to maintain the current ratio, working capital, or net worth, either at a minimum amount or as specified for various time periods. They may be keyed to projections made by the company; accordingly, care should be taken by the company in preparing the business plan to project financial results and conditions which management is comfortable in undertaking to attain on a contractual basis.

15. *Use of proceeds:* The use of funds may be broadly stated in terms of the business of the company, or it may be narrowly defined with reference to a specific financing plan.

In contrast to affirmative covenants, which generally exhort the company to undertake actions which it would ordinarily choose to take in the normal course, the negative covenants contained in the investment agreement serve to limit the company from actions it otherwise might be inclined to take, unless the investors have consented in advance. Typically these negative covenants relate to matters which would affect the fundamental nature of the business in which the investment has been made (e.g., mergers and acquisitions) or would alter the balance of control between the investors and entrepreneurs reached in the investment agreement. Since the negative covenants limit the scope of managerial flexibility, they are often the subject of sharp negotiation. As suggested above, there is a trade-off between the degree of investor control of the voting power and board of directors and the strictness of the negative covenants imposed on the company. Many typical negative covenants are described below:

1. *Mergers, consolidations, and sale or purchase of assets:* Mergers, consolidations, acquisitions, and the like are generally prohibited without the investor's advance approval. Liquidation and dissolution of the company and the sale, lease, or other disposition of substantial assets without consent may also be barred. Restrictions may also be placed on the company's purchase of capital assets.
2. *Dealings with related parties:* The company will covenant that no transactions between the company and any officers, directors, or stockholders of the company shall be effected unless on an arm's-length basis and on terms no less favorable to the company than could be obtained from nonrelated persons. Approval of all transactions with affiliates by either the board or the investors may be required.
3. *Change in business:* The company will not change the nature of its business as described in its business plan.
4. *Charter amendments:* The investor may prohibit the company from amending its corporate charter or bylaws without the consent of the investor. More narrowly drawn covenants might prohibit only certain specified actions (such as a change in the capital structure) without the investor's consent.
5. *Distributions and redemptions:* The company typically agrees not to make any dividend distributions to stockholders. Dividends may be prohibited until a given date or may be limited to a fixed percentage of profits above a set amount. In addition, the company may covenant not to repurchase or redeem any of its securities except in accordance with the terms of the securities purchased by the investor (e.g., redeemable preferred stock), employee plans (e.g., forfeiture of stock upon termination of employment), or agreements with stockholders (e.g., right of first refusal).
6. *Issuance of stock or convertible securities:* The investor may prohibit the company from issuing any securities that would result in dilution of the investor's position. This includes restrictions on the issuance of securities of the type purchased by the investor and any securities convertible into such securities at a price less than that paid by the investor. Alternatively, such an issuance could result in an improved conversion rate for the securities purchased by the investor. Frequently these covenants are included in the terms of the securities themselves.
7. *Liens and encumbrances:* The investment agreement (generally for debt-oriented securities, including redeemable preferred stock) may provide for restrictions on liens, pledges, and other encumbrances, with exceptions for such liabilities as real estate mortgages. Separate restrictions can be placed on leases of real property or equipment.
8. *Indebtedness:* The company may agree to restrictions on future indebtedness, with exceptions for institutional senior borrowings, indebtedness on personal property purchase money obligations, and trade indebtedness, up to certain limits in the ordinary course of business. Again, this provision is most typical of investments in debt-oriented securities.
9. *Investments:* Restrictions against investing in other companies may be imposed by the investor. Exceptions are made for investments in subsidiaries.
10. *Employee compensation:* The company may agree to limit employment and other personal service contracts of management or key personnel to a maximum term and a maximum amount of annual compensation.

11. *Financial covenants:* Negative financial covenants are frequently imposed upon a company in a debt-oriented investment, such as prohibiting key ratios or financial conditions from exceeding certain limits or limiting the company from incurring losses in excess of a certain amount. Semantics often determine whether a financial covenant is affirmative or negative in nature. Clear definition of financial and accounting terms is critical. In lieu of defaulting on securities, failure to comply with financial covenants may trigger adjustments in conversion ratios of securities or give rise to preferential voting or other rights for the investor.

In addition to the numerous affirmative and negative covenants described above, the venture capital investment agreement will customarily contain a number of more complex undertakings by the company, which are generally set apart in the agreement. Two of the more typical of these covenants pertain to registration rights and rights to participate in future financings. Another such provision, indemnification of the investors for breach of the investment agreement, is also discussed briefly below:

1. *Registration rights:* The right to register securities for public sale under the Securities Act of 1933 and state securities laws represents the most advantageous vehicle for a venture capital investor to achieve liquidity and realize a return on his investment. The potential of an enterprise to achieve a size conducive to a public offering is an imperative of most venture capital investments; accordingly, the right of the investor to participate in the public market for the company's securities is an area in which the venture capitalist will concede few limitations on his flexibility of action. Registration rights are intricately bound up in the complexities of federal and state securities regulation and must be thoroughly understood by the investor and his counsel. The key elements of a registration rights provision in a venture capital investment agreement generally include the following:

   a. *Securities available for registration:* Registrable securities will invariably be limited to common stock, including shares issuable on conversion of other securities. After-acquired common stock may also be included. If the investor is participating in a second- or third-round financing, he must consider to what extent his registration rights will be coordinated or "pooled" with registration rights granted to investors in previous financings.

   b. *"Piggyback" registration rights:* Investors will have the right to include shares in any registration which the company undertakes either for its own benefit or for the account of other holders of securities. Exceptions are generally made for registrations involving employee stock plans or acquisitions. "Piggyback" registrations will frequently be unlimited in number on the theory that no significant burden is imposed on the company by requiring it to include additional shares in a registration which it is otherwise undertaking. Except for the company's initial public offering, investors may be guaranteed a minimum participation in "piggyback" registrations.

   c. *Demand registration rights:* Investors frequently obtain the right to require an issuer to register their shares upon demand and without regard to the registration of shares for the account of any other person. Demand rights assure the investor access to the public market. Theoretically, unrestricted demand registration rights enable an investor to force a company to go public; as a practical matter, demand rights are rarely, if ever, used to this end, although their presence may influence the decision of a company to go public. Because of the expense involved, demand rights may be limited in number, unless registration is available on a short-form registration statement such as Form S–3. In addition, investors may agree to limit the exercise of demand rights to the holders of a minimum specified percentage of registrable securities to avoid unduly small registrations.

d.   *Marketing rights:* "Piggyback" registration rights generally contain provisions enabling the managing underwriters to cut back on a pro rata basis the number of shares to be registered by selling securityholders if, in the underwriters' opinion, such a cutback is necessary or desirable to market the public issue effectively. If securityholders other than the venture capital investors also hold registration rights, the relative marketing priorities of the various groups, including management, in the event of a cutback must be addressed.

e.   *Indemnification:* Each party will agree to indemnify the other against liabilities for which it is responsible arising out of a registration. Although the extensive indemnification provisions of an underwriting agreement will frequently supersede the terms of the investment agreement, they are nevertheless important because underwriters will typically look to the company and any major selling shareholders for indemnification on a joint and several basis and will leave those parties to their own devices to allocate any liabilities among themselves.

f.   *Procedural covenants:* Many registration rights provisions contain undertakings to comply with certain procedural matters involved in a registration, such as participation in the preparation of a registration statement, qualification under state securities laws, and entitlement to legal opinions and accountants' comfort letters.

g.   *Availability of Rule 144:* The company will agree that once it has gone public, it will file all reports and take all other action necessary to enable the investors to sell shares in the public market under the exemption from registration contained in Rule 144 under the Securities Act of 1933.

h.   *Expenses of registration:* Because of the cost involved in a registration of securities, investors will typically require the company to agree at the time of the initial investment to bear the expenses of registration, exclusive of underwriters' discounts or commissions.

2.   *Rights to future financings:* Venture capitalists often insist upon a right to participate in future financings by the company. On the upside, this offers the investor an opportunity to maintain or increase his interest in the success of the enterprise; on the downside, the investor receives some protection against dilution or loss of his initial investment in the event financing must be sought under distress situations. The right to participate may include:

a.   *Rights of first refusal* to assume the entire financing (each investor on a pro rata basis with other members of the investor group).

b.   *Preemptive rights* to participate in the financing on a pro rata basis with all other securityholders of the company.

c.   *Rights of prior negotiation* to discuss and negotiate financing opportunities with the company prior to the company making offers to others.

3.   *Indemnification for breach of agreement:* Particularly in the case of start-ups, venture capital investors may require founders and/or top management to share personal responsibility for the representations and warranties made by the company in the investment agreement and to indemnify the investors for any breaches thereof. From the investors' point of view, imposing the specter of personal liability on the insiders can be an effective means of assuring complete and accurate disclosure of all material business information. Indemnification by insiders also circumvents the anomaly of investors seeking indemnification from the company out of the capital which they have invested in the business. On the other hand, personal liability for disclosure matters which may be outside his reasonable knowledge may be an unfair burden to place on the entrepreneur. For this reason, in cases where personal responsibility for representations

and warranties is desired, care should be taken to focus that responsibility in areas of special knowledge of the entrepreneur (e.g., ownership of proprietary rights, compliance with prior employment arrangements, etc.) and to distinguish between the risks assumed by the company and those assumed by the individual (e.g., unqualified representations versus "best knowledge" representations). Termination of indemnification obligations often occurs after a stated period of time, usually not exceeding two years, or after the issuance of audited financial statements covering a one- or two-year period.

E. Conditions to Closing

The use of "conditions precedent to closing" in the investment agreement, or more appropriately the satisfaction of conditions at or prior to closing, is a device used for two principal purposes. The most obvious is to guarantee certain fundamentals relating to the securities and the particular transaction, with favorable legal opinions being a classic example. In addition, conditions are used as negotiating tools to change or affect the affairs of the company. For example, a common closing condition may involve the contemporaneous execution of a bank loan agreement satisfactory to the investor or the consummation of a significant commercial transaction with a customer.

Many venture financings contemplate a simultaneous signing of the investment agreement and closing. Consequently, there is no technical need for a set of conditions designed to cover the time period between execution of the agreement and a subsequent closing. Notwithstanding a simultaneous signing and closing, the use of express conditions serves to expedite the negotiations and to assist the closing process by serving as a checklist of actions to be taken in connection with the implementation of the transaction.

Conditions that are commonly seen in the capital formation process include: opinion of counsel for the company; opinion of counsel for the investor; execution of the several ancillary agreements, including employment, noncompetition, and stock restriction agreements; elections and resignations of directors; and compliance certificates by senior management. Descriptions of certain of these ancillary agreements and documents are included in Section IV below.

Section IV. Terms of Investment Securities

A. General Considerations and Descriptions

Selection of the appropriate investment security for a specific transaction will depend upon the relative importance to the venture capitalist and the issuer of a number of factors, including the level of risk of the venture, investment objectives of the investors, capital requirements of the company, the relative interests and contributions of other securityholders, the degree to which management control by the investors is desirable, liquidity of the securities, and so on. Among the securities which are commonly used in a venture capital financing are:

> Common stock.
> Convertible preferred stock.
> Convertible debt.
> Nonconvertible preferred stock or debt coupled with common stock or common stock purchase warrants.

Generally the venture capitalists will prefer to invest in a senior security which is convertible into, or carries rights to purchase, common equity. A convertible senior security affords the investor downside protection, in terms of the opportunity to recover the investment on a priority basis through redemption, repayment, or liquidation preferences, with the upside potential of a liquid equity security traded at significantly appreciated values in the public market. Discussion of the relative merits and disadvantages of the various types of investment securities is beyond the scope of this article. Described in the following sections, however, are certain of the principal provisions of typical preferred stock and debt securities.

B. Principal Terms of Preferred Stock

Preferred stock is the investment security most frequently involved in venture capital financings because of the flexibility it offers the company and the investor in tailoring the critical issues of the investment—principally management control and recovery/return on investment. Typically the preferred stock utilized in a venture transaction is convertible into common stock and contains redemption provisions designed to enable the investor to recoup his investment if the enterprise fails to achieve its anticipated success. Convertible preferred stock provisions should address the following major issues:

1. *Dividends:* "Plain vanilla" convertible preferred stock does not generally carry mandatory dividend rights. Preferred will, however, participate with common to the extent dividends are declared. If dividends are desired, they may be on a cumulative or noncumulative basis. Cash flow considerations will affect the ability of a start-up to pay dividends.
2. *Liquidation:* Holders of preferred stock will have a priority claim to assets of the corporation over the common stockholders in a liquidation. The liquidation preference will typically equal the original purchase price of the security plus accrued dividends. Participating preferred may also share pari passu with common stock after the liquidation preference has been distributed. Convertible preferred stock provisions usually permit the investors to elect liquidation treatment in the event of a merger or acquisition.
3. *Voting rights:* Convertible preferred stock votes with the common stock on all matters and is entitled to one vote for each share of common into which the preferred may be converted. In addition, the holders of convertible preferred stock, voting separately as a class, may have the right to veto certain corporate transactions affecting the convertible preferred stock (such as the issuance of senior securities, mergers, acquisitions, and amendment of stock terms). Other preferential voting rights may include:
   a. Class vote for election of directors.
   b. Extraordinary voting rights to elect a majority of the board of directors upon a breach of the terms of the convertible preferred stock, such as a failure to pay dividends or make mandatory redemptions or default in the performance of financial or other covenants which may be contained in the convertible preferred stock provisions or underlying investment agreement.
4. *Conversion:* Holders of convertible preferred stock may convert their shares into common stock at their discretion (except as limited by automatic conversion obligations). Conversion provisions should address the following matters:
   a. Automatic conversion upon the occurrence of certain events, principally the completion of a public offering or the attainment of specified financial goals.
   b. Mechanics of conversion.
   c. Conversion ratio, usually expressed by a formula based upon original purchase price, which initially yields a 1-for-1 conversion factor.
   d. Adjustment of conversion ratio to take into account (1) stock splits, stock dividends, consolidations, etc. and (2) "dilutive" common stock issuances, that is, sales of common stock at prices lower than those paid by the investors.

e. Certification of adjusted conversion ratios by independent accountants.

The nature of the antidilution adjustments can have a dramatic effect on the number of common shares issuable upon conversion. "Rachet-down" antidilution provisions apply the lowest sale price for any shares of common stock (or equivalents) as the adjusted conversion value.

"Formula" or "weighted average" antidilution provisions adjust the conversion value by application of a weighted average formula based upon both sale price and number of common shares sold. Antidilution provisions generally carve out a predetermined pool of shares which may be issued to employees without triggering an adjustment of the conversion ratio.

5. *Redemption:* Redemption offers the investor a means of recovering his initial investment and the issuer an opportunity to eliminate the preferential rights held by the holders of the senior security. Topics to be addressed include:

a. Optional or mandatory redemption.

b. Stepped-up redemption price or redemption premium designed to provide investors a certain appreciated return on the investment (NB: "unreasonable redemption premium" issue under IRC Section 305).

c. Desirability of a sinking fund.

d. Redemption call by the company.

It should be noted that the prospect of mandatory redemption or redemption upon call by the issuer may force the holder of convertible preferred stock to exercise his conversion privilege lest he lose the upside potential of his investment.

C. Principal Terms of Debt Securities

The purchase of debt securities will enable the venture capitalist to receive a current return on his investment through receipt of interest payments. In the case of a convertible debt instrument, the interest rate will be below market rates because of the equity feature coupled with it. Although the terms of convertible debt may be structured to resemble preferred stock in many aspects, significant differences between the two securities do exist. First, debt securities do not carry the right to vote for the election of directors or on other stockholder matters. Accordingly, the investor's ability to influence management of the company directly is diminished and he must resort to voting agreements and proxies in order to participate in the election of directors or, alternatively, rely on indirect means of influence such as the affirmative and negative covenants contained in the investment agreement. It should further be noted that the investor's status as a creditor of the company in any bankruptcy proceedings may be affected by principles of "equitable subordination" to the extent that such equity-like control is exercised. Second, the investor's right to receive interest under a debt instrument is more secure than the right to receive dividends on a preferred stock, inasmuch as payment of dividends may be restricted by state corporate laws relating to legally available funds and by the requirement that dividends must be declared by the board of directors. Finally, although a debt security may rank prior to preferred stock in terms of a claim on corporate assets in liquidation, this advantage is at the cost of creating a weaker balance sheet, which may have adverse effects in terms of trade and commercial bank credit, even where subordination provisions are present.

The following principal issues are generally addressed in the structuring of a venture capital investment in debt securities:

1. *Interest rate:* Interest will be at a fixed rate, below market if debt is convertible or coupled with common stock purchase warrants. Because of cash flow considerations of the issuer, interest payments may be deferred for a period of time.

2. *Repayment:* Repayment of principal is often scheduled in quarterly, semiannual, or annual installments commencing four to six years into the term, or in a single payment at maturity.

3. *Optional prepayment:* The company may elect to prepay the debt, often at a premium. Since prepayment will have the effect of extinguishing any conversion rights, the right to prepay will be deferred generally to such time as initial principal installments fall due. Issuance of stock purchase warrants in lieu of conversion will avoid this problem.

4. *Conversion:* The debt instrument may be converted into common stock at a fixed price at any time. Conversion terms, including antidilution provisions, will be similar to those of convertible preferred stock.

5. *Subordination:* Debt is generally subordinated to bank and other institutional borrowings and may thus be viewed as equity by lenders. Complex subordination provisions are often required to regulate the relationships between senior lenders and subordinated noteholders in the event of defaults, insolvency, etc.

6. *Affirmative and negative covenants:* Debt instruments are tied into extensive affirmative and negative undertakings by the company, which are usually contained in the purchase agreement. In addition to standard covenants used in a venture capital financing, these may include lengthy financial covenants of the variety typical in a commercial lending transaction.

7. *Defaults:* Defaults include material breaches of representations and warranties, breach of covenants which are not remedied within a cure period, nonpayment of principal and interest on debt instrument, acceleration (cross-default) of senior debt, insolvency, and events of bankruptcy.

8. *Security:* Generally a debt instrument will be issued to a venture capitalist on an unsecured basis, although collateral is sometimes given in asset-based transactions such as leveraged buyouts. Another common exception to the general rule is an SBIC financing, in which adequate collateral and personal guarantees are often required.

Section V.   Ancillary Agreements and Documents

A.   Stockholders Agreement

The stockholders agreement is designed to control the transfer and voting of the equity securities of the company so that stable ownership and management of the enterprise may be maintained for the term of the investment. This is accomplished through restrictions on the sale of stock by insiders, which have the effect of limiting the stockholder group to persons who are known quantities to the investors, and through voting agreements, which assure that the balanced composition of the board of directors will be perpetuated. The principal provisions contained in a typical stockholders agreement to achieve these results are:

1. *Right of first refusal:* Key management stockholders will grant the company and/or the investors the right to purchase their shares on the same terms as those contained in a bona fide offer from a third party. Investors participate in the right of first refusal on a pro rata basis and have oversubscription rights to acquire any offered shares which are not picked up by another investor. Rights of first refusal are generally *not* extended to the company or insiders by the investors since the existence of such terms would tend to chill any sale of an entire block of shares by the investors to a third party. Transfers of shares by way of gifts to members of an insider's family or as collateral in a bona fide loan transaction are permitted, provided the transferee or pledgee also agrees to be bound by the agreement.

2. *Buy-out provisions:* Some stockholder agreements provide that the company and/or the investors will have an option to purchase the shares of any insider at fair market value upon the occurrence of certain contingencies, such as death, personal bankruptcy, or attachment of shares by legal process. Detailed procedures, usually involving one or more appraisals by disinterested persons, are provided to assure a fair valuation of the stock.

3. *Right to participate in insider sales:* Although philosophically at odds with a right of first refusal, a stockholder agreement may provide that the investors have a right to participate alongside management insiders in any sale to third parties. Although rarely exercised, this right limits the ability of management to bail out of the company leaving the investors at risk to recover their investment. Often this right of cosale is triggered only by a sale which would have the effect of transferring actual or effective voting control to a third party.

4. *Voting requirements:* All parties will generally agree to vote all shares for the election of directors in favor of specified nominees of the respective groups.

Restrictions under applicable state law need to be examined to determine the legality of stockholder agreements in any given jurisdiction, as well as to verify compliance with state procedural and substantive requirements. Unless otherwise limited by state law (10 years in Massachusetts), stockholder agreements will generally terminate upon the earlier of a public offering by the company or the expiration of a stated period of time.

B. Employee Stock Purchase Agreements

Venture capital investors typically insist that appropriate equity incentives be implemented to attract, retain, and motivate key employees. Both the entrepreneurs and investors are willing to suffer dilution of their respective equity interests (anywhere in a range from 5 percent to 15 percent of fully diluted equity) to achieve this end. The investment agreement will specify a pool of shares to be set aside for employee purchases and exempt the issuance of those shares from the various negative covenants, antidilution provisions, and preemptive rights contained in the investment agreement and the terms of the investment securities. Establishment of appropriate employee stock plans is frequently a condition of closing of the investment. Incentive objectives and tax considerations play a significant role in determining the shape of an employee equity program. Among the typical employee equity incentives are the following:

1. *Stock purchase plans,* providing for an outright sale to key employees, often at a bargain price, with the company retaining an option to repurchase the shares on a lapsing basis (generally over four or five years) if the employee terminates employment for any reason.

2. *Incentive stock options,* enabling the employee to purchase shares with advantageous tax consequences at the fair market value on the date the option was granted.

3. *Nonqualified stock options,* which may be granted in amounts which exceed the aggregate dollar limitations for incentive stock options under the Internal Revenue Code and which may have exercise prices less than fair market value and other terms not available under incentive stock options.

4. *"Junior" common stock,* which is an equity security bearing only a percentage of the voting, dividend, liquidation, and other rights of a straight common stock and which is automatically converted into common stock upon the attainment of certain specified objectives, such as revenue and profit goals. Although "junior" common stock was a popular incentive vehicle through the end of 1983, its continued use and attractiveness as a method of compensating management have been called into question by recent actions taken by the Securities and Exchange Commission and proposed to be taken by the Financial Accounting Standards Board (FASB).

In all circumstances (other than incentive stock options) consideration must be given to the application of Section 83 of the Internal Revenue Code to issuances of stock to employees. Section 83 provides that an employee is required to recognize income in respect of property (including corporate securities) transferred to him in connection with the performance of services in an amount equal to the difference between the fair value of the property and the amount paid therefor. In the case of property subject to restrictions which lapse over time (such as forfeiture restrictions or repurchase options), the income is recognized at the time the restrictions lapse. Thus, an employee who acquires stock at a low purchase price in the early years of an enterprise and whose rights to those shares "vest" as forfeiture restrictions lapse over a period of years will recognize income based on the appreciated value of those shares as each installment lapses. Section 83(b) of the Code ameliorates the harsh effect of this provision by permitting a taxpayer to elect to include the value of the transferred property in income in the year of receipt by filing a special election.

In a recent decision (*Alves et al.* v. *Commissioner,* 79 TC 864, CCH Tax Court Reports Dec. 39,501 (1982)), the Tax Court applied Section 83 to a founding stockholder of a new company who acquired shares subject to a repurchase option granted to the company and exercisable upon his termination of employment prior to the end of a specified period. As a result of this decision, founding stockholders should consider taking the precaution of filing Section 83(b) elections when shares are initially acquired in order to prevent assessment of significant tax liabilities when those shares vest at appreciated values in later years.

C.   Employee Confidentiality and Proprietary Rights Agreements

Protection and preservation of the "intellectual capital" of an enterprise are of paramount importance to the venture capital investor, especially where the portfolio company is engaged in product development activities on the leading edge of technologies. To secure the company's claim to its valuable proprietary and business rights, investors are increasingly requiring that founders and other key employees enter into confidential nondisclosure and invention agreements with the company. These agreements typically provide that the employee (1) will not disclose company trade secrets or rights to third parties or use such rights for any purpose, in each case other than in connection with the company's business; and (2) will disclose and convey to the company all inventions developed by the employee during the course of employment. Such agreements often contain acknowledgement that the individual is not bound by any obligations to a former employer which would prevent or restrict his employment with the company and his performance of services for the company does not involve the violation of the proprietary rights of any former employer. Founding stockholders may also agree to noncompetition covenants.

D.   Legal Opinion

The favorable legal opinion of company counsel generally covers the legality of the securities, compliance with state and federal securities laws, and related matters. If the company is involved in litigation, company counsel may be requested to express a position. Likewise, if patents are critical to the company's business, a favorable opinion of patent counsel may also be required. A common error is to confuse the opinion of legal counsel with due diligence. Counsel is not a surety for business or legal uncertainties; the opinion is not a substitute for factual investigation.

APPENDIX IV—SAMPLE TERMS SHEET © *Jeffry A. Timmons, 1990*

BLACK BOX TECHNOLOGY, INC.
Summary of Principal Terms

Amount: $ _____

Security: _____ shares of Convertible Preferred Stock ("Preferred") at a price of $ _____ per share ("Original Purchase Price")

Rights, Preferences, Privileges, and Restrictions of Preferred Stock

1. *Dividend Provisions:* The Preferred Stock shall be entitled to dividends at the same rate as the Common Stock ("Common") (based on the number of shares of Common into which the Preferred is convertible on the date the dividend is declared).

2. *Liquidation Preference:* In the event of any liquidation of the Company, the Preferred will be entitled to receive in preference to the Common an amount equal to the Original Purchase Price.

3. *Redemption:* The Company will redeem the Preferred in three equal annual installments commencing six (6) years from the date of purchase by paying in cash a total amount equal to the Original Purchase Price.

4. *Conversion:* The Preferred will be convertible at any time, at the option of the holder, into shares of Common Stock of the Company at an initial conversion price equal to the Original Purchase Price. Initially, each share of Preferred is convertible into one share of Common Stock. The conversion price will be subject to adjustment as provided in paragraph 6 below.

5. *Automatic Conversion:* The Preferred will be automatically converted into Common, at the then applicable conversion price, in the event of an underwritten public offering of shares of Common at a price per share that is not less than five times the Original Purchase Price in an offering resulting in gross proceeds to the Company of not less than $10 million.

6. *Antidilution Provisions:* The conversion price of the Preferred Stock will be subject to adjustment to prevent dilution in the event that the Company issues additional shares (other than the Reserved Employee Shares described under "Reserved Employee Shares" below) at a purchase price less than the applicable conversion price. The conversion price will be subject to adjustment on a weighted basis which takes into account issuances of additional shares at prices below the applicable conversion price.

7. *Voting Rights:* Except with respect to election of directors, the holder of a share of Preferred will have the right to that number of votes equal to the number of shares of Common issuable upon conversion of the Preferred at the time the record for the vote is taken. Election of directors will be as described under "Board Representation" below.

8. *Protective Provisions:* Consent of the holders of at least two thirds of the Preferred will be required for any sale by the Company of a substantial portion of its assets, any merger of the Company with another entity, each amendment of the Company's articles of incorporation, and for any action which (i) alters or changes the rights, preferences, or privileges of the Preferred materially and adversely; (ii) increases the authorized number of shares of Preferred Stock; or (iii) creates any new class of shares having preference over or being on a parity with the Preferred.

Information Rights

The Company will timely furnish the investors with annual, quarterly and monthly financial statements. Representatives of the investors will have the right to inspect the books and records of the Company.

Registration Rights

1. *Demand Rights:* If investors holding at least 50 percent of the Preferred (or Common issued upon conversion of the Preferred) request that the Company file a Registration Statement covering at least 20 percent of the Common issuable upon conversion of the Preferred, the Company will use its best efforts to cause such shares to be registered.

   The Company will not be obligated to effect more than two registrations (other than on Form S–3) under these demand right provisions.

2. *Registrations on Form S–3:* Holders of 10 percent or more of the Preferred (or Common issued upon conversion of the Preferred) will have the right to require the Company to file an unlimited number of Registration Statements on Form S–3 (but no more than two per year).

3. *Piggyback Registration:* The investors will be entitled to "piggyback" registration rights on all registrations of the Company.

4. *Registration Expenses:* All registration expenses (exclusive of underwriting discounts and commissions or special counsel fees of a selling shareholder) shall be borne by the Company.

Board Representation

The Board will consist of _____ members. The holders of the Preferred will have the right to designate _____ directors; the holders of the Common (exclusive of the Investors) will have the right to designate _____ directors; and the remaining _____ directors will be unaffiliated persons elected by the Common and the Preferred voting as a single class.

Key Man Insurance

As determined by the Board of Directors.

Preemptive Right to Purchase New Securities

If the Company proposes to offer additional shares (other than Reserved Employee Shares or shares issued in the acquisition of another company), the Company will first offer all such shares to the investors on a pro rata basis. This preemptive right will terminate upon an underwritten public offering of shares of the Company.

Stock Restriction and Stockholders Agreements

All present holders of Common Stock of the Company who are employees of, or consultants to, the Company will execute a Stock Restriction Agreement with the Company pursuant to which the Company will have an option to buy back at cost a portion of the shares of Common Stock held by such person in the event that such shareholder's employment with the Company is terminated prior to the expiration of 48 months from the date of employment; 25 percent of the shares will be released each year from the repurchase option based upon continued employment by the Company. In addition, the Company and the Investors will have a right of first refusal with respect to any employee's shares proposed to be resold or, alternatively, the right to participate in the sale of any such shares to a third party, which rights will terminate upon a public offering.

Reserved Employee Shares

The Company may reserve up to _____ shares of Common Stock for issuance to employees of the Company (the "Reserved Employee Shares"). The Reserved Employee Shares will be issued from time to time under such arrangements, contracts, or plans as are recommended by management and approved by the Board.

Noncompetition, Proprietary Information, and Inventions Agreement

Each officer and key employee of the Company designated by the investors will enter into a noncompetition, proprietary information, and inventions agreement in a form reasonably acceptable to the investors.

The Purchase Agreement

The purchase of the Preferred will be made pursuant to a Stock Purchase Agreement drafted by counsel to the Investors and reasonably acceptable to the Company and the Investors, which agreement shall contain, among other things, appropriate representations and warranties of the Company, covenants of the Company reflecting the provisions set forth herein, and appropriate conditions of closing.

Expenses

The Company will bear the legal fees and other out-of-pocket expenses of the investors with respect to the transaction.

APPENDIX V — OUTLINE OF AN INVESTMENT AGREEMENT © *Jeffry A. Timmons, 1990*

What follows is a detailed outline of the contents of a venture investment agreement. The main sections of a typical agreement are briefly described, and many of the terms that might appear in each section are noted. However, not all of the terms listed will appear in an investment agreement. Venture capital investors select terms from among those listed (and some not listed) to best serve their needs in a particular venture investment situation. For more detail on investment agreements we recommend the papers by Gardner[1] and Stewart.[2]

1. Description of the Investment

This section of the agreement defines the basic terms of the investment. It includes descriptions of the:

a. Amount and type of investment.
b. Securities to be issued.
c. Guarantees, collateral subordination, and payment schedules associated with any notes.
d. Conditions of closing: time, place, method of payment.

When investment instruments are involved that carry warrants or debt conversion privileges, the agreement will completely describe them. This description will include the:

a. Time limits on the exercise of the warrant or conversion of the debt.
b. Price and any price changes that vary with the time of exercise.
c. Transferability of the instruments.
d. Registration rights on stock acquired by the investor.
e. Dilution resulting from exercise of warrants or debt conversion.
f. Rights and protections surviving after conversion, exercise, or redemption.

---

[1] W. F. Gardner, Jr., "Venture Capital Financing: A Lawyer's Checklist," *Business Lawyer,* January 1971, p. 997.
[2] M. D. Stewart, "Venture Capital: Semi-Industry," *Venture Capital,* Publication 44–1092 (New York: Practicing Law Institute, 1973), p. 29.

2. Preconditions to Closing

This section covers what the venture must do or what ancillary agreements and documents must be submitted to the investor before the investment can be closed. These agreements and documents may include:

a. Corporate documents (e.g., bylaws, articles of incorporation, resolutions authorizing sale of securities, tax status certificates, list of stockholders, and directors).
b. Audited financial statements.
c. Any agreements for simultaneous additional financing from another source or for lines of credit.
d. Ancillary agreements (e.g., employment contracts, stock option agreements, keyman insurance policies, stock repurchase agreements).
e. Copies of any leases or supply contracts.

3. Representations and Warranties by the Venture

This section contains legally binding statements made by the venture's officers that describe its condition on or before the closing date of the investment agreement. The venture's management will warrant:

a. That it is a duly organized corporation in good standing.
b. That its action in entering into an agreement is authorized by its directors, allowed by its bylaws and charter, legally binding upon the corporation, and not in breach of any other agreements.
c. If a private placement, that the securities being issued are exempt from registration under the Securities Act of 1933 as amended and under state securities law and that registration is not required under the Securities Exchange Act of 1934.
d. That the capitalization, shares, options, directors, and shareholders of the company are as described (either in the agreement or an exhibit).
e. That no trade secrets or patents will be used in the business that are not owned free and clear or if rights to use them have not been acquired.
f. That no conflicts of interest exist in their entering the agreement.
g. That all material facts and representations in the agreement and exhibits are true as of the date of closing (includes accuracy of business plan and financials).
h. That the venture will fulfill its part of the agreement so long as all conditions are met.
i. That any patents, trademarks, or copy rights owned and/or used by the company are as described.
j. That the principal assets and liabilities of the company are as described in attached exhibits.
k. That there are no undisclosed obligations, litigations, or agreements of the venture of a material nature not already known to all parties.
l. That any prior-year income statements and balance sheets are accurate as presented and have been audited and that there have been no adverse changes since the last audited statements.
m. That the venture is current on all tax payments and returns.

4. Representations and Warranties by the Investor

This section contains any legally binding representations made by the investor. They are much smaller in number than those made by the company. The investor may warrant:

a. If a corporation, that it is duly organized and in good standing.

b. If a corporation, that its action in entering into an agreement with the venture is authorized by its directors, allowed by its bylaws and charter, legally binding upon the corporation, and not in breach of any existing agreements.

c. If a private placement, that the stock being acquired is for investment and not with a view to or for sale in connection with any distribution.

d. The performance of his or her part of the contract if all conditions are met.

5. Affirmative Covenants

In addition to the above representations and warranties, the company in which the investor invests usually has a list of affirmative covenants with which it must comply. These could include agreeing to:

a. Pay taxes, fees, duties, and other assessments promptly.

b. File all appropriate government or agency reports.

c. Pay debt principal and interest.

d. Maintain corporate existence.

e. Maintain appropriate books of accounts and keep a specified auditing firm on retainer.

f. Allow access to these records to all directors and representatives of the investor.

g. Provide the investor with periodic income statements and balance sheets.

h. Preserve and provide for the investors stock registration rights as described in the agreement.

i. Maintain appropriate insurance, including keyman insurance with the company named as beneficiary.

j. Maintain minimum net worth, working capital, or net assets levels.

k. Maintain the number of investor board seats prescribed in the agreement.

l. Hold the prescribed number of directors' meetings.

m. Comply with all applicable laws.

n. Maintain corporate properties in good condition.

o. Notify the investor of any events of default of the investment agreement within a prescribed period of time.

p. Use the investment proceeds substantially in accordance with a business plan that is an exhibit to the agreement.

6. Negative Covenants

These covenants define what a venture must not do, or must not do without prior investor approval; such approval not to be unreasonably withheld. A venture usually agrees not to do such things as:

a. Merge, consolidate with, acquire, or invest in any form of organization.

b. Amend or violate the venture's charter or bylaws.

c. Distribute, sell, redeem, or divide stock except as provided for in the agreement.

d. Sell, lease, or dispose of assets whose value exceeds a specified amount.

e. Purchase assets whose value exceeds a specified amount.

f. Pay dividends.

g. Violate any working capital or net worth restrictions described in the investment agreement.

h. Advance to, loan to, or invest in individuals, organizations, or firms except as described in the investment agreement.

i. Create subsidiaries.

j. Liquidate the corporation.

k. Institute bankruptcy proceedings.

l. Pay compensation to its management other than as provided for in the agreement.

m. Change the basic nature of the business for which the firm was organized.

n. Borrow money except as provided for in the agreement.

o. Dilute the investors without giving them the right of first refusal on new issues of stock.

7. Conditions of Default

This section describes those events that constitute a breach of the investment agreement if not corrected within a specified time and under which an investor can exercise specific remedies. Events that constitute default may include:

a. Failure to comply with the affirmative or negative covenants of the investment agreement.

b. Falsification of representations and warranties made in the investment agreement.

c. Insolvency or reorganization of the venture.

d. Failure to pay interest or principal due on debentures.

8. Remedies

This section describes the actions available to an investor in the event that a condition of default occurs. Remedies depend on the form an investment takes. For a common stock investment, the remedies could be:

a. Forfeiture to the investor of any stock of the venture's principals that was held in escrow.

b. The investor receiving voting control through a right to vote some or all of the stock of the venture's principals.

c. The right of the investor to "put" his stock to the company at a predetermined price.

For a debenture, the remedies might be:

a. The full amount of the note becoming due and payable on demand.

b. Forfeiture of any collateral used to secure the debt.

In the case of a preferred stock investment, the remedy can be special voting rights (e.g., the right to vote the entrepreneurs' stock) to obtain control of the board of directors.

9. Other Conditions

A number of other clauses that cover a diverse group of issues often appear in investment agreements. Some of the more common issues covered are:

a. Who will bear the costs of closing the agreement; this is often born by the company.

b. Who will bear the costs of registration of the investors' stocks; again, the investors like this to be borne by the company for the first such registration.

c. Right of first refusal for the investor on subsequent company financings.

APPENDIX VI—SAMPLE VESTING AND STOCK RESTRICTION AGREEMENT © *Jeffry A. Timmons, 1990*

Agreement, dated as of September 30, 1983, between Venture *x,* a Massachusetts corporation (the "Company"), and Investor *y* (the "Stockholder").

Whereas, the Company has previously sold shares of its common stock ("Common Stock") to the Stockholder; and

Whereas, the Company is amending its Articles of Organization to remove certain provisions set forth therein which restrict the transfer of its Common Stock; and

Whereas, the parties desire to retain and impose certain restrictions on the shares of Common Stock presently owned by the Stockholders and on any new, additional, or different shares of the capital stock of the Company which may at any time be issued to the Stockholder as a result of a recapitalization, stock dividend, split-up, combination, or exchange of or on the Common Stock of the Company (collectively, all such Common Stock and any other such shares being referred to as "Shares");

Now, therefore, in consideration of the covenants and agreements set forth herein, and the mutual benefits which the parties anticipate from the performance thereof, the parties agree as follows:

1.   Repurchase of Shares on Termination of Employment Relationship. Subject to the lapse provisions hereinafter set forth, if at any time the Stockholder's employment or consulting relationship with the Company is terminated for any reason whatsoever, including death or disability, the Company shall have the right (but not the obligation) to require the Stockholder to sell to the Company all or any part of the Shares at the cash price paid by the Stockholder therefor.

The Company's right of repurchase set forth in this Section 3 to purchase part or all of the Shares shall lapse as follows:

a.   As to 100 percent of the Shares on November 30, 1983, if at least $180,000 in funding has not been received by the Company on or before such date.

b.   If such funding has been received on or before such date, at the rate of 25 percent of such Shares each year for four years effective annually on the anniversary of this agreement.

The Company may exercise its right of repurchase of such Shares by giving written notice to the Stockholder or to his estate, personal representative, or beneficiary ("Estate") at any time within 90 days of the termination of the Stockholder's employment with the Company, specifying the number of Shares to be sold to the Company. Such notice shall be effective only as to Shares as to which the Company's repurchase rights have not lapsed as of the date of such notice. Once such notice has been given, no further lapsing of such right of repurchase shall occur.

2.   Procedure for Sale of Shares. In any notice given by the Company pursuant to Section 1 hereof, the Company shall specify a closing date for the repurchase transaction described therein. At the closing, the repurchase price shall be payable by the Company's check against receipt of certificates representing all Shares so repurchased. Upon the date of any such notice from the Company to the Stockholder or his Estate, the interest of the Stockholder in the Shares specified in the notice for repurchase shall automatically terminate, except for the Stockholder's right to receive payment from the Company for such Shares.

3.   Right of First Refusal. If the Stockholder desires to sell all or any part of any Shares as to which the repurchase rights of the Company under Section 1 hereof have lapsed and an offeror ("the Offeror") has made an offer therefor, which offer the Stockholder desires to accept, the Stockholder desires to accept, the Stockholder shall: (i) obtain in writing an irrevocable and unconditional bona fide offer (the "Bona Fide Offer") for the purchase therof from the Offeror; and (ii) give written notice (the "Option Notice") to the Company setting forth his desire to sell such Shares, which Option Notice shall be accompanied by a photocopy of the original executed Bona Fide Offer and shall set forth at least the name and address of the Offeror and the price and terms of the Bona Fide Offer. Upon receipt of the Option Notice, the Company shall have an option to purchase any or all of such Shares specified in the Option Notice, such option to be exercisable by giving, within 30 days after receipt of the Option Notice, a written counternotice to the Stockholder. If the Company elects to purchase any or all of such Shares, it shall be obligated to purchase, and the Stockholder shall be obligated to sell to the Company, such Shares at the price and terms indicated in the Bona Fide Offer within 60 days from the date of receipt by the Company of the Option Notice.

The Stockholder may sell, pursuant to the terms of the Bona Fide Offer, any or all of such Shares not purchased by the Company for 30 days after expiration of the Option Notice, or for 30 days following a failure by the Company to purchase such Shares within 60 days of giving its counternotice of an intent to purchase such Shares; provided, however, that the Stockholder shall not sell such Shares to the Offeror if the Offeror is a competitor of the Company and the Company gives written notice to the Stockholder within 30 days of its receipt of the Option Notice stating that the Stockholder shall not sell his Shares to the Offeror; and provided, further, that prior to the sale of such Shares to the Offeror, the Offeror shall execute an agreement with the Company pursuant to which the Offeror agrees not to become a competitor of the Company and further agrees to be subject to the restrictions set forth in this Agreement. If any or all of such Shares are not sold pursuant to a Bona Fide Offer within the times permitted above, the unsold Shares shall remain subject to the terms of this Agreement.

The refusal rights of the Company set forth in Section 3 of this Agreement shall remain in effect until a distribution, if ever, to the public of shares of Common Stock for an aggregate public offering price of at least $3 million or more pursuant to a registration statement filed under the Securities Act of 1933, or a successor statute, at which time this Agreement will automatically expire.

Because the Shares cannot be readily purchased or sold in the open market, and for other reasons, the Stockholder and the Company acknowledge that the parties will be irreparably damaged in the event that this Agreement is not specifically enforced. Upon a breach or threatened breach of the terms, covenants, and/or conditions of this Agreement by any of the parties hereto, the other party shall, in addition to all other remedies, be entitled to a temporary or permanent injunction, without showing any actual damage, and/or a decree for specific performance, in accordance with the provisions hereof.

4. Adjustments. If there shall be any change in the Common Stock of the Company through merger, consolidation, reorganization, recapitalization, stock dividend, split-up, combination, or exchange of shares, or the like, all of the terms and provisions of this Agreement shall apply to any new, additional, or different shares or securities issued with respect to the Shares as a result of such event, and the repurchase price and the number of shares or other securities that may be repurchased under this Agreement shall be appropriately adjusted by the Board of Directors of the Company, whose determination shall be conclusive.

5. Restrictions on Transfer. The Stockholder agrees during the term of this Agreement that he will not sell, assign, transfer, pledge, hypothecate, mortgage, or otherwise encumber or dispose of, by gift or otherwise (except to the Company), all or any of the Shares now or hereafter owned by him except as permitted by this Agreement.

The Company may place a legend on any stock certificate representing any of the Shares reflecting the restrictions on transfer and the Company's right of repurchase set forth herein and may make an appropriate notation on its stock records with respect to the same.

6. Waiver of Restrictions. The Company may at any time waive any restriction imposed by any Section of this Agreement with respect to all or any portion of any of the Shares.

7. *No Obligation as to Employment.* The Company is not by reason of this Agreement obligated to start or continue the Stockholder in any employment or consulting capacity.

8. *Successors and Assigns.* This Agreement shall be binding on and inure to the benefit of the Company's successors and assigns and the Stockholder's transferees of the Shares, heirs, executors, administrators, legal representatives, and assigns. Without limiting the foregoing, the Company is specifically permitted to assign its repurchase rights under Sections 1, 2, and 3 hereof.

9. *Notices.* All notices and other communications provided for or contemplated by this Agreement shall be delivered by hand or sent by certified mail, return receipt requested, addressed as follows:

If to the Company:
If to the Stockholder: At his address set forth below

or to such other address as the addressee may specify by written notice pursuant to this Section 10. Notices or communications sent by mail shall be deemed to have been given on the date of mailing. In the event of the Stockholder's death or incapacity, any notice or communication from the Company may, at the Company's option, be addressed either to the Stockholder at his last address specified pursuant to this Section 10 or to the Stockholder's Estate.

10. *Governing Law.* This Agreement shall be governed by and construed in accordance with the laws of the Commonwealth of Massachusetts.

11. *Amendments; Waivers.* Changes, amendments, or modifications in or additions to or waivers of any provision under or of this Agreement may be made only by a written instrument executed by the parties hereto. Any waiver of any provision of this Agreement shall not excuse compliance with any other provision of this Agreement. Notwithstanding the foregoing, no course of dealing or delay on the part of either party in exercising any right shall operate as a waiver thereof or otherwise prejudice the rights of such holder.

The Stockholder acknowledges that the issuance of the Shares to the Stockholder hereunder satisfies and discharges in full any previous understanding between the Company and the Stockholder regarding the issuance of the Company's stock or option rights with respect thereto, and the Stockholder waives any preemptive rights he has to purchase any capital stock of the Company.

12. *Captions.* Captions are for convenience only and shall not be deemed to be a part of this Agreement.

In witness whereof, the undersigned have caused this Agreement to be executed as an instrument under seal as of the day and year first above written.

APPENDIX VII – SAMPLE LOAN AGREEMENT

BANK OF NEW ENGLAND, N.A.
TERM LOAN AGREEMENT

For value received and in further consideration of the granting by Bank of New England, N.A. ("Bank") to the undersigned ("Borrower") of a line of credit or of a loan or loans thereunder (all such loans, together with any existing loans from Bank to Borrower, being hereinafter collectively and separately referred to as the "Loan"), Borrower represents and warrants to and agrees with Bank as follows ("Agreement"):

SECTION 1. THE LOAN.

1.1 **Amount.** Bank will lend to Borrower, and Borrower will borrow from Bank $_____, with interest at _____% per annum.

1.2 **Evidence of Loan.** At the option of Bank, the Loan and the terms of repayment thereof, including the rate of interest, may be evidenced by a note or notes, or by Bank's books and records.

1.3 **Security and/or Guaranty.** The payment of the Loan may at any time or from time to time be secured and/or guaranteed wholly or partly separate and apart from this Agreement, but whether or not secured and/or guaranteed, all monies and other property at any time in the possession of Bank which Borrower either owns or has the permission of the owner thereof to pledge with or otherwise hypothecate to Bank, including, but not limited to, any deposits, balances of deposits or other sums at any time credited by or due from Bank, shall at all times be collateral security for all of the liabilities, obligations and undertakings of Borrower to Bank, direct or indirect, absolute or contingent, now existing or hereafter arising or acquired including, but not limited to, the payment of the Loan.

SECTION 2. WARRANTIES AND REPRESENTATIONS. Borrower hereby represents and warrants to Bank (which representations and warranties will survive the making of the Loan) that:

2.1 **Corporate Existence.** Borrower, if a corporation, is and will continue to be, a corporation duly incorporated and validly existing under the laws of the State of _____ and duly licensed or qualified as a foreign corporation in all states wherein the nature of its property owned or business transacted by it makes such licensing or qualification necessary. Borrower has obtained all required permits, authorizations and licenses, without unusual restrictions or limitations, to conduct the business in which Borrower is presently engaged, all of which are in full force and effect.

2.2 **Corporate Authority and Power.** If Borrower is a corporation, the execution, delivery and performance of this Agreement, any note or security agreement or any other instrument or document at any time required in connection with the Loan are within the corporate powers of Borrower, and not in contravention of law, the Articles of Organization or By-Laws of Borrower or any amendment thereof, or of any indenture, agreement or undertaking to which Borrower is a party or may otherwise be bound, and each such instrument and document represents a valid and binding obligation of Borrower and is fully enforceable according to its terms. Borrower will, at the request of Bank at any time and from time to time, furnish Bank with the opinion of counsel for Borrower with respect to any or all of the foregoing or other matters, such opinion to be in substance and form satisfactory to Bank.

2.3 **Financial Status.** All financial statements and other statements heretofore or hereafter given by Borrower to Bank in respect hereof are or will be true and correct, subject to any limitation stated therein, consistent with any prior statements furnished to Bank, and prepared in accordance with generally accepted accounting principles to represent fairly the condition of Borrower at the date thereof.

2.4 **Litigation.** There is not now pending or threatened against Borrower any action or other proceedings or any claim in which Borrower has any monetary or other proprietary interest nor do any of the executive or managing personnel of Borrower know of any facts which may give rise to any such litigation, proceeding or claim, except: _____

_____

2.5 **Subsidiaries Affiliates.** If Borrower is a corporation it (a) owns 100% or _____% of the issued and outstanding stock of the following subsidiaries and/or affiliates: _____

_____

_____

(b) such stock shall be free and clear of any pledges, liens, or other encumbrances.

2.6 **Events of Default.** No event of default specified in Section 5.0 hereof, and no event which, with the lapse of time or notice, would become such an event of default, has occurred and is continuing.

2.7 **Title to Property.** Borrower has good and marketable title to all property in which Borrower has given or has agreed to give a security interest to Bank and such property is or will be free of all encumbrances except: _____

_____

2.8 **Taxes.** Borrower has filed all tax returns required to be filed, has paid all taxes due thereon and has provided adequate reserves for payment of any tax which is being contested.

25-141-1 (5/82)

SECTION 3. AFFIRMATIVE COVENANTS. Borrower agrees that until payment in full of the Loan and performance of all of its other obligations under this Agreement, Borrower will, unless Bank otherwise consents in writing, comply with the following:

3.1 **Compensating Balances.** Bank shall be Borrower's main bank of deposit and Borrower shall maintain average aggregate collected balances in its deposit account or accounts with Bank of not less than _____ per centum (_____%) of the outstanding unpaid balance of the Loan or Loans; such collected balances to be calculated net of any balances required to support demand deposit account activity costs. Balances shall be averaged _____.

3.2 **Commitment Fee.** Subject to the terms of this agreement Bank commits itself until _____, 19_____, to lend to Borrower at any time or from time to time a sum or sums in the aggregate amount of $_____; and Borrower agrees to pay to Bank monthly in arrears a fee for Bank's said commitment in the amount of _____ per centum (_____%) of the unused portion thereof so long as the same be outstanding. Borrower shall also, in addition to requirements of Paragraph 3.1 above, maintain collected balances in its deposit account or accounts with Banks of not less than _____ per centum (_____%) of the unused portion of said commitment. Repayments on account of the Loan shall not operate to increase the unused portion of said commitment, except in the case of Revolving Loans.

3.3 **Financial Statements.** (a) Borrower will furnish to Bank quarterly statements prepared by Borrower within forty-five days of the close of each quarter, and within ninety days after the close of each fiscal year, an annual audit prepared by the equity method and certified by public accountants selected by Borrower and approved by Bank, together with a certificate by such accountants that at such audit date Borrower was acting in compliance with the terms of this Agreement. If Borrower is a corporation, consolidated and consolidating statements shall be furnished for Borrower and all subsidiary corporations, (b) Borrower shall indicate on said statements all guarantees made by it and (c) Borrower will upon request permit a representative of Bank to inspect and make copies of Borrower's books and records at all reasonable times.

3.4 **Insurance.** Borrower will maintain adequate fire insurance with extended coverage, public liability and other insurance as Bank may reasonably require as consistent with sound business practice and with companies satisfactory to Bank, which policies will show the Bank as a loss payee.

3.5 **Taxes and Other Liens.** Borrower will comply with all statutes and government regulations and pay all taxes, assessments, governmental charges or levies, or claims for labor, supplies, rent and other obligations made against it which, if unpaid, might become a lien or charge against Borrower or on its property, except liabilities being contested in good faith and against which if requested by Bank, Borrower will set up reserves satisfactory to Bank.

3.6 **Maintenance of Existence.** If Borrower is a corporation, it will maintain its existence and comply with all applicable statutes, rules and regulations, and maintain its properties in good operating condition, and continue to conduct its business as presently conducted.

3.7 **Notice of Default.** Within three (3) business days of becoming aware of (a) the existence of any condition or event which constitutes a default under Section 5.0 hereof, or (b) the existence of any condition or event which with notice or the passage of time, will constitute a default under Section 5.0 hereof, Borrower will provide Bank with written notice specifying the nature and period of existence thereof and what action Borrower is taking or proposes to take with respect thereto.

3.8 **Use of Proceeds.** Borrower shall use the proceeds of the Loan hereunder for general commercial purposes, provided that no part of such proceeds will be used, for the purpose of purchasing or carrying any "margin security" as such term is defined in Regulation U of the Board of Governors of the Federal Reserve System.

3.9 **Further Assurances.** Borrower will execute and deliver to Bank any writings and do all things necessary, effectual or reasonably requested by Bank to carry into effect the provisions and intent of this Agreement.

SECTION 4. NEGATIVE COVENANTS. Without the prior written approval of Bank, Borrower will not:

4.1 **Consolidation, Merger or Acquisition.** Participate in any merger or consolidation or alter or amend the capital structure of Borrower including, but not limited to, the issuance of additional stock, or make any acquisition of the business of another.

4.2 **Dividends.** Pay any dividends, **including stock dividends**, or make any distributions, in cash or otherwise, including splits of any kind, to any officer, stockholder or beneficial owner of Borrower other than salaries.

4.3 **Encumbrances.** Mortgage, pledge or otherwise encumber any property of Borrower or permit any lien to exist thereon except liens (i) for taxes not delinquent or being contested in good faith; (ii) of mechanics or materialmen in respect of obligations not overdue or being contested in good faith; (iii) resulting from security deposits made in the ordinary course of business; and (iv) in favor of Bank.

4.4 **Investments.** Invest any assets of Borrower in securities other than obligations of the United States of America.

4.5 **Disposition of Assets, Guarantees, Loans, Advances.** Sell, transfer or assign any assets of Borrower other than in the ordinary course of business or, except as hereinafter specifically permitted, (i) sell or transfer or assign any of Borrower's accounts receivable with or without recourse, (ii) guarantee or become surety for the obligations of any person, firm or corporation, or (iii) make any loans or advances except:

_____

4.6 **Working Capital.** Permit its inventory to exceed _____% of its Current Assets; permit its net Working Capital (excess of Current Assets over Current Liabilities) to be less than $_____ for the current fiscal year and for each subsequent fiscal year to be less than the amount for the prior fiscal year plus _____% of Borrower's net income earned for the prior year, after provision for taxes, provided that there shall be no reduction in the required working capital for losses; or permit its Current Assets to be less than _____% of its Current Liabilities, Current Assets and Current Liabilities to be computed in accordance with customary accounting practice except that Current Liabilities shall in any event include all rentals and other payments due within one year under any lease or rental of personal property.

4.7 **Liabilities.** Permit its total short and long term liabilities including borrowings to exceed _____% of Borrower's **tangible net worth, said percentage to decrease** _____% per year for the term of the Loan.

4.8 **Fixed Assets.** Make, or incur any obligation to make, any expenditures in any fiscal year for fixed assets by purchase or lease agreement the aggregate fair market value of which assets is in excess of $_____.

4.9 **Compensation.** If Borrower is a corporation, pay to its officers and directors aggregate compensation in any fiscal year which exceeds $_____.

4.10 **Employee Retirement Investment Secuirty Act of 1974 as amended ("ERISA"). Permit any pension plan to:** (a) engage in any "prohibited transaction"; (b) fail to report to Bank a "reportable event"; (c) incur any "accumulated funding deficiency"; or (d) terminate its existence at any time in a manner which could result in the imposition of a lien on the property of the Borrower. (The quoted terms are defined in Sections 2003(c), 302, and 4003, respectively, of ERISA.)

SECTION 5. DEFAULTS. If any one or more of the following "Events of Default" shall occur at any time, **Bank shall have the right to declare any or all liabilities or obligations of Borrower to Bank immediately due and payable without notice or demand:**

5.1 Any warranty, representation or statement made or furnished to Bank by or on behalf of Borrower or any guarantor or surety for Borrower was in any material respect false when made or furnished;

5.2 A failure to pay or perform when due any obligation, liability or covenant of Borrower or of any guarantor or surety for Borrower, under this loan agreement or any other indebtedness or obligation for borrowed money, or if such indebtedness or obligation shall be accelerated, or if there exists any event of default under any such instrument, document or agreement evidencing or securing such indebtedness or obligation, including, but not limited to, failure to perform the terms of this Agreement or of the note or notes evidencing the Loan;

5.3 The commencement of any proceeding under any bankruptcy or insolvency laws by or against Borrower, the appointment of a trustee, receiver, or custodian and, if any such proceeding is involuntary such proceeding has not been dismissed and all trustees, receivers, or custodians discharged within 30 days of its commencement or their appointment.

5.4 The service upon Bank of a writ in which Bank is named as trustee or Borrower or any guarantor or surety for Borrower;

5.5 If Borrower or any guarantor or surety for Borrower is a corporation, trust or partnership, the liquidation, termination or dissolution of any such organization or its ceasing to carry on actively its present business;

5.6 The death of Borrower or any guarantors or surety for Borrower, and if Borrower or any guarantor or surety for Borrower is a partnership, the death of any partner; or

5.7 A judgment or judgments for the payment of money aggregating in excess of $_____ is outstanding against Borrower or any guarantor or surety for Borrower and any one of such judgments has been outstanding for more than thirty (30) days from the date of its entry and has not been discharged in full or stayed.

SECTION 6. MISCELLANEOUS.

6.1 **Other Agreements.** This Agreement is supplementary to each and every other agreement between Borrower and Bank and shall not be so construed as to limit or otherwise derogate from any of the rights or remedies of Bank or any of the liabilities, obligations or undertakings of Borrower under any such agreement, nor shall any contemporaneous or subsequent agreement between Borrower and Bank be construed to limit or otherwise derogate from any of the rights or remedies of Bank or any of the liabilities, obligations or undertakings of Borrower hereunder unless such other agreement specifically refers to this Agreement and expressly so provides. This Agreement and the covenants and agreements herein contained shall continue in full force and effect and shall be applicable not only with respect to the Loan, but also to all other obligations, liabilities and undertakings of Borrower to Bank whether direct or indirect, absolute or contingent, due or to become due, now existing or hereafter arising or acquired, until all such obligations, liabilities and undertakings have been paid or otherwise satisfied in full.

6.2 **Waivers.** No delay or omission on the part of Bank in exercising any right hereunder shall operate as a waiver of such right or any other right and waiver on any one or more occasions shall not be construed as a bar to or waiver of any right or remedy of Bank on any future occasion.

6.3 **Expenses.** Borrower will pay or reimburse Bank for all reasonable expenses, including attorneys' fees, which Bank may in any way incur in connection with this agreement or any other agreement between Borrower and Bank or with any Loan or which result from any claim or action by any third person against Bank which would not have been asserted were it not for Bank's relationship with Borrower hereunder or otherwise.

6.4 **Notices.** All notices and other communications hereunder shall be in writing, except as otherwise provided in this Agreement, and shall be hand delivered or mailed by first-class mail, postage prepaid (in which event notice shall be deemed to have been given when so delivered or deposited in the mail), addressed (a) if to Borrower, to _____

and (b) if to Bank, to 28 State Street, Boston, Massachusetts 02106. Attention _____ The address of any party hereto for such demands, notices and other communications may be changed by giving notice in writing at any time to the other party hereto.

6.5 **Massachusetts Law.** This Agreement is intended to take effect as a sealed instrument and shall be governed by and construed according to the laws of the Commonwealth of Massachusetts.

6.6 **Successors and Assigns.** This Agreement shall be binding upon Borrower's legal representatives, successors and assigns and shall inure to the benefit of Bank's successors and assigns.

6.7 **Additional Provisions.** Borrower furthermore agrees to the following additional provisions: _____
_____
_____
_____
_____
_____
_____
_____
_____
_____
_____

IN WITNESS WHEREOF the parties hereto have caused this Agreement to be duly executed under seal this _____ day of
_____, 19_____, at Boston, Massachusetts.

_____
(Name of Borrower)

By _____
   Hereunto duly authorized
   Title:

ATTEST:

By _____
   Hereunto duly authorized
   Title:

_____

BANK OF NEW ENGLAND, N.A.

By _____
   Hereunto duly authorized
   Title:

ORIGINAL

BANK OF NEW ENGLAND, N.A.

SECURITY AGREEMENT

To secure the due payment and performance of all of the liabilities and obligations hereunder of the undersigned, herein called "Debtor", to Bank of New England, N.A., herein called "Secured Party", and all other liabilities and obligations of Debtor to Secured Party of every name and nature whatsoever, direct or indirect, absolute or contingent, now existing or hereafter arising or acquired, including without limitation the due payment and performance of all liabilities and obligations under a note of even date herewith and all notes given by way of renewal or extension of or in substitution in whole or in part for the same, all hereinafter called the "Obligations".

For value received, Debtor hereby grants to Secured Party a security interest in all property of Debtor which is now or may hereafter be in Secured Party's possession, including without limitation any deposits, balance of deposits or other sums at any time credited by or due from Secured Party to Debtor, and in Debtor's following described personal property:

A continuing security interest in all goods (excluding inventory) including but not limited

to all machinery, equipment, furnishings, and fixtures and other tangible personal prop-

erty (with all accessions thereto) used or bought for use primarily in business, wherever

located, whether now existing or hereafter arising, now or hereafter received by or belonging

to Debtor, and in the proceeds and products thereof, including any insurance proceeds.

and in any and all additions, accessions and accretions thereto and substitutes therefor, all hereinafter called the "Collateral", and in the proceeds thereof.

Debtor hereby specifies, warrants and covenants that:

1. Debtor's mailing address is:_____
   (Street and No. — Box)   (City or Town)   (State)   (Zip)

2. The Collateral is or will be used primarily for: ☐ Personal, family or household purposes   ☐ Business (including Profession)   ☐ Farming

3. The Collateral will be kept at:_____
   (Street and No.)   (City or Town)   (County)   (State)

4. If the Collateral or any part thereof is or is to become fixtures, Debtor will upon request furnish Secured Party with a disclaimer or subordination in form satisfactory to Secured Party of their interests in the Collateral from all persons having an interest in the real estate, the name and address of the record owner of and a general description of said real estate being as follows:

   _____

   _____

   _____

5. If the Collateral or any part thereof is or is to be used primarily for business, Debtor's (A) principal and (B, etc.) other places of business are as follows:
   (Street and No.)   (City or Town)   (County)   (State)

   (A) _____

   (B) _____

6. If the Collateral or any part thereof is or is to be used primarily for farming or for personal, family or household purposes, Debtor's residence is as follows: _____
   (Street and No.)   (City or Town)   (County)   (State)

7. Secured Party is authorized and requested to disburse the proceeds of the note of even date herewith, if any, to the following named person(s) from whom Debtor is acquiring the Collateral:

   _____

"Debtor" shall include all persons signing below as Debtor except those signing in a representative capacity, and all Obligations of Debtor, if more than one person, shall be joint and several.

THIS AGREEMENT IS SUBJECT TO THE ADDITIONAL TERMS AND PROVISIONS SET FORTH ON THE REVERSE SIDE HEREOF, THE SAME BEING HERE INCORPORATED BY REFERENCE AS FULLY AS IF HERE SET FORTH VERBATIM.

DEBTOR HAS RETAINED A TRUE AND COMPLETED COPY OF THIS AGREEMENT AT THE TIME OF DEBTOR'S EXECUTION AND DELIVERY THEREOF.

Signed, sealed and delivered at Boston, Massachusetts this   day of   19

Executed in Presence of: DEBTOR:_____

_____   By_____
                                 Hereunto duly authorized   (Title)

_____   By_____
                                 Hereunto duly authorized   (Title)

25-150-1 (5/82)

TERM NOTE

$ ....   Boston, Massachusetts, ... , 19 ....

For value received, the undersigned, which term wherever used herein shall mean all and each of the signers of this note jointly and severally, promises to pay to BANK OF NEW ENGLAND, N.A., or order, at said bank, the principal sum of ....

.... Dollars in .... instalments, as follows: $ .... on .... , 19 .... and the same amount (except the last instalment which shall be the unpaid balance) on the same day of each .... month thereafter until this note is fully paid, with interest from the date hereof on the unpaid balance of said principal sum from time to time outstanding at the — ☐ Large Business Prime Rate

☐ Small Business Base Rate — for commercial loans from time to time in effect at said bank plus .... per centum per annum, but in no event shall such interest be at a rate of less than .... per centum per annum. Such interest shall be payable .... in arrears, the first instalment thereof being due on .... , 19 ....

At the option of the holder, this note shall become immediately due and payable without notice or demand upon the occurrence at any time of any of the following events of default: (1) default of any liability, obligation or undertaking of the undersigned, hereunder or otherwise, including failure to pay in full and when due any sum due hereunder, or of any indorser or guarantor of any liability, obligation or undertaking, hereunder or otherwise, to the holder; (2) if any statement, representation or warranty made in or in connection with the application for the loan evidenced by this note, or in any supporting financial statement of the undersigned or any indorser or guarantor hereof shall be found to have been false in any material respect; (3) if the undersigned or any indorser or guarantor hereof is a corporation, trust or partnership, the liquidation, termination or dissolution of any such organization or its ceasing to carry on actively its present business or the appointment of a receiver for its property; (4) the death of the undersigned or of any indorser or guarantor hereof and, if any of the undersigned or any indorser or guarantor hereof is a partnership, the death of any partner; (5) the institution by or against the undersigned or any indorser or guarantor hereof of any proceedings under the Bankruptcy Code or any other law in which the undersigned or any indorser or guarantor hereof is alleged to be insolvent or unable to pay their respective debts as they mature or the making by the undersigned or any indorser or guarantor hereof of an assignment for the benefit of creditors; (6) the service upon the holder hereof of a writ in which the holder is named as trustee of the undersigned or of any indorser or guarantor hereof; or (7) if the holder hereof should at any time deem itself insecure.

The undersigned agrees to pay upon default costs of collection including reasonable fees of attorneys.

No delay or omission on the part of the holder in exercising any right hereunder shall operate as a waiver of such right or of any other right of such holder, nor shall any delay, omission or waiver on any one occasion be deemed a bar to or waiver of the same or any other right on any future occasion. Every one of the undersigned and every indorser or guarantor of this note regardless of the time, order or place of signing waives presentment, demand, protest and notices of every kind and assents to any one or more extensions or postponements of the time of payment or any other indulgences, to any substitutions, exchanges or releases of collateral if at any time there be available to the holder collateral for this note, and to the additions or releases of any other parties or persons primarily or secondarily liable.

The proceeds of the loan represented by this note may be paid to any one or more of the undersigned.

All rights and obligations hereunder shall be governed by the law of the Commonwealth of Massachusetts and this note shall be deemed to be under seal.

....
Borrower(s) - Print name or names

ATTEST:

     (by) ....
                                   Signature

....
Clerk or Secretary of Corporation   (by) ....
                                   Signature

25-148-3 (5/82)

DEMAND NOTE

$ .... Boston, Massachusetts, ... , 19........

  ON DEMAND, for value received, the undersigned, which term wherever used herein shall mean all and each of the signers of this note jointly and severally, promises to pay to BANK OF NEW ENGLAND, N.A., or order, at said bank, ...

.... Dollars, with interest from the date hereof on the unpaid balance from time to time outstanding

CHECK APPROPRIATE BOX AND COMPLETE ITEM	
☐	at the rate of .... per centum per annum,
☐	at the **Large Business Prime Rate** for commercial loans from time to time in effect at said bank plus .... per centum per annum,
☐	at the **Small Business Base Rate** for commercial loans from time to time in effect at said bank plus .... per centum per annum,

such interest to be payable .... **in arrears.**

  The undersigned agrees to pay upon default costs of collection including reasonable fees of attorneys.

  No delay or omission on the part of the holder in exercising any right hereunder shall operate as a waiver of such right or of any other right of such holder, nor shall any delay, omission or waiver on any one occasion be deemed a bar to or waiver of the same or any other right on any future occasion. Every one of the undersigned and every indorser or guarantor of this note regardless of the time, order or place of signing waives presentment, demand, protest and notices of every kind and assents to any one or more extensions or postponements of the time of payment or any other indulgences, to any substitutions, exchanges or releases of collateral if at any time there be available to the holder collateral for this note, and to the additions or releases of any other parties or persons primarily or secondarily liable.

  The proceeds of the loan represented by this note may be paid to any one or more of the undersigned.

  All rights and obligations hereunder shall be governed by the law of the Commonwealth of Massachusetts and this note shall be deemed to be under seal.

....
Borrower(s) - Print name or names

(by) ....
      Signature

(by) ....
      Signature

25-102-3 (5/82)

APPENDIX VIII—VASES AND FACES EXERCISE

The exercise[1] that follows is specifically designed to help you shift from your dominant left-hemisphere mode to your subdominant R-mode. The process could be described over and over in words, but only *you* can experience for yourself this cognitive shift, this slight change in subjective state. As Fats Waller once said, "If you gotta ask what jazz is, you ain't never gonna know." So it is with R-mode state: you need to experience the L- to R-mode shift, observe the R-mode state, and in this way come to know it.[2]

Vase-Faces Drawing 1

You have probably seen the perceptual-illusion drawing of the vase and faces. Looked at one way, the drawing appears to be two faces seen in profile. Then, as you are looking at it, the drawing seems to change and become a vase. One version of the drawing is shown in Exhibit VIII.1.

Before you begin. First, read all the directions for the exercise.

1. Draw a profile of a person's head on the *left* side of the paper, facing toward the center. (If you are left-handed, draw the profile on the right side, facing toward the center.) Examples are shown of both the right-handed and left-handed drawings (Exhibits VIII.2a and VIII.2b). Make up your own version of the profile if you wish. It seems to help if this profile comes from your own memorized, stored *symbols* for a human profile.
2. Next, draw horizontal lines at the top and bottom of your profile, forming the top and bottom of the vase (Exhibits VIII.2a and VIII.2b).
3. Now go back over your drawing of the first profile with your pencil. As the pencil moves over the features, *name them to yourself:* forehead, nose, upper lip, chin, neck. Repeat this step at least once. This is an L-mode task: naming symbolic shapes.
4. Next, starting at the top, draw the profile in *reverse*. By doing this, you will *complete the vase*. The second profile should be a reversal of the first in order for the vase to be symmetrical. (Look once more at the example in Exhibit VIII.1). Watch for the faint signals from your brain that you are shifting modes of information processing. You may experience a sense of mental conflict at some point in the drawing of the *second* profile. Observe this. And observe *how you solve the problem.* You will find that you are doing the second profile *differently. This is right-hemisphere-mode drawing.*

Before you read further, do the drawing.

After you finish. Now that you have completed the Vase-Faces drawing, think back on how you did it. The first profile was probably rather rapidly drawn and then, as you were instructed, redrawn while verbalizing the names of the parts as you went back over the features.

This is a left-hemisphere mode of processing: *drawing symbolic shapes from memory and naming them.*

In drawing the second profile (i.e., the profile that completes the vase), you may have experienced some confusion or conflict, as I mentioned. To continue the drawing, you had

---

[1] Betty Edwards, *Drawing on the Right Side of the Brain* (Boston: Houghton Mifflin, 1979).
[2] For those of you who can take the time, especially if you feel that you "can't draw a straight line," the author suggests that you find the book and try a further exercise.

Exhibit VIII.1

Exhibit VIII.2

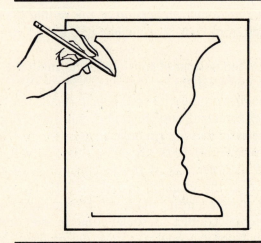 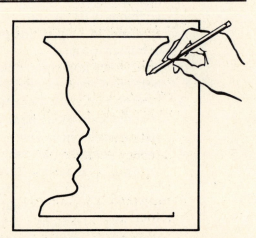

to find a different way, some different process. You probably lost the sense of drawing a profile and found yourself *scanning* back and forth in the space between the profiles, estimating angles, curves, inward-curving and outward-curving shapes, and lengths of line *in relation to* the opposite shapes, which now become *unnamed and unnamable.* Putting it another way, you made constant adjustments in the line you were drawing by checking *where you were* and *where you were going,* by scanning the space between the first profile and your copy in reverse.[3]

    In short, you began by drawing a symbol for a *face;* you concluded by drawing a *line* — the same result, but achieved by an entirely different process.

[3] Edwards, *Drawing.*

ANNOTATED BIBLIOGRAPHY

GENERAL BACKGROUND AND REFERENCE

Encyclopedia of Entrepreneurship, ed. C. Kent, D. Sexton, and K. H. Vesper (Englewood Cliffs, N.J.: Prentice-Hall, 1982).

A fine collection of research articles by the leading academicians on many aspects of the entrepreneurial process: the entrepreneur, the venture, the environment, the history, the nonacademic literature, and suggestions for further research.

The Encyclopedia of Small Business Resources, by David E. Gumpert and Jeffry A. Timmons (New York: Harper & Row, 1984). Published in hard cover by Doubleday in 1982 as *The Insider's Guide to Small Business Resources.*

A topic-by-topic listing of sources for information, consulting help, and capital for new and small enterprises. "This is a competent and comprehensive guide in a field in which information i scattered and hard to come by" (Forbes).

Entrepreneurial Behavior, by Barbara Bird, Case-Western Reserve University (Glenview, I ..: Scott-Foresman, 1989).

It provides a comprehensive discussion of what is known about the behavioral side of entrepreneurship.

The Entrepreneurial Mind, by Jeffry A. Timmons (Acton, Mass.: Brick House Publi hing, 1989).

A book about the title, which J. Willard Marriott, Jr., chairman of the Marriott Corporat on, calls "truly outstanding!"; and of which Peter Sprague, chairman of National Semicondu or, says, "Your book is a revelation. You could have saved me a great deal of trouble and mone if you had written it 20 years ago!"

Entrepreneurship: An International Journal of Economic and Regional Growth d. Gerald P. Sweeney (London: Taylor & Francis, 1988).

A new journal that reports on global research on entrepreneurship onomic development.

Entrepreneurship, Creativity and Organization, by John V , Harvard Business School (Homewood, Ill.: Richard D. Irwin, 1989).

A new book based a course by that title developed by he author. It is the first book to treat thoroughly the critical "creativity dimension" of entrep eneurship.

Entrepreneurship for the Eighties, by Gordon Baty (Englewood Cliffs, N.J.: Prentice-Hall, 1981).

A breezy, practical walk-through of starting a n w venture by someone who has done it.

Frontiers of Entrepreneurship Research: 1981 thro gh 1990, ed. J.A. Hornaday, J.A. Timmons, F. Tarpley, and K.H. Vesper (Babson Par , Mass.: Babson College).

These 10 volumes include the complete proceedings of five annual conferences on entrepreneurship research. The data-based papers cover every aspect of the venture creation process. The authors are from academia, government, and the private sector, both in this country and abroad. These documents are the most comprehensive existing compendium of research into entrepreneurship.

Note: Portions of the Annotated Bibliography are adapted from *The Encyclopedia of Small Business Resources,* by David E. Gumpert and Jeffry A. Timmons (New York: Harper & Row, 1984).

The Frugal Marketer, by Donald J. Weinrauch and Nancy Croft Baker (New York: Amacon, 1989).

This book is an excellent resource of ideas, information, and techniques for marketing when you are operating on a shoestring or bootstrapping the venture. It is full of examples of how entrepreneurs barter, beg, and creatively market their products and services on a limited marketing budget.

Getting to Yes, by Roger Fisher and Wm. Ury (Boston: Houghton Mifflin, 1981).

A useful book on the art of gaining agreement in negotiating without giving in.

Growing Concerns, edited by David E. Gumpert (New York: John Wiley & Sons, 1984).

This is a compendium of articles about emerging growth ventures that have appeared in the *Harvard Business Review.*

Journal of Business Venturing (Philadelphia, Pa.: Wharton Entrepreneurial Center).

A quarterly journal that focuses on new developments and research.

New Business Opportunities, by Jeffry A. Timmons (Acton, Mass.: Brick House Publishing, 1989).

Addresses how and why successful entrepreneurs always seem to get to the right place at the right time. Roger Enrico, President and CEO of the Pepsi-Cola Company says of it: "As practical as it is logical. NBO is a bible for the entrepreneur."

New Business Ventures and the Entrepreneur, by Howard H. Stevenson, Michael J. Roberts, and H. Irving Grousbeck (Homewood, Ill.: Richard D. Irwin, 1989).

This book, an update and revision of Patrick Liles's 1974 publication bearing the same title, contains cases and technical notes on specific aspects of venture creation.

The New Venturers, by John W. Wilson (Reading, Mass.: Addison-Wesley, 1985).

It is good reading about the entrepreneurs and investors in some of America's most famous new companies of the past 20 years.

Planning and Financing a New Business, by Jeffry A. Timmons (Acton, Mass.: Brick House Publishing, 1989).

It is the third of a three-book series. It covers the practicalities of planning the start-up, finding money, and negotiating a deal.

The State of Small Business: A Report of the President. Published annually by the U.S. Government Printing Office, Washington, D.C.

It is an excellent summary of the current state of small business in the country and includes useful summaries of facts and charts about new and job company formation rates, failure patterns, and other recent trends.

Trials and Rewards of the Entrepreneur, articles reprinted from the *Harvard Business Review* (Harvard College, 1984).

These articles, written between 1964 and 1982, deal with various aspects of the merging, growing, and maturing venture. It is nice to have them all under the same cover.

The Winning Performance: How America's High-Growth Mid-Size Companies Succeed, by Donald K. Clifford, Jr., and Richard Cavanagh (Toronto: Bantam Books, 1985).

Must reading for the growth-minded entrepreneur. The authors show evidence and examples of how and why new ventures "grow up big."

You Can Negotiate Anything, by Herb Cohen (Toronto: Bantam, 1980).

A short but invaluable aid for anyone who has to negotiate anything. Don't leave home without it!

EDUCATION AND TRAINING SOURCES

A. For Start-Ups

Entrepreneurship and Venture Management, by Clifford M. Baumback and J.R. Mancuso (Englewood Cliffs, N.J.: Prentice-Hall, 1975).

> A good book of readings on starting and operating a small business.

New Venture Strategies, by Karl Vesper (Englewood Cliffs, N.J.: Prentice-Hall, 1980).

> Informative discussion of start-up approaches that have worked for others. Liberal use of actual examples and anecdotes makes it readable and worthwhile. Vesper is one of the leading gurus of entrepreneurship.

B. For Existing Small Businesses

U.S. Small Business Administration
U.S. Small Business Administration
1441 L Street, N.W.
Washington, D.C. 20416

> SBA has about 300 publications covering all aspects of small business management for a wide range of businesses. These publications present facts, figures, and techniques in readable, nontechnical form. Some of the best-sellers include:
>
> *Management Training.* Excellent summary of SBA's publications and materials.
> *Management Aids for Small Manufacturers.*
> *Small Marketers Aids.* Suggestions, checklists, guidelines for small retail, wholesale, and service firms.
> *Small Business Management Series* (35 vols.). Covers various businesses and problems.
> *Starting and Managing Series.* Covers various businesses.
> *Managing for Profits.* A pragmatic, how-to guide.
> *Buying and Selling a Small Business.*
> *Protecting the Small Business Cash Flow Lifeline* (Office of Advocacy, January 1980).
> > Excellent discussion of 55 practices frequently used to cope with tight money conditions and a weak economy.

Non-SBA books for existing small businesses include the following:

How to Organize and Operate a Small Business, 6th ed., by Clifford M. Baumback and Kenneth Lawyer (Englewood Cliffs, N.J.: Prentice-Hall, 1979).

> Probably the leading college text on the subject.

Small Business Management Fundamentals, 2d ed., by Dan Steinhoff (New York: McGraw-Hill, 1978).

> A good nuts-and-bolts textbook.

Small Business Reporter (San Francisco, Calif.: Bank of America).

> An excellent collection of reports on starting and managing specific types of businesses and on the problems of such businesses.

CONSULTANTS AND MANAGEMENT ASSISTANCE

Six major associations and publications provide information and directories on management consultants:

Institute of Management Consultants
19 West 44th Street
New York, New York 10036
(212) 921-2885

Consultants News
Templeton Road
Fitzwilliam, New Hampshire 03447
(603) 585-2200

Association of Management Consultants
331 Madison Avenue
New York, New York 10017
(212) 687-2825

Association of Consulting Management Engineers, Inc.
230 Park Avenue
New York, New York 10017
(212) 697-9693

Consulting: A Complete Guide to a Profitable Career, by Robert E. Kelley (New York: Charles Scribner's Sons, 1981).

Kelley is widely recognized in academic circles as an expert on consulting. He is also a fine writer.

"How to Get a Good Consultant," *Harvard Business Review,* November–December 1977.

FEDERAL GOVERNMENT FINANCING SOURCES

Catalog of Federal Domestic Assistance. Issued by the Office of Management and Budget; available from the Superintendent of Documents, U.S. Government Printing Office, Washington, D.C. 20402; $20; published annually.

This approximately 1,000-page catalog is an exceptional document for the entrepreneur who wants to explore every possible source of federal assistance. It lists and briefly describes each and every federal loan, grant, training, and assistance program. Included within each program description are vital statistics, such as the total amount of funds available, expected future funds, the number of grants or loans made, and where to get further information. The one drawback to the volume is that it requires some patience to use, because business-related program information is mixed in with education, defense, and social welfare program information.

Business Services and Information, The Guide to the Federal Government, by Management Information Exchange (New York: John Wiley & Sons, 1979).

This 300-page book is a directory of federal services and information of specific interest to businesses of all sizes.

Small Business Guide to Government. Issued by and available from U.S. Small Business Administration, Office of Advocacy, 1441 L Street, N.W., Washington, D.C. 20416; free.

This 72-page booklet lists the names, addresses, and telephone numbers of government agencies that are of particular interest to small business owners. It provides a similar listing for small business trade groups.

Business Loans: A Guide to Money Sources and How to Approach Them Successfully, by Rick Stephan Hayes (New York: CBI Publishing, 1980).

This book about small business financing devotes some 60 pages to describing and advising about government loan programs, federal, state, and local. It also devotes more than 200 pages to the mechanics of preparing loan proposals. Much of the material on government loans reads as though it came straight from government manuals and has become outdated with the Reagan administration cutbacks, but the book contains some useful information on agency attitudes and approaches.

How to Finance Your Small Business with Government Money: SBA Loans, by Rick Stephan Hayes and John Cotton Howell (New York: John Wiley & Sons, 1980).

The first 24 pages of this 165-page book are devoted to explaining the various SBA lending programs. The remainder of the book is purportedly a guide to preparing SBA loan applications, but in reality it is a guide to preparing a loan proposal for any number of potential lenders. It instructs readers on putting together market surveys, pro forma balance sheets, cash flow statements, and other basic financial information required by any lender.

STATE AND LOCAL GOVERNMENT ASSISTANCE

Sourceguide for Borrowing Capital, by Leonard E. Smollen, Mark Rollinson, and Stanley M. Rubel (Wellesley Hills, Mass.: Capital Publishing, 1977).

This book contains two quite useful chapters on state financing sources. One chapter, by the late Stanley M. Rubel, is a description and listing of business development corporations and other organizations. A second chapter, by Mark Rollinson, examines in detail revenue bond programs in each state. Both chapters also contain useful advice about exploiting state financing sources. The book's only real weakness is that it is beginning to become somewhat outdated as new state programs are added and others are changed.

COMMERCIAL FINANCE

The Realty Bluebook, volumes I & II (San Rafael, Calif.: Professional Publishing).

The bible for real estate entrepreneurs and brokers. It contains all the checklists, tables, and tax considerations involved in buying or selling real estate, including how to do calculations on an HP 12C or HP 18C.

The Small Business Guide to Borrowing Money, by Richard L. Rubin and Philip Goldberg (New York: McGraw-Hill, 1980).

Conceptually similar to the Hayes book, though a little shorter and with fewer sample forms. Includes selected listings of venture capital firms and SBICs. Good discussion of how to work with different sources.

Financing the Growing Small Business, by Thomas J. Martin (New York: Holt, Rinehart & Winston, 1980).

An excellent book on financing the small firm. It contains many practical examples, guidelines, and suggestions. Also includes a glossary, valuation guides, and present value tables.

VENTURE CAPITAL

Financing and Investing in Private Companies, by Arthur Lipper, III (Chicago, Ill.: Probus Publishing, 1988).

A practical guide to financing private companies.

Financing and Managing Fast-Growth Companies, by G. Kozmetsky, M.D. Gill, Jr., and R.W. Smilor (Lexington, Mass.: Lexington Books, 1984).

A useful book on the challenges of financing rapidly growing ventures.

Venture Capital Investing, by Wm. Gladstone (Englewood Cliffs, N.J.: Prentice-Hall, 1988).

This is a very practical and detailed book about the venture capital investing process from the investor's perspective. Specific lists of questions asked by venture capitalists as part of their screening and due diligence, for instance, provide a useful insight into how they go about their business.

Venture Economics
75 Second Ave.
Neadham, Massachusetts 02194
(617) 431-8100

Capital Publishing Corporation has long been recognized as the most authoritative source of information on the venture capital industry, with its monthly *Venture Capital Journal,* reference books on business development, and seminars for entrepreneurs and investors. Capital Publishing has also recently developed an information services, research, and consulting division called Venture Economics, which uses a proprietary database built up over the past 20 years. Venture Economics clients are generally investors who are looking at industry trends, but entrepreneurs should find the *Journal* and the book *Guide to Venture Capital Sources* extremely valuable.

Pratt's Guide to Venture Capital Sources, 9th ed., ed. Stanley E. Pratt (1985).

Contains articles written by experts on such subjects as business plan preparation techniques, guidelines for working with venture capitalists, raising and using venture capital, and going public. It also contains information on more than 700 venture capital companies and more than 60 small business underwriters.

ASSISTANCE FOR MINORITY BUSINESSES

Black Enterprise
Earl G. Graves Publishing Company
295 Madison Avenue
New York, New York 10017
(212) 889-8820

Black Enterprise, published monthly, offers the most comprehensive and entertaining coverage of minority business of any publication. It provides updates of developments in government assistance to minority business, along with profiles of successful black entrepreneurs. It also includes articles, similar to those in *Ebony* magazine, on black lifestyles and neighborhoods. The annual subscription rate is $10.

National Minority Business Campaign
1201 12th Avenue N.
Minneapolis, Minnesota 55411

This nonprofit organization publishes three directories and booklets on an annual or semiannual basis. These are:

Try Us: National Minority Business Directory known simply as *Try Us*)

Guide to Obtaining Minority Business Directories (known simply as *Guide*)

Purchasing People in Major Corporations (known simply as *Purchasing People*)

Try Us lists 4,300 minority businesses that have at least regional sales, with a brief description of each company's products or services. Minority firms are listed without charge. The directory costs $14.

Guide lists by state 200 organizations that have compiled minority firm listings in their areas. It costs $3.

Purchasing People lists purchasing officials and minority vendor program coordinators of the 750 largest companies in the country. It costs $4.

ASSISTANCE FOR WOMEN

Superintendent of Documents
U.S. Government Printing Office
Washington, D.C. 20402

A Directory of Federal Government Business Assistance Programs for Women; free.

This guide was put together by several federal agencies.

The Guide to the U.S. Department of Commerce for Women Business Owners; $2.75.

Describes Department of Commerce efforts to aid women entrepreneurs just starting out and already operating businesses.

Women and the Small Business Administration and *Women's Handbook: How the SBA Can Help You Go into Business.*

Both publications, which describe SBA programs of potential use for women entrepreneurs, are available free from local SBA offices or the central SBA office:

U.S. Small Business Administration
Office of Women's Business Enterprise
U.S. Small Business Administration
1441 L Street, N.W.
Washington, D.C. 20416

The Women's Guide to Starting a Business, by Claudia Jessup and Genie Hipps, rev. ed. (New York: Holt, Rinehart & Winston, 1979).

This book offers advice on starting and operating small businesses, with chapters on evaluating business ideas, financing, advertising, accounting, and marketing. It also includes interviews with 30 entrepreneurs, along with a bibliography and an information source list.

Women and the Business Game: Strategies for Successful Ownership, by Charlotte Taylor (New York: Cornerstone Library, 1980).

A thoughtful and clearly written guide to starting and operating a small business. The title is misleading, though, since the book's advice is mainly the sort addressed to entrepreneurs in general by various other guides to starting small businesses. At the end the book lists information sources of particular interest to women entrepreneurs.

The New Entrepreneurs: Women Working from Home, by Terri P. Tepper and Nona Dawe Tepper (New York: Universe Books, 1980).

This book essentially consists of 40 profiles of women who started businesses at home, with their own accounts of how they learned to operate their businesses and the obstacles they encountered. Among the women profiled are a shoemaker, an antique dealer, a pastry chef, and craft specialists.

The Entrepreneurial Woman: How She Thinks and Copes: How She Starts and Succeeds in Her Own Business, by Sandra Winston (New York: Newsweek Books, 1979).

This book also consists mostly of case histories of women who have started small enterprises. *Inc.* magazine in its September 1979 issue was critical of the book for including "an endless series of self-help checklists" and for being "condescending" to readers.

Women's Networks: The Complete Guide to Getting a Better Job: Advancing Your Career and Feeling Great as a Woman through Networking, by Carol Kleiman (New York: Lippincott & Crowell, 1980).

This book offers an overview of the network concept together with advice on setting up and using networks of different types. It also lists women's organizations around the country that promote the network concept.

Working Together: Entrepreneurial Couples, by Sharan and Frank Barnett, 1989, by the National Association of Entrepreneurial Couples, Box 825, Belmont, Calif. 94002.

This is the first book that addresses the unique challenges and opportunities of entrepreneuring as a couple. It is for anyone who has or is considering going into business with a spouse or significant other.

FRANCHISING

For Prospective and Operating Franchisees

Franchise Opportunities Handbook, U.S. Department of Commerce. Available from Superintendent of Documents, U.S. Government Printing Office, Washington, D.C. 20402; $6.50.

This annual survey of about 900 franchisors probably provides more extensive information on the franchises it covers than any other publication. Information on each franchise includes number of outlets, length of time in business, capital needed for starting a franchise, financing assistance available from the franchisor, and training and managerial assistance available from the franchisor.

Your Fortune in Franchises, by Richard P. Finn (Chicago: Contemporary Books, 1979).

Finn's book is a worthwhile introductory text for prospective franchisees. It explains such things as how to investigate opportunities, financial elements to consider, franchisor rights, site selection, training, promotion, financial management, and special opportunities for minority and female franchisees. Among the several hundred franchisors listed in the book are detailed appraisals of the six best franchising opportunities; there are also examples of franchises in each business category.

The Franchise Annual Handbook and Directory, ed. by Edward L. Dixon (Lewiston, N.Y.: Info Press).

This sourcebook lists about 2,000 American and Canadian franchises in each annual edition, as well as general information and advice for potential franchisees. Though it has more listings, it provides less information than does *Franchise Opportunities Handbook.*

IFA Membership Directory and *Investigate before Investing: Guidance for Prospective Franchisees* (Washington, D.C.: International Franchise Association); $5 for both.

The *Directory* lists all IFA members, along with the number of franchises belonging to each, length of time in business, and investment required for enfranchisement. *Investigate before Investing* is a booklet that explains how to evaluate franchising opportunities.

Franchise Index/Profile, the U.S. Small Business Administration. Available from Superintendent of Documents, U.S. Government Printing Office, Washington, D.C. 20402; $2.

This book provides guidance on the pros and cons of franchising and on evaluating individual franchisors.

Franchising and Business Opportunities: Rules and Guides, Franchise and Business Opportunities Program, Federal Trade Commission, Washington, D.C. 20580; free.

This booklet explains the FTC's disclosure rules in the layperson's terms.

1980 Directory of Franchising Organizations (New York: Pilot Books, 1980).

This book contains a listing of only about 100 franchisors, with a one-or two-line description and oversimplified investment figures for each. It also has a superficial three-page discussion of franchising and a nine-point evaluation checklist. Overall, it contains the least amount of useful information of all the sources listed here.

For Prospective and Operating Franchisors

Franchising in the Economy, U.S. Department of Commerce. Available from Superintendent of Documents, U.S. Government Printing Office, Washington, D.C. 20402; $4.75.

Published annually, this book is mainly a statistical compilation of the influence of franchises in the American economy. It also provides information on foreign franchise markets and general advice for the franchisor on approaching different countries as potential franchise markets.

FTC Franchising Rule: The IFA Compliance Kit, by Carl E. Zwisler III and Andrew A. Caffey (Washington D.C.: International Franchise Association, 1979); $40 to members, $80 to nonmembers.

This book, which comes in a three-ring binder, contains a history and analysis of the Federal Trade Commission franchising disclosure rule so as to enable franchisors to comply with it. The book also provides an outline of state disclosure requirements.

How to Organize a Franchise Advisory Council (Washington, D.C.: International Franchise Association, 1979); $5 to members, $10 to nonmembers.

This book provides detailed advice and directions to franchisors on how to help set up trade associations of francisees to aid in communication and cooperation among franchisees and between franchisors and franchisees.

The Franchise Option, by DeBanks M. Henward III and William Ginalski (Phoenix, Ariz.: Franchise Group Publishers, 1980).

This book provides advice on franchising businesses, with a view toward planning and implementing franchising systems.

Franchising: Proven Techniques for Rapid Company Expansion and Market Dominance, by David Seltz (New York: McGraw-Hill, 1980).

This book discusses how to go about franchising a business. It also describes other types of business expansion techniques.

Franchising World, the International Franchise Association; $60 per year.

This monthly publication provides information on developing franchising trends, along with detailed information on IFA member public relations and advertising programs. It also includes updates on legal issues and industry profiles.

Continental Franchise Review, National Research Publications, Inc., 720 South Colorado Boulevard, Denver, Colorado 80222; $105 per year.

This newsletter is published twice monthly and provides an analysis of the existing franchising situation and climate.

For Prospective and Operating Franchisees and Franchisors

Franchising Today, Franchise Technologies, 1201 San Luis Obispo Avenue, Hayward, California 94544; $18 per year.

This magazine comes out semimonthly and features profiles of successful franchisors and franchisees. The magazine reports on legal developments, international franchising, and new technologies. It also offers advice to both prospective franchisees and franchisors on getting started in their respective endeavors.

GOVERNMENT PROCUREMENT

The $100 Billion Market: How to Do Business with the U.S. Government, by Herman Holtz (New York: AMACOM, 1980).

Offers a good overview of the federal procurement process. The writer's informal, breezy style makes for easy reading. His approach is hardheaded—he acknowledges the various obstacles to obtaining government contracts but argues that the businesses that are best prepared can make out profitably in the procurement game. Besides advising the reader on how best to understand and exploit the system, he provides an extensive appendix of relevant publications and government procurement offices.

Government Contracts: Proposalmanship and Winning Strategies, by Herman Holtz (New York: Plenum Press, 1979).

This book is more specialized than the previous one, concentrating on negotiated contracts as opposed to fixed-price contracts. Gives a good feeling for the breadth of opportunity available and amount of effort required to obtain negotiated contracts. Written in the same breezy style as the previous book.

How to Get Started in Government Business, by Eli Chappe (Suffern, N.Y.: Danbury Press, 1979).

This is a manual that provides detailed instructions on selling products to the federal government. Though services are not covered, much of the material applies to services as well. The book is intended for novices in the area of federal procurement, but it actually assumes that the reader has something of an overview of the procurement process. It sets out 27 steps for small business owners to follow in selling to the government, along with describing markets and listing agencies and other contacts. Without some background on the process, however, the reader quickly becomes lost in going through the details of the 27 steps. The 120-page manual is also packed with abbreviations that are confusing even though they're explained in a two-page listing. Readers who have some familiarity with the procurement process, however, can benefit from the details and advice offered.

Various subsets of regulations exist that aren't covered in the above two publications, however. Searching out all of the procurement regulations involves going through the multivolume *Code of Federal Regulations* and ordering the appropriate volume on procurement regulations. An index to the code can be ordered for $8.50; major libraries have the volumes of the code available for perusal. Specific volumes cost between $8 and $10 each.

U.S. Government Purchasing and Sales Directory (Washington, D.C.: U.S. Government Printing Office); $5.50.

Lists the products and services purchased by military and civilian agencies along with the appropriate purchasing offices to be contacted. Also lists types of surplus property sold with contacts.

GSA Supply Catalog; $5.50.

Lists items commonly purchased by the GSA.

Doing Business with the Federal Government; free. Available from GSA, Washington, D.C. 20405, or from local GSA Business Service Centers.

Provides an overview of the federal procurement process in fairly understandable language. Not surprisingly, it stresses all the assistance potentially available from the GSA.

Selling to the Military; $4.

Gives instructions on the procedures for selling to the armed forces and lists major buying offices within the military, along with descriptions of their purchasing activities.

Commerce Business Daily; $105 annually via first-class mail, $80 via second-class mail.

Ostensibly lists all purchases being planned by all federal agencies, so that any company that feels qualified can seek to bid on the work. In reality, it lists only about 10 percent of intended purchases. Still, it's a good source for the newcomer to discover potential government markets, since it's the most complete single listing of what government agencies are planning to buy. Available for perusal at all SBA, Commerce Department, and GSA offices.

Contractor Paths to Grief with Some Solutions; free.

This booklet, published by the SBA, describes some of the commonest problems that small businesses encounter in doing business with the government. It's surprisingly frank for a government publication and is valuable for this reason alone. This and several other SBA publications on selling to the federal government are available from the SBA, 1441 L Street, N.W., Washington, D.C. 20416.

FOREIGN TRADE—EXPORTING

World Trade Information Center
One World Trade Center
New York, New York 10048
(212) 466-3068

The World Trade Information Center does research for individual businesses to locate overseas contracts, statistics, and market reports. Its basic fee is $30 hourly for most services.

The federal government issues a variety of publications that track foreign economic and trading trends. The publications listed can all be obtained from:

Superintendent of Documents
U.S. Government Printing Office
Washington, D.C. 20402
(202) 783-3238

Among the publications are the following:

Foreign Economic Trends, a series of publications issued by the U.S. Foreign Service on business developments and economic indicators in more than 100 countries; $50 annually.

Overseas Business Reports, a publication issued irregularly that provides current and detailed marketing information, trade outlooks, and market profiles; $40 annually.

Global Market Surveys, a series of publications providing detailed information on 15–20 of the best foreign markets for the products of various American industries. Prices vary according to the survey.

Country Market Sectoral Surveys, a series of publications that pinpoint the best exporting opportunities in particular foreign countries. Prices vary.

International Economic Indicators, a quarterly publication that presents a wide variety of comparative economic statistics for the United States and seven major competitor countries for recent periods. Annual subscriptions, $10.

Business International Corporation
One Dag Hammarskjold Plaza
New York, New York 10017
(212) 750-6300

Business International Corporation issues a variety of publications on foreign trade trends around the world. Its publications also offer guidance on financing foreign operations and on investing abroad. Prices vary.

Foreign Trade Marketplace (Detroit: Gale Research, 1977).

This directory lists organizations, government agencies, and companies and provides export and import procedures, trading zones, and other information regarding foreign trade.

Committee for Small Business Exports
Box 6
Aspen, Colorado 81611
(303) 925-7567

The Committee for Small Business Exports is a lobbying organization that was formed in 1979 for the purpose of pressing federal legislators and bureaucrats to aid small business exporting. Its members in 30 states include small manufacturing, trading, export management, and consulting companies. Any company with up to $100 million in annual sales is eligible for membership. An internal newsletter keeps members informed of activities. Dues are $100 annually for companies with less than $3 million in annual sales and $200 for larger companies.

Complete Export Guide Manual, by Steve Murphy (Manhattan Beach, Calif.: SJM & Associates, 1980).

This book is concerned mostly with the documentation that must accompany exported products. It also offers exporting rules for over 150 different countries.

SMALL BUSINESS LOBBYING AND SERVICE ORGANIZATIONS

Encyclopedia of Associations (Detroit: Gale Research).

This three-volume annual publication lists and describes 14,000 associations in alphabetical order within broad categories. Besides providing addresses, phone numbers, and officials to contact, the publication includes number of members, staff sizes, and member services.

National Trade and Professional Associations of the United States and Canada and Labor Unions (Washington, D.C.: Columbia Books).

This volume lists 6,300 national trade associations, labor unions, and professional and scientific societies. The listings are in alphabetical order, but not by category. The volume provides names, addresses, phone numbers, membership sizes, annual budgets, staff sizes, and similar information along with one- or two-line descriptions.

NEWSPAPERS AND PERIODICALS

The Babson Entrepreneurial Review, organized and published by students at Babson College, Babson Park, Mass. 02157.

It is well written, with timely, practical, and informative articles for entrepreneurs.

For timely, often provocative, information for and about entrepreneurs we suggest the following publications:

Harvard Business Review, "Growing Concerns," Soldiers Field Road, Boston, Massachusetts 02163.

In Business, Box 323, Emmaus, Pennsylvania 18049.

INC. Magazine, 38 Commercial Wharf, Boston, Massachusetts 02110.

Small Business Reporter, Bank of America, San Francisco, California.

The Wall Street Journal publishes a regular feature on small business, and the *New York Times* frequently has items of interest to entrepreneurs.

VIDEOTAPES

Some excellent videotapes have become available since the publication of the last edition.

Beyond Start-Up, by William Sahlman, Harvard Business School (Boston, Mass.: Nathan/Tyler, 1987).

Provides a behind-the-scenes look at five of America's most successful founders and an analysis of the stages of business growth.

How to Really *Start Your Own Business,* by *INC.,* 1986.

A lively summary of the fundamental issues of new venture creation covered in this book.

The Shape of the Winner, by Tom Peters (Video Publishing House, 1988).

A talk to nearly 500 entrepreneurs attending a conference for high-growth ventures in Boston in the fall of 1988.

Index

A

A. C. Gilbert, 495
Accountant; *see* Resources
Actions; *see* Entrepreneur; Managing growth; *and* Planning
Adler, Fred, 39, 401
Advanced Energy Technology, Inc., 87
Administrative domain; *see* Entrepreneur
Administrator; *see* Entrepreneur
Air Florida, 81, 82
Alex. Brown & Sons, 442-43
Alger, Horatio, 292
Allen, Fred T., 298
Allen, Louis L., 553
Allied Chemical, 293
Altman, Edward, 534
American Electronics Association, 45
American Research & Development Corporation, 16
American Women's Economic Development Corporation, 46
AMF, 19
Amoco, 450
Amos, Wally, 22, 165
Analytical framework; *see* Entrepreneurship; Ethics; Financing; *and* Team
Angels; *see* Financing
Anthanas, Anthony, 274
Apple Computer, 10, 12, 16, 72, 78, 172, 548
Apprenticeship; *see* Entrepreneur
Artic Circle, Inc., 444, 446
Ashland Oil, 450

Assets; *see* Resources
Association of Collegiate Entrepreneurs, 46
Association of Women Entrepreneurs, 46
Atkinson, John W., 162, 168
Attitudes and behaviors; *see* Entrepreneur
Attorney; *see* Resources
Attractive small companies, 9

B

Babson, Roger, 511
Babson College, 43, 165, 323, 511, 516, 534, 549
Babson College Academy of Distinguished Entrepreneurs, 4, 165, 283
Babson Entrepreneurial Exchange, 46
Balance sheets; *see* Financing
Bank; *see* Financing *and* Resources
Bank of New England, 644-50
Bankruptcy; *see* Managing growth
Bankruptcy law, 249, 536
Baruch, Bernard, 545
Battelle Memorial Institute, 45
Bausch & Lomb, 44
Beantown Seafoods, Inc., case, 239-60, 280
Bechtel, Steve, 274
Bechtel, Steve, Jr., 274
Bechtel, Warren, 274
Bechtel Corporation, 274
Becton Dickinson, 497
Behaviors, and attitudes; *see* Entrepreneur
Bingham family, 271

Board of directors; *see* Resources
Boesky, Ivan, 298
Bok, Derek, 294
Booth's, 52
Boston Computer Society, 46
Boston Consulting Group, 450
Bowmar, 80
Boy Scouts, 293
Bread And Circus, 13
Breakeven; *see* Financing
Bricklin, Dan, 40
Bridge Capital Investors, Inc., case, 439-51
Bridge capital; *see* Financing
Budgeting; *see* Financing
Burr, Egan, Deleage & Company, 16, 330
Bush, George, 293
Bushnell, Nolan, 7, 331
Business plan; *see* Financing; Planning;
    Resources; *and* Strategy
Business Plan Guide, 378-97
Bygrave, William D., 323

C

California Institute of Technology, 45
Capital; *see* Financing
Capital cow; *see* Harvest
Career strategy; *see* Planning *and* Strategy
Carnegie, Andrew, 292-93
Carnegie Institute of Pittsburgh, 293
Carnegie-Mellon University, 40
Case studies
    Beantown Seafoods, Inc., case, 239-60
    Bridge Capital Investors, Inc., case, 439-51
    Family Venture Partners, Inc., case,
        279-81
    Fibercom Applications, Inc., case, 87-116
    Halsey & Halsey, Inc., case, 46-62
    Hindman & Company case, 411-20
    Kevin Mooney case, 176-79
    Michigan Lighting, Inc., case, 480-89
    Outdoor Scene, Inc., case, 24-32
    PMI, Inc., case, 196-202
    Rapidrill case, 340-75
Cash flow; *see* Financing
CB Company, 493, 494, 496
Cellular One, 337
Cetus, 429
Change Masters, The, 188
Charles Krug Winery, 276
Charm, Leslie, 231
Chartier, Alain Emile, 37
Childers, Sloan K., 293
Chrysler, 529
Chunks of experience; *see* Ideas
Churchill, Winston, 530, 542
Cisneros, Gustavo A., 227
Civil Service, 299
Climate; *see* Ethics *and* Managing growth
Cohen, Herb, 454

Command Performance, 231
CommnaComp, 477
Compaq, 6, 12, 78, 548
Competencies, managerial; *see* Entrepreneur
Competitive advantage issues; *see*
    Opportunity
Competitor intelligence, 83
Conditions; *see* Opportunity
Conner, John T., 293
Consultant; *see* Resources
Continental Cablevision, 16
Control Data, 165
Core management modes; *see* Stages of growth
Coster, Betty, 161
Crate & Barrel, 40-41
Creative Squares exercise, 63
Creative thinking; *see* Entrepreneurship *and*
    Ideas
Credibility builders, 507-9
    example; *see* Example
Crisis; *see* Planning, Managing growth; Stages
    of growth; *and* Team
Cuisinarts, Inc., 166
Cullinane, John, 39, 283
Cullinet, Inc., 39, 283
Culture; *see* Managing growth

D

Data General, 39
Deal structure; *see* Financing
Debt; *see* Financing
Dekalb Agrisearch, 429
Detroit Lions, 529
Digital Equipment Corporation, 12, 74, 165,
    429
Documents; *see* Financing
Doktor Pet Centers, 231
Domain; *see* Entrepreneur *and*
    Entrepreneurship
Doriot, General George, 16
Drexel Burnham, 298
Driving forces; *see* Entrepreneurship
Dun & Bradstreet, 8

E

Economic issues; *see* Opportunity
Edwards, Betty, 42
Egan, William, 16, 78, 330
Emerson, Ralph Waldo, 38
Employee Stock Ownership Plan (ESOP);
    see Financing *and* Harvest
Encore Computer Corporation, 160
*Encyclopedia of Small Business Resources,
    The,* 323
Endowment for International Peace, 293
Enrico, Roger, 188, 517
Entrepreneur
    actions, 22, 161, 493-509, 520

Entrepreneur—*Cont.*
  apprenticeship
    management competencies, 9, 23, 556,
      184, 185, 188-95, 195
      example; *see* Example
      exercise, 208-25
      influence skills, 191-92
      traditional skills, 193-95
    paradoxes and dilemmas, 173-74
    shaping and managing, 172-75
    strategy, 23, 174-75, 195; *see also*
      Planning
    timing, 173-74
  attitudes and behaviors, 161-71, 172,
    555-56
  converging on the entrepreneurial man-
    ager
    administrative domain, 182-84
    apprenticeship, 195
    entrepreneurial domain, 182-84
    factors, 182
    managing growth; *see* Managing growth
    stages of growth; *see* Stages of growth
    themes, 165-70
  entrepreneur versus administrator, 23
  entrepreneur versus inventor, 23
  entrepreneur versus promoter, 23
  entrepreneurial mind, 22-24, 165-171,
    555-56; *see also* Harvest
  ethics; *see* Ethics
  experience, 161; *see also* Ideas
  motivation, 162, 168
  myths and realities, 19-22, 161-62
  non-entrepreneurial mind, 171-72
  role models, 24
  who can be an entrepreneur, 3, 161
Entrepreneur's creed, 175-76
Entrepreneur's Roundtable, 46
Entrepreneurial domain; *see* Entrepreneur
  and Managing growth
Entrepreneurial finance; *see also* Financing
  critical financing issues, 402-4
  differences in entrepreneurial domain,
    404-6
  entrepreneurial versus corporate finance,
    404-6
  financing ventures, 401-2
Entrepreneurial mind; *see* Entrepreneur *and*
  Harvest
Entrepreneurship
  analytical framework
    driving forces, 12-19
    founders, 15-17; *see also* Team
    opportunity, 15; *see also* Opportunity
    resources, 18-19; *see also* Resources
  anatomy of iterative process, 493-509
  creation of value, 5, 8, 10, 17, 19
  culture/climate; *see* Managing growth
  definition, 5-6, 17
  destination, 543-46

Entrepreneurship—*Cont.*
  entrepreneurial wave, 3-5
  establishing business
    credibility builders, *see* Credibility
      builders
    example; *see* Example
    setting up
  failure
    failure rates, 8
    failure rule, 7-12
  family venture; *see* Family venture
  fit; *see* Fit
  impact of goals
    publicly owned corporations, 270
    closely held corporations, 270
    family owned/controlled corporations,
      271
  implementation, 19
  intellectual and policy agenda, 7
  intrapreneuring, 172, 188-90, 517
  journey, 543
  managerial domains; *see* Managing growth
  practical agenda, 7
  problems; *see* Managing growth
  role of harvest goal; *see* Harvest
  Silent Revolution; *see* Silent Revolution
  stages of growth; *see* Stages of growth
  success
    about solo entrepreneurs, 17
    backing of venture capital, 11-12
    definition, 9
    economic renewal, 9, 550
    exceptions to failure rule, 9-12
    lemons versus pearls, 73-74
    measure of success, 8
    problem of survival, 8
    promise of growth, 10
    role of apprenticeship, 172-73
    role of team, 16, 227-28
    secrets of success, 550
    survival rates, 10-12
    threshold concept, 10, 12
    types of firms, 9-12
  timing; *see* Timing
  traditional models, 14
  urgency, 6
Equity; *see* Financing
ERISA "prudent man" rules, 425
Ernst & Whinney, 439, 442, 445
ESOP; *see* Financing *and* Harvest
Esprit, 276
Establishing business; *see* Entrepreneurship
Ethics
  analytical framework, 296-97
  controversy, 291
  conventional disciplines, 291
  corporation, 296
  ends-and-means issue, 298, 299
  ethical climate, 292-93
  ethical quicksand, 298

Ethics—*Cont.*
  ethical stereotypes, 292-93
  exercise, 283-90, 300-301
  law, 291-92, 298-99
  overview, 291-92
  philosophical
    descriptive ethics, 297
    metaethics, 297
    normative ethics
      contractarianism, 297
      pluralism, 297
      utilitarianism, 297
  teaching of ethics
    controversy, 293-94
    Kohlbert construct, 295-96
    reasons for teaching, 294-96
  thorny issues, 298-300
Ethics Exercise, 283-90, 300-301
European Foundation for Entrepreneurship
    Research, 5
Evaluation of venture; *see* Opportunity
Example; *see also* Case studies
  Entrepreneurs in action, 493-505
  Rapidrill, Inc., business plan, 340-75
Exercises
  Business Plan Guide, 378-97
  Creative Squares exercise, 63
  Ethics Exercise, 283-90, 300-301
  Financial Statements Exercise, 323-28
  Idea Generation Guide, 65-69
  Managerial Skills and Know-How
      Assessment, 208-25
  Personal Entrepreneurial Strategy
      Exercise, 558-604
  Rewards Exercise, 261-65
  Take an Entrepreneur to Dinner exercise,
      32-35
  Vases and Faces Exercise, 651-52
  Venture Opportunity Screening Guide,
      118-58
Experience; *see* Ideas
External conditions; *see* Opportunity
Exxon, 429, 450
Eye-Natural, 231

F

Failure; *see* Entrepreneurship
Fair Employment Practice Acts, 299
Fairchild Semiconductor, 16
Family venture; *see also* Team
  forming and building team; *see* Team
  impact of goals, 271
  nature of involvement, 273-74
  timing of involvement, 272-73
Family Venture Partners, Inc., case, 279-81
Famous Amos' Chocolate Chip Cookies, 165
Fatal flaw issues; *see* Opportunity
Federal Express, 16
Feedback; *see* Planning

Fibercom Applications, Inc., case, 87-116
Finance; *see* Entrepreneurial finance *and*
    Financing
Financial analysis; *see* Financing
Financial life cycles; *see* Financing *and*
    Stages of growth
Financial resources; *see* Resources
Financial Statements Exercise, 323-28
Financial Statements; *see* Financing
Financing
  analyzing requirements, 316-23, 606-17
    balance sheets, 317, 323
    breakeven, 317
    budgeting, 317
    cash flow, 317, 323
    exercise, 323-28
    income statements, 317, 323
    spreadsheets, 317-23
  critical variables, 406-7
  debt
    banks and lending institutions, 470-71
    criteria for choosing lender, 469, 471-73
    finding lender, 469-80
    lenders, 313-14; *see also* Resources
    lending criteria, 470, 475-76
    lending documents
      cautions, 476, 478
      loan agreement, 476-77, 644-50
      loan proposal, 474
    lending instruments, 474
    lending relationship, 478-79
    other sources, 479
    role of business plan, 473-75
  entrepreneurial finance; *see* Entrepre-
      neurial finance
  equity
    costs of capital; *see* Stages of growth
    deal structure
      amount of investment, 456
      other elements, 459-60
      ownership share, 456-58
      return objectives of investors, 457
      role, 453
      stages of growth; *see* Stages of growth
    finding investors, 421-38
    investment documents, 435, 460-62,
        620-34
      investment (purchase) agreement,
          460-61, 637-40
      other, 460, 461-62, 640-43
      terms sheet, 460, 635-37
    investment instruments, 462-63, 629-32
    role of business plan, 330-31, 338, 424,
        431-33
    role of investors, 405, 422
    sources, 407-9
      friendly investors, 422
      informal investors (angels), 422-24
      professional investors, 425-35
        history of venture capital, 425-26

Financing—*Cont.*
 equity—*Cont.*
  professional investors—*Cont.*
   venture capital sources, 427-29
  types of investment
   ESOP financing, 436-37
   mezzanine and bridge capital, 437
   private placements, 435-36
   public stock offerings, 437-38
 existing businesses, 406-7
 financial life cycles
  stages of growth; *see* Stages of growth
  types of capital, 407-9
 financial strategy framework, 409-10
 investor preferences, 410
 negotiating
  cautions, 460, 476, 478
  equity, 454, 456-60
  debt, 476-78
 new ventures, 406-7
 opportunity screening, 75
 sand traps, 463-67
 strategy; *see* Strategy
 timing, 406, 421, 469, 474
Finding
 opportunity; *see* Ideas *and* Opportunity
 information; *see* Information
Fisher, Ken, 159
Fishery Conservation and Management Act, 259
Fit, 14, 18, 75, 165, 191, 232-35, 305, 557
Ford, Edsel, 274
Ford, Henry, 274
Ford, Henry, II, 274
Ford Motor Company, 274
Forum Corporation, The, 72
Foster, Bill, 230
Foundation firms, 9
Founders; *see* Team
Framework; *see* Entrepreneurship; Ethics; Financing; *and* Team
Fuld, Leonard, 83
Fund raising; *see* Financing *and* Strategy

G

Gallo Vineyards, 274
Gallo, Ernest, 274
Gallo, Julio, 274
Gaps; *see* Fit
Genentech, 430
General Foods, 250
General Mills, 52
General Motors, 254
Geodyne, 502, 503, 504, 505
Girl Scouts, 293
Goals; *see* Planning
Goodpaster, Kenneth E., 296

Gorton's, 52
Grease Monkey, 444
Great mousetrap fallacy; *see* Ideas
Greylock, 430
Growing up big; *see* Managing growth *and* Stages of growth
Growth; *see* Managing growth *and* Stages of growth
Gulf and Western Invention Development Corporation, 45
Gumpert, David, 84, 323

H

Halsey & Halsey, Inc., case, 46-62
Halsey, Daniel, 47, 58, 240-55, 279-81
Halsey, George, 47, 58, 241-55, 279-81
Halsey, Michael, 255-58
Hammer, Armand, 293
Harnett, Susan, 13
Harnett, Tony, 13
Harriman, Edward, 292
Harvard Business Review, 291, 315, 329
Harvard Business School, 3-4, 163, 169, 173, 231, 291, 293, 294, 296, 305, 310, 317, 331, 333, 550
Harvard University, 162, 294
Harvest, 19, 79-80, 229-30, 544-49
 creation of value, 544
 goal, 544
 beyond harvest, 549-550
 harvest options
  capital cow, 546-47
  employee stock ownership plan, 547
  management buy-out, 547
  merger and strategic alliance, 547-48
  outright sale, 548
  public offering, 548-49
  wealth building vehicles, 549
 opportunity screening; *see* Opportunity
 relation to entrepreneurial mindset, 229
 relation to team philosophy, 230-31
 strategy; *see* Strategy
 timing, 545-46
Haslett, Brian, 236, 378
Hayes, John L., 236
Head, Howard, 19, 37, 41, 306
Head Ski, 19, 41
Heritage Merchandising, 441
Hewlett-Packard, 80, 184
High potential venture, 9
Hill, James, 292
Hindman & Associates, 411
Hindman & Company, case, 411-20
Hindman, James, 411-20, 439-51, 453
Honda, Sochio, 165
Honda Motors, 165
HTC, Inc., 545-46
Hugo, Victor, 117

I

IBM, 10, 38, 72, 250, 272
Idea Generation Guide, 65-69
Ideas
  creative thinking
    control of modes of thought, 42-43
    creativity blockers, 43
    enhancing, 41-43
    entrepreneurship, 5
    example; *see* Example
    exercise, 63
    team creativity, 43
  definition, 37
  exercise, 65-69
  Great mousetrap fallacy, 38-39
  idea versus opportunity, 37-40
  pattern recognition
    chunks of experience, 40
    experience factor, 40-41
  relation to reward system, 239; *see also*
    Team
  role, 37-38
  sources
    consulting, 46
    existing businesses, 43-44
    former employers, 46
    franchises, 44
    industry and trade contacts, 45-46
    networking, 46
    patents, 44
    product licensing, 44
    professional contacts, 46
IMEDE, 5
Implementation; *see* Entrepreneurship
In Search of Excellence, 190
Inc., 10, 182, 310, 323
Income statements; *see* Financing
Industry issues; *see* Opportunity
Industry Norms and Key Business Ratios, 618-20
Inetron, 525, 527
Information
  other sources, 43-46, 86-87, 279, 424, 430,
    471, 475, 479
  publications, 44, 83-86, 323, 430, 471, 475,
    637, 653-65
Intel, 12, 16
International Franchise Association, 44
International Telephone & Telegraph, 81
Intrapreneuring; *see* Entrepreneurship
Inventor; *see* Entrepreneur
Investment; *see* Financing
Iowa State University, 45
IRS Code, 351, 440
Iterative process; *see* Entrepreneurship
ITT Research Institute, 45

J

Jiffy Lube International, 411-20, 439-51, 453
Jobs, Steven, 172

Johari Window, 554
Johnson, John, 22
Johnson Publishing Company, 22

K

Kanter, Rosabeth Moss, 172, 188, 190
Kapor, Mitch, 172
Kaspar, 269
Keilor, Garrison, 469
Kelley, Ed, 411-12, 414, 443-44, 450
Kentucky Fried Chicken, 8, 171
Kevin Mooney case, 176-79
Kleiner Perkins, 430
Know-how; *see* Entrepreneur *and* Managing
    growth
Kohlberg, 295
Koran, The, 553
Kraft Corporation, 45
Krentzman, Harvey, 23
Kroc, Ray, 165
Kwik Change, 444

L

Land, Dr., 38
Lane, Bobby, 529
Lawyer; *see* Resources
Lead entrepreneur; *see* Team
Lemons and pearls; *see* Entrepreneurship
Lender; *see* Financing *and* Resources
Life cycle models; *see* Stages of growth
Lifestyle firms, 9
Lionel, 495
Litton, 185
Loan; *see* Financing
Lockheed Corporation, 45
Lotus Development Corporation, 12, 39, 172,
    236, 548, 620
Lube Pit Stop, 444

M

Management buy-out; *see* Harvest
Management modes; *see* Stages of growth
Management tasks; *see* Stages of growth
Management team; *see* Team
Manager; *see* Entrepreneur
Managerial competencies; *see* Entrepreneur
Managerial domains; *see* Managing growth
Managerial Skills and Know-How
    Assessment, 208-25
Managing growth; *see also* Stages of growth
  approaches to management, 518-19
  core management modes; *see* Stages of
    growth
  growing up big, 511-27
  managerial domains
    entrepreneurial domain, 182-84
    management competencies, 184

Managing growth—*Cont.*
  managerial domains—*Cont.*
    principal forces, 182-84
    venture modes, 182-84
  problems
    anticipating problems
      monitoring variables, 520-25
      Net-Liquid Balance-to-Total Assets
        Ratio, 534-35
      non-quantitative signals, 535
      Z-Score model, 534
    bankruptcy
      bargaining power, 536-37
      involuntary bankruptcy, 536
      role of bankruptcy law, 535
      voluntary bankruptcy, 536
    causes of trouble
      management issues, 531
      patterns and actions, 520-24
      planning and financial/accounting issues,
        531-32
      strategic issues, 530
    culture/climate, 187-88, 517
    diagnosis of problems
      analysis of management, 537
      numbers, 537-38
      strategic analysis, 537
    effect on organizational morale, 533
    example; *see* Example
    gestation period of crisis, 532-33
    paradox of optimism, 532
    problem areas and crises, 186-88, 519-20,
      529-30
    solving problems
      attitudes, 525-26
      intervention (turnaround), 537-42
      steps, 526-27
Marcus, Herbert, 277
Marcus, Stanley, 277
Market issues; *see* Opportunity
Marriott, Willard, 272
Marriott Corporation, 272
Mars, 269
Maryland National Bank, 445
Massachusetts General Hospital, 46,
  497, 498
Massachusetts Institute of Technol-
  ogy, 45, 497, 549
MassComp, 430
Massey-Dickinson, 497-503, 527
Massey Ferguson, 497
Maugham, W. Somerset, 421
McClelland, David C., 162, 168
McDonagh, James, 445
McDonald's, 165, 441, 443
McDonnell Douglas, 269
McKinsey, 164
McQuick Oilube, 444
Merck and Company, 293
Merger; *see* Harvest

Mezzanine capital; *see* Financing
MGA Technology, Inc., 44
Michigan Lighting, Inc., case, 480-89
Milken, 298
Minitlube, 439, 443, 444, 446, 450
M.I.T. Enterprise Forum, 46
Mondavi, Cesare, 276
Mondavi, Peter, 276
Mondavi, Robert, 276
Mondavi Vineyards, 276
Morgan Library, 292
Morgan, J. P., 293
Motivation; *see* Entrepreneur
Mousetrap Fallacy; *see* Ideas
Mrs. Paul's, 52
Myths; *see* Entrepreneur

N

National Distillers, 429
National Labor Relations Act, 537
National Patent Development Corpora-
  tion, 44
*National Petroleum News Factbook Annual
  Issue,* 444
National Semiconductor Corporation, 181
National Technical Information Service, 44
Naylor, George, 506
Negotiating; *see* Financing
Neiman-Marcus, 277
Net-Liquid-Balance-to-Total-Assets Ratio,
  534-35
New Bedford Seafood Co-op, 258
New Product Development Services, Inc., 44
New York Times, 291
New York Yankees, 493
Non-entrepreneurial mind; *see* Entrepreneur
Normative ethics; *see* Ethics
Norris, Bill, 165
Northeastern Business School, 241

O

Occidental Petroleum, 293
Old Court Savings & Loan, 439, 441-51
Olsen, Ken, 74, 165
128 Venture Group, 46
Opportunity
  conditions, 71-72
  definition, 17, 71
  driving force of entrepreneurship, 15
  fit; *see* Fit
  opportunity versus idea, 17-18, 37, 71
  screening opportunities
    attractiveness scale, 76
    example; *see* Example
    exercise, 118-58
    opportunity focus, 75
    process, 117
    recognition, 17-18

Opportunity—*Cont.*
  screening opportunities—*Cont.*
    relation to business plan, 377
    relation to financial analysis, 75
    relation to team formation, 233
    relation to strategy, 75; *see also* Strategy
    relation to valuation, 75
    role in planning; *see* Planning
    rules of thumb, 75
    screening criteria, 75-82
      competitive advantage issues, 77, 80-81
      economic issues, 77, 79-80
      fatal flaw issues, 77, 81-82
      harvest issues, 77, 79-80
      industry issues, 77
      market issues, 77
      personal issues, 82
      team issues, 77, 81
    valuation; *see* Valuation
  sources
    gathering information, 83
    other sources, 86-87
    published sources, 83-86, 618-20
  window of opportunity, 71, 73-74; *see also* Timing
OPR (other people's resources); *see* Resources
Organizacion Diego Cisneros, 227
Organizational climate/culture; *see* Managing growth
Osborne, Adam, 6, 40
Osborne Computer, 6, 77
O'Shea, Neil, 440
Outdoor Scene, Inc., case, 24-32
Outside resources; *see* Resources

P

Partner; *see* Team
Pattern recognition; *see* Ideas
Pegasus Corporation, 44
Pennzoil, 413-16, 420, 444-45, 447-88
Pepsi Cola Corporation, 188, 517
Personal Entrepreneurial Strategy Exercise, 558-604
Personal issues; *see* Entrepreneur; Opportunity; Planning; *and* Strategy
Peters, Tom, 190
Phillips Petroleum Company, 293
Pier, 4, 274
Pillsbury Company, 45
Pitney-Bowes, 298
Pittsburgh Steelers, 529
Planning
  actions, 336-38
  business plan
    definition, 329
    example; *see* Rapidrill, Inc., case
    guide, 378-97

Planning—*Cont.*
  business plan—*Cont.*
    implementation, 19
    process
      complete business plan, 377-78
      dehydrated business plan, 330, 377-78
      sample table of contents, 378-79
      segmenting and integrating information, 339
      skills needed, 337
      strategy, 330-31, 338
      tool to guide growth, 330-31
      using Venture Opportunity Screening Guide, 377, 380
      who develops plan, 338
      writing, 339
    relation to opportunity screening, 117
    relation to resources, 305-7
    relation to reward system, 239
    role in financing, 330; *see also* Financing
  crucial ingredients, 338
  definition, 329
  do's and don'ts, 336
  goals, 336-38
  impact of goals; *see* Entrepreneurship *and* Harvest
  personal plan
    apprenticeship, 174-75
    exercise, 558-604
    fit, 557
    guidelines for receiving feedback, 556-57
    impact of goals, 270-71; *see also* Entrepreneurship *and* Harvest
    personal "business plan," 553-58
    reasons for failure, 554
    reasons for not planning, 554
    reasons for planning, 554
    relation to opportunity, 82
    relation to team, 232-33
    self-assessment, 554
    setting goals, 557-58
    strategy, 195, 232; *see also* Entrepreneur
    timing, 553-54
  pitfalls, 333-36
  problems, 333; *see also* Managing growth
  process, 329, 339
  reasons for failure, 333-36
  reasons for not planning, 333
  reasons for planning, 330-31, 331-33
  role in resources, 330-31
  role of opportunity screening, 336, 377
  venture action plans, 505
    example; *see* Example
PMI, Inc., case, 196-202
Polaroid Corporation, 37-38
Price-Babson Fellow, 4
Prime Computer, 159-60, 187
Prince, 41
Principal forces; *see* Entrepreneurship
Private placements; *see* Financing

Problems; *see* Managing growth; Planning;
    Stages of growth; *and* Team
Promoter; *see* Entrepreneur
Public offering; *see* Financing *and* Harvest
Purdue, Franklin P., 166
Purdue Farms, Inc., 166
Purdue University, 45

Q

Quadram, 37
Quaker State, 414, 439-44, 446-48, 450-51

R

Rabb, Sidney, 543
Raiffa, Howard, 293-94
Rapid-American Corporation, 274
Rapid growth; *see* Managing growth *and*
    Stages of growth
Rapid Oil Change, 444
Rapidrill, Inc., case, 340-75
RCA Corporation, 45, 52
Reality Income Corporation, 451
Remey, Don, 446
Research Corporation, 44
Resources
    assets, 302
    business plan; *see* Planning
    custodial viewpoint, 306
    definition, 302
    driving force of entrepreneurship, 15,
        18-19
    entrepreneurial approach
        advantages, 305-6
        control, 18, 305
        difference, 302-7
        example; *see* Example
        minimizing, 18, 306-7
        other people's resources (OPR), 307
        relation to team formation, 233
    financial, 18-19; *see also* Financing
    information, 323
    people, 302, 307-16
        accountants, deciding and selecting,
            314-15
        attorneys, deciding and selecting,
            310-13
        board of directors
            alternatives, 310
            deciding and selecting, 308-9
            investors, 308
        consultants, deciding and selecting,
            315-16
        lenders, deciding and selecting, 313-14
        role, 307
        team, 307
    strategy; *see* Strategy
Reward; *see* Harvest; Planning; *and* Team
Rewards Exercise, 261-65

Rich, Stanley, 8
Right Stuff, The, 6
Riklis, Ira, 274
Riklis, Meshulam, 274
Risk capital; *see* Financing
RJR Nabisco, 405
Robert Morris Associates, 84, 317, 610
Rock, Arthur, 16, 19
Rockefeller, John D., 292
Rockefeller Foundation, 292
Role models; *see* Entrepreneur

S

S. C. Johnson & Sons, 269
Sale of venture; *see* Harvest
Sanders, Colonel, 8, 171
Sasser, John, 443
Schlenger, Jacques, 443
Schumpeter, Joseph, 9
Scientific Data System, 16
Screening; *see* Opportunity
Secrets of success, 550
Securities and Exchange Commission, 193,
    294, 299, 404, 436, 507, 548
Self-Assessment; *see* Planning
Shaw, George Bernard, 19
Shearson Lehman Brothers, 439, 441-42, 444,
    445-51
Shulman, Joel, 534
Siegle, Harold, 229
Silent Revolution, 3, 5
Simon, Herbert, 40
Skills; *see* Entrepreneur
Small Business Administration, 8, 10, 298,
    316, 407, 428-29
Smaller Business Association of New
    England (SBANE), 46
Smollen, Leonard E., 378
Solving problems; *see* Managing growth *and*
    Planning
Sontheimer, Carl, 166
Sources; *see* Financing; Ideas; Information;
    Opportunity; *and* Resources
Southwest Research Institute, 45
Spinelli, Steve, 411
Sprague, Peter J., 181
Spreadsheets; *see* Financing
Stages of growth
    core management mode, 512, 518-19
    culture/climate; *see* Managing growth
    financing
        costs of risk capital, 407-9, 456-60
        financial life cycles, 407-9
        principal sources, 407-9
    key management tasks, 184-85
    life-cycle models, 511
    managing rapid growth; *see* Entrepreneur
        and Managing growth
    problems and crises, 186-88, 511-16, 519-20

Stages of growth—*Cont.*
    problems and crises—*Cont.*
       industry turbulence, 516
       rate of growth, 512
    realities, 512
    stages
       high growth, 184-85
       maturity, 185
       stability, 185
       start-up, 184
       theoretical view, 184-85
    transitions, 184-85, 512
Stancill, James, 317
Stanford Research Institute, 45
Stengel, Casey, 493
Stevenson, Howard H., 173, 175, 188, 291,
    305, 306
Stock; *see* Financing *and* Team
Stop & Shop, 543
Strange, F. Leland, 37
Strategic alliance; *see* Harvest
Strategy
    business plan; *see* Planning
    example; *see* Example
    family venture; *see* Team
    financial, 402, 406; *see also*
       Financing
    harvest, 545-46
       guidelines and cautions, 546
    opportunity screening, 75
    personal; *see* Planning
    problems; *see* Managing growth
    resources, 305-7
    strategies for success; *see also* Team
       back-door policy, 506
       bandwagon effect, 506
       business or venture action plan,
         505
       communication, 506
       involvement, 507
       simplicity, 506
    team, 232
Stratus Computer, 230
Success; *see* Entrepreneurship; Strategy;
    and Team
Sun Microsystems, 78
Sunmark Companies, The, 229
Survival; *see* Entrepreneurship
Synectics, 41-42
Syrus, Publilius, 377

T

Take an Entrepreneur to Dinner exercise,
    32-35
Tandem Computer Corporation, 430
Tandon, 16
Tax Reform Act (1986), 549
Taylor, Sandy, 454

Team, 81, 187-88
    connection to success, 228
    creativity; *see* Ideas
    forming and building teams
       additional considerations, 234
       common pitfalls, 235-36
       evolution of team, 231
       example; *see* Example
       family venture
         critical issues, 274-75
         unique problems
           control, 275
           credibility, 275
           family dynamics, 275-76
           succession, 276-77
           strategies for success, 277-79
       fits and gaps, 232-34
       framework for formation, 232-33
       lead entrepreneur, 232-33
       philosophy and attitudes
         anchor, 228-31
         basis of reward system, 229
         entrepreneurial mindset, 229
         harvest, 230-31
    opportunity screening; *see* Opportunity
    problems; *see* Managing growth
    resources; *see* Resources
    reward system
       critical issues, 237
       exercise, 261-65
       mechanisms, 238
       relation to vision, 228
       rewarding outsiders, 237
       rewards and incentives
         financial rewards, 236
         personal rewards, 236
         role of reward system, 236
         timing of rewards, 236-37, 238
         valuing contributions, 239
    role in strategy; *see* Strategy
    role of team, 228
Teledyne, 16
Terms; *see* Financing
Testa, Hurwitz & Thibeault, 620
Testa, Richard, 235, 620
Threshold concept; *see* Entrepreneurship
Thurston, Phillip, 331
Timing, 14, 18, 19, 71, 73-74, 173-74,
    184-85, 186-87, 231, 236-37, 238,
    272, 403-4, 405, 406, 421, 456, 469,
    545, 553-54
Tobin, Paul J., 337
Tompkins, Doug, 276
Tompkins, Suzie, 276
Transitions; *see* Stages of growth
Trilogy, 429
Trouble; *see* Managing growth
TRW Corporation, 45
Turnaround; *see* Managing growth
Twain, Mark, 5, 71

U

Union Carbide Corporation, 45
United Nations, 255
United States Department of Commerce, 44, 47, 53, 259
United States Department of the Interior, 259
United States Public Health Services, 503
United States Senate, 260
United States Steel, 293
UNIVAC, 39
University of California, 45
University of Chicago Business School, 294
University of Michigan, 162
University of Minnesota, 411
University of Oregon, 45
University of Southern California, 317
University of Wisconsin, 45
University Patents, 44

V

Valuation, 456, 547, 612-17
  critical variables, 456
  methods, 405-6, 455-56
  opportunity screening, 75
Value; *see* Entrepreneurship *and* Harvest
Van de Kamps, 52
Van Slyke, John, 310
Vases and Faces Exercise, 651-52
Veasy, Brian, 258
Venture action plan; *see* Planning
Venture Capital Journal, 425
Venture capital; *see* Financing
Venture Economics, 429, 430
Venture Founders Corporation, 236, 378
Venture modes; *see* Entrepreneurship
Venture Opportunity Screening Guide exercise, 118-58

Venture screening; *see* Opportunity
Vesper, Karl, 43
Viatron, 81
VisiCalc, 40, 317
Vogel, Robert, 445
Voltaire, 329
von Oech, Roger, 43
VSOG; *see* Venture Opportunity Screening Guide Exercise

W

W. J. Hindman, Ltd., 420, 439
Wall Street Journal, The, 293, 294
Waller, Fats, 651
Wang, An, 165, 293
Wang Laboratories, 165, 293
Waterman, Bob, 190
Watson, Thomas, Jr., 272
Wealth building; *see* Harvest
Western Maryland College, 411
Wetzel, William, 422
Window of opportunity, 18, 71, 73-74
Winning performers, 12
Winters, O. B., 38
Whitney, J. H., 430
Woods Hole Oceanographic Institute, 257, 500, 501, 502, 505

X–Z

Xerox, 38, 45, 80
Yankalovich, 5
Yeager, Chuck, 6
Youngman, Carl, 231
Z-Score, 534